THE LAND AND
LITERATURE OF
ENGLAND

By Robert M. Adams

Ikon: John Milton and the Modern Critics
Strains of Discord
Stendhal: Notes on a Novelist
Surface and Symbol
Nil: Episodes in the Literary Conquest of Void
during the Nineteenth Century
James Joyce, Common Sense and Beyond
Proteus: His Lies, His Truth
The Roman Stamp
AfterJoyce, Studies in the Post-Joycean Novel
Bad Mouth: Fugitive Papers on the Dark Side
The Lost Museum
Decadent Societies

Translated and edited by Robert M. Adams

Voltaire, *Candide,* a Norton Critical Edition
Stendhal, *Red and Black,* a Norton Critical Edition
Thomas More, *Utopia,* a Norton Critical Edition
Niccolò Machiavelli, *The Prince,* a Norton Critical Edition
Villiers de l'Isle Adam, *Tomorrow's Eve*

Edited by Robert M. Adams

George Meredith, *The Egoist,* a Norton Critical Edition
Ben Jonson's Plays and Masques, a Norton Critical Edition
and
with M. H. Abrams *et al., The Norton Anthology of English Literature*

THE
LAND AND
LITERATURE OF
ENGLAND

A Historical Account

Robert M. Adams

W·W·NORTON & COMPANY

NEW YORK · LONDON

Library of Congress Cataloging in Publication Data
Adams, Robert Martin, 1915–
The land and literature of England.
Bibliography:p.
Includes index.
1. English literature—History and criticism.
2. Great Britain—History.   3. Literature and
society—England.   I. Title.
PR83.A3   1983   820'.9   82-14141

ISBN 0-393-30343-8

W. W. Norton & Company, Inc., 500 Fifth Avenue, New York, N.Y. 10110
W. W. Norton & Company Ltd., 37 Great Russell Street, London WC1B 3NU

4 5 6 7 8 9 0

Contents

Illustrations following pages 23, 80, 175, 230, 314, 370, 399, 429, 489

Foreword

The intent of this book is to set forth the outlines of English history so that they may serve as background for the study of English literature.

Mention English literature, and it's clear within quite definite limits what you mean; mention English history, and it's much less clear. There are constitutional, political, social, economic, military, diplomatic, and cultural histories; most general histories are a medley of all these varieties. Considered as a background to English literature, however, English history is almost required to assume a certain character. Like most of the world's literatures, the literature of England has mostly been written for and by the educated, who commonly are the leisured and relatively wealthy classes. History as it affects them provides the most relevant background for literature written with their tastes and values in mind.

The leisured and wealthy classes, to be sure, are only a fraction of the whole society; and in some stages, even the literate are only a small minority. A short history covering a long period of time cannot possibly give full attention to those silent throngs whose lives rose only rarely to literary expression. But this should not be an excuse for forgetting them. They are the background to the background, millions of people engaged in routine chores such as milking the cow, tending the pig, tanning the leather, grinding the flour, hewing the wood, and drawing the water. For thousands of years, most men and all women fell into this class; interest in sonnets or allegorical romances may distract attention from them, and sheer lack of space prevent an author from constantly reminding his readers that there they are. But there they were, throughout the entire history; and it was only because of their obscure and unceasing labors that history as a narrative of public events, and literature as the free expansion of the imagination, became possible at all, for anybody.

As there are two long stories to tell, and very little space to tell them, other elements of the background must be treated only intermittently. Literature presupposes people who can read and write; there's more than one way to acquire these skills, and different individuals do it differently. For much of England's history, her educational "system" was the reverse of systematic; many even of those who attended the best schools and universities got an education (if they did so at all) through their own initiatives. Some of England's greatest writers were self-taught; the "system" often hindered as much as it helped. This is a general if not a universal fact of life. Accordingly, the educational backgrounds of individual authors (unless exceptionally interesting or illustrative of a general point) can't be explored in the intimate detail which alone would make them meaningful. There are biographies, there are histories of education as such, and thither the curious student is referred. In the background of English literature, there is much that we do not and cannot know. Who bought and read *Paradise Lost?* Why did so few competent English writers take up where Chaucer left off? Why did any individual or group choose to dissent, or not to dissent, from the church of England? Who exactly supported the king and who the Parliament during the civil wars—and was that what they thought they were doing? Specialists can investigate these questions far more deeply than a general history can afford to do; but even they must often be reduced to speculation. For the general historian, with thousands of years to cover and 500 pages to do it, speculation is a rare luxury.

Again, institutions may exist for hundreds of years, performing their primary functions well, indifferently, or badly, but not impinging on the story of English literature till relatively late in their lives. That, then, is when they must come in, though the sensitive reader will be aware that they must have a previous record and the curious student will want to look into it. A case in point is the system of guilds or craft organizations, which had a long and various history before they enter the world of literature in connection with early drama. That previous history, like the full functioning of guilds as economic organizations, is for another volume or volumes. As England expanded her power in the nineteenth century, she became involved in the affairs of many "colonial" peoples, all of whom had previous histories and, of course, subsequent courses of development after the English came in contact with them. Each relationship is a volume in itself, but the historian who is mindful of his scope and intent can spare only a peripheral glance at the most important. The word "important" in this context implies a bushel basket of judgments about the events themselves and about the perspective of the presumed reader.

I may seem to be saying that the book I have undertaken to write can only be written badly. If it undertook to pronounce some sort of final, definitive word on anything, that would doubtless be true. But at the stage in a student's studies for which this book proposes itself, the alternative to presenting the subject concisely is not presenting it more fully, it is not presenting it at all. History I take to be a matter of fascinating interest in itself and a frequent resource for understanding the literature which is part of it and within which it often plays a major part. Neither study need be cramped to coexist with the other. And, as Professor Gilson put it with fine irony and exquisite reserve: "Historical events are sometimes whimsical enough to fall into a pattern and simulate an order." Getting things in order is one of a student's first jobs. I have tried to supply background material for a one-year introduction to English literature, amounting to reading of no more than 175 pages per quarter or 250 pages per semester. Illuminating the main documents of the literature and explaining some sequences of the history have been primary objectives. If, in addition, the book proves entertaining in itself and suggests further lines of reflection and study, it will have fulfilled all its purposes.

I make no apology for having introduced my own enthusiasms into the literary commentary. Nothing would be duller than a book which recited only accepted opinions about accepted masterpieces. I hope that among my divagations about Davies's "Orchestra," Borrow's *Lavengro,* or Peacock's *Crotchet Castle,* the student will hear a note that suggests to him buried treasure, for which, if he has a mind to be diverted, he'd better dig.

When, in the course of text or footnotes, allusion is made to a book listed in the Suggestions for Further Reading, the reference will take the form SFR, A.29— i.e., the twenty-ninth item in the first group.

A WARNING

Just to make explicit the amount of precision that can be expected of a highly compressed history, let the author here remind his readers that:

(1) all population figures and economic statistics are rough estimates—the earlier the period and the bigger the figure, the rougher the estimate;
(2) technical inventions, economic processes, and cultural changes, though often dated for convenience to a single year, are commonly prepared for, modified, and spread out over several;
(3) an action explained as the outcome of a single predominant motive is generally the result of several concurrent, subordinate motives as well;
(4) no general statement about the mood of a nation, the interests of a social class, or the beliefs of a group is true without exception.

The popular historian is not on his oath to tell the truth, the whole truth, and nothing but the truth—were he to attempt any such wild enterprise, his book would be interminable and unreadable. His highest hope is to weave a tissue of coherent probabilities, through which an interested student will readily pass in his search for more precision, greater certainty. May he frequently do so.

Robert M. Adams

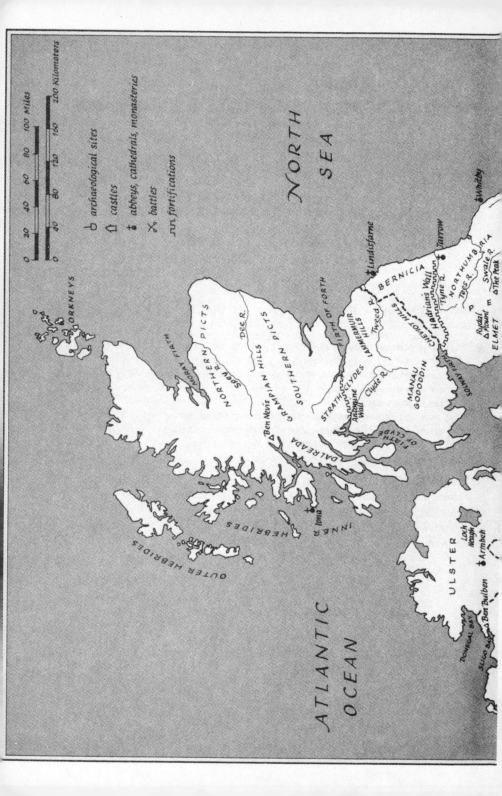

ATLANTIC
OCEAN

NORTH
SEA

ORKNEYS

MORAY FIRTH

NORTHERN PICTS

Spey R.

Deer

GRAMPIAN HILLS

Ben Nevis

SOUTHERN PICTS

OUTER HEBRIDES

INNER HEBRIDES

Iona

DALREADA

FIRTH OF CLYDE

STRATHCLYDE

Antonine Wall

Clyde R.

FIRTH OF FORTH

LAMMERMUIR HILLS

CHEVIOT HILLS

MANAU GODODDIN

Tweed R.

Hadrian's Wall

BERNICIA

Lindisfarne

Jarrow

Whitby

NORTHUMBRIA

Tyne R.

SOLWAY FIRTH

Tees R.

Swale R.

Rydal

Mount

ELMET

The Peak

ULSTER

DONEGAL BAY

Sligo Bay

Ben Bulben

Loch Neagh

Armagh

archaeological sites
castles
abbeys, cathedrals, monasteries
battles
fortifications

0   20   40   60   80   100 Miles
0   40   80   120   160   200 Kilometers

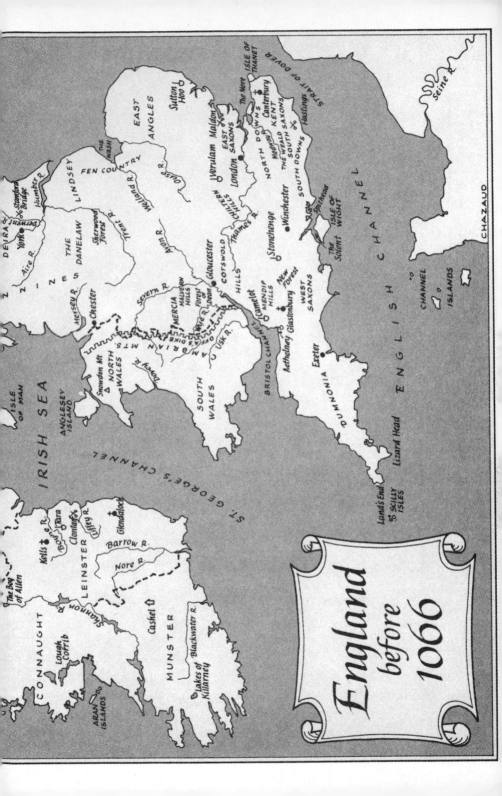

England before 1066

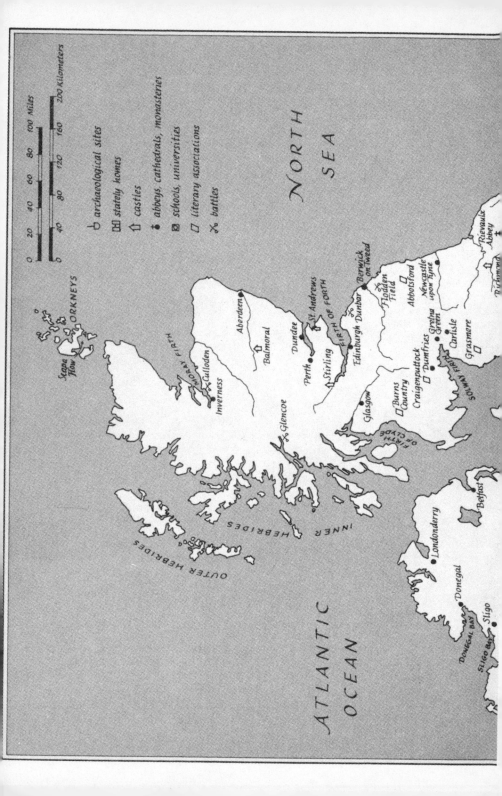

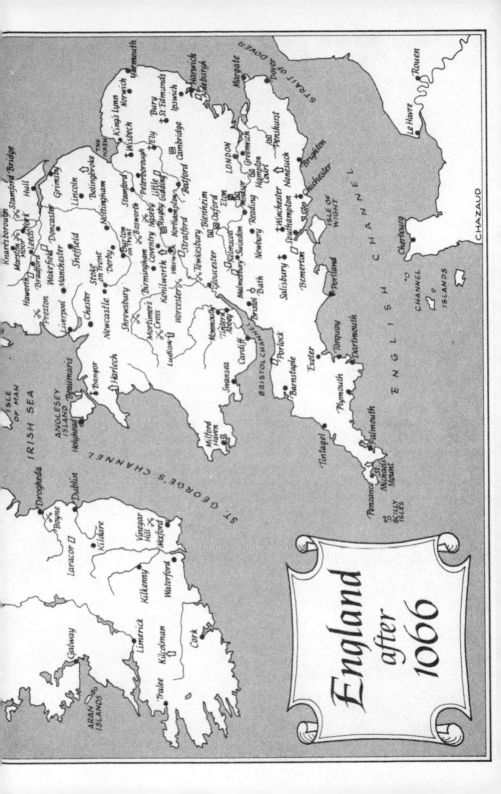

England after 1066

THE LAND AND LITERATURE OF ENGLAND

1

Celtic Britain, Roman Britain, and Their Fate (1500 B.C.–A.D. 600)

The rock-bound, rain-drenched islands which are now divided into the four ancient nations of England, Ireland, Scotland, and Wales lie off the northwest coast of Europe, with the English Channel to the south of them, the North Sea to the east, the Norwegian Sea to the north, and the broad sweep of the North Atlantic to the west. Across the English Channel at its narrowest, France lies about 20 miles away; Belgium and Holland are less than 100 miles from the southeast tip of England. From Scotland to Norway, across the stormy North Sea, is a full 300 miles, while from Ireland to Newfoundland via the Great Circle route is just about 2,000 miles of open ocean. Near Belfast, Ireland is less than 20 miles distant from Scotland, but the southern route from Dublin to Holyhead in Wales crosses 70 miles of rough sea water. From its narrowest point, where the white cliffs of Dover can be seen from the beach at Calais, the English Channel widens to the west, so that Penzance at the tip of Land's End is a full 125 miles from Brest, the seaport city in which the Breton peninsula, pushing far out into the North Atlantic, comes to an end.

Looked at as a unit, England and Ireland form a rough triangle with its base along the English channel, its apex far to the north in the Shetland Islands. From Land's End, where the long combes and rocky promontories of Cornwall point a skinny, stony finger into the Atlantic, to the last outlying islands of Scotland, not far south of the Arctic Circle, the country extends nearly 800 miles from south to north. Of a midsummer midnight, you can read print in the Shetlands without artificial light; it is the land of the midnight sun. On the southwest coasts of both England and Ireland, where the Gulf Stream from the Caribbean washes against the island shores, the climate is semitropical. Palm trees grow in Devon, hydrangeas at Penzance, and at Glengarriff, on the far western shore of Ireland, tropical bushes flourish year round. " 'Tis a soft day," say the country folk in the Killarney district of southwest Ireland; and generally it is—soft, wet, misty the year round, with hardly a trace of winter snow. In such circumstances one easily forgets how far north the islands lie. At 50° north latitude, their southern portions are about opposite Labrador; at 60° north latitude, most of the northern islands lie above the southern tip of Greenland. A few thousand feet of altitude and a little distance from the warming influence of the Gulf Stream, and one is in a different climate entirely—colder, drier, more wintry.

Taking for the moment England, both Irelands, Scotland, Wales, and all the peripheral islets as a single land mass, it includes about 121,000 square miles— that is, slightly less total area than the state of New Mexico (which ranks fifth among American states, after Alaska, Texas, California, and Montana). Each of three Canadian provinces, Ontario, Saskatchewan, and Alberta, is by itself twice as large as the British Isles. France is today about one and three quarters times as big, territorially, as Britain; Italy is a bit smaller and Spain a good deal bigger. These are the modern nations that are being compared; and the figures for Britain are taken to include Eire or the Republic of Ireland, though politically that region is not and does not want to be incorporated with England. To make a nation the physical size of the United States or Canada would require thirty Great Britains.

Though the islands are relatively small, they include a great variety of different countrysides and topographies. Broadly speaking, the high country of England is in the west and north—as if, while those two corners of the triangle had been tilted up, the southeast corner had been pushed down by the same force which sank parts of Holland, across the channel, below sea level. In that southeastern part of England lies the district around Cambridge known as the "Fen country"; as its name implies, it is very low and watery indeed, with many dykes and ditches and even today some wet, marshy areas. The Thames, which drains out this corner of England, is a typical "drowned" river valley, being tidal for a distance of about 20 miles above London Bridge and throughout the entire estuary below it. When tides are unusually high, or when a strong east wind piles up masses of water in the estuary, the Thames is quite capable of flooding a good part of its lower valley.[1] This low country continues along the east coast of

---

1. As I write, a gigantic and immensely expensive project is under way to build an adjustable barrier dam across the Thames below London. If successful, it will hold back flood tides while allowing the river and its traffic easy passage in normal circumstances. It is required because the ground around London is gradually subsiding, while the level of the sea, because of shrinking polar ice caps, is rising.

England, north through Suffolk and Norfolk as far as the Humber.

The mountains of Britain are found to the north in Scotland and to the west in Wales. They are not towering peaks; Snowdon, the highest point in Wales, rises about 3,500 feet above sea level, and Ben Nevis, in the highland shire of Inverness, is the loftiest mountain in the British Isles, at a shade more than 4,400 feet. These are not Alpine, far less Himalayan altitudes. Still the mountains of Scotland and Wales, just like the bogs and swamps of southeast England and of Ireland, served as refuges for some of the island's early inhabitants. Many social and cultural differences that will be encountered in the history of the islands go back to these broad and simple facts of geography.

But the greater part of England is neither mountainous nor boggy. It is rolling hill country, deeply indented by inlets of the sea into which empty the land's many rivers, dappled with ponds, and marked with a thousand little ridge-and-valley combinations for which the English tongue has such a loving variety of names. There are downs, dells, dingles, vales, glens, glades, heaths, moors, denes, straths, crofts, cloughs, garths, leas, wolds, wealds, combes, meads, fells, hams, warrens, bourns, chases, and dozens of other local familiar names. As one rises out of the Thames valley, pushing westward from London, the land also rises and opens out into the great plain surrounding Salisbury where Stonehenge still measures the solar years, falling off then into the southern downs—those rolling hills of Dorset, Somerset, and Devon, of which Thomas Hardy gives so deep an impression in his Wessex novels. Westward through Devon and Cornwall, the road dips to meet the channel as it widens toward the open Atlantic, at a run of little harbor towns and villages cut into the rocky cliff stretching out toward the Scilly Islands. Somewhere on the other side of this Cornish peninsula was Camelot, seat of King Arthur and the Table Round. But, turning still more to the north, one follows another series of ridges and hills—the Mendip, Cotswold, and Malvern Hills, which outline the Bristol channel and lead into the narrow valleys and rough, broken countryside of Wales. The Welsh hills occupy the entire middle region of England's west coast, pushing their craggy points far out into the Irish sea and forming a striking counterpart to the low, marshy terrain on the east coast. But they cut off abruptly, leaving the island of Anglesey barely a stone's throw off the mainland; and the next group of northward hills lies farther to the east, about in the center of the island. It is the Pennine range, a line of low rises reaching north like a backbone as far as Scotland. They are a very moderate range of hills, and no great obstacle to east-west travel because there are many gaps in them. But the Pennines form an important watershed in northern England, where the streams of Yorkshire, pouring down the steep western slope and the gentler eastern slope, provided a major source of power during the early industrial revolution. The Pennines are also a significant weather screen. The storms that rage and whistle over Wuthering Heights in Emily Bronte's novel are Pennine storms; the bleak and savage Yorkshire moors on which that novel takes place are products of Pennine weather. At the very northern end of the Pennine chain, just before the border with Scotland and on the west side of the mountains, is the region known to literary history as the Lake District, the habitat primarily of William Wordsworth. It is a secluded corner of England, cut off by mountains to the east and south, with the Irish sea to the north and west.

Perhaps to the disadvantage of both countries, the border between England and Scotland is low, level, and easy to pass. For centuries, Scottish cattle raiders found it easy to put the snatch on English flocks and herds, then retreat from English vengeance to hiding places north of the border. Border warfare became legendary; it is the very stuff of Walter Scott's novels. Geography granted the Scots one distinct advantage. Below the border, the Pennines run north and south, leaving travel to either side relatively unimpeded. But north of the border the Cheviots and other ranges like the Moffet Hills and the Lammermuirs run east and west, interdicting or impeding passage. North of the great trough constituting the ridges and valleys of Lowland Scotland lie the still higher and less passable mountains of Highland Scotland, the Grampian Hills and their ancillary ranges. Until recently, no roads and only a few trails crossed this country.

Thus for many centuries it was hard to penetrate the fastnesses of Scotland; and, worse than hard, it was unprofitable. For as we move north, the ground typically gets stonier, the soil poorer, the vegetation more scant. Even when the rest of England was swathed in deep forests, northern Scotland seems always to have been a land of gorse and heather. The uplands are particularly sparse; pine and birch grow in the valleys along the clear trout streams, but the mountains are often bald. And naturally as we go farther north and climb higher, the climate becomes colder. A little south of the present boundary the emperor Hadrian, about A.D. 122, caused a wall to be built from the Tyne River on the east coast to Solway Firth on the west. A century later, another wall was added some 50 miles to the north, across the narrow waist of Scotland. Forts and blockhouses studded both walls. The Roman generals knew the hostile tribes to the north could be defeated in battle, but thought the effort not worth making. Walling out the tribes was the traditional solution; it was crude but, for a couple of centuries, effective.

THE OTHER ISLAND

Ireland, as it is about a quarter the size of England, is less various geographically. There are mountains, or rather hills, in Ireland, but they are neither high nor steep; unlike the mountains of Scotland, they form neither a barrier nor a refuge. Mostly the Irish mountains seem to form a backward letter Ɔ around the largest and most obvious geographical feature of the land. This is a wide, low-lying, watery plain in the very center of the country. It consists mostly of bogs and lakes (loughs), drained by slow-moving streams which gradually assemble toward the largest of Ireland's rivers, the Shannon. The bogs have been here for a very long time, though perhaps they once supported more trees than they do now. Bog water soaked in peat is rich in tannic acid, and preserves just about anything that falls into it—a tree, an animal, a person, a leather bucket of butter with somebody's hand-print on the butter. Much that we know about ancient Ireland (and we know a surprising deal) comes from artifacts dredged out of the bogs

Though colder on the east coast than the west, Ireland's climate is generally milder than that of England, and the abundant moisture that blows in off the Atlantic makes Irish fields not only green (hence the "emerald isle") but splendidly fertile. Especially in the midland counties and in Wales, England has natural resources of iron and coal, and now she has access to oil from the North Sea. Ireland has none of these commodities so valuable for an industrial society. What she does have is peat from her bogs; cut and dried, it glows gently and fragrantly in a fireplace. But it is not very concentrated; one couldn't smelt iron with it or use it to generate steam. Ireland has never developed an industrial economy or an industrial population; and, being small (only a little bigger than West Virginia in land area), the island's proper interests have many times been subordinated roughly to those of her bigger, stronger, richer neighbor.

WATER, WATER EVERYWHERE

In this thumbnail sketch of British geography, one feature that cannot be overlooked is the universal proximity of the sea. No place in all England, it's been said, is more than a hundred miles from salt water. The innumerable rivers of England provide easy access to and from the ocean.[2] Whether one thinks of the little harbors of Devon and Cornwall, the shipbuilding centers of Belfast and Liverpool, the many fishing towns of the North Sea off which men trawl for herring or venture as far as Iceland for bottom fish, the average-sized commercial centers like Cork, Bristol, Southampton, Glasgow, and Swansea, or the superport of London with its miles of docks, Britain has everywhere access to the sea and to the trade that plies on it. From Scotch salmon to Dover sole, from Colchester oysters to Dublin Bay prawns, from kippers to trout, fish and shellfish make up a major part of Britain's diet. The chant of "Cockles and mussels alive, alive-o" resounds not only through Dublin's fair city, but through half the towns in the islands. So it is and has been throughout history. From her earliest days, the story of Britain is the tale of arrivals from the sea, adventures on the sea, sea life and sea power; salt of the sea flavors every aspect of the national life.

2. In one romantic meander of the wide-wandering *Faerie Queene* (Book IV, canto 11), Spenser celebrates the marriage of the robust Thames with the buxom Medway, a watery ceremony to which all the rivers of England, Ireland, and indeed of the world lend their plashy, murmuring presence. (The Medway flows into the Thames just before they both pour into the North Sea; so their "marriage" was a matter of daily observation for London readers of Spenser's poem.)

FIRST EVIDENCES

Let us now turn back in imagination, via Mr. Wells's time machine, to a period before the Angles and Saxons invaded England, before the Romans came, far back in the pre-Christian era, where the light of recorded history glimmers and starts to fade into archaeological murk and mythical darkness. Just a little while ago, a few thousand years, a mere yesterday, the huge ice cap which had pressed down on the entire northern hemisphere for many millennia, started to retreat and dissolve. Why it had come in the first place we do not know, any more than we know the reason for its retreat. What it left behind was the British Isles, roughly as they are now in size, shape, and position, but covered, especially in the southern regions which had not been scalped of their topsoil, by a thick layer of forests. Because of these forests and those which covered all of northern Europe, the climate was much colder than it is now. Possibly it was colder anyway, as a result of those world conditions which produced the Ice Age;[3] but the deep forests, by keeping winter snows from melting till late in summer, sufficed by themselves to keep the climate cold. Through these forests roamed an abundance of wild and unfamiliar creatures—ferocious wolves, gigantic elk, enormous mammoths, and a hairy, violent, crafty creature in whom we can recognize our universal ancestor, prehistoric man.

Stone Age man seems to be much the same wherever you find him; partly that is because all that survives from these very early ages is an occasional flint tool and a heap of split marrow bones. Perhaps if he had had caves to decorate, like those in southern France and northern Spain, prehistoric man would have left in Britain some of his paintings and fetishes. But he did not, and mostly we must follow his footsteps dimly and at a distance through the flint scrapers and crude axes that he left behind. Late in the Stone Age, as his mental aspirations and technical capacities increased, early man began building rough fortifications for his family, and tombs for his dead. The forts were built by laying sods one on another to form a circular wall; these rings, surviving for millennia and long overgrown with grass, are likely to be enshrined in folklore as "fairy rings," created by elves and leprechauns for their midnight revels. As for the tombs, they took a simple but very distinctive form. Several stones were set upright in the ground and a big flat stone laid atop them to create what is called a *dolmen* or a *cromlech*. Some of the capstones of these structures are extremely heavy; the tribesmen must have groaned and sweated to raise their primitive tombs. Perhaps, like the Incas in South America, they had slaves to do the backbreaking work; the forts or raths behind which they lived suggest a need for defense, and even in primitive wars human beings reduced to slavery represent a useful and

3. During the Neolithic age (roughly 10,000 to 3000 B.C.), the ice cap had reached down to cover most of Europe. Cave men living in southernmost Spain, within fifty miles of Gibraltar, drew in the dank recesses of their caverns unmistakable pictures of reindeer. Nowadays these creatures are rarely seen south of the Arctic Circle.

portable form of wealth. Sometimes we find huge stones arranged in rings; the best known of these is Stonehenge on Salisbury plain, and while religious rites may have been performed there, its crucial shape was determined by the sun; it was an astronomical calendar and timekeeping device. But not all megalithic (big rock) arrangements had this function. Perhaps they were simply theaters of ritual observances, such as acts of worship to deities embodied in the stars and planets; perhaps human sacrifices were performed there; perhaps special priests, calling themselves Druids or calling themselves something else, officiated; perhaps everyone was a priest. We simply do not know.

Over the long centuries, it is likely that tribal alliances were formed, and cattle raids led to something like small-scale wars. Tribes from one area may have attacked tribes from another, tribes from the Continent may have joined in the mix, fighting with the natives and then intermarrying with them, after the immemorial pattern. Somewhere in this dark pool of time, perhaps around 1000 B.C. (but this is an almost random date), one of the new arrivals brought with him something small and portentous: a dagger of bronze, that is, copper hardened with tin. Copper and tin are found together in Cornwall, but it is not likely that bronze was an indigenous British invention. Once discovered, though, the technique of bronze casting was soon copied and became relatively widespread, without, however, changing the basically Stone Age character of the British tribesmen. For many years they still used flaked flints to make their points, but as their numbers gradually increased, they began to need more tools to clear forests and plough fields. And to satisfy this need, they turned gradually to the iron ore of England, which they smelted in wood fires and hammered into weapons. Growing in sophistication, they learned to kill one another with stones flung in slings, and to attack one another in war chariots drawn by horses. To get horses across the channel, they must have known how to build large and tolerably steady boats. Celebrating the new arrivals, they carved giant white horses in some of the chalk hills of southern England; the largest and oldest is titled, not unreasonably, White Horse Hill in western Berkshire.

THE COMING OF THE CELTS

Somewhere over this thousand years before the birth of Christ, Britain started to be invaded by a new group from the Continent, who supplanted the indigenous (or at least the older) population. These newcomers were a fair-haired Germanic group known as Celts; not the northern Teutons, but of southern, "Alpine" stock. The assumption is that they were quite different from the smaller, darker people whom they replaced.[4] Some of them came from the Low Countries, or

4. The small, dark peoples are sometimes called Iberians on the assumption they came from Spain; there are legends to this effect, there is some ethnographic and a little archaeological evidence. But the argument is far from conclusive.

had at least passed through them, as we now guess, because they used certain pots ("beakers") like those customary in Holland. We are on surer ground when we distinguish two different waves of Celtic invaders, speaking cognate but not identical languages. First came the Goidels, whose language developed into Gaelic, and who wound up inhabiting Ireland, Scotland, and the Isle of Man. After them came the Brythons (Britons) who, if they did not move by preference into Wales, Brittany, and Cornwall, at least wound up preserving their cultural identity and their language patterns there.

In the late nineteenth century a romantic view developed, which represented the gallant Celts being pushed inexorably back to the far fringes of Europe (to the peninsula of Brittany, the remote valleys of Scotland and Wales, and the trackless bogs of Ireland) by those Germanic tribes who in the second or third century A.D. started to become known as Franks. This is probably too simple. There's some evidence that the Bretons-Britons-Brythons who settled on the peninsula of Brittany were Cornish and Welsh refugees from the Saxon invasions of about 450, while the Picts and Scots were not just driven north from England proper, but also crossed over from Ireland. As the Roman Empire expanded into Gaul, pushing the tribes around and squeezing them back toward those eastern enemies whose pressure was unrelenting in the other direction, there was ample opportunity for the peoples to be stirred up and mixed together, for alliances to be made and broken, for new names to be assumed and old identities shed. All these peoples were without the use of letters; their history, such as they had, was handed around by word of mouth; and, as they moved from place to place or changed one leader for another, they might be known by different names. Some linguistic evidence enables us to distinguish, for example, the Goidelic from the Brythonic Celts; but the legends and stories that are told about the origins of the various tribes are almost all picturesque nonsense.

This is not wholly negligible nonsense, since the tales flourished and were recited, either as true histories or just as interesting narratives, over a period of many centuries. The Celts had a brilliantly inventive gift of imagination. Their decorative work was intricate, formal, yet full of animistic detail; their mythology was equally full of grotesque and vital figures laced into an elaborate pattern of fable; and they often exercised their imaginations on stories about their own origins. These stories would be repeated by serious historians during the middle ages and adapted by poets from the Renaissance onward to provide the dramatic core of their romantic legends. A few of them are presented here, not in the least as history, but as illustrations of mythology with a special function, to make connections with some famous figure of the past who might serve as sponsor and (as it were) authority figure for his latter-day descendants.

MYTHS AND LEGENDS

The British myth, unique among these legends in having a late origin and a distinct author (Geoffrey of Monmouth in the twelfth century), reminds us that

Virgil's epic hero Aeneas had a son, Ascanius; from him descended a grandson Sylvius, whose son was named Brut or Brutus. Through a hunting accident, Brutus killed his father, and fled Rome with a few friends, descended from the Trojan associates of Aeneas. Finding Britain uninhabited "except for a few giants," they settled there, founding a "New Troy" or "Troynovant" where London now stands. Their descendants were a line of British kings, including Bladud, Gorboduc, Ferrex and Porrex, Lud, Cymbeline, Coel, Vortigern, Lear, Uther, Arthur, and many others whose names and stories are alluded to in Book II, Canto 10 of Spenser's *Faerie Queene*. Gorboduc and his descendants Ferrex and Porrex were heroes of an early English tragedy, Lear is the central figure of Shakespeare's grandest play, Old King Cole lives in a nursery rhyme, and Lud, by raising a wall around Troynovant, changed its name to Lud's town, hence London. Because there had to be a gate in Lud's wall, a district of London is still called Ludgate.

The men of Cornwall make much of their descent from Corineus, one of Brut's companions. Among the aboriginal giants of Albion, a specially large and obnoxious one bore the Biblical name of Gogmagog (Revelation 20:8); Corineus wrestled with this outsize villain, and threw him into the sea, where he drowned. As reward, Corineus was given the land of Cornwall, where the men have, ever since, been specially fond of wrestling. Debon flung Coulin into a pit and was rewarded with the county of Devon; and Canute destroyed Godmer, receiving therefor the county of Kent with its chief city Canterbury. Meanwhile Albion, father of all these giants, incautiously crossed the channel, where he met Hercules, with the inevitable result—Hercules killed a giant a day without so much as thinking about it.

Many of these stories are obvious back formations from a geographical name already in existence. "Kent" suggests "Cnut" or "Canute," a historic Danish king who lived about A.D. 1000, so by easy transposition he is made a companion of Brut (600 B.C.?) and given a giant to kill. Giants, like dragons, are stock props for testing heroes. To common sense the tales are ridiculous. Yet the fact is that Irish bogs have yielded a good number of ancient skeletons belonging to quite respectable "giants," men over seven feet tall. Perhaps the Celts (who had nothing at all to do with Brutus and Aeneas except for being displaced wanderers like them) really did have to dispose of some giants when they landed on the shores of what was not yet Britain.

Another elaborate set of legends presents the origins of the Irish—i.e., Celtic or Gaelic people. Various invasions by various invaders make up the first part of the story.[5] The first of these visitants was a Greek named Partholan (son of Seara, son of Sru, son of Easru, son of Framant, son of Fathocda, son of Magog,

5. All the episodes of ancient Irish history are precisely dated in the old chronicles; as these dates are calculated on the "year of the world," which is an extremely vague concept at this time, they don't mean much any more. But they lend an air of splendid precision to the chronology, as if someone had actually been present, calendar in hand, in the year of the world 2520, to record Partholan's arrival from Greece (where, by the way, nobody ever heard of him).

son of Japhet, son of Noah, whose descent from Adam can easily be traced in the first few chapters of Genesis). He came, fleeing like Brut from the guilt of a parricide, and settled near Dublin, where his offspring ruled for three hundred years till they all died of the plague—proper, if misplaced, punishment for Partholan's original sin. The next arrival was a Scythian warrior named Nemed, whose followers fought a mighty battle with some African sea pirates calling themselves Fomorians. A few of the Nemedians survived, and late in the eighth century B.C. they were joined by a third wave of Greek immigrants known as Firbolgs. The Firbolgs were shortly supplanted by the tribes of the god Danu (Tuatha dé Danaan), who arrived from Greece via Scandinavia and Scotland, establishing a kingdom at Tara and fighting a savage battle against the Firbolgs at Moytura. Then, after some two hundred years of Danaan rule, the climactic invasion took place. Miletus of Spain, whose ancestor was Fenius Farsaigh, king of Scythia (direct descendant through Magog and Japhet of Noah), had eight heroic sons. They invaded Ireland, and though some were slain by the magic spells of the Danaans, others by the treachery of the mean-spirited Firbolgs, two survived. Heber and Heremon divided the kingdom between them and established a succession of Milesian kings with whose difficult names, in the absence of distinct identities, we need not be concerned. But ever since, the Irish have been a people divided between noble Milesians and treacherous, underhanded Firbolgs, heroic leaders of the people and malignant informers.

RELIGIOUS MYTHS

Myths of origin may also have religious coloration. After the Crucifixion, we read that Joseph of Arimathea, owner of the holy cup from which Christ drank at the last supper, which had also been used to gather His blood at Golgotha, entered a little boat which was directed miraculously across the Mediterranean, out the straits of Gibraltar, and across the bay of Biscay to the Celtic settlement of Glastonbury in Somersetshire.[6] There, weaving wattles and willow branches together, he built the first Christian church in England; there he deposited the Holy Grail, which king Arthur's knights would later spend so much time in seeking; and there, placing his staff in the earth, he saw it miraculously flower into the fabulous Glastonbury thornbush. During the middle ages, thousands of

---

6. With the decorative addition of the three Marys (Mary the wife of Cleophas, Mary Magdalen, and Mary the mother of God), a very similar story is told by the French about *their* holy place, Les Saintes Maries de la Mer, near the mouth of the Rhone. The improbabilities of both tales are patent. But during the age of Elizabeth, apologists for the Reformation (including the queen herself) used the myth to argue that England never owed anything to Rome except priestly corruptions and papal usurpations. From the wellhead in Palestine, England received her Christianity pure and undefiled, with Joseph of Arimathea. England was Christian long before the first missionaries came from Rome to convert her. Whether or not Elizabeth believed this story, she found it handy.

pilgrims came to visit the sacred spot and touch the marvelous thornbush. As it happened, this was the very spot to which King Arthur retired after his final, fatal battle with the traitor Mordred: Glastonbury was really the isle of Avalon. (In fact, the town had been built, as the Celts were fond of building for defensive purposes, in the middle of a swamp; hence Glastonbury, though fifteen miles from the sea, might be an "isle," just as the town of Ely, near Cambridge, is set on a little rise of solid ground in the midst of the fen country, and so constitutes "the isle of Ely.") Glastonbury was therefore twice sacred and remained so till the Reformation of the sixteenth century, when Henry VIII murdered the last abbot, tore apart the ancient church, and chopped down the sacred thornbush, all in the name of religious "purity."

One institution of the ancient Celts calling for particular mention because it has been so lavishly romanticized is the class of priests-poets-prophets known as Druids. Roman historians, Tacitus particularly, describe them, not very sympathetically, but in broad, clear outlines. They were not a caste or group inheriting special privileges, but a college of individuals who had earned their position through an arduous and protracted training program. They had to memorize and recite unprompted the long heroic poems which constituted the history of the race; they also intervened with the presiding deities to implore guidance or favors. Their sacred services were conducted in oak groves, where they performed sacrifices and offered prayers. Originally the sacrifices were probably of human beings, prisoners or criminals; later, their place was taken by animals or other symbolic figures. Within the tribal society, Druids wielded wide power; they advised the king on questions of war and peace, they acted as diplomats and ambassadors, they led the tribe into battle. Their blessings and imprecations were accepted as having immense, immediate power; they could blast an enemy or shower blessings on an ally. When, in A.D. 61, Suetonius Paulinus led his Roman legions against the sacred island of Anglesey (Mona) off the coast of Wales, he was met by a line of screaming women and Druid priests, hurling divine maledictions and advancing fearlessly against the Roman discipline. After a moment of superstitious hesitation, the leaders were cut to pieces, the sacred groves hacked down, and the order exterminated—except in the imaginations of men. People who feel, with Shelley, that poets are the unacknowledged legislators of the world are impressed with the fact that the Druids were *acknowledged* legislators. They have lived on, in the poetry of Milton, Gray, and Yeats, not to mention the grand opera of Bellini (*Norma*).

ROMANS IN BRITAIN

From the clouds of myth we emerge, if only briefly, into the clear light of day, with Julius Caesar's two invasions of Britain, in 55 and 54 B.C. These were not serious efforts at conquest; during his first visit, Caesar scarcely moved off the

Kentish beaches on which he landed with a single legion, and in the next year he pushed only a few miles north of the Thames with five. Caesar, it would seem, was not much impressed with the British; he had seen brave, disorganized barbarians before and evidently concluded that there was no profit, material or political, to be had from a full-scale conquest. He made a few short marches, declared the country conquered, imposed on it a heavy fine (never collected), and withdrew to winter quarters in Gaul, to compose another chapter of his military memoirs.

The Britons, however (meaning by them the two recent breeds of invading Celts, still very little mixed in with the previous mixture of indigenous and invading peoples), were rather more impressed with the Romans, especially the creature comforts of life in Roman Gaul. There had always been some trade across the channel, now there was more; and when, about a century later, the emperor Claudius decided to have a proper conquest of England, the island had already been partly Romanized. Claudius was not himself a warlike or aggressive man; he was actually invited into Britain by a tribal chief who felt himself aggrieved by one of the sons of Cunobelin, whom we know, after Shakespeare's play, as Cymbeline. Claudius not only sent 40,000 crack troops into Britain; after they had conquered London, or the place where that city now stands, he appeared there in person, and for a while took charge. Splitting into three groups, the Romans fanned out through the flatlands and undulating hills of southern England, conquering the natives or leaving them under the control of puppet rulers. For some time they were held up by fierce resistance in the Welsh mountains; in the slaughter of the Druid bards we noted above a grim terminal episode of that struggle. And they never did eliminate the Celts whom they drove across the Irish sea or up into Scotland, where they became distinguished as Picts and Scots.[7] Having cleared the flatlands, the Romans built a wall to keep out barbarians in the north, and planted garrisons to watch over restless remnants of the old civilization in the mountains of Wales.

ROADS, TOWNS, COMFORTS

Where they prevailed, the Romans installed a typically Roman civilization (SFR, A.4). That meant armed camps which developed into towns—a real novelty for

---

7. "Picts" from the Latin word for "painted," because the warriors were in the way of painting their bodies blue with the juice of the woad plant. The reason for "Scots" is less clear, though an origin in the Greek word for "dark" has often been satirically proposed. Some of the Scots were early or late immigrants from Ireland, which the Romans never captured or even attacked. (About A.D. 80 Julius Agricola looked hungrily toward Ireland but was never granted leave to make a move.) Likely the absence of Romans is one reason for the richness of ancient Irish art and the fullness of Celtic mythology in Ireland (SFR, A.14).

the natives, who were used to tribes, not cities. All English towns with names ending in -*caster* or -*chester* (Doncaster, Winchester, Gloucester, Chester) take those names from Latin "camp," *castrum*. Romanization also terminated Celtic styles of ornament and design; they were not forbidden, that we know, but went out of style. Out in the country, it's likely that the Roman conquest disturbed little; field hands must have dressed, talked, and worshiped as they always had. There was an active commercial life; there must have been some intermarriage. Britain also rejoiced in a system of roads, splendid roads, well paved and engineered. The Romans were the supreme road builders of antiquity, and the roads they built in Britain were the best the country would know till the middle of the nineteenth century. Some stretches of Roman road are still usable to this day, after almost 2,000 years. A few of them were simply Roman improvements of pre-existing routes; others were engineered from scratch. Among the most famous (by their later English names) are Ermine Street, which ran due north from London through York to the Scottish wall; Icknield Street, an older road connecting with several more modern extensions, running west from London along the southern coastline; and Watling Street, which ran northwest through Verulamium (modern Saint Albans) to Wroxeter near Shrewsbury. These three roads can be seen as three fingers splaying out from London; and a fourth road, called the Fosse, cut diagonally across their outer ends, from Ilchester in the southwest to Lincoln, just south of York. There were hundreds of other roads in Britain, and some of them the Romans made. But these four laced together the central lowlands of England, tying the outlying districts to the capital at London, as well as to each other. In the uplands and outlands, however, beyond the area they chose to civilize, the Romans built few roads and founded no towns (SFR,A.2).

Within their chosen boundaries, the Romans settled down to be comfortable, and comfortable they were. Their little towns were built, just as in Italy, around forums; they raised temples, erected statues, and paved their floors with decorative mosaics. At Verulamium, they put up the one and only outdoor theater in Britain; in Bath, where the mineral waters invited it, they built baths, just as luxurious though not as grandiose as those in Rome. Out in the countryside they built villas from which, with the help of native labor (slave or half-free), they directed farms. Finding lead and iron beneath the soil, they operated mines and small metal-working shops. But the true prosperity of the land rested on the export of wheat and wool. Plentiful English rainfall, well-drained English soil, and mild English weather cooperated to make these products the best of their kind in Europe. They were eagerly bought up, and in exchange the semi-assimilated Romano-Britons acquired luxuries like wine, olive oil, objects of glass, oriental spices—the delicacies and amenities of civilization. From soldiers garrisoned in Britain, they picked up as well a flavoring of the many religions prevalent in the empire. Mithra, the Persian sun god, was familiar among the legions, but an eastern rival was making headway against him: the crucified god,

Jesus. Perhaps because they shared many points of similarity, the two cults were bitterly hostile; but here in Britain, where both were tiny minorities, there was no reason for conflict. About what their soldiers believed, the Roman officials knew little and cared less.

The land was at peace, give or take a sporadic revolt here, a hit-and-run incursion there. Outcast barbarians sulked in their mountain retreats, but dared not challenge the legions guarding Roman Britain. The use of Latin became general among proprietors, *possessores;* such people dressed in the Roman fashion, did their business with Roman coins, traveled freely across the short seas to Roman Gaul. The famous Greco-Egyptian astronomer-geographer Claudius Ptolemy, who wrote in the middle of the second century A.D., knew a good deal about southern England and Ireland. He had never visited these outlandish places, but he talked with men who had done so; and while he makes ludicrous errors about the northern parts of the islands, he is surprisingly exact about the southern districts. No doubt the Roman tax collector was not greeted with shouts of joy; still, the protection of Roman soldiers and the advantages of Roman roads must have been worth a good deal. The prosperity of Roman Britain came to a peak in the third century. But toward the end of that period, sinister developments started to overshadow this brief era of light and urbanity—and, it may be added, of cultural torpor. Early in the fourth century, it was necessary to establish along the east coast of England a special military guard against Saxon pirates. As Goths, Huns, and Vandals increased their pressure on the empire's heartland, as the Roman road system across Gaul became infested with tribes of murderous nomadic barbarians, the troops garrisoning Britain were needed for service closer to home, and the province was increasingly left to its own devices. About the middle of the fourth century, the walls to the north were breached, and Pictish invaders started to raid the once peaceful fields and villages of Roman Britain. As word spread of the easy pickings to be had, Scots from Ireland[8] crossed over to raid on their own, and to battle with the Welsh and Picts over the spoils. Word of these barbaric goings-on reached Rome in time for Claudius Claudianus, last of the truly classical poets, to include a few words about them in his poems of servile compliment to the barbarian general Stilicho, then in service to the weakest and most contemptible of Roman emperors, Honorius. Thanks to the mighty Stilicho, Claudian has grateful Britain declare, "I need not fear the Scottish arms or tremble at the Pict or keep watch along my coasts for the Saxon who would come on any vagrant wind." So the poet, a supple Alexandrian Greek polishing his flattery for a rough barbarian patron; but the truth was very different. Neither Picts, Scots, nor Saxons had ever heard of the mighty Stilicho, nor did they care a rap for him, as long as he stayed in Rome. And meanwhile it was grim weather

8. They are known as the Dalriad Scots; they came at first, as on summer vacations, to loot and murder; later they settled into western Scotland. If it seems odd that the early Scots were really Irish, one should recall that an early scholastic philosopher, John Scotus of the ninth century, was born in Ireland, as his sobriquet "Erigena" (*Erinn-genitus,* Irish-born) indicates.

blowing up in Britain for the helpless sheep and their equally helpless herdsmen. By 410, the last of the legions had left the island.

SAXON WOLVES

Who were these Saxons, of whom we start to hear at the end of the fourth century? Like the Celts before them, they were a Germanic tribe from somewhere in the east, occupying, in the later stages of their wanderings, the middle part of that peninsula which today we call Denmark. Their neighbors in the province of Schleswig were called Angles or Angli, and the two tribes, mingling and intermarrying in the process, seem to have made common cause against tribal enemies in nearby Germany, like the Franks, Salii, and Hermunduri, dwellers in the deep Thuringian forest. The part of Denmark where the Angles and Saxons settled is low and boggy; and from these bogs has been recovered a good deal of material from which we can get an idea of their civilization. They had the use of iron, from which they forged long swords and heavy battle-axes; and because they lived on the offshore islands as well as the mainland, they were quite at home on the water. Complete ships from a much later age survived in grave mounds and can now be seen in historical museums, like that at Oslo, Norway; and from them we can surmise what these early Saxon vessels were like. High in the prow and at the stern, they were low in the waist where the rowers sat on benches; they were broad in the middle, pinching to a point at each end, so they were almost as easy to move backward as forward. When the wind was favorable, they could hoist a single square sail and skim over the water; to go against the wind, though by ever so little, the mariners had to down sail and row. For the vessels had little draft and hardly any keel; though this limited their sailing possibilities, it was advantageous in other ways: the ships could be rowed up shallow inlets and required practically no harbor facilities. And as each vessel could carry about four times as many warriors as it had oars (we may assume these early boats had not fewer than thirty oars), each ship was like a floating garrison.

The men who crossed the wild North Sea in cockleshells like this were very tough customers indeed. Fighting was just about their only interest in life— fighting and getting enough loot to support them in glorious idleness till it was time to fight again. Their social organization emphasized the absolute importance of kinship and loyalty to the head of one's tribe; the most potent of all their gods was Ty or Tyr, the god of war. About the afterlife they did not think very much; probably most of them imagined it as a place where successful warriors got together, drank mead, and boasted of their prowess. In battle, their weapons were swords, spears, and heavy axes; they wore helmets and coats of mail (birnies), they carried shields. To begin with, they crossed the seas during the favorable summer season, caught the crops just as they were ripe for harvesting, and returned before winter; such a short campaigning season limited them to attacking settlements near the coast. About the middle of the fifth century a band of vagrant Saxons, or perhaps they were Jutes,[9] led by warriors to whom later ages assigned, on doubtful authority, the names of Hengist and Horsa, came to England. They landed at Ebbsfleet on the Kent side of the Thames estuary, and were granted by King Vortigern a permanent home on the nearby island of Thanet. (It has not been an island since the channel silted up in the sixteenth century.) Vortigern wanted to use these dangerous acquaintances to fight off some troublesome Picts to the north. But the crafty barbarians said that without reinforcements they were unequal to so large a task; they would have to send home for more warriors. Vortigern took the bait. Angles, Saxons, and Jutes arrived in quantity, and before long they had defeated not only the Picts, but their host and his band of disorganized warriors, driving them back into the swamps and mountains of western England. This was a relatively easy job because the Romans had set up their defenses against enemies coming from the west and north; the new invaders came from the south and east, and once ashore there was nothing to stop them. When they found themselves securely settled in the new land, they promptly acquired horses, which enabled them to make long, swift raids inland.

ARTHUR THE BRITON

A victim of the Saxons who hid away in remote Cornwall and southern Wales was a leader named Uther or Arthur. We know him as King Arthur, lord of the knights of the Table Round, the original of Tennyson's mournful gentleman in the *Idylls of the King*. What the historic Arthur was like is an agreeable if idle speculation; hardly anything can be seen through the mists of time except that he rallied the Welsh and Cornish outlaws, fought sundry battles, and was destroyed, perhaps by a traitorous friend or deceitful wife. Whether the tale of his exploits was carried directly to French Brittany by Britons fleeing the Saxon onslaught or ripened for centuries in Wales before crossing the channel has been much mooted. There can be little question that it germinated for a long time in darkness, getting confused here and there with sundry vegetation myths, solar legends, and fertil-

9. The evidence that the Jutes, also called Geats, came from Jutland lies mainly in their name. Bede says that in Denmark they were on one side of the Angles, the Saxons on the other; but Bede had no first-hand knowledge of Denmark, and was writing nearly three hundred years after events of 450. Indeed, there was for a while a separate Jutish kingdom in Kent and southernmost England, so it's probable that Hengist and Horsa, if they existed at all, were of that stock. (There is also some evidence that the Jutes did not come directly to England, but stopped off in the Rhineland where they picked up some Frankish institutions.) In the early pages of *Finnegans Wake,* James Joyce imagines a hilarious dialogue between an indigenous Mutt and an invading Jute; despite many linguistic problems, they are astoneaged to make each other's acquaintance.

ity rites; it accumulated episodes and used up heroes.[10] Over the centuries, it got heavily Christianized, and in Geoffrey of Monmouth's *History of the Kings of Britain* (early twelfth century), it swelled briefly to monstrous proportions. (Arthur not only becomes emperor of Britain, he carries his career of conquest abroad, and expands his sway as far as Rome.) Early or late, the saga crossed the channel to Brittany where professional minstrels picked it up, broke it into a number of short, interlaced narratives, and passed them along to Chrétien de Troyes (late twelfth century), who made of them the substance of his poetic life work. Legendary materials based on the story of Arthur and his companions now became the common property of Europe; and, as different artists selected different parts of the story for use as diverting fable or pseudo-history, they naturally invented new characters or gave new coloring to old ones. Arthur himself was sometimes the boldest of all his knights, sometimes a sleepy old dotard, like Charlemagne in the other great cycle of romantic legends. The story of the Holy Grail, mixed with various Celtic fertility rituals and tales of pre-Christian heroes, was grafted onto the basic story of the Table Round. The story of Tristan and Iseult, once quite independent, also got built into the larger cycle of Arthur stories; the jointing was perfunctorily done, and you can still see that the story doesn't quite "belong" in Arthurian company. Other additions and changes were freely made as the tales went their rounds. In a word, the Arthur legend is a tiny grain of fifth-century fact around which have been deposited layer upon layer of other miscellaneous material from every kind of random source. We shall have more to say of it later, in connection with Sir Thomas Malory particularly; but as the Anglo-Saxon tide sweeps over Roman Britain, we have no business thinking of Lancelot and Guinevere, Galahad and the Holy Grail. The Germanic horde is at the gate; they have driven off the cattle, torched the farmhouse, slaughtered the pig, raped the women, and are even now torturing the landlord—you can hear his choked screams—to find out where his money is hidden. For the old proprietors, it is lights out; whether the ragged, semistarved serf working his field in a lonely forest clearing recognized or regretted the Saxon invasion, we cannot know.

CELT AND SAXON

The social, cultural, and literary doings of the Anglo-Saxons are reserved for the next chapter; for the moment, we must concentrate on the imaginative achievements of the Celts. This split may create a false impression of chronological

---

10. Heroes of romances have a tendency to deteriorate with use; from an immaculate knight in the early tales, Gawain degenerated to a very soiled and battered character in the later ones. He is, among other things, a curious example of a solar myth domesticated in a chivalric tale; in Malory, his strength increases till noon, then declines (SFR, C.11).

sequence, as if Celtic literature came first and Anglo-Saxon literature afterward. That is only partly true. Indeed, Celts had been on the British Isles long before the Saxons came in the fifth century; but they were not completely supplanted at that time. By absorbing the Saxon invaders as formerly she had absorbed the Romans, the island of England protected that of Ireland. Celts also survived in Wales, on the Cornwall peninsula, and across the channel in Brittany—and in these places Celtic literature survived alongside the Saxon. To be sure, the manuscripts in which all these materials are recorded date from periods much later than the fifth century. They may reproduce still earlier manuscripts, but those manuscripts, or the manuscripts from which *they* were copied, mostly go back to an oral tradition, the "real" date of which is unknowable, since oral traditions are unlikely to have any precise point of origin. Of one thing we can be pretty sure: some of the Saxon stories go back before the time this tribe came to England. So priority is hard to establish, and it's a mere matter of convenience to describe Celtic literary legends first and Anglo-Saxon ones second. But separate they must be, because they are so very different. And because Celtic legends are all difficult to date, as well as because many of them remained a long time on the fringe of English literature, relatively inert, we shall describe them here as a group, without trying to be nice about their chronology.

CELTIC MYTHOLOGY

The first thing to note about the Celtic material produced or preserved in Ireland is its immense quantity. The libraries of Europe contain thousands of pages of old Irish materials. But a great deal of this material is reduplication—the same material recopied. A great many pages are devoted to those fantastic genealogies and accounts of prehistoric invasions noted above; and still others are filled with annals (the events of Ireland, year by year) and historical records; though unreliable as formal history, these pages may be of human interest. There are a good many books of saints' lives, martyrologies, Irish commentaries on Biblical texts—again, not without interest, but patently of an age much later than the earliest. Finally, there is a mass of narrative materials, more or less epic in form, more or less fragmentary as it has come down to us, relating the deeds of gods and heroes in the primitive era of Celtic society. These are the pre-Christian years, the years of heroic tribal warfare; the similarity of these Irish heroes and their war deeds to the heroes and deeds of the Homeric poems is a commonplace. The largest and best known of these fragments, which may serve as a sample of the rest, is preserved in a twelfth-century manuscript known for sacred reasons as "The Book of the Dun Cow."[11] It is a miscellany of stories which were already

11. Saint Ciaran's favorite bovine at Clonmacnoise sacrificed her pelt to make the vellum in which the original manuscript of these texts was bound. The vellum has long since disappeared, the grateful memory remains.

ancient when the book was assembled; most of them belong to the "Ulster cycle" of stories about kings of the northern "Red Branch," notably King Conchobar and the fiery young hero Cúchullin. *The Cattle Raid of Cooley* (Tain Bo Cualnge) is a main feature of this collection; it describes how Maeve, queen of Connaught, organizes a raid to carry off the great Brown bull of Cooley. She is warned by Fergus the Druid that Cúchullin, though only a boy of seventeen, possesses supernatural strength, capable of confounding all her warriors. She pushes forward anyway, but after a series of preliminary conflicts, the marvelous boy goes into one of his preternatural rages or frenzies, and after killing his old companion Fer Diad, puts to flight the hosts of Maeve. The story ends with a general melee of the peoples, in which both the sacred bulls of Ireland (Maeve's original White Horn bull and the Brown bull she was trying to steal) are killed.

The story is ancient. Druid Fergus is the supreme religious authority, and the emphasis on cattle rustling suggests we are back in an age when kine were the chief form of portable wealth—before the invention of money, in other words. The warriors fight in chariots; typically, they behead a defeated enemy, and sling the heads they have accumulated over the necks of their horses. In battle they are accompanied by savage war dogs. Much of the story's action turns on a supernatural curse laid on the men of Ulster by a powerful witch-woman. As in Homer, there is a great deal of heroic bragging, and there are occasional touches of grim or grotesque humor. These are more marked in one of the smaller appended epics of about the same period, *Bricriu's Feast*. At a feast given by the mischief-maker Bricriu, three Ulster heroes and their wives vie, first in boasts, then in deeds, for the title of bravest and strongest. Cúchullin is generally successful; but the tests are prolonged, and culminate in a grotesque "beheading contest" similar to that in the English story of "Sir Gawain and the Green Knight."

There are a great many more stories in the "Ulster cycle" of Celtic legend, and there is another entire cycle of primitive stories from the south of Ireland, dealing with Finn MacCool, his trusty band of Fenian comrades, and his son the warrior-poet Ossian. Readers of Yeats and Joyce will recognize, again and again, in the characters and episodes of ancient Irish legend, the originals of persons and events, as well as the point of hundreds of allusions, in these modern writers. A major reason for the revival of this material starting in the nineteenth century was the activity of scholars who searched out and edited the old texts, while men of letters retold in modern English the old Gaelic stories. The work of Kuno Meyer, Ernst Windisch, Arbois de Jubainville, Eugene O'Curry, Standish O'Grady, Patrick Weston Joyce, Douglas Hyde, and Eleanor Hull, to mention no others, amounted to rediscovery of an entire buried culture. Meanwhile, the archaeological evidence for this entire period of prehistory was accumulating as scientific exploration, augmented by a number of lucky finds, brought to light more and more of ancient Irish civilization. At a time when many of the themes familiar to English literature since the Renaissance were starting to play out, a

Celtic revival was far from mere nostalgia, it was a recovery of fresh and vital imaginative impulses (SFR, A. 15).

EARLY CHRISTIAN IRELAND

The extended period of eclipse between the epic age and the nineteenth-century revival of its glories is palpable but not as vast as it seems, for the language and its culture continued to flourish well into the modern era. We hear of schools and books being widespread in the land when Saint Patrick arrived (A.D. 432 is the traditional date), bringing a fresh access of Christianity to the Irish. It seems likely that Patrick was a Welshman by birth, and had spent some involuntary time in Ireland as the captive of some pirates. It is pretty definite that Pope Celestine I chose Patrick to convert Ireland after the failure of an earlier envoy, Palladius; and it is probable that Patrick had some disputes with the local Druids. But the huge folklore of miracles and supernatural feats, the banishing of reptiles, the visit to purgatory, the demonstration of the Trinity from a shamrock, call for several grains of salt. Of his practical success there can be no doubt at all. Ireland was Christianized quickly and thoroughly, well before England.[12] Indeed, the Irish found something deeply congenial, not only in Christianity, but in the monastic ideal. They formed religious schools and communities which attracted as many as 5,000 aspirants; they retreated from the world into solitary hermitages on the northern islands or deep in the Irish bogs. With Christianity came the introduction of a Roman alphabet, replacing the very cumbersome Ogham script;[13] the combination of many monks with undisturbed time and a new flexible technique of writing resulted in that immense volume of manuscript material noted above. It also resulted in the most beautiful hand-lettered and hand-illuminated books that the world has ever seen. The eighth-century Book of Kells, long preserved in the monastery of that name and now in the library of Trinity College, Dublin, is so intricately decorated and elaborately patterned that a single page must have taken years of precise labor to complete. Almost as splendid is the Book of Armagh. The designs are never stiff or mechanical, despite their complexity; they are alive with little creatures and people, with vines and lines that bewilder yet gratify the eye that tries to follow them. A

12. Bede is responsible for the famous story about Saint Gregory, that passing through the Roman forum, he saw some handsome young slaves for sale, was told they were Angles, and produced his celebrated pun: "not Angles, indeed, but angels." He set off to convert their land in person, but was recalled to become Pope Gregory I, sending instead Saint Augustine (to be distinguished carefully from the earlier, more famous Saint Augustine, author of *The City of God*). Augustine became first archbishop of Canterbury; but he did not set foot in England till 597, 165 years after Patrick came to Ireland.

13. Ogham has an alphabet of twenty characters, represented by combinations of horizontal or vertical lines with dots. These can easily be carved on stones, but we don't find many extensive texts of Ogham; it was apparently as hard to read as it was easy to write.

medieval visitor, seeing one of these manuscripts, could only suppose it had been done with divine assistance. Yet when Viking pirates started to raid Ireland in the eighth and ninth centuries, these splendid books had to be buried in the earth, while the monasteries in which the scribes had worked year after patient year were burned to the ground. For safe keeping, many Irish books were removed at this time to Europe; with them went Irish scholars, who brought to the still-dark Continent the light of learning long preserved in Irish monasteries. The Benedictine house of Saint Gall in Switzerland, famous for its library in which there are many Celtic manuscripts, owes its foundation to an Irish hermit who settled there in the seventh century; Virgil, abbot of Aghaboe in Leinster, went abroad in 745 to become archbishop of Salzburg and to be canonized (Saint Virgil) after his death. He was famous as an astronomer, his Irish name was Fergil, and his family, under the name of O'Farrell, are active in Irish affairs to this day. Or so a believing man may believe. Irish teachers not only returned to the Continent, with interest, the light they had borrowed with the coming of Patrick; they crossed the Irish seas to teach in Saxon England during the ninth and tenth centuries. At Glastonbury, there was a regular college of Irish professors.

THE SLOW DEATH OF CELTIC CULTURE

Even after the Reformation, when Gaelic was a despised tongue and Irish Catholic priests a pariah breed to be exterminated like vermin, historians and chroniclers continued to work in the language of the outlaw.[14] Geoffrey Keating accumulated in Gaelic an immense if overcredulous history of early Ireland; he wrote while on the run from Protestant priest-catchers of the early seventeenth century. About the same time, the so-called "Four Masters" (three O'Clery's and an O'Mulconry) were collecting their annals of events on the island from the beginning to 1616. These compendia are valuable, less as guides to the past, than as gatherings of ancient records and legendary traditions which in their original forms have disappeared. Even Gaelic poetry continued, though in diminished and sometimes vulgarized form. Turlough O'Carolan, the blind harpist and singer who died in 1738, was reputed at the time to be the last of the bards; but Yeats saw in a Dublin street singer of his youth yet another, and the tradition may not be altogether dead, even now.

We might speak at greater length of Irish civilization as it was before Viking raids and English conquests destroyed it—might elaborate on the amazing achievements of Irish goldsmiths, the fame of Irish musicians, the many Irish translations from classical tongues, or the mysterious round towers, which are needles of stone with a few tiny windows and no conceivable practical functions. But we must hasten forward to note that Wales too had a culture of great antiq-

14. That Gaelic was for long considered "the language of the outlaw" probably helps explain why relatively few Celtic words have been adopted into English.

uity and variety, which suffered general neglect for many years but then revived in the nineteenth century. Perhaps Welsh writers suffered neglect because of a tendency to violent obscurity which has afflicted their poets down to and including Dylan Thomas. An early epic remains, in chaotic form; it seems to describe battles between Saxons and their Welsh foemen, but is very dark. The master-piece of early Welsh literature is the collection of romantic prose tales known as *The Mabinogion;* eleven of these stories survive in a single miscellaneous vol-ume, *The Red Book of Hergest,* and of these eleven, four seem to be primitive beyond the others.[15] These are true *mabinogi,* stories for the instruction of young bards. The others are later, chivalric additions to the mythology, some of them Arthurian, others actual translations from the French. About the basic *mabinogi* there is a wild, fantastic energy; the stories deal with passionate blood feuds, mysterious enchantments, dark bargains with the underworld, magical transfor-mations. As in Ireland, this strain of grotesque and primitive feeling survived in Wales to fuse with chivalric tales of King Arthur's court—the rituals of animistic religion transfusing their queer vitality into tales of knights, ladies, and the rare-fied passions of Christian mysticism. The same strains of natural feeling flowered also in a school of Welsh poetry, of which Dafydd ap Gwilym was the most admired representative. He flourished in the last half of the fourteenth century, an almost exact contemporary of Chaucer; his verses are the despair of translators because of the subtlety with which the ladies who are his ostensible theme blend into the natural landscape which is apparently only their setting. An eloquent appreciation of his poetry may be found in the nineteenth chapter of George Borrow's autobiographical novel *Lavengro.*

Welsh poetry retained its vitality in part through a peculiarly Welsh institution, the eisteddfod, or national poetry festival. This was no routine "festival of the arts," but a national assembly convoked from time to time when the poet-priests of the nation felt the need for it. Harps were tuned, songs sung, prizes awarded; in addition, the deep history of the folk was called to mind and the present situation of the nation discussed. The eisteddfods were not without strong polit-ical implications, and English governments were sometimes reluctant to permit their calling; they did much to prevent Welsh poetry from degenerating into that merely verbal word play which in "civilized" societies it sometimes becomes. As a footnote, we may add that during the eighteenth century the more inspira-tional connections of Methodism made great headway among the Welsh, and converted their lyrical impulses to hymn singing. They promptly turned this often-dreary practice into an exhibition of virtuoso vocalism. Welsh choirs are world famous, and it's often been noted that any time half a dozen Welshmen get together, it won't be long before they're singing in harmony, and probably a hymn.

15. Lady Charlotte Guest, a versatile and tireless Victorian lady, made the earliest translation of the *Mabinogion;* it is still standard. Her version appeared from 1838 to 1849, at a time when interest in things Welsh was reviving.

Scotland produced a little early literature in Gaelic, and the language never wholly died out; nowadays, a conscious effort to revive it, paralleling a similar effort in Ireland, is being made by nationalists. But most of the Scottish contribution was made in the fifteenth century and in that dialect of English (northern English) used by the Scottish followers of Chaucer, notably Gavin Douglas, William Dunbar, Robert Henryson, and Sir David Lindsay. There will be occasion to consider them in due chronological order. Meanwhile, let us register the small but special gift of Scotland to early Celtic literature, along with even smaller contributions from Cornwall and the Isle of Man. For linguists and archaeologists, these cultural fragments are of great interest; for a broad history of English they are undoubtedly peripheral.

Technically, no writings in languages other than English make a part of English literary history. But the wild strains of Celtic fancy intertwine so regularly and richly with the solid Saxon stock, that one cannot neglect or minimize them. Pure native English is as much an artificial fantasy as the true-born Englishman; like the society, the language has grown by a process of accretion, picking up whatever stuck, from whatever source. There is nothing unique about the English example, except, perhaps, the number and variety of directions in which the culture's imaginative roots can be traced. In future, we shall be following for the most part the single story of English in its passage through the centuries. Before starting that trip, it's well to be reminded of the rich variety of Celtic elements which both underlie the Saxon tree trunk and twine lovingly around its spreading branches.

Though mythical and magical stories have been told about Stonehenge ever since it has stood on Salisbury plain—that is, for close to four thousand years—speculation about its origins started only in the seventeenth century. Some early students thought it a Roman structure, others attributed it to the Danes, still others said the Druids erected it, while a final theory assigned it to the Saxons. All these guesses fell far short of Stonehenge's real age and the complexity of its ancient history. John Constable, when he sketched Stonehenge in 1820, did not know, any better than anyone else, who wrestled into place these immense monoliths. (Some weigh as much as thirty tons.) But his picture somehow captures both the immensity and the sense of hoary antiquity which in Hardy's novel *Tess of the D'Urbervilles* bring the tormented Tess to gaze on its misty, elemental magnitudes, and find there a sort of peace.

While the prehistoric constructions known as dolmens are found throughout Europe, they are particularly numerous in Ireland and on the peninsula of Brittany. Though they can be dated only approximately, some may well go back to 3500 B.C. or thereabouts. Folklore has, naturally, invented hundreds of stories to account for these rude, massive constructs, but we do not know for sure what sort of people put them up, or why—only that, as the stones are very heavy and the workmen had few tools, shaping, moving, lifting, and putting them in place must have required enormous expenditures of energy.

The little Saxon church of St. Lawrence at Bradford on Avon is no more than 25 feet long, dark as a pocket, and quite unadorned. From the twelfth to the nineteenth century, it was not recognized as a church at all. But someone reading in the old chronicles learned that Saint Aldhelm, in the seventh century, had built a church in Bradford; and this apparently was it. So St. Lawrence was reconsecrated, more as an antiquity and a curiosity than as a working church. Aldhelm himself was a shining light among the scholars of his day, but the Saxon sense of architecture was rudimentary.

Thirteen centuries underground have, understandably, left the helmet found in the Sutton Hoo ship grave rather badly disintegrated; but a tentative reconstruction of the remaining fragments yields a piece of armor rather like this, suggestive of a formidable fighting man.

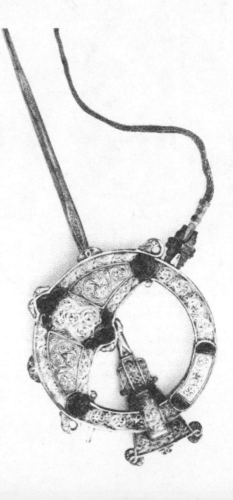

The hill of Tara in County Meath was the primeval seat of the *ard-ris* (high kings) of ancient Ireland; this was well before Scarlett O'Hara's family bestowed the name on their palatial Georgia plantation in *Gone with the Wind*. But, apart from its obvious splendor, the so-called "Tara brooch" has no more real connection with one place than the other. It was found in 1850 by a boy playing on the beach near the seaside town of Drogheda; there was absolutely nothing around it to explain its presence there. It consists of fine filigree goldwork, ornamented with amber, glass, and enamel; our picture shows the reverse side, which is slightly less damaged than the front surface. The brooch is a marvel of workmanship, but its strange reappearance after a millennium of total obscurity comes close to the miraculous.

The Book of Kells, a manuscript copy of the four Gospels, was probably written and drawn—illuminated, in a word—on the holy island of Iona in the eighth century. Carried for "safekeeping" to the monastery of Kells (County Meath), it survived numerous stormings and burnings by Viking raiders, once by lying buried for some years in the ground. This page contains, in Latin, the first two words of the first verse of the first chapter of the Gospel according to Matthew. They are "Liber generationis," i.e., the book of the generation of Jesus Christ, his genealogy from Abraham to Joseph the husband of Mary. Most of the letters making up "generationis" can be found in the rectangle lower right; the "Liber" is harder to assemble. Early readers wrote the two words in ordinary script at the bottom of the page to help later readers. The wide-eyed Irishman at the left is not the reader, but Saint Matthew himself, holding his book.

For seventy miles, from the river Tyne and the North Sea to Solway Firth and the Irish Sea, the first and greatest Roman wall, called Hadrian's, stretched across northern England. Three Roman legions worked on it for ten solid years (123–133); they produced a masonry barrier some twelve feet high, with a wide ditch in front of it. Turrets and blockhouses studded the wall, as well as sixteen forts, which were in effect little towns built into the wall itself. Such a massive structure to protect against roving tribes neither numerous nor well armed may seem disproportionate. But by Hadrian's day the empire was everywhere on the defensive; domestic tranquillity was one of the main values it had to offer. The wall helped maintain that tranquillity for not far short of three centuries.

Mosaic floors surviving in Britain from Roman times are surprisingly numerous; we know of almost a thousand sites. Most of them conform so closely to standard patterns visible elsewhere that scholars suppose they must have been made from pattern books which laid out geometric designs and a few outline figures. Some of the British mosaics use specifically Christian emblems and symbols; most of the figures represent pagan gods or heroes. A particularly elegant mosaic in a country villa at Lullingstone (Kent) portrays the rape of Europa by Jove in the form of a bull. The design is accompanied by a Latin inscription referring jocosely to the jealousy of Juno; it is the kind of joke that implies knowledge of Virgil and Homer—as if an exile from the Mediterranean were comforting himself, in foggy Britain, with thoughts of that remote, familiar mythology.

This great silver dish from Mildenhall on the border of the Suffolk fens (not far from Cambridge) was uncovered in 1942 along with a group of other silver vessels. With prowling Saxons in the area, some wealthy family evidently buried its plate in the bogs, and never lived to reclaim it. The salver, nearly 2 feet across, shows the triumph of Bacchus over Hercules, a frieze of sea nymphs inside it, and at the center a mask, probably of Oceanus. It was made in the third century, most likely at Rome itself, and for a patrician family. When the Saxons came, patrician families got all the worst of it.

2

Saxon England
(600–1066)

By about 600 the Saxons had finished conquering the Romano-Britons as far as they wanted to. When the Romans overcame the Britons, they left some client-kingdoms in existence to save themselves the bother of conquering and governing troublesome people. The Saxons likewise found it unnecessary or impossible to occupy places that were inconveniently located or toughly defended. Little British kingdoms held out here and there: the kingdom of Strathclyde, north of the river Clyde, the even smaller kingdom of Elmet in Yorkshire's west riding, for examples.[1] Saxons sometimes set up mini-kingdoms of their own; the Hwicce in lower Mercia once numbered 3,000 households; in western Essex a few folk calling themselves Hrothingas may have occupied only two or three villages; some Gyrwe in the fen country were too scattered and furtive even to be counted; and a little enclave called Manau Gododdin, south of Strathclyde, evaporated early, leaving few marks of its identity—it may well have been British. As was already traditional, Scotland, Wales, and western Cornwall (the high country of England, as opposed to the southeastern flatlands) resisted more or less successfully the new invaders. There were intervals, as well as districts, of co-existence, where the level of organized violence was lower, the level of disorganized violence perhaps higher. The tide of conquest did not flow regularly or all in one direction; some Saxons wandered back to the continent, some Britons fled to

1. Yorkshire, being large, was divided by its early occupants into three parts, north, east, and west thirds or *thridings*. Dropping the *th* because it was hard to pronounce "north *th*riding," men soon began to call the districts *ridings*, and still do.

western Gaul. The earliest English historian, Gildas, tells us that Britons, perhaps led by Arthur, though he doesn't use that name, won a sort of victory at Mons Badonicus (when or where that was, he doesn't say), and a truce of sorts resulted. But over the last half of the sixth century, a new Saxon push began; battles became more frequent, and the record of Saxon victories almost unbroken.[2] As these conflicts occurred in a kind of ring from Northumbria west along the Welsh border, and farther south against the seagirt fastnesses of Cornwall, they suggest a push to the north and west by Saxons from bases in the south and east already under their control. But this was at least 150 years after Hengist and Horsa landed on Thanet—if, indeed, they were the first arrivals or even existed. These highly hypothetical "first Saxons" may perfectly well have come to Britain even before the Romans left, as part of the Second Legion protecting Britain. For in the provinces, and in the years of the empire's decline, "Roman" soldiers were most often Germans of one sort or another. The Saxons who came to destroy Britain were perhaps following and joining uncles or cousins who had first been called to defend her.

Once they made up their mind to it, the Romans had conquered Britain quickly and easily; in three or four years they took as much of the island as they wanted. Their legions were highly disciplined, the enemy troops much less so; their culture had permeated the country before they came; the benefits they offered, from roads to luxuries to domestic tranquillity, were genuine; they granted easy terms to capitulators; they had a central strategic and administrative plan. By contrast, the Saxon takeover was slow, hard, and cruel. The Saxon invaders were not an organized and disciplined army; they came in bands, as tribes or family groups. They had no technical or organizational superiority; no political idea unified them. They came in the first place for loot, and only after all the portable loot had been picked up did they start to take land, which would be valuable only if worked. (Work, in that sense of the word, did not come at all naturally to men whose lives had been spent in piracy.) Since they had little political or legal machinery at first, what they took must have been taken piecemeal, at sword's point, about as hatefully and horribly as can be imagined.

SAXON SOCIAL LIFE

Historians have a professional impulse to organize and arrange their material; and we can describe how, over some centuries, the Saxons divided themselves

2. "Battles" in these dark conditions should not be exaggerated. Many must have involved as few as a hundred warriors or so on a side; the "armies" likely consisted mostly of pickup troops: local farmers, ex-slaves, leftovers from Roman legions. Throughout the disintegrating empire, it was common for the poor and dispossessed to make cause with barbarians against their former oppressors. Gildas, alas, was a bad historian because he was an eager moralist; in his zeal to rally Romano-Britons against the invader, he neglected to lay out clearly who was who, what what, and when when. This entire period is complex and obscure; almost everything one says of it is conjectural (SFR, A.7).

into three major and a number of minor kingdoms. But in the early stages most of these "kingdoms" were not much like organized governments at all. The Saxons did not like to live in cities, they did not build in stone and cement, they did not want elaborate laws. Their unit was the tribe, the folk, not a defined piece of dirt called a "nation." The center of their social and political life was the mead hall, like Heorot in *Beowulf;* it was a long hall built of timber (thus likely to catch fire from the roaring blazes they lit to heat it), surrounded by huts for retainers, servants, women, and slaves.[3] This was far from a permanent city. Warriors and counselors lived with the king in the mead hall, all together, their armor on the wall ready for use, their intimacy with the king a matter of daily personal contact.

The king was supposed, of course, to be descended from a long line of royal forebears, and sometimes he was; sometimes also, after he had held power for a while, a distinguished ancestry was arranged for him. Written records of any sort were few; beyond a few generations, most family trees must have been compounded of folk tales, high imagination, and fierce-sounding names. In reality, the king was often just the strongest and most successful warrior of the group, who had muscled his way into the kingship. Apart from leadership in war, the royal office did not amount to much; sometimes the same Anglo-Saxon tribe would have two or three kings or sub-kings at once, sometimes the kingship would be allowed to lapse. The king's counselors (in Latin, his *comitatus*) were a miscellaneous group—his chief warriors in the first place, his relatives, his friends.[4] They were not elected or formally appointed; they had no specialized functions. They were the court, the government, the general staff, the diplomatic corps, and the judiciary; what they decided was the law, and as they were also the police and a good part of the army, they enforced the law as they made it. Between the king and his counselors relations were strict and simple. They owed him total fidelity, especially in times of war and danger. While he was alive, they must be ready to die for him, and after his death they must take every action possible to avenge him. To shirk either obligation was an absolutely unforgiveable sin. This is the disgrace that Wiglaf predicts for the unfaithful followers of Beowulf, who deserted their master in his hour of need. In the other direction, the obligation of the king or lord was to be generous. He was the giver of rings,

3. These huts, known as long houses, were narrow structures without windows or chimneys; cattle occupied one end, people the other. Dark, smelly, and smoky year round, they must have been freezing cold in winter (SFR, A.5).

4. The early Anglo-Saxons did not have an elaborate hierarchy of nobles; anybody who was a professional warrior in the service of a lord qualified as a thegn or thane. Naturally, some thanes were richer and more important than others, but all were just thanes. Sometimes a thane was expected to have a certain amount of land, to support him in dignified idleness; more often he depended on the king to lend him a horse and armor (when he died, it had to be returned, and that was *heriot*), and expected to live on his share of the plunder. When assembled, the king's conselors were known, hopefully, as the *Witan,* or wise men; collectively, the *Witena-gemot,* or assembly of wise men. There are places today where they would be known as the good old boys.

the provider of war gear, the father of his people, and (in what amounted to a joint-stock enterprise) the declarer of dividends. All these loyalties being strongly concentrated within the tribe, there was very little consideration for anyone outside it. A Briton appealing for "justice" before an Anglo-Saxon king and his thanes would be lucky to escape with his sconce uncracked.

For the different Saxon kingdoms were instruments, not so much of government, as of conquest and defense. They fought against the Britons, the Picts, the Welsh, and any other outsiders; also, constantly and intricately, against one another. Certain kings, now of one tribe, now of another, seem to have been granted the special title of "Bretwalda," perhaps "Brytenwealda," meaning sole ruler of all the Britons and including Saxons, rather confusingly, under that heading; in any event, it carried some implication of distinction and perhaps superior authority. But if it existed at all, that authority did not extend to making peace between tribes. The Saxons did not expect peace to prevail, or care very much when it didn't; for the influential among them, war was a game and a business which they enjoyed more than anything else in life. They were encouraged in their warlike habits by the fact that most boundary lines between kingdoms were indefinite. While they remained seminomadic, Saxon tribes "controlled" areas much larger than they could or wanted to occupy, that is, settle and cultivate. Raiding parties were constantly pushing across hazy boundary lines and getting into fights with gangs on the other side. Where there was so little order, there was also very little law; the reason one didn't murder the neighbor was not fear of the policeman or the king, but fear of the victim's kinsmen, who would feel bound to avenge him. Blood feuds were common, and a primitive device for stopping them was the institution of *wergild:* it was a fixed sum of money or amount of property to be paid by the murderer or his kinsmen to the kinsmen of the victim. Wergild was more for a king than a thane, more for a thane than a ceorl (churl, commoner), more for a Saxon ceorl than for a mere Briton. But for any killing a price had to be paid, otherwise the string of revenges and counter-revenges would never stop. That was a fixed principle, though it must have been hard to carry out when the supply of currency failed. For though Roman coins continued to circulate for a while after the Romans themselves left, nothing took their place till the late eighth century when Offa, king of Mercia, reinstituted a currency. For a long time in there, most of the nation's business must have been transacted by barter.

A BIT OF SAXON SPLENDOR

Much in Anglo-Saxon life strikes us as primitive; much also, about which we have only recently learned, was rich to the point of opulence. In 1939 investigators uncovered, on a sparse field in Suffolk called Sutton Hoo, an Anglo-Saxon burial mound. At a guess, the Sutton Hoo find dates from the seventh century; it is the tomb of a man of importance, a king or lord comparable to Scyld Scefing, whose funeral is proudly described in the first lines of *Beowulf*. He was buried with an entire ship, something like 80 feet long, which had been dragged up half a mile from the sea and lowered into a vast grave pit. In the middle of the boat was built a covered room within which were deposited mounds of gold ornaments and jewelry, exquisite in workmanship and sophisticated in design. There were also gold coins from Gaul, pieces of silver plate, plus remains of ironwork, textiles, and leather objects. This material, now in the British Museum, evidences not only the wealth of the individual, but the high skill of his craftsmen.[5] We had not previously been altogether ignorant of Anglo-Saxon skill at jewelry making; but the riches of Sutton Hoo came as a revelation because they were so many and so splendid. The find is England's equivalent to the tomb of Tut-ankh-amun.

CONVERSIONS IN SAXON ENGLAND

Though in many respects the Anglo-Saxon settlers were coarse, greedy, and violent, the Christian faith made steady progress among them, taking two slightly different forms and approaching them from two distinct directions. Patrick's successful mission to Ireland in 432 created a number of missionary priests who promptly set off to convert, first the Scots their countrymen, then any heathen they could find. For 165 years they had the field to themselves before in 597 Saint Augustine (not, as noted, the great church father, but the first archbishop of Canterbury) arrived direct from Rome to convert the island.

The first group, of Irish missionaries, was the more picturesque. From a monastery founded by Saint Columba on the island of Iona in the Inner Hebrides, disciples of the saint spread out, tramping over rock and fell, through moor and glen, to preach, baptize, convert, and perform the odd miracle. Loose discipline in the Irish church encouraged these brawny, poetic priests to go on solitary pilgrimages among the tribesmen. A wandering Irish priest named Fursa did yeoman work among the East Anglians, while a Northumbrian named Cedd or Chad, who had been trained in Ireland, converted the East Saxons. Then when Augustine arrived to take up residence at Canterbury, his first task was to convert Aethelberht king of Kent, after which he sent his assistant Paulinus to Northumbria, where he worked earnestly to convert the king of that nation and keep him converted. Thus to a degree the two strains of Christian influence, Irish and Roman, worked hand in hand.

5. There is apparently no positive evidence that the grave at Sutton Hoo ever had an occupant. Perhaps the corpse, like Scyld Scefing's, was cast adrift in an open boat, while the grave mound was entrusted with the boat and treasure which would serve him in the afterlife. Some of the designs on the jewelry are said to suggest Christian themes; that wouldn't necessarily imply that the hero himself was a Christian (SFR, A.17).

The Irish, however, having been little supervised by Rome since the fifth century, had retained some old-fashioned practices of their own. Irish monks tonsured their heads in a special way, and calculated the date of Easter by a special formula.[6] The first difference seems trivial, the second only a little less so; but one can imagine the confusion in Northumbria, when King Oswiu celebrated Easter with a feast at the very moment when his queen Eanfleda was still deep in the austerities of Lent. And there was another difference, deeper than either: Irish bishops had no fixed jurisdictions, being free to roam around and exercise their functions where they chose, while English bishops, though vested with ample powers, were limited to their dioceses. These disparities easily could, and in fact did, develop into a series of conflicts; and in 664, at Whitby on a crag overlooking the North Sea, a summit conference was held. Most of the questions were resolved in favor of the Roman and against the Celtic faction; and in due course even the most remote monasteries of Ireland began cutting their hair and celebrating Easter like everyone else. The Whitby decisions were further consolidated in 669 by the arrival in England of a new and vigorous archbishop of Canterbury. Theodore of Tarsus had spent most of his life in worldly Byzantium; what he felt when ordered to the land of the Saxons we can only guess. But he was a good soldier and went about his work briskly, dividing the country into dioceses, touring the provinces to ensure that things were in order, and making the various bishops, as well as all the monks and abbots, responsible to himself at Canterbury. By the end of the seventh century Christianity was not only established throughout the land, it was organized doctrinally and administratively into a single solid corporation. And that corporation was united, doctrinally as well as administratively, with the church on the Continent.

What is described here, for brevity's sake, as a simple, straightforward process was, naturally, neither simple nor straightforward. Some kings and kingdoms converted to Christianity and then changed back; there were ugly scenes of Christians butchering other Christians with the help of pagans. An epidemic of sickness which swept the country was attributed to the new religion, and produced a mass revulsion to paganism. Wives often converted first, and dragged their husbands reluctantly after them. One indecisive king had a Christian shrine in one room and an altar to the "demons" in the next. Pagan observances and customs remained intertwined with Christian formulas placed beside or atop them. Eostre's day, the spring festival, was converted to a celebration of the resurrection, and the pagan name for midwinter, Giuli, survives as our season of Yule. Charms, curses, spells, proverbs, recipes, riddles, and nursery rhymes built out of the old pagan lore and its belief in magical properties continued to be part of the common stuff of life long after a community had ostensibly become Christian; in the same way, pagan motifs and figures of animistic deities continued to

6. Rome itself had changed its way of calculating Easter in 457, but neglected to notify the Irish. The dating of Easter is a topic almost as complicated as the nature of the festival itself. Bede apparently did not think it a Christian occasion; he relates it to Eostre, Anglo-Saxon goddess of spring.

be worked into the decorative schemes of illuminated manuscripts, though the text on the page might be from Scripture. We still carry into the days of our week a memory of the old Saxon gods, in Tig's day, Woden's day, and Thunor's day.

THE KINGDOMS: NORTHUMBRIA AND MERCIA

Having duly emphasized the chaos of Saxon England, we must now try to describe the different groupings as they settled on English soil or developed there. In the southeast corner of the island, we've noted an early Jutish kingdom in Kent, spreading along the channel coast as far as Hampshire. Though it established many enduring social practices in Kent (which made it in many ways unique among English counties), it never grew strong or expanded far, and was overrun by stronger powers late in the seventh century. To the north and west of the Jutes, county names like "Sussex," "Essex," and "Middlesex" preserve the memories of groups called "South Saxons," "East Saxons," and "Middle Saxons." Not a county name but a recognized district of England is the spacious region covering parts of Hampshire, Wiltshire, Somerset, Dorset, and Devon; it was known as Wessex, the country of the West Saxons, who as the last-formed of the Saxon nations, ultimately became the most powerful. In the flat fen country of Norfolk, Suffolk, and Cambridgeshire, the invader-settlers were primarily Angles; hence that district is still known as East Anglia. And north of the river Humber, north of the East Anglians, beyond a little barrier kingdom called Lindsey which occupied much of modern Lincolnshire, stretched the first of the three major Saxon kingdoms, Northumbria.

Northumbria was first, chronologically; it was also, for many years, first in terms of power. It was formed by gluing together (after an eventful series of coups and counter-coups) two smaller states, Bernicia to the north and Deira to the south.[7] These various names are not particularly Saxon, and it does not appear that the Saxons left in this northern kingdom very many of their distinctive marks. (These include place names ending in -*ing,* like Gedding, Stebbing, or Cressing; and burial in urns, generally after incineration, with some personal belongings included.) Likely the core of the Northumbrian state was German soldiers from the northern wall mixed with guardsmen who had kept watch along the North Sea. In any event, Northumbria was a large state with a mixed population; and under Edwin, who ruled 616–632, it was not only organized but pacified: that was a rare event indeed in seventh-century Europe. The Venerable Bede, who was a native of Northumbria and wrote his history a century or so after Edwin's death, looks back on that earlier period as an age of gold, of universal peace and prosperity. A woman with her newborn babe, he tells us, might have walked

---

7. Deira provided Pope Gregory, who made the pun about "angels, not Angles," with an occasion for another. Told that the handsome young slaves came from Deira, he saw it as a hint to rescue them from the wrath (*de ira*) of God.

from sea to sea without molestation, so perfect was the public discipline. About thirty years after Edwin's death, Bede was also able to record, in Northumbria, the first faltering voice of English poetry. The story itself of Caedmon assures us that he was not absolutely the first English poet; the other fellows all sang like larks, and Caedmon, because he could not, was humiliated—till a still voice from on high stirred him to praise, and emulate, the Creator. But Caedmon's is the first English poem we have in full, the first to which we can attach a personal name and an approximate circumstance. A haze of monkish morality hangs over the story (too edifying, perhaps, to be true); but the Hymn itself could not be more fitting as the germ from which a mighty literature was to grow.

Perhaps because it did not suffer as much from the Saxon conquest as other districts of England, Northumbria rose early to political and intellectual eminence. Caedmon may have been an accident, as inspired plowmen generally are; but Bede was a man of great intellectual distinction, and he was no isolated figure. In the eighth century Alcuin of York became so famous as a result of his study in the schools of Northumbria that he was invited to become cultural adviser to Charlemagne and in that capacity to bring Latin letters to the untutored Franks. A particular center of learning was the abbey of Lindisfarne on a tiny island off the Northumbrian coast; the Lindisfarne Gospels, which owe much to the Celtic schools of illumination described above (p. 20), rival even the great Book of Kells. And in addition to this flamboyant masterpiece, the scriptoria (writing rooms) of the monasteries produced many simple practical texts for the daily use of the church. But though Northumbria flourished during the seventh and eighth centuries, its physical situation exposed it to attack from northern Picts and Danish pirates from across the North Sea. The holy island of Lindisfarne was sacked in 793 and Bede's own monastery of Jarrow in 794, less than sixty years after his death. Domestic turmoil added to the troubles of Northumbria; and still another difficulty was the popularity of that monastic life which marked one of the kingdom's major achievements. Bede himself tells us, too many men entered the cloister, not enough stayed outside to defend it. As the central authority of Northumbria weakened, little kingdoms around its periphery took occasion to expand their boundaries. One of these was the still-British kingdom of Strathclyde in southeast Scotland; another was the midlands kingdom of Mercia, taking its name from Mierce, the borderers or March-men. Where the Mercians came from we cannot confidently say; but they rose to a position of strength in southern England under their fierce pagan king Penda (seventh century) and their even abler Christian king Offa (eighth century). On one frontier Mercia had, in the Welsh, neighbors just as likely to be troublesome as useful; King Offa marked this precarious relation by drawing an indelible dividing line along the border, where it can be seen to this day, under the name of "Offa's Dyke." It was not a defensive wall, just a set of indelible markers, a firm reminder. Actually, the Mercians sometimes used Welsh help to push back the Northumbrians; but then they went on to expand their borders eastward by taking Lindsey, East Anglia, and Kent. At one point, they controlled a good deal of southern England, felt stable enough to issue their own currency (the first in England since about 430), and began to develop trading relations with Europe. It was a pardonable exaggeration when Offa in several of his charters inscribed himself as king of the English or king of the whole land of the Angles.[8]

THE MERCIAN EPIC, BEOWULF

The prosperity of the Mercians did not long outlast that of the Northumbrians, both nations being ground down in the ninth century between Danish invaders pushing in from the east and the third great Saxon kingdom, Wessex, expanding in the south and west. But in a literary history we must pause with special interest over the court of Mercia because very likely it is where the finest of Old English (i.e., Anglo-Saxon) poems took form. *Beowulf* survives, and just by the skin of its teeth,[9] in a single manuscript which was evidently copied in the tenth century by a Wessex scribe. He introduced some Wessex dialect forms into the poem but without altering its basic character; and from that basic character, the deduction is that the poem took shape in Mercia around 700. Not that the world it describes is the world of western England under King Penda. *Beowulf* almost certainly depicts a world long past for the Mercians, a world they might have known long before they migrated to England. The poem may take us back as far as the fourth or fifth century, when Swedes, Franks, and Frisians were the enemies to be feared, and when, if there was any layer of Christianity on the old Germanic traditions, it was thin and intermittent. The funeral which concludes *Beowulf,* like that which opens it, is stripped clean of any Christian trappings, though elsewhere there are Christian allusions which may be late interpolations. Much of the poem's point, for those Mercian warriors who heard it recited, night after night, by the gleeman or *scop* of the Mercian court, would have resided in its distance. Like the Homeric poems, it is a tale of ancestors and the heroic deeds men did *then,* before they became degenerate, as they are *now*.

At the same time, the poem as it took crude shape around 700 called for considerable sophistication, both in the bard who told it and in the audience that heard it. For the bard, recounting three dragon fights without making them monotonously similar was a feat of some skill; while the various genealogies and narrative digressions which lent the poem historical interest represented a true feat of memory. From the audience's point of view, the poem is thick with tough

8. About the distinction between Angles and Saxons, Bede is more specific than most modern historians like. Still, he specifically assigns Mercia to the Angles, and a point in his favor is that the name "East Anglia" almost implies the existence somewhere of a "West Anglia"; that could only have been Mercia.

9. The *Beowulf* manuscript was badly damaged and nearly destroyed altogether, before it had even been properly transcribed, by a fire in 1731.

traditional metaphors (known to the Anglo-Saxons as *kennings*) which must be grasped in passing: hate-bites are wounds, the wave-way the sea. In short, though *Beowulf* began as a primitive poem (or more likely three primitive poems about dragon fights), it acquired a measure of unity and complexity as it was shaped by the Mercian artists; and either then, or in the tenth century when it was copied into the manuscript that partly survives, it acquired a veneer of Christianity. On the way, the poem picked up all sorts of blots, blurs, and confusions. Oral transmission from speaker to hearer is notoriously inexact;[10] the copyist who made our manuscript did not speak the same tongue as the original poets; and that fire of 1731 left holes in the text that can only be filled with conjecture. Still, *Beowulf* is a heroic, an epic poem, if ever there was one, and without it we should have a vastly diminished image of human life in those darkest of the dark ages. Nowhere else in the literature do we have the same sense of rude nobility. For partial analogues we must turn to the ice-clear, rock-hard world of the Icelandic sagas (*ca.* 1100–1200).

WESSEX

After Northumbria and Mercia, the third of the major Saxon kingdoms was that of Wessex or the West Saxons. Like the others, Wessex had its mythic progenitors, Cerdic and Cynric, who are said to have come ashore behind the isle of Wight and made their way northwest late in the fifth century and early in the sixth; by the end of the sixth century, the tribes had taken Gloucester, Cirencester, and Bath, setting up a little enclave for themselves just south of the Bristol Channel. But for many years they were hard pressed by the Mercians on the north, and limited their conquests to a community of Britons surviving in Cornwall under the name of Dumnonia. Only in the late seventh century did the West Saxons start expanding down the Thames valley and into the old Jutish kingdoms where Sussex and Kent now lie. Most of the eighth century was spent in fluctuating battles with the Mercians. King Offa of that large warlike kingdom was a formidable leader, and so long as he lived, Egbert, who claimed to be king of Wessex, had to live abroad as an exile in Gaul. But Offa died in 796; Egbert resumed rule of Wessex in 802, and quietly built up his forces till they were in a position to defeat the Mercians under Beornwulf at the pitched battle of Ellandun (825). Beating the Mercians enabled the West Saxons to advance faster to the east, till they were able to claim control over most of southern England. They levied tribute from Mercians and Northumbrians; their power was great and

10. In its formative years, *Beowulf* was almost certainly chanted from memory to the accompaniment of a harp; one gleeman would learn the story from another, and modify it to satisfy his tastes or the demands of his audience. But even after the poem started to be written down, the standard way for it to be transferred from one manuscript to another was for the old manuscript to be recited by a reader and copied by a scribe. (We have no way of guessing how many times this process was repeated to make the single manuscript that now survives.) Thus there was always an aural element in the transmission of the poem, even after it became a manuscript.

growing, they seemed on the point of uniting most of England under a single political authority. But just then the entire country had to bow before a new and terrible storm in the shape of those Viking raiders from Scandinavia,[11] whom we have had occasion to mention before (p. 21).

BLOOD AND FIRE: THE VIKINGS

These Vikings were not very different from what the Anglo-Saxons themselves had been three or four hundred years earlier. They were pirates and looters, a wolfish, pagan, predatory crew, driven from their homeland by meager harvests and increasing populations, their leaders avid to be known as generous ring givers and distributors of treasure. They sacked the northern monasteries toward the end of the eighth century; three of their ships appeared off the coast of Dorset while Egbert was still king of Wessex, killed the king's reeve who came down to ask what they wanted, and made off unscathed. These new invasions caught the Anglo-Saxons just as they were starting to develop some civilized amenities (which made them worth plundering) and some gentle manners (which made them easy to plunder). With a sure instinct, the Vikings went after the monasteries first, grabbing the sacred vessels and images, burning the laboriously illuminated manuscripts, and selling the hapless monks into a short, wretched life of slavery in a Spanish mine or at the oar of a Mediterranean galley. After they had snatched all the portable loot, the Danes, like the Anglo-Saxons before them, settled onto the land, formed a regular, year-round army, and began pressing westward. Checked briefly by Egbert's successor Aethelwulf in 851, they regrouped and reinforced their armies, and between 865 and 870 fought a series of battles which wiped out the old kingdoms of East Anglia, Mercia, and Northumbria. Danes now controlled most of England except for the rising and fast-consolidating kingdom of Wessex. In 870 the two forces came into direct collision at Ashdown in Berkshire, not far from White Horse Hill. Among the West Saxon leaders was the fourth son of Aethelwulf, a bold, intelligent young man of twenty-two named Alfred. Less than a year later, his older brothers having died, Alfred succeeded to the throne. He would become known to history, and deservedly, as Alfred the Great.

THE GREAT KING, ALFRED

The circumstances under which Alfred came to the throne required him to buy time from the Danes; though he had won the big battle of Ashdown, he lost many more of the lesser engagements than he won. For five years an uneasy

11. To the English, they were all "Danes," but in fact they were a mixed bag of unsorted Scandinavians.

truce prevailed, while the Danes were busy consolidating their positions elsewhere in England. Then a series of surprise raids during the late 870s drove Alfred and a few loyal followers into the fort of Athelney, deep in the fens and swamps of Somerset. Here is supposed to have taken place the famous incident of the burnt cakes: Alfred, hiding in the hut of an old woman, was asked to watch some scones that were baking by the hearth. But his mind was on pursuing Danes and upcoming battles, so he let the cakes burn, and was duly scolded as a dunderhead. The truth of legends like this is wholly immaterial; they are the kind of story that springs up around a folk hero (which Alfred quickly became), and if they did not happen, they would have to be invented.

In due course Alfred emerged from his hiding place at Athelney to rally the shire levies of Somerset, Wiltshire, and Hampshire; in 878 he won the crucial battle of Edington, and forced the Danish king Guthrum, with thirty of his chief swordsmen, to receive baptism. It is an interesting ceremony, not untypical of the age: the church was called on to ratify a peace achieved in the first place by brute force. (For the pagan Danes it was not, perhaps, a matter of prime religious importance; they had plenty of gods before, and did not much mind adding another. But the implication that accepting the Christian faith meant keeping one's word and not looting or killing like a wild animal seems to have been understood and honored with surprising fidelity.) Not all the Danes, of course, accepted Guthrum's truce; both Alfred and his son Edward (nicknamed "the Elder") had to fight frequently and remain ready to fight all the time in order to keep the peace. But Alfred developed two new practices to solidify the military situation. Against the quick and active Danes, who could call up an army overnight and move it swiftly by sea, he devised a system of forts called *burhs,* big enough to hold not only a garrison but most of the people and cattle of the surrounding district. The Danes had no interest in prolonged sieges; they wanted to grab and run. So these "burhs" which later became "burgs," "boroughs," or fortified market towns, were very effective temporary shelters. Alfred also divided the *fyrd,* or host, in two, so that one part could work the fields while the other part dealt with invaders. Thus the Danes were always sure of meeting an army, and crops did not have to be neglected. Alfred even built some ships with which to intercept Danish boats; and he carefully planned his battles, not to kill Danes in quantity (which would have involved Saxon losses in equal numbers), but to starve them out, make them uncomfortable, encourage them to go away. Some he shunted off to Ireland, some to Gaul; gradually the remainder retired to an area north and east of Watling Street (above, p. 13); and there, for lack of ready plunder, they settled on the land and domesticated. Their district became known as the Danelaw.[12] And as they settled down to raising swine and oats,

---

12. Saxon law outside, Danish law inside. The fact that the Danes had a fairly well-developed code of laws marks them already as something distinct from simple freebooters. Place names mark a fairly distinct boundary between Saxon and Danish territory: Saxon names often end in "ham" (home) or "tun" (town), Danish in "by" (village) or "thorpe" (town).

brewing good Danish beer, and munching on salt herring, it must have seemed, at least for the moment, that they were not much different from other invaders of England, and would soon be indistinguishable from them.

In fact, the Danes proved themselves admirably adapted, not only to farming, but to trading and town life. Five of their military and market towns (Lincoln, Stamford, Leicester, Derby, and Nottingham) became particularly prosperous. All these towns, as it happens, are on rivers; the Danes had a lot of practice in shallow-water navigation, and turned readily to gardening, livestock raising, and barging around the backwaters as the basis of an active commercial life. Before long, they were in a position to teach their stolid Saxon neighbors a thing or two about salesmanship and sharp business practice.

THE CULTURAL WORK OF ALFRED

At the start of his reign, Alfred had had no chance to be anything but a war leader, and a splendid one he had proved; his later career brought out another side of this remarkable man. Years of intertribal fighting and battling against the Danes had left the land practically destitute of scholars, meaning by that term men who could write something more than their name. Alfred himself declared that when he took power in 871, there was nobody south of the Thames who could conduct a church service in Latin or translate a Latin letter into English— nobody south of the Thames, very few south of the Humber, and not many north of it. Singlehandedly he set about educating his kingdom. He sent for scholars and translators; they came from the Continent, from Ireland, from schools that the king himself established. He translated Pope Gregory the Great's Latin treatise on *Pastoral Care* (it advised a bishop how to care for his spiritual charges), and ordered that a copy of it be placed in every cathedral church. Under his influence the Anglo-Saxon chronicles were begun, so that men could have a record of events in their own land. He had Bede's history of England and the Latin treatise of Orosius on the history of the world translated into Anglo-Saxon; he personally translated the classic philosophic treatise of Boethius, *On the Consolation of Philosophy.*[13] In addition, he took steps to codify and register the laws and customs of the past. He added nothing of his own; he submitted all to the opinion of his counselors; but when he and they found something they did not like, they omitted it from the collection. Such a combination of strong common sense and personal restraint is rare in any age, extraordinary in a man brought up, like Alfred, to fight for his life against brutal savages.

13. Boethius, who lived early in the sixth century in Italy, was a Roman patrician put to death by king Theodoric the Ostrogoth. Theodoric was a Christian of sorts, Boethius a pagan; but the middle ages so admired the book of Boethius that they practically canonized him, while Theodoric was degraded accordingly. As a translator of Boethius, Alfred was followed by Chaucer, Queen Elizabeth, and many others.

ALFRED'S DESCENDANTS

Alfred's reign saw out the ninth century (he died in 899), and the political supremacy of the West Saxons was upheld by his able son Edward the Elder and his grandson Aethelstan. Their work was not easy; they had to weave together the miscellaneous populations of Wessex, hold back the restless Danes, yet keep from overburdening their people with fiscal and military demands. At Brunanburh (937), Aethelstan won a crushing victory over a coalition of Celtic, Scottish, and Strathclyde forces; but this was a high-water mark, and Aethelstan's successors, though they presided over a vigorous program of monastery building and manuscript copying, were forced to remain generally on the military defensive. Partly, the new cultural developments rose out of Alfred's earlier stimulus to learning; partly they came from increased contact with the culture of the Continent. Across Europe, the monastic movement was gaining impetus, led by the great house of Cluny in France;[14] its counterpart in England became the monastery of Glastonbury under Abbot (later Saint) Dunstan. Glastonbury was but one monastery of many renewed or founded in the late tenth century; in these Wessex monasteries were produced almost all the manuscripts through which we know Anglo-Saxon literature. Yet these cultural achievements could not conceal the structural weakness of the Saxon monarchy.

Edgar, nephew of Aethelstan, was apparently a man of energy and imagination, who saw the need to tighten his hold over the lands he ostensibly ruled; but he had no legal or social tools to do the job. At his coronation, he improvised a little ceremony, hardly more than a charade, to show what he wanted. Eight crowned kings of minor (some *very* minor) Saxon kingdoms rowed Edgar across the river Dee in a boat, while he sat back and steered. Cooperation and subordination were vaguely symbolized; but what in fact did the gesture mean? Nobody knew; and Edgar, who died after only three years on the throne, never had a chance to spell out his intentions. His death threw the kingdom of the West Saxons into chaos. Edward, who succeeded, ruled just two years before being murdered by his half-brother Aethelred, quick to grab the throne but utterly inept on it. Having begun his reign with a murder (Edward was quickly given the name of "the martyr"), Aethelred proceeded to earn contempt for his general weakness, and fear for his occasional streaks of violence. The name "Aethelred" means "noble counsel," and the nickname he soon acquired, "the Unready," means "the man with no counsel." But Aethelred was unready in the sense of "unprepared" as well. What he was unprepared for was a second wave of Viking invasions, not hit-and-run raids this time, but systematic invasions. They were

14. From their central house near Mâcon the Cluniac order reached out to gain control of nearly 2,000 lesser abbeys and religious houses; the Musée de Cluny in modern Paris is lodged in what used to be the town house of the order. Cluny is of special interest to modern historians for the high level of its financial and industrial organization; its pattern of propertyless communal productivity may have suggested overtones to Sir Thomas More's *Utopia* (SFR, B.4).

led, not by warlords, but by national monarchs; they came to bleed the country white. In 994 Olaf Tryggvasson, a future king of Norway, arrived in England with Sweyn Forkbeard, a legal king of Denmark. Aethelred and his counselors, consulting only their weakness, chose to bribe these greedy intruders rather than fight with them. The trouble was that they came back every year for another bribe, and the size of the payment, known as *Danegeld* or Dane money, increased every year. Aethelred and his tax collectors had to devote their full energies to piling up cash for next year's Danegeld. Growing desperate, they tried in 1002 to organize a massacre of all the Danes in the land; and in some districts, where Danes were in a small minority, the massacre took effect. Most escaped, however, and in no cheery frame of mind. Danegeld continued to be collected under threat of brutal reprisals; the tax effectively drained England of all her silver coins and much of her movable property. Even in the twentieth century, hoards of old English currency are occasionally discovered under the sods or deep in the root cellars of old Scandinavian houses.

A DANISH KING OF ENGLAND

For worse and for better, these eleventh-century Danes were different from the first Viking raiders of the ninth century; they were greedier for money, but sometimes used it to buy English land which they then cultivated. Socially, they were better organized, and many were even Christians. Some of Sweyn's men thought it appropriate to murder the archbishop of Canterbury; offended by this crudeness, a thane named Thorkell the Tall shortly led off some of his warriors to join up with Aethelred. At the same time, the feeble leadership of the Unready one had so disgusted many of his thanes and ealdormen[15] that they began to cooperate with the Danes. This wasn't base betrayal; Danes and Saxons alike were eager for a competent king, whatever his nationality. When Sweyn died abruptly in 1014 and Aethelred in 1016 (long after everybody else was ready for him to go), the only successor to take over was Sweyn's young son Cnut, who accordingly became king of England, his name anglicized as Canute.

As king, Canute had three constituencies to satisfy: the Anglo-Saxons, the old established Danes of the Danelaw, and the "new" Danes of the second installment. Pleasing them all was not as hard as it sounds. The first two groups were grateful for a truce and a chance to improve their properties; the more recent Danes were pacified with an enormous Danegeld.[16] Wulfstan, the intelligent and

15. The Anglo-Saxon *ealdorman*, whose name is all that relates him to a modern alderman, was a figure of superior dignity and authority among the thanes, but his power varied widely. One might be ealdorman of a vast or a very petty district. Close advisers and legal representatives of the king tended to be ealdormen; under Canute, they started to be called *eorls*, or in modern English, *earls*.

16. With a Danish king on the English throne, the rationale for Danegeld evaporated; but taxes, once instituted, are hard to remove, and Danegeld was not abolished for good till 1163. It was always a bitterly unpopular tax.

persuasive archbishop of York, preserved the English church largely unchanged under the Danes; and Canute tactfully married Aethelred's youthful widow, a Norman princess named Emma. In 1018 a formal peace treaty at Oxford endorsed both the English church and the laws as established by the late King Edgar. Canute thus became a great man in his generation at a very early age; for he was king, not only of all England, but of Denmark, Norway for a while, and a bit of Sweden as well. In these various capacities, he was able to keep further Scandinavian invaders from devastating England, and his reign was long remembered as one of unusual prosperity. Indeed, he was the most powerful monarch in northern Europe, and when he made a pilgrimage to Rome in 1027, both the pope and the German emperor were pleased to make his acquaintance. In short order he became more an Englishman than a Dane, refusing to confiscate English land for the benefit of Danish subjects, and keeping many English advisers in his intimate circle. One important change he did make. Because he came young to power and in troubled times, Canute had to rely heavily on the *eorls* or earls who represented the first rank of Norse nobility; indeed, he promoted a number of Anglo-Saxon ealdormen to this new rank, and gave them a new function. They and their sons formed a royal bodyguard, first seen in Canute's time, under the name of *housecarls*. These were not the *Witan*, or wise men, familiar in Saxon society. The housecarls were primarily fighting men, and they were aristocrats, like the barons who would be the chief support of William the Conqueror in his 1066 invasion. They might be sent out as a company, to be billeted on troublesome districts of the country; some always remained by the king as his personal bodyguard. They were his men. Thus, even before the conquest, Anglo-Saxon administration was tending to become more centralized, even, one might say, more feudal. The main thing lacking was the strict contract: military service from the vassal for land tenure granted by the lord. In this respect Saxon social fabric remained loosely knit (SFR, A.13).

EDWARD THE WEAK CONFESSOR

The rule of Canute, being personal, proved transitory. Having taken the throne when young, the king died young (1035); a short period of confusion followed, during which Canute's bastard and legitimate sons squabbled; when they both died within two years, the *eorls* could think of nobody to put on the throne except an unworthy descendant of unworthy Aethelred. This was Edward, known from his piety as "the Confessor"; and though likely he was not a bad man, he was definitely a bad king. Having been raised in Normandy, he had a fondness for foreigners, to whom he freely granted offices, estates, and positions of power. Yet at the same time he inherited a situation where his English and Danish earls (who detested the foreigners) had an unusual measure of power and influence. The result was a reign full of muffled, and sometimes overt, strife, which Edward was neither able nor willing to pacify. He put much of his energy into building Westminster Abbey, a pious project but of limited interest to most of his subjects; and because he refused to make love to his wife, he left no direct heirs. Finally, he lived an unusually long time for a king of that age; his death was long and eagerly anticipated, and a number of pretenders gathered, ready to put in their claims the minute the old king died. He did so on the fifth of January, 1066, and the battle royal was on.

PRETENDERS TO THE THRONE

Genealogically speaking, the best claim probably belonged to a boy named Edgar, popularly designated "the Aetheling."[17] But genealogy was only one of the elements determining an Anglo-Saxon succession; also to be considered were the voice of the dying king, the vote of the *Witan,* and—basic to the whole business, though not of much theoretical import—who was closest with the biggest army. Of all the late king's intimate council of earls, the strongest and most independent had always been Godwin, earl of Wessex; when he died in 1053, his son Harold became earl in his turn, and actually assumed something like the powers of a joint monarch with Edward the Confessor. Genealogy was against him, but he had the king's dying voice, and he had plenty of soldiers to back him up. A third claimant was the king of Norway, Harald Hardrada; his genealogical links were of the slightest, but he too had many soldiers, though they were in Norway. He also had an agent on the spot, in Harold of Wessex's jealous, conspiratorial brother Tostig.[18] And finally the fourth claimant was William, duke of Normandy, bastard son of an earlier duke known ominously as Robert the Devil. On paper, William had the worst prospects of all. His genealogy was terrible: he had no connections with any of the English royal families, though his wife Matilda could trace a sort of connection with Alfred the Great through the female line. He did not have the support of the Witan; he did not have the dying word of the old king. He had soldiers, but they were in Normandy, and even with buildups they would probably not be adequate to invade England. All William had to sustain his claim on the throne was two promises, one of them old and dubious, the other extorted under duress. On the other hand, he was a Norman; and in the eleventh century, that counted for a lot.

The Normans were not very remote descendants of Vikings (Northmen); dur-

17. Though born in Hungary, where his parents had fled for safety from Canute, Edgar the Aetheling was a great-grandson of Aethelred the Unready. He was but sixteen years old in 1066, and never figured seriously as a contender till it was too late.

18. The eldest son of Earl Godwin had been the aptly named Sweyn, but he got into one set of troubles by seducing the abbess of Leominster, and then into another by murdering his cousin Beorn. While off on crusade to atone for these crimes, he was killed in 1052, leaving Harold unchallenged heir to the earldom.

ing their stay in France of about 150 years, they had picked up a good deal of intellectual finesse without losing any of their original barbaric energy. They were Christian knights now, organized along feudal lines;[19] they had fought and married with the best aristocracy of Europe, capturing control of kingdoms by both processes; they had gone on crusades, where they earned a European reputation as fearless swordsmen and brash yet subtle negotiators. Over the years they had had some dealings—commercial, diplomatic, cultural, and matrimonial—with the Anglo-Saxons, whom, from their more cosmopolitan point of view, they had learned to despise. The Normans were keen, cruel predators by nature; they were now armed with modern military expertise; they thought the Saxons uncouth and inept; and besides, there was the matter of those promises.

The first promise to support William's claim had been made (if it was made at all: there was nothing in writing) by Edward the Confessor in 1051, when William had visited England to adjudicate a quarrel over the English king's Norman advisers; on that occasion, he had made a lasting enemy of Earl Godwin whose son Harold was now, in 1066, the leading on-site aspirant for Edward's crown. But meanwhile, in 1064, a curious and crucial incident had occurred involving Harold and William. For no reason that anyone could calculate then or can fathom now, Harold went sailing on the English channel, wandered ashore on the coast of France, and fell into the hard hands of William. As a condition of his release he was forced to swear, by the holy relics in Bayeux Cathedral, that he would support William's claim to the succession. It was a public commitment, more public than Edward's promise of 1051; but, being made under what amounted to blackmail conditions, it wasn't hard for Harold to repudiate. He did so, and the day after Edward's death, Harold of Wessex ascended the throne of England. That was January 6, 1066.

WAR, NORTH AND SOUTH

At once, a sequence of swift, interrelated developments started to unfold. In May, Harold's brother Tostig launched raids against the isle of Wight and the coast of Kent. Harold naturally supposed these were preliminaries to an attack in force by the Normans, so he summoned the *fyrd* or host of the southern counties and gathered a fleet of ships to repel the attack. They waited through the summer, while crops spoiled in the field; but the attack never came. In Septem-

19. When Edgar of Wessex took his royal rowboat ride, his eight kings were enacting a personal relationship of compliment and courtesy. The harder, more contractual relations between Norman William and his barons provided that they hold their land from him on condition of military service. No service, no land; it was a point on which William tolerated no nonsense. Even bishops holding land from the king were expected to fight in the Norman army. Fortified stone castles and heavily armored knights on horseback were less important to the Norman power than their stiff, legalistic social structure. It wasn't by any means their invention; they had picked it up on the Continent. But they made good use of it, especially against the less contractual Saxons.

ber, however, the treacherous Tostig sailed north and joined with the king of Norway, Harald Hardrada, in an attack on Northumbria. It was no small armada with which the Norsemen came ashore; more than 300 ships were crowded to the gunwales with warriors who disembarked, formed up, and defeated the local militia in a sharp engagement at Fulford. But word of their coming quickly reached London, and Harold swept north at the head of his housecarls. These were the earls, thanes, and personal retainers of the king. They fought under his eye and felt directly responsible to him; and fearful fighters they were. Though they might ride to the battlefield, they preferred to fight on foot behind a wall of shields,[20] wielding heavy battle-axes. They were the most formidable infantry in all Europe—big, grim men, who entered into battle with savage gaiety, and thought death infinitely preferable to the ignominy of defeat. At Stamford Bridge, on the 25th of September, they fell on the Norsemen, and cut them to ribbons; Earl Tostig and Harald Hardrada died on the field of battle, and a scant twenty-five vessels sufficed to carry the survivors back to Norway. Harold of Wessex had won his first tremendous victory and secured England forever from the threat of further Scandinavian invasion. Meanwhile, however, William of Normandy had slipped across the English channel, landing at the broad bay of Pevensey but pitching camp a few miles to the east at Hastings. His troops were ashore just two days after Stamford Bridge.

A good deal of evidence suggests that William's advisers did not think well of his chances to capture England by force of arms. He had at his disposal the forces of a single duchy which had been busy for some years fighting scrappy territorial wars on the Continent. England was a big country, and Harold a warrior almost as tough and determined as William himself. When they were first consulted, most of the Norman barons spoke against the venture. But William was determined; he got the approval of the pope, a promise of neutrality from the German emperor, and hearty endorsement from the guardian of the youthful king of France—who just happened to be William's father-in-law. Most important of all, he let it be known throughout Europe that England was to be invaded, and that there would be land as well as loot for the successful invaders. With promises of this sort, he sharked up from Brittany, Sicily, Gascony, and other odd corners of Europe a splendid crew of landless, land-hungry knights, to reinforce a core of native Norman warriors. The invading army actually contained two of these ringers for every natural subject of William's.

HASTINGS FIELD

Luck was all with the Normans. William had wanted to invade earlier in the summer, but had been held up by adverse winds; had he encountered the house-

20. These heavy, kite-shaped shields were a recent innovation. Big enough to shelter a man, they were too heavy to carry around easily; but they locked one to the other to form a palisade (SFR, A.16).

carls before their long gallop up to Stamford Bridge and back, the result on the beaches of Hastings might have been very different. Had Harold not been over-confident after Stamford Bridge, he might have moved more slowly against William, giving the *fyrd* time to reassemble after their long summer of fruitless waiting, and the housecarls time to catch their breath. The involuntary delay was a blessing for William; the tremendous impetus and hurry of Harold was his downfall. The two armies met on the 14th of October, with the Saxons standing to defensive positions atop a ridge rising out of the great Sussex forest of Andredsweald, the Normans charging uphill to beat against the Saxon shield wall. The tone of the battle was set by the Norman minstrel Taillefer, who had begged permission of William to strike the battle's first blow; he rode against the enemy line, tossing his sword in the air and catching it, singing of Charlemagne, Roland, and the legendary battle of Roncevaux—until the Saxon axe men caught him and hewed him to bits. It was to be a battle to the death.

The armies were relatively small; six or seven thousand men on each side took part in the battle. The victory of the Normans was determined by two weapons they wielded with particular force. Their heavy cavalry had the effect of tanks against footsoldiers, because an armored knight with a long spear on an armored horse charged with fearful impact. And their foot soldiers used bows and arrows to rain death from a distance on the Saxons, who had no way to reply. As long as the shield wall stood unbroken, neither cavalry nor arrows could do much execution; but sometimes, after an unsuccessful cavalry charge, the Saxon foot could not resist the temptation to pursue, and then the archers did deadly damage. After a full day of heavy fighting, Harold lay dead with an arrow in his eye, his brothers Gurth and Leofwin dead beside him, his gallant band of housecarls scattered over the ridge. For the conqueror, it was crucially important that Harold of Wessex be unmistakably, unequivocally dead; his mistress, Edith Swanneck, was summoned to make identification, and though the face was mutilated beyond recognition, she knew, by certain marks on the body, that indeed it was Harold.

William waited a few days on the battlefield to see what the English Witan would do. They were foolish enough to think he was a casual adventurer who would take some plunder and go away; they declared for Edgar the Aetheling, and were followed in their declaration by a number of earls, bishops, and dignitaries. Somebody clearly needed a lesson, and William became its teacher. At the head of his army, he marched slowly and circuitously toward London, burning, looting, hanging, and confiscating as he went. For the first time now the English saw what manner of man they had to deal with; their dismay was unbounded, but there was no power in the land to withstand the Bastard of Normandy. On Christmas Day of 1066, in Edward the Confessor's much-prized church of Westminster Abbey, William was crowned king of England.

THE SAXON TONGUE

When we think of the permanent contributions of the Anglo-Saxon period, the first thing that comes to mind is the language we use, every day, all the time, in the common business of life. When I say, "The roots of our English tongue lie buried in old Anglo-Saxon speech," there is not a word in the sentence that does not illustrate the point it's making. Of course, over the centuries the language has grown enormously. An old Anglo-Saxon would be amazed and appalled at the sight of a modern dictionary, containing half a million entries or more. Most of the new words would be completely strange to him, referring to objects he never dreamed of, and using Latin, Greek, or French components to build weird hybrid compounds, like "television" and "automobile." He would probably be surprised too at our capacity to make ourselves understood with so few inflections. Old English was a highly inflected language with many more declensions and verb forms than modern English; most of these inflections fell off during the centuries when Saxon was a despised and neglected tongue, spoken only by the lower social orders. Our modern English would doubtless seem to an ancient Saxon both simplified in its structure and overwhelming in its vocabulary. He would also find its word order strange and its syntax complicated; Saxon prose tended to be paratactic, the clauses strung together on a series of "ands," the sentences invertebrate. Yet for all these differences, an Anglo-Saxon carried magically into our age would hear echoes of his tongue in ours, as we hear echoes of ours in his. Saxon is the heart wood of the English language; its toughness, simplicity, and infinite range of metaphorical application are resources upon which we draw daily, with scarcely a thought for the donors.

Effectively, Anglo-Saxon literature disappeared with the conquest. The Normans took no active steps against the old language, they simply despised and neglected it. Manuscripts of old Saxon poems, being written on sheepskin (vellum), the only paper available in those days, were erased and used to write something else; or they were used to polish brass, or cut up to line pie pans. Monasteries, where nobody could or wanted to read the old material, discarded it as junk. What survived by accident in the vault of an Italian cathedral, on the back shelf of a Swiss library, in an antiquarian's collection, was the merest fraction of a once vast literature. Only in the seventeenth century did men start to be interested once more in the old literature;[21] they invented our word Anglo-Saxon, a compound that had been used, but only sparsely, in Alfred's day, and made it apply to the entire period of Old English, that is, the period before the

---

21. Sixteenth-century ecclesiastical and seventeenth-century political controversy produced much rummaging after precedent in the old records. Laurence Nowell compiled an Anglo-Saxon dictionary in the earlier period, though it was never published; Sir Henry Spelman compiled and published another in 1626. Interest in poetry came later. The manuscript of *Beowulf,* discovered by Sir Robert Cotton in the 1620s, was not described till 1705 or transcribed till 1786.

conquest. Slowly they learned to read the old codices and ultimately to take an interest in them for their own sake. In our time, writers of both prose and poetry have turned back to Old English for inspiration and renewal; out of many possible instances, we need note only the deliberately severe, Saxonized prose of Charles Doughty (*Travels in Arabia Deserta,* 1888), the alliterative verse of W. H. Auden (*The Age of Anxiety,* 1947), and the imaginative cosmos of an Anglo-Saxon scholar turned fabulist, J. R. R. Tolkien.

THE SAXON LAW

Another heritage from the Anglo-Saxon age, less general than our speech, is an attitude toward the law, and some of our specific legal institutions. For Anglo-Saxons, law was not the recondite study of complicated texts in big compilations; both Roman law and church law had this character, but the law of the Saxons was something else. They did not have professional lawyers, professional judges, or encyclopedic codes. Their law, which started to be written down only after they were Christianized and of which the church was a major custodian and guarantor, was expressed in the vernacular, not in Latin. Mostly men carried their grievances to the local courts, originally called folk-moots; from there they could appeal to the shire court, presided over by the shire reeve (sheriff). Common procedure was for plaintiff and defendant to take oaths and summon supporting witnesses, who also took oaths. If that process yielded no decision, the case went to trial by ordeal—boiling water, red-hot iron. It was not a very efficient system, and many cattle thieves, housebreakers, and assorted malefactors escaped punishment for long periods. But it made for popular, accessible justice. In areas like family life, Saxon law was flexible enough to recognize the property rights of women; because the church bore a hand in them, penalties commonly stopped short of capital punishment. After the conquest, a custom long established in the Danish district of England (the Danelaw) started developing toward what we can vaguely recognize as an incipient jury; that made law still more the expression of popular tradition, popular sentiment. And overall, the frequent meetings of the folk-moot (or, as it came to be called, the hundred court), combined with less frequent assemblies at the shire court, did much to knit these local districts, the hundred and the shire, into stable and effective units of government.[22]

22. It is a notable circumstance that the division of England into shires (counties) was substantially complete by the end of the Saxon period, and has not changed materially to this day. Formally (because it is represented as a unit in parliament) and informally (because "county society" is often a closely knit group), shires are basic components of the English political system, and their stability over the centuries is a matter of some importance.

Hundreds (known in the Danelaw as "wapentakes") were administrative units, smaller than shires

THE SAXON CHURCH

The monastic revival of the tenth century (above, p. 37), led by men of unusual intelligence and energy, had been tonic for the Christian church. Abbot Dunstan and his disciples Oswald and Aethelwold laid material and spiritual foundations for the work of an eleventh-century scholar-teacher like Aelfric, who raised Anglo-Saxon prose to the precision and fluency, almost, of Latin. From the monasteries, learning radiated widely if not always deeply. By the eleventh century, Danes as well as English had been securely Christianized, and priests were a natural part of the domestic landscape. Domestication could go too far. It would be idle to pretend that the Saxon church before the conquest was a beehive of intellectual activity; no more was it a model of good discipline and Christian austerity. Stigand, archbishop of Canterbury, insisted on holding the rich bishopric of Winchester as well; the pope denounced his avarice, but he paid no heed. With few exceptions, the Saxon clergy were mentally mediocre at best. A good many priests were still only semiliterate, and some lived in open concubinage—a sin that would have appeared more grievous if the Norman clergy who replaced them had not been even more notoriously addicted to this fault. Still, the Saxon clergy must have been doing something right, for we find their influence holding steady among the laity. The saintly Wulfstan was even able, after the conquest, to stop that pernicious traffic in English slaves which had plagued the country for centuries.[23] And as early as the reign of Edward the Confessor, we find the central government starting to rule, in some degree, by writ.

A writ is simply a letter sent by higher authority (say the king) telling someone inferior (say the sheriff) to do something. But in the art of government its coming is a portentous event. It implies that the recipient can read, or has someone in his service who can. The message comes word for word; it obviates the clumsy, imprecise business of trusting to someone's memory. The messenger doesn't have to carry a ring or physical token to prove his authority; the writ itself can be sealed in wax or lead with a distinctive seal. Carrying on government becomes infinitely easier when a good proportion of the king's servants can read and write. The only place they could have learned those tricks in the eleventh century was from the clergy (SFR, A.12). In a word, Anglo-Saxon society was developing, even under feeble leaders like Aethelred and Edward the Confessor, toward a centralized monarchy; when the king was strong, like Canute, centralization

---

but generally comprising several towns. A hundred hides of land, a hide being the amount of land a man needed to support his family, would be the usual loose measure. A chief function of the hundred was to hold a frequent small-claims court; by the time of the Tudors, hundreds and their courts were largely obsolete.

23. "Traffic in slaves" (the capture and selling of people) was easier to stop than slavery itself; unfree forms of land tenure like serfdom and villeinage continued under many different forms into the fourteenth century, and it was the late eighteenth century before the last native British slaves—a few remote Scottish miners, drudging half naked in the black pits with iron collars round their necks—were finally manumitted.

went even faster. Much that would be characteristic of English society after the conquest was in the making before it.

CHARACTER

In an indefinite matter like the national character and its components, it is hard to know if one is talking about Angles, Saxons, Jutes, or Danes; they are all Scandinavians (Scandiknavery, as Joyce says) of slightly differing flavors, stirred up in the giant salad bowl of English society with many other seasonings. But the Germanic element has been a deep, persistent strain in the nation's history. It is the base on top of which other colors are applied; the Anglo-Saxons laid it down. Their temper was not on the whole airy or imaginative; their humor tended to be grim, their minds far from mercurial. (Anglo-Saxon doesn't make much use of those balancing and concessive clauses which enable modern English, even as it makes one main point, to consider and compare two or three others. Saxons took their ideas one at a time.) In its coloring, Anglo-Saxon literature is prevailingly dark, not to say pessimistic. It was an Anglo-Saxon mind which compared human life to the brief instant of warmth and light experienced by a sparrow as he darts into the mead hall through a window on one side and out through a window on the other.[24] They most often saw life as hard and grim, sometimes mourning the destruction that they themselves had wrought. A Saxon poem (*The Ruin*) laments the destruction of Roman Bath in the same spirit as Spenser would bewail, in *The Ruins of Time,* the downfall of ancient Verulam. The Saxon mind pays little attention to women, much to war and money. (Germanic and Homeric epics are often contrasted in this respect. The war in Troy was caused by a lover stealing Helen from her husband; the action of the *Nibelungenlied,* Germany's chief epic, is motivated by a bag of stolen treasure. Women, though not a male preoccupation, were not abused in Anglo-Saxon society; they could own money and land, they could not be sold or forced into marriage.) Saxon tenacity, fidelity, and endurance are the qualities of which their literature speaks most movingly. In the year 991, the first of those Viking raids which were to fill the eleventh century with misery and murder descended on the tidewater village of Maldon in Essex. It was a small episode in an obscure place at a dark period of history; but a poet knew of it. A fragment of his poem has come down to us in the same manuscript as *Beowulf.* Boatloads of Vikings landed on a tidal island in the river Pant, now the Blackwater; ealdorman Birhtnoth and his hastily assembled *fyrd* came out to meet them. The Viking spokesman demanded gold, Birhtnoth answered defiantly; the fighting began. Birhtnoth was

24. The comparison occurs in Bede's *Ecclesiastical History,* II, 13. It was made by an anonymous counselor of King Edwin of Northumbria when Paulinus, first archbishop of York, was inviting the king to convert.

an old man, the pirates chopped him down, and some of his retainers fled, to their everlasting shame. (The poet makes sure to mention them by name.) But a band of faithful ones remained shoulder to shoulder, encouraging one another to the end; and as their numbers shrank, old Birhtwold spoke perhaps the most famous, certainly the most characteristic, lines of Anglo-Saxon poetry:

> Hige sceal the heardra, heorte the cenre,
> Mod sceal the mare, the ure maegen lytlath.[25]

> Aim shall be harder, heart the keener,
> Manhood the more, as our might lessens.

That is the essential Saxon scene. Under a darkening sky on a lonely beach the dwindling group stand defiantly over their dead leader, without hope of victory, dream of reward, or thought of flight. Without knowing it, old Birhtwold spoke those last words for the housecarls seventy-five years later on the ridgetop at Hastings, and for his whole people.

25. This pattern of verse was standard in Anglo-Saxon; it is the meter of *Beowulf* and of Caedmon's "Hymn." The line is measured by four strong or accented syllables, the first three of which alliterate. There is no rhyme. The line tends to be slow and weighty, the more so because Saxon poets liked to repeat the same idea several times in different words.

3

From the Norman Conquest to the Age of Chaucer (1066–1399)

The army that conquered at Hastings field was largely mercenary in its motivation—no worse, in this respect, than most medieval armies, but basically out for plunder. What determined the peculiar character of the Norman conquest was that William didn't have much ready cash to pay them off, and wouldn't have given it if he had. What he gave instead was land taken from the Saxons. The Danes had been content with outrageous sums of money, raised by taxing the land; William took the land itself. That was what determined the depth and bitterness of the conquest. By the time William ordered the compiling of the Domesday Book in 1086,[1] more than 80 percent of the land in England had

---

1. Compiled mostly for tax purposes, Domesday was an encyclopedic listing of all the landed properties in England. The name represents Saxon awe at the majestic finality and inclusiveness of the book. It is in fact the nearest thing we will get to a census for the next 700 years. For each shire it lists the holdings of the king, of the churchmen and religious houses, then of the barons, of women, of the king's sergeants, and finally of those few Saxon thanes who still had any land left (SFR, B.20).

changed hands. The change was simple, swift, and brutal. If they had not died on the ridge at Hastings, Saxon thanes were replaced out of hand by Norman barons; it was straight confiscation. In the first days after the conquest, a few of the old landholders who could prove they had not supported Harold were permitted to buy back their own lands at an exorbitant fee and so to retain possession. But when the conquered districts started to revolt, as they did sporadically, ineffectually, out of sheer desperation, then the full cruelty of the conqueror came out. He hanged, he beheaded, he blinded, he cut off hands; the thanes of Harold were killed, mutilated, outlawed,[2] or reduced to the lowly estate of villeins, half-free serfs on land they had once owned. By removing an entire population (we had better not ask how), William created open space to plant the New Forest in southwest England; two of his sons were killed while hunting there, from which the Saxon countryfolk got a grim satisfaction. In Yorkshire, where there had been a particularly troublesome rebellion, Norman soldiers wasted the entire countryside, leaving a geographical blank. Partly this was "good policy," partly it was natural cruelty; partly also it occurred because William and his gang thought the native Saxons subhuman, refused to learn their language, assigned them only the most servile tasks. Norman French became the language of the law courts, by which Saxons who could not understand it were fleeced and oppressed.[3] Normans replaced Saxons in the church, as fast as the latter could be kicked out and the former pushed in. Marks of the old discrimination remain embedded in our modern English. In a famous passage of *Ivanhoe*, Walter Scott has a couple of resentful Saxons describe how a domestic animal in the field is known by its Saxon name, but when it appears on the table to be eaten assumes a French title. A swine in the sty becomes pork when brought to table, a sheep in the fold becomes mutton when served in the castle, an ox for the herdsman is beef for the cook. Production is Saxon, consumption French. As for the producers, the nasty connotations of "villain" and "churl" survive to remind us what Normans thought of the common Saxon countryman—*villanus* in Latin, *ceorl* in Saxon. (In early Saxon days, churls had been quite respectable fellows; they had sunk quite far in the world before the Normans came along to sink them still deeper.)

2. Among the outlaws was the legendary Hereward the Wake who joined with some Danes lurking in the fen country around the isle of Ely, and for a while raided Norman settlements. Like king Arthur 500 years before, he became a focus of patriotic feeling and the hero of a myth. More practically, a good number of Saxon warriors crossed Europe to take service with the Byzantine emperor, who formed them into a crack unit, the Varangian Guard.

3. Law French still lingers in bits and scraps of legal terminology, in *torts, bail,* and *sergeants,* as well as the call for silence in the court, *Oyez! Oyez!* It was 1363 before the lord chancellor opened a session of the English parliament with a speech in English; always before it was in Norman French. So long as England and Normandy remained closely tied, Norman French was simply French with the Norman accent; as the ties relaxed, other dialects entered the Anglo-Norman mix.

KEEPING THE PEACE

Most of the troubles that were to plague England for centuries after the conquest were direct consequences of it. In the first place, William in becoming king of England had not ceased to be duke of Normandy; those of his followers who had Norman estates did not lose them when they got English ones. Norman England had responsibilities on the Continent such as Saxon England never knew; and barons[4] who were discontented on one side of the channel could often scrape up enough sympathizers on the other side to make trouble for the king. On the other hand, the king himself, seeing this tendency to anarchy, had a chance to guard against it. The clean slate with which he started after 1066 made his position in England relatively strong. Everything in England was his. He gave lands to tenants-in-chief, his barons, on the understanding that they would serve him; they granted pieces of their estates to subtenants (*their* barons) on the same condition. And "serving" in these contexts meant one essential thing: military service in the form of private armies of well-equipped retainers, instantly available at the king's call. In actual practice, Norman knights might be less obliging than in theory; but by feudal theory, they were bound to answer the king's summons.

Again, the English barons were relatively manageable because they were given their estates a piece at a time, one piece here, another there, as the Norman power spread north and west from its center in London. Barons were not generally allowed to own immense domains all of a piece, as feudal lords did on the Continent. The only exceptions were at the border with Wales, where the earls of Chester, Shrewsbury, and Hereford were given specially large estates and broad powers, obviously to strengthen them against the unruly Welsh. Barons might, and often did, grow discontented with the royal government; but their ability to rally their tenants against it was lessened by the deliberate diffusion of their estates. And where William saw that the old Saxon ways made for his interest, at the expense of the barons, he did not hesitate to retain them. The Saxon *fyrd,* for example, came directly under the king's command, without any feudal intermediaries; as the shire levies, it was the nearest thing to a nation in arms. William providentially retained this institution, despite the system of feudal loyalties and subloyalties; several times it saved his successors.

Feudalism also strengthened and formalized a custom infrequent among the Saxons, the institution of primogeniture. This custom decrees that real property (not chattels or movable goods, but land) shall ordinarily descend undivided from father to eldest son. This was good for the feudal lord because it gave him at the first possible moment a loyal thane capable of heading up a private army. It also kept farms and estates from being subdivided down to the point where they could no longer support the owners. Where primogeniture never took root,

4. Norman barons were the rough equivalent of Saxon earls; for further titles of honor introduced after the Norman conquest, see Appendix B, "The British Baronage."

as in Wales and parts of Kent, an older custom known as "gavelkind" prevailed; it allowed, under certain conditions, for equal division of an estate among the heirs; and it really did result in smaller holdings. Primogeniture is obviously hard on younger sons; in every generation, they are pruned away, to prevent their draining energy from the main line of growth. On the other hand, when thrown young into the world, with no real hope of succeeding directly to the title or estates, but with backing and connections from the family interest, they often thrive on their own, and may establish separate lines of which they are heads in their own right. Over the centuries since the conquest, primogeniture has been the prevailing custom in England, and the keystone of the English aristocracy.

Finally, when he dismissed Saxon churchmen and replaced them with Normans, William had a chance to get rid of dullards and install men of intelligence. But he also got men who took the church seriously, asserted its rights vigorously, and could not be bullied. Conflict between the rights of the church and those of the state was particularly sharp in the late eleventh century. In 1073 archdeacon Hildebrand became pope under the title of Gregory VII; he was such an extreme advocate of papal authority over secular rulers that this doctrine has been known ever since as the "Hildebrandine" position. His dispute was mostly with the Holy Roman emperor, and it came to a climax when Heinrich IV, a truculent German emperor more exalted than any king, was forced to do public penance at Canossa (1077), where for three days the pope refused imperiously even to see him. Some of the men whom William placed in the English church shared the pope's jealousy of secular encroachments on religious power. They wanted churchmen to be tried before special church courts; they wanted their church to be in direct communication with Rome; and they wanted churchmen to receive their offices from the pope, not from secular rulers. This was important because, if secular rulers could bestow offices, they could also withhold them; some had been known to do just that, and to collect the revenues attached to the office for years on end, while it stood vacant. These disputes paved the way for yet more bitter quarrels between the conqueror's son, William Rufus, and his saintly archbishop of Canterbury, Anselm. Festering over the years, they led finally to that mortal struggle between Henry II and Thomas Becket which came to a head about a century after the conquest.

Having captured England, William ruled it for twenty-one years, busy for the most part with continental adventures, but active as well putting down Saxon rebels and discontented Norman barons. When he died in 1087, he left Normandy to his older son Robert and England to his younger son William, nicknamed Rufus (Redhead). Inevitably the two brothers came into conflict, and because Robert was the weaker, the English barons supported him, almost to a man. (The feudal system, which is really the absence of a system, always prefers, when given a choice, a weak over a strong central authority.) But William Rufus had a recourse against the barons, placed in his hands by his father's shrewdness. It was the *fyrd* or shire levies which turned out to support Rufus, not from love of him particularly, but from hatred of the barons, who would be many tyrants in place of just one. Ultimately, William crushed his domestic enemies, wearied out his brother, and fought off some troublesome Scots till his throne was relatively secure. But all these wars were fearfully expensive. To raise money, William Rufus used every nasty trick in the tax book (at his approach, we are told, his loving subjects used to flee into the hills as before an invading army), and there was little sorrow in the realm when a hunting accident (or was it really an accident? the circumstances were highly suspicious) cut him off in 1100 at the age of only forty. This was one of two royal deaths in the New Forest, alluded to above; men also noted with sour pleasure that soon after William Rufus was buried in Winchester Cathedral, the church tower collapsed on his tomb. Divine displeasure could hardly be made more manifest.

THE FIRST HENRY

Technically speaking, the older brother Robert should have succeeded to the throne, William Rufus being childless; but Robert was off on pilgrimage to Jerusalem, and even if he had been closer, the third brother Henry would have beaten him to the prize. No sooner was William Rufus cold than young Henry dashed into Winchester with a few soldiers and seized the royal treasury. He had a glib tongue, commanding presence, tangible troops; and nobody was in position to withstand him. Within three days he was king as Henry I; and because his legal title to the throne was not very strong, he had to make a lot of popular promises, which, to a surprising degree, he kept. He retrenched taxation; he promised, and actually effected, some redress of grievances; and by a master stroke of policy, he married a Saxon princess, Edith, niece of Edgar the Aetheling.[5] Thus when the inevitable baronial rebellion came along (fomented by Robert of Normandy, supported by barons descended from the original conquerors), Henry was able to call on the shire levies as his older brother had done, and drive many of his most troublesome subjects from the land. He replaced them with less arrogant types, more amenable to his influence—constables, sheriffs, and castellans who are wardens of castles, but not independent noblemen. Such men could be counted on to carry out royal policy; and under Henry an organized central administration started to take shape. Its chief agency was a group of royal counselors known as the Curia Regis or Royal Court; from this central council in time split off certain traveling investigative bodies which over the next century became the courts of assize. The word, Norman French in origin, means simply "sitting"; cognate to it is our modern word "assess" with its double meaning of "count" and "take." These were courts of inquiry or inquest, circuit courts.

5. Snobs among the Norman nobility sneered at Henry's marriage, but it set a fashion; by the middle of the twelfth century, so many intermarriages had taken place that hardly anyone could claim to be exclusively of one race or the other.

Another subcommittee became the court of exchequer, charged with supervising government receipts and expenses.[6] Some royal counselors were men of independent authority, big landowners, high church officials; others were chosen for their executive and administrative ability. Henry I's part in developing this governmental machinery was a real and permanent contribution to the national life.

THE COMING OF THE PLANTAGENETS

Unhappily, at his death in 1135, Henry left the succession in a muddle of which the barons were only too ready to take advantage. There was a profusion of bastards, but no legitimate male heir.[7] Given several alternatives to choose among, the barons shifted from one to the other, gaining special privileges from each and building unauthorized castles throughout the realm from the security of which they could defy their rivals and the monarch himself, whenever there should be one. Though not in direct line of succession (he was a nephew of Henry I), Stephen had the first advantages, but he proved so weak and indecisive that the country under his guidance slipped close to total anarchy. His first opponent was the equally erratic Matilda, daughter of Henry I and wife, by a second marriage, of Geoffrey of Anjou.[8] Geoffrey himself was hated and feared by the Norman English because of his Angevin connections; but his son, through whose veins flowed a reassuring mixture of blood from the conqueror and from Edgar the Aetheling, was less objectionable. Stephen was allowed to wear the crown during his lifetime, but after his death in 1154, Matilda's son came to the throne as Henry II. In many ways he carried on the work of his grandfather the first Henry, strengthening the bureaucracy, suppressing unruly barons, and tearing down their illegal castles. In two important ways, however, the situation of Henry II differed from that of Henry I. Through his father Geoffrey of Anjou and his wife Eleanor of Aquitaine he was embroiled in constant dynastic wars on the Continent; they kept him abroad for much of his reign. And the quarrel with the church which

6. "Exchequer" from the checkered tablecloth which served these early accountants in their ciphering; it was particularly useful with Arabic numbers, which, though introduced in the twelfth century, were not generally adopted till the sixteenth.

7. Henry's one legitimate son, William Aetheling, had drowned in 1120 while crossing the English channel in a vessel known as the "White Ship." A ballad of that name by Dante Gabriel Rossetti (1881) tells the story.

8. Through Geoffrey two names of wide application and great importance enter English history. *Angevins* were members of the many-branched family of Anjou, stemming from the ancient Frankish conquerors of Gaul; they were hereditary enemies of the independence of Normandy. *Plantagenets* took their name from Geoffrey himself, who had a trick of wearing in his cap a sprig of broom ("genet" in French). These nicknames were frequent and necessary when many members of the same family shared the same surname; they implied no disrespect. Henry I because of his book learning (specially proud he was of his Latin) was called "Beauclerc." The last Plantagenet king of England was Richard III ("Crookback"), and the line, Geoffrey's line, became extinct in 1499.

had always fretted, sometimes enraged, the first three Norman kings had now with time shifted ground and become even more ferocious.[9] What most infuriated Henry II was that the archbishop with whom he had to cope was his own man, a former servant who had been rewarded with high church office, and now seemed determined to use that office against the king who had put him in it. The insubordinate archbishop was Thomas Becket.

THE DEATH AND TRIUMPH OF THOMAS BECKET

Apart from the clash of two headstrong personalities, the quarrel between Becket and Henry focused on the authority of church courts and the applicability of church law. Indeed, the right of clergymen to plead before ecclesiastical courts was generally recognized; so was the need for certain cases, involving heresy, matrimony, divorce, and church property such as tithes, to be heard by churchmen. But like all special privileges, these had been widely expanded during the years of baronial anarchy. A major public nuisance, obvious to the eye, was the right of any cleric, convicted of a crime in the king's court, to appeal to Rome. There his case would be heard by a tribunal of fellow clerics, probably sympathetic and in any case perfectly ignorant of English law; it was likely he would get off. A recent case could be cited in point. In 1088, with William Rufus newly enthroned, the bishop of Durham took part in a futile rebellion against him; the other participants were promptly punished, the bishop appealed to Rome. There was no equity in that, and after some negotiation a compromise was reached, very much like that reached over lay investiture. The king's court tried the bishop as a lay baron, holder of lands in fief to the king, while letting him go as a cleric. This probably didn't satisfy the bishop, as he was heavily fined, though it may have gratified his sense of logic.

But even in the ordinary course of justice, church courts proceeding by the rules of canon law, tended to acquit clerics of crimes for which laymen had to pay dearly.[10] Because one could count on this, a lot of people took pains to have

9. The early issue of lay investitures had been compromised in England as it would be, a few years later, on the Continent. The king lost the power of direct appointment to church offices and with it the power to leave them vacant for long years while collecting the revenues for himself; on the other hand, he retained feudal rights over abbots and bishops as their secular protector and overlord. The new issues had to do less with ecclesiastical appointments than with the routine legal processing of churchmen who broke the law.

10. The canon law, an immensely complicated subject in itself, began as a set of traditions slowly hardening into rules by which Christian churches governed themselves. To these were gradually added, piecemeal, decisions of church councils, decrees of popes, and sundry guidebooks and codes—for example, lists of the penances to be assigned for particular sins. This miscellaneous and often contradictory material was partly organized about the middle of the twelfth century by an Italian monk named Gratian, though it continued to be supplemented long after his time. Canon law was not only bewilderingly complex, it was a great deal gentler than secular law.

themselves defined as "clerics," even though they had never taken holy orders and never intended to do so. Becket, defying the king to abate the clergy's special privileges, was tried for crimes with legal Latin names, amounting basically to insubordination, and condemned by the Curia Regis or royal court. But of course the jurisdiction of that court was part of the basic question. Becket's power against the secular state was only spiritual, the king's power was material, and there was a lot of it. Becket had to flee the country, but after six years he returned to renew the struggle. (An unintended but important result of this tug-of-war was the establishment of the university of Oxford [SFR, B.11]. To deprive the archbishop of material and moral support abroad, Henry ordered home all the English students who had gathered at Paris; almost immediately, they started a university of their own [1167], from which, in 1209, a rebellious group split off to form the university of Cambridge.) Against Henry's blunt political authority, Becket appealed to the pope, and the pontiff, after some hesitation, allowed Becket to excommunicate the king's chief counselors; the next step would be an interdict, a ban on all church services in England. The enraged king, who was campaigning in France when the ban was threatened, spoke some words that his rough, impatient soldiers construed as an invitation to murder. Four of them crossed hastily to Canterbury, attacked Becket in his cathedral, and cut him down (December 29, 1170). This is the action of T. S. Eliot's 1935 play, *Murder in the Cathedral*.

The outcry was immediate and tremendous. Becket martyred was far more influential than Becket alive and kicking; it was a consequence on which he had certainly counted. Henry, though himself put under papal ban, held to some of his legal claims; but on the central one, he lost. Special justice for "criminous clerks" was finally and firmly established; any man who could read qualified as a cleric, and was entitled to the benefits of canon law. (The test of reading was a single verse of the Bible, generally verse 1 of Psalm 51, known therefore as the "neck verse"; among thousands of others, it saved Ben Jonson's neck when he was on trial for murder.) Clerical appeals to Rome continued unabated. And meanwhile, Becket's shrine at Canterbury became one of the most gorgeous, and most visited, in all Europe. He was canonized in 1173, and pilgrimages began immediately, Chaucer's storytellers being only a few of the thousands who flocked to Canterbury. Pilgrims came from overseas as well as from England, reversing the ancient pilgrimage paths of Europe, which previously all ran from north to south. Looking forward a moment, we note that when Henry VIII destroyed the Canterbury shrine (because he loathed the very thought of Becket, who had defied royal power), eight strong men were required to carry off the gold and jewels adorning it; they went straight to the royal treasury, of course. As for Henry II, he was able to escape from his excommunication only by doing public penance barefoot at Canterbury, where the monks inflicted on him three lashes apiece. They were supposed to be purely symbolic, but some of the brothers may have felt impelled to lay it on a bit.

NORMANS IN IRELAND

So far as his troubles with the church allowed him to be, Henry II was an aggressive and expansionist king. He worked to subdue the perennially unsubdued Welsh; by a clever combination of wars, dynastic marriages, and arranged inheritances, he gained control of most of western France; and in 1169, at the height of the Becket dispute, he encouraged a few of his barons to cross the waters and take part in the interminable tribal feuds of Ireland. Easily and quickly, they conquered the entire island, without more than minimal help from Henry. The plum had been ripe for picking. For centuries Viking raiders and warring tribal chieftains had been tearing the society of old Ireland to bits. The Danish invaders especially established a permanent presence on the east coast of Ireland. (Humphrey Chimpden Earwicker, who is one phase of Joyce's epic hero in *Finnegans Wake*, descends from the ancient Danes of Dublin; though he has lived in Ireland for 1,100 years and maybe more, people still think of him as an outsider!) At the battle of Clontarf in 1014, Brian Boru was able to regain, at the cost of his own life, some power for the native Irish. But it was not power to construct an organized society; the surviving Danes and surviving Irish settled into a state of permanent tribal anarchy which ended only when the Normans came to Ireland in 1169.

They were mounted knights in steel armor, with a developed instinct for building stone castles; they fought Irish soldiers who wore linen shirts to battle, carried wicker shields, protected their heads with leather caps, and built no structures more solid than wattled huts. No wonder, as the most plaintive of modern Irish verses says, "They went forth to battle but they always fell." The chief of the invading Normans was Richard de Clare, earl of Pembroke (nicknamed "Strongbow"); among his advance agents was one Maurice Fitzgerald, whose parents had been Gerald de Windsor and a famous Welsh beauty, Nesta ap Tudor. From Maurice, son of these two portentously titled people, sprang a numerous progeny known after their begetter as the Geraldines. Their names would be written across Irish history for the next six centuries; and the first thing to be noted about them is how Irish they were. Being far fewer than the Normans in England, they absorbed far more readily into the native population. Indeed, the conquest lacked none of the usual episodes of blood, torture, rape, and murder, but its consequences did not rankle quite so long. Settling into their castles, the Geraldines became in the words of the chronicler, "Hibernis ipsis Hiberniores," more Irish than the Irish themselves. From Fitzgerald Mor (Big Fitzgerald)[11] to Silken Thomas Fitzgerald (hanged for treason in 1537) to Lord Edward Fitzgerald who led the doomed rising of 1798, they are among the heroic and unfortunate names

---

11. Charged before Henry VII with burning down the cathedral of Cashel (1495), he offered a frank and manly excuse. "By Jesus," said he, "I never would have done it if I had not been told the archbishop was within."

of Ireland. A gallant and tragic American president, John Fitzgerald Kennedy, bore the name as well.

TWO BAD KINGS: A HERO AND A VILLAIN

Henry II's last years were made miserable by his sons. The eldest, Henry, died in 1183 while waging war against his father; it was for encouraging this unnatural strife that Dante placed Bertran de Born (carrying his severed head in his hand) in a lower circle of nether hell. Richard and John both made trouble for the old king, but showed the full measure of their incapacities only after his death in 1189. Richard, nicknamed "Coeur de Lion," or "Lion-Hearted," was a fighter and nothing else. He quarreled with practically everyone he knew, and when Europe had not fights enough to satisfy him, went off on the Third Crusade to fight for the Holy Sepulchre. Military operations in Palestine were muddled by political scheming, and when Richard headed home in disgust, he was captured in Vienna, and turned over to the Holy Roman emperor. That worthy extorted from him the promise of an enormous ransom, the first installments of which were naturally passed on to the English taxpayer (later installments were simply forgotten). When he did get home, Richard lingered only a few weeks before setting off to prosecute some French feuds, in the course of which he was killed after ten absolutely useless years on the throne. Only the strong administrative system set up by the first two Henry's and the devoted service of a faithful official, Hubert Walter, kept the kingdom from falling apart.[12]

Richard was succeeded in 1199 by his brother John, who proved an even worse king, being neither brave, honest, nor particularly intelligent. But, as sometimes happens, the vices of the king proved advantages for the kingdom. John was a poor soldier; accordingly, in 1204, the king of France snatched from him the dukedom of Normandy, which had caused so much trouble and so many divided allegiances. England was better off without it. Then, John was so clumsy and aggressive in his attacks on the rights of the church, that in 1208 Innocent III put the entire English church under a ban. That action, combined with further threats, enabled the pope to impose on King John and his church, in 1213, an archbishop who proved to be an able administrator and a real patriot; his name was Stephen Langton. John had so disgusted his subjects that when they got a good man like Langton, they instantly rallied to him. He called an unprecedented national assembly on the river-island of Runnymede near Windsor, and there the barons and prelates of England assembled in the warm English summer of 1215. They trooped to attend, and not one was friendly to John; they presented to him

12. Walter was archbishop of Canterbury, but more significantly the king's justiciar. This officer acted in place of the king when he was out of the country, and also heard appeals from subjects who spoke no French. While it was of the greatest convenience for everybody, the post bestowed on its holder more authority than was always safe; it did not long survive the thirteenth century.

a document in which their demands and his obligations were spelled out; and after some negotiation, on June 15, he signed it. It has been known ever since as the Great Charter, *Magna Charta* (SFR, B.12).

THE CHARTER AND ITS USES

The fact that this document provided essentially for the rights of English barons, only incidentally for the rights of common folk, is as unimportant as the fact that John began scheming to evade and destroy it the minute it was signed. (He actually got the pope to declare it null and void only two months after it was drawn up.) Thus the charter had to be fought for, and desperately, before it could be accepted as a basic part of the constitution. But over the years it established its authority; what it did not explicitly say was fleshed out by legal interpretation. And in fact it placed a number of limitations on the executive power (to use an anachronistic term) which remind the modern reader of the American Bill of Rights. Only a ruler as generally loathed as King John could have inspired such a document; and the king climaxed his services to the nation by dying a little more than a year after Runnymede. He had done what he could to make trouble for the land, and it took some years of civil war to get rid of the worst consequences he left behind.[13] But at length his son, who had been only nine years old when his father died, grew up enough to assume royal responsibilities as Henry III; and the fifty-six years of his reign (1216–1272, a very long period for an English king in those turbulent times) were, in the main, years of tranquillity, steady growth, and reconciliation. "In the main" is a qualification we will have to expand; and though the realm prospered, Henry III was not personally responsible for much of its growth. To put the best possible face on it, his vices were, on the regal scale, minor. He was a habitual liar, pathologically unstable, and a fussy, feeble man without any sustained sense of purpose; he was extravagant, and bestowed the high offices of the land on foreigners, regardless of merit. This offended the national pride, but on the other hand it showed there was a national pride to offend. Among the politically alert, affection had attached itself, like moss, to stable institutions, and now made possible their further development. About the middle of Henry's reign we start hearing of a new institution (or, more properly, an occasion, a meeting to talk things out) called "Parliament," to which, in addition to the great barons and high administrative bishops, delegates chosen by the different counties are summoned. The concept of an established body of law, to which even the king can be held, is growing in the land;[14] the

13. At one stage the barons were so enraged with John that they invited over a French prince, who later became Louis VIII, to be king of England as well. Only the papal legate, Cardinal Gualo, prevented an obvious disaster.

14. Magna Charta had a strong influence here; one of its major demands is for predictability in government. Men should know what their duties are and are not, what fines they will incur under

old precedents are being codified and rationalized into a standard, uniform, universal legal system. And so when Henry made a ridiculous commitment to the pope, the barons, instead of resorting to civil war, appealed to paragraph 61 of Magna Charta and formed a council of control to supervise future royal idiosyncrasies. Indeed, this operation was not managed well; the counselors managed to insult, not only Henry, but his abler, tougher son, Edward.[15] There was fighting between the barons under their leader Simon de Montfort and loyalists led by young Edward; after considerable bloodshed, the prince was able to restore his father to the throne, while himself remaining the power behind it. So great was Edward's authority, indeed, that though he was away on crusade between 1270 and 1274, while Henry died in 1272, there was not a murmur or a question about the succession. England sat still and waited peacefully for Edward to come back and claim his own, as he ultimately did.

EDWARD THE FIRST: CONSOLIDATING THE KINGDOM

It was an impressive display of loyalty to an impressive man. Edward was big, strong, and resolute, the finest figure of a man among the royalty of his day. He took as his motto "Keep Your Word" (it is engraved on his tombstone), and not only did so himself, but expected everyone else to do so too. Much of his reign was devoted to pacifying, i.e., conquering, Wales and Scotland. Llewelyn ap Gruffydd for the Welsh, William Wallace and Robert Bruce for the Scots were stubborn and persistent opponents; in prolonged conflicts with them, Edward honed a new set of military tactics which would prove their ultimate value under his grandson sixty years later in the amazing successes of Crécy and Poitiers. The English long bow, adapted from Welsh practice, sounded the doom of mounted chivalry before ever guns and gunpowder arrived to make steel armor permanently obsolete.[16]

---

what circumstances. Paragraph 40 of the charter says bluntly, "To no one will we sell, to no one will we refuse or delay, right or justice." The barons who dictated Magna Charta were not unusually enlightened; it was the king's irresponsible government to which they objected, not their own. But by writing down the principles in categorical form, they mowed a wider swathe than they altogether appreciated at the time. In 1297, for instance, Edward I tried on his own authority to impose a tax on the wool merchants. His loyal subjects forced on him a Reconfirmation of the Charters (including Magna Charta), which spelled out that taxation must be an act of the entire kingdom, and specifically granted Parliament (not mentioned in Magna Charta itself) authority to approve or disapprove taxes.

15. We note here for the first time since before the conquest a monarch with a Saxon name. Trivial in itself, the name counted in terms of national feeling. Henry's basic blunder had been to promise an enormous sum of money to help Pope Innocent IV conquer Naples and Sicily (1254); it was an absurd promise because the proposed war was widely unpopular throughout Europe. As things turned out, Innocent died within the year, and the whole venture collapsed.

16. Edward's domestic enemies were in his eyes just preliminary obstacles to the serious task of conquering France; the French, seeing that engagement down the road, encouraged Scottish resistance, and so formed a long-lasting alliance. The Scottish-French connection had its ups and downs,

Though limited in scope, Edward's military successes at home indirectly strengthened his hand abroad; political and social changes during his reign were even more noteworthy. The Parliament of 1295 became known as "the model Parliament" because its system of representation was the one followed thereafter. Its members included representatives of the different shires, representatives of the cities and boroughs, representatives of the lesser clergy. Its root idea, summarized in the phrase "that which touches all should be approved of all," was to be the watchword of parliamentary reformers for centuries to come. On another level, Edward weakened the power of the baronage to dispose in their wills of the land they held by tenure from the king. What weakened them strengthened him. Direct heirs were not touched, but if the direct line failed, leaseholds would revert to the landlord. The biggest landlord of all was, naturally, the crown; and when the king got his hands on a big estate through a failure of inheritance, his interest clearly called him to break it up into a number of smaller parcels. (There would be fewer intermediary landlords to cut into his rent receipts, and less chance of an independent baronial authority to make trouble for him.) Thus, gradually, the power of the baronage diminished as the power of the central monarchy increased; and this change depended, not on the king's personal character, but on principles of law.[17] Finally, Edward weakened the power of baronial and manorial courts, many of which existed simply on the basis of ancient custom. Edward started issuing in quantity writs inquiring *quo warranto,* by what warrant, what particular royal charter, a court was being held. If you could produce your warrant, you could hold your court; and it should never be forgotten that dispensing justice was a highly profitable activity because fines and forfeitures went to the entity holding jurisdiction. But, no warrant, no court. And where the old manorial courts had been, the king's courts took over, to his great profit and the increase of his authority within the nation.[18]

Thus Edward II, a weakling prince, provided only a momentary interruption to the centralizing tendencies set in motion by his strong ancestors. He tamely surrendered his father's conquests in Scotland to the irrepressible Robert Bruce;

---

all but disappearing in the sixteenth century when John Knox and his covenanters sided with England against Catholic France; but it lingered, ghostlike, into the eighteenth century, when French support was all that rendered possible the Stuart risings of 1715 and 1745.

17. A special aspect of this legal reform was a statute known as "mortmain" against donating lands to the church. Church lands were tax-exempt, and the church, being a corporate body, could hold onto them forever, as the title of the statute says, in its "dead hand." For the vigor of the country and the prosperity of the government, a limit had to be put on land going to the church, and by the statute of mortmain it was.

18. The odd and sometimes absurd baronial court survived into the sixteenth century, with its quaint, unchanging customs. William Harrison, in his *Description of England* (1577), mentions one which met in a tavern at midnight. Some time in the proceedings, the steward was bound to steal away to a certain hilltop, and there, by lantern light, to call the roll in a whisper. Tenants sharp enough to follow him and answer "Here!" to their names, escaped the fine inflicted on all others. The court, popularly known as "the lawless court," was petrified punishment for a tenants' revolt in the remote past.

the one battle he tried to fight (Bannockburn, 1314) was an utter rout because he misunderstood the application of his father's tactics. Worse, he turned over the real business of government to a frivolous companion, one Piers Gaveston; and when Gaveston was murdered by some irritated barons, he resorted to even more dubious advisers, who succeeded in alienating him from his wife Isabella. She promptly fled to France with her infant son, the future Edward III. There she became the mistress of Roger, earl of Mortimer, and in due course the lovers returned to England with an army which overcame Edward II; flung into a dungeon, he was finally murdered, while his fourteen-year-old son ascended the throne.[19] But Mortimer and Isabella had been far from discreet; as soon as he reached the years of understanding, young Edward saw he must make a break with them. Mortimer was beheaded, and Isabella forcibly retired to one of her estates. In this way the third Edward, having come to the throne by remarkably crooked paths, partially legitimized himself by murdering his mother's lover (1330); he was not long in making good the rest of his title by prompt and vigorous actions on the battlefield.

A WARRIOR KING, EDWARD III

For a number of reasons, Edward's ambition took the form of war with France. France was a piece of unfinished dynastic business which the first Edward had wanted but been unable to despatch. Though deprived of Normandy, England still retained a foothold in the region around Bordeaux known as Gascony; that was a mutual irritant. Then, in the various troubles that the Plantagenets had with Scotland, France was always suspected, and sometimes rightly, of instigating the Scots and supplying them with arms. Besides, Edward had a specious genealogical argument, too intricate to recite, that he really ought to be king of France. Finally, he was a natural warrior, and the French, weak at the moment, provided a tempting victim. The result was what came to be called, with hindsight, the Hundred Years' War; less neatly but more accurately, it could have been called the Hundred and Sixteen Years' War, for it lasted, with intervals of truce, from 1336 to 1453.

Conspicuous success did not greet Edward III's first military ventures abroad; in fact, they fell little short of disaster. With some Dutch and German allies, he tried to invade France through the Low Countries, but his allies were halfhearted, and except for the naval battle of Sluys (June 1340), in which English seamen destroyed a much bigger French fleet, Edward achieved nothing.[20] But when he

19. Almost three hundred years after these events, Christopher Marlowe wove them into a splendid historical tragedy, *Edward II* (1593); that play, two or three years later, inspired Shakespeare to *his* historical tragedy, *Richard II*, also about the deposing of a monarch.

20. Sluys, though part of a generally unsuccessful campaign, left its mark. England gained command of the seas for years to come, and laid the foundations for her commercial prosperity later in

took sole command and shifted operations westward to Normandy and Brittany, the king fared better. With a tough little army he marched up the Seine valley nearly to Paris, and when the French king came charging out with a much bigger army, Edward retreated carefully north to the little village of Crécy, where the English stood and fought (June 1346). It was one of the world's classic battles. The English were outnumbered three to one, and they fought almost without cavalry. Their foot soldiers planted long lances butt-end in the ground, the points forming a bristling hedge against cavalry charges, the soldiers waiting behind with broadswords. On either side, each of these blocks was defended by companies of English archers, drawn up at an angle to the line of battle. It was in effect a saw-tooth line that the French attacked with their heavy cavalry, in the fashion that had worked at Hastings and unfailingly throughout Europe since the battle of Adrianople a thousand years before. At Crécy, it did not work at all, and the reason was the English archers. They carried a long bow originally used by the fierce warriors of south Wales; it was a polished piece of yew about five feet long, firing a yard-long, razor-sharp arrow. Gerald de Barri, writing before Crécy, tells us that the archers of his day could drive such an arrow through a heavy oaken door so that it would stand out a hand's breadth on the other side. Bows of such power naturally had tremendous range, and when turned against charging cavalry, could hardly fail to do deadly execution. Whether they hit horse or rider mattered little; they mowed down the French chivalry before they could even come close to impaling themselves on the English lances.[21] Sixteen times the gallant if not very imaginative French knights charged the English lines, and sixteen times they were driven off with murderous losses. For the entire battle, the English lost fewer than 50 killed; French losses were over 1,500 knights and an uncounted but much larger number of common soldiers.[22]

---

the century. In addition, the English picked up in the Low Countries knitting and weaving techniques which were the key to the really profitable part of the wool trade. Having been previously mere exporters of raw wool, Englishmen now started to export woven cloths from which garments had only to be cut; they were helped in this enterprise by the fact that Edward I had established, in the last years of the thirteenth century, staples (i.e., permanent commercial centers for the sale of English goods) in Dordrecht and Antwerp. Goods sold at the staple had to meet certain quality standards; and when taxes were due, they were easy to collect there.

21. A special advantage of the long bow over the arbalest or cross bow was the speed with which it could be fired. Cross bows had to be wound up with a crank; long bows could be fired as fast as arrows could be pulled from the quiver. A miserable troop of Genoese cross bowmen was shot down by droves while laboriously turning their cranks at Crécy.

22. From about the middle of the fourteenth century, perhaps from festivities celebrating Crécy, we date the institution of the most noble order of the Garter. What lady's leg the amorous token slipped from, history recordeth not; but that Edward picked it up, placed it on his own knee, and uttered the deathless words "Honi soit qui mal y pense" (Shame on him who thinks evil of it), there is no reason to doubt; and what there's no reason to doubt may conceivably be true. The order became, for long remained, and still is, one of the most honorable and exclusive of knightly companionships.

THE COMING OF THE BLACK DEATH

It was a famous victory, but Edward was too shrewd to press his luck. He retreated toward Calais (the French armies in no shape to challenge his passage), and after a year's siege starved out that important town. For more than two hundred years it would remain an English possession, long after the rest of England's territory on the Continent had been lost. Calais exhausted both Edward's army and his treasury, but he would doubtless have returned to the wars immediately, for his success at Crécy had been capped by that of an army under Henry Percy and the archbishop of York, which at Neville's Cross (October 1346) defeated the Scots and captured their king. But in 1348 all war was interrupted by something worse than war—a terrible epidemic of plague borne from the east by fleas living on rats, seeming to the inhabitants of Europe like the chastising hand of an angry god. Even today there is not much that science can do for anyone who catches the bubonic plague; in the fourteenth century, there was no cure, nor a single practical means of prevention. Plague spread unchecked through the crowded, unsanitary towns; it spread like wildfire across the countryside, wiping out entire communities so completely that not a soul was left to bury the dead. Though bubonic plague was the main killer, other epidemic diseases joined in; so many waves of disease passed back and forth across Europe that a wretch escaping from one was merely left a prey to terror of the next. Estimates of mortality are very rough indeed; it was not a statistically minded age, and in circumstances of total terror, who counts? Probably in western Europe between a quarter and a third of the entire population perished in frightful agonies—on the order of 25 million people, rich and poor, laymen and clergy, the strong and the puny, absolutely indiscriminately.[23] The king's daughter Joan and two successive archbishops of Canterbury died of the plague. One strain of the disease seemed to take a malignant delight in killing mainly children. In addition to the physical effects of the disease, the popular imagination was oppressed, overwhelmed. From this period date the first of those gruesome artistic sequences known as "The Dance of Death"—images of capering skeletons still clad in the rags of their rotten flesh, whirling giddily on the brink of the grave. For later generations, such macabre images were too horrifying, and they were often destroyed; but throughout Europe a few still linger in evidence of the ghastly world of the fourteenth century.

23. One slight variation was noted; monks crowded together in abbeys and monasteries suffered worst of all. Once given a foothold in such crowded quarters, the disease could not be controlled till it had exterminated everyone. It was during this epidemic that the events of Boccaccio's *Decameron* are represented as taking place. The young people who tell those merry tales did the best thing possible: they left the crowded town to dwell for a while in a villa on a little hill, removed on every side from the roads. Not everyone could escape so readily; and even in Boccaccio the background of plague provides a grim undertone for the droll stories. The introductory "Preface to the Ladies" gives a cruelly detailed account of what a plague epidemic was really like.

NEW DISCONTENTS, NEW PROSPERITY

In England, for those working men who survived the scourge, the plague brought many changes, not all of them disagreeable. Labor, being scarce, became expensive beyond all precedent. Landlords and the government they dominated tried hard to hold down wages and keep workers on the land; they invoked such extreme penalties as whipping and branding. But not even the savage Statute of Laborers (1351) availed much against heavy economic pressure. Laborers fled from the farms if they were employed there under traditional terms, as villeins;[24] knowing they could be caught if they just moved to another farm, they often escaped to the towns, where labor was also short and where it was easier to drop out of sight. "The air of the town," said an ironic adage of the day, "makes a man free." As for replacing villeins with day laborers, the landlord who offered the old pre-plague rate of two or three pence a day was likely to be shunned as if he had the plague himself. Three or four times that sum was the going rate; and as the price of commodities had increased too, who could blame the workman for asking a living wage? Landlords who previously owned a big farm mostly cultivated by villeins (plus a few day laborers in busy seasons) now found they could work the land only by leasing farm-size plots to independent tenants. As villeinage diminished, the class known as "yeomen" started to appear. The word is Saxon in origin, meaning perhaps "villager," perhaps "young man"; it does not antedate the thirteenth century. It denotes a very imprecise class of men, sometimes owning land of their own, sometimes not, but generally working it themselves, not renting it out. Definitely below gentry, definitely above day laborers, yeomen never fitted tidily into the feudal pattern of lord and underling. Such an independent rural lower middle class tended slowly to roll up feudalism from the bottom, even as the king was extending his control over it from the top. And the influx of laborers from the country made hamlets grow to villages, villages to towns, and London (uniquely in the British Isles) to something like a city, its population estimated roughly, very roughly, at between 40,000 and 50,000. Such numbers suggest the possibilities of specialization, a trade in luxuries, a class with some leisure for literature, a modest measure of urban variety. In addition, the new arrivals from the countryside, being mostly laborers, gave fresh impetus to the use of English, a dialect slowly being compounded from a mixture of Saxon and French. The courts of law, the royal court, and some of the Norman nobility clung to the use of French, but English gradually became the ordinary speech of ordinary people. It was by no means the Old English of

---

24. Neither chattel slaves nor freemen, villeins can be thought of as slaves to their lords and free in relation to others. Sometimes they were attached to the land, and passed with it when it was sold; sometimes they had to get the lord's permission, or pay him a fee, before marrying; almost always they had to perform a certain amount of unpaid labor. In addition, villeins might have to pay more or less rent for the use of a certain amount of the lord's land.

Alfred and Aelfric; inevitably, over a period of almost three hundred years, during which Saxon was the dialect of unlettered men, much of the old vocabulary, and most of the fine points of Saxon grammar, had died away. Words of Norman French origin replaced Saxon words wherever elevation or abstraction was called for; sometimes the French word drove out the Saxon, sometimes simply duplicated it. The old inflections disappeared, their place taken by prepositions or auxiliary verbs. Because there was no rule of uniformity, a great many different dialects appeared; but about the middle of the fourteenth century, the midlands dialect gained predominance, and when in 1362 English was made the standard language in courts of law, it was midlands English that prevailed. The language of Chaucer is not quite standard for his day, being still a little influenced by a southern dialect; but it can fairly represent what later times have christened Middle English.

As they drew together in their language, so the men of Chaucer's day drew together under the influence of that genial sense of bourgeois prosperity that radiates through the *Canterbury Tales*. Chaucer himself was the son of a dealer in luxuries for gentlefolk; his father was a wine merchant, selling most likely wines from the Bordeaux region, where Edward III had been busily enlarging English hegemony. And the merchant in Chaucer's company, we note, is a great enthusiast for that freedom of the seas which had been won at the naval battle of Sluys in 1340, just about the time Chaucer was born.

MORE WARS, LESS SUCCESS

The Black Death imposed a short, uneasy truce on western Europe, but in 1355 the French wars started up again; and at first English power seemed on the verge of disintegrating the French monarchy altogether. At the battle of Poitiers (September 1356), Edward's son, known as Edward the Black Prince, repeated even more stunningly the success of Crécy.[25] At Poitiers he even captured King Jean of France, from whom, in return from his liberty, he was able to extort enormous concessions. But after imposing the brutal treaty of Brétigny on the French in 1360, the English found things beginning to go downhill. Edward III, though not yet fifty, had been involved in wars and intrigues since the age of seven; his health was failing. The Black Prince, eighteen years younger, was already suffering from a fatal disease, akin to dropsy, which he had contracted during a campaign in Spain. Accordingly, one of the king's younger sons, John of Gaunt, duke of Lancaster, took over as field commander in France.[26] But John was not

25. The Black Prince probably got his name from the color of his armor, but he got it for the first time some years after performing his chief exploits. Since Edward II, the male heir to the throne has been named prince of Wales, a title designed to gratify that proud and restless principality which had developed archery from a toy to a deadly weapon.

26. Edward III had twelve children, seven sons (of whom two died in infancy) and five daughters. John of Gaunt (so called because he was born at Ghent in Belgium) was the fourth son and founded

the soldier that Edward his father or Edward his elder brother had been. Besides, the French armies had learned their lesson at Crécy and Poitiers; they sulked behind stone walls, and refused to come out for a pitched battle. "Free companies" of international mercenaries, first recruited to help the English cause, started to wander off on smashing, murdering, and plundering expeditions of their own. So the war dragged on, ruinous for both sides, with the English gradually losing control of France and the English people gradually losing patience with the whole wasteful process. The royal household thus entered the 1370s in extremely uncertain shape; and much depended on the order in which they chose to die. The Black Prince went first, in July of 1376, leaving, however, a son, Richard of Bordeaux, aged just nine. Edward III died less than a year later; and though there was much apprehension that John of Gaunt would seize the throne for himself, in fact he threw his support to the youthful Richard, who accordingly, in 1377, became king as Richard II.

THE HOUSE OF BOLINGBROKE

Not surprisingly, considering the dark and violent age into which he was born, Richard was a complex, unpredictable character. For some years he was too young to do much, but about the age of fifteen, he began to take a strong, not very wise, hand in government. His first excesses were put down to youth, but in 1386 Parliament felt called upon to vote for that useful device contained in the sixty-first paragraph of Magna Charta, a council of control. This constitutional bridle seemed to settle Richard down, and for nine years he ruled quietly, according to the laws. But in 1397 he turned abruptly on his advisers, imprisoning and executing some, exiling others, and taking absolute power into his own hands. His coup appeared a total success, for the only great lords who had not succumbed to his vengeance had abetted it. Feeling secure, he therefore crossed over to put down a minor revolt in Ireland; and while he was gone, Henry Bolingbroke, who had been banished to France, landed in England. Henry was the elder son of John of Gaunt, recently deceased (he got his name of Bolingbroke from the castle in Lincolnshire where he was born). The pretext for his return was that he had come to claim his father's estate, which Richard had confiscated. Indeed, Henry had not come with armed force, but not much time passed before he had it. The baronage had grown weary of erratic Richard; they hoped for better things from Henry, and he, without committing himself to much, had given them reason to hope.[27] Armies sent against Henry by desperate Rich-

the house of Lancaster; Edmund of Langley, the fifth son, founded the house of York. The struggles of these houses in the later fifteenth century will be described in the next chapter as the Wars of the Roses.

27. Shakespeare, in *Henry IV, Part I* (Act III, scene 2) brilliantly sketches the arts of popularity by which Bolingbroke gained the favor due to Richard. Richard's point of view, more somber, more lyrical, is given in *Richard II*.

ard melted away as they marched; new access of strength flowed to the usurper from every corner of the realm. Within a month (July 1399), Henry was master of England; and now Richard, instead of fighting or fleeing, abjectly capitulated. He was made to sign a document in which he declared himself "insufficient and useless," and his life was promised, with those of his adherents; but the promises were writ in water. Before Henry was fairly crowned as Henry IV (October 1399), steps had been taken to eliminate Richard and his followers. They were tried for treason and, as a matter of course, convicted; the former king, shut up in a dank Yorkshire castle, was allowed to perish of cold and hunger. Realistically, he could have anticipated nothing else. As royal politics was played in those days, Richard's surrender of himself into the hands of his cousin Harry Lancaster was nothing but an act of suicide.

A PEASANT RISING

In following out the troubled tale of dynastic succession to the moment when the house of Lancaster in the person of Henry Bolingbroke took the throne, we passed over two major events of the late fourteenth century which lie quite outside the circle of court intrigues and foreign wars, seeming to enter history from another angle entirely. These are popular, even vulgar, movements, one social, one religious; they are the Peasants' Revolt of 1381, led by Wat Tyler and John Ball, and the religious impulses fanned by John Wyclif which in the last half of the century became popularized as Lollardry. As the simpler of the two events, and the one with fewer consequences, the Peasants' Revolt invites our attention first.

It blew up in 1381 very largely in protest against a government which imposed heavier and heavier taxes to support an unpopular war in France, while passing harsher and harsher laws to keep villeins and rural laborers at underpaid drudgery in the fields. Immediate discontents were thus immediate occasions for the rising of 1381. But in the background lay an ancient, deep-seated rancor against the heavy weight of feudal overlords and the enormously wealthy, vastly overprivileged church. While princes, dukes, and bishops were strutting around the foreground of our stage, it has been easy to forget the poor plebeians in the background, who did the dirty work of society—and very dirty it was. Field labor in those days before farm machinery was brutal and exhausting; the expressive old English word for it was "swink," and Norman French, significantly, has no equivalent. Men, women, and children who performed this grinding labor grew old before their time, and they died at appallingly early ages. They wore rags, ate acorns, went barefoot, lived in huts and hovels; they never saw a doctor, exchanged words with a priest, or fingered a coin as big as a shilling. Sometimes the men were rounded up and shipped off to war for reasons wholly beyond their comprehension; returning, amputated or blinded, they were given a begging-bowl and told to sit in front of the church. Their lined, weather-beaten faces, their wens and goiters and crooked backs are to be seen in old Flemish paintings, as by Pieter Breughel, which we think deliberately ugly or grotesque, but which were apparently just realistic. And at the same time a deep, underground strain of Christian thought and feeling told them that things need not be thus. Though the Bible was locked up in learned languages, even in the age of faith, so called, some word of its contents had become public, and the communist element which was evident to Saint Ambrose could not be concealed indefinitely from everybody else. Revolutionary messianic thought had a long tradition in Europe;[28] when people contemplated the second coming of Christ, they assumed almost instinctively that on that glad day all distinctions between high and low, rich and poor—being essentially considerations of this world—would automatically be canceled. From there it was only a short step to the argument that distinctions should be abolished first so the kingdom of Christ could follow after.

In England particularly, the weight of the conquest and the burden of the Norman aristocracy continued to be felt and resented by the lower orders. In the common course of life they could not, dared not, rebel; but the Black Death and the depopulation it caused made them aware of their importance to society, at the very moment when society through the harsh Statute of Laborers was bearing down on them more heavily than ever. Perhaps there had been some excuse for a lord of the manor in the old, bad days when his castle offered protection and his military training a bulwark against marauders; but not in the fourteenth century, when the worst marauders in view were the barons themselves. Thus the soil was well prepared for teachings like those of John Ball, an itinerant, much-jailed friar, who preached on the popular doggerel verse,

> When Adam delved, and Eve span,
> Who was then the gentleman?

In Eden, as among the apostles, social equality and community of property had prevailed; why not here and now? Ball's point was sharpened, for the farm laborers of Kent and Essex, by the commercial prosperity of nearby London. Toward the end of May 1381 crowds of men began assembling throughout the Thames valley; they talked for a number of days, then marched into the city. About this point, their organization got out of hand; they bullied the aldermen, burned a number of houses, caught the archbishop of Canterbury and killed him. Not unnaturally, there was a good deal of panic. Richard II, a fourteen-year-old boy, showed more presence of mind than most of his ministers. He met with a relatively moderate group which demanded the abolition of villeinage; he conceded it. Next day he met with the men of Kent under their leader Wat Tyler; and they

28. It has been traced in a fascinating volume by Norman Cohn, *The Pursuit of the Millennium* (New York: Harper, 1961); Professor Cohn goes on to demonstrate lines of essential similarity between these programs of primitive communism and modern totalitarian movements (SFR, C.2).

had some pretty radical ideas. They wanted to abolish all social ranks except for one king and one bishop; they wanted church property confiscated and given to the poor. Richard granted their demands too, then watched as the lord mayor of London rode up behind Wat Tyler, pulled him off his horse, and killed him. The king ordered the crowd to disperse and they did—whether in sullen despair, in confusion, or under the delusion that they had gained something, nobody knows. John Ball escaped, was captured and executed. Some of the rank and file were punished; the king's promises were never kept. The revolt was over almost as fast as it had begun; just for a moment, it had revealed something of what lay beneath society's surface—the hot lava of social discontent, the stirrings of aspiration for a more just order. Compared with the court and courtiers, the chivalric games and dynastic intrigues of the Plantagenets, we seem suddenly to be in another world with Wat Tyler and John Ball.

WYCLIF AND THE LOLLARDS

Akin to the revolt is a larger and more complex event which spreads out on both sides of it. This is a movement stemming from the thought of John Wyclif, who died just three years after the Peasants' Revolt, a movement for which he was certainly not responsible yet which would hardly have occurred without him. Wyclif was an Oxford theologian, the most distinguished lecturer of his day, but not particularly a reformer, much less a heretic, till the last dozen years of his life. Most of his new ideas sprang from a single early position, that to exercise ecclesiastical authority one must be in a state of grace. The church has never looked kindly on this position;[29] church authorities did not look kindly on Wyclif's version of it, especially after he began drawing from it the strong conclusion that the civil governor is a proper judge of a churchman's righteousness and may deprive a cleric whom he thinks profane of his office and his property. This position dovetailed with certain anticlerical views of the duke of Lancaster, John of Gaunt; and he, by stirring up a brawl in St. Paul's Cathedral, saved Wyclif from an inquisition about to be conducted by the bishop of London. Pope Gregory XI, appealed to, ordered Wyclif arrested and silenced, but patriotic feeling in England, combined with a series of accidental distractions, prevented the orders from being carried out.[30] And just about this time the papacy itself split apart, in what has been called the Great Schism. Since 1305 a succession of French

29. Whether an individual at any given moment is or is not in a state of grace is hard to resolve on this earth. As the virtue of the sacrament resides, not in the priest's inward intent but in his office, so the church has always taught that a pope may be a true pope though personally a reprobate. Wyclif's views derived from the thought of Marsilius of Padua, as the church noted at once; Marsilius' most notorious book had appeared in 1324.

30. Edward III died on June 21, 1377, leaving his grandson Richard, a boy of ten, on the throne; Gregory XI died on March 27, 1378. And the university of Oxford, refusing to surrender Wyclif, stood on its privileges and immunities, which the papacy only dimly understood.

popes had chosen to live in French Avignon rather than Italian Rome; now, from 1379 to 1417, there would be two rival popes, one in Rome, one in Avignon, thundering anathema at each other and bidding for popular support. The patriotic feeling that saved Wyclif resented not only the pope's ordering an Englishman arrested, but a *French* pope's doing so; and no pope ever looked good when there were two of them, fighting with each other.

As a result of the schism, Wyclif was safer, and in his new security he developed the radical implications of his thought. His attack on the Roman hierarchy deepened into an assertion that the papacy was antichrist itself, and widened into an attack on the power of priests in general. That led to a flat denial of the doctrine of transubstantiation (i.e., the substantial presence of Christ's body and blood in the sacrament), thus to a radical de-emphasizing of the mass and the role of the priest in administering it. The positive side of Wyclif's doctrine was a strong appeal to the religious conscience of the individual enlightened by Scripture. He exalted conscience and the Bible at the expense of clerical intercession. This is close to the basic Protestant position as developed about 140 years later by Martin Luther. Men sympathetic with Wyclif's views, if not directly inspired by his teachings, began a program of popular propaganda throughout the countryside. One of them was John Ball, leader of the Peasants' Revolt, and there were many others. They denounced luxury and laziness among the higher clergy; they preached a simple, earnest Christianity based on equality, personal zeal (i.e., sincerity), and the direct teachings of Christ in the New Testament. At first Wyclif relied on the mendicant orders of friars to spread his teaching, then he turned to priests of his own, known as "poor" or "simple" priests, who might even be laymen. To help them along, he and two of his disciples translated the Latin Bible (that is, the Vulgate) for the first time into English. These preachers and disciples of Wyclif's, who despite social disapproval and active persecution rapidly multiplied in numbers, were given the derisive nickname of "Lollards."[31]

Wyclif's radicalism developed late in life, and we can't be sure how much it amounted to. John Ball, who claimed to be his disciple, had already been excommunicated in 1366, when Wyclif was still a staid professor of theology at Oxford. Indeed, the Peasants' Revolt lost Wyclif the support of John of Gaunt, who had no wish to be associated with anything so radical. But the revolt was one logical outcome of Wyclif's thinking, and he never repudiated it. In less troubled times, when a grown man occupied the throne of England and a single pope sat in Peter's chair, Wyclif would surely have been burnt at the stake. But he was popular with the poor folk; he was old and ailing; he got off. Apparently he was

31. Professor Skeat in his *Etymological Dictionary* traces the word to Dutch and German sources; one of its root meanings is apparently "God praiser" or "hymn singer." Wyclif's translation of the Bible was not absolutely the first, since in the dark days of Danish disorder, when few priests knew any Latin, Saxon trots for their use were indispensable. But Wyclif was the first to put a vernacular Bible in the hands of the laity.

advised to retire to his parsonage at Lutterworth in Leicestershire; and there, on the last day of 1384, he died in his bed. For years Lollards remained a secret and persecuted sect, dying out only after a century and a half, when many of their principles were already accepted, as Protestantism. But the main force of Wyclif's ideas was felt by the reformer and martyr of Bohemia, John Huss, who was burned in 1415; from him, the impetus passed to Martin Luther, and Milton was not wrong in praising "the divine and admirable spirit of Wyclif" as the first bright taper of the Reformation, from which others took their light.

MEDIEVAL ART AND THOUGHT

Our period has extended from 1066 to 1399, from Harold of Wessex to Harry Lancaster; and English literature proper takes classic shape only in the last fifty years of it, with the work of Langland and Chaucer. It is a birth of strikingly unlike twins, an earnest evangelical Lollard paired with an ironic, sophisticated Anglo-French courtier. Both writers use English for complex literary ends, boldly and freely; in no sense are they tentative. These are the founding fathers, no doubt about it. But though the strictly literary work of the earlier centuries is a good deal sparser, we cannot neglect it or look too narrowly at England's medieval past. For though little or nothing was written in English when Saxon was the despised tongue of an oppressed people, French the speech of a cultured minority, and only Latin the language of the learned, England was never ignorant of the great intellectual and spiritual movements on the Continent.

We should note, for example, that when the Normans arrived, they started almost at once building Gothic cathedrals and constructing stone castles on continental models. Saxon churches had been small and dark; few of them survive intact after all these years, though there is a tiny typical one at Bradford-on-Avon in Wiltshire. Mostly the Normans tore them down or incorporated them in newer and larger structures; an old Saxon church is built into one end of Winchester cathedral. At first the Norman work followed Romanesque style, with rounded rather than pointed arches; but the prelates William imported for his new church were the brightest and best, and very soon they were building in the Gothic manner churches bigger and more innovative than any they could have seen on the Continent.[32] Again, the first castles the Normans built were pretty crude, mere mounds of earth surrounded by a ditch and crowned with a wooden palisade. But as soon as they had time, they began to build stone castles with roofs, several rings of walls, and "keeps" (central citadels) for defence in depth. The wall now had projecting towers, so that fire could be directed against ene-

---

32. Looking ahead a little, we remark that English Gothic followed a distinct line of development toward a style known as the "perpendicular." Used only for ecclesiastical buildings, it was widely adopted in the age of Chaucer; but its emphatic vertical lines and delicate tracery continued in general use till the early Tudor period. Magdalen College at Oxford and the chapel of Henry VII in Westminster Abbey provide examples.

mies at the foot of it; access was through a complex structure of gates. On their way to the holy land, the crusaders had seen castles and forts built by the Byzantines against Turkmen raiders; they had developed their own style of castle-building in Palestine; and when they got home, they began busily capping the hills of France and England with bristling turrets. Harlech and Beaumaris in North Wales and the famous Tower in London still stand, massive and stern, to show the solidity of Norman building.

SCHOLASTICISM

The kind of mind that built those intricately proportioned and subdivided cathedrals, those ingeniously defended castles, was also at work developing the most elaborately and methodically rationalized theology the world has ever known.[33] Powerful contributors to this philosophical theology over a period of three or four centuries were a group of clerics known as the schoolmen, or more formally as the scholastic philosophers. Many of them taught in the universities; all used the techniques of formal logic as studied there. They included a ninth-century Irish monk named John Scotus Erigena, Peter Lombard and Peter Abelard at Paris, two famous Italians, Saint Thomas Aquinas the Dominican and Saint Bonaventura the Franciscan, and three important thirteenth-century Englishmen, Roger Bacon, Duns Scotus, and William of Ockham. All these men wrote in Latin, and none on topics that we would recognize as specifically literary. They exercised the academic dialectic, saying what could be said in favor of a proposition, then what could be said against it, and reconciling the two views. During the Renaissance, it was customary to dismiss the schoolmen as empty verbalizers and their method of dialectic analysis as mere crabbed pedantry. The formula was that they should have talked more about real things and less about mere words. But that was one of the things they talked about most acutely: whether things were real and words mere. Nobody can pick up Peter Abelard's provocative discourse titled "Sic et Non" ("Yes and No") or Saint Bonaventura's twenty-page mind bender "On the Reduction of the Arts to Theology" without recognizing that here are minds of the highest subtlety, delicacy, and distinction. This Latin Christian culture, narrow at times but deep, flourished in monasteries, cathedral closes, and university classrooms, while outside baronial chaos raged. The shaky rule of Edward II, through which they both lived, cast not the shadow of a reflection across the thought of Duns Scotus and William of Ockham.

Though it was created by and for clerics, the Latin culture was not necessarily or entirely theological. John of Salisbury, who died in 1180, was a disciple and admirer of Thomas Becket, whose life he wrote and for whose canonization he

---

33. A parallel between "Gothic Architecture and Scholasticism" is brilliantly worked out by Erwin Panofsky in a little essay of that title published by Meridian Books, 1957. One by-product of scholasticism was the transformation of the Latin language itself from a rather rigid and literal instrument into a flexible and intricate vehicle for highly abstract thought (SFR, X.22).

was partly responsible. As a result of his studies with Abelard and perhaps Bernard of Chartres, he was well read in classical authors; he modeled his prose style on that of Cicero and produced several books—stylish, erudite, sometimes even jocose—of which his *Policraticus* is probably the best known. Two other men of general learning who lived about a century later were Robert Grosseteste, bishop of Lincoln, the foremost mathematician of his day,[34] and a man named Bartholomew (Bartholomaeus Anglicus) who wrote an encyclopedia of universal knowledge. Bartholomew was a compiler, not an original thinker, but his book, as was common in those days, had a long history. Translated into English and printed form in the fifteenth century, it enjoyed the honor of a commentary and continuation in the late sixteenth and was still current in Milton's time. The continuation, by Stephen Batman, is often cited concisely and picturesquely as "Batman upon Bartholome."

HISTORIES AND PSEUDO-HISTORIES

Bede, at the beginning of the eighth century, had been an authentic historian, lucid and critical; Nennius, at the end of that century, was a compiler of other men's work; and thereafter not many formal histories were even attempted, the problems of organization and perspective being too difficult for the Anglo-Saxons. But they kept chronicles of events as they happened, year by year, and the last of these did not peter out till about a century after the conquest. Of the conquest itself we have a remarkable contemporary record; it is not written, but in a form as close to moving pictures as the eleventh century could hope to come. The Bayeux tapestry is a thin strip of linen about 230 feet long, embroidered in several colors with scenes leading up to and resulting from the conquest, as well as of the invasion itself. These pictures are vigorous if necessarily schematic; half a dozen soldiers represent an army, two or three ships a navy; they are supplemented by simple captions in Latin. The tapestry was made for William's half-brother Odo, bishop of Bayeux, who is shown riding into battle with a heavy mace instead of his episcopal crozier. Survival of the tapestry is one of the marvelous accidents of history; though others like it were made to commemorate other occasions, this is the one above all we should want to have survived. It is a historic document of unique importance (SFR, A.16).

In connection with the Arthur legend, we have noted the line of historian-

---

34. Grosseteste's protégé of the next generation, while possibly the greater mind, is the more dubious reputation. Roger Bacon, a studious Franciscan friar, put so much trust in experiment at the expense of logic that he was several times accused of heresy and in our time has been credited with anticipating scientific method. His popular reputation was that of a necromancer. All three views are exaggerated. Much of Bacon's science was alchemy, much of his "heresy" common sense, and the necromancy stories are mostly naïve folk tales. Bacon was an advanced thinker for his time; how great a mind he was can't be said for sure.

mythologists who carried the story forward and expanded it to fabulous dimensions; for convenience let it be summarized here in tabular form:

- Gildas (about 545) does not mention Arthur at all;
- Nennius in his Latin *Historia Britonum* (about 795) gives the germ of the story;
- Geoffrey of Monmouth in his Latin *Historia Regum Britanniae* (about 1150) follows the basic story of Nennius but gives it a thick coating of Welsh legend and imaginative coloring;
- Robert Wace in his *Roman de Brut* (about 1155) translates large parts of Geoffrey's *Historia* into French couplets;
- Layamon, a Worcestershire mass priest, in his *Brut* (about 1200) translates Wace's poem, with additions, into Middle English verse;
- from these sources and some others—filtered, most likely, through one or more intermediate compilations—Sir Thomas Malory would draw, in the fifteenth century, materials for his English prose classic, the *Morte d'Arthur*.

Standing well apart from this legendary material is the work of William of Malmesbury, who lived into the middle of the twelfth century. He wrote two long histories of Britain, one secular, the other religious, both in Latin, and both making some effort, not only to separate fact from fiction, but to organize the facts into a coherent story. William is rather contemptuous of mere chroniclers, though he concedes that Eadmer, who wrote a Latin life of Anselm, archbishop of Canterbury under William Rufus and Henry I, had an agreeable prose style. The kind of thing he dislikes can be exemplified in the *Ecclesiastical History* of Orderic, who died about 1142; it consists of a list of popes, a history of the author's abbey with digressions on the deeds of William the Conqueror, and an account of the French monarchy with heavy emphasis on recent events. One can learn something from a book like this, especially where the author is copying a manuscript otherwise lost; but a work of historical art it isn't. There were many local chroniclers in England who recorded the events of their abbeys; Jocelin de Brakelond, chronicler of Bury St. Edmunds who lived around 1200, became famous in the nineteenth century when Thomas Carlyle, in *Past and Present*, made a lay sermon out of his chronicle. Like Jocelin, most of the chroniclers deal with local events from a local point of view; Matthew Paris, around the middle of the thirteenth century, saw things a little more widely because he was in the monastery of St. Albans, where he could pick up gossip from distinguished visitors. But the very greatest of these chroniclers does not appear till the last part of the fourteenth century, and he is a figure of French, not English, literature. Jean Froissart was a contemporary of Chaucer, born in France but at home on both sides of the channel, who chronicled the wars between France and England. His was a chivalric, idealistic soul, animated less by patriotic spirit than by admiration for gallant knights and audacious deeds. Lord Berners translated Froissart's *Chronicles* into English early in the sixteenth century, and the book had a strong influence on later English chronicle writers, including Holinshed; but in himself, Froissart is only on the fringe of English literature.

STIRRINGS OF ENGLISH

Froissart, writing in French, and for knightly readers, marks a step away from the chroniclers and historians, who still wrote in Latin, though of a most unclassical character; a third option now began to open before men who felt the ferment of literature within them. During its long underground sojourn, when French and Latin seemed to have relegated it permanently to the linguistic subcellar, English had lost most of its literary sophistication. What emerged now was a group of primitive but vigorous dialects which began to exist side by side with more established languages. Layamon's *Brut,* being a translation from the French, shows that somebody felt a need for literature in the indigenous tongue; in addition, the poem is said to show the stirrings of literary energy. The same cannot be said about the long moral poem known as the *Ormulum,* after its author, a monk named Orm; it was written in the middle of the thirteenth century. About the same time, an anonymous poet had a better idea; he versified a debate between a solemn owl and a giddy nightingale over the benefits they confer on man. "The Owl and the Nightingale," in rough English couplets, is not without touches of humor, and might have grown to a full-scale allegory. During the twelfth and thirteenth centuries the universities of Europe and the students who wandered from one of them to the other produced a group of lyrics on bawdy or satiric themes, written in Latin but using the rhythms and rhymes of modern languages. These are called the "goliardic" poems, "golias" or Goliath being an epithet hurled against Peter Abelard by Saint Bernard. Wine and women are the themes of the goliardic songs; the singers, though wickedly anticlerical, are understood to be clerks themselves. But since they are students on the loose together, they naturally use the student language, Latin. (Carl Orff has made a brazen, bouncy modern cantata out of some of their ditties.) There are English lyrics which date back to this period, some curious, a few haunting, most clearly intended to be sung. But they are bits and scraps accidentally preserved; they do not bear the impress of a single personality or represent a coherent body of work. Finally, we must mention a group of vernacular romances, longer than ballads but far from epic in size or style. They make use of mythical material from the European scrap pile of themes and characters; they often read like translations from works originally in other tongues, and they have not as a rule been much improved by translation. "Sir Orfeo" is the best of them and an enchanting, a magical, poem it is; others, like "King Horn" and "The Lay of Havelock the Dane" are not much better than old wive's tales in verse. The heroic dream world of the London shopkeeper produced tales not much sillier in the story of the four gallant prentices who by their prowess defeated the wicked paynims in one of the crusades.[35]

35. We glance aside and backward to note the work of a really sophisticated, courtly writer of "lays." About the end of the twelfth century, Marie de France wrote in Norman French a series of verse narratives, after the manner of Brittany. Twelve of her poems survive. They are brief romances on the themes of adultery and enchantment. Dryly sophisticated and utterly unpretentious, they ring

That story was very popular, and ultimately rose to the dignity of a play by Thomas Heywood. Prentices loved it.

THE GAWAIN POET

Quite of a different order is the mind we encounter in the anonymous author of four poems preserved in a single manuscript of about the age of Chaucer. The poet who wrote "Pearl," "Patience," "Purity," and "Sir Gawain and the Green Knight" was definitely a single individual; and from the dialect he used, we can locate him near north Wales but outside it, probably around modern Liverpool and Manchester—incongruous as that seems. (The district, incidentally, is that where the main part of "Sir Gawain and the Green Knight" takes place.) Though we do not know the poet's name, we can make a number of guesses about him. He was a layman with deep religious convictions, a man of some wealth and position in his community, old-fashioned in his tastes (his language would have been incomprehensible to Chaucer and that smart London set), and quite without ambition, literary or otherwise. He was a countryman, and had some contact with his Welsh neighbors and their folk tales; he took chivalry seriously but not solemnly. This is a good deal of guesswork about a man whom we know only through his poems, but the poems are distinctive, and a man with any other personality could hardly have written them.[36]

Exquisite as they are, the poems of this anonymous craftsman entered the main stream of English literature only five hundred years after they were written. During that long period they existed in a single manuscript which, because of its provincial and archaic dialect, nobody could read. Not till 1864 was the manuscript transcribed, published, and translated into modern English. His combination of smiling sophistication with deep, quiet privacy makes the Gawain poet one of those we should most want to summon up from the past for a half hour's conversation.

LANGLAND: NEARLY A VISIONARY

Some kind of divine comedy was evidently in the mind of William Langland, author of *A Vision Concerning Piers the Plowman*. It is a poem he never quite

---

like silver coins, while the vulgar romances clunk like lead. But, being in Old French, their relation to English literature is marginal. They were first published in 1819, first translated toward the end of the nineteenth century.

36. The importance in "Sir Gawain" of a lady's "favor," her green scarf, has led some scholars to connect the poem with the founding of the Order of the Garter (above, p. 63n.); but this hardly accords with the retired, contemplative life of the author. We don't know if he ever visited court or cared a rap about the tight circle of the aristocracy—or, if he did, why he wrote the poem in a dialect no courtier could read and kept it completely to himself.

succeeded in writing, an arraignment of society as a whole by the everlasting standards of Christian justice and Christian mercy; but the shadow of it provides the element of fascination in what he did write. Langland came from much the same western districts as the Gawain poet, and lived about the same time; they might have known, but could only have hated, one another. Like the Gawain poet, Langland used the old alliterative line of Anglo-Saxon origin, and followed an old medieval convention, that of a dream-vision.[37] But there all resemblances cease. Langland is a passionate social critic, with a feeling as deep and angry as Wyclif's for the way in which the rich and powerful, abetted too readily by the church hierarchy, are grinding the faces of the poor, and rendering impossible a truly Christian life. Christ is with us every day (Langland feels) in the person of Piers the Plowman; and every day we crucify him anew. Langland has no words harsh enough for the proud prelates who profess Christianity with their mouths and betray it in every act of their lives; his tenderness goes out to the folk, whom he loves, not in the abstract, but in their disorderly, homely multiplicity:

> Bakers and brewers and butchers many,
> Woolen-websters and weavers of linen,
> Tailors and tinkers and tollers in markets,
> Masons and miners and many other trades.

Langland is at his best with what we could call genre scenes, with ragtag folk in tavern squabbles, vivid bits of colloquial dispute; structure, on the other hand, gives him trouble. His allegory is too bald for modern tastes, with many barely personified abstractions, like Falsehood and Conscience, stating their cases at length; in these edifying debates what action the poem has dissipates, along with some of its moral energy. *Piers Plowman* has the qualities of a great book without those of a good poem. It has warmth and depth of feeling; what it lacks is clear focus. Langland never cast the poem in definitive form; it exists in three different versions (1362, 1377, 1392), varying widely in length and in character. And though it gained great popularity among the oppressed classes who swarmed behind Wat Tyler in 1381 and kept the Lollard movement alive thereafter, it still lives mainly in scraps and fragments.

THE CROWN OF ENGLISH MEDIEVAL VERSE

Chaucer represents the full flower of the fourteenth-century renaissance. Not too long before, his family had been humble folk; the name itself derives from the

37. We pause to register amazement at the survival of Saxon-style alliterative verse into the fourteenth century and beyond: the last such poem was written on the occasion of Flodden Field in 1513. Between "The Battle of Maldon" in the late tenth century and the poets of the fourteenth, alliterative verse had seemed utterly dead. But obviously it had maintained a hidden existence subsurface, changing indeed but never altering its basic character. Its emergence after long silence reminds us how deep the stream of a nation's culture runs.

French word for shoemaker, *chausseur*. But his father was a prosperous tradesman, and Chaucer enjoyed throughout his life many diplomatic appointments
and employments. In those days kings did not always pay the pensions they
promised, and late in life we find Chaucer addressing to Henry Bolingbroke a
polite "Compleynt to his Purse," which needed filling. But on the whole he had
patrons and patronage aplenty; he was related by marriage to John of Gaunt, and
his children are found intermarrying among the gentry and lesser nobility of
future generations. Chaucer himself was widely traveled and widely read. He
certainly read and probably spoke competently at least four languages: French,
Italian, Latin, and English. He may well have conversed with Petrarch and Guillaume de Machaut. It's probable that he considered himself one of a European
community of writers, in a way that would be very hard indeed to realize during
the Reformation and the terrible wars of religion that ensued. Chaucer wrote for
courts, and courts were cosmopolitan.

The career of Chaucer divides easily and naturally into three parts. In the first
or French stage he wrote mostly octosyllabic (four-beat) couplets, as exemplified
in "The Book of the Duchess" (a lament for the death of Blanche, first wife of
John of Gaunt), and a translation of Jean de Meung's *Romaunt de la Rose*. In
the second or Italian stage, Chaucer's great achievement is the narrative poem,
in rime royal stanzas, *Troilus and Criseyde*.[38] This is, in effect, a novel in verse.
The core of the story is traditional, though not Homeric; it reaches back to Dictys
Cretensis and Dares Phrygius (of the fourth and sixth centuries respectively),
who both wrote Latin prose epitomes of the Trojan war. Benoît de Sainte-Maure
in his *Roman de Troie* greatly enlarged the story of the loves of Troilus and
Criseyde, and in the thirteenth century Guido delle Colonne retold the tale in his
Historia Trojana. Boccaccio picked it up in his *Filostrato* (1338), and Chaucer
translated from Boccaccio about a third of his *Troilus and Criseyde*. Thus in the
middle ages a theme was worked and reworked; and perhaps this long history
accounts for a certain sense of ripeness in Chaucer's poem—as if, the obvious
features of the story being long established, the poet were free to develop the
nuances, to give Pandar a genial, jocose character, to provide a sonnet by Petrarch
for Troilus to warble soulfully in his love throes. The gift of civilized sympathy,
combined with the no less civilized gift of detachment, marks Chaucer's special
way of relating to his young lovers. And *Troilus and Criseyde* itself represents
the highest achievement of Chaucer's constructional powers, not simply in telling the story, but in manipulating complex feelings toward a harmonious and
satisfying conclusion.

In plan and in execution *The Canterbury Tales,* which represent Chaucer's last
or English phase, are more ambitious but also looser and more episodic than the

---

38. Rime royal stanzas consist of seven pentameter lines rhyming *a–b–a–b–b–c–c*. Chaucer was
the first to make use of the form in English. It was used in a poem written about 1424 by King James
I of Scotland, but isn't called "royal" for that reason. Best guess is that "rime royal" got its name
because someone thought it a splendid stanza. James's excellent poem was not printed till 1783.

Troilus. They are written prevailingly in the pentameter couplets which would become widely prevalent in English at a later date;[39] and their appeal is to a popular, even a vulgar audience. Some of the stories Chaucer had written in his youth; others he translated anew or retold, with increasing freedom (it would seem), as he gained confidence in his powers. Whether he could ever have finished as many stories as his plan called for is doubtful, but those he completed were, from the first, widely popular. *The Canterbury Tales* survive in a great many manuscripts; they were printed by the first English printer, William Caxton; and the expression "a Canterbury tale" became proverbial for a light, amusing story. Of the whole medley nobody has spoken more eloquently than Dryden, when he said of the *Tales* simply, "Here is God's plenty." Chaucer was still at work on them when he died in 1400.

The fullness or (so to speak) catholicity of vision that we find in both Langland and Chaucer is a special and wonderful medieval quality. One sees it, not just in the literature, but in medieval cathedrals, which—alongside the saints and prophets sculptured on the porticoes, in addition to the kings of Israel and the worthies in the stained glass—cover their flying buttresses with grotesque gargoyles and hide impish little decorative obscenities under the seats in the choir. In Our Father's house are many mansions; all men are His children, some bad, some good, the guzzlers and lechers no less than the pious and sanctified, because all men are weak and fallible. Only the Church, like the Virgin Mother she represents, gathers humankind in under the sheltering folds of her voluminous blue skirt—all human beings, not one left out. There have been, and will be again, religions more notable for those they kept out than for those they let in. The medieval church saw men as one before it saw them as many, and could revel in their multiplicity because it knew that in the end they must all be subsumed in a unity.

39. From the sixteenth to the nineteenth centuries, Chaucer was thought to have been a slovenly, roughshod craftsman in verse; for that reason, John Dryden in the seventeenth century paraphrased several of the tales into more "correct" English. Indeed, without its vestigial plural forms, a line like "And smale fowles maken melodye" shrinks to a lame tetrameter; pronouncing them as it's to be supposed Chaucer did, we got a smooth and fluent pentameter.

The ladies who stitched the history of their time into the Bayeux tapestry were not present at the battle of Hastings, but they got an amazing amount of accurate detail from the warriors and put it into their vivid, if necessarily sketchy, pictures. Among other things, Halley's comet returned to the neighborhood of the earth just before the invasion; it does this routinely about every seventy-five years, but the Normans saw it as a good omen, and the ladies portrayed the blazing star in one of their panels. Probably because he was paying to have the tapestry made, they showed William's half brother, Bishop Odo, in vigorous action; they showed Harold's brothers, Gurth and Leofwin, being struck down; and climactically they portrayed the death of the Saxon king himself, the subject of this picture. The tapestry is an epic in embroidery.

Like its neighbor, Fountains Abbey, Rievaulx Abbey in the North York Moors was founded in the twelfth century by monks of the Cistercian (Benedictine) order. Its architecture was, therefore, particularly austere and undecorated; but its commercial power was immense. With over a hundred monks and four times as many lay brothers, Rievaulx sold raw wool in quantity to itinerant Italian buyers, and its name is often found in the registers of far-off companies in north Italy. But by the sixteenth century, when the heavy hand of Henry VIII put an end to its activities and ruined its buildings, Rievaulx housed only twenty-two monks and no lay brethren.

The quiet town of Wells, with its ancient and spectacular cathedral, stands in the western county of Somerset, sheltered by a crook of the Mendip Hills. Whether Bath or Wells should be the seat of the diocese was long in dispute till in the twelfth century the matter was sensibly settled by making it the bishopric of Bath and Wells. Most of Wells cathedral dates from the twelfth and thirteenth centuries; but in the fourteenth century a central tower, 160 feet high, was added. Its weight threatened the four pillars on which it stood, and a distinctive double set of arches, shaped like an hourglass, was added to the interior. The arches are not only a striking engineering achievement, but aesthetically superb, indeed unique, among the cathedrals of the world. And the pillars they reinforced have stood unwavering for better than five centuries.

Monks who illuminated manuscripts often exercised their talents as artists on the side. What they drew might or might not pertain to the text they were copying. Very often the free sketches they made are the most interesting, because they show conditions of everyday life (the costume of a day laborer, the construction of a plow) which don't generally get into the formal art of the day.

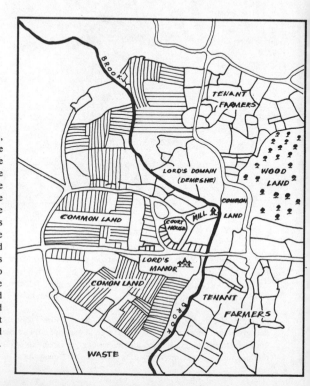

A simplified sketch of a medieval village, with the lord's mill, the lord's law court, the lord's personal domain or demesne at the center of it. Probably the church could be called the lord's as well, since he had the power, in event of a vacancy, to nominate the new parson. The ordinary worker on the common land farmed several strips of it; plots took the form of long strips because the plow was heavy and had to be turned round at the end of each furrow. In this diagram enclosers can be seen reaching into the common land just above and below the main road running through town (dotted areas). Besides his parsonage and the land directly attached to it, the clergyman might receive rent from several other parcels of land assigned to his living as the glebe.

Medieval engineers have not always been given proper credit for their achievements; in the arts of war as well as those of peace they developed much ingenious machinery. But they did not have enormous concentrations of force at their disposal, and until the coming of gunpowder, castles remained hard nuts to crack. When a castle contained several concentric layers of wall, enjoyed a strategic defensive position, and was commanded by a man of courage, it might hold out for months. Many of England's finest medieval castles (Basing, Pembroke, and Arundel, for example) served as strong points in the seventeenth-century civil wars, when they crumbled, indeed, under artillery fire, yet not without giving a good account of themselves. Arundel, in our picture, has been for the last five hundred years the seat of the dukes of Norfolk.

The Tower of London was erected by the Norman conquerors for their own protection barely a decade after the conquest. Two lines of fortification, each studded with towers, surround the central keep, known as the White Tower because of the white French limestone of which it is constructed. (Apparently the Normans did not think that English rock could be trusted to protect them.) Apart from its original function as a fortress, the Tower has served, at different times, as a royal residence, a prison, a menagerie, and a treasure house. At present the crown jewels are kept in one apartment and the royal collection of armor in another; but the many historic associations of the old building qualify it uniquely as a tourist attraction.

Medieval battles were almost all decided by charges of heavily
armed cavalry; and when the knight bestrode a powerful
stallion, he could be very heavily armed indeed. (Heavy armor
added to his impetus in a charge, and mobility was the horse's
problem.) But Crécy, Poitiers, and Agincourt demonstrated
the vulnerability of the armored knight; and during the
sixteenth century body armor became increasingly ceremonial
and ornamental. This suit of mail for Robert, earl of Leicester,
is designed exclusively for jousting in tourneys; the wearer had
very limited vision and, if forced to walk any distance, would
have been stifled by his airtight helmet. But the decorations
are magnificent, as befitted the gallant courtier for whom the
suit was made.

Between the thirteenth and the seventeenth centuries, English families of status often commemorated deceased members with portraits engraved on sheet brass and either set in the church floor or mounted in a niche against the church wall. Monumental brasses, as they were called, could be quite elaborate and beautiful; they were practical as well because they did not take up much space. Unfortunately, the metal of which they were made was valuable, and many of the brasses were stolen. Others fell prey to iconoclasts, who smashed them as "idolatrous" and "papistical." Many survived, however, and for years it used to be a popular antiquarian pastime to take "rubbings" of the old brasses by putting a sheet of paper over them and rubbing it with graphite to obtain a tracing.

The Ciuill Irish Woman · The Ciuill Irish man · The Wilde Irish man · The Wilde Irish Woman

Early Irish art, as represented mainly by drawings in illuminated manuscripts, was wonderfully rich and beautiful, but so highly schematized that one cannot tell very assuredly what the original figures looked like. John Speed, the cartographer who published his maps of the world in 1611, surrounded each map of a country with what he put forward as representative images of the inhabitants. His engravings of upper-class Irish personages are not very different from equivalent English figures of the day; but the peasants (kerns, as they were known in Ireland, or woodkerns) look much like the sort of shaggy creatures who startled and amazed Londoners when they appeared in town (1562) in the train of Shane O'Neill. Speed, like other Englishmen of his day, called them the "Wild Irish"; it is a term for which Ireland's people have never been grateful.

4

The Fifteenth Century
(1399–1509)

The England over which Harry Lancaster had just come to rule as Henry IV, and over which Chaucer looked out with dying eyes, was a land within which the process of social change had been vastly accelerated. Most of these changes stemmed from the impact of the Black Death and pointed toward the centralizing of government. Before the 1340s, England had been land-poor, and the great move had been to open up new lands, arable or pasture, for use by new tenants. Only large landlords had the capital for such expansion, and they used their money to bind villeins and tenants to their service. England was thus a land of castles and manor houses, each surrounded by fields complexly divided into strips farmed by dependents; whether free or serf, they were all socially subordinate to the lord of the manor, who might be distinguished as a knight or an abbot.[1] These nuclear estates were the basic units of society; their slow rotation

---

1. Dividing the land into strips was supposed to ensure equal division of good and bad land; but when a man had many little strips to work, he wasted much time getting from one to the other. At sowing and harvest time, he had to wait his turn for the use of draft animals and such primitive tools (plows, flails, harrows) as the lord could lend him. Wooden plows scarcely scratched the surface of the ground; crop rotation was hardly understood, so fields simply stood fallow every third year. Because no effort was made to breed them selectively, sheep, cows, and pigs were dwarfish and sickly; as there was no way to winter-feed them, most had to be slaughtered in the fall. Because herds were turned loose to graze on the stubble after harvest, everyone had to grow the same crop, or crops ripening at the same time. The extreme inefficiency of this early agriculture was one reason why so large a part of society had to devote full time to it (SFR, B.7).

through the cycles of the agricultural year proceeded untouched by the central government or anything else. Neither visitors nor news from the outside world penetrated such quiet rural enclaves. The parson was very likely the only man in the district who could read; solidly indoctrinated with awe for the hierarchy and respect for the landlord, he required no policing. Custom and tradition played major roles in the old life; an elder son generally inherited his father's leasehold and performed as part of his rent the same duties his father had performed. Little money circulated in the manor; obligations were defined as so many days' labor at plowing time, so many piglets of a farrow, so much wood for the lord's fireplace. The unfree, who constituted perhaps a quarter of the whole society, were forbidden to leave their land; landlords had little reason to do so, and tenants with good leases would not want to. So hardly anybody in England moved from his native district. The few towns, with their muddy streets and high prices, offered little incentive to leave the farm. From generation to generation hardly anything changed. Change was not desired or encouraged. In the cathedrals and abbeys monks recited, day and night throughout the year, a liturgy that was always the same, always consolatory, the image of a cyclical existence.

But after the great plague, England was a labor-poor instead of a land-poor society. Many villages simply disappeared. Modern aerial photography can trace their outlines—rows of houses, circling walls, intricately stripped fields—under six centuries of turf. What took the place of these abandoned towns? Sometimes nothing. Forests overran once-cultivated fields, forests being prized by the gentry as deer parks. Alternatively, the fields might be grassed over and converted to sheep runs. A single shepherd with his dog could watch over meadows that formerly a dozen families had farmed. During the sixteenth century we hear many complaints about this change, and laws are passed against it, but most of the harm was already done in the fifteenth. What worried social theorists was the disappearance of the sturdy agricultural laborer, who would swink for years uncomplainingly at minimal wages, then march off uncomplainingly to war. Such men are always popular.

Wool, moreover, is a cash crop; in the fifteenth century, much of it was sold to weavers and clothmakers living abroad. Commonly it was collected in England by Italian merchants who had brought spices and silks for sale in England; on their return trip, they carried the wool to Flanders where the best weavers were. Italian merchants monopolized the trade because Italy had the best banking system in Europe, and in this business large sums of money had to be tied up for months on end. Commercial houses in north Italy had long lists of English graziers, including particularly the big monasteries and abbeys of Yorkshire, from whom they bought their annual quota of wool. Meanwhile, the former tenant or villein, whether dispossessed by sheep or simply out to get a better price for his labor, moved to a town or city. In one of the boroughs which had won or bought its liberty[2] from the feudal baron or bishop who was nominally its overlord, he

2. "Liberty" for medieval man meant, not just freedom in general, but a specific exemption from obligations to which other people were held. One spoke of "a" liberty or of certain specific liberties.

could often find anonymity and employment. Thus towns grew in size and prosperity, especially where their position at a port or on a river gave them trading advantages. Technically and to some extent actually, they stood outside the feudal system, owing no service, military or manorial, beyond payment of a fee, to anyone. Under these favorable conditions, many burgesses grew rich, got themselves knighted, called themselves gentlemen, and married their children into the landed gentry. Their social rise was hastened by the fact that English, rather than French or Latin, was rapidly becoming the language of business; and with the fading of Latin, the monopoly position of the clergy also weakened. Though still useful, they no longer wielded the sort of independent authority that had enabled Anselm and Becket to challenge kings. Wool merchants who had dealt for years with Italian wholesalers and Flemish manufacturers could serve better in diplomatic posts than the average bishop. And when the king needed a loan, there was no question where he would turn. The clergy professed poverty, the landlord's capital was all tied up in his estate; only the merchant could raise money quickly and be paid off gradually, for example, with a grant for two or three years of the customs receipts at a particular seaport.

Thus we see in effect one society growing up inside another. Perhaps it appears paradoxical that the plague, by killing off so many of the laboring classes, strengthened the position of the survivors. But so it was; and though the course of dynastic politics grows ever rougher and more violent through the fifteenth century, we shall find the import of these noble feuds slowly diminishing as the real strength and practical energies of the country develop outside the feudal system altogether.

THE REIGN OF HENRY IV

Henry Bolingbroke, though through his father John of Gaunt he could claim a share of royal blood, was actually a usurper from Richard II, and the crown never sat comfortably on his head. Only the fact of possession could justify his title, and his relatively short reign (from 1399 to 1413; he was only forty-six when he died) was disturbed by many revolts and risings, mostly in the north and west of the country, which kept him busy fighting for power. For purposes of dramatic presentation, Shakespeare in *Henry IV, Part I,* has compressed two or three of these separate revolts into one; but the essential truth of history is in that account of Owen Glendower, Harry Percy, and the archbishop of York, who rebelled against the Lancaster monarchy and were defeated at Shrewsbury in July of 1403. The plot to partition England belongs to a later episode; but the resentments leading to the revolt are very accurately represented in the play.[3] The king

---

The "liberties" of London town were districts outside the city proper, where city legislation did not apply.

3. Shakespeare also soft-pedaled a specially disagreeable consequence of the later (1405) revolt. By direct order of Henry IV, Richard Scrope, archbishop of York, was beheaded. It was a ruthless act, morally shocking and politically unpopular; his part in it troubled the king to his dying day.

had refused to ransom Mortimer when he was captured by Glendower, and he had demanded that the Percys turn over to him certain Scottish prisoners whom they had taken at the battle of Homildon Hill in 1402. Both acts violated the feudal code of a lord, who was supposed to relieve his thane's distress and not to deprive him of his proper booty. Glendower's grievance was economic; he resented the taxes demanded by the new government. So all the resentments of feudal separatism were represented among the rebels. Besides, Bolingbroke had deposed and murdered a legitimate king; a mixture of violence and deceit was necessary to consolidate his power. Such behavior hardly made for popularity, and the king's life was a troubled one, particularly after he began to suspect that his elder son, soon to be Henry V, was impatient to supplant him. In his youth, Henry IV had been an active and practiced warrior; after 1405 a wasting disease was on him, and he was able to govern only with the help of a special council. For a while the prince of Wales dominated this council, not altogether to his father's satisfaction; on one occasion he was dismissed and replaced by his younger brother, Thomas. But when the "old" king died, there was no doubt at all that Prince Henry would succeed.

THE SHORT, GLORIOUS CAREER OF HENRY V

Like Edward III before him, Henry V was a warrior king. There has been speculation that he saw foreign adventure as a way of uniting factions that had troubled his father, but the ingenuity is unnecessary. Henry had as many reasons as Edward III to war on France; and like Edward's reasons, they all come down to the fact that he wanted to. France was now ruled by a king (Charles VI) who was not only weak but periodically insane; the country was torn by political feuds; and besides, Henry seems sincerely to have believed in his title to the French throne.[4] All these motives came together within a couple of years after his coronation.

One measure of Henry's confidence was the fact that most of the royal family accompanied him on his cross-channel expedition; a sign of the nation's support was the fact that most of the powerful aristocrats (including some whose families had been no great friends of Henry IV) came along too. Landing at Harfleur near the mouth of the Seine, Henry paused unwisely to besiege the town. Its capture cost him heavily in troops killed or disabled by sickness; but at last the garrison capitulated. Henry then marched, with unusual quickness for a medieval army, toward Calais, till he was intercepted near Agincourt by a French army three or four times larger than his own little troop of 6,000. The French, who since Crécy had learned nothing and forgotten nothing, once more attacked the English army

---

4. From a modern perspective it seems strange that anyone could ever have thought England and France would make a single rulable nation. But with the Norman example in mind, Henry thought himself justified in a campaign as hopeless as it was, ultimately, miserable and destructive. At least he tried to justify himself, repeatedly.

frontally, slogging across plowed fields in heavy armor under withering fire from English archers. When they reached the English lines, they were so exhausted by their struggle through the mud, and so burdened by their armor, that the agile English yeomen hacked them to pieces. Henry returned home in the late fall, having captured a fabulous prize, the duke of Orléans, chief guardian of the null king Charles. Agincourt took its place in heroic English legend (25 October 1415).

So confused and disordered were the affairs of France that Henry had no trouble returning in 1417 to secure a base in Normandy. This was no hit-and-run raid; the English besieged and took walled cities like Caen and Rouen, from which Henry's captains carried off mountains of booty. By making a shrewd alliance with the duke of Burgundy (still, and till 1477 an independent sovereign), Henry was able to widen his influence till the French king controlled only a small southern fraction of his own kingdom. Burgundy and England split up the rest; and by a treaty signed at Troyes (May 1420), they agreed that Henry would marry Catherine, daughter of Charles VI, and on the French king's death succeed to the throne of France. Naturally, this arrangement did not gratify the dauphin, legitimate son and heir of Charles; and to strengthen his claim he had the support, among the French, of the Armagnac faction, a group based in southeast France and ferociously hostile to the Burgundians.[5] Had Henry V lived, however, he might (disastrously for both countries) have swept France clean as far as the Mediterranean. But in August of 1422, less than two months before Charles VI, he died abruptly of dysentery. He was only thirty-five years old, and the son he left behind, to become Henry VI, had not yet seen his first birthday. By contract, the poor baby was committed to become king of England and France as soon as he grew up.

AN UNEASY OCCUPATION OF FRANCE

During the minority of Henry VI, the two countries were ruled by a council of the great barons and potentates of England under the leadership of the late king's brothers, John, duke of Bedford, and Humphrey, duke of Gloucester. To the misery and distress of the French, Henry V's captains were almost as tough as the king himself had been; they carried out in France, to their own enormous profit, the program of indiscriminate loot and carnage into which "knightly prowess" was always apt to degenerate. Holding to the alliance with Burgundy, they expanded their control over France until, five or six years after Henry's death, they controlled everything north of the Loire, plus Gascony to the south

---

5. Not far from Gascony, where the English had long kept a political and commercial foothold, Armagnac is the home of a famous brandy. When the Armagnac party allied with followers of the duke of Orléans (after Agincourt, he was held captive for fifteen years, but his followers remained active in support of the monarchy), they became in effect a French national party in opposition to the Burgundy-England alliance.

of it. Some of this "control" was the result of organized warfare carried out by regular armies; but a good deal of it amounted to no more than bands of desperadoes roaming about and killing or torturing for plunder. It was a terrible period for France because her own population seemed so abject before the bullies. And whether it happened by accident or design, it was of the greatest advantage to the peaceful farmers and more peaceful burghers of England to have those insatiable, murderous noblemen out of the country and bringing misery to someone else.

A SAINT IN ARMOR

In 1428 the earl of Salisbury, pushing southward against the forces of the dauphin, laid siege to the city of Orléans; its fall would have been all but fatal to the nation of France. But at the last minute an inspired peasant girl appeared from nowhere, convinced that she had a divine mission to save the nation. Joan of Arc put new spirit into the dauphin and his armies; they lifted the siege and drove the English back. Two months later (July 1429) the dauphin was crowned at Rheims as Charles VII, king of France. It is true that the French commanders who thought themselves professional soldiers deeply resented Joan's success. They did as little as possible to help her, and were more pleased than otherwise when within a year she was captured by the Burgundians, who turned her over to the English, who burned her as a witch.[6] But her influence remained vital; the French were emboldened, and the English, having stripped the countryside bare, found the war hard to continue. While it was bringing home rich booty, the war had been tolerated and even supported by the Parliament at home. But, like all freebooting expeditions, this one had to be successful to keep going; the minute the English went on the defensive in France, their cause was lost. A good part of the English army had grown up with war as a way of life; they resisted grimly, smashing and burning what they couldn't carry off. Yet gradually they had to give way, abandoning cities and regularly losing battles. After 100 years the French had finally learned not to make frontal attacks on English armies; instead, they waylaid the English while they were on the march, or forced them to fight in a town, where their archers did not have a clear field of fire.

DISINTEGRATION AND DEFEAT

Worst of all, during the 1430s, the crucial alliance with Burgundy began to deteriorate. At the heart of it had been the duke of Bedford's marriage with Anne, sister of the duke of Burgundy. But in 1432 that lady died; and though

---

6. Five hundred years after her execution, the Catholic church canonized this "witch" as a saint. George Bernard Shaw's *Saint Joan,* inspired by this event, makes much of English hypocrisy in executing for "witchcraft" a girl who had beaten them fairly on the field of battle. With some justice, Shaw compares the private "voices" which inspired Joan to the inner inspiration that would be characteristic, a hundred years later, of Protestantism.

Bedford, with patriotic vigor, took another French wife within five months, the political alliance was crumbling. In 1435 the duke of Burgundy made peace with France and recognized Charles VII as sovereign. Henceforth the English were limited to fighting a rear-guard action in Normandy. The character of young Henry VI as he grew up offered little incentive to do otherwise. He had inherited none of his father's dynamic qualities as a leader of men; rather, he was physically weak, personally mild, and better suited to a classroom or a monastery than a throne.[7] The barons, trying to make such use of him as they could, married him in 1445 to Margaret of Anjou, niece of Charles VII; the political aim was to stabilize what was left of the English presence in France and ease out of the war. But only a brief truce resulted. In 1450 Normandy was retaken for France as a result of the catastrophic battle of Formigny, in which an English army was annihilated almost to the last man. (In the desperate last stages of this hideous struggle, neither side took prisoners.) When Normandy was lost, it was the turn of the centuries-old English enclave in Gascony; it had been English since 1153 when Henry II married Eleanor of Aquitaine, but was now doomed. The dreaded John Talbot, first earl of Shrewsbury (a man feared by his own soldiers quite as much as by the enemy), rushed to defend it, and died fighting in Castillon. Bordeaux had been captured, lost, recaptured, and reduced to a heap of rubble when in 1453 the English were finally driven out. Nothing now remained of English holdings on the Continent except the fort of Calais, to which England would cling for another century. After nearly forty years of atrocious bloodshed and blind destruction, the English were considerably worse off than they had been in 1415, when young Henry V set sail gallantly for France. On this sour note ended the Hundred Years' War, actually begun in 1336. Also in 1453, after eight years of marriage, Henry VI surprised everybody by actually generating a son, Prince Edward; in the same year, he unfortunately went mad. To be sure, the difference between Henry sane and Henry mad was negligible; in either case, he was the creature of his hardheaded advisers. But to their number was now added, because she had a son to fight for, one of the fiercest of the lot, Queen Margaret. In the first act of *Richard III,* Shakespeare has left us a memorable portrait of her in old age—a savage hag, despoiled of husband, son, power, influence, and beauty, but still raging, still unreconciled, laying on her enemies the many furious curses that it will be the work of the play to fulfill.

DUBIOUS ORIGINS: THE HOUSE OF TUDOR

Before considering events leading up to the Wars of the Roses, we must turn aside to consider a romantic little episode which would, in due course, flower

---

7. Two telling details of his behavior are preserved. He wore a simple blue velvet gown, and only that—as if, men said, he had no other clothes to his name. And when he was shocked at something, he said simply, "Fie, for shame! Forsooth ye are to blame." Shakespeare's Hotspur would have been appalled, who wanted even his ladies to swear "a good mouth-filling oath" (*Henry IV, Part I,* Act III, scene 1).

into a supremely significant historical event. Catherine of Valois, widowed by the death of Henry V, and consigned by the undoubted succession of Henry VI to the stuffy role of queen mother, was barely twenty-one years old, and by no means the sort of lady to spend the rest of her life pining. Among the courtiers surrounding her infant son, she took note of a sturdy and very handsome young Welshman named Owen ap Mereddyd Tudor. In north Wales Tudors had held respectable if not distinguished offices, as seneschals, stewards, and the like. Owen's father, having killed a man under criminal circumstances, was hiding in the deep mountains around Snowdon; not to put too fine a point on it, he was an outlaw. But Owen Tudor put a bold face on things (he had rather a knack for this), came to court, and about 1428 was accepted as the lover of Catherine, an unofficial post. Humphrey, duke of Gloucester, brother to the duke of Bedford, procured a special order forbidding Catherine to marry without council consent. But lack of proper papers proved no obstacle to the endeavors of the happy couple; they quickly produced three sons and two daughters. And though the bold young Welshman was several times questioned and jailed because of the intrigue, he bore it out, and years after Catherine had retired to the traditional abbey, he met death by beheading while supporting the forlorn cause of Henry VI at the battle of Mortimer's Cross in 1461.[8] Edmund, the elder son of Owen and Catherine, was brought up a knight, created earl, legitimized belatedly, and married young to Lady Margaret, daughter of John Beaufort, duke of Somerset. (The Beauforts were also a left-handed family, being descended from John of Gaunt's liaison with Catherine Swynford, extralegal at the time though later legitimized.) Their child, born to a fourteen-year-old widow three months after her husband's death, was Henry, who as Henry VII became the first Tudor monarch and founded a famous royal line.

YORKISTS AND LANCASTRIANS

The royal council which ran the kingdom during the long reign of Henry VI consisted mainly of his extended family, who derived their lineage from that splendidly fertile man John of Gaunt, duke of Lancaster. The dukes of Bedford and Gloucester, both uncles to the king, were grandsons of Lancaster; Henry Beaufort, bishop of Winchester, was a great-uncle to the king via that illegitimate Swynford connection, which had also produced the duke of Somerset, who exercised great influence on the council. Rich, powerful, and unpopular, Wil-

---

8. Catherine entered Bermondsey Abbey (where she shortly died), and Owen Tudor was summoned to London for questioning, in 1436; the date suggests that the duke of Bedford had been their protector, and that after his death in 1435, powerful men in the council took steps to break up the liaison. After his execution in 1461, the head of Owen Tudor was set on the market cross in Hereford; and there (says tradition) a mad woman came to wash the face, comb the hair, and set wax candles alight before this macabre relic of one who had loved a queen.

liam de la Pole, earl of Suffolk, was also of the council; he gained eminence by arranging Henry's marriage with Margaret of Anjou, and as the exponent of a peace policy. But the most powerful of all the family outsiders on the council was Richard, duke of York. He had estates, retainers, money; he also had a pair of connections with the blood royal which did not involve John of Gaunt at all.

Shakespeare, who worked hard to make an intricate matter seem straight, laid out the genealogies painstakingly in *Henry VI, Part 2,* Act II, scene 2:

> What plain proceedings is more plain than this ? [says the earl of Warwick]
> Henry doth claim the crown from John of Gaunt,
> The fourth son [of Edward III]; York claims it from the third.
> Till Lionel's issue fails, his should not reign.

Lionel's issue is the family of Lionel, duke of Clarence, the third son. Through his mother Anne Mortimer, Richard of York could claim to be of that prior line, while through his father he descended from the fifth son, Edmund Langley, duke of York. Of course, if Henry VI had been half the man that Henry V was, these antiquarian quibbles would never have been raised; and at first Richard of York, being a moderate and sensible man, did not press his claims. In fact, while Henry VI was temporarily mad, York acted as his protector and, when the king recovered, laid down his authority quietly. But he was always suspect to the Lancastrians. Aware that their king was weak and their French war record unpopular, they tried to keep York on the defensive. When he held a command in France, they refused him necessary support; when he returned to England, they tried to shelve him by sending him off to Ireland. Because of popular discontent with the war and with the quarrelsome Lancastrian chiefs, and because Richard of York, by marrying the wealthy and well-connected Cecily Neville, had himself become wealthy and well connected, he grew to be popular in ways that were not altogether safe. An ill-conceived and ill-starred revolt of 1450, called Jack Cade's rebellion, had a notably Yorkist character, forcing York himself to take part in repressing it.[9] But the Lancastrian party, animated by Queen Margaret and Edmund Beaufort, duke of Somerset, would not be reconciled; the king himself pleaded weakly for peace, and was derided. Banishments, impeachments, and accusations of treason were the early weapons of the factions; then there was the occasional assassination or mysterious disappearance; and at last, in May of 1455, the two sides met at St. Albans in open battle. This is generally regarded as the start of the Wars of the Roses. It is a misnomer because, though a white rose was the emblem of York, a red rose was the emblem of Tudor, not Lancaster. Still, we will not try to correct an error so old and so picturesque; the Wars of the Roses let them be.

9. Cade, a restless, violent man well represented in *Henry VI, Part 2,* Act IV, had few positive aims. His people, mostly from Kent and Sussex, looted where they could, and opened the jails to get quick recruits. Though they got briefly into London, the citizens promptly threw them out. Cade was wounded while being captured, and died in the cart carrying him to the gallows.

THE CIVIL WARS

The outstanding fact about these wars was their limited and superficial character. They were not wars of principle, wars between districts, wars between racial groups, social classes, or religious sects; they were intermittent gang fights between small groups of aristocratic professionals. (With some pardonable exaggeration, it's been said the Wars of the Roses pitted Lancastrian bastards against Yorkist impostors.) Bitter these struggles certainly were, but neither wide nor deep. Neither faction wanted, or was able, to rouse the countryside, so that most of the battles were fought between "armies" of retainers amounting to no more than 1,000 men on a side. Plain folk found it hard to be concerned with the genealogical hairsplitting over who should be king of England. The real core of the boil was feeble Henry VI, who for thirty-nine long years occupied the throne without filling it—simply, by his presence, preventing anyone else from really ruling.

Military actions may be summarily described. After the first battle of St. Albans, an uneasy truce prevailed until the Lancastrians, victorious at Ludlow field in October 1459, took full command of the central government. Their victory sent the duke of York to seek refuge in Ireland, while his kinsman Richard Neville, earl of Warwick, took defiant command of the garrison at Calais. In 1460, Warwick, with the duke of York's son Edward, crossed the channel, defeated the Lancastrians at Northampton, and forced them to accept Richard, the old duke of York, as heir to the throne after Henry VI. Within a year, however, Richard of York was dead, killed in a battle at Wakefield. Young Edward, already earl of March and now by his father's death duke of York, gathered an army, fought and won the battle of Mortimer's Cross (February 1461), and marched on London. He was joined by Warwick (who earned in the process the nickname of "kingmaker"), and crowned as Edward IV. Within a month he had sealed his victory with a battle at Towton near York which scattered the last army of Henry VI and drove him with his protectress, Queen Margaret, into exile in Scotland.

As a replacement for Henry VI, Edward, the first of two Yorkist kings, was not bad. His genealogical qualifications were as good as anyone's, he was brave, handsome, and intelligent. But he was also very lazy and more than a little dissipated. From the defeated Lancastrians he inherited a bitter legacy of hatred, and he owed a heavy debt of gratitude to Warwick the kingmaker, behind whom stood the numerous and hungry clan of Nevilles. Edward could not even trust his own brothers, George, duke of Clarence, and Richard, duke of Gloucester, whom his enemies, perhaps unfairly, nicknamed "Crookback."

A PRECURSOR OF THE TUDORS

Lingering groups of sullen Lancastrians, lying low in Scotland and Wales, helped keep Edward's forces united during the first part of his twenty-two-year reign (from 1461 to 1483). Queen Margaret proved herself clearly the fiercest warrior in the Lancastrian camp; using her French connections, she strove to win French support for her inert husband, and she stirred up her son to think himself deprived of his proper rights. But not even the threat of these intrigues could halt the gradual alienation of Edward from his chief supporter, the earl of Warwick. Against the wishes of Warwick, who had hoped for a French alliance, Edward married Elizabeth Woodville; and to the family of Woodvilles he distributed the offices and estates that the Nevilles had wanted for themselves. Again, Edward pursued a foreign policy of alliance with Burgundy rather than France, which Warwick favored. Warwick thus sought out support from the king's brother, the duke of Clarence and, when he had it, made open alliance with Margaret and the Lancastrians to raise an insurrection against Edward (September 1470). It was for the moment successful, and poor old Henry VI (who had been kept in the Tower of London since 1465, when he was captured in a north-country skirmish) was brought forth to serve for six months or so as figurehead for Warwick's personal government. But Edward, in exile on the Continent, raised an army with the help of his ally Burgundy, returned to England, and in two smashing battles (Barnet, near London, April 14, and Tewkesbury, near Gloucester, 4 May 1471) crushed Lancastrian hopes forever. At Barnet Warwick was killed and Henry VI recaptured, an event which he survived only briefly. At Tewkesbury Margaret was captured and her only son killed. Thus Edward IV remained triumphant, his enemies defeated and his right to the succession unchallengeable.[10]

A compressed account like this doesn't properly represent the ragged texture of the fifteenth-century wars. They were localized, in time and space: a furious battle might be raging in a back-country field, while half a mile away cows grazed placidly. Dozens of country houses and castles were besieged, but not a single real town or city; the towns, as a rule, took no sides. Nobody controlled at any given point a significant amount of contiguous territory. Atrocious murders were committed secretly in the midst of an ostensible peace. Corpses were insulted, sanctuaries violated, poison and necromancy invoked, natural feelings outraged. Traitors switched sides again and again. Raiding parties slipped secretly across peaceful landscapes to storm, burn, and massacre an enemy stronghold. There were episodes of wild, despairing flight and lost causes suddenly redeemed, of children murdered because of their position on a genealogical chart. It was like an insanely complicated and very brutal private game played at a furious pace by a few totally absorbed players in the midst of a largely oblivious countryside.

Growing up in the midst of this turmoil, Edward IV turned into a tough and wily monarch. Having learned the importance of money as an engine of policy,

10. At Tewkesbury we hear for the first time of artillery playing an important role in fighting on English soil. Smaller hand-held guns remained ineffective for some years to come, but Edward, a skilled tactician and a man of alert faculties generally, used cannon to good effect only a few years after they had first proved their value in Europe.

he collected all he could by confiscating the estates of enemies and squeezing Parliament to raise taxes. Even war was made to turn a profit. In 1474 Edward agreed with his lifelong friends the Burgundians to undertake a joint invasion of France. For this occasion loans were levied, taxes raised, and troops shipped off to Calais. The Burgundians, confident in their old ally, marched off to war. But at the last minute Edward, in return for a large bribe, canceled the invasion, left the Burgundians to their fate, and kept both the French bribe and his own subjects' taxes in return for not fighting a war he had never seriously contemplated.[11]

Within England, the chief source of royal anxiety was the king's brothers, unhappy at the distribution of the many estates forfeited by the earl of Warwick and his kinsmen of the Neville tribe. The duke of Clarence, who had once already deserted to Warwick and returned to his brother's cause just in time to be forgiven, showed himself restive again. It was dangerous to agitate against the king, but much more dangerous to agitate against the other royal brother, Richard, duke of Gloucester. Charges of doing just that were brought against the duke of Clarence, and while they were pending he was mysteriously but very conveniently murdered (1478). Edward had five more years, and they were years of relative tranquillity; he died at Westminster, without seeing his forty-first birthday. He had inaugurated many policies to strengthen the monarchy and make it self-sufficient, the full success of which it was left to Henry VII to realize.

THE ULTIMATE GAMESMAN: RICHARD III

At his early death, Edward IV left, in addition to a daughter, two sons, the eldest of whom, at the age of twelve, automatically became king as Edward V. But Richard of Gloucester was not satisfied with that arrangement. From his estates in the north country, he moved swiftly south, and without a moment's hesitation captured the youthful king and his protector, earl Rivers. Shortly thereafter, Richard put forward in Parliament the argument that Edward IV had not been legally married, because, before his marriage nineteen years ago to Elizabeth Woodville, he had been engaged to another girl. If this were so, Edward's children were illegitimate, and the rightful king of England was Richard of Gloucester. Without any further argument, he had himself crowned as Richard III, while Edward V and his younger brother were placed "for safe keeping" in the Tower of London. Earl Rivers and other strong supporters of the late king were quickly sent to the block. As for the two little princes in the Tower, nobody knows for sure what happened to them, though it's not hard to guess. They were never seen alive again. Many years later a pair of youthful skeletons were found under a

---

11. In 1492, Henry VII played much the same trick, with equal success, on Maximilian of Germany and Ferdinand of Spain. In the *Utopia,* Sir Thomas More deplores this device as typical of dishonest courtiers.

staircase where they had been walled up, but at the time there was simply a quiet, and rather sinister mystery. Since the two princes had disappeared so completely, and at such a youthful age, later impostors found it easy to impersonate one or other of them.

Because Shakespeare lived and wrote under a Tudor monarch, the legitimacy of whose line he was bound to justify, he portrayed Richard III in the blackest of colors. In this he was simply following the regular Tudor propaganda line. By genealogy the first Tudor king, Henry VII, had the weakest claim that any English king has ever advanced; for though he claimed royal blood through his mother and his father's mother, on both sides it was through the female line and with the stigma of illegitimacy (see above, p. 87). If Henry's usurpation of the throne in 1485 was to be justified, it must be through the misdeeds of the monarch he replaced, Richard III. When all this is said, it remains that Shakespeare had plenty to build on in making Richard an unscrupulous villain. Perhaps he did not kill with his own hands his brother Clarence and his two little nephews in the Tower; but he held them all in his power, he had much to gain by their deaths, and in an amazingly convenient way, they all turned up dead. Still, Richard was a man of courage and genuine intelligence; he might well have made an able king. But as he ruled only two years, during most of which he was busy fighting off rebellions, he was hardly able to make much policy. An early but embittered supporter, the duke of Buckingham, collected some helpers and raised a revolt in the west country (autumn 1483). The revolt collapsed and Buckingham was executed, but many of his followers crossed the channel to Brittany, where they rallied round Henry Tudor. He had fought unsuccessfully at Tewkesbury in 1471, and would have been proclaimed king if Buckingham had succeeded. The name of Tudor was popular in Wales, that of Richard everywhere tainted. Still, when Henry landed at Milford Haven on the farthest western tip of Wales in August of 1485, his success was far from assured. At the battle of Bosworth (22 August 1485), Richard might well have beaten back the invader. But he was betrayed by Thomas, earl of Stanley, who had married, as his second wife and her third husband, Margaret Beaufort, mother of Henry Tudor.[12] Richard died, sword in hand, facing his enemies; Henry, out of gratitude to his stepfather, created him earl of Derby. And as a gesture toward reconciling long-divided factions, the new king took early opportunity to marry Elizabeth of York, eldest daughter of Edward IV (and sister, accordingly, of the two princes in the Tower). Thus Henry VII united in his own close family the foremost representatives of the Yorkist and Lancastrian parties.

12. There is irony in the fact that Richard the arch-conniver was himself deceived as a result of a family connection that he ought to have suspected. Stanley's betrayal of his sworn allegiance was shocking even to an age well versed in the double cross: "Who can trust anybody now?" was a frequent sentiment. Personal allegiance had been the cement binding together feudal society; its adhesive power was now loosening, a fact of which the Bosworth betrayal was a sign, not a cause.

A NEW KIND OF MONARCHY?

It is often said that Bosworth field marked the end of the Wars of the Roses; and with historical hindsight, we can see that it did. But at the time things were not so clear. Richard had left behind nephews (a son of the murdered duke of Clarence, for one) with claims to the throne at least as good as Henry's; years of civil war and weak government had left many factions and a long tradition of contempt for the central administration. Henry worked furiously to unify his kingdom, and repeatedly took the field to defend his throne. As a first step, he multiplied arguments to justify his own title, getting it confirmed by Parliament, reinforcing it by his marriage, buttressing it with the judgments of genealogists and propagandists, who labored to make the best of a weak pedigree. All this was needed to supplement his title by conquest at Bosworth; yet it was a dozen years before he could feel really secure.

A first and fundamental step in Henry's policy was to put down the private armies which had done most of the fighting during the Wars of the Roses. About this he was absolutely ruthless. Time out of mind, it had been the custom of great men to be followed by crowds of "retainers," burly, belligerent, idle fellows who lounged around the castle or manor house in time of peace but in time of war were always ready for a bout of loot and murder. After the French wars ended, they made nuisances of themselves at home. Pitched battles were fought—at Stamford Bridge in 1453 between the Percy and Neville families, at Exeter in 1455 between those legendary feudists the Bonvilles and the Courtenays. These private armies were harmful in many different ways. Their intimidations made it practically impossible for a poor man to win a lawsuit, or for the king's justice to be carried out, or for taxes to be collected equitably. All this Henry ended as fast as he could.[13] His royal justice was strict, and the fines collected for trifling offenses enormous; potential malefactors were terrified and the treasury enriched at the same time.

Other ways of building up the fisc were not neglected. During the wars, many estates had been forfeited; it was the traditional penalty for losing, and the royal exchequer gained by it. But the exchequer had not before had personnel to supervise the management of royal estates, which accordingly paid most of their profits to local overseers, very little to the king. Under Henry that changed, along lines first laid out by Edward IV. Royal officers no longer accepted unquestioningly the accounts submitted by stewards; they went out to inspect fields and tenements, formed their own estimates of what the property should yield, and made heavy trouble for the steward who came in with less. A major source of royal income was from tenants whose leases lapsed and became forfeit to the

13. He couldn't completely abolish armies of feudal tenants, gamekeepers, huntsmen, and the like; in the remote districts, such manorial gang gatherings continued to exist till the middle of the seventeenth century. But they were extremely careful to lay low, not interfering with the king's peace or his justice.

crown (above, p. 61). Weak kings, intent on currying favor with courtiers, had given those properties away as fast as they came in. Not so Henry: he incorporated them in the royal estates. Before long he had enough money to do as Edward IV had promised—live off his own income without asking Parliament for extra money. (War, of course, was another matter, whether real or fake; Henry avoided real wars and took his profit from fake ones.) For centuries the English monarchy had been in the habit of borrowing money from its wealthier subjects. Because of the prejudice against usury, interest rates were often concealed, but we hear of rates up to 50 percent a year. Suddenly the monarchy was not only free of debt, but in a position to make loans itself.

Another economy: the new king chose his high officials, not from great barons who had vast establishments to maintain and extended families to support, but from humbler groups, clergy, gentry, and bourgeois. They could be had cheaper than barons, they were more reliable, worked harder, and in the end they proved more intelligent. Richard Fox, who held several bishoprics and rose to lord privy seal, came from a family of yeomen; Cardinal Morton, archbishop of Canterbury and lord chancellor, from a family of lesser gentry. Morton's protégé Thomas More was son of a London barrister, a bourgeois agent of London merchants. One of Henry's typical minor officials was a Welsh yeoman named David Seyceld, Scisseld, or Cecill; he may have fought at Bosworth, later became mayor of Stamford, rose to M.P. and sheriff of Northamptonshire. He was a devoted servant of Henry VII and of his son Henry VIII; and the next three generations of the Cecil family were, with increasing distinction, officials and advisers to the royal house—rising finally in the seventeenth century to be earls of Salisbury. Less dramatically but many times over, the story of the Cecils was repeated during the forging of the Tudor monarchy's civil service.

Henry was particularly fortunate in presiding over a revival of the wool trade, long depressed because of wars foreign and domestic, but suddenly picking up in the late fifteenth century. An ignorant or a lazy prince would have seen in the reviving wool trade simply a source of new taxes; Henry saw in it an industry to be cherished and encouraged. He made treaties with the Low Countries, with the Scandinavian nations, with the Italians; and in every case his agents drove hard bargains to the advantage of English businessmen.[14] If what he ran was not a businessman's government, it was more like it than anything England had known before. Evidence of Henry's busy, practical mind was his readiness to finance expeditions by John Cabot of Genoa to explore the northeast coast of America. This occurred barely five years after Columbus first discovered the American continent; Cabot thought he was getting to China, but had to settle for discovering the rich fishing grounds off the Grand Banks of Newfoundland. Though it was many years before Cabot's discoveries could be exploited, Henry's interest

14. The first of his treaties with the Flemings (1496) was called the *Intercursus Magnus* (Big Treaty); the second, made just ten years later, was so favorable to English interests that the Flemings called it *Intercursus Malus* (Bad Treaty).

in such practical ventures was an important side of his character. No wonder he became, after a shaky start, a solidly entrenched, if never a very popular, monarch. Having received from his predecessors a treasury deep in debt, he left it when he died with an enormous cash surplus. In his last years he was unquestionably the richest monarch in all Europe, and probably the most avaricious; he was deeply respected, but not much liked. An early and influential biography is that of Francis Bacon (1622).

IMPOSTORS

Legacies from the bad days of civil war, when new pretenders to the throne sprouted like weeds, were a couple of adventurous young men who troubled Henry's early reign. Lambert Simnel of Oxford was coached by an intriguing Yorkist priest to pretend that he was one of the young princes in the Tower; later it seemed better to change this story and have him pretend that he was the son of the murdered duke of Clarence. There was a hitch here in that the real son of the duke of Clarence was alive, imprisoned in the Tower. But for the quick coup the Yorkists had in mind, a false figurehead would be almost as good as a true one; if they could get to London, switching pretenders would be easy. And they had means to get to London—German troops recruited abroad and some Irish enthusiasts whom they enlisted by crowning Simnel (as Edward VI) in Dublin. That happened on 24 May 1487; and two weeks later the invading band, having landed in Lancashire, attacked a royal army under the personal command of Henry VII. Simnel's mercenaries put up a surprisingly good fight (the Germans had some new guns called hackbuts: they were like primitive muskets), and the king's troops left something to be desired; but after a struggle the loyalists prevailed, most of the rebel leaders were killed, and Simnel captured. Henry talked with the young man, found him simple and harmless, and gave him a job as kitchen scullion (potboy) in the royal household. After some years of service, he was promoted to royal falconer.

   The other pretender, a grosser fraud but a bigger nuisance, was named Perkin Warbeck; he came to notice seven or eight years after Simnel's charade. Mostly, he claimed to be the younger of the two princes in the Tower. Warbeck was really the son of a French burgher and spoke English haltingly; but his resemblance to Edward IV was so marked that it's conceivable he was one of the king's several bastards. (He had in fact been born in London when his father was briefly in business there.) The exiled Yorkists saw he could be coached, paraded him about Europe, and raised yet another army in his support. Henry's spies infiltrated the movement, learned who its English supporters were, and, before Warbeck could cross the channel, had caused most of his reception committee to be arrested and executed.[15] The pretender thereupon tried a feeble landing in

15. Among those beheaded was Sir William Stanley, the king's chamberlain, who had fought with him at Bosworth; he was brother of the Thomas Stanley whose betrayal of Richard gave victory to Henry. In those days, one could never be sure how high even a harebrained plot might reach.

Kent, skipped across to Ireland, where he got another hot reception, and so on to Scotland. There James IV, who had been inveigled by the emperor Maximilian into making war on England (Maximilian was still smarting from the double cross of 1492), gave him a measure of support. But the Scots were much hated in England, and a projected invasion, with Warbeck at its head, fell flat. Only an insurrection in Cornwall, against taxes imposed to pay for war in the north, gave the pretender his last chance. In the summer of 1497 the Cornish rebels marched on London, gaining strength as they went; they were stopped at Blackheath only when the London trained bands (militia) went forth to meet them and, after a hard fight, beat them. Warbeck arrived late and tried to rally the survivors, but in vain. Captured, he was offered his life if he would make full public confession; and this he did, several times. Then he was lodged in the Tower with Edward, authentic son of the duke of Clarence. Warbeck was negligible, but his fellow prisoner, though personally meek and mild, represented a direct threat to Henry Tudor, because he was a real live, legitimate Plantagenet, the last in England. In 1499 the two young men tried to escape together; they were easily caught, and the false Plantagenet executed alongside the true one. From then on, Henry was not bothered with impostors. Though Yorkist plots continued to be hatched, mostly abroad, they were handled by Henry's efficient secret police.[16]

TYRANNY BY CONSENT: THE FIRST TUDOR

The government of Henry Tudor was highly authoritarian. There were, at first, excellent reasons for this. For half a century feuding barons had done their best to create chaos; they had to be put down with a firm hand. Henry had not been two years on the throne when he created the extraordinary court of Star Chamber (1487) to do justice on malefactors of great wealth and power. Star Chamber (so called from the ceiling of the room where it met) was staffed with members of the king's council, lay and ecclesiastic; it did justice by its own rules, swiftly and without appeal; it was bound by no heavy burden of precedent. It was at the same time a court of law and an executive body for carrying out the king's policies. County bigwigs who could bully a sheriff or terrorize a tax collector cringed at the thought of appearing in Star Chamber.

At the same time, Henry took what seems a directly contrary way of bringing local magnates into line; he incorporated them in the peacekeeping apparatus itself. The traditional office of Justice of the Peace took on new importance. This

16. Henry was not a bloodthirsty man; when plots were uncovered, he commonly reacted by jailing or executing a couple of leaders and mulcting every suspected sympathizer for an enormous fine. This was good for the treasury, and didn't let anyone think he was getting away with anything. The last pretenders to the throne were members of the de la Pole family (Edmund, Richard, and their cousin William Courtenay); the minute they became serious threats, misfortune befell them. An illegitimate Plantagenet did survive till 1542: Arthur Plantagenet, Viscount Lisle, who wrote a set of famous, recently published letters. He was a bastard of Edward IV (SFR, D.25).

was an unpaid official post bestowed on a man of standing in the community; the specific requirement was phrased in terms of income and property. The JP was responsible for settling petty disputes, investigating riots, jailing vagabonds, summoning grand juries, calling out the posse. Much of this work the squire might have done before, as judge of his own manorial court; but as JP he had the king's commission, which gave him more authority and bound him to observe peace and good order more strictly himself. If he exceeded or violated his commission, he could be complained of to London, with expensive and disagreeable consequences. If he did acceptably, his reward would be prestige in the district, perhaps a knighthood: he would be "Sir John," his wife "Lady Eleanor."[17]

Thus Henry effectively combined stick and carrot to pacify the troubled land over which he reigned. As England grew accustomed to the ways of peace, as commerce flourished and tenantry replaced villeinage, as castles gave way to country houses and armed retainers to a domestic staff, the need for tough disciplinary machinery diminished. But the machinery remained in place; it was supplemented by a secret police and a network of informers; and one note of the king's independence was very remarkable. He called few Parliaments and asked little money of them; accordingly, they had little chance to question his rule. Not having to pay heavy taxes was doubtless agreeable at the time; but it removed a major control that elected representatives had over their monarch, the power of the purse. Henry governed less through Parliament than through his royal councils and royal courts; and he lived cannily on his own income, gained by his own means.

NUPTIALS

A smattering of matrimonial matters, all centering on the year 1503, may conclude the history of the seventh Henry. In this year the king married his daughter Margaret to King James IV of Scotland. For the moment, this bond brought welcome peace to the two countries; exactly a century later, it would enable James I of England (but James VI of Scotland) to inherit peacefully the throne left vacant by Elizabeth, last of the Tudors. (Stuart succession to the throne of England was actually discussed in 1503; it did not worry Henry VII.) In 1501

17. Both Henry VII and VIII steadily augmented the list of problems with which JP's were empowered to cope; they were an efficient first approximation to justice. A specially useful extension of their power flowed from an agreement negotiated by Henry VII with Pope Innocent VIII, limiting the right of sanctuary. When malefactors could take refuge in abbeys or shrines and there be exempt from pursuit, all law took on the character of a lottery.

Shakespeare, who may have had reasons of his own for disliking justices, caricatured the class in Justice Shallow of *Henry IV, Part 2;* other literary JPs, brutal and overbearing rather than weak and silly, are found in Fielding's *Joseph Andrews,* II, xi, and IV, v. Most justices were neither morons nor monsters but honorable men with the prejudices of their class who wanted the respect of their neighbors.

Henry's elder son Arthur had been married to Catherine of Aragon, princess of Spain; but, Arthur dying prematurely in 1502, the girl was abruptly transferred in 1503 to the king's second son, Henry. Doubts were expressed at the time about the ecclesiastical legitimacy of this arrangement; but the engagement stood till 1509, when Henry VIII, newly installed on his throne, fulfilled the contract and married the lady. It was this ill-starred marriage, broken by divorce in 1533, that gave rise to the English Reformation. Finally, in 1503, the old king's wife, Elizabeth of York, died, and the king himself went onto the marriage market. Joanna of Castile was the older sister of Catherine, now engaged to the king's son. A slight impediment appeared, in that Joanna was said to be insane; but her dowry would have been enormous, and in the presence of large sums of money, Henry was not a man to higgle. Perhaps fortunately, nothing came of this odd project;[18] Henry died, 21 April 1509, a widower.

On the positive side, the major achievements of Henry VII were impressive: (1) he made peace with Scotland; (2) he crushed the Yorkist pretenders and settled the succession; (3) in behalf of the wool trade, he drove advantageous bargains with the Low Countries; and (4) he avoided a major war with either France or Spain, both of which would have been delighted to use England in their quarrels.

SOUNDING THE LITERARY DEPTHS

The fifteenth century is commonly spoken of as the low-water mark of English literature, and despite some qualifications this is about right. In the mid-century those long-lived Arthurian legends were at last given classic form by Sir Thomas Malory, and the later century saw some promising developments in popular drama, such as the morality play *Everyman*. But the immense achievements of Chaucer and the great promise of Langland were not really followed up. Those authors were respected and imitated, but so clumsily, in works so mannered and monotonous, as actually to degrade the originals. Nor was the fifteenth century a period of great architecture; little building took place during the civil wars, and what did tended to be repetitious and imitative. With exceptions here and there, the age was not distinguished by artistic achievement of any sort.[19] By comparison

18. There is a tradition, ill-confirmed but too interesting not to be mentioned, that Joanna the Mad was not mad at all. For a fact, her four children by a first husband were all perfectly normal. Perhaps she had just picked up—through that husband, Philip the Handsome, to whom she had been passionately attached—some unorthodox religious ideas which were widespread in the Low Countries under the generic name of the *devotio moderna*. Rather than convict the lady of heresy, with the attendant scandal, the Inquisition put her away in a madhouse. Certain it is that because of his wide intellectual interests (rare indeed in a king of Spain), Philip the Handsome could have been called Philip the Intelligent; and perhaps Joanna the Mad deserved that title too.

19. Between 1350 and 1500, Englishmen mined in the midlands counties great quantities of alabaster; it is a variety of gypsum like onyx—soft, easy to work, and translucent. English craftsmen

with the art of the Italian Renaissance at the same time (Mantegna, Masaccio, Ghirlandaio, Lippi, and Ghiberti are only a few of the major artists working during the fifteenth century), English art simply did not exist. Many Englishmen visited Italy, and some must have passed their eyes across the great works of art, though paintings were much less accessible then than they are now. But as they were unprepared to look at them, few could see what was there.[20] The verbal arts were more available, and toward the end of the century, numbers of English scholars visited Italy to learn the ancient languages and acquire the new polished modes of speech and thought. Poise, elegance, and eloquence took on new importance when gentlemen, instead of sulking in their castles preparing war on their neighbors, were encouraged to attend the royal court, where, inevitably, they became courtiers. For the moment, it was mostly a matter of imitating Italian styles, Italian manners. England was still a very provincial society; not even the royal court of Henry VII, rich and powerful though he was, could compare with the brilliant and learned societies of city-states like Urbino and Florence. Chaucer had been able to converse on terms of relative equality with the continental writers of his day; for the hundred years after his death till the coming of age of Thomas More, England had no equivalent figure.

Speculation may play with the reasons for this abysmal decline in the quality of English literature. The noble classes were absorbed in foreign and domestic wars that left little time to invest in culture. The commercial classes flourished, sometimes despite baronial battles, sometimes because of them; but most were not yet ready for literature in the sense of *belles lettres*. Still less were the working classes. Ballads they liked, simple, sharp, and clear of outline; minstrels called crowders (because they accompanied themselves on a fiddle, a crowd) collected and sang them in the streets or at fairs. Though these folk poems often came from remote climes and distant periods and were not written down in many cases till centuries later, a good many took shape in the fifteenth century (SFR, C.4). If he was a real person at all, Robin Hood probably lived in the late twelfth and early thirteenth centuries; he is mentioned in *Piers Plowman* as the subject of rude rhymes. By the fifteenth century, he was a popular folk hero, idealized in a cycle of folk ballads on the verge of organizing themselves into an epic; he was also celebrated in rural festivals of the May as an embodiment of Robin Goodfellow and perhaps of even older nature and vegetation deities. The same

---

made of the stuff many small religious images, sometimes painted, sometimes left clear. Though most of those that were placed in English churches were smashed by the iconoclasts of the sixteenth and seventeenth centuries, others were exported to Portugal, Spain, and France, where they are still to be seen. After images fell under a ban in England, the center of alabaster working shifted to Florence, Italy, where it largely remains.

20. Linear perspective, to which our modern eyes are trained almost from birth, was a difficult discipline for north European eyes to recover. Hugo van der Goes, a Dutchman who about 1475 painted an immense altarpiece (now in the Uffizi gallery, Florence) was a marvelously talented artist; but he makes some of his figures very big, others very little, based not on what his eye told him, but on abstract ideas about the relative importance of his personages.

popular impulses produced lyric poems in honor of holidays, the change of seasons, and the girls with whom fifteenth-century poets were in love. These poems were for the most part sung, and transmitted from singer to singer with modifications; the stiff, cold medium of print preserves them only meagerly. Yet as they appealed to basic emotions of plain folk in the fifteenth century, they may still, though from a distance, appeal to ours.

Another popular genre was the book of manners that taught folk how to behave in better society than they were used to. Vulgar romances flourished; books of scientific lore, generally antiquated, were in demand, and so were histories of England, mostly legendary, but popular nonetheless. The universities were, by and large, stagnant; but many grammar schools were founded during the fifteenth century. Elementary education made great strides; besides grammar schools, the simpler "petty schools," which taught English instead of Latin grammar, sprang up in quantity. Writing in 1530, and under circumstances where he would be inclined to minimize the literacy of the population, Sir Thomas More says 60 percent of Englishmen could read in his time. Writing was another matter; it is much harder. But the figure is still impressive. We find the women as well as the men of an average squire's family to be capable of a vigorous, ill-spelled letter, though no doubt they would have been amazed to learn that they were creating English prose.[21] But for people of this class, existence was hard; they had to scratch and claw to hold onto the property they thought they possessed; there was no room for sentiment in arranging marriages, indulging friendships, or working up an "interest" at court—far less, for imaginative literature. Law counted for very little in their world if it was not backed by hard force, a gang of armed friends and retainers. With all these various wolves at the door, one can understand that such folk wouldn't be much interested in literary elegancies.

On the other hand, fifteenth-century translations into English from French or Latin are so numerous, it's apparent that a largely unlanguaged class is starting to demand access to what, in its terms, are classics. *The Golden Legend,* an ancient collection of saints' lives, was several times translated, either from its original Latin or from a French version. The simple, devout *Imitation of Christ,* written in Latin about 1425 by a Dutch monk Thomas a Kempis, was put into English by 1450. *Gesta Romanorum,* a twelfth-century collection of classical stories with appended morals had long been useful to preachers seeking simple stories with pious points; three different translators, working independently, Englished it during the fifteenth century. These multiple translations show how little communication there was between various districts; in fact local dialects were sometimes so extreme that people from one region could not understand those of another. When the century began, there were still people who had not

---

21. The Paston letters, a cache of over a thousand items of domestic correspondence from the period from 1422 to 1509, give us an intimate view of the life of a Norfolk family in the fifteenth century. They were collected, arranged, and published in six volumes at the beginning of the twentieth century (SFR, C.3).

decided between English and French, and who in their everyday communications used a hodgepodge of both.[22] And yet, confidence in the power of English was steadily growing. Reginald Pecock turned the English language to the purposes of religious controversy with his anti-Lollard tract, *The Repressor of Over-Much Weeting [Blaming] of the Clergy* (written about 1455, not printed till 1860). Pecock wanted to convince heretics, not by fire and hanging, but by reason; it was a bold attempt, and he got into bad ecclesiastical trouble for some of his incautious ideas; but his use of the vernacular in serious argument was a landmark. Sir John Fortescue, chief justice of England, mostly wrote for his brethren learned in the law, hence in Latin; but about 1471 he also produced an English book on *The Governance of England*. It did not have much influence; Sir John had his hands full maintaining the Lancastrian cause against the Yorkists, and in those days before printing, books of this sort did not circulate easily. But again, the fact of his writing his book in English was significant.

Scraps and bits of miscellaneous prose, such as we can dredge up from the dark pool of the fifteenth century, are far from making a literature. Yet we should beware of thinking that because common folk had so little and such threadbare material to read, they were mentally torpid. Books sought out readers when readers were rare; there was much lending around and reading aloud to the neighbors. Toward the middle of the fifteenth century, John Shirley developed a kind of primitive lending library. More important, an oral, popular tradition of culture was widespread; folk knew what they knew, and talked it out at the alehouse or around the hearth. This was how the tradition of alliterative poetry survived; this was how the Lollards remained a vital influence without printed books to speak of. Simple men with strong prepossessions (against the hierarchy, for example) could seize on incidental phrases in thoroughly orthodox books, and twist them to the service of their own opinions. Out of no more than a dozen commonplace, miscellaneous books, read searchingly in the light of a popular tradition, a complex and very individual world view might be constructed.

SUB-CHAUCERIANS: LYDGATE AND OCCLEVE

On the poets who pretended to continue the work of Chaucer we shall not need to linger. John Lydgate who died about the middle of the fifteenth century was a monk of Bury St. Edmunds who combines two unenviable distinctions; he is the dullest poet in English and the most long-winded. His language is turgid, his syntax clumsy, his versification doubtful at best. He wrote dozens of poems, mostly in imitation of Chaucer, whom he had known as a youth. His masterpiece is said to be *The Fall of Princes,* more than 36,000 lines long. It is a much expanded version, via a French intermediary, of an original in Latin prose by

22. For a striking example of what modern Frenchmen call "franglais," see H. S. Bennett, *Chaucer and the Fifteenth Century* (Oxford, 1947), p. 177.

Boccaccio. Lydgate did it during the 1430s for his patron of the moment, Humphrey, duke of Gloucester. How the duke liked it, and whether he read it, he was too much of a gentleman to say.

Thomas Occleve or Hoccleve, Lydgate's almost exact contemporary, was a layman and a Londoner, for thirty-five years a clerk in the office of the privy seal. Like Lydgate, he admired Chaucer this side idolatry; as a poet, he was, like Lydgate, the victim of his own carelessness and prolixity. As a youth, before he married and became respectable, Occleve suffered the poverty and enjoyed the scruffy freedoms of London low life, and he often enlivened his tedious, moralistic poems with such details. The Prince Hal who played around with Falstaff might have relished Occleve's tales of tavern revelry; but the poem that the bard produced for the reformed prince of Wales was an immense didactic treatise called *The Regiment [Rule] of Princes* (1412). Most of it was a translation into incongruous rime royal of a Latin prose treatise by Aegidius Colonna of the thirteenth century. If he ever looked at it, no doubt it put Henry V to sleep.

Lest it be thought that gentle Geoffrey laid a fatal blight on all his followers, let us recall briefly the Scottish Chaucerians: William Dunbar, Robert Henryson, and a royal romantic, King James I of Scotland. The monarch was captured at sea in 1406, when only twelve years old, and kept in confinement for nineteen years, during which he met and married Lady Jane Beaufort. His poem "The Kingis Quair" ("quair" means "book") describes this experience. It is written in rime royal, and includes many conventional elements (a dream sequence, allegorical visits to the lands of Venus, Minerva, and Lady Fortune), culminating in the poet's marriage with his lady. But it is a deeply personal poem for all that, worthy of the gallant monarch who wrote it. Had he not been so busy in later life with his high office and quarrelsome subjects, he might have become one of the major poets. Dunbar and Henryson, who lived toward the end of the fifteenth century, are authors of great verve and originality. Dunbar was a Rabelaisian figure, satirical and grotesque by turns, with a deep sense of sin and mortality. His "Lament for the Makaris" ("makaris" or "makers" are the poets who preceded him) is in the spirit of François Villon, the balladeer of the Paris gutter. Henryson is a more homely and country author; he versified the fables of Aesop into broad Scots, with many a touch of droll wit, and in his best-known poem provided a dramatic epilogue to Chaucer's *Troilus and Criseyde*. None of these three authors belongs more than marginally in a history of England and its literature, but one is bound to mention them, if only to provide a contrast with Lydgate and Occleve.

THE REBIRTH OF ARTHUR

Sir Thomas Malory, who cast the tales of Arthur in definitive form, is a shadowy presence for whom no fewer than four historical identities have been proposed.

If he was the Warwickshire Sir Thomas, not the Yorkshire one or either of the other two, our author was a rough case who was jailed semipermanently after a career of assault, robbery, murder, extortion, jailbreaking, poaching, rape, and assorted other felonies. While doing time for these misdeeds (if he did them) in the 1460s, Malory acquired a "French book," not otherwise described and not now identifiable.[23] Using this book, augmented by his own strong intuitions, Malory created, in the *Morte d'Arthur,* the first real masterpiece of English prose. By the time he got to it, the Arthur legend had grown like a banyan tree into a wild tangle of roots, stems, and narrative branches. Total order was impossible, and even local structure is not the long suit of Malory's book—at least not until the final chapters when the Table Round is fatally diminished and finally brought down. Nothing surpasses the scene when, after the last terrible battle in the west, only Mordred and Arthur are left to settle accounts in the gathering gloom, while wolves, crows, and robbers creep out to rifle the scattered corpses. The moment that follows that last doubly fatal encounter is one of those slow, sad, dignified processionals for which Malory is famous. The mysterious ceremonial by the lake is accomplished; with restrained awe, and a deep sense of loss, Arthur fades from sight leaving a permanently darkened world behind him. The ending of the book, which gave its title to the whole, is as pure and mysterious as the passing of Oedipus in the final play of Sophocles' trilogy. But Malory is also to be admired for the sharpness and concision of his dialogue, his severe avoidance of the highfalutin. In descriptions and narrative passages where the author speaks in his own voice, the sentences tend to be long and murmuring; so many of them begin with "and," "so," "when," or "then" that they seem to flow over the periods, carrying an unbroken thought from sentence to sentence. But the dialogues are crisp and firm, sometimes laconic; their quality comes out when one compares a scene by Malory to one by Lord Tennyson. Like Tennyson, Malory is romantic and nostalgic; but he knows how a knight should talk. His is the last major voice of authentic feudalism. It is natural for readers to feel uneasy on finding that a noble book was written by a lawless scoundrel; but a good deal of chivalry wears both faces, and Sir Thomas may be more interesting as an enigma than as a paragon. In any event, who he was matters less than what he wrote—or, more accurately, than the way in which the legend of Arthur, using him as an instrument, finally wrote itself.

STAGED DOCTRINE

While medieval romance reached its climax, the English stage started to grow toward independent existence (SFR, C.9). A long, slow process lay behind this

---

23. It was probably a compilation based on several of those tellings of the Arthur legend noted above, p. 75. Malory relied on it heavily, and at one point tells us that he cannot go on with the story of the Knight of the Chariot (Lancelot) because he has lost the "very mater," that is, the true substance of it.

change. As in Europe generally, the first English plays (miracle or mystery plays) developed out of church holidays as a way of recreating the original event. Easter plays and Christmas plays were particularly popular, marking the resurrection and the nativity; each town put on its own, first in the church, then in the church-yard, and finally in the streets. Sometimes the play was staged on trestles and boards in a marketplace, sometimes on a wagon which drove around town, paus-ing from time to time to put on the play. Originally these plays were very static affairs, not much more animated than tableaux. (Christmas *crêches* are miniature tableaux, much like these early plays.) But as the different craft organizations (guilds) began competing with one another to have the best show, popular ele-ments increased; and the name of them all was action. Something simple and diverting had to happen: Noah got drunk, his wife scolded and beat him, Herod roared aloud. Since the same play was repeated, using the same actors, before the same audience, year after year, there was a powerful impulse for each actor to fill out his part each year with a new bit of business. Moralists disap-proved, and the priest sometimes disavowed what was ostensibly "his" show; but the impulse to ham it up before an audience was irresistible. Actors who were particularly clever at devising such material became, after a fashion, play-wrights.

The Second Shepherds' Play at Wakefield was the outcome of such a process. Evidently a first shepherds' play had served at Christmas for many years, and worn itself out. The second version is the boldest of all these miracle plays in padding out the basic scene of the shepherds' adoration at the nativity with comic business; it comes closest to the dramatic creation of character. We note in pass-ing that it reduces the nativity itself to a momentary charade at the end of the show; how the Wakefield parson liked that we have no way of knowing. Besides the one at Wakefield, there were other cycles of plays at York, Coventry, Ches-ter, Beverley, Norwich, and Newcastle; some of these survive only in part, the Beverley plays not at all. (The Protestant Reformation was particularly hard on the old dramas.) But clearly a giant gap separates even the most advanced of the miracle plays from the kind of professional theater that would be the glory of the Elizabethan age.

At first glance, *Everyman* seems even stiffer and more church-bound than the miracle plays, which undertook to humanize a Bible story already known to the audience. The roots of the morality play lie, on the other hand, in the homily or sermon, which often represented human life as a struggle between good and bad moral qualities.[24] Allegorical elements tend to be the basic stuff of morality plays, to the point of overwhelming the human individual under a load of abstractions. In its favor, the morality play is not tied to performance on a single

24. Very influential in this respect was a poor but interesting poem called "Psychomachia" writ-ten in the late fourth century by a Spanish Christian poet named Prudentius. The name means "soul struggle," and the poem depicts a conflict between Christian virtues and pagan vices. Soul struggles are the prime concern of Christian autobiography from Saint Augustine to John Bunyan.

day, and its theme is not dictated in advance; to some extent, it can be what the playwright makes it. The story of the summoning of Everyman is more preachy than today we are likely to find palatable; it uses the figure of Everyman and his potential companions with the directness of a pile driver to make its relative simple point. It seems further from free imaginative drama than the best of the old miracle plays. But when the powerful impulse to score direct moral points has subsided a little, one can see how the structure of the morality play might lead toward the debate in Marlowe's *Doctor Faustus* between the hero's good and bad angels.

TECHNOLOGY AND HUMANISM

The early years of the fifteenth century saw the first general introduction into England of writing paper; its last years witnessed the first instance of printing from movable type. Before the days of paper, writing was done on vellum or parchment (the treated skins of sheep);[25] the stuff was durable, could be shaved fairly thin, and could be erased for reuse. But animal skins were expensive, and could never be used in printing presses. Papermaking reached Europe from the orient through the Arabs and partly as a result of the Crusades. Mills were first set up in Spain and Italy; and by the fifteenth century, a family of rural squires like the Pastons were habitually writing to one another on paper. It was probably better paper than most of what we use nowadays, for it has survived 500 years, as very little modern paper would do; but it was expensive, and they used it sparingly.

As long as books had to be copied out by hand, they too remained expensive and therefore relatively scarce. Chaucer's Clerk of Oxenford in the fourteenth century was said to have sacrificed all the luxuries of life to have

> at his beddes head
> Twenty bookés clad in blak or reed
> Of Aristotle and his philosophie.

Rich Sir John Fastolfe, who in the middle of the fifteenth century made the Paston family his heirs, left about two dozen books; by contrast, Sir William More, making his will in 1556, listed 140. During most of the middle ages, a monastic library holding a thousand volumes was thought to have about as much reading matter as any man could want. (But some of those volumes might contain in one binding several different works.) About the middle of the fifteenth century, Humphrey, duke of Gloucester, gave his collection of books to Oxford

---

25. Papyrus, though perfectly feasible in Egypt, where the plants grew, the climate was dry, and the ordinary form of the manuscript was a scroll, could not be adapted to other circumstances. In the cold of north Europe the reeds would not grow, in a damp climate the scrolls disintegrated, and in the form of sheets papyrus wasn't strong enough to be bound into a book. England had to get along with imported paper till in 1588 a German named John Spilman founded a successful paper mill at Dartford in Kent; at least, we don't know of any permanent English mill earlier than Spilman's.

and built a room to house it; most of the collection has been lost, but Duke Humphrey's room survives, and a few thousand books would fill it. Yet the library was thought magnificent, unparalleled in England, and probably it was. As for the value of books in those days, it speaks in the fact that they were often chained to the desks of early libraries.

All this changed with the introduction of printing (SFR, C. 14). It too had been an early oriental invention, but developed independently in Europe out of the practice of printing pictures from wood blocks. From woodblock printing to the use of movable type (first wooden, then metal) was a short step taken early in the fifteenth century by German and Dutch printers, of whom Johann Gutenberg is the best known. Gutenberg produced his first books in the 1450s, and in 1477 the craft was first practiced in England. By modern standards, early printing presses were slow and clumsy. The sheet of paper was laid on a forme (frame, tray) of inky type and pushed into a screw press which squeezed it to make an impression; the press was then unscrewed, the sheet pulled off, the type re-inked (with a mop of rags on a stick), and the process repeated, while the first sheet, printed only on one side, was hung over a wire to dry. When enough copies of that page were printed, the type was distributed, another page set up and printed; and finally all the pages were assembled to make a book. The process would seem to us unbearably tedious. Still, slow as it was, the printing press could produce hundreds of volumes, employing artisans, not calligraphers, in a fraction of the time that hand copying of manuscripts had taken. The price of books diminished; the accuracy of texts improved. For manuscripts had multiplied in scriptoria (writing rooms), where one man read an original text aloud and others copied. Aural transmission is notoriously inexact because many words sound alike but are spelled differently, and because copyists rarely pay constant attention to what they are writing. But a single man could read proof on a page of type, and if he got the page right the first time, one was bound to get an unlimited number of pages of identical accurate copy.[26]

The development of printing in the second half of the fifteenth century lent wings to a movement which took its rise in northern Italy, mainly Florence, and (as nearly as these matters can be dated) in the fourteenth century. *Humanism* has by now become a word of many meanings, but as it began in Italy it implied a new attitude toward the Greek and Roman classics, and toward the education which would enable one to read and apply them intelligently. A first stage in this

26. Other advantages of printing are too many to list; a few may be briefly noted. Having a lot of texts in one place enables scholars to compare and combine them; knowing that all other scholars have substantially the same text before them makes emendation a matter of general, not just private interest. Indexes (which suddenly throw into prominence the alphabet and the need for uniform spelling) are crucial devices of ready reference and textual comparison; the possibility of listing errata and improving the text from edition to edition makes scholarship more a collective, less an individual, enterprise. Systematic bibliography becomes possible, reducing duplication of effort (SFR, D.3).

The literary consequences of a vast, slow, and largely unconscious shift from the values of oral to those of printed communication continued to exercise pressure on authors through the seventeenth and eighteenth centuries; the topic is of great interest to modern criticism.

process was to discover what actually remained to us from the classical world; and in this enterprise the early humanists did heroic work. Poggio Bracciolini, during the first half of the fifteenth century, singlehandedly recovered dozens of classical manuscripts where they lay neglected on dusty monastery shelves. But then these new manuscripts must be circulated quickly and accurately through the learned world; and for this purpose printing was ideal. The famous Venetian printing house of Aldus Manutius was founded around 1490 and rapidly gained eminence in the production of Greek texts; it published important Latin and Italian works as well.

In addition, the ethos of humanism and the demands of printed publication forced on men a new critical attitude toward classical texts, and ultimately toward Biblical texts as well. The most ancient manuscripts we possess stand at a distance of several hundred and some as much as several thousand years from the original authors. During that period, manifold corruptions and errors crept into even the best preserved texts. The authentic work of classic authors was also overlaid with a vast mass of later material—popularizations, glosses, interpolations, imitations, outright forgeries. To correct the errors of the manuscripts, fill in their gaps, and clear off corrupt later additions was a work of special scholarship. It required one to enter into the mind of the original author, to appreciate the nuances of his language and culture.

Medieval man, viewing all texts (the book of nature, the book of Scripture, the book of Virgil) as more or less directly inspired by God, thought them all bound to mean much the same thing; he read them as if they were all written in the same timeless present, and by "interpreting" them vigorously, he could in fact often reduce them to uniformity. The humanists, discriminating historical periods and phases of languages, were able to see the classical world in its own light (SFR, D.16). Some interpretations, some texts, and some entire authors, they were able to show, must be discarded because the concepts and the very words involved were not current when the texts were supposed to have been written. Lorenzo Valla demonstrated conclusively that the so-called "Donation of Constantine," on which the church had grounded its claim to universal temporal dominion, could only be a late and clumsy forgery because the words used in it did not exist in the age of Constantine. Thus the new learning sought to purify the ancient texts, to discriminate different ages of the classic past, and to use the best of ancient materials for educating liberal and humane minds. In some degree this was a reaction against the theological Latin and intricate abstractions of the scholastic philosophers. But it was also a movement in favor of a liberal aristocratic ideal, that of the urbane and intelligent man, capable of fulfilling all the offices of peace and war in a civilized secular state. It tended to substitute the open palm of rhetoric (the gentle art of persuasion) for the clenched fist of formal logic.

The deep appeal of humanism can be read in the first book of François Rabelais's giant satire, *Gargantua and Pantagruel* (1535). Here we see young Gargantua brought up under the old system, a slovenly, lazy lout stuffed with memorized gibberish out of monkish commentaries. With him is contrasted Eudemon, of the same age but brought up under humanist principles. He is clean, articulate, well behaved; his Latin is so good, he seems to be "a Tiberius Gracchus, a Cicero, or an Aemilius Lepidus of old." Confronted with Eudemon, Gargantua can only bawl like a sick cow.

Eloquence was much prized by the early humanists, and Cicero, greatest of Roman orators, was for many the supreme stylist. Through eloquence a man might influence his fellow citizens, might gain access as a counselor to his prince, might serve as an ambassador representing his country. In France, Spain, and Germany, as well as in England, new monarchies were forming up, far more powerful than the common run of feudal chivalry. Now that the old warlike ways were dying out, men thought or hoped, kings and their courts would need men of wisdom and eloquence, for diplomatic counsel, for civilized conversation, for what the age called "magnificence." So it was not remarkable that a few English aristocrats went to Italy, to investigate the new learning and its applications, even before (in the century's last years) a flock of English scholars and men of letters started to make the Italian pilgrimage, to bring back the sweets of humanist scholarship.

John Tiptoft, earl of Worcester, and Anthony Woodville, who was successively Lord Scales and Earl Rivers, were the pioneering noblemen. Their visits to Italy were made during the 1460s, partly for religious, partly for diplomatic reasons. Both were warriors, both courtiers and scholars as well as travelers; both came to violent, untimely ends.[27] In a small way, both wrote, and Woodville actually produced copy for the first book printed on English soil. It was a modest pamphlet, titled *Dictes and Sayings of the Philosophers,* and it appeared in 1477. As a sample of the new humanist learning, this little anthology of adages is not very impressive, but important it was, for its mode of production. Its printer was William Caxton; and it is for their protection and encouragement of Caxton that both Woodville and Tiptoft are remembered today.

AN ENGLISH PRINTING PRESS

William Caxton had been born in Kent about 1422, and spent the first forty-seven years of his life in the wool trade, mostly at Bruges in Flanders. Over the

27. In 1467 Woodville had distinguished himself by successfully encountering, singlehanded in the lists, the dangerous Bastard of Burgundy; it was the climax of a famous tournament. But in 1483 he attracted the enmity of Richard III, and was executed by that implacable foe. Tiptoft was such an eloquent Latinist that on his embassy to Pius II, he is said to have reduced that humanist pope to tears by the magnificence of his discourse. But English politics was a crueler pastime; during the brief Lancastrian restoration of 1470 (above, p. 91), he was hunted down as a Yorkist and executed. On the scaffold, he made the unusual request that, in honor of the Trinity, his head should be severed in three separate strokes. It was.

years, he got to know many English exiles, of all parties; he also got to know a number of Flemings, just entering the new trade of printing. More by accident than design, he took up the craft himself. For diversion he had translated a medieval French romance on the Trojan war, the *Recuyell of the Historyes of Troye*. Friends asked him for copies, he grew weary of writing them out, and so turned printer. After doing three books at Bruges, he moved to Westminster in the London suburbs and set up there as writer and printer, continuing busy in both trades till his death in 1491. He was an industrious if undistinguished prose stylist, confining himself mostly to translations; but he published, in the fourteen years of his activity, nearly a hundred different books and editions.[28] Considering that he was in his fifties when he started, had little help, and worked at a press that demanded great physical exertions, it was an amazing achievement. He printed Chaucer and Malory, translations of Boethius and *The Golden Legend,* and a steady stream of chivalric romances which apparently paid the rent (SFR, C.6). His success paved the way for other printers, some of whom were actually his pupils. No early English books approach the typographical level of early books in Italy; some of the Aldine editions rank among the most beautiful books ever created. But simply having publishers on the island was a good omen for English authorship. For several decades after Caxton's death, they were all foreigners; but then a shrewd law was passed requiring them to take English prentices, and shortly, without major pain to anyone, they were mostly English. Printing and publishing were major contributions of the fifteenth century, itself so poor in literature, to the ultimate emergence, in the sixteenth century, of a bookish and ultimately a literary culture.

28. As he didn't have a big enough press, or enough type, to set more than a page at a time, it's remarkable that he printed nearly 20,000 pages, each in sufficient quantities to make an edition of several hundred copies.

5

Henry VIII and the Reformation (1509–1557)

Like Henry Bolingbroke (the fourth Henry) at the start of the fifteenth century, Henry Tudor (the seventh Henry) at its end held his throne by a bad title, which gave him many restless nights. Both reigns present the picture of an anxious monarch, uncertain of his position and avid to consolidate it in every way possible. Both men were then succeeded by confident and aggressive sons. Henry VIII in particular was trained, if not from the cradle, at least from the age of eleven, when his brother Arthur died, to think himself a royal paragon. There had been a still younger brother, Edmund, who died within a few weeks in 1499; there were sisters (Margaret, who married James IV of Scotland; Mary, who married as his third wife Louis XII of France). But essentially Henry, from the age of eleven, had the spotlight to himself. He inherited by unquestioned right from his father; he did not have to endure a regency or protectorate; he did not have to wait many tiresome years for his crown. At the age of eighteen, in the full flush of his youthful spirits and good looks, Henry became king of England.

A FLY IN THE OINTMENT

No young prince ever seemed to deserve it more. Educated along humanist lines, Henry was handsome, eloquent, learned in many tongues and disciplines. He was a subtle student of theology and law, the most polished of courtiers, the most jovial of good fellows, an accomplished sportsman and musician, a dazzling presence, bold and decisive in action, subtle and wary at the counsel board. And yet, almost from coronation day, there was a rift in the lute of Henry's happiness. Catherine of Aragon had been married briefly to Henry's brother Arthur; they were but sixteen at the time, and whether the marriage had been consummated remained questionable. Catherine vigorously denied that it had. But Henry VII kept the child-widow in England after her child-husband's death. Even though Ferdinand had paid out only half his daughter's dowry, Henry did not want to give it back; he also wanted a Spanish alliance against the power of France. Thus Catherine was betrothed to Henry, subject to the payment of the rest of the dowry, over which haggling and recrimination developed. Her position was far from comfortable, and it seems she did not really expect Henry to marry her. But the old king demanded on his deathbed that the contract be fulfilled; and Henry, though he raised some scruples over marrying his brother's widow, was calmed by a special dispensation from the pope. So the marriage took place shortly after the coronation; and though the bride was some six years older than her husband, they lived happily enough, till her troubles in producing a male heir began to mount. In the first nine years of her marriage, Catherine gave birth to six children, but only one daughter, Mary, survived infancy; the rest were either stillborn or died within a few weeks. Without a male heir, England might relapse into the wild violence of the Wars of the Roses. Perhaps to make a point, Henry took a mistress, Elizabeth Blount, and begat upon her an authentic, if illegitimate, male, Henry Fitzroy, later made earl of Richmond. Catherine's seventh child was also stillborn; in 1524 she reached the age of thirty-nine; the chances of a male heir for this monarch who looked so strappingly virile, began to appear dim indeed.[1]

In the early years of his reign, however, the worst of these troubles lay far in the future. Henry cut a dashing figure, spending money faster than his father had been able to amass it, and letting agents do the grubby work of government. In his late years, when avarice grew upon him like a wen, Henry VII had made use of extortionate fines, forced loans, and "contributions" from his subjects.[2]

1. Why couldn't Henry have been satisfied with Mary as his heir? No law forbade a woman to sit on the English throne, as the Salic law was supposed to forbid a female ruler of France. But the island had never had a successful female ruler (Matilda, daughter of Henry I, and Isabella who murdered Edward II might count as unsuccessful ones). Besides, if women were eligible to rule, then Henry VII had been a usurper, since Margaret Beaufort, through whom he claimed succession, was still alive at his coronation. (The Lady Margaret, celebrated at Cambridge university for her generosity, died only in 1509.) Thus the problem was left in limbo. It was acute, because the male genes of the Tudor line carried a fatal flaw; two of Henry's brothers died young, and of his two sons (one legitimate, one not), neither lived to the age of 18.

2. "Morton's fork" was one such device, named afer Archbishop John Morton but probably the contrivance of Bishop Richard Fox: if the designated victim lived lavishly, he could well afford to contribute to the royal treasury; if he lived meagerly, he was bound to have immense savings, and could contribute even more.

Especially notorious for their exactions had been a couple of the king's ministers, Edmund Dudley and Richard Empson. What they did to extort money for the king was pretty ugly work; but they had done it with the king's knowledge and at his orders. No matter: they were unpopular and Henry VIII was no man to protect them at the cost of his own prestige. They were tried, convicted, executed. Their deaths set a precedent of which future servants of Henry VIII might well have taken notice. But for the moment, euphoria ran high, especially among the humanists. Lord Mountjoy wrote rhapsodically, inviting the famous Dutch humanist Erasmus to visit England:

Oh, my Erasmus, if you could see how all the world here is rejoicing in the possession of so great a prince, how his life is all their desire, you could not contain your tears for joy. The heavens laugh, the earth exults, all things are full of milk, of honey, and of nectar! Avarice is expelled the country. Liberality scatters wealth with bounteous hand. Our king does not desire gold or gems or precious metals but virtue, glory, immortality. . . .

THE HUMANISTS

Henry VIII was, in fact, well educated himself and interested in bringing humane letters to England. Two concurrent developments made this feasible. Starting in the early 1490s, Italy, which previously had been a society of relatively balanced powers and small-scale conflicts, became the theater of massive and terribly destructive international wars. France, Spain, Switzerland, and Germany sent hordes of marauding mercenaries into the peninsula; they took part in the ongoing squabbles of the city-states, but raised the level of violence a thousandfold. They battered down city walls, devastated the countryside, and looted Italy's splendid artistic heritage. Under the circumstances, it was natural for Italian humanists to go traveling. A number came to England, where they held offices in the church, acted as tutors and secretaries in great houses, and served in the universities as teachers of Greek and the new "correct" Latin. The best known of them was Polydore Vergil of Urbino, who wrote an authoritative history of England; there were perhaps a dozen others.[3] These birds of passage were supplemented by a generation of English scholars, mostly born in the 1460s, who had visited Italy and studied there (SFR, C.1). Dean of the group was William Grocyn, who, though born in 1446, did not visit Italy till he was over forty. When he went to Italy, Grocyn found there Thomas Linacre (b. 1460), primarily a medical doctor but also a classical scholar. After his return to England, Linacre taught Greek at Oxford and tutored those children of Henry VIII who lived long enough to become his charges. John Colet (b. 1467) was in Italy from 1493 to 1496 or 1497; though his Greek was never more than rudimentary, his piety was exemplary, and his position as dean of St. Paul's in London enabled him to

3. Among them were Stefano Surigone, Cornelio Vitelli, Domenico Mancini, Pietro Carmeliano, Adriano Castelli di Corneto, Silvestro de' Gigli, and Andrea Ammonio of Lucca. Visiting Greeks included Demetrius Cantacuzene, John Sorbopolous, and Emanuel of Constantinople.

forward vigorously the cause of the new learning. When he founded a school on humanist principles, he placed in charge of it William Lily, an almost exact contemporary, who had studied in Italy and knew more about instilling the classical tongues than any man alive. Latin was the basis of the curriculum because Latin was the language of diplomacy, scholarship, theology, and in large part law, as well as medicine. For scholars who did not aspire to the learned professions, there were other schools which taught less Latin or none at all. But at Dean Colet's school, it was Lily's Latin Grammar or nothing; the book became a classic, and for centuries to come schoolboys would learn their Latin from it.

Finally, though a full account of them cannot be given here, we must note the two most remarkable of the humanists, Desiderius Erasmus and Thomas More. Erasmus was born (out of wedlock) in 1466, at or near Rotterdam; much against his will, he was put into a monastery and became a monk. But he was restless in the cloister and soon abandoned it for the life of a wandering scholar, first at Paris, then in Italy, England, Switzerland, Brussels, Louvain, wherever he could do his own work and enjoy his much cherished independence. He was a tireless writer, an audacious wit, an editor of painstaking erudition. His collection of adages or popular sayings was a monument of the new scholarship; in editing the Greek text of the New Testament, he for the first time freed discussion of it from dependence on the Vulgate, the old Latin translation done by Saint Jerome in 405. He was a schoolmaster to half of Europe, and (like Voltaire in the eighteenth century) a scandal to the other half.[4] And from the first he was a close friend and admirer of Thomas More, twelve years his junior and the crown of English humanism.

The son of a London lawyer and himself a man of practical affairs, More was a prodigy in letters, compared in his own day to Pico della Mirandola, the youthful genius of Italy. He never traveled to Italy, did little serious work on classical texts, and wrote only one classic work of literature, the *Utopia,* but his reputation was spectacular. Unlike the rootless Erasmus, More tried to put his humanist learning to the service of his own society—i.e., his king, his church, the community of London merchants. This division of humanists into the politically active and the politically detached can be traced back to the Florentine divisions within the movement in the very first years of the fifteenth century. But more interesting than the contrasts between More and Erasmus is the common ground they share. A glance at their most famous books will make this clear.

Both Erasmus's *Praise of Folly* (1509) and More's *Utopia* (1516) are serious

4. Erasmus never left the Catholic church, though he mocked many of the abuses against which the Protestant movement protested. A Catholic view was that "Erasmus laid the egg that Luther hatched." Though much too simple, the phrase contains a germ of truth. In the history of western thought, Erasmus is a portentous figure because, to an unusual degree, he owed no allegiance to any corporate body, whether nation, church, party, or patron. His native turf, so far as he had one, was the printing press. Like Petrarch before, and Voltaire after him, he was a citizen of the republic of letters. In the darkening fanaticism of the sixteenth-century wars of religion, his example was particularly important.

jokes, both written in Latin for the special delight of humanist circles, both published on the Continent. Mistress Folly delivers a speech in praise of herself; it is ambiguous to start with, since self-love is, by definition, folly itself, and folly is the lady's name. Still, she is a shrewd and worldly minx; we laugh easily as she singles out lawyers, theologians, professors, courtiers, and monks (the learned classes) as signal examples of her influence. But when she goes on to propose that the Christian religion is, on the word of Saint Paul, a model of unworldly folly, it's clear her attitude, and with it that of her creator, has shifted. If false wisdom is folly, and real wisdom is folly too, what's wrong with our definition of folly? Apart from her "real" opinions, if any, this slippery agility of a foolish lady in manipulating her point of view is the very reverse of foolish—so much so that for nearly half a millennium now it has left readers feeling foolish in the face of Folly's elusive subtlety.

More's *Utopia* also tests the reader's quickness and insight. Raphael Hythlodaye who tells More (and us) about the island of Utopia, is, according to the Greek roots of his last name, a peddler of nonsense. But as we first meet him, he is an acute and rational critic of English society. What he says about abuses of the criminal code and absurdities of the social system is incisive and unanswerable; his judgment of the Utopian way of life will therefore be authoritative. And in many of their details, Utopian institutions do contrast directly and favorably with those of Europe; there is neither poverty nor extravagance, the legal code is simple, punishments are humane, exploitation and aggression are unknown, a spirit of rational economy prevails. But the whole structure stands, as we learn, on the abolition of private property: that is the indispensable preliminary. For More, as for his readers, it was evidently a hard nut. No doubt More himself believed, after a fashion, in communism as an ideal social arrangement. It had apostolic sanction, in monasteries it was practiced daily, it was an obvious way to root out that pride and self-love to which private property and selfish appetite ministered. Communism was an ideal; but More, in addition to being an idealist and a potential saint, was a hardheaded and very prudent lawyer who knew that in Henry VIII's England, communism was out of the question. Like Folly's vision of Christianity, it was divine nonsense. Both authors were brilliant, subtle, wide-minded, and elusive; both exploited, in ways that anticipate the most sophisticated developments of the novel, indecision between divided and conflicting points of view.

HIGH HOPES, HARD REALITY

It was a fragile but tantalizing humanist dream, therefore, which young Henry VIII was to fulfill; and hardly anything he did during his long reign was not, one way or another, a betrayal of the humanism Erasmus and More espoused—that is, humanism tempered by Christian humility, Christian moderation. As a young man, he was much given to frivolities—sports, dances, tourneys, feasts, gorgeous apparel. In a single day's hunting he rode eight different horses into total exhaustion. By French standards, Henry's court was morally strict and severe; but nobody dared tell the young king to eat less, and his naturally full figure soon became unwieldy. His mind may have been set on "virtue, glory, immortality," but it was also set on foreign conquest. In his many intricate wars he was occasionally successful on the field but always a financial loser; in the diplomatic and dynastic bargaining that accompanied warfare in those days, he was generally outwitted. And while he divided his time between the pleasures of peace and those of war, the running of the country devolved on a man quite ready to undertake it. This was Thomas Wolsey, originally the son of an Ipswich innkeeper. Before he died in 1530, at the age of fifty-eight, Wolsey the son had risen to be archbishop of York, cardinal, papal legate, lord chancellor, and incomparably the most powerful man (but one) in the kingdom.

WOLSEY'S UNEASY DIPLOMACY

Under Henry VII, Wolsey had proved his fitness in minor posts, but his career took off only after the advent of Henry VIII. Within the church he accumulated quickly and easily a great many offices, mostly rewards for his service in the secular administration. As lord chancellor, he made himself responsible for much of the high-level legal business in the realm, using the powers of Star Chamber so freely that many people thought he had created that court. He also conducted the king's foreign policy, and worked furiously to keep the king in money. With time, he became arrogant enough to write that "I and my king" wish this or that to be done; foolish people opined that he was the real head of state, Henry just a figurehead. How wrong they were was slow to appear, but terrible in the event.

Meanwhile, Wolsey gathered domestic power into his hands, from which it would one day be roughly removed, and Henry took part in the wars of the Continent. They were continual and inconceivably complex; but the main enemy was generally France, the secondary enemy her devoted, unfortunate ally, Scotland. Between 1512 and 1514, Henry was at war with both at once, not very successfully with France, even though she was then busily warring in Italy with Julius II plus his Swiss and Spanish allies. But early losses in northern France were partly avenged at the battle of Guinegatte (13 August 1513), while Henry's lieutenant in the north, the earl of Surrey, gained a crushing victory over the Scots at Flodden Field (9 September).[5] Only the second victory amounted to

5. By an odd coincidence, Flodden occasioned both the first purely English ballad, by John Skelton, and the last English poem in alliterative verse, written by a retainer of the house of Stanley, and known simply as "Scottish Field." Skelton's "Ballad of the Scottish King" is a typical bit of boasting, but "Scottish Field" is a fine, strong poem in a verse form which by rights should have been obsolete centuries before (SFR, B.17).

much; Scottish losses at Flodden, which included their warlike king James IV, kept the northern kingdom quiescent for the next quarter century. But in Europe things changed too fast for Henry to keep up. Ferdinand of Spain died and was replaced by his grandson Carlos; when, three years later, in 1519, the German emperor Maximilian died, Carlos, who was also *his* grandson, absorbed his authority.[6] Louis XII of France died in 1516, and was replaced by François I; Julius II died in 1513, and was replaced by Leo X. There was a brief moment in 1519 when the pope's leadership, a temporary balance of power between France and Spain, and Wolsey's eloquence seemed likely to produce a general European peace. But the moment passed, leaving as one of its memories a glittering meeting on a field in Flanders between Henry VIII and François I (June 1520). On "The Field of the Cloth of Gold" the two young monarchs—envious at once and admiring—met in a setting of unprecedented splendor. Fine words were exchanged and expensive clothing paraded about; there were feasts and tourneys. Much of the palaver was directed by Wolsey to the end of having him elected pope; but when the tents were struck and the showmen departed, most of the promises that he had garnered proved weak and ineffectual. Leo X died in December 1521, but Wolsey got only a fraction of the necessary votes, and when a new pope was again to be elected in October 1523, he got none at all. Within two years of the glamorous meeting between Henry and François, the two nations were at war again. This time England was ostensibly allied with Spain. Henry's daughter Mary was to marry Carlos V when she was old enough (she was just six when the papers were signed); and meanwhile a joint strategy against François was elaborately designed. But the alliance fell apart when at the battle of Pavia (25 February 1525) François was utterly defeated by the hardbitten Spanish infantrymen and tough German *landsknechte,* thus opening the door for the notorious and barbaric sack of Rome in 1527. When Carlos V found himself so spectacularly successful, with both the pope and the king of France his prisoners, he had no further need of Henry. He cast off the English alliance, broke his engagement to little Mary, and married Isabella of Portugal, who was not only immediately nubile but brought with her a dowry of a million crowns. Thus Wolsey's foreign policy and the maze of intrigues supporting it, brought him and his royal master to an absolute dead end.

PAPACY AND PROTESTANTISM

Shortly after the Field of the Cloth of Gold, while Wolsey's papal hopes were still alive, Henry VIII had written a book of theological controversy on the seven sacraments. Against the new doctrine of the German monk Martin Luther, Henry defended the validity of all seven: baptism, confirmation, the Eucharist, penance,

6. As king of Spain, Carlos was first of his name, hence Carlos I; as Holy Roman emperor, he was Carlos V, and is commonly known in Spain as Carlos Quinto.

extreme unction, holy orders, and matrimony. Luther wanted fewer; he was not yet quite sure how many fewer.[7] He was not declared an outright schismatic till the conclusion of the Diet (conference) of Worms (May 1521), but he was definitely obnoxious to the pope, and Henry's ponderous pamphlet defending the orthodox position earned him from Leo X the formal title of "Defender of the Faith." Gratifying at the moment, the new title proved something of an embarrassment later, when questions arose as to what faith Henry and his successors were actually defending.

For the moment, Henry had proved himself, and as late as 1527 he remained, a dutiful and docile son of the church. This role was not always easy, because different popes often switched their alliances from one to another of the nations invading Italy, in an effort to get rid of them all; but, to the best of his ability, Henry followed from a distance the papal lead. His pamphlet against Luther was, if anything, overenthusiastic; Thomas More, to whom he showed it, suggested mildly that the monarch had conceded rather more secular authority to the papacy than was safe. Henry would have none of that; one couldn't possibly exalt the pope's authority high enough, he said, because that of the king himself depended on it. More disagreed, but was tactfully silent. During the hideous sack of Rome, in 1527, Pope Clement VII appealed for help to the powers of Europe; that Henry sent his prayers for the pope's safety surprised nobody, but that he actually delivered 30,000 cash ducats absolutely amazed the worldly cardinals of Rome. By comparison with those practiced, instinctive deceivers the kings of Spain and France, Henry was a naïve, even chivalric son of the church. Perhaps that was why few of his continental projects bore fruit.

But as Catherine reached the end of her childbearing years without producing a male heir, the king's worries increased. He had objected to the marriage in the first place; suspicions grew in his mind that in marrying his brother's widow he had committed incest, and that lack of a male heir reflected God's displeasure with that sin. (Unhappily, Biblical texts point both ways: Leviticus 20:21 *forbids* a man to marry his deceased brother's wife and says they shall be childless, while Deuteronomy 25:5 *requires* the brother of a deceased husband to marry the widow.) Henry consulted appropriate ecclesiastical authorities; perhaps the pope would annul the marriage or grant a dispensation permitting a divorce. There were precedents for both these actions; popes had been particularly liberal in allowing monarchs to patch and mend their diplomatic marriages in view of

7. Sacraments are the visible means through which divine grace is sought by and conferred on the believing Christian. Luther began his revolt by denouncing the sacrament of penance, as exercised in the selling of papal indulgences. Indeed, he conceded, the church could impose strictly ecclesiastical penalties, and then remit them, for money or otherwise. But an ecclesiastical rule is not a sacrament; and that the church could forgive sins decreed to be such by God, he utterly denied. Likewise he denied that the church could remit sins after death, for example by shortening anyone's stay in purgatory as a result of money given or masses said by the living. Most Protestant churches nowadays recognize only two sacraments, baptism and the Eucharist, which they prefer to call the Lord's Supper.

altered circumstances.[8] But when the emperor Carlos V, nephew of Catherine, held the pope as hostage, it could hardly be expected that the emperor would allow his aunt's marriage to be invalidated. Catherine herself protested bitterly against her husband's new projects. Her marriage had lasted for twenty years, her first engagement went back a quarter of a century; in all that time, there had been no charges of incest. The objection had in fact been foreseen and fore-stalled; Pope Julius II had granted a dispensation, specifically allowing Henry to marry his deceased brother's widow. How could a union be declared incestuous in 1527 which the pope himself in 1503 had declared not to be so?

To Cardinal Wolsey Henry assigned the impossible task of negotiating with Clement VII a release from his oppressive marriage. Even had he been so inclined, the pope could not possibly have granted the dispensation without infuriating the emperor; and the emperor was close at hand, while Henry was far away. Nego-tiations were complex and protracted; but the king was a man whose mind hard-ened the more obstacles it met. His eagerness for a divorce was heightened by the fact that he had fallen in love with another woman, Anne Boleyn or Bullen, who he was quite sure would produce for him the long-sought male heir. Besides, he was about to get rid of Cardinal Wolsey, whose foreign policy had been expensive and unproductive.[9] Wolsey's negotiations over the divorce put him in a no-win situation. If they succeeded, he had placed on the throne Anne Boleyn, who hated him because he had advocated a French bride for Henry; if they failed, Henry would lose no time in getting rid of him.

The negotiations failed definitively in 1529. For more than two years, Henry and Catherine had been living apart, to satisfy Henry's tender conscience, con-vinced by now that their cohabitation was "sinful."[10] While Wolsey was in France, trying to patch up an alliance there, Henry sent his private secretary to Rome, trying to arrange a deal whereby, without the pope's direct involvement, a marriage with Anne could be approved. A "court" consisting of Wolsey and the papal legate Campeggio actually began meeting at the Blackfriars in London during the summer of 1529; but Catherine boldly protested against it, and appealed to Rome. Spanish power forced Clement to recall the case, and take charge of it

8. An imposing list of the precedents for and terrible obstacles to Henry's divorce will be found in the Introduction to Henry A. Kelly's *The Matrimonial Trials of Henry VIII* (Stanford, 1976).

9. After trying for years to poise Spain against France, he was no longer trusted or valued by either of the great powers. Henry, whose view of international politics was always of the shortest, exulted in the defeat of François at Pavia, not seeing that it left England without any leverage at all in her alliance with Spain.

10. Curiously, Henry had few such scruples about his new love, Anne Boleyn, though in fact he had had sexual relations with her sister Mary, and the canon law makes no distinction between affinity by matrimony and affinity by fornication. (For a brilliant comic exposition of the various impediments to marriage, see Ben Jonson's *Epicoene,* Act V, scene 3.) Henry was widely suspected of having meddled with Anne Boleyn's mother, as well as her sister; he denied the mother. Less public but potentially more explosive was the fact that Anne Boleyn had an earlier husband still living. In divorcing his first wife and marrying his second, Henry was treading an unmarked mine field.

himself—a clear sign that Catherine would block the divorce. Within six months, Wolsey had been deprived of all his secular offices, and indicted under the ancient, sweeping statute of *praemunire;*[11] he made his submission, forfeited his immense estates, and retired to his see as archbishop of York. There he might have lived quietly, but he could not quiet the suspicions of his enemies or of Henry; he was arrested and on his way to the Tower, when he cheated the headsman by dying en route (November 1530). Two major things he had done, unwittingly, to forward the coming English Reformation. He had gathered so much power in his hands that Henry found it easy to seize the entire package; and by arrogating power in the pope's name to the church and himself, he had rendered the establishment deeply unpopular. His splendid rise and sudden fall furnished moralists with material for years to come.

ANNE BOLEYN AND THE KING'S SCHISM

Henry's need for a male heir was the occasion, not the cause, of the English Reformation; but it was a powerful occasion. All over Europe, the new Protestant doctrine was making headway, in Germany, France, Switzerland, even in some of the mediterranean countries. Henry was not sympathetic to it, at least not consistently so; but he was not consistently opposed to it, either. He wanted to be rid of Catherine so as to beget a legitimate male heir on Anne Boleyn. The papacy interfered with that purpose of his, but the Protestants as a group offered him no particular help. The great powers of Europe, busy with their own intricate quarrels, troubled by complex new religious difficulties, struggling in the throes of a continent-wide inflation, paid little heed to Henry's domestic anguish. For him, the issue became suddenly urgent when in late 1532 Anne proved to be pregnant. Perhaps, at last, this was the male heir himself. In January of 1533 Henry secretly married his new lady; in May the marriage to Catherine was declared null (by the archbishop of Canterbury and a convocation of the English church, never mind the pope); and in June Anne was crowned queen. In September, she gave birth to a daughter, who later became Queen Elizabeth. Thus "the king's great cause," his divorce and remarriage, was settled by the cleaver of royal authority rather than the logical finesse of a legal code.

The rest of Anne Boleyn's career is briefly told. She had a miscarriage in 1534, gave birth to a dead male child early in 1536, was accused, during the summer, of manifold adulteries (with her own brother, among others), had her

11. The word means "warning"; the statute is a bundle of several fourteenth-century laws aimed at limiting papal authority in England. The chief one was passed in the sixteenth year of Richard II's reign (1393), and forbids "translating"—i.e., transferring cases under dispute in the royal courts to the jurisdiction of Rome. Obviously, application of a law like this depended heavily on political circumstances; when Henry was in his phase of papal "docility," *praemunire* was never heard of; later it swelled to giant proportions.

marriage annulled, and was executed by the headsman.[12] Less than three weeks elapsed from the first hint of royal displeasure till her head rolled on the scaffold. The day after her execution, the king announced his engagement to Lady Jane Seymour, and the marriage followed posthaste.

THE REFORMATION FROM BELOW: CRANMER, TYNDALE, AND THE MEN OF CAMBRIDGE

Well before Henry forced the issue of his divorce to the point of an open break with the papacy, Protestant ideas and practices had made their way to English shores. English merchants trading in Germany, German merchants trading in England, carried some of them; but most seem to have traveled, via exchange students, from German to English universities, particularly Cambridge. In late 1520 Luther flatly defied the pope and issued three pamphlets of justification. His views about the supremacy of individual conscience and the financial extortions of the ecclesiastical hierarchy chimed to a considerable extent with those of the old "Lollard" party in England, still surviving in obscurity and official reprobation. There were book burnings and inquisitions against the Lollards before the name of Luther was ever heard in England; in 1515 there were ugly riots when a man named Richard Hunne, who was being held prisoner in an ecclesiastical jail, was found dead in his cell.[13] An ecclesiastical court found that he had committed suicide and was a heretic besides; thus his family could not inherit his property. A lay court found the jailer and three other men, including a priest, guilty of murder. After a time Wolsey smoothed things over; but events of this sort not only created anticlerical feeling, they showed how much anticlerical feeling already existed among the people.

The first of the "new" reformers were Cambridge scholars. Thomas Cranmer did not originally intend to take orders at all, for he married; but his wife died, and he was ordained in 1523. Like many Lutherans after the great crisis of the Peasant War in Germany (1524–1525), he gave a great deal of authority in ecclesiastical matters to the secular ruler; and a word he dropped on the topic of

12. That a woman so busy with pregnancies could have taken (in Anne's perilous position) such a multitude of lovers, may seem unlikely. But she was under terrible pressure to produce the male heir, and may well have despaired of Henry. What more natural than to turn elsewhere? Of course, the charges may have been trumped up; evidence in such matters is generally scanty. All the men with whom she was accused went to the block the day before she did. Annulling the marriage made nonsense out of the charges of adultery, in any case, since no one can be false to a marriage that never existed. The grounds for annulment were apparently the same as those for the divorce from Catherine: too close an affinity to a previous sexual partner (that would be Anne's sister Mary).

13. Hunne, a respectable tailor, had refused to pay a mortuary fee to the priest who buried his child; he was also accused of attending private prayer meetings, perhaps private religious services, with his fellow businessmen. He might have been guilty of this, and much more, without coming close to the heresy charged against his memory (SFR, C.7).

divorce caught Henry's ear almost by accident, in the fall of 1529. The monarch was delighted with a man who gave him just the doctrine he wanted on the topic closest to his heart.[14] Cranmer was clearly not ambitious, for he married again in 1532; but the king, afire as usual with a fresh enthusiasm, overlooked that inconvenience, and nominated Cranmer in 1533 to be archbishop of Canterbury. More strikingly still, he either kept the pope ignorant of the archbishop's recent marriage or got him to ignore it. Cranmer's life as archbishop was far from easy; his principles called for him to support royal authority, but Henry's ideas shifted rapidly, and Cranmer sometimes had to disavow what he had recently asserted. On becoming archbishop, he took an oath of obedience to the pope, but an equal and potentially conflicting oath to the king, realm, laws, and prerogatives of England. Consulted about the sacraments, he gave his opinion, but concluded, "This is mine opinion and sentence at this present, which I do not temerariously define, and do remit the judgment thereof wholly unto your majesty." Cranmer was deeply loyal to Henry, and Henry was exceptionally loyal to Cranmer; but it was only after the monarch's death that the full depth of Cranmer's Protestant commitment made itself felt.

William Tyndale was another of the Cambridge reformers, but more radical than Cranmer, and consequently less congenial to Henry. He studied Greek in classes which had been initiated by Erasmus, and about 1521 took orders. Tyndale's ministry in the west country of England brought him into conflict with the hierarchy as a suspected heretic; but he was simply warned and dismissed. A bit naïvely, he asked the humanist bishop of London for help in translating the New Testament from Greek into English;[15] but help was not forthcoming, quite the contrary; so Tyndale turned for support to a London merchant, one Humphrey Monmouth, in whose house he resided for a while and with whose help he sailed in 1524 to Germany. There he continued to work at his task till forced to move on by ecclesiastical pressure. By 1526 he had finished his translation (a truly excellent job, which has left many traces on the work of the King James trans-

14. What Cranmer actually suggested was that the canon lawyers and university professors of England could declare illegal any marriage with a deceased brother's widow. That would suffice for Henry's purposes, and put off an appeal to Rome for a long time, perhaps, under the statute of *praemunire*, forever. Cranmer was not a committed Lutheran; though he was at Cambridge when the new doctrines were being eagerly discussed at the White Horse Tavern, he did not attend the meetings there. But he was subject to strong influence from admirers of the German church.

15. The Catholic position emphasizes the value of the church (with its doctors, bishops, councils, and supreme pontiff) as a *guide* to the conduct of human life; Protestants emphasize as a corrective the *rule* laid down in Scriptures and interpreted by the individual conscience. Hence Protestants are eager to have the Bible translated, diffused widely, and popularly read; Catholics, fearing this process will lead to conflicting interpretations and general confusion, preferred to keep the Bible in the learned tongues so that a learned clergy could provide a single, uniform, authoritative interpretation of it. Here as elsewhere the humanists played ambiguous roles. Erasmus published a carefully researched Greek text of the New Testament, which implied that the Latin Vulgate was questionable; he spoke out in favor of translations; but he did not himself translate the New Testament into any vernacular. When Tyndale did just that, it was the Greek text of Erasmus that he used.

lators who worked eighty years later); but it had to be smuggled into England, where authorities burned copies as fast as they could capture them. Archbishop Warham, Cranmer's predecessor, even sent abroad to buy copies in order to destroy them, and Henry tried to have Tyndale himself brought to England as a subversive. It would have gone hard with him there, for the lord chancellor, Thomas More, was eager to identify and "punish" (burn at the stake) "heretics" of Protestant persuasion.[16] Tyndale exchanged polemics with More at a distance, but kept out of his reach. Unhappily, in 1535 (that was three years after More himself had fallen from power), he was caught near Brussels by agents of Carlos V, and, in October of 1536, strangled. The fires that he had started burned underground, however. Henry did nothing to encourage them; whatever reforming the English church needed, it had had at his hands, and no further volunteers were wanted. And yet when Parliament, under Henry's urging, began cutting back on the power of the clergy, and cutting off their access to the supreme authority of Rome, it was creating a climate in which Protestant opinion, especially as it was anti-ecclesiastical, could hardly fail to flourish. The pope thundered his anathemas on Henry and on the Lutherans alike; their case was in that measure common, whether they liked it or not.

PARLIAMENT: FULCRUM OF THE REFORMATION

Like his father before him, Henry VIII in the early days of his reign made little use of Parliaments; Wolsey, who was naturally uncomfortable with them, discouraged the practice. But with the Parliament which sat from 1529 to 1534, earning itself the name of the "Reformation Parliament," everything changed. For a little while, Henry was able to make use of Thomas More as his chief agent; when the limits of More's tolerance were reached, he turned to a rough, resourceful fellow named Thomas Cromwell. This was a man who, though short on formal education, had soldiered on the Continent and picked up business procedures from the Florentine bankers; intellectually quick and versatile, he caught at ideas where he found them, and translated them into instant action (SFR, D.28). In the hands of Henry, he became a deft and deadly weapon; and the political body through which he worked was the House of Commons. A first step was to reform ecclesiastical abuses at the visible, popular level; these were mostly privileges and exemptions, exorbitant fees demanded by churchmen for service to the laity, and the "pluralist" practice of holding a number of offices in the church to the detriment of some or all of them. Reforms such as these,

16. More may have been unusually fierce against those he called heretics from a feeling that his earlier *Utopia* had done something to encourage them; it was not usual for a lord chancellor to take personal part in such prosecutions. In any case, his badgering helpless men and women whose "sin" lay in the free exercise of their Christian consciences is not, for us, the most attractive side of his character.

which brought relief to common people, were instantly popular; they also served
to warn the pope that an English Parliament could take measures against his very
vulnerable purse. As the message did not get through, Henry in December of
1530 sued the entire body of the English clergy for an immense sum of money,
on the score that in recognizing Wolsey as papal legate, they had violated the
statute of *praemunire* (see above, p. 120). The charge was ridiculous; Englishmen had recognized papal legates for centuries, Henry VIII had recognized Cardinal Wolsey, he would have punished brutally any churchman who didn't. But
impoverishing the clergy was a way of enriching the crown; and in the process,
Henry forced the clergy to acknowledge the absolute supremacy of the royal
authority. They had to admit that he was "their Supreme Lord and, so far as the
Law of Christ allows, even Supreme Head." Supreme Head was what the pope
had claimed to be; that title now belonged to Henry. In 1532 Cromwell pushed
through Parliament another set of laws rendering all the clergy's legal and legislative authority subject to the approval of the king. Next, Henry moved to cut
off payment to Rome of the "annates" or "first fruits," representing the first
year's revenue of any ecclesiastical post. Instead of to Rome, this money was to
be paid to the crown; but the king suspended application of the law till he had
collected papal authority for placing Cranmer in the archbishopric of Canterbury.
Then he pushed through an act reaffirming his supremacy while completely sev-
ering the English church from Rome, legally, disciplinarily, financially, but not—
a curious exception, passed over in almost complete silence—doctrinally. Doctrinal differences would have been hard to define in an act of Parliament; they
were ignored. The other reformations in Europe (those made by Luther, Calvin,
Zwingli, Knox) were the work of theologians, and had doctrine at their very
heart; England's Reformation was made by a king operating through Parliament
and was essentially administrative in character.

In this way England broke with the papacy, and during the year 1534 Parliament worked long and hard to tie up the legal threads thus severed. Essentially,
Henry had cut away the papacy as head of the English church and put himself in
its place. He, a layman, must now appoint bishops, enforce discipline, collect
tithes, ordain ritual, and define belief; he, far from celibate himself, must decide
if priests should remain celibate. Finally, the word "treason" must be greatly
expanded, since it must henceforth include the use of words decribing the king
as a heretic, a schismatic, and a usurper. Disagreeing with the king on a point of
abstruse theology could now be called "treason"; and Henry went even further
by having Parliament declare that the mere secret wish to deprive the king of the
privileges he had asserted was treasonous. All public officials must swear an
oath promising total support to the king in all his ecclesiastical pretensions. Over
this oath Sir Thomas More came to grief. Foreseeing trouble, he had resigned as
lord chancellor (10 May 1532); but he was too prominent and too much admired
to be left in peace. That the king was rightfully king of England he would swear;
that others might swear loyalty to the king as head of the church he granted, and

he would not discourage their doing so. But he himself could not and would not take that oath. Imprisoned and tried on the grotesque charge of treason, he was beheaded on 7 July 1535; Bishop John Fisher and eight abbots of Carthusian monasteries suffered with him. In 1886 Sir Thomas More was beatified and in 1935 canonized as Saint Thomas More.

All these extreme and ruthless events, violent new laws, and patently unjust executions might seem to bespeak a paranoid habit of mind in Henry. Perhaps they do. But we should not forget that he had the support of the House of Commons in what he did; and behind the Commons stood the burgesses and gentry of England, or at least a good part of England. Not everybody thought More a martyr; hardly anybody thought Cromwell, much less Henry, a monster. Much was forgiven the men who had liberated England, however roughly, from what was widely perceived as an oppressive system. Still, the Reformation stirred spontaneous protests in parts of the country where old ways and old loyalties remained strong. The great Irish house of Fitzgerald was roused to revolt in 1534; by a combination of force and guile the revolt was put down, and not only the leader ("Silken Thomas" Fitzgerald) but five of his uncles suffered at Tyburn the frightful death, by hanging, disemboweling, quartering, and beheading, reserved for traitors. (This was directly contrary to the royal promise of clemency—but who would dare to remind Henry of his royal promises?) More serious was a gathering in the north country two years later under the pious name of "The Pilgrimage of Grace." The "pilgrims" who gathered in the autumn of 1536 were in fact armed soldiers; many were veterans of Flodden Field. There were some 30,000 of them, and their demands were essentially for less taxation, less central authority, and no ecclesiastical changes at all. Had they been led by real militants, they might have made serious trouble for Henry; the pope and some of the Catholic powers on the Continent might have been persuaded to lend them aid. But they were talked out of their revolt, such as it was. The king, when things were under wraps, hanged a couple of hundred participants, mostly poor men. And to keep order in this still largely feudal district, he erected a new and powerful arm of the very central government against which the "pilgrims" had been protesting. The Council of the North was a special prerogative court like the powerful Star Chamber in London. But its sittings were mostly in York, and it kept a close eye on troublemakers. Henry learned his political lessons very quickly.

THE RUIN OF THE MONASTERIES

A major motive stirring the "pilgrims" in the north to action was a new and sweeping act of the king's agent, Cromwell. During the summer of 1535, he and his operatives visited all the monasteries in the land, and decided that all those with an income of less than £200 a year were iniquitous; they were accordingly dissolved, their lands and buildings declared forfeit to the crown. The reasons for this action were severely practical. Protestantism, indeed, is not sympathetic to the contemplative life. Monks in their cloister are easily represented as drones, useless to God and society; their communities seem to the wayfaring, warfaring Christian of Protestantism mere nests for the lazy and luxurious. In 1535 this may even have been partly right, for the monasteries and abbeys, richly endowed during the middle ages, were now attracting few monks, and could accordingly spread the jam thicker. But Henry's reasons for the expropriation were none of these; he needed money, quickly, and in large quantities. Politically, the church was weak, so the church went to the wall; the middle classes, realizing that they could get some of the loot themselves, and that if the church was not looted, middle-class men would have to pay Henry's bills, cooperated. Henry picked on the little monasteries first as a way of getting legislation through Parliament. Most of the big abbeys sent representatives to the House of Lords; they could be bribed, by a momentary exemption for themselves, into condemning their less affluent brethren. But all the monasteries, abbeys, and major shrines were doomed.

Nothing in the Reformation did more to change the countryside than the ruin of the monasteries. Many had been established for centuries; some were architectural jewels, and their libraries were rich in ancient manuscripts and works of art. Pilgrims had brought offerings to the shrines at Glastonbury and Canterbury till they were religious treasure chests more opulent by far than the throne rooms of kings. Within the countryside, monasteries were traditional sources of charity and hospitality; the traveler, unable to find an inn, could stop and sometimes linger in a monastery. The homeless vagabond could get a handout there and a warm bed for the night. They were not all admirable. Some of them had been, in effect, country clubs for the rich; others had been privileged, tax-exempt commercial houses; as a group, they monopolized in perpetuity a very large fraction (perhaps as much as a third) of England's best land. Yet for all that, their brutal and indiscriminate expropriation violated something precious in the English countryside. Chapels were converted to pigpens, cloisters to horse stables. Stained-glass windows were smashed, vellum manuscripts used to wrap fish. Lead guttering was stripped from roofs, and ancient walls mined for cheap building stone. Simultaneously, the Parliament passed a new statute, harsh beyond all precedent, for the treatment of vagabonds and "sturdy beggars."[17] The middle class, proud

17. The act of 1531 (22 Henry VIII, cap. 12, is the technical reference) allowed the "impotent poor" (those physically unable to work) to beg, with a license, in their own districts; able-bodied poor, caught outside their district, were to be whipped and sent home by the most direct route. If they strayed from that route, they were to be whipped again; once home, they were to get a job or— if they refused or were unable—to be put to forced labor for the parish. That usually meant road work for meager meals and no pay.

Another aspect of the Protestant work ethic, now gaining control over the land, was a radical diminution in the number of holidays, saints' days, and rural feast days. One contemporary estimate has it that the old regime celebrated some 95 saints' days and 30 more *profesti* (half holidays, we should probably call them); under Protestantism, this was reduced to 27 holidays in all. (For the sake of comparison, modern America celebrates about a dozen real holidays.)

of its own industry, naturally identifies idleness with wickedness. Those who abolished the monasteries felt they were striking a double blow at idleness, and so at Satan. Idle monks who sheltered idle vagabonds would be no more; nor would charity be, any more, one of the three theological virtues.

Of course, the distinction between big and little monasteries was only temporary; hardly a measurable interval separated completion of the first operation from the start of the second. The ancient institutions of Glastonbury, Malmesbury, and Bury St. Edward's, rich with ancient, hand-illuminated Irish manuscripts, were looted and ruined; so was the Augustinian convent at Canterbury, cradle of Christianity for the entire island. Henry went with particular zest after the Canterbury shrine of Saint Thomas Becket, goal of Chaucer's pilgrims. It was rich in votive objects of gold and silver, adorned with precious stones—the king had it stripped bare, the precious metals carried off to his treasury, the most famous ruby set in a ring to adorn his own fat finger. The monks, if they were docile, were not much brutalized. Some were pensioned off, others absorbed into the regular hierarchy, still others sent off to find secular jobs. But if they showed the slightest sign of resistance, their fate was swift and savage. The last abbot of Glastonbury was accused, absurdly, of desecrating his church; he was tried, convicted, and hanged in a trice. The king's agents then showed their respect for the vast and ancient edifice by ripping it apart, smashing, plundering, and burning till practically nothing was left above ground.

Those who did the work of destruction did not fail to profit by the spoiling of the English church; they took outright or bought cheap the best of the lands for themselves, becoming established quickly as a new generation of gentry and aristocrats. But the greater part of the money went to Henry himself. Part of it he spent on ambitious building programs. There were several enormous pleasure houses on the scale of Nonesuch in Surrey; the vast palace at Hampton Court, begun by Wolsey, was taken over and completed by Henry; the chapel of Henry VII at Westminster was finished in splendid style by his son. Splendid as it was, however, Henry's building program cost but a fraction of the sums he squandered throughout his reign on wars with Scotland and France. Between 1541 and 1546 these struggles cost the nation more than £2,000,000;[18] and to carry them on, Henry exhausted his treasury, borrowed to the limit from German bankers, and during the 1540s systematically debased the national currency by almost 50 percent. He succeeded only in solidifying hatred in both France and Scotland against the English. The Scottish Reformation did not take place till 1560, so that in both countries Henry was not only a foreign aggressor but a heretic. He could not hope to conquer or annex either nation. Why then did he persist? By now the king was so corpulent and gouty that when cased in armor he had to be

18. The pound, in those days, was a very large sum of money. We note that a lancer with two attendants would be paid 18 pence a day, an archer 8 pence if mounted but 6 pence if afoot. The ordinary seaman got 1 shilling 3 pence a week at sea; Sir Thomas Wyatt, appointed high marshal at Calais in 1528, received the splendid stipend of 2 shillings a day! Plenty of people did not see £5 a year in hard money. See Appendix A.

hoisted atop his horse with block and tackle. Still he persisted in thinking himself a gallant knight. Years of effort went into besieging Boulogne and raiding the French coast. Halfway through the war, Henry's major ally, Carlos V, pulled out (18 September 1543); with some sense of practicality, if not generosity, he offered to include England in the peace, but Henry, headstrong as always, refused, and a ruinous war, of which nobody could have defined the objective, dragged on till June of 1546.

WIVES, WIVES, WIVES

We must not overlook Henry's last three matrimonial adventures, but there is no reason to linger over them—*he* certainly did not. We left him, newly married to Lady Jane Seymour (30 May 1536); on 12 October 1537, the long-anticipated son was born. He was a sickly lad, who was to rule briefly as Edward VI, but never to see his sixteenth birthday. His mother died in giving birth to him; and Henry, out of respect, waited two years before seeking another spouse. In October of 1539 Thomas Cromwell recommended to him a German princess, Anne of Cleves, and early in 1540 (though Henry found the lady shockingly ugly, and she thought him rude and crude) they were married. By June this inauspicious marriage was on the rocks; Cromwell was beheaded for it (a lesson to matchmakers!), Parliament annulled the marriage, Henry pensioned the lady off, and on the very day of Cromwell's execution married Catherine Howard, niece of the duke of Norfolk. Once more the unhappy monarch was deluded; while he was away in Scotland, in 1541, the new queen took occasion to misbehave with her cousin, Thomas Culpeper. Investigation disclosed still other lovers in the back corridors; and the familiar routine of hangings and beheadings had to be repeated. After eighteen months in the single state, Henry made a final effort with Catherine Parr, whom he married on 12 July 1543.[19] She was a kindly young woman, twenty years the king's junior but already twice widowed, and by temper pious and patient. For three years she put up with Henry's increasing ill humor and invalid complaints; she was particularly kind, if tradition tells true, to his three children. By the fall of 1546, it was clear that the king was dying. At fifty-five he was not an old man, but for years he had been crippled by gout, for which until the nineteenth century there was no known remedy. It affected his circulation, his legs became gangrenous, and only at the last minute did one bold courtier, disregarding the king's positive orders, venture to say that death was at hand. Henry died, comforted by one of the few servants against whom he never turned, his archbishop, Thomas Cranmer.

19. The fate of Henry's six wives can be summarized in a brisk formula as: divorced, beheaded, died, divorced, beheaded, survived. Anne of Cleves was annulled or dismissed rather than formally divorced, but the general import of the formula is about right.

A PROTESTANT KING—OR WAS HE?

When he finished spoiling the monasteries in 1539, King Henry VIII had struck his last major blow against the Roman Catholic church. Pope Clement VII had excommunicated him over the royal divorce in 1533, and Paul III, responding to the execution of More, Fisher, and the Carthusian abbots, threatened to depose him in 1535. Technically speaking, the king was an outlaw, a pariah, an outcast. But, practically, excommunication hardly bothered him. The last years of his life were devoted to a curious balancing act, in which the king encouraged alternately the Catholic and Protestant factions of his nation. In 1536 he devised the so-called Ten Articles, to establish Christian quiet in the realm; they proposed much traditional doctrine, but mentioned only three sacraments instead of the traditional seven, and expressed strong approval of a vernacular Bible. They also warned against images, prayer for the dead, belief in purgatory, and, of course, papal supremacy. In 1539, the relatively tolerant Ten Articles were followed by a more stringent statue of Six Articles; they decreed the death penalty for anyone questioning the doctrine of transubstantiation, the value of auricular confession, of clerical celibacy, or of communion under one kind—i.e., bread without wine.[20] At the same time, steps were taken to limit access to the Bible; it was to be read only by discreet and understanding people. Men might be punished for being too Protestant, but also and equally for being too Catholic. On 30 July 1540, three Lutheran clergymen were executed, alongside three Catholic believers, for different but equally fatal offenses against the Six Articles. Henry seemed to delight in tantalizing everybody; on a famous occasion in 1543 (used by Shakespeare as the climax of his play on the monarch), he invited the council to accuse Cranmer as a heretic and imprison him in the Tower. Then he called Cranmer late at night, warned him of the impending threat, and gave him a royal ring to secure his immunity from the accusers. Next morning at the crucial moment, Cranmer produced the ring, baffled his enemies (who thought they had cleared everything with the king and were fulfilling his wishes), and brought down on them a furious royal reprimand, full of threats and angry menaces. For Henry it was like a royal diversion. He loved to converse in a friendly, "confidential" way with one individual, and then with another unsay everything he had said to the first. People were reduced to guessing his views. Anne of Cleves, as a German and a project of Cromwell's, was supposed to be a good omen for Protestants; her replacement by Catherine Howard encouraged the Catholic faction; Catherine Parr was good

20. These are all Catholic positions based on traditions of the church, not explicit Scripture, and emphasizing the crucial role of the priest as dispenser of the sacraments leading to salvation. Transubstantiation is supremely important among these beliefs because it proposes that the priest, in consecrating the communion wafer and wine, converts them to the actual body and blood of Christ. The Protestant view is that Christ is in the spirit of the communicant, the worthiness of the communicant determining the real presence in the sacrament. Thus some Protestants hold that the bread and wine are mere symbols, the true sacrament being wholly spiritual.

for Protestants again. About Henry himself we do not know if he considered himself a Catholic in bad standing, a Protestant in good, or—since neither of these definitions would have satisfied his gigantic ego—simply a king too big to be hedged in by petty theological definitions.

EDWARD AND MARY, CONTRASTING HEIRS

The children of Henry VIII succeeded to his throne in strict and proper order— the male heir first, and after his death without an heir, the two daughters of Henry, in order of seniority. Edward VI and Mary were the first two successors before Elizabeth; they ruled for five and a half years apiece, Edward in the Protestant interest, Mary in the Catholic. Their reigns were troubled and unhappy, and both ended in untimely death. Edward, a child of but nine, inherited from his father a wretched constitution, a divided kingdom, an exhausted treasury, and a desperate diplomatic situation. Though a precocious scholar, the solemn little boy was frail from birth and in obvious need of a protector. His uncle, Edward Seymour, duke of Somerset, promoted himself to this profitable position, and held it till he was deprived of power (late 1549) and executed (January 1552) by John Dudley, duke of Northumberland. This sort of infighting among the "counselors" followed naturally from the abrupt power vacuum at the center after so many years of Henry's authoritarian presence; it was encouraged too by a surge of economic discontent rising to the surface after years of suppression. Europe was suffering an international wave of inflation, caused partly by the influx of gold and silver from America, partly by expanding populations. Rising commodity prices eroded the position of those on fixed incomes. As hard-pressed landlords had been doing for centuries, sixteenth-century landlords began enclosing land, and converting it from tillage to pasture; that, of course, enraged tenants. There were rural revolts, of which the most violent flared up briefly in East Anglia under the leadership of a man named Robert Kett (summer 1549). And meanwhile the magnates from their seats of power squabbled over the loot and privileges of government. More remarkable than their differences is the fact that they generally agreed on a Protestant church for England. Chief responsibility for this policy, which within wide limits held constant for the years of Edward's reign, belongs to Archbishop Cranmer.

THOMAS CRANMER AND THE CHURCH OF ENGLAND

While the old king lived, Cranmer had followed his lead implicitly, even to the point of putting away his wife at the king's suggestion (1539). But he opposed the statute of Six Articles, and at some point he became deeply convinced that transubstantiation was wrong. He was not a very positive man, and he picked his way slowly, seeking new light where he could find it. Protestant scholars visited England in great numbers, from Poland, Italy, Germany, Switzerland, France, the Low Countries. Cranmer talked with all and learned from some. Within the church itself, he pressed for less ritual and ceremonial, fewer "superstitious" decorations, a plainer service more accessible to the people; he made it legal for English clergymen to marry, and many did. Working with colleagues, and using the model of an older Latin breviary, he developed a Book of Common Prayer; it climaxed a movement for the use of English in religious services, and has endured, with only minor modifications, to the present day.[21] Cranmer also strove to define the doctrinal position of the church which Henry had left without a coherent rationale. This he did in Forty-two Articles (reduced during Elizabeth's reign to Thirty-nine, and somewhat modified in the process); apart from bearing the mark of Cranmer's tolerant spirit, the new Articles also profited from being the work of a professional theologian. They gave the English church for the first time a solid intellectual substructure.

Less agreeably, action was taken to deprive the Catholic bishops of their positions in the church. A few were imprisoned, others lost their jobs. During this process some of the powerful political magnates laid greedy hands on church property.[22] When laymen got involved in church matters, money seemed almost invariably to stick to their fingers. But to give little Edward's advisers their due, few people died for religion during this short reign. Two who did were a woman who denied the humanity of Christ and a man who denied His divinity; persons professing such opinions would have been persecuted by almost any church of that age. The relative tolerance of the Protestants during Edward's reign made it easier for them to assume the role of martyrs under Mary's.

THE BURNING QUEEN

For Edward did not live to celebrate his sixteenth birthday, and despite deep uneasiness at the prospect of a Catholic sovereign his half sister Mary was legally bound to succeed. Northumberland, who felt himself endangered, tried to get

21. Because it steered a middle course, Cranmer's Prayer Book was hateful to extremists of both left and right. In 1549 some angry Catholic traditionalists in Devon and Cornwall demanded a return to the Latin mass and rejected the Prayer Book as a "Christmas game" written in a language (English) they said they could not understand. Perhaps because of Kett's simultaneous agrarian revolt, the government handled them very severely. For the Scottish Presbyterian revolt, objecting to the Prayer Book as "papistical" and sparking the English civil wars, see below, p. 214.

22. At the same time, another wave of reformation mingled with plunder swept out of the English countryside a great many chantries, free chapels, colleges, hospitals, guilds, and fraternities. These were quasi-ecclesiastical institutions, charitable, devotional, or commemorative. Though they were generally small, many had been sanctified by time and custom; their abolition cut even deeper than the earlier dissolution of the monasteries. Buildings and endowments alike went to enrich local landlords.

Edward to name a Protestant successor, and for this dangerous role he tapped the Lady Jane Grey.[23] Feeling no enthusiasm for the role into which she had been pushed, she naturally aroused none. The plot failed, Northumberland was executed at once, and poor Lady Jane not long thereafter. Mary took the throne without major conflicts.

The new queen, it will be recalled, was the one living child of Henry's first wife, Catherine of Aragon; she had been born in 1516. Like all royal children of that day, she had to suffer the bickering and bargaining of sundry matrimonial treaties, all of which fell through because of Henry's determination to prove his marriage illegal and his poor little daughter, consequently, illegitimate. Mary, naturally, sided with her mother; her father, not quite so naturally, did his best to make her young life intolerable. She was publicly proclaimed a bastard, and forbidden to visit her mother's deathbed; Anne Boleyn, the new queen, tried to ingratiate herself with Henry by being as disagreeable as possible to Mary. And though Anne did not last long, Mary had, literally, to crawl on her knees to win back a meager bit of her father's favor. She had to renounce the pope, proclaim her father's absolute supremacy, declare herself illegitimate, and denounce her mother's marriage; it goes without saying that she did not believe a word of this cruel rigmarole.

This was the grim and troubled history that lay in the background of Mary's life, and one should recall it before using lightly the nickname, under which she has gone down to history, of "Bloody Mary." She was thirty-seven years old when she ascended the throne, old for a spinster in those days and at the outer limit of her childbearing years at any period. Her aim in life, almost her obsession, was to redeem her mother's good name, restore her mother's religion, authenticate her own good birth, and cleanse the nation from what she saw as the taint of heresy. The means to these several ends were all the same: an alliance, preferably matrimonial, with the imperial house of Hapsburg, represented at the moment by Carlos V of Spain.[24] Carlos himself was sixteen years older than she, and not inclined to matrimony; but his son Philip, though eleven years younger than Mary, might be had. The emperor, still embroiled with France, needed allies; a bargain was struck; and in 1554, Mary was married to Philip, soon to become Philip II of Spain.

In England, the marriage was intensely unpopular. The Inquisition was active in Spain; it might easily be extended to England, with its hooded inquisitors, torture chambers, and *autos-da-fé*. The nation had never before been ruled by a

23. The Lady Jane was the great-granddaughter of Henry VII by way of his second daughter, thus only weakly qualified by pedigree for the throne. Intelligent, gentle, beautiful, and, alas, all too docile, she allowed herself to be drawn into deep and dangerous political waters, and perished there, barely seventeen years old.

24. Since the death of his first wife Isabella in 1539, Carlos Quinto had been a widower; but, having been king of Spain since he was eighteen and Holy Roman emperor since he was twenty, he was a weary man, as he showed by abdicating in favor of his son (1555) and dying in 1558. He had been born in 1500.

queen, and to have that queen subject to a foreign husband offended the national sense of independence.

Elaborate conditions and provisos were written into the marriage contract, but hardly anybody expected them to be observed. Almost from the first, it was noted that Mary's policies were being directed from the Spanish embassy; and though the first steps were gradual, they accelerated rapidly. Preaching was limited to those who had received licenses from Catholic bishops; the mass was publicly celebrated; Protestants who protested against it were arrested; visiting Protestants from abroad were ejected, and with them went a number of native Protestant leaders who felt the weight of the gathering storm. Then the famous Protestant preacher Hugh Latimer was jailed, and with him went the former archbishop of Canterbury, Thomas Cranmer. Married priests were deprived of their offices, then all clergymen holding Protestant opinions and refusing to recant them, as much as a fifth of the entire English clergy (1,500 out of about 8,000 parsons). And on the fourth of February 1555, the first Protestant martyr, John Rogers, was burned alive. He had denied the real presence of Christ in the sacrament.

THE BURNINGS

It seems likely that Mary, like most persecutors, thought she could make her point with a little timely severity, and thereby cow so many Protestants that few or no further burnings would be necessary. In this judgment, she and her advisers were quite wrong. As with the Christian martyrs in pagan days, those who suffered in Mary's time inspired others to follow them. Bishops Latimer and Ridley, burned at Oxford in October 1555, advanced boldly into the fire, confident that the truth to which they were witnessing would never be allowed to die. Cranmer had great trouble with his conscience, for he had supported Henry VIII's supremacy so vehemently that he did not see how to deny equal authority to Henry's daughter. He signed several recantations of his Protestant views, but at the last minute, when asked to sign still another, he withdrew them all, saying that the hand which had signed them against his conscience should suffer first of all in the flames. And so it did; he held it forth till the flames consumed it and him (Oxford, 21 March 1556). First and last, approximately 300 people died in Mary's fires.

The burning of "heretics" in England blackened the reputation of Roman Catholicism for centuries to come. The memory of the sufferers was preserved, almost on the spot, by a vehement Protestant partisan, John Foxe, who gathered together the stories of persecution, held them till after Mary's death, and published them in 1563 under the title *Acts and Monuments*. Foxe's book, known generally as *The Book of Martyrs*, was immensely popular and extremely influential; by law, a copy of it had to be kept in every parish church, alongside a copy of the English Bible.[25] The two massive volumes had almost equal authority. For Foxe, the parallel between Mary's martyrs and those of Nero and Diocletian was no accident. God had chosen to test the early church as a way of assuring himself of its worthiness; in the same way, he had tested the faithful of England, under Mary, in order to open the way for a glorious destiny to come. Thus Protestantism wove itself, in England, tightly together with a sense of national destiny, to create a very potent mystique.

Apart from her religious problems, Mary met with many troubles abroad and in her personal life. Her marriage with Philip was mostly political,[26] and his duties to an immense empire kept him abroad much of the time. Still, she hoped for offspring, and twice announced her pregnancy, only to be disappointed. Spain, taking the lead in foreign policy, dragged England into yet another war with France. Philip was an unenterprising commander, the war was intensely unpopular in England, and its chief result was the loss (January 1558) of the city of Calais. England had held this bridgehead on the channel coast for more than two hundred years, since Edward III captured it in 1347; its loss was a matter of pride for the English rather than of real interest, but no less painful for that. At the peace table, England was not represented, and Philip showed what he thought of his new possession by making no effort whatever to consider English interests.

By every criterion, Mary had been an unmitigated disaster; but there was no constitutional way to change things, and the situation might have dragged on indefinitely, if the queen—exhausted, disheartened, and neglected by her husband—had not sickened and taken to her bed. What her ailment was we do not know; the Tudor blight manifested few symptoms. But sick to the death she was, too sick even to take any action against her half sister Elizabeth, Protestant to the core, who stood next in the line of succession. When Mary died, on 17 November 1558, Elizabeth, the last Tudor, took her place on the throne. She was just twenty-five years old, with little experience of government, but a great deal of practice in the hard craft of survival.

ENGLISH IN THE MAKING

Sophisticated works of wit and wisdom, like the *Praise of Folly* and the *Utopia* give the impression of great literary activity in the early sixteenth century; but these books were written in Latin and published abroad for the benefit of an international readership. Erasmus's mock oration was not translated into English

---

25. Though his book accumulates hideous cruelties, and dwells on them almost ghoulishly, it is well to recall that Foxe himself was the most tender-hearted of men, gentle and compassionate far beyond the standard, the very low standard, of his contemporaries (SFR, D.6).

26. The happy couple had been engaged at long distance, without ever meeting. When first he laid eyes on his bride, Philip is said to have cursed the ambassadors and portrait painters who had deluded him. In the Isabella Gardner collection at Boston there is a large portrait which may or may not be accurate but is certainly not alluring.

(by Sir Thomas Chaloner) till 1549; More's fantasy remained in Latin till the English version of Ralph Robynson in 1551. Latin, in those days, was the established language for addressing the educated public; by writing in any of the vernacular tongues, one limited one's audience to a mere corner of Europe and implied a special interest in reaching people who weren't normally readers of good books. Most of the "worthy" subjects had for generations been discussed only in Latin. Polydore Vergil, the Italian humanist, adopted England as his second country; he worked at his *History of England* for almost thirty years, but when it appeared in 1534, it was written in Latin and published at Basel, in Switzerland. Practical treatises on medicine, agriculture, and the mechanical processes were naturally written in English. But the readers of Roger Ascham's *Toxophilus* (1544), a dialogue on the moral and physical benefits of shooting the long bow, must have been surprised to find it written in smooth and fluent English. Ascham, who was famous as a classical scholar and tutor of Greek (for a while he was tutor to the Princess Elizabeth), knew he had committed an innovation, and felt it necessary to defend himself for having "written this English matter in the English tongue for English men."

POLEMIC AND CONTROVERSY

A major and deliberate exception to this rule of Latin predominance was provided by early reformers of the English church, who made it a point to write in the vernacular. One of the earliest, a man named Simon Fish, had offended Cardinal Wolsey, and wisely fled to Germany, from where in 1529 he addressed to Henry VIII a short, forceful piece of propaganda called *The Supplication of the Beggars*. His blunt argument was that the religious orders should be suppressed for the benefit of the poor people of England; and his book, though it had to be smuggled into the country, was widely popular. Wolsey came to the king to complain about it, and the king from under his robes produced a copy of his own. Tyndale too had written religious tracts in English, and one in particular, *The Obedience of a Christian Man* (1528), sorely galled the church establishment. These were forerunners of a great storm of religious polemic which blew up later in the sixteenth century and overcast the entire heavens in the seventeenth. What is striking is that the orthodox bishops of England did not feel themselves equal to answering these tracts in their own native tongue. Instead, they asked Sir Thomas More to be their spokesman; and he, loyally and single-handedly, so far as his powers allowed, answered the "heretics."[27] The bishops

27. More began the task with a sense that he must entertain, as well as refute error; but as he proceeded (he wrote seven books in all), his temper worsened, and he neglected the warm and human touches which livened his first efforts. A particularly awkward problem for More and all defenders of orthodoxy was whether to represent the opponent's arguments at large. It is well known in theological circles that most of the errors assailed by the industrious and orthodox Irenaeus would be totally unknown today except for the book he wrote refuting them.

were not, as a class, stupid or inarticulate men, but the kind of attack being launched against them was unprecedented. It appealed to blunt common sense; it was laced with wit and derision; it rose occasionally to lofty moral indignation; it borrowed from pulpit rhetoric the devices of brief moral narratives (*exempla*) and simple, pointed allegories. Theological Latin was useless against such argumentation; what one needed was the common touch, and the bishops were at least sharp enough to realize that they didn't have it. Even More's prose was more wordy, his sentences more unstructured, than those of his chief antagonist, Tyndale. His jokes and funny stories came to sound hollow when trotted forth against the hard moral indignation and cutting sarcasms of the Protestant casuists.

LITERACY AND THE ENGLISH BIBLE

Though the Reformation did not immediately forward the cause of literature, it did much for the cause of literacy.[28] The old Catholic system had encouraged men to rely on the guidance of the church and the reassuring availability of the sacraments, without seeking to grasp the moral foundations of religion. An inquiry into the conditions of the clergy in Edward VI's day revealed that many ordained and beneficed priests could not repeat the Ten Commandments; one man said confidently that the Lord's Supper was so called because it was instituted by Our Lord the King of England (SFR, D. II). Protestantism, a "book religion" if ever there was one, demanded that clergymen, and laymen too, know a lot more than that; it put into the hands of laymen, as many as possible, the text of the sacred Scriptures, translated as eloquently and accurately as possible into their own native tongue. Each new translator profited by the errors and infelicities of his predecessors as well as by their triumphs.[29] Protestantism encouraged the faith-

28. It's sometimes said of men like Bunyan, that the Bible had an uncommonly strong influence on them because they read so little else. The rule is general: any book which is a man's sole reading will influence him strongly; print loses much of its impact when commonplace and various. Short-term, Bible reading strengthened religious convictions; by opening interpretive problems and encouraging collateral reading, in the long run it diffused them. So early Protestant churches were commonly more severe and restrictive than the Catholic church from which they rebelled, but developed over the years toward a much more relaxed discipline.

29. In capsule chronological summary, the early English Bibles were:

    ·1382 and 1388: the Wycliffe or Wycliffite Bibles, done under the influence but probably not by the hand of John Wyclif, and from the Latin Vulgate.

    ·1525–1526: Tyndale's Bible, not complete, but done from the original tongues.

    ·1535: the Bible of Miles Coverdale, complete but not done from the original tongues—rather from the Vulgate, the German of Luther, and with the help of Tyndale's previous English translation. Printed in Zurich.

    ·1539: the Great Bible or Cranmer's Bible, prepared by Coverdale. Printed in Paris and London.

    ·1560: the Geneva or "Breeches" Bible, so called because of its version of Genesis 3:7: "They sewed fig leaves together, and made themselves breeches." The marginal notes on

ful flock to search the Bible, that huge miscellany of Jewish history, moral admonition, and metaphorical prophecy, for clues to their own salvation. Thousands of Bibles, printed abroad when necessary or by English printers when it was safe to do so, were put into circulation. Men carried the Bible in their pockets to consult in every emergency of life; in the evening at the fireside, families read the Bible aloud, and discussed its intimate application to their lives. Children were required to commit long sections of it to memory. Phrases from it and allusions to it became part of the common texture of life. Every Sunday, preachers expounded on it. Sermons, spoken or reprinted, were particularly welcome to Protestants intent on extracting from the Holy Word every last grain of divine wisdom. Nothing was more precious than the sacred text which alone taught one the way to the gates of heaven. While this study preoccupied the minds of men, the exercise of worldly prose and poetry naturally languished. In the first half of the sixteenth century, more than half of the books published in England dealt with theological subjects.

SCATTERED NOTES OF EARLY VERSE

Thus, such literature as we find in the early century seems to consist mostly of bits and pieces. John Skelton was "poet laureate" under both Henrys, VII and VIII; but whether the office amounted to anything in those days we cannot tell. Our poet was a parson, rather a ribald one if legend tells true. He evidently spent little time at court and in his verses moralized against the perils of high place. Skelton is remembered now for his bawdy satirical poems, written in a meter peculiarly his own. The lines are short (irregular six-syllable), and rhyme on the same sound as long as the poet's ability to find another rhyme word holds out. The effect is colloquial, hasty, random, and the verse often hovers on the brink of doggerel; Pope, who valued correctness in verse, had no better epithet for Skelton than "beastly." On the other hand, only part of Skelton's total output was in Skeltonics; much of his work was linguistically pompous and grammatically contorted, like Lydgate's imitations of Chaucer. And quite a lot of Skelton's verse was so unimpressive that nobody even tried to preserve it; we know many poems only by their titles. The "good" Skelton poems are playful and

---

this Bible were much influenced by Calvin's theology and proved a source of future controversy. First printed in Geneva and often reprinted.

·1568: the "Bishops' Bible," promoted by the English establishment, to counter the popularity of the Geneva Bible.

·1582 and 1609: the Rheims-Douai Bible, put out by English Catholic priests resident in France. Feeling uneasy with the whole process of vernacular translation, the Catholics when they translated from the Vulgate left a great many words in Latin or markedly Latinate forms.

·1611: the "Authorized" or King James version of the Bible, still standard in many parts of the English-speaking world.

brimming with energy; they are bold and funny in a way that hardly anybody has tried to imitate: they have remained idiosyncratic.

Portents of better things are two court poets whose names are inseparably linked, Sir Thomas Wyatt, and Henry Howard, earl of Surrey. Wyatt died in 1542, Surrey was beheaded for generally uppity and refractory behavior in 1547; their poems, though circulated in manuscript, did not appear in print till 1557, and then in a book which bore only Surrey's name on the title page. Richard Tottel had acquired a monopoly on printing law books in England. He was a conscientious fellow, and did a good job at his very profitable specialty. But law books did not satisfy him, and in 1557 he took a flyer into literature by issuing a small volume of poetry called *Songs and Sonnets.* The book was very popular and soon became known simply as *Tottel's Miscellany:* it was many times reprinted. About half the volume consisted of poems by Wyatt and Surrey, the rest was contributed by one Nicholas Grimald, and sundry anonymous hands. Tottel had apparently scraped up poems where he could get them. Of the two major contributors, Wyatt had been about fifteen years the elder (born 1503); he was the bolder and more inventive talent. His poetic speech is often colloquial; he can suggest with great delicacy the wildness of love, as in the famous "They flee from me"; his imagination is dramatic, as when he writes a poem to his falcon Lux, or a moral essay on the fable of the town mouse and the country mouse. In addition, Wyatt during his diplomatic travels had visited Italy and discovered there a great variety of poetic forms new to England, as well as the fashions in love developed by Petrarch to celebrate his lady Laura.[30] Of the poems that Wyatt and Surrey contributed involuntarily to Tottel's *Miscellany,* many are direct translations from the Italian of Petrarch or one of his imitators. Surrey added to Wyatt's original achievement a gift for graceful versification; but as he died before thirty, his poetic talent never developed fully. One thing he did achieve, in his partial translation of Virgil's *Aeneid,*[31] was the first use in English of blank verse, such as would later sustain the greater weight of Milton and Wordsworth.

30. Francesco Petrarca (Petrarch in English) was one of the very early Italian humanists; he saw Laura for the first time, he tells us, at Avignon on 6 April 1327. Whether she really existed cannot be proved, and it certainly was convenient for Petrarch's poetic purposes that the poet's crown is traditionally woven of laurel leaves. But the story of his love for her, developed with enormous subtlety and intelligence through a sequence of sonnets, drew for his readers a map of a whole new countryside, the human mind. In addition, Petrarch's poems in the vernacular (he wrote rather more Latin than Italian verse) showed how the techniques and materials of classical verse could be adapted to "modern," fourteenth-century use; and his elegant sense of form set an example for poets in many lands.

31. Though Surrey's was an important early effort to get Virgil into English, we should not overlook Gavin Douglas's earlier (1513) rendition of the entire *Aeneid* (plus a thirteenth book contributed by Maphaeus Vegius, a fifteenth-century Italian humanist) into Scots. For a modern reader, the Scots of Douglas is not much less difficult than the Latin of Virgil; an appreciation of its many virtues will be found in C. S. Lewis, *English Literature in the Sixteenth Century* (Oxford, 1954), Chap. 1.

PROSE GROPINGS

There were, therefore, some English poets under the first four Tudors, but not many, and those who had most to teach the first generation of Elizabethan poets were not published till the very dawn of Elizabeth's reign. In prose the story is much the same. Roger Ascham, who in 1538 wrote that book about archery, waited a quarter century before writing the other book by which he is known; in fact, the *Schoolmaster* appeared posthumously, in 1568. Ascham intended by the word "schoolmaster," not a classroom pedagogue, but a private tutor for young gentlemen; and while his book is of interest as it sets forth the humanist program of education, by the time it was published, many of its ideas had become familiar, if not commonplace. In 1531, for example Sir Thomas Elyot had published *The Book Named the Governor,* consisting of instructions for educating young people to positions of authority. Elyot had lived in the circle around Thomas More, and imbibed humanist principles from that society. He was a translator of note, and put great stock in the classic authors; many of their sayings and stories are repeated in the course of his book. He was also urbane enough to suggest that his young rulers practice, in addition to the usual manly exercises such as hunting and archery, the social skill of dancing, to which he attributed by emblematic interpretation moral and humane virtues. In the twentieth century, T. S. Eliot, who claimed kinship, made courtly allusion to old Sir Thomas in his *Four Quartets.*

The popularity of books on how to behave in positions of authority suggests that many folk were finding themselves so situated, without a family background for the job. Perhaps so; the Tudors preferred to use agents of middling status rather than members of the great houses, who wouldn't have to learn manners from a book. But it is also true that the standards of polite behavior were changing fast. The great Italian courtesy book, which defines the ideal of an aristocrat and the fervent spiritual love in which that ideal flowers, was Baldassare Castiglione's dialogue *The Courtier* (published 1528); by 1552, Sir Thomas Hoby was at work on an English translation, which because of Mary's censorship couldn't be published till 1561. Apart from describing the serious training required of a diplomat, an adviser to princes, and a leader of men, *The Courtier* sets an example of easy, intelligent conversation between the sexes, serious but not solemn, witty but not buffoonish. Its influence, though subtle, ran wide and deep.[32]

SERMONS, BIOGRAPHIES

In religion, we must emphasize once more the great influence of Thomas Cranmer, whose Book of Common Prayer has sunk almost as deep into the English

---

32. The cultural supremacy of Italy did not always go unresented. Ascham was but one of several authors who denounced Italian sophistication as dangerous to English innocence. A frequent innuendo was that Italians were given to homosexual practices.

consciousness as the Bible itself. Extreme Protestants disliked the prayer book because it was much indebted to the Latin ritual developed during the thirteenth century at Salisbury Cathedral, and known therefrom as the Sarum Missal; and of course Catholics disliked the very idea of an English prayer book. Cranmer's middle course justified itself here as elsewhere; the Church of England has found in his eloquent rhythms and lofty but unforced diction just the right tone for its public ceremonies. On a lower plane, we must note the teeming and often violent activities of the English pulpit during the Reformation. Sermons at that time were followed with a passion modern folk find hard to comprehend; they offered information of vital interest to each man's most inward concerns. Preachers who had talked for two hours, and offered to stop, were begged to continue; Bishop Ridley once preached all afternoon at Paul's Cross, and had to be escorted home through the cold November dusk by a torchlit procession of his hearers. Parsons and bishops preached regularly; itinerant preachers preached wherever they could assemble an audience, and strong language was a recognized way of gathering a crowd. Most of these sermons were never printed or preserved; but Hugh Latimer was so famous for his eloquence that a number of his discourses were written down, as he delivered them. Latimer, who was burned at Oxford with Ridley in 1555, spoke a nervous, direct, colloquial English, very personal, with a gift of homely wit and vigorous metaphor. Even now, more than four hundred years later, his prose rarely seems archaic; it is a model of the plain and forceful style. Latimer was exceptional, but only in degree; there were powerful preachers of his kind in many parts of the land, and they contributed to the growth of a modern prose style.

Two biographers left manuscript accounts of extraordinary men they had known. William Roper described his father-in-law Sir Thomas More in a memoir written about the end of Mary's reign though not published till 1626. Apart from being firsthand information about a fascinating man, Roper's study is largely free of the sanctifying mystique that began to surround More long before he was officially canonized by the church. Roper's is an authentic document, human and full of precise detail, as the biography of a saint should be. His fellow biographer was a kind of sixteenth-century Boswell. George Cavendish was only a young man when he took service with Cardinal Wolsey, but already he had in mind to know some famous men and write about them. During Wolsey's last days, he stuck steadfastly by his patron, and was much admired for his fidelity. But one famous man was enough for Cavendish; and even though he had many materials for his life of Wolsey, he did not try to assemble them till thirty years later, in 1557. The *Life of Wolsey* was then copied out by hand in several versions, one of which Shakespeare evidently used in composing his drama of *Henry VIII*. The book was printed at last in 1641, but in badly garbled form; and the authentic text finally appeared only in the early nineteenth century. It may seem curious that with the classic examples of Plutarch and Suetonius before them, Englishmen should have been so little interested in the art of biography. (Sir Thomas

More's *History of Richard III*, an important exception, did not see print till 1557.) But political animosities ran deep, and trying to tell the truth about great men was often radically unsafe. Besides, there may have been a certain hangover from the middle ages, when individual achievements and personalities seem to have been of little interest. As the great cathedrals are not (with rare exceptions) the work of any single dominating personality, so many great literary works of medieval times are anonymous or of communal authorship. Thus biography, which seems to us so natural and normal a literary form, was of slow growth and sparse achievement, at least till the seventeenth century.

COMEDIES AND TRANSLATIONS

We should note, finally, the appearance during the 1550s of a couple of rough vernacular comedies with titles that would look good on a Broadway marquee even today. *Ralph Roister Doister*, written about 1553, and the almost-anonymous *Gammer Gurton's Needle*, about 1556, are both farces of the simplest sort. Loutish Ralph tries to seduce the buxom widow, but is beaten off with kicks and cuffs; Gammer Gurton's long-sought needle makes itself felt at last in the seat of Hodge's pants. Nothing very artistic here, nor are we yet in sight of professional companies; schoolboys at Westminster and Cambridge probably acted out these comedies for the amusement of their fellows. (There is a chance that *Roister Doister* was acted at court; though the author Nicholas Udall had been a schoolmaster and an academic aroma of Plautus clings to his farce, in 1553 he seems to have been on forced leave from school for beating his boys too cruelly and otherwise misusing them.) Here the drama has liberated itself entirely from church festival and moral preachment; in these farces it deals with the raw, smelly stuff of vulgar existence, unsanitized and unedifying. But out of such stuff it will one day weave subtler and richer tapestries of mimic life.

The literary record of the early sixteenth century is not only scant, it is prevailingly drab and utilitarian. Some of this mediocrity may be due to political and religious uncertainties. Or again, England may have had trouble recovering from the wars, foreign and domestic, of the fifteenth century. Whatever the reasons, a man standing in the year 1550 and looking back over the record of English literature, would have found precious little, apart from Chaucer, to look at. *Beowulf* would not be discovered till the eighteenth century and the "Gawain" poet not till the nineteenth. Malory would have had to stand for the entire art of prose fiction; there was no drama worthy of the name, little history, and in lyric poetry little that was visible but ballads and carols. (Middle English lyrics would languish in scattered manuscripts till collected and published in the twentieth century.) Even in the humble endeavor of translating from other languages, England could show only a spotty record. Thomas Phaer, not much of a poet but doggedly persistent, did most of the *Aeneid* into hobbling fourteeners (rhyming couplets of seven-stress iambic lines); some years later, Thomas Twyne finished the job, and England had Virgil's entire epic in lamentable verse. Translations from the Greek were slower in appearing, though many Greek texts were available in Latin, and Latin was known by every serious pretender to learning. While gradual, the process was incremental. The last years of Elizabeth's reign and the first of King James's were a golden age of translation, when such authors as Ovid, Plutarch, Apuleius, Livy, Pliny, Suetonius, and, climactically, Homer, in the versions of George Chapman, entered English in appropriate dress. Indeed, books that had a popular smack to them got translated earlier. Lord Berners translated Froissart, the French chronicler of chivalry, in the 1520s, and popular stories like *Reynard the Fox* or satires like Sebastian Brant's *Ship of Fools* had no trouble passing into English. Still, the record was thin; and our imaginary mid-century observer (unless he had a touch of prophetic vision) might well have concluded that his countrymen were a hopelessly unliterary race. In fact, the poverty of the fifteenth and early sixteenth centuries was so exceptional in the history of the island that it invites us to look for concrete and specific causes.

Politics did not yet exist as a subject of general discussion; having too pronounced an opinion on religion could easily get one burned alive; few people had both the leisure and the education to read for amusement. Printing was a marginal economic enterprise at best. Learned books in the learned languages were better printed on the Continent, where Dutch printers like Plantin and (later) Elzevir had learned workmen, fonts of Greek type, and widespread commercial connections. English printers naturally turned to books with practical functions or prefabricated reputations. Mechanics of publication apart, the language itself was not ready for *belles lettres;* even the best prose was still ungainly, and fundamental decisions had yet to be made about the rhythms and meters most appropriate to the tongue. Amid all these anxious uncertainties, it's no wonder that English literature remained embryonic. The new printing press served quite as much to disseminate old trash as to diffuse new light. At the very birth of printing, Johann Gutenberg had plunged immediately into the great work of printing the entire Bible; it was 1539 before the first English Bible was printed on English presses. Nor should one underestimate the courage—intellectual, commercial, and in the most direct sense, personal—that went into such an enterprise at such a time.

6

Intrigues, Conspiracies, and an Almost-Invasion (1558–1588)

Elizabeth Tudor was twenty-five years old at her coronation. As the daughter of Anne Boleyn, whose marriage to Henry had been annulled, she had no hereditary claim to the throne, and the succession act of 1537, passed in a moment of euphoria when Edward VI had just been born, repudiated her and her older sister Mary as illegitimate; but seven years later, a second statute, without repealing the first, declared Mary next in line after Edward, and Elizabeth after Mary. Henry's last will also placed her in line for the succession. After the debacle of Mary's reign, popular opinion welcomed Elizabeth, since the only alternative was civil war.

THE TWO CATHOLIC MARYS

But before she was in a position to reach the throne, Elizabeth had a perilous path to tread. Relations with her sister Mary were ambiguous in the extreme. Henry had used the infant Elizabeth and Elizabeth's mother Anne Boleyn to humiliate Mary and Mary's mother; then there was a period when both daughters were out of favor; and under Edward VI, Elizabeth, who was fond of her owlish half brother, had her Protestantism confirmed, while Mary, who was passionately Catholic, had to defend her religion tooth and nail. By the same logic that Mary was Catholic, evidently, Elizabeth was Protestant: out of loyalty to her mother. All her training served to strengthen this commitment; she studied humanities and languages with Ascham, philosophy and theology with Ochino and Acontio, a pair of those Italian Protestants brought to England by Cranmer. Baptista Castiglione, who tutored her in Italian, was jailed by Mary on suspicion of writing a Protestant pamphlet. Thus the period of her sister's reign was a period of intense danger for Elizabeth. Pious hypocrisy was her chief refuge; she attended mass when she had to, expressed Catholic sentiments on convenient occasions, and borrowed from her sister some books of religious instruction, with which to improve her attitude. Nobody, least of all Mary, doubted that this was hypocrisy; but as public behavior, no fault could be found with it. The problem was to catch the Princess Elizabeth in an overt act of treason; and she was too sly a bird to be caught that way. In 1554 there were some difficult moments after Sir Thomas Wyatt, son of the poet, was caught fomenting a conspiracy. For a while it seemed almost demonstrable that she had known of it; but at the crucial moment, evidence failed. Secretaries could be blamed for documents that looked like complicity, while not a word of her speaking or writing could be adduced to make her guilty. Still, she spent two extremely disagreeable months in the Tower, while her fate was being decided; and after that, she did her best to keep out of sight, mostly at one of the lesser royal estates, Hatfield House. Several circumstances protected her there. Mary, newly married to Philip, was convinced she must have children, and went through a complete phantom pregnancy; it ended in bitter disillusion, but while it lasted Elizabeth was safe enough, since any child born to Philip and Mary would take precedence of her. Various of Mary's Catholic advisers wanted Elizabeth eliminated from the succession by act of Parliament; but the House of Commons, with whom she was very popular, would not hear of it. And Philip of Spain, a cautious, intricate man, had reasons of his own not to want his sister-in-law done away with. His wife was clearly not going to have any babies; she was not in very good health herself and (given the history of the Tudor family) not likely to live long. If she should die, and Elizabeth not succeed her for whatever reason, the person with the best claim would be another Mary, Mary "Queen of Scots." Her claim, it could be argued, was better than that of Elizabeth herself; her grandfather, James IV of Scotland, had married in 1503 Margaret, the older sister of Henry VIII. Margaret had thus been Elizabeth's aunt, and the queen of Scots was her cousin. Since Mary's father, James V of Scotland, had died when she was only an infant, she had been brought up in France, under the special guidance of her mother, Mary of Lorraine; she was a convinced, indeed a fanatical, Catholic. The French connection was what frightened Philip. Mary had every right to become queen of Scots; the alliance of France with Scotland was an old one, and did not contribute much to French strength. But if the queen of Scots became also queen of England, then, in view of the fact that she was already engaged to the dauphin of France, soon to take the crown as François II, she became the potential keystone of a triple alliance very disagreeable indeed to Spain. Philip therefore had an interest in keeping Elizabeth available as queen of England when Mary died, though, of course, as she was a heretic, he detested her. Thus, amid lowering storm clouds of fear, jealousy, suspicion, and her sister's pathetic faith in offspring, Elizabeth followed her dangerous path to the throne.

THE COMING OF PURITANISM

One group of Englishmen on whose support it was tempting but dangerous to rely were the people soon to be known as "Puritans." Though they were never a single organized group, and were known by a variety of names, "Puritans" being just one of them, they agreed in a broad way that the English Reformation as carried out by Henry VIII had not gone far enough. They wanted to "purify" the English church of its remaining Catholic observances and institutions; and many of them accepted as ideal a model of church government which they found set forth in *The Institutes of the Christian Religion* (1535) by the French reformer John Calvin. The ideal church described by Calvin existed not only in his book but (after 1541) in the city of Geneva, Switzerland, where, after many disputes, the people had invited Calvin to be their minister. A major feature of Calvin's church was that it had no bishops, archbishops, or authoritative subordinated hierarchy such as the pope ruled in Rome and Elizabeth controlled in England.[1] In the Calvinist church there were no organs or stained-glass windows, no rich robes for the priest, no pictures, no statues of saints or crucifixes, nothing that might lead to "superstition," the ultimate word of Calvinist condemnation. Like the Lutherans and like most other Protestant sects, the Calvinists deplored the idea of salvation through *good works*, such as gifts to the church, ascetic practices, acts of conspicuous piety or benevolence. Their hope lay in salvation through *faith*. But to ensure that faith would not be distracted by worldly considerations, the Calvinists not only insisted on strict austerity in church services; they accorded the religious discipline once exercised by bishops to special assemblies (synods) of clergymen (presbyters). These synods tended to be severely censorious themselves; they were also free of all lay control. Their superstructure resembled democratic centralism; local congregations elected ministers, district ministers met in a local synod to elect to a higher synod, and the various higher synods elected to a national synod, governed by an elective president. Within this solidly

---

1. Puritan polemic concentrated on the wicked institution of bishops; but in the name of "bishop" was comprised hostility to deacons, archdeacons, archpresbyters, and the several varieties of deans. All these were essentially assistants and coadjutors of bishops. Most deans serve as presidents of chapters, which are councils to advise bishops; rural deans are in effect inspectors general within a particular see; and there are a few deans, like the dean of arches, whose function is to hold a particular ecclesiastical court for the service of the archbishop of Canterbury.

clerical church structure, the secular ruler occupied no special position whatever; king or queen, prince or duke or baron, was simply one member of the church and, like other members, bound by its instructions.[2] Thus, though the Puritans (and among them the Calvinist Presbyterians) were fierce antagonists of the church of Rome, none fiercer, they were not safe allies for Elizabeth because the system they proposed to establish left no room for her royal authority, at least as she proposed to exercise it. At first they objected only to minor customs; they did not want to wear the traditional black gown (surplice) and square cap. But the trifling question hid a bigger one: Who was to be boss in the church? If her path to the throne had been dangerous, Elizabeth still had to step warily through a field of friends as dangerous as enemies.

THE USES AND DANGERS OF SCOTLAND

When British Protestants fled Mary's persecutions and settled in European towns like Frankfort and Geneva, they came in close contact with Calvinist churches; many were deeply impressed by what they saw, none more than a Scottish preacher named John Knox. He was a veteran of what amounted to civil-war conditions in Scotland. With a group of direct-action reformers he had taken part in storming the episcopal castle at St. Andrews, and killing the bishop (1547). The Catholic regency of the land (Mary queen of Scots was still an infant) called on French soldiers to besiege the castle; it fell, Knox was captured, and spent two years under the whip in French galleys. Edward VI redeemed him, but Mary drove him abroad again, where he took part with Calvin in preparing the influential "Geneva Bible." His heart remained in Scotland, however; and in 1559 he returned there to begin the work of converting the kingdom. Mary queen of Scots being still only seventeen years old, the land was ruled by her mother, Mary of Lorraine, as regent; and against the two Marys, as Catholics and therefore limbs of Satan, Knox mounted nothing less than a popular revolution. It was a most instructive lesson for Elizabeth, newly seated on her throne, and watching events from the other side of the border. On the one hand, the queen of Scots was her cousin and a fellow monarch; a successful revolt in Scotland might spread sparks in her own kingdom. On the other hand, cousin Mary was in process of being married to the king of France; Catholic herself, she was allied to the most extreme Catholics in the French kingdom. By supporting Knox and the Protestants, Elizabeth would win popularity with Puritans in England, and might even hope to wean Scotland from her ancient alliance with France. Yet

2. Indeed, the Presbyterians admitted some laymen to the government of the church under the title of "elders"; but they were subordinate to the clergy and exercised a strictly ecclesiastical authority. James VI thought himself king of Scotland but his Calvinist tutor called him, contemptuously, "God's silly vassal." Early Puritans did not endear themselves to Elizabeth by praying that God would open her eyes to the need for obeying His ministers—i.e., themselves.

she did not want to do too much for revolutionaries[3] because, politics apart, war was just too expensive for England at present. But, urged on by her advisers, Elizabeth lent enough aid to the Covenanters to enable them, in 1560, to establish Presbyterianism in Scotland. In the middle of that year the queen regent (Mary of Lorraine) died; at its end, so did François II, the boy-husband of Mary queen of Scots. In 1561, she returned to rule over a kingdom, the most powerful member of which, John Knox, profoundly hated her "proud mind, crafty wit, and indurate heart against God and His truth."

Into the complex and violent struggles of the next seven years we cannot enter in any detail. Mary was as ruthless a partisan for her cause as Knox for his; and for neither was Scotland much more than a momentary field on which was being fought out a battle in the great war between Christ and the devil. Knox, owing much to Protestant England and hating Catholic France, did his best to maintain peaceful relations with Elizabeth; but Mary queen of Scots thought she could serve her church best by becoming queen of England—as successor to Elizabeth if necessary, as replacement for Elizabeth if possible. Had she played her cards shrewdly, she might even have negotiated an agreement of sorts. But, though an intriguing, devious woman, she had more passion than judgment; and she threw away the game. Her first big mistake was to marry a man named Henry Stuart, Lord Darnley, who through his mother was a great-grandson of Henry VII.[4] She thought a second connection with the house of Tudor would strengthen her claim on the English throne. But Darnley proved a miserable weakling, whose only achievement, and that dubious, was to give Mary a child, the future James VI of Scotland and James I of England. Even before the infant was born, Mary, disgusted with Darnley, had taken another lover in David Riccio, an Italian musician.[5] Behind a gang of bravos, Darnley burst in on them at dinner, and had Riccio stabbed to death (9 March 1566); Mary promptly took a new lover, the earl of Bothwell, and with him arranged to have her husband murdered (February 1567); then, as soon as she could (for Bothwell had an inconvenient wife to dispose of) she married him. For Knox and the Covenanters, this swift sequence of events put her beyond the range of human decency; in England, it ended any prospect of her succeeding to the throne. Before long, Bothwell was a forlorn exile in Scandinavia, and Mary was forced to seek refuge with Elizabeth in England. She was not exactly welcome, especially to the Puritan faction; her

3. The Scottish Protestants called themselves "Covenanters" because they had all pledged to support the Presbyterian system by taking an oath, a covenant. The first covenant was signed in December 1557; only nobles were allowed to subscribe. Later versions were circulated more widely in 1581, 1590, 1596, and 1637, and the sharp division between those inside and those outside the godly party became a constant feature of Scottish life.

4. In Don Carlos of Spain, cretinous son by a brief first marriage of Philip II, Mary might conceivably have found a worse husband than Darnley, and with a sure instinct she went after him; but destiny preserved her for Darnley.

5. With Gallic malice, Henri IV of France used to say that James Stuart was rightly called the modern Solomon, being the son of David the musician.

Catholicism, her immorality, her intriguing disposition, all made her suspect. But for Elizabeth to have her hands on this dangerous, attractive woman was not all bad, even though, for the moment, nobody knew quite what to do with her. Elizabeth put her in a number of very comfortable castles, treated her with utmost respect, and had her discreetly watched. The troubles she got into there will appear later.

ANGLICAN COMPROMISES

The violent conflict between extreme positions taking place in Scotland during the decade 1557–1567 was exactly what Elizabeth was bending every effort to avoid in England. Having observed a good deal of fanaticism in her life, she was not much given to it, and was always ready to urge a practical accommodation instead of scrupulous orthodoxy enforced by persecution. Accordingly, when she chose a new archbishop of Canterbury, to replace Cranmer, it was a moderate and docile man to whom she turned. Matthew Parker had been chaplain to Anne Boleyn, and a steady though not eminent Protestant under Henry VIII and Edward VI; he was married, a point that bothered Elizabeth, but he had suffered under Mary, just the right amount and in just the right way. He had not courted martyrdom, he had not gone abroad, had not been infected by continental Calvinism; he had been deprived of his church positions, and he had bowed before the storm. He was not in fact eager to be archbishop of Canterbury, and did his best to duck the job. But Elizabeth got him, and got from Parliament an Act of Uniformity (1559) which marked out the broad outlines of a practical compromise later formalized as a "middle way." Her church would be the church of England, with herself as ruler, with an English liturgy based on Cranmer's prayer book, and with the Protestant articles as its doctrinal foundation. All that by way of pushing aside the pretensions of the church of Rome. Her church would also be governed in the traditional authoritarian way, by archbishops, bishops, and deans; it would retain a modicum (undefined) of ritual and ceremony. So much for the democratic synods and stripped spirituality of the Presbyterian style.

The work of renewing yet tempering the Reformation proceeded gradually. Mary had burned some bishops and converted others to Catholicism from which they dared not reconvert; many had died and not been replaced. It was not easy to find four legal bishops to consecrate Archbishop Parker, but found they were, and the new administration began. Cranmer's Forty-two Articles of 1553 were mulled over, tightened somewhat, and reduced to Thirty-nine, though they did not take final form and receive parliamentary approval till 1571. Henry VIII's title of "Defender of the Faith," received from Leo X for his book against Luther, sounded too splendid to let go; but since England was not very far from Lutheranism these days, it was not easy to retain. It was therefore abbreviated; and instead of "Defender of the Faith, Roman, Catholic, and Apostolic," it now read simply, "Defender of the Faith, &c." When Elizabeth wanted to be blurry and vague, her mind was razor sharp. Faith was something she wanted to keep nice and vague. Being "mere English," as she bragged, she liked things to be done decently and in orderly manner, without any strained theorizing.

POLITICIANS, MATCHMAKERS, FAVORITES

Her chief political adviser was William Cecil, grandson of that David Cecyll or Sitsyllt who had first gained the favor of Henry VII. As a rising young lawyer, a Cambridge graduate and a good Protestant, Cecil had held office under Edward VI; but the caution which was always his hallmark guided him safely through Mary's reign with no more than a little twisting and some notable moments of silence.[6] Well before Mary's death, he had shifted his hopes to Elizabeth; and the fact that he had made no trouble for Mary actually commended him to her sister. Like Parker, he was a Protestant but not an agitator, a man of independent intelligence but also of deep loyalty. He was a devoted, untiring instrument of her royal wishes, and she used him for every ounce of energy and intelligence he possessed. In two matters chiefly, he showed that he had a will and mind of his own. Cecil was largely responsible for sending that bit of aid to Scotland which tilted the scales in favor of the Covenanters, and transformed the Scottish power from an agency of French policy to an ally of Protestant England. And he never ceased to urge—patiently, respectfully, insistently, in the face of sulks and temper tantrums and labyrinthine evasions—that his royal mistress should get married and have children.

At first, the pressure to matrimony rose from traditional ideas of woman's innate mental inferiority. (John Knox, ever tactful, published just a few months before Elizabeth's accession a *First Blast of the Trumpet against the Monstrous Regiment [Rule] of Women*. He had in mind the three Catholic Marys—Mary Tudor, Mary of Lorraine, and her daughter Mary queen of Scots—but Elizabeth heard the blast all too clearly and, despite awkward apologies, would never be reconciled to Knox.) Later, when it became clear that Elizabeth had all the brains she needed, and more by far than any husband she was likely to find, the argument shifted to the need for offspring to settle the succession. Cecil became a nag on the point; the Parliament remonstrated, repeatedly. Elizabeth played it coy. She was the most eligible match in Europe; but nobody was going to push her into matrimony. It was she and she alone who had to be pleased; and she was hard, indeed impossible, to please. The list of her suitors is long, and complicated by the fact that several of them, after being once rejected, came back

6. Cecil, it's been said, committed the first and last indiscretion of his life when at twenty he married, against his father's wishes, Mary, daughter of Sir John Cheke the humanist. It was the mildest of indiscretions, and when amortized over seventy-seven years of unfailing prudence may even appear a fault to be admired. Unhappily, his first wife survived her marriage by only two years.

and tried again. The Archduke Charles of Austria was put up several times; but he spoke no English, he was Catholic, he would not do. Charles IX, king of France, was all right, but his feet were too big. When Elizabeth wanted to recruit some help for the Scottish Protestants, James Hamilton, earl of Arran, was mentioned as a possible husband; he presented himself, served his turn, and was dismissed, not contemptuously, not gratefully, with indifference. Philip II (her deceased sister's husband, but that was no obstacle) let it be known that if she would change her religion, he might condescend to marry her. She smiled, and because of the political situation at the moment did not reject him out of hand; but when he was kind enough to marry the French king's daughter, she greeted the news with a joke. Eric, son of the king of Sweden, came back for four separate rejections; at one time, there were a dozen different royal suitors, or agents for the same, cooling their heels in the English court. The queen would have none of them. The last to appear, when Elizabeth was at the very outermost verge of her childbearing years, may have had, just for that reason, a slightly better chance than the others. He was the French duke d'Alençon (after 1576, duke of Anjou), not very tall, not very handsome, Catholic but no bigot, brave as a lion, and amusing to the queen. He made one venture in 1570, another in 1579. By then, she was forty-six years old; not, apparently, without a regret or two—for she liked younger men when they had some spunk in them—she let him slip away.

ELIZABETH AND LEICESTER

Much less to Cecil's liking, much more to Elizabeth's, was an English favorite whom she might even have married, if . . . . Robert Dudley was a bold, fluent, handsome young fellow when Elizabeth first took note of him in 1559. He was married to, but separated from, an unwelcome wife, Amy Robsart. Other problems lurked in his background. He was the son of that earl of Northumberland who had tried, by using Lady Jane Grey, to deprive Mary Tudor of the throne, and who, for his pains, had been executed as a traitor. Northumberland's father was that Edmund Dudley, too-zealous servant of Henry VII, who had been executed for treason in the first years of Henry VIII. Two generations of traitors in a row was a bit much; and the qualities that made them such—vanity, ambition, instability—shone forth in Lord Robert. Elizabeth did not care; she fell in love with Robert Dudley, poured honors and offices on him, and saw so much of him, in such intimate circumstances, that people began to talk. If some reputable way could have been found to disengage him from Amy Robsart, the queen might have married him, probably with disagreeable consequences, for she was infinitely smarter than he. But at a time when the whole world was wondering how he would escape from Amy, when rumors that he was poisoning her were widespread, it was too much of a coincidence that Amy Robsart should be found one morning, at the foot of a staircase, dead, with her neck broken (9 September 1560).[7] A storm of scandal broke; it was mostly speculation, but the more fatal for that, and in the teeth of that scandal, it was clearly impossible for Elizabeth and Dudley to marry.

She did not therefore dismiss him from her service; indeed, when she lay deathly ill in 1562, it was Lord Robert whom she appointed to be protector of the realm in the event of her death. She gave him the splendid estate of Kenilworth, unoccupied today and for the past three centuries, but baronial in its grandeur when Dudley entertained there. She made use of him on military and diplomatic missions, and scolded him like a bad schoolboy when he exceeded his commission or spent too much of her money. But of anything more personal between them, there was never any question after 1560. When she created him earl of Leicester in 1564, it was only in the hope that he could be converted to a husband for Mary queen of Scots, and used to tame that restless lady. But there was nothing doing that way, and Leicester lingered about Elizabeth's court, always charming, always unreliable, never quite free from the touch of scandal, until his death in 1588. He was perhaps the only man Elizabeth ever really loved.

In the aftermath of Leicester, and even during his lifetime (for Elizabeth hated a complacent lover), there were other flirtations with other favorites. But none were of much importance or long duration till the affair with the earl of Essex blew up in the 1590s; and then the difference in ages (Elizabeth was thirty-four years older than her handsome young flatterer) made it another game entirely. But through all these fancies, passing or profound, dangerous or merely diversionary, Elizabeth's constant companion and best source of advice remained William Cecil. She named him Lord Burghley in 1571, giving him estates and profitable offices to support the dignity; she pensioned his worthless son and took the clever one into her service as his father's successor. Plotters occasionally tried to shake her trust in him; it never wavered; and as the old man lay dying (1598), his queen came to sit by his bed and feed him with a spoon.

CATHOLIC CONSPIRACIES, GOVERNMENT COUNTERMEASURES

As was traditional, Elizabeth's Catholic troubles came from the north; they came in direct response to the intrigues of Mary queen of Scots. Though technically imprisoned, she found ways to get in touch with the Spanish ambassador, Guerau d'Espes, who in 1569 concocted an elaborate scheme. As usual, it involved marrying her to somebody; and as a preliminary to this step, Bothwell the third husband was disposed of (marriage annulled; Bothwell died insane in a Danish dungeon). Next, the duke of Norfolk, son of Surrey the poet, was canvassed for

---

7. A little bit of ambiguous evidence suggests that Elizabeth knew of Amy's death before it happened, or at least before word of it could possibly have reached her, starting from the moment when the body was discovered.

the dangerous job of being the lady's fourth husband; he not only agreed, but recruited into a larger scheme the heads of two ancient and powerful Catholic families resident in the north. The earl of Westmoreland was a Neville, the earl of Northumberland a Percy; both had at their disposal large armies of retainers; and there was hope that the duke of Alva, then busy slaughtering Dutch Protestants, could be landed in England with his Spanish veterans. But before the full plot could reach a head, Norfolk came under suspicion and was arrested (September 1569). The northern lords, fearing they might be implicated, rose prematurely, and were as quickly scattered. While the plotters fled into Scotland, their English properties were all confiscated, and some 600 of their wretched retainers hanged. Clearly the plotting had suffered from a lack of coordination; and in 1570 an Italian banker resident in London, one Roberto Ridolfi, tried to assemble an even bigger plot from the broken pieces of the old one. He communicated with Mary in her castle and with Norfolk, who had been released; he talked with Alva at Brussels, with Pius V at Rome, and with Philip II at Madrid, enrolling them all. But most of his too-many communications were intercepted by English counterspies. On 25 February 1570, the pope went through with his excommunication and deposition of Elizabeth, but as there were no military or political forces to give it effect, nothing happened.[8] Norfolk, rearrested in September of 1571, was beheaded in June of 1572. Ridolfi, who was lucky to be in Paris when the plot blew up, got away. But with Mary, who had been at the center of all the plotting, Parliament was absolutely infuriated. Her instant execution was demanded; even cautious Cecil cried out for it. Elizabeth, however, had barely brought herself to go through with the execution of Norfolk, and could not contemplate the killing of Mary. Mary had made clear, in her correspondence with Ridolfi, that if the plot succeeded, it would be sealed with the death of her cousin; but the cousin could not reciprocate. Cecil and the other advisers raged; the Parliament was all but mutinous; still, Elizabeth contented herself with transferring Mary to a castle more remote from the flammable north, and keeping her under closer guard. Her new residence was to be Sheffield Castle; she stayed there for fourteen years, watched over by the earl of Shrewsbury. But, as time would tell, not closely enough.

PAPAL INTRIGUES

The popes of the Counter Reformation, Pius V (pope from 1566 to 1572) and Gregory XIII (pope from 1572 to 1585), were cut out of much the same cloth. Pius had his training in the Inquisition, and made no bones of wanting to see all Protestants, wherever they could be caught, converted or killed; his bull of

8. Even among Catholics, it was not clear that Pius V had legal authority to depose Elizabeth; that he tried to do so, and in unmeasured language, had the effect for years to come of rendering every English Catholic a suspected traitor.

excommunication absolved all Englishmen of their loyalty to Elizabeth. Gregory was not only delighted with the infamous St. Bartholomew's massacre of 24 August 1572, in France;[9] he allowed his secretary to tell a couple of Englishmen who were thinking of assassinating Elizabeth that, not only would they be committing no sin, but their deed would earn them merit in heaven. Both popes actively encouraged Spain to invade England. In face of these threats, English policy gradually changed from a tepid alliance with Spain and active hostility to France, in the direction of active hostility to Spain and tepid alliance with France. Not even the massacre of St. Bartholomew could prevent this shift from taking place. Elizabeth detested sectarian slaughter, she showed her displeasure at that black night of treachery; but some sort of ally on the Continent England must have, and if it was not Spain it would have to be France. Indeed, there was a third force, smaller but significant, which both France and England could unite in fostering. These were the Protestants of Holland. The Roman Catholic council of Trent, which finished its work in 1563, laid down a strict line for Catholic princes to follow regarding "heretics," and Philip of Spain, who was the narrowest and least imaginative of men, chose to follow it rigidly in the Netherlands. Here his power was technically supreme, and there were many Protestants on whom to exercise it. The duke of Alva, a man of iron, was sent to exterminate heresy by exterminating heretics; and this he proceeded to do, as best he could.[10] France, though Catholic herself, could not want to see the military power of Spain bristling all around her borders. Thus the Catholic duke d'Alençon, last of Queen Elizabeth's suitors and a son of Catherine de' Medici herself, had fought with the Dutch against their Spanish masters. The English too were naturally sympathetic to Protestants fighting for their lives against the Inquisition. In a practical way, there was not much they could do. They offered shelter and a few supplies to the hardbitten Dutch sailors who proudly called themselves Sea Beggars. (The title, given to them in contempt by the Spanish, they wore as a title of honor; and savage opportunists they were, who worked hand in glove with Huguenot privateers operating out of La Rochelle, to sweep the seas clean of "papist" shipping.) In addition, the English printed and circulated through the Netherlands much anti-Spanish propaganda; and during the years 1585–1587,

9. On this night the French Catholics made a sudden, unprovoked effort to extirpate physically all the French Protestants (Huguenots) on whom they could lay their hands. It was but one episode, though the most ferocious, in those merciless wars of religion which turned the entire continent into a bloody slaughterhouse in the name of Christ. An incidental consequence of the massacre, by no means unwelcome in England, was that thousands of Huguenots, many of them skilled and enterprising craftsmen, sought refuge in England, as an even larger group would do again after the toleration granted by the edict of Nantes (1598) was revoked in 1685.

10. In six years, Alva estimated, not without complacency, he had had 18,000 persons put to death—"not counting men slain in battle and executed after victory," i.e., not counting the massacres performed in captured cities. The duke's total bag must therefore be multiplied by a factor of perhaps twenty. By way of contrast, Queen Mary earned her nickname of "Bloody" by executing fewer than 300 Englishmen over an equivalent period of time.

Elizabeth sent some money and a small contingent of troops to keep the Dutch rebellion alive. (Leicester was the commander, and immediately infuriated Elizabeth by flagrantly exceeding his commission; Sir Philip Sidney was one of the soldiers, and got himself heroically killed at Zutphen.) But the Dutch did not need a great deal of help; under their great commander William of Orange and his equally implacable son, Maurice of Nassau, they developed into tough, resourceful, and determined soldiers.[11] The war dragged on; in Holland itself it was a nightmare, and it brought neither glory nor profit to Spain. The flower of the Spanish infantry was consumed in the Netherlands, the treasures of America vanished. For Carlos V, in the early century, the Netherlands had been a gold mine, for his son Philip II they were an open wound. The golden age of Spain was the sixteenth century; the golden age of Holland, the seventeenth. The wars of Dutch independence were the fulcrum on which this change pivoted.

PRIVATEERING

In addition, the English were able to cut a major artery of Spanish economic circulation by raiding Spanish shipping as it carried gold and silver bullion from the new world. Early in the sixteenth century, Cortez had taken Mexico and Pizarro Peru; both conquests yielded large amounts of bullion. Spain and Portugal thought themselves possessed of indisputable monopolies because Pope Alexander VI, in 1493, had divided the new world between them, assigning the eastern section to Portugal, the western areas (of whose size he had not the faintest idea) to Spain. Thus it was a profound shock to Spain when Francis Drake, cruising around the world in 1577–1580, raided at will Spanish shipping off the coast of Chile. Of all places in the world, they never expected to see a foreign ship *there!* Before long, there were few parts of the world where they did not have to be on the lookout. The English vessels which swarmed the high seas hijacking Spanish treasure were a typical piece of social improvisation. They were not vessels of the navy, they were not exactly pirates either. Most of them were manned by sailors from Devon and Cornwall, and most of their captains (Drake, Raleigh, Frobisher, Hawkins) came from that part of the world. They took commissions as privateers, often going shares with the queen or one of her courtiers on the loot of their trips. The risks they ran were very great; if captured by the Spaniards and not killed on the spot, they would certainly be turned over to the Inquisition as heretics. The vessels they sailed, though quick and maneuverable (by the standards of the day), were very small. Drake's *Golden Hind,* in which he sailed around the globe and brought home a colossal fortune, was a vessel of about 100 tons. There were bigger ships in the royal navy, one

11. William was nicknamed "The Silent"; in fact, he talked as much as anybody. The nickname came from an episode in his youth, when the French were trying to pump him for some military information, and found him too much for them.

or two as big as 1,000 tons; but the privateers were small. Their strong points were speed and gunnery. English guns could outrange the heavier guns of Spanish warships, and thus, sailing outside the enemy's range, pepper him at leisure. Against heavily guarded convoys they were less effective; they were never able to capture the entire Spanish treasure fleet and drown England in a golden stream. But they were a serious nuisance to the king of Spain. And the queen was happy because, without putting out any of her own money, she was building a naval force second to none (SFR, D.17).

THE QUEEN'S ECONOMY

For Elizabeth resembled her grandfather, Henry VII, in being stingy, rather than her father, Henry VIII, in being extravagant. She played the game of European diplomacy, none better, but avoided as much as possible the sort of open warfare that would require levying and equipping an army. Her court was splendid, but the splendor was mostly at the expense of the courtiers. Sir Henry Sidney, Philip's father, thought himself ill rewarded for a long life of difficult diplomacy, successful enough, but very poorly recognized by the royal mistress. Edmund Spenser lost everything serving the queen, and wrote an immortal poem in her honor as well, but failed to receive more than a pittance. Except for an occasional lucky favorite like Leicester—and he undeserving—she tended to dispense honors but not material rewards. Low taxes and domestic peace made England prosperous; they contrasted starkly with conditions on the Continent, where Spain was tottering on the verge of national bankruptcy, Italy was prostrate, France torn by religious war, and Germany so feeble that the Turks were able to make large inroads in eastern Europe. These disasters were not just measured in soldiers killed on the battlefield; wars of religion all involved, as a matter of course, looting, burning, torturing, and murdering members of the other party. Armies, whether "friendly" or otherwise, fed their soldiers on what they stole from the countryside, and soldiers all expected to supplement their scant pay with loot. By contrast, most of the plots and conspiracies that blew up during Elizabeth's reign were taken care of by police actions.

THE JESUIT MISSIONS

This was possible because the English Catholics, though numerous (perhaps the largest group in the kingdom), were divided and out of touch with one another. Because Elizabeth made it easy for them to lie low and keep their opinions to themselves, they were politically inert. The 1569 rising in the north was poorly supported, and the fate of those who joined it did not encourage anyone to try again. The papal excommunication of 1570 remained a dead letter. Before another major effort could be made against England, some sort of basic preliminary propaganda work would have to be done; and, starting about 1580, the most militant order of Catholic missionaries, the Jesuits, undertook to do it.[12] Had the missionary priests sent to England by the Jesuit order been mere connivers and political troublemakers, they would not have been very dangerous. Some such there were; but there were also men of pure lives, sacred convictions, and utter selflessness, who sincerely (by their lights) professed to be loyal subjects of Queen Elizabeth. (They were able to do this because the pope, *with regard to them,* had *temporarily* set aside his ban of excommunication against Elizabeth. This deft, but somewhat technical, manipulation of good faith was the sort of thing that raised deep distrust of the Jesuit mission.) For Elizabeth's secret police, however, all priests were dangerous because, as they traveled through the countryside, they organized and united the Catholic community. They were therefore forced to live hunted lives. After a short and hectic career in England, Father Robert Parsons was able to escape to the Continent, where he spent the rest of his life at the safer work of concocting pamphlets. Father Edmund Campion was less fortunate; captured, he was interrogated at length, Queen Elizabeth herself coming to plead that he would accept some formula that would save his life. He would not do so; nor, under the fierce duress of torture, would he reveal any of his associates. And so, by the logic of the day, he had to be executed; the English government calling him a traitor, the Catholic church just as naturally bestowing on him the title of martyr. His fate did not deter other passionate young Englishmen, mostly students in the Catholic seminary at Douai in France, from seeking to carry on the work. Both the pope and the king of Spain lent their support; and after 1585, when Spain finally declared open war, the police services operated by Cecil and his chief assistant Sir Francis Walsingham had their hands full chasing about a hundred secret priests.

THE LAST PLOT OF THE QUEEN OF SCOTS

The plot of Anthony Babington, in 1586, brought matters at last to a head. Babington had been from childhood a covert Catholic; he had served as a page to Mary queen of Scots, and was devoted to her. Before he was twenty, he had joined a secret society supporting Parsons, Campion, and the Jesuit missionaries from the Continent. After their failure in 1580, he went to Paris where Mary's agents were at work trying to get her released from her captivity; and there he met a priest named John Ballard with whom he formed the standard Catholic plot, to kill Elizabeth, crown Mary, and keep her on the throne with the help of Catholic soldiers and inquisitors from Spain. Philip II, not satisfied with the

12. The Society of Jesus, or Jesuits, had been founded in 1534 by Ignatius Loyola, as an arm of the Counter Reformation. Its rigid discipline and absolute loyalty to the pope made it, for many years, the object of great suspicion and distrust in some Catholic as well as all Protestant countries.

ghastly butchery his troops were inflicting on Holland, entered into the plot with alacrity; as soon as Elizabeth was assassinated, he would provide an army. But Babington, who was only twenty-five and romantic, wanted Mary to appreciate his services while they were being performed. His letters to her were intercepted, and the plotters rounded up. Questioned separately, and doubtless under torture, they incriminated one another. Babington tried to squirm and wiggle, but suffered the inevitable frightful penalty of treason. And in the wake of his execution, Elizabeth's advisers pushed her slowly, reluctantly, and unhappily into ordering the trial and execution of Mary. The queen of Scots had been well informed of Babington's plot; like most of her earlier plots, it had required the death of Elizabeth. Still, the queen was in great pain at the need to execute her royal cousin.[13] She gave orders for the execution, then stayed them, finally passed them on to her secretaries, and pretended, when they had been carried out, that the execution was against her will. Cecil took a tongue lashing; his assistant, a young man named Davison, was sent to the Tower, to be released—though not rehired—when political circumstances allowed. This anger was largely play-acting, to be sure; but its aim was not simply to make Elizabeth look good. James VI of Scotland, Mary's only child, was by now a young man of twenty-one; he had been offered a pretty straight choice between sticking by his mother or else inheriting the English throne from Elizabeth after her death. And in a letter that would have shamed him forever had it been made public during his lifetime, he wrote privately to the earl of Leicester, "How fond and inconstant I were if I should prefer my mother to the title, let all men judge." To save the young man's "honor," Elizabeth had to pretend that the execution of Mary was without her consent. Whoever was responsible, Mary was beheaded on 8 February 1587. She was just forty-four.

MARSHALING THE ARMADA

If there had been any doubt before that Philip of Spain would try to attack England, the death of Mary made it certain. Mary had been the center of the Catholic cause; her death must be avenged. Conspiracies had failed; a massive blow must be attempted. Always a methodical man, Philip began to assemble in the ports of Spain a huge Armada to attack England. Gathering vessels, supplies, soldiers, and sailors for an enterprise on this scale was a slow process. Francis Drake,

13. Rather than try and execute her publicly, Elizabeth would have preferred to have Mary secretly assassinated. She suggested as much to Sir Amyas Paulet, the Puritan soldier who was guarding Mary; he was horrified, and said it was against his conscience to do anything outside the law. Elizabeth was horrified too, pointing out that it was the reforming party, including Sir Amyas, who were eager for Mary's blood, yet they insisted that she, who did not want to kill Mary at all, must do the job and take public responsibility for it. Interestingly, the Catholic princes of Europe felt much as the queen did; they blamed her for having Mary executed by the common headsman instead of discreetly assassinated, as they would have done.

alerted to the situation, sailed into the harbor at Cadiz with all guns blazing, and sank or burned some 10,000 tons of shipping for the Armada. Early in 1588 the fleet's designated commander, the marquis of Santa Cruz, died; his place was taken by the duke of Medina Sidonia, a man of slight military experience. Still, despite many difficulties, the Armada did get in motion, and about mid-July 1588 made its way into the broad Atlantic mouth of the English Channel.

THE GREAT SEA FIGHT

Many of England's sea captains, including Drake, would have preferred to take the offensive, and crush the Armada in Spanish ports; Elizabeth thought that plan too risky. When the enemy appeared, the English fleet was divided—one half off the western ports of Devon and Cornwall, the other half in the narrow eastern part of the channel, where, with a small but tough Dutch squadron, they were blockading the Flemish ports. That was to prevent the Spanish army, already in Holland under the able duke of Parma, from crossing to English soil. As Philip and his advisers had planned the operation, the Armada itself was simply to secure a beach head; the hard fighting would be done by veterans from Holland, with the help of a hoped-for insurrection in the Catholic north. So the English fleet had to be divided, and as the Armada entered the channel, there seemed little the English could do to stop the invasion. Drake, knowing the prevailing winds there are westerlies, insisted that the English vessels not get in front of the Spaniards, but keep advantage of the wind and attack the Armada from behind. This they did; but English guns, though they outranged those of the Spaniards, were not very heavy. They peppered the Armada, but did not break it up or slow its majestic progress.

On July 24, the Spaniards prepared to attack the isle of Wight, which would have been hard to defend, and an ideal staging area for Parma's infantry. But while the Spanish vessels were lining up to enter the estuary which would have given them access to Wight, Drake with a pickup group of fifty vessels made a slambang attack from behind. Before the Armada could maneuver to meet him, he had driven it downwind from Wight to a position from which, under the circumstances, the slow, high galleons could not recover. So they sailed on down-channel, and on July 26 anchored off Calais. But Parma's Spanish veterans were still blockaded in Holland and unable to move. The Spaniards paused to make new plans, and while they were thinking, on the night of July 28, the English command sent fireships among them. These were old hulks, charged with tar barrels, flares, and occasional heavy charges of gunpowder. Skeleton crews steered them upwind of the enemy, lit the fuses, and abandoned ship, while the fire ships blundered into the enemy anchorage, blazing and blasting unpredictably. Their effect was frightening. Many Spanish captains cut their cables in panic and drifted off into the night; the great Armada fell into confusion, and at daybreak the English attacked in force. Before long the Spanish were running low on powder and shot; English ships could therefore approach closer, and, firing at close range, their culverins raked the galleons to terrible effect. At this point the duke of Medina Sidonia lost heart and began looking for a way out. But the winds that had wafted him gently into the channel now blocked him from getting out. For lack of an alternative, he decided to sail north beyond Scotland, turn west into the broad Atlantic, and so run for home.

It was a desperate scheme at best, disastrous in the event. The Armada was short, not only of powder and shot, but of food and water; the pilots had no charts to guide them through the northern seas, and the weather was stormy. Many vessels ran aground on the craggy reefs of Scotland, others came to grief on the northern and western coasts of Ireland. Overall, the Spanish lost in the Armada venture over 20,000 men and fifty vessels; the English lost no vessels, one junior officer, and about 100 seamen. Just as striking was the fact that the English Catholics, whom Spain had been expecting to revolt in support of the invasion, lay very low. Whether they were fearful or loyal or just unorganized, the Catholics never moved. The failure of Spain was an international turning point. For half a century England had been in something like a state of siege; suddenly, she was safe, and not only she, but the entire cause of Protestantism in northern Europe. The English cast a medal for the occasion, with the motto, *Flavit Jehovah et dissipati sunt:* "The Lord blew and they were scattered." Armada year was taken as a clear sign of England's manifest destiny.

TUDOR ENGLAND, A SNAPSHOT

The nation which the Lord had rescued (with the help of Sir Francis Drake and a North Sea tempest) had enjoyed domestic tranquillity for better than a century, since the battle of Bosworth. While religious wars were devastating Europe, English circumstances remained relatively easy. The wool trade, long a center of commercial activity, flourished; increasingly, it was concentrated in London, and, increasingly trade and credit lines came to be drawn between London on the one hand and Antwerp on the other. Iron works, dirty but profitable, were starting up around Sheffield, and coal from Newcastle was lightered down to London to glow in winter grates. Merchants from that collection of Baltic port cities known as the Hanse had been established in England since the thirteenth century; now they enlarged their trade, and regularized its conditions. London itself during the Tudor period tripled its size. Provincial centers also expanded. Bristol was the second city in the kingdom; Hull, York, Gloucester, Plymouth, Norwich, and Winchester were among the other established towns. But predominantly, England was still a rural and village society; roads were bad, communications poor, most people spent their lives in, or not far from, their place of origin. Because the industrial potential of the midlands and north country was barely tapped, much the greater part of the population lived in the south—three parts in four, by the roughest of rough estimates. As a way of binding this expanding population more closely to the central government, the Tudors drastically increased the size of the House of Commons; from 297 members at the accession of Henry VIII, the lower house had risen to 458 by the death of Elizabeth.

Though broadly the kingdom was prospering, areas of stagnation, misery, and darkness persisted. It goes without saying that sanitary facilities were everywhere primitive, disease was prevalent, diets (for all but the very rich) meager and monotonous. The plowboy in the fields was likely to be illiterate and ignorant of even the rudiments of religion; as late as the nineteenth century, "polite" opinion held that book learning could only spoil the working class. A very small percentage of English men and no English women at all attended the two universities, and what they learned there amounted, often enough, to little more than a degenerate form of semi-Aristotelian logic chopping in bad Latin. Grammar schools existed to convey the rudiments of Latin syntax, petty schools provided basic instruction in English; often the local minister would (for a fee) teach what he knew to a few of the brighter boys in the neighborhood. But clearly these procedures could not and did not create a large reading public. Books, published in small editions, were available mainly in London, the university towns, and only a few places besides. Poor children went to work very young; they were apprenticed to a trade, and if they learned to read, write, and cipher did so on their own, or in the course of their business training. Folk tales about industrious apprentices who rose to lord mayor of London encouraged their aspirations. And rising in the world was not an impossible dream; it was a stratified society, but not marked by rigid castes. A poor boy could become a shopkeeper, a thriving shopkeeper a merchant, a rich merchant a squire, a solid squire (or at least his son) a member of the lesser nobility. Society had its paupers and its princes; those who were neither, whatever the name or names we call them by, were numerous in the country as in the towns.

IRISH MISERIES

As often in history, England's triumph in 1588 simply filled to overflowing the cup of Ireland's woes. That unhappy land had never taken kindly to the Reformation, which it tended to view as an alien English movement. As we noted (p. 125), the great house of Fitzgerald suffered cruelly in 1534 when one of its members was rash enough to rebel against Henry VIII. Since then the Irish peasantry, unshakably loyal to its priests, had been further alienated by the Tudor habit of sending unwelcome rulers to Ireland, and paying them off with grants of Irish land. In fact, there were and had been for many years, two distinct Irelands, known since the fourteenth century as "the pale" and the rest of Ireland. Within the pale lay an enclave around Dublin, sometimes embracing more and sometimes less of the nearby counties; here English law, English language, English business practices, and sometimes even English religion prevailed. Beyond the pale were the "wild Irish," warring tribes, controlling ill-defined districts, in accordance with their own immemorial tribal traditions.[14] Not even Henry's severest deputies could expand the English-controlled area very far or fast, and under Mary the instinctive Catholicism of the people reasserted itself. Elizabeth thus inherited a chaotic situation in Ireland: Protestants were at daggers drawn with Catholics, the Desmonds were in open feud with the Ormondes, the O'Neills with the O'Donnells, and even within individual tribes there were fierce fights between different claimants to the headship. Papal delegates slipped in and out of the country, fomenting trouble for Elizabeth; and most of the English deputies sent over to keep order simply added to the chaos. The best of them was Sir Henry Sidney, father of Sir Philip; he strove bravely against a rising tide of violence before which he was finally impotent. The civil war that gradually developed during the late 1560s, and then flared into a wild melee during the early 1580s, was a many-sided, many-issued, many-directional war of such total savagery and universal destruction that it died down only when the land was an empty desert. Spenser, who was there, describes Munster after its devastation:

Out of every corner of the woods and glens they came creeping forth upon their hands for their legs could not bear them, they looked like anatomies of death, they spake like ghosts crying out of their graves, they did eat the dead carrions, happy where they could find them, yea and one another soon after, insomuch as the very carcasses they spared not to scrape out of their graves.

It was these starving wretches upon whom the bedraggled survivors of the Armada fell when a lucky remnant dragged themselves ashore in Ireland. Which group was more pitiable would be hard to say.

Such desperate conditions prompted Elizabeth to try the classic but hateful expedient of "colonizing" Ireland with peoples of non-Celtic stock. Giving Irish estates to English landlords was an old expedient, but it did not strike at the root of the problem. An entire new population was needed, and certainly at first, perhaps permanently, it would have to be a garrison population. If it was to do its job, it would have to be firmly Protestant, and if it was not to cost too much, it would have to consist of small, independent farmers. The first such experiment was tried in Munster, the beautiful southwest corner of Ireland; though it failed, the memory remained to suggest to Elizabeth's successor the idea of settling Scottish Presbyterians in Ulster. The Scots were violently anti-Catholic; thus they would "balance" the Catholic majority in the southern part of the island.

14. Most Londoners had only the vaguest notion of what life was like in back country Ireland. In 1562 Shane O'Neill came to court to plead a case, accompanied by a troop of shaggy gallowglasses (tribal retainers) from his district in Ulster. Their strange Gaelic speech, bare heads with long hair falling over their shoulders, and rough yellow shirts (their only garments) created a great impression.

Besides, Scotland was overcrowded, underemployed, and feud-ridden; transferring excess Scots to Ulster would solve these problems and keep a tight rein on the Irish Catholic population as well. At the time, these must have seemed like smart ideas; in light of the misery they have caused over the centuries, and are still causing today, they look a lot less smart.

FRACTIOUS FACTIONS

The murderous religious wars on the Continent, which Englishmen felt themselves so lucky to have escaped, took in England the form of plots and polemics, muted disputes punctuated by an occasional execution, but nothing like the mass bloodshed abroad. The Catholics who failed to support the Armada in 1588 earned by their inaction an extra measure of tolerance from the government. We do not know how numerous they were; as long as they kept quiet, nobody tried to find out. The longer they were left in peace, the less inclination they had to disturb a situation which for many was not uncomfortable at all.[15]

By and large, then, the religious disputes which from small and remote beginnings rose to overcloud the seventeenth-century landscape, took place not between Catholics and Protestants, but between different groups of Protestants. Originally, indeed, they were hardly even disputes. The party which came to be called "Puritan" knew itself for a long time as the party of "reformers"; those supporting the established church, which was episcopal (ruled by bishops) and came to be called Anglican, hardly had any proper designation at all. They were the national church. For a long time doctrinal differences played almost no part in the controversy; discipline was the heart of the matter, and particularly the question whether the church should be governed by royally appointed bishops. The Scriptures make no mention of bishops; that alone was enough to condemn them in the eyes of John Calvin and his still stricter successor Theodore Beza. If bishops had not been instituted by the apostles or their immediate successors, then they were of human or even diabolic invention, and so (according to the reformers) should be abolished. That would leave the church to be governed (disciplined) by the fundamentally undifferentiated clergy, the "presbyters." But getting rid of the bishops was hard, because Elizabeth, who ruled the church through their influence and controlled their appointment, would not hear of it. The Puritans addressed a pair of *Admonitions to Parliament* (1571, 1572), telling

15. The Gunpowder Plot of 1605 brought to light a split between "old" Catholics who wanted to leave well enough alone, and "new" Catholics who were ready to resort to violence. The split went back to a decision by the English government, not to make martyrs of captured priests, but to intern them on an estate named Wisbech near Ely. There, being men of quick wit with much leisure, they began to quarrel; the radical wing was isolated, and so resorted to desperate measures. The Gunpowder Plot (for which, see more below, p. 208), though much denounced as a piece of malignant villainy, was really a confession of weakness and despair (SFR, D.8).

it just what to do; but Elizabeth, through her practiced and worldly ministers, had no trouble persuading it to do nothing of the sort. Puritan controversialists, of whom the most famous was the redoubtable Thomas Cartwright, preached powerful sermons against the bishops, and wrote heavy treatises demonstrating that their office was contrary to the word of God. They provoked other treatises, demonstrating contrary positions, but changed nothing. The Puritans also got themselves expelled from their positions in the episcopal church; this was not always unwelcome to them because, as martyrs, they attracted a great deal of sympathy. But the several techniques of propaganda need concern us here no more than the intricate arguments marshaled out of texts from the fathers of the early church. Elizabeth did not want the kind of reformed church which would give committees of clergymen power over an organization which she, like her father before her, claimed the right to control as she saw fit. The reformers cried out for a "godly discipline"; Elizabeth thought the discipline they had was already quite godly enough, and in this view she was, naturally, encouraged by her bishops. But she was not by nature a persecutor. When the reformers became very troublesome, they were therefore suppressed or silenced; they were not, as a rule, persecuted further; and many were accommodated within the church. There they were free to preach. They had influential protectors, not only in the cities but among secular magnates like the earl of Leicester and the earl of Bedford. Preaching, which they far preferred to the ritual parts of the service, was a way of gaining more friends; thus, instead of making laws in England to establish the discipline they wanted, the Puritans were reduced to making propaganda. Instead of seizing power, which was their aim, they had to ask for toleration—which, in fact, if they could have had power, they would never have thought of exercising.

Matthew Parker's successor as archbishop of Canterbury was the gentle Edmund Grindal, who assumed the primacy in 1575. He was so considerate of Puritans within the church that he got into trouble with Elizabeth, who at one point wanted to deprive him of his office. She was dissuaded, but when the archbishop soon died, being old and feeble, she replaced him with a much tougher man, John Whitgift. With the help of new laws, new oaths, and new court procedures, he cracked down hard on the Puritans; and they, feeling their legal resources exhausted and their cause further than ever from success, began resorting to direct action. Though Robert Browne was but a single individual, he saw the dilemma of the Puritan position more clearly than most. He had been deprived of his office in the church, imprisoned for preaching outside the church, and had emigrated briefly to Holland to escape the law. In 1582 he proposed a new course, sufficiently indicated by the title of the book he published: *A Treatise of Reformation without Tarrying for Any*. Individual congregations, he thought, should reform themselves when and as far as they wanted; national churches and secular governments should be ignored. Behind this apparently simple shift in tactics lay a very deep change in objectives; Browne did not want the church to include everybody, or indeed anybody but the spiritual elite. The world was too wicked; all that the few true believers could do was huddle together and try to preserve a tiny spark of the true faith. The fewer they were, the purer they would be, and the safer the faith was. Robert Browne's basic attitude reached an ultimate a few years later when John Smyth, an English Puritan living in Holland, began to doubt whether he was in fact a Christian man, in the sense of having been baptized in the true faith. If not, where could he acquire true baptism? He could find only one man of whose righteousness he could be assured, himself; so he baptized himself (October 1608), creating thereby a church of one. It was the logical conclusion of the Protestant process, separation based on conscience; in future, many sectarians would follow the same logic, though self-baptism would always remain an exceptional procedure.

MARTIN MARPRELATE AND THE AGE OF SATIRE

Of more immediate import was the rise, just after the Armada scare in '88, of a popular prose satirist hostile to the bishops and frankly favorable to the Puritan cause. His activities being highly illegal, he concealed his identity under the name of Martin Marprelate and provided no clues to his address or that of his printer. He attacked the bishops directly and personally, with invective, derision, and a gaudy line of patter that nobody else in the age, least of all the bishops, could match. Like Tyndale before him, Martin Marprelate appealed to popular tastes for the lively, the funny, and, incidentally, the ethical. As he noted himself, a lot of people calling themselves "Puritans" disapproved of his raw, rowdy jesting; Thomas Cartwright the "serious" Puritan controversialist deplored this handling of sacred matters in the manner of a stage farce, and the government tacitly endorsed his judgment by hiring stage writers like Nash and Lyly to write answers. But nobody was quite as good at Martin's game as Martin Marprelate. He was not only quick of wit but light of foot. Elizabeth's secret police chased him cross-country for a year or two before they caught up with the printing press, which in the meanwhile had produced no fewer than seven Marprelate tracts. (It turned out to have been hidden on a haywagon, which every so often drew up in a grove or abandoned barn, and ran off another tract.) A Welshman named John Penry was accused of being Martin himself, and hanged in 1593; perhaps he was not the right man, for he denied it steadfastly, and if he was he had accomplices, one of whom died in prison, while another professed repentance. In any case, the Marprelate tracts came to an abrupt end. But the author, whoever he was, had written the finest comic prose of the late sixteenth century, and deepened appreciably the bitterness of the Puritan-Anglican conflict. To differ with a bishop over technical questions is one thing; to mock his verbal mannerisms, impugn his motives, and make him look like a fool is something else. Martin Marprelate inaugurated the age of satire, cynicism, and darkening passion that was to embitter the last fifteen years of the queen.

THE QUEEN'S GRACE

Though a new order of troubles was brewing at home, Elizabeth after the defeat of the Armada seemed ready to enjoy the unbounded admiration of her countrymen. In the hour of peril, she had stood forth unflinchingly as the leader of her people, appealing to their chivalry, their patriotism, their sense of destiny.[16] As queen, she had been from the first a great actress, always on stage. In the hour of her coronation, the Spanish ambassador had tried to tell her that Philip II had put her on the throne; she cut him off with a tirade. It was not the king of Spain or the church or the nobility to whom she owed the throne, she said; it was the people, *her* people. She had a natural gift for popularity; diplomatic fogies called it undignified, the common folk loved it. During summers, she made a practice of going on long, leisurely "progresses" from one stately home to another. Aldermen made speeches to her; she thanked and complimented them. Children came forward to be patted on the head; municipalities gave state dinners. She thanked her loving subjects, was delighted at their gifts, ate their dinners, and asked to have an extra piece of the special cake sent to her quarters so she could enjoy more of it. When a farmer asked the royal driver to stop so he could exchange a few words with her majesty, the procession stopped; when rural speechmakers stuttered over their elocution, she calmed and encouraged them. All the gallant young men of one district dressed up in special velvet robes and rode out on their best horses to greet her—a brave show advancing across the fresh fields to cheer her carriage; she was enchanted. Introduced to young Lord Herbert of Cherbury, who thought himself a very proper figure of a man, she looked him over, and said what a pity it was he had married so young.[17] Her rages were sulphuric; she could swear like a trooper, and often did; when she was disappointed in something, she sulked and cried like a little girl. She had private nicknames for all her special friends and favorites; she loved pageants,

16. Her lifelong stinginess also manifested itself in the summer of '88. Whenever she could, she held back on pay and supplies for the maritime heroes whom she was urging to defend her; against the advise of all her military men, she disbanded the armed forces before it was safe to do so, because she feared having to pay them for a single extra day. But these were secret actions; her public posture was a mixture of dauntless defiance and feminine helplessness. She was always good at playing the weak woman in need of male protection, whereas she was really much tougher and craftier than most of the crowned heads in Europe. Sixtus V, a bold and wily pope, was bound to oppose her theologically, but he could not help admiring her as a ruler.

17. He was the brother of George Herbert the poet, and later a philosopher of substance; indeed, he had married when but sixteen, and Elizabeth was fifty years older than he; but what a compliment from what a queen!

parades, and horseback riding. When she did not want to do something, or even talk about it, she had a thousand different ways of changing the subject or confusing the issue or putting her interlocutor in the wrong. Foreign ambassadors, whom she could outtalk, either in their own languages, or in *extempore* and often vitriolic Latin, went away mumbling in their beards; ten thousand devils, said the Spanish ambassador, lurked in this one woman. She worked her secretaries into exhaustion and beyond; she enraged her advisers and filled her noblest adversaries with admiration. For many years, November 17, the anniversary of her accession, was kept in England as a public holiday.

Somewhere during the 1570s—when she was being excommunicated by the pope, vilified by the Catholic powers, betrayed by her cousin Mary, and threatened daily with assassination—Elizabeth started to become a cult figure. Protestantism had diminished, if not destroyed, worship of the Virgin Mary; without intention on her part, or much awareness on the part of her people, the virgin queen of England took on many of the attributes of the virgin mother of God. In some ways, the legend outgrew the woman; but that is a story for the next chapter.

TUNING UP FOR A LITERATURE

War, religion, and political intrigue dominate the story of Elizabeth's early reign, drowning out the relatively sparse and scattered notes of literary endeavor; during the much shorter period after 1588, the proportions will be quite reversed. To that period we also assign a description of the drama, which could hardly flourish in a major way till the building of the first public theater in 1577. But the earlier decades, though marked by few outstanding literary achievements, are a period of vital fermentation and decision reaching. The instruments are not yet ready to play, but they are being tuned. In one respect, preparation for the great Elizabethan achievements may reach as far back as 1556, when the stationers' guild was elevated to the status of a livery company and charged with maintaining a record of English coyprights.[18] The motive for this change was not altogether liberal. To be sure, the printer owning a copyright could make money on it, but he and his company could also be counted on to safeguard it, to prevent interlopers from infringing on it. The necessity to register a copyright made censorship much easier. Most publishers, and the registry office of the stationers' company, were in London, so the duties of censorship were entrusted to the bishop of London and inspectors appointed by him, occasionally to the arch-

18. "Stationers" were booksellers, taking their name from the stalls or stations they set up, commonly around the great cathedrals. So long as they were simple book and paper sellers, they needed no special organization; but as printing became widespread, their functions expanded to include printing and publishing. Then both they and the government saw the need for further regulation (SFR, D.1).

bishop of Canterbury. Under Mary the laws had sharp teeth, but Elizabeth, apart from one or two particular points, did not enforce them severely, and during her reign the more positive side of copyright began to emerge. Publishers could now invest money in a major project and hope to get it back. Raphael Holinshed, for example, came up to London from the university about 1560, and found employment as a translator for a publisher just starting work on a universal history of the world. He would not have conceived such a project had there not been an appetite for handy compendia of general knowledge, had there not been some self-consciousness about England as a specially significant enterprise, and had he not been protected by copyright laws. Not the least important part of Holinshed's *Chronicles* (on which, as is well known, Shakespeare drew liberally for the materials of his history plays) was a full-length description of England by a clergyman named William Harrison. In those days of extreme provincialism, when most Englishmen had never set foot outside their native county, and some had never ventured beyond the bounds of their parish, such a description of England must have opened many eyes. Harrison was a zesty, positive-thinking patriot; his favorite expression, entering on a description of a district, is "we have." We have excellent wood, we have admirable stone for building, we have splendid mineral deposits, we have the best dogs in the whole world; he is all enthusiasm and appreciation (SFR, D.9). There had, of course, been accounts of England before (about 1500 the Venetian ambassador wrote a notable one), but they were by foreigners, for foreigners, and aimed only to give a summary "character" of the country. Harrison saw what there was to see, but he also read what there was to read; and he was lucky to have access to the papers of John Leland, an English antiquary, who lived in the first part of the century. They were in extremely bad shape, tattered, disordered, moldy, and decayed. Harrison thought they had deliberately been muddled to frustrate plagiarists, but, alas, it was not so; poor Leland had died insane. Leland's omnivorous labors lent depth to Harrison's book; and Leland's true successor was already at work on his own great book of exploration and discovery. William Camden put years of travel and study into the preparation of a book he would call *Britannia*. It was first published in Latin (1586) and not translated into English till 1610, but it was influential from the first. Camden never really stopped writing it, for each new edition was more copious than the last. What it provided was a view of the island in depth, with an account of its ancient ruins, charters, history of invasions and feudal wars. Antiquarianism became a general vogue in the last years of Elizabeth; John Stow published a general chronicle of England from the legendary beginnings of Brut down to the present (1580), and also the work by which he is best known, the *Survey of London* (1598). John Speed was another antiquarian, whose *History of Great Britain* was published in 1611; and dozens of handy abridgments and summaries of the chronicles were available for the reader who wanted to know something but not too much. A society of antiquaries took root and flourished, till King James, uncertain of what they might discover, discouraged them. It was a nation deeply oriented toward history, particularly its own history; we find poets like Michael Drayton writing archaic ballads on battles like Agincourt, which took place two hundred years previous, and, of course, playwrights like Marlowe and Shakespeare making dramas of the national history.

John Foxe's *Book of Martyrs* (1563) contributed mightily to this interest of the English people in themselves; they had only to recall the reign of Mary to realize that they were protagonists of a mighty drama engaging all the forces of light and darkness. Their naval exploits were not just stirring adventure stories but testimonials to the divine wisdom guiding the universe. About 1577 a clergyman named Richard Hakluyt began to collect stories of early voyages to America; this interest of his put him in touch with Raleigh, Drake, Frobisher, Hawkins, and the other great captains of England. He described their adventures in a prose style remarkably free and vigorous for its day, and published them, just one year after the armada, as *The Principal Navigations, Voyages, Traffics, and Discoveries of the English Nation*. Some of the stories that Hakluyt collected (and, like Camden, he kept collecting long after the first edition of his book appeared) had already been published. But many had not, and having them all gathered together gave to Englishmen an intimate sense of the epic that they had never known before.

CRITICAL QUESTIONS

Having all these rich new materials freshly assembled, along with the courtly verse forms popularized by Wyatt and Surrey, it might seem that the Elizabethans should have found it easy to turn out great literary works. But there was no way to put Drake's voyage around the world into Italian love sonnets; and a surprising number of problems confronted the early Elizabethan poets before they could settle to their work. That these problems were solved long ago makes them look terribly obvious now; but in those days it was not so. Before assured and elegant verse could be written, the criticisms of puritanism against imaginative literature as such had to be answered. The question of whether, and in what spirit, men should imitate their great classical predecessors had to be resolved; and the crucial matter had to be faced of what diction should be used in English literature. Overfancy, "aureate" diction was one trap; archaic English was another; still another was the use of "inkhorn" terms, neologisms coined out of Greek or Latin words and sounding uncouth in English. Should one use rhyme, for which the precedents were all in the barbaric modern tongues, or follow the more elegant Virgil and Horace, who used none? Should English verse be measured, like classical verse, by quantity, or rather (as we now know is natural to English) by accent? Why was it that certain metrical forms like the six-footed hexameter or the curious "poulter's measure"[19] did not work well in English? Critical issues of this character filled a number of books and pamphlets by Ascham, Gascoigne, Lodge, Sidney, and Gabriel Harvey; but the published documents can represent only a small fraction of the shoptalk that must have been going on among the poets. Vaguely, and as from a great distance, we hear rumors of a sort of literary club, calling itself (after the high judicial council in ancient Athens) the "Areopagus." If we surmise that they met during the 1570s, it would doubtless have been to discuss the question of quantitative verse, and other burning issues of the day; among their members were (apparently) Sir Philip Sidney, Fulke Greville, Sir Edward Dyer, and Edmund Spenser.[20]

THE SHEPHERD'S CALENDAR

Thus when Spenser brought out his *Shepherd's Calendar* in 1579, it was not just another poem, but a new sort of poem, accompanied by a manifesto announcing and explaining what was new about it. The author of this manifesto signed himself simply "E.K.," and a great deal of scholarly study has been invested, not very conclusively, in discovering his identity. Perhaps he was Edward Kerke or Kirke, an otherwise undistinguished college friend of Spenser's; perhaps he was Spenser himself or Gabriel Harvey in a mood for mystification. In any case, the little book contained hardly less annotation than text. The poems, twelve in number, one for each month in the year, are declared to be "well grounded, finely framed, and strongly trussed up together." They are dedicated to Sir Philip Sidney, who will guard them from detraction, introduced by a letter from E.K. to Gabriel Harvey, prefaced by a General Argument, provided with a woodcut and an astrological sign for each individual idyll, and given a set of glosses which explain the hard words, point up the beauties, and invite speculation about the allusions. Much of this commentary is by now merely quaint. Confronted with the lines

> I love thilke lass (alas, why do I love?)
> And am forlorn (alas, why am I lorn?),

19. This verse form, popular in the sixteenth century and visible in Tottel, alternated lines of twelve and fourteen syllables; it may have been intended to imitate the Latin elegiac meter, which alternates hexameters and pentameters. But "poulter's measure" (a name reflecting, perhaps, on the honesty of chicken dealers) was never anything but a lame meter.

20. Most of the Areopagites were gentlemen of quality and fortune: Spenser was not. His family was obscure and evidently needy; only the will of a charitable London citizen enabled him to attend Cambridge, and so, through friendship with Gabriel Harvey, to become inward with the Areopagites and to hope for favor from the earl of Leicester himself. But no patronage was forthcoming, Spenser's services as an official in Ireland were rewarded no better than his poetry, and he died (1599) an embittered man, if not in actual penury.

we scarcely feel the need of a commentary which tells us we've experienced "a pretty Epanorthosis in these two verses and withal a Paronomasia or playing with the word."

And yet in a large way, E.K. is right in his claims for "the new poet." *The Shepherd's Calendar* is a key work in the development of English poetry. It is filled with the idyllic spirit of classical pastoralists such as Theocritus and Virgil, not to mention their recent Renaissance imitators on the Continent; at the same time, it represents real English soil and English climate. It deals with moral, political, and religious issues of immense import; its shepherds stand for lords and prelates, its shepherdesses for countesses and queens. Yet it maintains, if only precariously, its pastoral fiction; and in a splendid poem, like that for October, it confronts the problem of an audience for poetry in England, answering it in lofty style. Poetry may be scorned by the humble reader and neglected by the great and powerful; but it rises on its own visionary wings to become a voice of prophecy for which, in another sphere, rewards are reserved. This is the true accent of that Christian humanism for which More and Erasmus had stood, which would resound through the work of Milton, and which, in the immediate present, was most fully exemplified in the life and writings of Sir Philip Sidney.

SIR PHILIP: A MASTER OF THE ROLES

For in Sidney a number of strains from the past came briefly together to create a popular and romantic ideal. He was a humanist scholar, at home in many languages including the Greek; he was a staunch Protestant, who died fighting against the hated Spaniards. He was a knight-courtier, gallant and successful in the jousting-lists; amid the courts of kings he was an urbane diplomat, polished to the highest Italian gloss. He was a melancholy Petrarchan lover after the fashion brought to England by Wyatt and Surrey; and, except for the Protestantism, he took none of these poses with utter seriousness. Natural and negligent grace was the hallmark of his style; Castiglione had named it *sprezzatura,* that slight touch of disdain which implies that the actor is above any particular role he happens to play. *Astrophel and Stella* is a sequence of sonnets alluding loosely but persistently to the progress of a love affair; it follows in the tradition of Petrarch's sonnets to Laura. But the idea was new in England, and led to a considerable vogue. Sonnet sequences allowed the poets to play variations on a single form, and one susceptible of many tonal and rhythmic changes. They were both conventional and confessional, with room for the personal, yet so much of the traditional that anything halfway indiscreet could always be disavowed.[21] In fact,

21. From its beginnings in the eleventh century, courtly love always envisaged an adulterous affair which had to be concealed even as it was revealed. Concealment might be necessary either because the affair amounted to nothing whatever and was therefore absurd, or because it amounted to a great deal and was therefore criminal by the laws of God and man. The concept of married love represents

Sidney's sequence alludes rather clearly to the progress of an attachment to Penelope Devereux, who in 1580 married Lord Rich. (He was, be it noted in passing, grandson of that Richard Rich who gladly perjured himself to get the conviction which led to the execution of Sir Thomas More.) The precise mixture of convention and autobiography in *Astrophel and Stella* is a matter for every reader to estimate for himself, as Sidney certainly intended it to be. Nothing requires the poem to be one thing or the other. Whatever the ingredients entering into it, *Astrophel and Stella* brings a new fullness of feeling and ease of expression into English poetry. Its verse is supple, assured, alive with the strong emphases and nervous rhythms of colloquial speech. Astrophel, for example, describes himself at a tourney:

> When Cupid, having me his slave descried
> In Mars's livery, prancing in the press,—
> "What now, sir fool?" said he. "I would no less—
> Look here, I say!" I looked, and Stella spied. . . .
> (Sonnet 53)

The sonnets are wonderfully agile; even when they seem, like number 9, to develop a deliberate, artificial conceit almost cold-bloodedly, the last line's sudden turn to the direct and colloquial enacts a turn against the tradition—a turn that the tradition itself is constantly inviting. Sidney's poetry becomes more taut and elevated as the sequence advances; at its finest, his verse has an assured dramatic vigor which makes it, more than any other poetry written before 1590, a harbinger of mighty presences to come.

Though ostensibly slight and occasional, Sidney's two major works in prose fulfill Castiglione's definition of *sprezzatura* by promising little and then, as if unintentionally, performing a great deal. The *Arcadia* is a pastoral prose romance of the sort for which there were several models in Italy and Spain. Sidney wrote it for the amusement of his sister, and it is still known as "The Countess of Pembroke's *Arcadia*." But the author, though he wrote two versions of it, still was not satisfied, and asked on his deathbed that it be destroyed. Instead, it was preserved, published in 1590, and has proved, for a deliberately artificial and mannered work, surprisingly durable.[22] For its political insights and psychological complexities, some modern opinion ranks it among the most impressive of early English fictions.

---

a minority strain in English literature before Spenser and Milton. (Chaucer's Troilus and Criseyde, for example, never even consider matrimony: they're in love *par amour*.) Puritanism, with its deep conviction that woman too has a soul to be saved, created by a kind of pun on Genesis 2:18, the notion of woman as a helpmeet for man, after marriage as before, and thus helped convert marriage itself to a sacred partnership.

22. Sidney has a way of recurring to the literary mind. The heroine of Samuel Richardson's early novel *Pamela* (1740) takes her name from one of the *Arcadia*'s persecuted heroines; and Dickens's *Great Expectations* draws on *Astrophel and Stella* for its title (number 21), its theme, and the names of its two protagonists.

The "Apology for Poetry" was provoked by a book which it disdains to mention, Stephen Gosson's *School of Abuse* (1579). Gosson was an ex-actor and ex-playwright who, without asking permission, rudely dedicated to Sidney his sweeping assault on entertainments in general. Sidney's "Apology," dignified yet playful, orderly in developing its theme and deft in balancing its clauses, was built on the model of a Ciceronian oration; its view of poetry as an inspired form of creation or recreation owed much to earlier continental criticism. At least superficially, it demolished the unfortunate Gosson and the outright puritan hostility to worldly diversions which alone made Gosson more than an isolated crank. Hostility to literature as such became particularly hard after puritan sympathizers had their own great poets in Spenser and Milton. Yet a grumbling undertone persisted, the hostility focusing particularly on stage plays and stage players. There will be "rationalist" arguments against poetry as such in the nineteenth century, and at that time Shelley will pick up Sidney's argument for the visionary and prophetic character of the poet. There is in fact no answer to Sidney's *Apology* except that it raises the tone of the discussion a little higher than, for everyday purposes, poetry can stand. The poet as prophet may be a little too good for everyday use; nowadays, at least, we do not mind his talking occasionally, as Falstaff says, "like folks of this world."

THE HUMBLER PATH: LATE SIXTEENTH-CENTURY PROSE

With Spenser's first promising poems and Sidney's accomplished sonnets, we are fairly launched on the golden age of Elizabethan verse. The suddenness of this birth contrasts with the slow, easy development of Elizabethan prose. Like the chronicles of Holinshed, the heroic narratives of Hakluyt were written as if by men who did not know what prose was; the story lay before them, and the language yielded itself into their hands. The dramatic martyrologies of Foxe, like the fine, airy elegance of Sidney's *Apology,* display the expansion of English, its command of several registers and tones of feeling. In its exuberance, the language seemed bound to try new tricks, regardless of good sense or good taste. Two self-conscious semifictions by John Lyly sparked a brief vogue for a highly mannered style modeled on the rhetorical tricks of Greek sophists like Gorgias. Lyly's chief character betrays his ruling passion in his name, Euphues, the Fine Speaker. Metaphorical, antithetical, allusive, and wordy, Euphuism in its full-blown form was little more than a fop's fad. Lyly himself exhausted the vein in two books (*Euphues: the Anatomy of Wit,* 1579; and *Euphues and His England,* 1580). But though the experiment failed, it was as we say now, "a learning experience" for practitioners of the language. The ornate style of the seventeenth century owed at least a cautionary debt to Euphuism, and often something more.

When Martin Marprelate turned the tricks and japes of a stage buffoon to the ends of theological controversy (above, p. 164), it was striking evidence that different styles could be adapted to different occasions. Translators, who by nature are chameleons, were also quick to exploit varieties of English style. When he was translating the Spanish wit Guevara in 1557, Sir Thomas North set an example of the ornate, rhetorical, antithetical style; when he translated Plutarch's *Lives of the Eminent Grecians and Romans* in 1576, his manner was quite different. North could not get at Plutarch's original Greek, but worked from Jacques Amyot's rather stately and formal French version; what he added to it was a touch of Elizabethan zest and informality. The result was one of the classics of translation, a version so eloquent that in several of his Roman plays Shakespeare had to change no more than a few words to create glowing and vivid passages of blank verse. Not only the classics got translated. William Painter, in *The Palace of Pleasure* (two volumes, 1566, 1567) started a vogue by bringing into English a great number of short stories originally written in Latin, Italian, or French. These stories were popular in themselves, and writers of dramas or poems had no hesitation about using Painter's plots. Imitators followed. Geoffrey Fenton translated *Certain Tragical Discourses of Bandello* (1567) and George Pettie rounded up other stories into the ornately titled *Petite Palace of Pettie His Pleasure* (1576). In view of the fact that there was a translation of Apuleius's naughty fable of *The Golden Ass* as early as 1566, it is an oddity worth noticing that the first English version of Boccaccio's *Decameron* did not appear till 1624.

Poetical translators were not as a rule so venturous, or so successful in their ventures. Richard Stanyhurst's translation of the *Aeneid* (1582) made use of a Latinate hexameter, or something pretending to be such, which hardly anybody has failed to find ludicrous. Even Arthur Golding, though sometimes homely and humorous in his translation of Ovid, can't be said to have done much for English verse. But the prose translators tuned their instrument as they used it, and expanded its range as they applied it to new topics. The language was growing fast during the sixteenth century, attracting words from the continental tongues and from the newly popularized studies of Latin and Greek. Some of the words that the Elizabethans picked up or created for themselves never really made themselves at home in English, and they read strangely now. But a great many other words, which seem perfectly natural to us, sounded awkward at their first introduction. In one of the earliest discussions of metaphorical language (1550), a man named Richard Sherry undertook to defend such strange novelties as the words *scheme, trope, homily, usurped,* and *abolished.* With the language changing so fast under so many different pressures, it is remarkable indeed that English prose was able to consolidate itself as successfully as it did. At any rate, somewhere in the course of the century (depending on the author, his dialect, perhaps even the subject of which he is writing), it becomes clear that we have entered the world of modern English. Nobody thought or said so at the time, but historical hindsight finds convenient the triple division of the language into Old, Middle, and Modern.

A GRACE NOTE ON ENGLISH ART AND MUSIC

The age of Elizabeth gives us—not to be overlooked—the first native English painter of distinction. His name was Nicholas Hilliard, his dates are from 1537 or thereabouts to 1619. He worked entirely in miniature, painting portraits small enough to be carried in lockets, set in brooches, or held in the hand. After early training as a goldsmith in his father's shop, he worked for a while in France, but returned to England with the duke d'Alençon. He was a great favorite at court, where Elizabeth warmly endorsed his old-fashioned preference for line as against shading and modeling. The portraits he painted are among the most lovely, as they are also the rarest, artifacts that have come down to us from the Elizabethan age. Before Hilliard's time, many foreign artists visited England, of whom the most distinguished was the Swiss Hans Holbein, who did many portraits, in the "linear" style Elizabeth liked, of Henry VIII and his courtiers. About the same time as Holbein, Pietro Torrigiano the Florentine sculptor was imported to work on the tomb of Henry VII; and many foreign craftsmen of lesser stature worked on construction projects like Henry VIII's royal hunting lodge of Nonesuch. During the seventeenth century as well, foreign artists of major stature, like Peter Paul Rubens and Anthony Van Dyck, continued to be brought to England briefly. But not till the eighteenth century was there another native Englishman who could paint at the level of Nicholas Hilliard.

In sketching the background of Elizabethan poetry, we should not overlook the very advanced state of English music. Foreigners sometimes described the Elizabethans as "a nest of singing birds," and one reason was that their composers were talented and prolific. Men of that age made few sharp distinctions between popular and "serious" music; they never assembled in a concert hall, but they sang and played at home, on holidays, and in church. They had inherited many tunes from the medieval past, and picked up others in France or Italy. The art of singing madrigals, to the accompaniment of a set of virginals or a chest of viols such as no cultured family would be without, made music an integral part of English life.[23] The contrapuntal style of madrigals trained ordinary English folk from an early age in part singing, which Thomas Tallis developed into extravagantly intricate compositions, some for as many as forty voices. His colleague and successor was the stiffly Catholic William Byrd, who wrote mostly church music; *his* colleague and successor was Thomas Morley, who wrote mostly secular music, in the form of madrigals, canzonets, and ballets.[24] The

23. Virginals were small harpsichords, viols the ancestors of our violins and violas. Other instruments to be found in an Elizabethan household were lutes, mandolins, and recorders in several sizes and tones.

24. In 1510, we learn, a guild in Boston (Lincolnshire) hired Thomas Cromwell (the same who was later to be Henry VIII's inflexibly Protestant servant) to represent them at Rome in seeking certain privileges from Pope Julius II. With two retainers, he advanced into the papal presence, singing a three-part harmony and bringing as a gift for his Holiness some fine English jellies made with his own hands. The guild got its dispensations; Cromwell showed he knew the specialties of his native land.

songs were passed from singer to singer and group to group by word of mouth, they were copied and recopied by hand, and they were collected in volumes, of which one of the first was the pleasantly titled *Handful of Pleasant Delights* (1587). Miscellaneous collections of verses as well as songs were frequent in the age of Elizabeth; it was a sign of the fabulous artistic richness of the age that even the dust swept up in these catchall collections contained a goodly quota of diamonds.

The 1537 fresco for which this Holbein drawing of Henry VIII was a preparatory sketch no longer exists; it was, apparently, a terrifying image of a monarch. A foreign visitor who saw it in 1604 said he felt overwhelmed; and from the sketch, one can see why. Henry had just disposed of his first two wives and was about to take a third; he was at open odds with the pope and with a good many Protestants, he had just executed the entire Fitzgerald family and put down the "Pilgrimage of Grace." He was in no placatory mood, and Holbein caught the full charge of his rampaging energy.

Some of the money he did not waste on French wars Henry VIII spent erecting a chapel in Westminster Abbey to the memory of his late father. It was a gigantic undertaking. French designs were assiduously copied; Italian artists were imported to work for years on the bronze and marble adornments. The result is almost a church of its own, comprising a nave with aisles lined with carved oak stalls and ending in a constellation of small subchapels. From the ceiling with its intricate fan-shaped traceries hang the banners of the knights of the Bath, this being the special chapel of the order. Their colors add a blaze of spectacular display to an already ornate and opulent structure.

(Facing page) Hans Holbein the Younger came to England in 1528, bearing a letter of introduction to Sir Thomas More from his friend Erasmus. One immediate result was a large painting of More in the bosom of his family. A fire destroyed the painting itself more than four hundred years ago, but a preliminary sketch for it, marked with the names of the various persons and their ages, survives. More's many domestic bonds and plain middle-class circumstances (as revealed in this sketch) make a picture more genial and domestic than tidy. Because Holbein's gifts as a portraitist were much appreciated in England, he stayed for fifteen years, during which time he painted almost everyone of note at the court of Henry VIII.

Medieval castles were generally built for defense; when predators were on the loose, one had to be ready to fight them off. But with the establishment of domestic peace under the Tudors, more relaxed and comfortable building became possible. Compton Wynyates in Warwickshire was built with brick, not massive masonry, and its spacious windows open onto a garden, not a set of battlements. The many chimneys suggest a practical concern for keeping the interior warm; the topiary garden, with its many geometrical shapes, is a distinctive feature, but it is of recent origin. The Compton family, now earls of Northampton, have owned it for more than five hundred uninterrupted years, which perhaps accounts for its unusually fine state of preservation.

PALATIVM REGIVM IN ANGLIÆ REGNO APPELLATVM NONCIVTZ,
Hæ sði nusquam simile

Henry VIII built Nonesuch in Surrey as a royal hunting lodge; it was not only immense but very expensive, for the king imported the best foreign artisans to work on it. But death prevented the monarch from making much use of it himself, and though Elizabeth stayed in it from time to time, during the seventeenth century it fell into disrepair, was abandoned, and finally sold for the building material it contained. The engraver of this picture was a Dutchman, Joris Hofnagel, and his spelling of "Nonesuch" as "Nonciutz" is euphonic but not accurate; he made up, however, by explaining the word in Latin, "nusquam simile."

Crucial changes in the design of sixteenth-century ships are illustrated by a contrast between the *Mary Rose* of the early century, and the *Ark Royal,* which served as Lord Howard of Effingham's Armada flagship. The very lofty prow and stern of the earlier vessel made her hard to maneuver into the wind; the lower, longer, speedier *Ark Royal* carried many more guns—she was in effect a floating gun platform—and because she could be worked with fewer men, they could be better paid and more highly trained. The *Mary Rose* sank in 1545 because her crew neglected to close the lower gun ports in a high sea. The crews that fought the Armada were experienced, disciplined men; and the vessels in which they fought had been transformed, by the reforming hand of Sir John Hawkins, into first-rate fighting machines.

The English admiral victorious over the Armada. Lord Howard of Effingham, had a set of tapestries woven to commemorate his triumph. This one shows the Armada, in its crescent-moon formation, moving steadily up the channel as the smaller and less tightly knit English fleet hangs behind it, harassing, sniping, and ready to pick off the straggler, but not attempting for the moment any major action. To atone for the lack of drama, one notes, the tapestry artist has introduced a couple of highly imaginary whales, at play in the middle background.

An essential character of masques was expensive display. Courts were gaudy places in the normal course of things; masques were in effect fancy-dress balls organized around a sketchy plot and a good deal of flattery. These costumes were designed by Inigo Jones for some dancers in Ben Jonson's *Oberon* (1611), a masque which employed in addition such trick effects as a transparent palace and a chariot drawn by two white bears. The professional theater, where actors were trying to make money, not squander it, could dispose of few equivalent effects.

Our only contemporary picture of an Elizabethan theatrical interior was made by a Dutch visitor to London, Johannes De Witt, in 1595. He sent this crude sketch of the Swan theater, with a descriptive letter, to his friend Arend Van Buchel, who copied both into his journal—how accurately we cannot know, since De Witt's original document is lost. The open stage protruding into the pit (labeled "planities sive arena") is clear; behind it is the tiring house (labeled "mimorum aedes"). A second story of the house constitutes a gallery, which seems to be filled with spectators—the only ones shown in the theater. But since they can only be seeing the play from behind, and since many Elizabethan stage directions refer to an "upper" as well as a "lower" stage, it is possible that De Witt or Van Buchel misunderstood the function of the gallery. The roof ("heavens") above the gallery and supported by two pillars in front is plain in the drawing and confirmed by many stage directions. Three tiers of spectator seats seem to have been standard; De Witt estimates the seating capacity of the Swan as about three thousand spectators. He was particularly interested in the resemblance of English theaters to those of ancient Rome (as he envisaged them); this concern, as well as his own lack of skill at drawing, may have influenced a sketch done casually and perhaps from memory—which is, nonetheless, the basis of almost everything we know about the architecture of the Elizabethan theater.

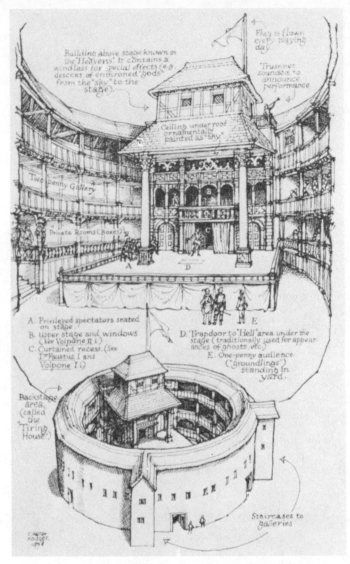

Hardly anything in C. Walter Hodges's modern reconstruction of the Globe theater is inconsistent with De Witt's crude contemporary sketch of the Swan; but Mr. Hodges is a far more careful student than De Witt as well as a much better draftsman. Besides, he shows a theater which had been rebuilt about twenty years after the De Witt drawing was made, and which, as a result of much accumulated experience, had many features which De Witt could not or did not see. (The curtained recess at the back of the stage and the trap door in its center are examples.) As for scenery, neither drawing shows very much; but lists of the "props" owned by acting companies show that they possessed or could improvise a good deal of it. And the costumes worn by actors, almost everyone agrees, were frequently magnificent.

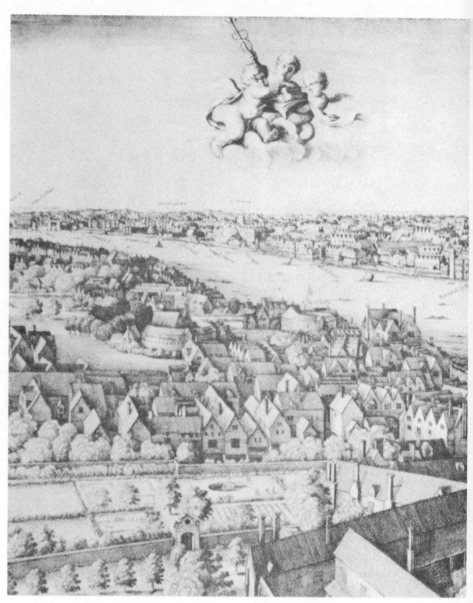

A section of an engraving of London in 1616 by J. C. Visscher shows the Bankside (south bank of the Thames) with the Globe theater alongside the Bear Garden and in the background, across the Thames, old St. Paul's with its truncated spire. The first Globe had burned down in 1613, so this is probably the second; it shows an octagonal three-story structure, with the flag flying over it to announce that a play will be given today.

7

Gathering Shades: The Last Years of Elizabeth (1588–1603)

With the defeat of the Armada, the focus of Elizabeth's reign shifts from foreign to domestic affairs. It is true that the king of Spain continued to plan new armadas for the subjugation of England, though his calculations faded further and further from the realm of reality. Occasionally, as in August of 1592, a rich Spanish or Portuguese vessel might be captured by English privateers;[1] but after 1588, Philip saw a gleam of light, armed his galleons with long-range culverins as well as heavy, short-range cannon, and had the American treasure fleet escorted by powerful convoys. The last fight of the *Revenge* (1591), which under Sir Richard Grenville stood off fifteen Spanish warships in an all-day battle, was a great piece of heroic English saga, but it also marked the end of easy plunder on the high seas. The fleet of which the *Revenge* was a part had done what every English naval force wanted to do, they had intercepted the main body of the Spanish treasureships. But the bullion was too well guarded to be reached; the battle fought by the *Revenge* was an accident, the result of faulty communications; the Spanish treasure reached Spain safely. Again, the wars in France

---

1. Elizabeth, who was a partner in the venture of Sir John Burgh that captured the *Madre de Dios* in 1592, made somewhere between 2,000 and 3,000 percent on her original investment; but this was a lucky stroke. Pickings were generally slim, and after Sir Richard Leveson got another galleon in 1602, there were no more.

required English intervention, especially after they brought Protestant Henri of Navarre into the dynastic picture: he took the throne in 1589, as Henri IV, though only after converting to Catholicism. But the main pressure that all these foreign involvements exerted on England came about through the existence of a war party gathered around the magnetic, unsteady figure of Robert Devereux, earl of Essex.

THE DASHING YOUNG FAVORITE

Queen Elizabeth was fifty-five in Armada year; Robert, earl of Essex, was just twenty-two. He appeared in the royal court, a bright, bold, ambitious young man, just when the queen's life had been darkened by the death of her old favorite, Leicester. Perhaps Raleigh had expected to be the new favorite; Essex stepped in to snatch the position and the rewards that went with it. They included lucrative offices (Master of the Horse), honors (the Garter), favors, easy access to the queen's ear; but the solid center of them all was money. Essex was extravagant, and the queen paid his debts; and when she conferred on him the right to share in the customs duties levied on imported sweet wines,[2] she made him a splendidly rich young man.

He was good looking, he was well connected (his sister Penelope had been Sir Philip Sidney's beloved "Stella"); he was master of that half-erotic, half-political innuendo in which the queen's courtiers expressed their devotion; when his spirits were high, he was a lot of fun. But from the first he was a jealous and demanding favorite. If he was to have the queen's favor, then Raleigh must not be countenanced; if Elizabeth bestowed a trifle on Charles Blount, later to be Lord Mountjoy, Essex was bound to say something snide that led to a duel. More ominously, the young man was determined not to be a carpet knight; he wanted to fight in the wars, and in 1587 tried to run away to help the Dutch against the Spanish; a little later he ran off with Drake and Norris to serve in an unsuccessful raid against Portugal. Courtiers were not supposed to leave court without the queen's permission, but these were youthful escapades, little more, and she forgave him. More serious were the events of 1591, when Essex got himself formally appointed to command a little troop of soldiers being sent to help Henri IV of France. All sorts of things went wrong. Gallant and irresponsible, Henri promised to pay for the English troops, then neglected to do so; Elizabeth had to pick up the tab. Essex wasted time on trivial and irrelevant adventures. He was brave enough for two, but boyish, foolish. Elizabeth ordered him home with his "army"; he obeyed, but before leaving France, knighted twenty-four of his followers, not because they had done anything to deserve it, but because they would

2. Technically, this was "farming" the customs; having paid a lump sum for his privilege, the farmer appointed agents, and tried to make sure the receipts would reimburse his original expense, take care of costs, and yield him a handsome profit.

have if given the chance. It was an impulsive, "popularity" gesture, redounding much to the young commander's credit with the new knights, much less agreeable to his royal mistress. Making knights was her prerogative, of which she had been deliberately chary; she did not like to have her honors cheapened. The jolly expedition to France had been expensive, and had accomplished nothing. She was distinctly cross, and she kept Essex at home till 1596, when with Raleigh and the Admiral, Lord Howard of Effingham, he was allowed to lead an expedition against the Spanish port city of Cadiz. Of all these raiding expeditions, it was by far the most successful. Raleigh sailed the English fleet into Cadiz harbor, Essex stormed ashore at the head of a landing party, and all the miserable duke of Medina Sidonia could do was incinerate the Spanish vessels, which had crowded into the inner harbor, before the English could loot them. That deprived the expeditionary force of much booty, on which Queen Elizabeth was counting to recoup her expenses. Worse yet, the soldiers and sailors who pillaged Cadiz took most of the plunder for themselves and never declared it to their commanders. On the positive side, Essex had impressed everybody with his courage and his courtesy—a "verray parfit gentle knight" in truth. Nuns had been led gently to safety, priests and churches were spared, there was no raping or burning. Essex had got along with everybody, even Raleigh; the very loot that he took for himself bespoke a man of culture.[3] After occupying Cadiz for two weeks, the expedition returned home, well pleased with itself—to face Queen Elizabeth, in a towering rage. She had paid out £50,000 to equip the expedition; all she was to receive from it, apparently, was a stack of bills representing wages for unpaid seamen. One circumstance only saved Essex's standing with the queen. After the sack of Cadiz, he had wanted to wait offshore and intercept the Spanish treasure fleet; he was overruled, and submitted. Now came word that he had indeed been right, that the treasure fleet had sailed safely into harbor just two days after the English raiders left. No doubt it was well armed, and would have been hard to take, but at least Essex had been right in wanting to wait. That softened Elizabeth's rancor against him personally; but still a contrast remained in his mind. To the country at large he was, after Cadiz, a hero, young, valiant, honorable, successful; to Elizabeth, he was a gaudy extravagant. Feeling undervalued, he cast about for ways to impress the cross, stingy old woman with his own immense merits.

THE BRAINS BEHIND ESSEX: ANTHONY AND FRANCIS BACON

Well before the Cadiz expedition, a number of young men, some bright, others just bold, had gathered behind the favorite, anticipating that he was or could be

3. The library assembled by Bishop Jerome Osorio was one of the most extensive in Europe. After his return to England, Essex gave it to Sir Thomas Bodley, who presented it to the university of Oxford as part of those munificent donations which caused the library there to be known as the Bodleian.

made a man of power and influence. They knew the queen was aging and had no direct heir; they saw that her chief agent, William Cecil, now Lord Burghley, grew every day more frail, while the son who was to take his place had been weak from birth, a hunchback. They admired Essex as the champion of the Protestant cause, a bold leader. And their minds turned to the way in which Henry IV had deprived Richard II of his throne, to Henry VII's timely intervention against Richard III. Most of them, no doubt, did not contemplate treason against the queen; but when the queen should die . . . well, what then? and why not? Among the keener and subtler spirits backing the still-vague intentions of the earl were two brothers, cousins to Sir Robert Cecil.[4] Anthony, the elder of the Bacon brothers, was a cripple, but he had an independent income; Francis, the younger, was a barrister and after 1593 a member of Parliament, but he was badly strapped for money. Both were sharp as razors. Having tried in vain to get help from their uncle Burghley, they switched their loyalties to Essex, encouraging him to consolidate his position by taking high office in the administration. To help him do this, they organized an extensive private intelligence service, which enabled the earl to know things, happening far and wide, before even the chief ministers of the queen did.[5] Naturally, a man well established in the seats of power would put his followers and sympathizers in office with him. But in practice the plan broke down. Essex would have liked to have William Cecil's job as principal secretary to Elizabeth; but while the gallant earl was away at Cadiz, Elizabeth formally appointed Robert Cecil to take his father's post. Essex tried to get Francis Bacon the post of attorney general, but after long delays it went to Sir Edward Coke; Essex pushed Bacon for solicitor general, but again there were delays, and the office went elsewhere. It was the same with the post of master of the rolls. One reason for these repeated failures was that in 1593 Bacon had rashly spoken out against granting certain taxes to the queen. But another reason was the queen's mistrust of Essex. Leicester had been able to influence her policies through the many friends he had got appointed to posts in the government; she was not going to repeat that mistake. Bacon wrote to Essex a cold, clear, intelligent letter, laying out the way to calm her suspicions and solidify her good opinion.[6] But calculated policy was no part of Essex's charac-

4. The brothers were sons of Sir Nicholas Bacon, lord keeper of the great seal under Elizabeth, whose second wife, Anne, was the sister of Burghley's second wife, Mildred.

5. Intelligence, in those distant days, was a matter of maintaining not only domestic informers but foreign correspondents in great number. Sir Francis Walsingham, Burghley's chief aide, received information regularly from every part of England, from forty-five cities on the Continent, as well as from undercover police agents. Unhappily, when amateurs, even very clever amateurs, assumed the job, they were likely to make bad mistakes. Essex was led by his informants to suspect Dr. Roderigo Lopez, the queen's physician and a Portuguese Jew, of plotting to poison the queen. Though almost certainly innocent, the wretched man was tried and executed in 1594. There were anti-Semitic riots at the time, and a strong argument suggests that the figure of Shylock, in "The Merchant of Venice," written about this time, derives from Dr. Lopez.

6. Essex must present himself as a judicious and informed administrator, and by no means a man of exclusively military interests. He must show himself supple and obedient to the queen's commands, developing a number of ostensibly "important" projects simply so that at her command he

ter; he crossed the queen instead of placating her, sulked and raged till he got himself appointed to a military position—in short, made clear to her that he thought of himself not as an adaptable servant but as an aspiring master. Bacon, lucid and practical as always, read the signs; slowly and cold-bloodedly he moved away from his devotion to the headstrong young favorite and aligned himself with that cousin, Robert Cecil, whom he had once despised.

FALL OF A FAVORITE

In the summer of 1597, Essex insisted on heading another naval expedition to attack the ports of Spain; John Donne, like many another young man of fashion, took part in it, and described in two early poems the storm which battered it and the dead calm which followed. Later in the summer, when the fleet was refitted, Essex led it to the Azores in search of the Spanish treasure fleet, but the fleet was missed, a shore attack was botched, the expedition ended in fiasco. Again there were bickerings with Elizabeth; and they intensified next year, when a rebellion by Hugh O'Neill, earl of Tyrone and ruler of Ulster, created a crisis in Ireland. There was talk of intervention by Spain (within two years it was to become a reality); councils were divided. During a discussion, the queen proposed to send one man to Ireland as lord deputy; Essex insisted on another. He made a gesture of contempt, and turned his back on her; she boxed his ears. He nearly drew his sword on her; courtiers intervened. And yet he found his way back into her favor, or partly so; at any rate, she appointed him to bring order to Ireland, and in March of 1599, with an army of 16,000 men and 1,300 horse, Essex left for the Irish wars. It was exactly what Bacon had told him not to do; and the circumstances were perilous. Any sort of failure would bring him down, and success could only augment Elizabeth's suspicions. In the event, his expedition was the worst catastrophe anyone could have envisaged. He wasted months in trivialities while his army dwindled from disease and desertion. When he finally moved against Tyrone, his forces were too weak to offer battle. The two leaders met apart, and negotiated in secret, some said with treasonous intent, at any rate to Tyrone's complete satisfaction. Essex, half insane with frustration and anxiety, crossed the Irish sea with a small band of friends (abandoning his command, of course) and galloped to the royal castle of Nonesuch where Elizabeth was staying. Mud-spattered and haggard, he burst into her boudoir while she was dressing (28 September 1599). She had not yet put on her wig.

She received him quietly, but soon sent him away and had him confined to quarters. After a few days he fell ill; she kept him under surveillance. But he really was sick, and in his sickness said ugly things of the queen, which were reported to her. His command in Ireland was given to Charles Blount, Lord

---

might lay them aside. He should be careful of his dress and language, showing himself always composed and prepared. Excellent advice for anyone but the man to whom it was addressed!

Mountjoy, who calmly and confidently inflicted a crushing defeat on Tyrone and captured a Spanish contingent sent to help him. Essex was brought to trial on charges of mismanaging the Irish campaign and returning to England without the queen's orders. He humbly pleaded guilty to the charges, begged for mercy, and was let off. And then she withdrew from him that grant for farming the customs on imported sweet wines which had made him rich. The infatuate man tried to raise a rebellion with a group of his old military friends; he was counting on the Puritans of London town to support him, and on King James to come from Scotland with help. Nothing worked. The city refused to rise, his gang of bravos melted away, King James had no time to move.[7] Only the old queen, nearly seventy now, was completely fearless. With hardly a trace of hesitation she had Essex jailed, convicted of treason, and executed. He was only thirty-four years old when he went to the block (25 February 1601). Like Wolsey before and Buckingham after him, Essex in his meteoric career blazed wide across the heavens the power of monarchs and their courts to make and break subjects.

SUNDERING AND RECONCILIATION: THE HOUSE OF COMMONS

After 1588 Queen Elizabeth was at odds with her Parliaments almost continually. Troubles with Essex disturbed her personally; he was like a spoiled child, till finally he became just too bothersome and dangerous to endure. But the Parliaments also made trouble for her, on a more mature level. The House of Commons was dissatisfied with the religious settlement. Those fires in which Queen Mary consumed living men and women at Smithfield (fires of which Foxe's book was a constant reminder) had left deep scars on the consciousness of the survivors; they wanted nothing to do with a church which retained even a rag or shred of Roman Catholicism. Comparing the church of England with the ideal purity of the church founded by Christ, they found it seriously compromised by flaws, all of which they attributed to its incompletely repudiated "papistical" past. The bishops were proud, luxury-loving men, popes in miniature; the prayer book had been modeled on a Catholic missal; some priests were still ignorant, some statues and stained-glass windows (graven images) still adorned British cathedrals. And indeed, partly for other reasons having nothing to do with the church of Rome, the condition of the English church was not good.

Long-continued inflation had severely eroded the income of a parson who had to depend on fixed rents; whenever the value of money deteriorated, his income shrank, and, as a man of the cloth, he was thought a brute to raise rents. Also many tithes had been commuted—that is, instead of amounting to a tenth of a

---

7. About James's complicity in Essex's plot (though it was feeble and indecisive) there was no doubt; but Elizabeth, who had settled on him to inherit the throne at her death, had nowhere else to turn, and so concealed his guilt. He had denied his mother and tried to betray his benefactress, and was thus, between meanness and incapacity, the only candidate for the British throne.

farmer's actual increase (which might mean, say, 1.3 piglets and 10 percent of a calf), the tithe was figured as a flat sum, say, 2 shillings. Once that had doubtless approximated a 10-percent tithe; but now, after inflation, it might amount to no more than 1 percent. Worse, tithes, being a tax like any other, could be sold and bought; so the sixteenth-century parson might find that one of his predecessors, hard up for cash, had sold to the local squire or merchant tithes intended to support the ministry. Thus the condition of the clergy deteriorated. Fewer young men took orders, because they had better opportunities elsewhere; those who did enter the church received such miserable wages (especially now that the clergy could marry and have families) that they could survive only by getting several different benefices and serving them all inadequately.[8] When the Puritans complained that the church was full of "dumb dogs"—semiliterate, inarticulate parsons—they were right; when they complained of superstitious practices and profound ignorance among the laity, they were generally right again. Many of these evils went back to the grabbing of church lands under Henry VIII; but that was not a very good point for Puritans to raise, since it implied that things would be better under Catholicism.

Another cause of complaint was the deteriorating condition of the churches themselves. Many of the ancient structures, including St. Paul's Cathedral in London, had become shabby and half ruinous after centuries of neglect. Peddlers, booksellers, pimps, idlers, gossips, and general London riffraff thronged "Paul's Walk," making such a noise ("like that of bees," as a contemporary described it; "a strange humming or buzz . . . a kind of still roar or loud whisper") that services could hardly be heard. The Puritans themselves did not much mind this moneychanging in the temple, and in the seventeenth century they opposed efforts to cleanse and beautify Paul's. They wanted less money spent on the fabric of the church, more on the provision of learned and godly preachers. But the sad state of church structures, combined with an insufficient clergy, made the church a fair target for critics, who shot, sometimes, from opposite directions.

POINTS OF PRIVILEGE

The standing difficulty was that Queen Elizabeth did not want the Parliament to meddle in matters that she and her bishops could, as she thought, perfectly well

8. Pluralism was an ancient practice and widespread. The parson might reside at one of his livings, and hire curates for the others, paying them a fraction of the living's income and keeping the rest for himself; or he might preach alternate Sundays at one living and then another. One might hold a living along with a university professorship, serving the two offices simultaneously. Simply to survive, some rural parsons had to do so much farming that they made very rude preachers; for them, and for the hopelessly unlearned, the church provided a book of homilies, or made-to-order sermons, from which they were to read one homily per week through the year, and so through the book again, year after year (SFR, E.6).

handle. She was by law the head of the church, as her father had been before her. Parliamentary agitation for church reform was just one step away from popular agitation; and to that she would not submit. So far as they could, therefore, her ministers and council members shut off debate on the floor of the Commons. But when they met with a bold, determined man like Sir Peter Wentworth, they could not quiet him. His free attack on the church establishment got Sir Peter in trouble in 1576 and 1587; both times he ended in the Tower, protesting that the traditional freedom of the Parliament to speak its mind was being curtailed. It was and it wasn't. Parliament members did care tremendously about the state of their souls; on the other hand, it was hardly likely that issues of salvation and damnation were going to be decided in the House of Commons by majority vote.[9] The theater of discussion, for matters of dogma and discipline, was not properly political but theological. Just at this point, by no coincidence whatever, the Puritans came up against one of the most massive and impregnable books of theological polemic ever written. *Of the Laws of Ecclesiastical Polity* was its title; its author was a clergyman of the English church named Richard Hooker. The first four books appeared in 1573, a fifth in 1597; the author died in 1600, leaving three other books unfinished.

RATIONAL AUTHORITARIANISM: THE BOOK OF HOOKER

Hooker's book is entirely directed against one basic premise of the Calvinist argument: that the Presbyterian system of church government is exactly prescribed in Scripture and must be precisely followed. Gently, but with a touch of verbal acid, he points out that Calvin, though "incomparably the wisest man that ever the French church did enjoy since the hour it enjoyed him," was brought up in the study of civil law, not theology. "Divine knowledge he gathered not by hearing or reading so much as by teaching others." (In fact, Calvin never took a degree in divinity, or received holy orders; his extraordinary instant authority rested on the *Institutes*, published when he was just twenty-six years old; the printing press was his pulpit to Europe.) Thus the system he proposed, Hooker argues, was founded like all other social structures on the deductions, inferences, and practical judgments of a human, not a divine, intention.

The fundamental doctrines of Christianity, Hooker allows, are laid down in Scripture; but churches, being associations of human beings seeking prudential human ends (such as a measure of order, uniformity, and seemliness in public worship) can and must make for themselves rules founded ultimately on reason

9. The lord keeper, Sir John Puckering, had a point when he said, in 1593, that parliamentary liberty of speech allowed every man to say yea or nay to bills "with some short declaration of his reason therein," but not "to speak of all causes as him listeth and to frame a form of religion or a state of government as to their idle brains shall seem meetest." Freedom, in other words, was not absolute but relative to the function of the institution claiming it.

and common sense. Thus the church of England justifies separation from Rome because under Catholicism the fundamentals of Christian faith were being obliterated, yet exercises the usual privilege of human societies in asking that its members conform to certain common usages and uniform observances, the ground of which is not a Scriptural text but human reason. Neither Hooker nor any of his contemporaries (except, perhaps, Robert Browne: see above, p. 163) had any idea of general toleration in the modern sense. It was a first premise of all the disputants that there must be only one church in a society, to which everyone should belong. In practice, Hooker's *via media* (middle way) between Rome and Geneva was not half as tolerant as it sounded. For it called on the Puritans to suppress the voice of conscience in many matters which they thought (rightly or wrongly) crucial to their salvation, and to follow (right or wrong) the reason of a legally appointed bishop. But the basic position of Hooker's book set the tone for the Anglican establishment down to the present day. No small part of the book's lasting effectiveness can be assigned to its prose style. It is dignified, yet flexible and various, calm yet often touched with quiet wit. Hooker writes like a man determined to say nothing that cannot be demonstrated; he avoids the shrill partisan ferocity of vulgar controversialists. There are no scoffs, no caricatures of the opponent's position, no nagging point-by-point refutations of an argument. Hooker builds his position on deep-laid foundations, and makes a point of himself seeming open to rational conviction. His pages, though free from the least hint of rhetorical artifice, bring into English and adapt to close polemical argument, not only the structures of Ciceronian style but its capacity for sustained discourse, deep-rooted and many-branched. Hooker's sentences are filled with concessive and balancing clauses; he considers ideas, not one at a time, but comparatively, weighing them. Not for nothing did his generation refer to him as the "judicious" Mr. Hooker. Zealous Puritans, of course, would never be convinced that "judicious" could possibly define a proper attitude toward religion. But Hooker had captured for the establishment the voice of what was called "reason." His reputation stood high and lasted long.

SUCCESSION AND MONOPOLIES

Brave and honorable man that he was, Sir Peter Wentworth got into permanent trouble when he turned in 1593 from reforming the ecclesiastical establishment to settling the question of who should succeed Queen Elizabeth on the throne. This was a question that had dogged the queen since the first day of her accession; and like the governance of the church, it was a matter that she took to be her own particular business. (She distinguished "matters of state," on which she wanted parliamentary advice only when she asked for it, from "matters of commonwealth," on which members could speak their minds any time.) Puritans were terrified that some Catholic potentate would get control of the English throne;

Elizabeth, viewing the matter in a hard political light, knew that as soon as she publicly named someone to be her successor, English political factions would start making up to him. In any case, her dignity was involved, as a lady and a monarch; she would not be dictated to.[10] Accordingly, when Sir Peter tried to tell her what she should do in the matter, he went to the Tower, and for good. But this repeated jailing of a member for speaking his mind on the floor of the house sat ill with the whole Commons. What exactly were their rights? Voting yea or nay on a bill was all very good; but there were bills which the queen's known displeasure, and the influence of the queen's council in the Commons, would not allow to come to a vote. Could individual members introduce and debate such bills or not? For the moment, the plain answer was no, the individual member could not. For the future, the question was whether a group of members, without rendering themselves subject to the treason laws, could meet together and agree in advance to push a bill disagreeable to the royal authority and the royal administration. That was a question, however, for the next reign.

More urgent in the last Parliament of Elizabeth was the question of royal monopolies. These were forms of indirect taxation, money-raising devices which became more prevalent in the last years of the reign because, despite Elizabeth's penny-pinching, the costs of government continued to rise. Partly this rise was due to inflation, partly to the increasing complexity of government itself. In the early days of her reign, Elizabeth had enjoyed the services of Sir Thomas Gresham, a financial wizard and unscrupulous diplomat, who knew the ins and outs of the European money markets like no other man of his day. But Sir Thomas had died in 1579, and no equivalent magician took his place.[11] In any case, borrowing was not the answer; government in England was starving because the system of taxation, on which everything depended, was inadequate and antiquated. Elizabeth had only a fraction of the annual income that Spain and France could levy, and four-fifths of this came from her own royal estates, only one-fifth from taxation. Nagging over money thus became a regular and disagreeable feature of every parliamentary session, and to get away from this Elizabeth turned to a form of hidden taxation, the granting of monopolies. Against these hateful and fundamentally unprofitable taxes Parliament mounted a campaign; and here at least Elizabeth could, and wisely did, give way. She promised a royal procla-

10. In 1579 a rash Puritan printer named John Stubbs had tried to dissuade her from marrying the duke d'Anjou by printing an outspoken pamphlet against this or any other French marriage. For the offense to the queen as well as to a friendly foreign power, he was condemned to lose his right hand. (After it was cut off, he removed his hat with his left, waved it, and cried, "God save the queen!") We are appalled, no doubt, at the savagery of the sentence; but the idea of conducting delicate diplomatic negotiations subject to loud interruptions by crude moral stereotypers was an unwelcome novelty in those days.

11. Apart from "Gresham's law," which states that bad money drives out good, Sir Thomas left a major legacy to the English nation in "Gresham College," a vernacular and popular academy in London, to which may be traced an enormous number of the scientific inventions of the age to come. See below, p. 229.

mation to remedy the abuse. When it was issued, the house begged permission to come and express their thanks; they crowded into the presence, and heard the speech which was remembered for generations as Queen Elizabeth's "golden speech." In accepting the thanks and affections of the members, she assured them of her own, saying that whatever they bestowed on her, she accepted only to bestow it on them again. "It is not my desire," she concluded, "to live and reign longer than my life and reign shall be for your good. And though you have had, and may have, many mightier princes sitting in this seat, yet you never had, nor shall have, any that will love you better."

It was a magnificent finale, in the grand theatrical style of a great queen. In fact, her proclamation did not really solve the problem of monopolies, and we shall hear much more of this unpopular practice, over the next forty years. But the end of the queen's time was at hand. She celebrated the forty-fourth anniversary of her accession, 17 November 1602; but early in the new year, she fell ill of a bronchial infection, refused medication, and refused to eat. As her last royal duty, she nodded assent to James of Scotland as her successor, something she had intended to do all along. He was a safe choice—doubtless a little shifty, but an English Parliament could watch over that; and if one went back to Margaret, daughter of Henry VII, he had a bit of Tudor blood in his veins. He had been expecting the inheritance for years, not very patiently at times, and his reward came when on the morning of 24 March 1603 Queen Elizabeth died.

AN AGE OF GOLD

The sudden flowering of accomplished and inspired literature that took place during the last fifteen years of Elizabeth's reign, and spilled over into the reign of James, occurred in two main areas—drama and poetry. Significant work was done in prose: the treatise of Hooker, the essays of Bacon, some tentative ventures at prose narrative. But the big achievements which have made "Elizabethan" suggestive of an age of gold took the form of poems and plays. Why the English language, with such a scrappy background of achievement, suddenly exploded into imaginative brilliance is an intriguing question.

THE NASCENT STAGE

For the creation of great drama, it's apparent, a goodly number of social conditions had to come together, as in fact we can find them doing during the 1570s and 1580s. The opening of public theaters in London ("The Theater" in 1577, "The Curtain" shortly thereafter) took drama out of the academies and out of courtly assembly rooms (where it might have lost all its vitality in attenuated allegories and learned allusions), and brought it into the presence of a larger, rougher audience.[12] This was not pure gain; London audiences, or at least the "groundlings" who got in cheap and stood in the pit (we would call it the "orchestra"), had an unbounded appetite for rant and melodrama. There is many a phrase in Shakespeare to suggest that he thought ill of the crude swaggering and roaring too frequent in the popular theater of his day.[13] But the universality of his appeal derives from the fact that he had to engage a vulgar as well as an erudite audience. Creating that audience for which Shakespeare wrote and played was much more than a matter of opening a gate and selling tickets for tuppence.

In the first place, the audience had to be persuaded that playgoing was not immoral or detrimental to salvation.[14] We take such an attitude for granted, but the Elizabethan theater could not; indeed, throughout this period, theaters were generally relegated to the "liberties"—i.e. to the outskirts of London town, where they kept company with bear-gardens, bowling greens, low taverns, and bawdy houses. A good part of London society, the Puritan middle class, never did reconcile itself to theatergoing; their absolute ignorance of the simplest dramatic conventions is burlesqued in *The Knight of the Burning Pestle* by Beaumont and Fletcher (1613). Subtract the Puritan middle class from Shakespeare's audience, and subtract most women, whose respectability would be compromised by appearing in a theater;[15] those who came out of an afternoon to see a play would be mostly the idle poor and the idle rich, gentry and riffraff. Yet these were not illiterate yokels, far from it; living in a metropolis, they were informed (as rural plowmen would not have been) about the world, the history of their own land, current events. Above all, they could be trusted to exercise their imaginations. When they witnessed the battle of Shrewsbury being fought onstage, the Elizabethan audience had to transform four or five actors with wooden

12. An Elizabethan playhouse like "The Globe" probably held up to 2,000 spectators; most theaters were smaller, and those which were roofed over, like the indoor theater at the Blackfriars, must have been much smaller. But a play could be repeated in the public theaters till everyone in London who wanted to had seen it. Plays given at court or in the halls of private houses used up their audience the first night. Being able to repeat a play made steadier employment for the actors and bigger profits for the company.

13. "Oh," says Hamlet, "it offends me to the soul to hear a robustious periwig-pated fellow tear a passion to tatters, to very rags, to split the ears of the groundlings, who for the most part are capable of nothing but inexplicable dumb shows and noise. I would have such a fellow whipped for o'erdoing Termagant. It out-herods Herod. Pray you avoid it" (Act III, scene 2).

14. Superstitions about the stage ran very deep. The legend goes that when *Dr. Faustus* was being played at Exeter, and various actors impersonating devils appeared on stage, they all faltered and fell silent because it appeared *there was one more of them than anyone could account for.* They called off the play, fled the town, and spent the night praying in the open fields. For decades after the event allegedly occurred, the story continued to be told.

15. Whether the players provoked the bourgeois by insulting middle-class values or the bourgeois were basically hostile to the stage has been disputed; but of the mutual dislike there's no doubt. Naturally, this hostility did not prevent an idle prentice from pleading sick grandmother and sliding off of an afternoon to visit the playhouse. That was a point his employer was likely to make in denouncing the players. Some bourgeois were obviously more strait-laced, and some plays more scandalous, than others. But middle-class hostility to the plays was a very general fact.

swords and leather helmets into two clashing armies; the Chorus introducing Act III of *Henry V* summons the audience to imagine an entire fleet laden with an army sailing across the Channel to Harfleur. More startling yet, when he went to see *Julius Caesar*, the Elizabethan playgoer would have nothing to look at but an actor in the common trunk hose and doublet, orating on a bare stage, with at most a signpost at one side saying, "The Roman Forum." Yet he would be expected to imagine togas and temples, a senate house, an imperial capital. It was an audience in whose minds many moral and social commonplaces could be taken for granted, acquainted with a good deal of history but mixing it with legend, knowing the catchwords of theology but not necessarily taking them very seriously. They laughed at Falstaff's wit but also at his grossness, had a quick ear for metaphorical language, a sharp eye for the absurd, and no very solid commitment to the proprieties.

To appeal to such an audience, one needed a special sort of author—young, as a rule, and clever; educated, but possessing the popular, even the vulgar, touch. Such men might in former days, when the social structure was more rigid, have entered the church; there are stories of John Skelton's behavior in the pulpit which suggest he was a comedian who missed his vocation. In London now (a city of 200,000 in 1600, almost three times its population of a century before) there were many bright young men who came to town and tried to live by their wits. When they were con-men with actual criminal intent, they were called cony catchers (rabbit trappers), and there was quite a literature about them; when they wrote popular amusements, they might be more respectable, but they still felt an affinity with criminal tricksters. An odd character named Autolycus strolls through Shakespeare's *The Winter's Tale;* he sells ballads to dolts, and under that cover picks their pockets. Possibly in that figure Shakespeare has delineated sardonically his own literary vocation. Making money by the use of a pen, it should be recalled, was a brand-new experience in England. A few writers had expected, and some had even got, gifts from patrons; but that was indirect payment. Taking money direct from the public was something else, and the playwrights evidently felt a bit of wicked glee at getting away with it.

Perhaps because the procedure was new, the actual amounts involved were meager. Most plays were sold for a lump sum, to the theatrical producer of a particular company. Account books survive which show that authors were paid somewhere between £3 and £10 per play; and in most cases, that was it. The play could run for a while, be revived, be sold to another company, or simply pirated. (Writers of the newly invented shorthand sometimes sat in the audience and wrote down the text during a performance; or, after a play's run was concluded, one might assemble the actors in a tavern, have them go through their parts, and emerge with a fairly complete script at the cost of a few ales.) A specially successful play might even be brought to court for a command performance. But few of these fortunate circumstances brought any extra money to the playwright. His sale of the text generally constituted his reward. A fast, adaptable writer could survive on this sort of money, but barely. Thomas Dekker wrote or collaborated in some 44 plays (of which six survive); but he spent a good deal of his later life in jail for debt. Thomas Heywood claimed to have had a hand in 220 plays, mostly lost now; but for long periods of time, he had to work at other trades to make ends meet. Only Shakespeare retired from the business with a comfortable sufficiency, and that because he had been a shareholder in a major company (the Lord Chamberlain's, later the King's) and a successful actor as well as a playwright. The folio volume in which his plays were collected appeared only seven years after his death; of the 36 plays it contains, 17 had never before been printed in any form.

Early plays had alternated between raw, rude farces like *Gammer Gurton's Needle,* and bloody oratorical tragedies modeled on those of Lucius Annaeus Seneca.[16] John Lyly lifted prose comedy to the level of deft and witty verbal exchange; he was able to do this, and interested in doing it, because he aspired mainly (and, as it turned out, vainly) to a post at court, where wit was much appreciated. Quite different was Christopher Marlowe, who raised tragedy out of the horrors of Senecanism and established a lofty but not ranting mode of blank verse. The vaulting ambition of Marlowe's heroes, the proud march of his iambic rhythms, anticipate the more complex psychology and intricate rhythms of Shakespeare's later tragedies. These predecessors of Shakespeare began to write their plays within a few years after the opening of the public theaters, during the 1580s; in addition to Lyly and Marlowe, they included George Peele, Robert Greene, Thomas Lodge, Thomas Nash, and Thomas Kyd. All these writers but Kyd had at least attended a university, and it seems they looked with no friendly eyes on the competition of William Shakespeare, an actor from Stratford with no academic credentials to speak of.[17]

A QUICK SURVEY OF THE BARD

So much has been written about Shakespeare that a history of England and its literature must plead limitations of space, and remain frankly perfunctory. We know very little of his literary apprenticeship, and probably it was not extensive.

16. Seneca was a Stoic philosopher and tutor of the emperor Nero who, in gratitude, forced him to commit suicide. Though crude and bombastic, his tragedies were written in Latin, and consequently all ten of them were translated into English between 1559 and 1581, while the much finer plays of Aeschylus, Sophocles, and Euripides remained in their original Greek. *Titus Andronicus* is Shakespeare's venture at a Senecan tragedy; it is a mode from which he soon liberated himself, and there is some feeling that he was not even the author of this one example.

17. One must mention here, simply in order to be rid of it, the ridiculous argument that Shakespeare was not Shakespeare but somebody else. Francis Bacon is usually advanced as the alternative author of Shakespeare's plays, though a number of different literary noblemen have also attracted adherents. The subject is of interest only as it illustrates the power of an *idée fixe* to dominate otherwise rational creatures.

His first plays (*Henry VI* in three parts, *Titus Andronicus,* and *The Comedy of Errors*) are, surely, no finished masterpieces. But when the theaters were closed by plague from June 1592 to April 1594, Shakespeare took advantage of the forced leisure to publish two sophisticated erotic narrative poems, "Venus and Adonis," and "The Rape of Lucrece." Poems of this character, witty, polished, rhetorical, and vaguely obscene, were much the vogue at court; that Shakespeare wrote such poems and dedicated them (on terms implying some personal acquaintance) to Henry Wriothesley, earl of Southampton, suggests that already he was more than a hack dramatic author. And it is a notable fact that as Shakespeare asserted his full presence, his predecessors all dropped away,[18] leaving him, till the advent of a new generation which flourished almost entirely in the seventeenth century, the supreme dramatist of his age.

It's customary to divide Shakespeare's dramatic career into three convenient parts. During the 1590s he wrote mostly comedies and histories, with a first romantic tragedy, *Romeo and Juliet,* in 1594. At the century's end, the comedies turn very sour; *Troilus and Cressida* and *Measure for Measure* are plays so muddied with sexual anger that they still baffle interpretation. They are followed by a series of majestic tragedies, starting with *Hamlet* in 1600 and ending with the savagely misanthropic *Timon of Athens* in 1607. The last four plays, over the period 1608–1611, are commonly described as "romances." They have many elements of artifice and spectacle, they are cheerfully indifferent to literal realism, and the note of reconciliation is impossible to overlook. Speculation about biographical facts capable of "explaining" this pattern has naturally been rife; even if we knew much more than we do about Shakespeare's personal life, it's doubtful that mere domestic details would "explain" the vibrant exultation of *Antony and Cleopatra* or the special air of precious mystery surrounding those lost princesses Perdita and Miranda of *The Winter's Tale* and *The Tempest.*

For centuries, the acute and rational French used to describe Shakespeare as an unpolished and careless barbarian. Sometimes they granted him native genius, sometimes not, but the rudeness they insisted on. Anglo-Saxons used to bristle at this; but if we say simply that Shakespeare's plays tend to have an expressive or suggestive shape, rather than a formal structure, the distinction remains and the invidium disappears. Shakespeare's management of form is, in a word, psychological; the harmonies he creates are defined in terms of the reader's response, rather than in structures of objective action. To pick a single example from *Henry IV, Part 1:* scene 1 of Act II takes us into an inn yard at Rochester to savor a colloquy between two carriers and an ostler. The conversation in no way advances the action of the play, it is vulgar to a degree, and in a fundamentally serious drama about the making of a monarch, it seems out of place. But this is only if we define very formally the unity of the play. The scene of the carriers deepens

18. Of the seven predecessors of Shakespeare mentioned above, only Lyly was as much as ten years his senior; but their mortality was heavy, and most drifted, before their death, into activities other than the stage.

and complicates our feelings, not altogether antipathetic, about the vulgar life through which Prince Hal is now moving to find his princely self. At any rate, since the French have become accustomed to psychological form (it is the principle of symbolist poetry), one hears less talk of Shakespeare's incorrectness.

DRAMAS ON THE STAGE AND ON THE PAGE

The staging of Elizabethan plays is a complex and conjectural subject. Only one sketchy drawing of an Elizabethan theater has come down to us, done by a visiting Dutchman named DeWitt; from this we can see that the stage was raised about to the eye-level of the groundlings, and pushed forward into their midst (we would call it an apron stage, except that behind it there was no proscenium arch or curtain). The groundlings stood in the open air, before and around it. Part of the stage was covered by a roofed structure (the "heavens") supported on posts; angels could descend from heaven on a wire, as devils could rise out of the ground through a trapdoor. At the back of the stage was a little alcove, "the room behind the stage," which could be screened off or used to represent an inner room. But though this much is pretty clear, we must guess at the number of exits and entrances, imagine the way in which the stage could be divided into two rooms, and conjecture about what scenic props, machinery, and costuming were available to the stage manager. We know that locations were often indicated simply by a hand-lettered sign, "Thebes" or "Rome," set at the side of the stage. Scenes which in printed scripts are labeled "another part of the forest," and the like, were probably not dressed up at all on stage. But most of what we know or imagine about the staging of Elizabethan plays has to be reconstituted painfully from the stage directions in the plays themselves. Most of the public outdoor theaters, it is supposed, had generally the same sort of construction. But plays were also put on indoors, at the Blackfriars, presumably by candlelight; they were also acted in court assembly rooms and other halls which ordinarily served other purposes, some even in an old chapel of St. Paul's. In all these different venues different problems of staging had to be faced; and it's not surprising that under different circumstances, plays sometimes took on different shapes. Stage managers had to be a lively, inventive crew in those days, and so did actors. They often memorized (as the players are asked to do in *Hamlet*) special speeches for special occasions, and they certainly threw in topical allusions to events of the day, whenever they seemed good for a laugh or might serve to deepen the reality of an illusion.

As to how many plays were written altogether during Elizabeth's reign—300, 500, or more—we can only speculate. When printed, they had to be licensed at the Stationer's Register, and theoretically they all had to be approved by a censor before presentation. But only a few of those written were printed, and the censorship records are far from meticulous. Hundreds of plays must be pronounced "lost," and as they enjoyed no great popularity even in their own day, their loss represents no great misfortune. Plays were printed when an enterprising publisher saw a chance to make money. Ordinarily, he would go to the company and negotiate to buy a copy of the script in the company's "library." In addition, as already noted, a play could be pirated or resurrected from the memories of the actors ("traitor actors") who first performed it. But all these methods of transmission are insecure and precarious; they may leave us at some distance from the script as the author wrote it. Companies which owned a script cut and changed it at will, hiring play doctors to fix it up, eliminating passages they thought would not play well or for which at the moment they had no suitable actor. When a play was being reconstructed by an assemblage of actors, one or two might be missing; their parts would naturally be sketchily represented. Thus all sorts of mistakes, in addition to the usual quota of printers' errors, crept into the texts of published plays. Emending the text, of Shakespeare particularly, has developed into a craft of great fascination and rigor.[19]

Even when an Elizabethan play survived in print and in fairly good shape, we must not suppose that stage managers and directors, in the years following its publication, treated it with any great reverence. During the seventeenth and eighteenth centuries, actors and directors patched and interpolated new materials into even the greatest of Shakespearean plays. Songs and dances enlivened the Shakespearean tragedies; the comedies were converted into frank operas; star performers were allowed to build up their own parts at the expense of the rest of the play. Cibber, Garrick, Kemble, Kean, and Mrs. Siddons all wreaked their will on the old scripts, following in many cases "acting versions" only remotely related to the original. Garrick, for example, hashed up the ending of *Hamlet* by throwing out Osric and the gravediggers, having Gertrude go mad, and capping the duel between Hamlet and Laertes with another between Hamlet and the king. An extended and theatrical dying speech for Laertes proved so popular that Garrick simply took it over for himself, and let the prince of Denmark fatten his part with it. Producer-managers avid for self-display continued to play havoc with Shakespeare throughout the nineteenth century. Sarah Bernhardt when she was fifty-five years old insisted on undertaking the role of Hamlet, and the history of Shakespeare travesties is still far from complete.

ELIZABETHAN POETRY

Many of the Elizabethan playwrights were notable poets as well; while discussing drama and poetry separately, we shouldn't let it be thought that the two

19. One famous effort at emendation may stand for many. When the Hostess, in Act II, scene 3 of *Henry V*, reports the death of Falstaff, she says, "his nose was sharp as a pen and a table of green fields." Lewis Theobald the eighteenth-century editor emended to read "and 'a babled of green fields." But "a table of green fields" may make sense as "the very picture (table) of a cemetery (green fields)." You had only to look at his sharp nose, the Hostess says, to see where he was headed. The emendation makes easier, more literal reading; the bold metaphors of the basic text may be more akin to the Elizabethan way of thinking.

modes were unrelated. In addition to his narrative poems, and the marvelous little songs studded through his plays, Shakespeare was the author of a famous and much-analyzed sonnet sequence, printed in 1609 but written (at least parts of it) as much as fifteen years earlier. Marlowe, Lodge, Jonson, and Chapman were other poet-playwrights. But when we look at Elizabeth's England, it seems that amost everyone was writing poetry. Raleigh the daredevil sea pirate was a poet of note; so was Sir Henry Wotton the diplomat, and so was Sir John Davies, the solicitor- and attorney-general for Ireland. Chidiock Tichborne, waiting in the Tower to be executed for complicity in the Babington conspiracy, wrote a mournful, resonant elegy, which still stirs the mind to reflection; Robert South-well, if he had not been hanged at Tyburn as an undercover Catholic priest, might have lived to be one of England's greatest poets; he was only thirty-four at his execution, and already the admiration of fellow poets, whatever their creed. The shoemakers in Thomas Dekker's *Shoemaker's Holiday* warble merrily at their lasts; the author known as "Anonymous" was more than usually busy, and his works are preserved for us in the songbooks and miscellaneous collections, of which the most famous is *England's Helicon* (1600).

WHY?

Unmistakable social and technical changes combined to create the English drama. Building public theaters freed the companies from exclusive dependence on court and aristocracy; the social freedom of a big city developed in audiences tastes, attitudes, and a measure of sophistication which made them a fit instrument for dramatists of talent to play upon. But in the history of poetry no equivalent reasons for a suddenly heightened standard of taste appear. There is no abruptly expanded or newly enlightened audience for poetry. The "lower orders" are reading, to be sure, more than they used to; but their taste runs to ballads, moral tracts, and marvelous tales, works despised by gentlemanly authors with gentle-manly tastes (SFR, D.5). Gentlemen, either achieved or aspiring, were the class from which most of the Elizabethan poems came, and for whose delight they were intended. The rewards of literature were no greater than before, that is, they were meager and uncertain. Writers of prose as well as poetry might dedi-cate their works to a wealthy and influential man, and hope in return for patron-age—an office, pension, secretarial post—tangible reward of some sort. Elizabeth's favorite, Leicester, was the most munificent of Elizabethan patrons, and indeed he encouraged a wide range of authors. But among the many volumes dedicated to him, works of literature play a small part. Translations, histories, books of religious controversy, and books of propaganda predominate. Leicester was acquainted with Spenser, who dropped many broad hints that he would welcome employment. None was forthcoming. We can hardly think the scant and chancy system of patronage did much to encourage the rise of letters.

Again, more printers and publishers were active in the later century than in earlier years. But publication carried few rewards, and many of the best poems were not written for publication at all. They circulated in manuscript for years before being printed, and the coterie within which they circulated was not much bigger than it had ever been. There were, of course, more poets at work, and they had more and better models to imitate; but to say this is simply to say that the Elizabethan poets wrote much and wrote well because some of them wrote much and well, and others did the same. Somewhere in the background we note the grammar schools of England, which gave a thorough linguistic and a less thorough literary training, most of it in Latin; but their influence could have confined writers to a strict and perhaps deadening imitation of the classics, as happened all too often on the Continent. Why it happened only rarely in England is a question with perhaps as many answers as there were authors.

SPENSER'S EPIC ROMANCE

In part, it was the magnitude of Edmund Spenser's ambition that made him of central importance to the Elizabethan poets. His elegant erotic sonnets (*Amoretti*), his two romantic, yet classical, nuptial songs ("Epithalamion" and "Prothalamion"), his lofty hymns to Platonic beauty, all were authenticated by the gigantic undertaking of *The Faerie Queene*. For in this vast allegory Spenser challenged comparison, not only with Italy's epic romancers Ariosto and Tasso, but with the giants whom *they* had challenged, Homer and Virgil. Size was not unimportant: till it had produced a heroic poem, English must be set down (by the critical tenets of the time) as a weak language, incapable of supporting the massive structure of epic. To this challenge Spenser's poem was an indirect response, combining two potent, semicompatible components, Protestant Christianity and medieval chivalry. As to size, the project left nothing to be desired. The plan was to construct an ideal knight by following the adventures of twelve separate heroes, each representing one of the moral virtues.[20] Each knight (or lady; for Britomart in Book III combines both characters) was to undergo adventures to fill twelve cantos, each canto amounting to fifty or sixty nine-line stanzas. The completed poem would thus have amounted to at least 65,000 lines of verse, more than six times the length of *Paradise Lost*. To cast such a poem in an intricate nine-line stanza requiring two triple rhymes was adding audacity to ambition; but Spenser was led to it, as to many other qualities of his vast poem, by the Italian example.

Though typically Elizabethan in his exuberant and fluent versification, Spenser was distinctive in his passionate Calvinist morality, and downright idiosyncratic in the archaic language that accompanies his theme of knightly chivalry. His

20. The virtues represented in the part of the poem that was written are (1) Holiness, (2) Temperance, (3) Chastity, (4) Friendship, (5) Justice, (6) Courtesy, and (7) Constancy. (Of the seventh book we have only two cantos, on "Mutability.")

knight-adventurers face an almost unresolvable set of moral enigmas; only a shining inner idealism guides them, as it guides that later and rather similar prototype of Puritan morality, Bunyan's unstoppable Pilgrim. But neither Spenser nor his characters are wholly single-minded; their adventures often allude to figures in Elizabeth's court or events in the political life of the day. At some point in the composition of the poem, Spenser saw the danger of writing twelve separate adventure stories, and began to interlace his narratives after the fashion of his major Italian model, Ariosto. Rather to the distress of classical purists like Gabriel Harvey, he also started to enrich his tale with episodes from classical mythology, to which he gave his own twist. Thus the seduction of Hellenore by Paridell in Book III cannot help reminding us of the Homeric legend of Helen and Paris, though in fact the end of Malbecco, Hellenore's ex-husband, turns the whole theme of sexual rivalry in a most un-Homeric direction. (Malbecco tries to commit suicide by jumping from a cliff but has become so shriveled with anxiety that he is blown into a cave where he frets endlessly till he becomes Jealousy itself.)

Straining the Spenserian allegory toward some ultimate intricate moral consistency is probably not the best way to approach this author. If one follows the verse, with its insinuating rhythms and moments of idyllic beauty, its frequent black pits of horrid despair, one may well catch at moral points here and there. But where they don't lie ready to hand, or don't seem to form an elaborate theological construct, one may be sustained by the adventure of Faerie Land. The reader who catches Spenser's vital charm can safely leave knotty and intricate points of the allegory to specialists. A comparison with Byron's *Don Juan* may seem odd, for Byron is remote indeed from the sort of moralist that Spenser is. But both poems give one the sense of a long trip in a light boat over rippling, cool waves that are always fresh, always new, however similar they look from a distance (SFR, D.26).

STURDY PATRIOTS: DRAYTON, DANIEL, DAVIES

The sonnet sequences of Sidney, Shakespeare, and Spenser invite us to extend the listing with a reference to Drayton and Daniel. Both men wrote a great deal of poetry other than sonnets, and Drayton in particular was a voluminous and various author. By now, much of his work is of merely historical interest, and his lengthy poem on the beauties of Britain, *Poly-Olbion*[21] (1613 and 1622) is actually painful to read. He wrote other long and often tedious poems; yet when one starts to say, "on the other hand," one finds an amazing number of fanciful and spirited poems to Drayton's credit. There is the stirring ballad of Agincourt,

---

21. The title actually means, in Greek, "many blessings," but includes a buried pun on Albion, an ancient name for Britain. The poem is chiefly of interest nowadays for the extensive and erudite antiquarian notes by John Selden, one of the great seventeenth-century scholars.

celebrating Henry V's victory over the French; there is a dainty little fantasy of Fairyland, "Nimphidia"; just once, he hit the exact right note in a sonnet, the famous, "Since there's no help, come let us kiss and part." But then we are led on to "England's Heroical Epistles," a series of imaginary letters in verse between historical English personages, to his cheerful pastorals, "Idea, or the Shepherd's Garland," and to the naïve little "Letter to Henry Reynolds" on poets and poetry. Though Drayton, it seems, generally wrote on a humble plane, he rose above it often enough to earn our respect.

Samuel Daniel, son of a musician, struck a higher level on average than Drayton, but never rose much above or sank far beneath it. His sonnet sequence is addressed to a lady named Delia, apparently from the country near Stratford, and is notable for its early date of publication, 1592, as well as for a few lovely, limpid poems. At the death of Elizabeth, Daniel was welcomed (unlike Drayton) to the court of James, for which he composed a number of masques, triumphs, and entertainments. Like Drayton, he wrote a long historical poem on the civil wars between York and Lancaster, and went on to write a prose history of England from earliest times through the reign of Edward III. It was popular (evidence once more of England's interest in her own past), but Ben Jonson meant no compliment when he dismissed Daniel as a good, honest man, but no poet. In fact, most readers, whether explicit on the matter or not, felt a certain lack of fire in Daniel. He comes down in literary history under the half-complimentary title of "the well-languaged Daniel."

The two chief poetical productions of Sir John Davies seem more different than they are. "Orchestra" (1596) is a delightful poem in praise of dancing. The body of the poem is supposed to be spoken by Alcinous, one of the suitors of Penelope, in hope of getting that lady to tread a measure. Our sympathies should by rights lie with the faithful wife of long-suffering Odysseus; Alcinous is supposed to be a treacherous weakling. But his argument is beguilingly persuasive. The entire world, he declares, is dancing; the tides, the seasons, the creatures all have their dances, the planets and stars do nothing but dance. How then can the queen of Ithaca refuse? No more enchanting demonstration of cosmic harmony came out of the Elizabethan age, yet the special elegance of the poem is that it is only half serious. Sir John's other poem, more somber in its tonality, is "Nosce Teipsum" ("Know Thyself") (1599); it describes the physical and psychic condition of man, to the end of demonstrating the soul's immortality. Though very different from the poem in praise of dancing, it too is a poem about harmony, and shows the author as light on his philosophical as on his literal toes.

All three of these poets, Drayton, Daniel, and Davies, were very much of the court and religious establishment. When we put their verses together with those of the miscellaneous song writers who produced luminous trifles like "It was a lover and his lass," "My mind to me a kingdom is," "There is a lady sweet and kind," and "Though Amaryllis dance in green," we may get the impression that Elizabeth's last years were an unbroken period of hey nonny nonny and begone dull care. Indeed, the note of good cheer and unthinking delight is struck again and again. We don't know, of course, whether that means people were all cheerful or just in need of cheering up. Probably, when families gathered round the fire of an evening to sing ballets and madrigals together, even plaintive, melancholy airs took on a cheerful social aspect. In any event, the reader who is weary of sour, cynical, and contemptuous writing can readily find naïve joy and high good cheer in an Elizabethan songbook.

SHADOWS ON THE GREEN

And yet . . . and yet. . . . We said above that the last years of Elizabeth were years of discontent and bitter satire; and if these are the qualities we seek, they can be found without prolonged search. The black comedies of Shakespeare inaugurate the even darker period of his tragedies; alongside his savage *Troilus and Cressida* (1602) we may set a bitter tragicomedy like *The Malcontent* (1604) by John Marston, and Jonson's sullen Roman tragedy *Sejanus* (1603). During the 1590s Joseph Hall and John Donne were both writing, if not publishing, the first poetic satires in the language after the aggressive mode of Juvenal. In the case of Jonson and Donne, it's probably not unimportant that these men were brought up among, and felt sympathetic to, those Roman Catholics who represented the one actively persecuted religious sect of Elizabethan England. But the sense of intellectual strain and dissatisfied anxiety reached beyond the persecuted Catholics, involving in some instances a measure of muffled intellectual ferment. It is not easy to understand what was involved in the rumors of atheism and occult practices that clung to a group surrounding Sir Walter Raleigh. They have a romantic name, the "School of Night," but what these people believed and who exactly they were we cannot confidently say; they were clearly not eager for publicity. That Christopher Marlowe the dramatist was one of the group seems definite; others were, or may have been, astronomers and mathematicians such as Walter Warner, Robert Hues, and Thomas Hariot; they may have had contact with Giordano Bruno, the tough and witty Italian philosopher who would ultimately (1600) be burned by the Inquisition at Rome.[22] About all these people

22. In Raleigh and the "School of Night" learned forms of radical anticlericalism may have reverberated briefly against the chords of a deep popular tradition. The pomposity of formal theology, the wealth and comfort of the clergy, and their fondness for persecution and religious wars, all were old peasant themes, openly expressed during the Peasant Revolt, simmering subsurface since then. The very idea of a "school of night" carries reverberations from Nicholas Cusanus and his doctrine of "learned ignorance"; and Cusanus exerted major influence on Giordano Bruno. The direction of all this thinking is toward a simplified Christianity, directly available to the sincere heart and uncluttered mind of the true believer (SFR, D.22).

   Almost everything we say about the doctrines of the Raleigh "school" is conjectural; in the solemn, formal sense, they may not have had any doctrines at all. But their sense of restless discontent with the established culture is very clear, and their tendency to set themselves apart is what Shakespeare mainly seized on when he ridiculed the "School of Night" in *Love's Labors Lost*.

there lurked the somewhat vague scandal of "atheism"; it was a loose charge loosely made in those days when the use of algebraic symbols laid one open to the suspicion of "conjuring." In any case, there were poets well acquainted with Raleigh and presumably with the school; and it is interesting that they often use a style of complex and knotty abstraction, argumentative yet at the same time strongly metaphorical, and often homely in diction. Spenserian language tends to fit loosely over Spenserian thought; one often feels that, at a crunch, an idea will be stretched over two lines (by means of expletives and redundant adjectives) instead of compressed into one. George Chapman and Fulke Greville, both intimates of the Raleigh circle, cram their language full of meaning, and hammer it out of shape to make it express their full sense. The rough, masculine energy of Chapman's verse is best known from his rumbustious translations of Homer; but his original poems (not surprisingly) do more to reveal the dense twistings of his strenuous rhetorical mind.[23] One looks vainly in Chapman for strikingly new or original ideas; but the sense of mute strain and choked urgency is unmistakable. Chapman is at least half a metaphysical poet, lacking perhaps only the quality of verbal economy to equal Donne; concision often fails him.

SIR WALTER

In leaving the age of Elizabeth, let us invoke the complex and saturnine figure of Sir Walter Raleigh. He is everywhere in the age, a dashing privateer on the high seas and at the capture of Cadiz, a friend of Sidney and patron of Spenser, the first (though unsuccessful) colonizer of Virginia, a greedy land pirate in Ireland (where he introduced the cultivation of potatoes and tobacco), an insinuating courtier of the queen, an eloquent poet, something of a speculative philosopher, a universal historian, an explorer of South America, a fabled amorist, a soldier. Yet with all his panache and versatility, there was always something rash and wild about Sir Walter. He was a chance taker. His voyage to South America in 1595 produced a splendid narrative but not that gold which was the main point. On his return, he may have taken some minor part in the petty intrigues surrounding the accession of James. For these he was tried, convicted of treason, and sent to the Tower. But execution was stayed, and he lived on to dabble in chemistry and write the first volume (from the creation to 130 B.C.) of a projected *History of the World*.[24] Finally, in 1616, he was let out to search

23. The dark, hermetic side of Chapman is expressed in a couple of early poems, "The Shadow of Night" and the "Hymn to Cynthia" (1594), the heraldic-erotic side in "Ovid's Garden of Sense" (1595) and the four sestiads continuing Marlowe's "Hero and Leander" (1598). One could perhaps think of these as Chapman's inside and outside poems; but the formula, like most formulas applied to this elusive author, is inadequate. Around even the posed and burnished nudities of his classical poems gust swarms of particulate and furiously energized words (SFR, D.20).

24. James disliked Raleigh's *History* even more than his person, because Sir Walter went well out of his way to sneer at all the royal sodomites in ancient history. Contemporary applications were left to the knowing reader, but they were not hard to make.

again for gold in Guiana, but with the sharp proviso that he not attack any Spanish settlements. The king's greed led to his release, the king's timidity to the proviso. Raleigh knew from the first (*must* have known) that he could not perform what he had promised. The expedition to the Orinoco was a miserable fiasco. Raleigh found no gold; his men attacked a Spanish settlement, and succeeded only in getting Raleigh's son killed. The second in command committed suicide. Raleigh himself returned home, sick and despairing, to inevitable execution. And yet, though he had been a proud, greedy, and violent man—though it was more than twenty years since he had done anything of note—he went as a hero to his death, and lived long in the memory of the land. For he was the last of the Elizabethan adventurers, the survivor of a great age; its splendor covered his faults, and when he was gone, after so many others, Englishmen felt that the world presented a diminished spectacle.

8

The Early Stuarts
and Their Revolution
(1603–1649)

Long before the term was applied to the twentieth century, the early seventeenth century deserved to be called "the age of anxiety." At the time, people preferred the word "melancholy," and melancholy is everywhere in the literature of the early century. It doesn't mean simply "sad." Technically, melancholy is the predominance, among the four humors of a person's temperament, of black bile. (The other three humors are blood, phlegm, and choler; they give rise naturally to the sanguine, phlegmatic, and choleric tempers.) The melancholy man is thoughtful, introspective; not a man of action, he is likely to be a scholar, a questioner of himself and the world. Hamlet is melancholy; so, in a very different vein, is Malvolio of *Twelfth Night*, so is the melancholy Jaques of *As You Like It*, so is Bosola the dissatisfied and malignant agent of Webster's *Duchess of Malfi*. The metaphysical poets in their dark and self-questioning lyrics express melancholy sentiments; so do the satirists; and Robert Burton's immense *Anatomy of Melancholy* is a classic attempt to describe, analyze, and provide therapy for the condition. It was an age of worry and doubt. Behind even its massively erudite undertakings, such as the giant collections of Burton and Sir Thomas Browne, Raleigh's vast *History of the World*, and the antiquarian erudition of scholars like Coke, Selden, Spelman, and Ussher, one feels the pressure of a deep uncertainty, a thirst for assurance. For all its striking diversity, the literature of the early seventeenth century rarely strikes that note of happy and relaxed confidence that had been dominant in the previous age. There are partial exceptions to this rule (Robert Herrick is one of them), but a second reading may reveal a touch of deliberate archness, of conscious limitation, which makes of him the exception that proves the rule.

No longer an age of unquestioning faith; not yet, though soon to become, an age of scientific assurance and technical accomplishment, the seventeenth century is gnawed by a need to understand the shape of the cosmos and man's place in it.

THE OVERWHELMING QUESTION

If they did not cause, two major events helped trigger this deep and rather surprising shift in the national mood: the rout of the Armada and the death of Elizabeth. For nearly a century, since Henry VIII broke with Rome, the social order had been aligned against Catholic aristocrats in the north and the Catholic powers of Europe animated by the pope. Against these two menaces from the medieval past, the Tudors had made use of servants primarily from the lower gentry and the middle classes; families like the Cecils, Walsinghams, Greshams, Bacons, and Sidneys shaded down into west-country semipirates like Drake, Frobisher, and Hawkins. They gave their devotion to Elizabeth as a shield against feudal disorder and Catholic reaction. But after 1588, when these dangers no longer threatened, new worries began to arise as to the material and spiritual patterns of English life, particularly the operation of the court system as a whole. Royal monopolies cramped economic enterprise, royally appointed bishops stifled popular religious opinion, the royal prerogative was felt to restrict the privileges of Parliament. Nobody had yet reached the stage of questioning the monarchy or the church as such. But that something new was needed many people felt; and what form this "something new" should take, now that the first need of the nation was no longer self-defense, was a question that suddenly arose in the 1590s. From small beginnings, doubts and disputes swelled like a black cloud over the next half century. A tone of dark feeling and strenuous thought marked a new era of resentment, questioning, criticism, and self-analysis—out of which, in the thunder of battle, amid the strange, strident cries of fanaticism, the liberal era (of mutual toleration, common sense, material interest, and experimental evidence rationally interpreted) would be born. What at first appeared a social disease at last revealed itself as a pregnancy.

ROOTS OF A CRISIS

Under shelter of an authoritarian monarchy, England had in fact developed a rudimentary but vigorous capitalist society. Its leaders had served the Tudor monarchy and prospered by their service; now, like the earl of Essex in another sphere, they aspired to be more than servants. Their companies, syndicates, and partnerships united in a single enterprise folk from many different communities (for example, in the wool trade, graziers, spinners, weavers, warehousers, shippers, and bankers). As they expanded, entering into new credit arrangements and reaching out after new opportunities, they found their operations hampered by ecclesiastical restrictions on usury and engrossing, by monopolistic restraints, by government taxation and regulation. The whole structure of Tudor government had been geared to the concept of personal morality supervised by paternal authority; the Stuarts tried to continue, and even rigidify, the structure they found. In a small community, where each man acts on his own responsibility as an individual, this scheme might work, but it can hardly apply to the actions of a joint-stock company (which is an artificial personality, a legal fiction) or to a bank which is largely controlled by the fluctuations of a distant money market. Old values applied to new situations inevitably bred rancor.

One last question crucial to the early seventeenth century added a fresh disturbance to the strains of nascent capitalism. The scientific study of nature and nature's works, most boldly commended by Francis Bacon, threw into instant oblivion a long-established body of popular lore and received morality. The phoenix no longer emblematized the resurrection; in fact the phoenix turned out not to exist. Neither did the deadly basilisk (which killed at a glance) or the moral gryphon (which demonstrated the evils of greed). The very position of the earth in the heavens came under question as the theories of Copernicus and Galileo became known. In "The First Anniversary," Donne complains that the new world is "all in pieces, all coherence gone," and Milton illustrates the point by using in *Paradise Lost* two separate and unequal universes, one hidden away in a corner of the other.[1]

Science found a welcome in England because devices like the watch and the compass promised to be commercially useful. But the implications of mechanical thought were unsettling to traditionalists. Doing away with so many superstitions so fast suggested to the fearful that the fabric itself of religion might be next to go. Whether because of this fear or not, an age of growing scientific discovery was also one in which superstitions about witchcraft were defiantly published.[2] King James who, though credulous, was by no means ignorant, wrote a fierce *Demonology* (1599) calling for the active prosecution of witches. (Shakespeare

1. The universe across which Satan struggles in Book II of *Paradise Lost* is not only vaster, it is less defined in shape than "this pendant world, in bigness as a star," through which he sails easily in Book III.

2. While Protestantism, with its double emphasis on preaching and active, individual faith, stimulated the zeal of literate, ambitious classes, it often bored and oppressed unlettered plowmen, who had been at ease under Catholicism with its easier pattern of pervasive ritual and auricular confession. Magical beliefs, insensibly grown up around Catholic practices, were cast away by Protestant churches and therefore flourished more visibly outside them, as supplements and sometimes as rivals to the worship of God (SFR, D.27).

took the cue, and shortly after the accession produced *Macbeth;* Jonson outdid him, in 1609, with *The Masque of Queens,* which has more witches than one could shake a broomstick at.) Sir Thomas Browne was one of the most civilized men of the age, a skeptic and a wit; but he proclaimed his belief in witches and took part in a witch trial. It was an age of profound and various uncertainty, the more agonizing because everyone agreed that in the Holy Scriptures an infallible rule lay to hand which need only be interpreted correctly to yield correct answers to all the questions of life. That habit of thought proved hard to break.

THE TROUBLES OF JAMES

James Stuart, the sixth King James of Scotland, was duly crowned James I of England in high summer of 1603. He came from a very poor country into a relatively prosperous one; he was thirty-seven years of age, and had been a king (though at first without much real power) since the age of one. To his new subjects, he was far from impressive. His legs were weak, his appetites strong; he stammered and slobbered, and his fondness for handsome young men was so marked that not even a wife and three authentic children could muffle the gossip. He was a physical coward. Yet he was literate, learned, and in his own way adroit. His troubles in England, and they were many, came from the fact that he inherited many difficulties which he worsened by failing to understand his new subjects.

Because James had been raised under Presbyterian tutors, English Puritans assumed he must be sympathetic to their cause. Promptly they presented to him a petition, signed by a thousand ministers and known thereby as the "Millenary" petition. In January, James summoned a delegation of the petitioners to a conference at Hampton Court, where he sat in judgment, surrounded by his bishops. The meeting was not altogether futile, since the proposal for a new translation of the Bible met with approval and in due course (1611) produced the "King James" version, which we still read. Ever since the Reformation, the English have been a nation of Bible readers, and as the King James version soon superseded all others, its images and rhythms quickly became embedded in the language. Even today, when Bible reading is in decline, we cannot get along without phrases like "a good Samaritan," "whited sepulchres," "new wine in old bottles," and a thousand others. One does not exaggerate in saying the King James version is the most influential book ever published in English.

But the central request of the Puritans, that the clergy of each district might have a regular meeting to discuss doctrine and discipline (and by implication to censure anyone disagreeing with them), really enraged James. In his view, which exactly duplicated that of Elizabeth, doctrine and discipline were the business of bishops, whom he appointed and could dismiss. From bitter experience in Scotland he knew what it was worth to be king when tough-minded clergymen had power to censure and correct him at every turn. His position as head of the English church made him master in his own house, and master he would be. So, to conclude the conference, he swore to make the English Puritans conform, or else to harry them out of the land. Both sides were in desperate earnest; and the Puritans, who had waited long and hoped greatly, tasted bitter gall and wormwood. Some three hundred of their number chose to leave their posts in the church; and for conscience' sake some of these emigrated, first to Holland, then in 1620 to the rock-bound coast of New England, where they became the Pilgrim Fathers of American history. Ben Jonson, who loathed Puritans, caricatured them on the stage of *The Alchemist* as pastor Tribulation Wholesome and his disciple Ananias; James and his bishops were glad to see them go. But many Puritans and Puritan sympathizers remained; and though they could not agitate directly for a Presbyterian church government, they could and did propagandize in a general way for what they called "a godly discipline."[3] They were zealous and voluble men, they yearned mightily for a better order of things; but stiff laws kept them from ever giving their vision concrete form or distinct outline. Instead of creating their new discipline at a stroke (as Calvin had done at Geneva or Knox in Scotland), they had to talk about it; and the more they talked, the more glittering but indistinct it became. Thus the Puritans remained a sore spot in the body politic, bitterly discontent with the establishment and cherishing splendid, incompatible fancies of what an ideal church would be like.

THE NEED FOR MONEY

James alienated his new subjects by touching their purses as well as their consciences. Because England looked, and really was, rich, James assumed that as its new king he must be rich too. But under Elizabeth, Englishmen had got used to low taxes, and James soon found he had to make use of indirect devices to raise money. Fresh from Scotland, he distributed knighthoods freely among his subjects; in theory, it was an honor to be knighted, but so many of these honors were given out that the title became a joke. (In *Volpone,* Sir Politic Would-Be swears "by his knighthood," and a bystander remarks sarcastically that he has nothing better to swear by.) The title was not only cheap for James to give, it was expensive for the new knight to assume; heavy fees went with it. When subjects realized the honor was negligible and the expense considerable, some

3. Veiled language of many different sorts could be used to advocate puritan ideas. Rich merchants could appoint puritans as tutors or household chaplains. In addition, any group of laymen could collect money and endow a lectureship; unless he grew really scandalous, the lecturer was not under the bishop's control. Thus the same pulpit could resound to anglican doctrine on Sunday morning and puritan doctrine Sunday afternoon. Finally, tithes could be bought up for cash by laymen ("impropriated") and assigned by the new owner to a puritan sympathizer. James's bishops were much exercised by these evasions of their episcopal authority, and took appropriate steps.

of them tried to decline the honor; but James pushed through a law that knighthood could be forced, under penalty of a heavy fine, on anyone worth more than £40 a year. In May of 1611 the king also created a new title of baronet, in order to raise money by selling it for the considerable sum of £1,095. But so many of the titles were made available that the price fell to £200; one man even bought a baronetage who could not be certified as a gentleman. Cheapening the honors in this way made the monarchy hateful, especially to the older aristocracy.

Again, the crown angered its subjects by maintaining obsolete feudal regulations involving the nobility and gentry. When a gentleman died leaving a minor child, the king by law was entitled to appoint a guardian to administer the property. This had been useful in the old days, when a main reason for the king's granting an estate in the first place was to have a grateful nobleman at his back with a private army. But in the seventeenth century, wardship was nothing but a moneymaking device. It took two forms. The royally appointed guardian could milk the estate for his own advantage, order the youthful heir to marry one of his own hungry kinfolk, and, to punish a refusal, assess a huge fine on the estate. Or else, to avert such disaster, a family might influence the king to appoint one of them as guardian; the name of this influence was, once again, money. Either way, a family might be ruined forever by once getting into a wardship situation. Despite repeated pleas for reform of this abuse, James needed money too much to give it up.

Though Elizabeth had promised to end them, James continued and expanded the practice of rewarding courtiers by giving them monopolies to deal in particular commodities. When economic life was slower, monopolies had not been much resented; in bustling England, they irked not only consumers, who were many, but potential competitors, who were influential. Practically all the items of everyday consumption yielded profit to a monopolist. Salt, soap, starch, spices, butter, bread, beer, linen, leather, and hundreds of other items all cost more because a monopolist had to make a profit on them. The system stifled enterprise while taxing the poor to benefit the rich; a steady stream of petitions was directed against it.[4] But the Stuart court felt no sympathy for the commercial classes; its ideal seemed to be the centralized economic bureaucracy which controlled business life in France. Thus the Stuarts expanded the court's economic role as widely as they could. The king claimed a right to raise or lower customs duties without consulting Parliament or anyone else. He tried to capture the crucial wool trade by setting up a rival royal company; it was a catastrophe, but the intent was clear—to get the major center of capitalist development under state control. Prerogative courts, appointed by the king and responsible only to him, acted to

---

4. Another ancient and irksome royal privilege was known as "purveyance"; it entitled the king's purchasing agent to fix the price for anything needed by the royal household, and buy it at that price. The purveyors could also commandeer horses, vehicles, and supplies whenever needed for the royal travels. Complaints against the system had been voiced as early as the 1370s, but the Stuarts clung to it as long as their authority lasted.

mulct enclosing landlords, to punish usurers, to fine trespassers in the royal forests. The administration took particular and unfriendly notice of men who seemed to have got too rich too quickly; such a man might be pressured to lend the king £20,000 without interest, and count himself lucky to get off for a mere £12,000. Why did James need money so desperately? His income was suffering the wasting effects of inflation; and besides, he was extravagant. He and his court spent money on a regal scale to stage private theatricals for which not only poets like Jonson but musicians, designers, painters, and costumers had to be paid. Above all else, the king loved hunting; it was an expensive sport, requiring royal game preserves, royal huntsmen, royal lodges, royal wardens, royal stables, royal journeys with a royal retinue from one venue to another. The king was lavish in bestowing gifts on favorites. George Villiers was a handsome but far from affluent young fellow when he was brought to the king's attention; within four years, he had been successively created knight, viscount, earl, knight of the Garter, and marquess, while receiving the equivalent of millions of dollars in property; and he was still to be created duke of Buckingham, which made him even richer. At twenty-five he had become, with just one exception, the richest nobleman in England. Royal favorites were nothing new, but favoritism on this scale was unprecedented, and for such giving the king needed big money. But his supply of that useful commodity was short because of a running dispute with the House of Commons.

BLOCKADE

By an acknowledged law dating back to 1297 and rooted in Magna Charta (see above, p. 60), Parliament was the only body entitled to raise money through taxation; but it could also refuse to do so. Refusal could be used to pressure the monarch into investigating grievances and correcting abuses. An "abuse" could be an exorbitant monopoly, an offensive minister, a bishop too zealous or not zealous enough in his office; it could be an unpopular foreign policy. Refusing to vote supply was Parliament's lever for getting such abuses corrected. Already in the last Parliaments of Elizabeth, quarrels over abuses were starting to hold up the voting of supply, and under James this became a regular procedure. For one thing, the reformers in the commons learned to organize so that *their* interests and concerns took priority.[5] For another, James did not understand what a strong, well-entrenched body the lower house had become. An observer of the 1628 Parliament estimated that the Commons could buy up the Lords three times over; this was the exact reverse of the situation in Scotland, which James knew perhaps too well. Moreover, the Commons in England had developed some tra-

5. This process was brilliantly described for the first time by Professor Wallace Notestein in his Royal Historical Society lecture of 1924, "The Winning of the Initiative in the House of Commons" (SFR, E.22).

ditional privileges, on which they insisted stubbornly. James thought he could tell the members what they might and might not discuss; having now come over to the position of Sir Peter Wentworth (above, p. 185), they most vigorously disagreed. The king, they conceded, might refuse to summon them at all and do without the money they alone could vote; he might dismiss (prorogue) them when he chose, on the same terms. But while they sat, so they emphatically declared, they were free to discuss what they chose as long as they chose, like it or not. When grievances were fully satisfied, they would vote supply; but not till then. Through the first forty years of the century, one Parliament after another insisted on investigating grievances, refused to vote taxes, and was dismissed in a storm of royal indignation. In short, the system of centralized government was being slowly starved at the taproot.[6] And as sullen discontent grew throughout the countryside because genuine complaints were being smothered, the king's need for money and the desperation of his search for it increased together.

Starving the central government made it more authoritarian and more ecclesiastical than it might otherwise have been. Even before he came to England, James had declared his belief in the divine right of kings; but that was abstract theory. Constant financial pressure forced him to assert his royal power in concrete ways, often disagreeable to his subjects. When the king was deprived of his regular income, he began to argue that the royal power (prerogative) was greater than the law of the land, and that the monarch might, to meet an overriding need, levy taxes without consent of Parliament. Here he encountered bitter opposition, notably from the common lawyers, who constituted an influential and well-connected body of opinion. Sir Edward Coke, a crusty and truculent chief justice of the king's bench, did not scruple to tell James to his face that the king was, and ought to be, subject to the law. For James this was a bitter pill, and he took early occasion to dismiss Coke from all his offices. But then, giving up on the common-law courts, he turned to the prerogative and ecclesiastical courts, which dispensed a different brand of justice altogether.[7]

Time out of mind, there had been ecclesiastical courts in England to try cases

6. We should not attribute to these successive Stuart Parliaments too clear a design against the king or too absolute a control over his purse. The members did not sit long or regularly enough to be well organized; they had no revolutionary ideology. The structure of taxation included many different levies—import and export duties, fifteenths, tenths, subsidies, benevolences, forced loans—each with its own rationale and procedure. Occasionally the king collected a little of this money, plus of course the income from his royal estates; but it was never enough, and his income shrank as his debt service rose. The steadiness with which Parliament year after year withheld adequate supply bespeaks a certain stubborn determination—inarticulate perhaps, but implacable.

7. The common law is the general law of England. It is distinguished from statute law (created by the sovereign authority), from canon law (created by and for the church), from international and local law (different areas of application), and from equity law, which proceeds on different principles. The great emphasis of the common law falls on the rule of precedent; it grows out of judicial decisions and general customs, not always written down, but given the force of law by long observation. As their subject is complex and hallowed by time, common lawyers often form a tight corporation.

involving the clergy; Becket's martyrdom at the hands of Henry II had sealed the fact. The first two Tudors had created the prerogative (royal) courts of Star Chamber, High Commission, and Council of the North. With the common lawyers hostile and need for new revenue pressing, ecclesiastical and prerogative courts now began to expand their jurisdiction and serve as the king's "enforcers" in a wide variety of cases. In addition to their usual concerns, they began probing economic crimes; and while they looked darkly on private economic enterprise, they supported the king's right to levy fees and taxes without authority from Parliament. That stirred bitter resentment among subjects who felt their lives were being controlled and their property taken without due process of law. Comparisons were made with the Spanish Inquisition. Young John Milton bitterly renounced the ecclesiastical career for which he had been trained, saying he had been "church-outed by the prelates." And the popular mind acquired a profound hostility to clergymen in offices of secular government. It sank deep and lasted long.

APPEASEMENT

Another sore point was foreign policy. The peaceful succession of James, a safe Protestant, was a bitter blow to those aggressive Catholic partisans whom Elizabeth had interned at Wisbech (p. 162, note, above); after the coronation, a few fanatics formed a conspiracy to blow up James and his first Parliament, and actually moved barrels of gunpowder into the cellar. On 5 November 1605 they were discovered and shortly hunted down, tortured, and executed.[8] It was a terrible scare; but after James's terror subsided, he moved steadily toward rapprochement with Spain. There were prudent reasons for this. Peace was cheaper than war, and France, resurgent under Henri IV, an uncertain quantity. But a series of unwise acts made it seem as if James were actually leading England back into the Catholic camp. In 1618 Sir Walter Raleigh, symbol of patriotic resistance to Spain, was executed on blurry charges of treason; the decision to kill him was reputed to have been taken at the request of the Spanish ambassador, Gondomar. In 1619 England refused to aid the Bohemian Protestants, menaced by Spain in the area now known as Czechoslovakia. Frederick, the Elector Palatine whose proper kingdom lay in the Rhineland, had been asked to rule in Bohemia as well precisely because of his Protestantism. He was James's son-in-law, having married his daughter Elizabeth; and after the disastrous battle of White Hill (8 November 1619), his situation was truly desperate. But James

8. Guy Fawkes, who gave his name to the plot, was a soldier of fortune who had served with Spanish troops in Flanders; the real leader was Robert Catesby, a daring bravo with a history of involvement in violent causes. November 5 is still celebrated throughout England with squibs, firecrackers, and bonfires in which an effigy of the "Guy" is burned. The modern slang word "guy" meaning "fellow" comes from the effigy.

refused to help even his own kin; and to ardent English Protestants, that seemed a clear case of appeasing Spain.[9] Throughout the 1620s French Protestants (Huguenots) were under fierce attack from the Catholic party in their land; James did little to help them, and in 1628 the last Huguenot stronghold, La Rochelle, was allowed to fall. In 1623, negotiations to have England's Prince Charles marry Maria the infanta (princess) of Spain went so far that Charles and the duke of Buckingham rode across Europe to visit the court at Madrid. In the event, the marriage treaty came to nothing, much to the relief of English Protestants. (But Charles then proceeded to marry Henrietta Maria, ardently Catholic daughter of Henri IV of France, who was just as great a political liability for him as the infanta would have been.) And all this dealing with Spain and the Catholic powers could only increase popular suspicion of a court whose gentleness toward Rome was bound to be contrasted with its harshness (as at Hampton Court) toward English Puritans.

The posture of the Stuart regime toward domestic dissent slowly hardened, as we can see by noting in summary form what happened to end the sittings of the various Stuart parliaments. In 1611 James angrily dismissed his first parliament because it insisted on discussing matters disagreeable to him; in 1614 he called a second one which sat only a couple of months, passed no acts, voted no supply, and was abruptly dismissed, having fully earned its nickname of the "Addled" Parliament. A third parliament was asked to vote money for relief of Protestants in the Palatinate; members were not unwilling to do so, but urged that the Spanish alliance on which James had embarked was at the root of the trouble. James said he had not asked their advice on that matter, and it was not wanted; the Commons formally declared that they had a right to discuss anything which concerned the commonwealth—and they entered this declaration in the journal of their proceedings. King James called for the offending document (a breach of privilege in itself), and with his own hands tore that page out of the journal, then dissolved parliament. The Parliament that was summoned in 1624 might have voted money for the continental Protestants, but before it could do so, James died and Parliament was automatically dissolved. His son Charles summoned three parliaments in the first four years of his reign. The first two, in 1625 and 1626, were summarily dismissed after very short sessions because the Commons insisted on acting against Charles's chief minister and best friend, the duke of Buckingham, whom they declared to be incompetent, criminal, and treasonable.[10] The third Parliament, summoned in 1628, found Charles in desperate straits

9. The confused state of German political-economic life, the crucial situation occupied by Frederick, and the disastrous consequences of his weakness, are vigorously sketched in the first 136 pages of C. V. Wedgwood, *The Thirty Years War* (Garden City, N.Y.: Anchor Books, 1961).

10. Though not as they expected, the Commons' accusations against Buckingham did bring about the duke's downfall. A man with an old grudge against him was inflamed by the repeated charges, lay in wait, and fatally stabbed the duke on 23 August 1628; he was just thirty-six, two years older than his predecessor, Essex (above, p. 181).

for money and forced him to sign a document called the Petition of Right, which listed recent abuses of royal power, and promised to correct them in future. This general declaration, which passed after much angry debate and was signed by the king, obviously aimed to clear the air, and to some extent did so. But the Parliament at once fell into other disputes with the king, and Charles angrily dismissed it. The furious members of the Commons, however, refused to disband, and forcibly held the speaker in his chair while they passed a series of resolutions condemning the king's government. After this spectacle, for eleven years, until bankruptcy and an invading Scottish army forced him to call another parliament, Charles governed without one. Unless it was called by the king, parliament could not meet, and Charles had had enough of that particular form of trouble.

THE KING'S MINISTERS

During the eleven years without a parliament, Charles (basically a weak man in an authoritarian position) ruled through the agency of two ministers, William Laud, archbishop of Canterbury, and Thomas Wentworth, earl of Strafford. Though very different in character (Strafford a soldier and tough-minded administrator, Laud a scholar and student of divinity), they were united in their loyalty to Charles. He had few trustworthy servants, but these two were the best a monarch ever had or could want, better surely than their master deserved. In their private dispatches to one another, they called their common program "Thorough."

When he first entered parliament, Strafford was thought to be of the popular party;[11] but the Petition of Right struck him as unnecessarily vindictive in its marshaling of complaints against the king. He soon took service with the administration, first as president of the Council of the North, then as lord lieutenant of Ireland. Both jobs involved him in military matters; but in Ireland, where he stayed more than six years, his rule also brought remarkable tranquillity and prosperity. He encouraged trade and industry, brought order and common sense to the Irish Parliament, and built up a competent Irish army. It is one of the rare bright spots in Irish history. To be sure, Strafford was working to benefit his master Charles I; moneys raised in Ireland helped make the king independent of parliament in England, and that Irish army, largely Roman Catholic, seemed to many a threat against English liberties. But Strafford was no vulgar tyrant's tool; he was an able, a dangerously able, man in the eyes of the king's enemies. When they gained power in 1640, they paid Strafford the dubious compliment of cut-

---

11. He was a kinsman of the puritan Sir Peter Wentworth who made so much trouble for Queen Elizabeth during her last parliaments (above, p. 185). But Sir Peter, like many another man who differed with Elizabeth, was deeply loyal to her; he would not have her referred to save as "our gracious lady the Queen." Strafford too, though he would doubtless have been of the king's party anyway, took offense at something rude and hectoring in the manner of his original associates.

ting off his head, by fair means or foul, as quickly as they possibly could. The story of his undaunted defense at his mockery of a trial is one of the most dramatic narratives in English history.

Strafford's fellow minister Laud was a diminutive, soft-spoken, acutely intelligent man of limited human sympathies. Much of his work lay in administering the church, which he wanted to see restored to authority and adorned with "the beauty of holiness." Laud worked hard to rebuild the physical fabric and increase the social prestige of the church. He put the architect Inigo Jones to work cleansing and beautifying St. Paul's,[12] he shored up church finances, enforced press censorship, badgered recalcitrant Puritans to conform with the church or leave it, and created, especially among the bishops, a learned and persuasive set of spokesmen for the Anglican position. (The works of these divines are collected in a weighty nineteenth-century gathering, "The Library of Anglo-Catholic Theology"; though for most of us the arts of theology are obsolete nowadays, these volumes must impress anyone simply as intellectual exercises.) Laud himself was a deft writer and skilled theologian; but his most dangerous and unpopular work for Charles was done on that super-court of Henry VII's creation, Star Chamber.

The phrase "star chamber proceedings" is still in general use to describe secret and arbitrary trials which deny a defendant his rights; and there can be no doubt that Star Chamber as Laud ran it deprived a defendant of his right to counsel, and sometimes issued cruel sentences. But the court aimed to render equity justice based, not on precedents like the common law, but on the rights and wrongs of a particular case. It had no use for legal counsel because it aimed at simple procedures and quick decisions. Property rights and social privilege carried less weight before Star Chamber than before regular courts. This justice might be cruel or arbitrary, but it provided a corrective to local tyrannies exercised by JP's, and dangerous competition to common lawyers whose respect for property rights was often excessive. What Laud and Strafford aimed at might have turned ultimately into a kind of corporate state, ecclesiastical, authoritarian, restrictive of property rights, and very interesting to contemplate. In any event, "Thorough" never reached fruition, and Laud followed Strafford to the block in 1645.

PURITAN AGITATION

Whatever their positive aims, Laud and Strafford spent most of their eleven years of unparliamentary government in suppressing dissent and trying to squeeze money

12. This was not the present structure, built by Christopher Wren after the fire of 1666, but an earlier building nearly six hundred years old. Jones's designs, combining a neoclassic porch and façade with an ancient Gothic structure, are of great artistic interest. Socially, their aim was to get the money-changers out of the temple, where they had been ensconced for years (above p. 182). It is curious that the puritans were bitterly hostile to any such separation.

out of a reluctant population. As their trials proved, such behavior could not be made to add up to high treason, but it made their cause, and them personally, unpopular in the extreme. In 1633, for example, William Prynne, a puritan lawyer, published a long, violent attack on stage plays, *Histriomastix*. It was a crude, ill-written book, full of learned ignorance, on a topic which had been trite since Tertullian, in the third century A.D., wrote a similar diatribe. By a strained interpretation of a few words, one passage was construed to reflect on the queen, who had recently acted in a masque. Prynne was brought before Star Chamber and condemned to a huge fine, a prison term, loss of his academic degrees, disbarment, the pillory, and amputation of both ears. The sentence, savage in itself, was specially offensive because it violated an old taboo against physically disfiguring members of the learned professions. Three years later, in the company of Henry Burton a parson and John Bastwick a doctor, Prynne got in trouble again over a libelous pamphlet printed in Holland and imported into England for clandestine circulation. All three men were fined, imprisoned, and mutilated, Prynne having the last stumps of his ears cropped off. Again the severity was self-defeating; the law under which the men were tried was well established, their guilt was flagrant, but the penalties were seen as inordinate and savage. Such cruelty cried aloud for martyrs and agitators to protest against it, and in 1638 a young man named John Lilburne stepped forward who had talents in both lines. Whipped through the streets of London and stood in the pillory for publishing a libel, he converted the event into a public spectacle, boldly denouncing his persecutors and appealing in strong, direct speech for the sympathy of all freeborn Englishmen. He was a mighty portent. The puritans who stood before James I at Hampton Court in 1604 had been clergymen, meek of deportment, pleading for small indulgences to be shown the tender consciences of their brethren. Lilburne was a new type, the defiant soldier-saint, as ready to advance the standard of Christ on the field of battle as on that of martyrdom. We shall see many like him in the ranks of Oliver Cromwell's far-famed, much-feared "Ironsides," the New Model Army.

John Hampden was another new and portentous human type who rose to prominence under the rule of Laud and Strafford. He was a tax resister. Among the statutes of England was a law that in time of war the king, to reinforce the navy and channel ports, might levy on all maritime counties a tax known as "ship money." In 1637 Charles proposed to levy this tax on the entire country, and in time of peace; he wanted the money, it was plain, not to defend the realm, but as a source of ordinary income. Hampden was a wealthy man, and the sum assessed on him was trivial, to be counted in shillings, not pounds; but it was a principle for which he stood, one affecting every property holder in the land. The modest firmness with which Hampden sustained his case before the court of Exchequer made a folk hero out of a quiet Buckinghamshire squire. In the event, a bare majority of the judges ruled against Hampden; but the furore over ship money was so great, and popular support for Hampden so clamorous, that collection of the tax fell off sharply.

The emergence from obscurity of men like Hampden and Lilburne marked a new militancy in the mood of the nation. But the mainspring of the Puritan-parliamentary party was a man so little known that he was and remains practically anonymous. In the entire life of John Pym it is hard to find a single memorable phrase, a single striking deed. He was a quiet man with a few threadbare ideas and endless determination who acted as organizer and party leader in the Commons. During the eleven long years when parliament never met, he kept in touch with other opposition leaders through an American colonizing venture, the Providence Island Company. The project, for settling an island in the Bahamas, was never successful, but the group taking part in it is found, as soon as parliaments start to meet again, acting in close concert under the leadership of Pym. That was his gray style, to work behind the scenes. He was so skillful at wielding unseen power that people began referring to him as "King Pym." In fact the revolution he guided through its first phases was notable mostly for its lack of revolutionary slogans and programs. The great institutions of the land discouraged men from looking into the future or thinking of progressive change. Common law stood on a massive foundation of judicial precedents reaching into the darkest of the dark ages. Puritanism aimed at returning the church to the condition in which the apostles left it, in the first and second centuries. The squires, parsons, and businessmen who animated the revolution had no use for theoretical speculation; their whole training had been to leave matters like foreign policy and social goals to the king and his council. Thus it was that the English nation backed down the road of history toward a revolution it neither wanted nor foresaw under the guidance of a colorless parliamentary tactician without a slogan or a program. Though he was a master at manipulating the mood of the house, King Pym was the least revolutionary revolutionary the world ever saw; it is our misfortune, in trying to understand this curious man, that he died in 1643, before events could force him to decide how revolutionary he was really going to be (SFR, E.21).

A PSEUDO-WAR WITH SCOTLAND, A REAL WAR BETWEEN ENGLISHMEN

Charles's system of personal government broke down on a folly of his own devising. Since being reformed by John Knox in the mid-sixteenth century, the Scottish kirk had been presbyterian at heart, and passionately so. In the last years of his residence, just before he came south to rule in England, James Stuart had reestablished episcopacy there, though very shakily indeed. (He counted on Scottish bishops, as he would count on English bishops, to free him from domineering presbyterian preachers.) In the early part of his reign, Charles did a number of minor tactless things to irritate the Scots; but in 1637, the king decided fatally to enforce the uniformity of the Scottish with the English church by introducing Cranmer's Book of Common Prayer. It was a bad move every way.

Immediate rioting broke out in Edinburgh against the "idolatrous," "anti-Christian" "mass-book." Scottish patriots flocked, as in the sixteenth century, to subscribe the solemn league and covenant, pledging everlasting support for a presbyterian system; and Charles, seeing their defiance as flat rejection of his royal authority, took steps to "reduce Scotland to obedience." That meant war. But war meant money, and money meant reaching agreement with an English Parliament which tended to think of Scots as northern friends. The king was caught, as they say, between the rock and the hard place.

While armies marched, maneuvered, and negotiated, Charles tried through 1638 and 1639 to gain English support for war against the Scots. But nothing could be done without parliament. In April 1640 he summoned a parliament, hoping to appeal to the patriotic feelings of members, but they would have none of it. Instead, they listed their grievances, demanded to investigate the king's ministers, and called for complete reform of the church. Within a scant three weeks they were dismissed, earning the nickname of the Short Parliament. Promptly the Scots invaded an unarmed and penniless kingdom, occupied two counties, and demanded to be paid for their trouble before they would leave. In November Charles was forced to summon another Parliament; this one, which sat through storm and stress for nearly twenty years, earned the name of the Long Parliament.

Because they were deathly afraid of him, the managers of the Long Parliament began by demanding the head of Strafford. Unable to make a case of treason against him, and secretly aware that he could make one against them, they passed a bill of attainder, which is simply a polite phrase for judicial murder.[13] Once safe from the man they feared most, they proceeded to dismantle the whole structure of "Thorough." They passed a bill declaring that Parliament could not be dissolved except with its own consent; they jailed Archbishop Laud and abolished all the prerogative courts. Customs duties were placed under parliamentary control, ship money was annulled. Prynne, Burton, Bastwick, and Lilburne all came back from exile to triumphant receptions in London; their fines were revoked, they were indemnified for their sufferings. The House of Commons, deftly urged forward by Pym, moved to consider the question whether only a few bishops had done evil, or the office was corrupt in itself and should be abolished "root and branch." Opinion in the house was evenly divided, but a Catholic rising in Ireland converted the religious question to a question of raw power. An army was needed, and Parliament would not trust the king with it. Charles panicked, and on 4 January 1642 came into the Commons with armed troopers, intending to arrest Pym, Hampden, and three other radical leaders. The coup failed, its victims having been forewarned; but trust, it was clear, had

13. Technically, an act of attainder inflicts a penalty (usually death, forfeiture of estates, and corruption of blood) without judicial trial. The king had solemnly promised Strafford immunity; but, seeing his master in danger of suffering from his own unpopularity, Strafford released Charles from his promise. Signing Strafford's death warrant was the most craven, unkingly thing Charles ever did.

broken down completely. Charles promptly left London, and through spring and summer wandered across northern England gathering support and laying plans. On August 22 he raised his royal standard at Nottingham; civil war had begun for the first time in 150 years, the last time in history.

CRUEL CHOICES

The outbreak of the English civil war is much more interesting than the fighting of it. Five years of maneuver and negotiation intervened between the first instinctive revulsion of the Scots against the prayer book and the appeal to arms in 1642. During that interval Englishmen had been making up their minds, slowly and obscurely. Where they finally stood showed, as vividly as a social X-ray, what areas and classes were satisfied or dissatisfied with Stuart rule.[14] Broadly speaking, the king's strength lay in the north and west, the Parliament's in the south and east. Parliament had the support of the Puritan clergy and of those laymen whom they had been able to influence: city merchants, tradesmen, small businessmen, prentices, as well as gentry living in the "home counties" near London and connected by family or business ties with London money. East Anglia was solid for the Parliament because the wool trade there depended on London capital and sold on the London market, also because many refugee Huguenots had settled there to ply the weaver's trade. On the other side, the king had active support from the upper clergy (this often included cathedral towns, where the hierarchy had influence), from courtiers and Roman Catholics secret or avowed, whose existence depended on exercise of royal favor. And for the sinew of his armies the king drew on landowners of the west and north countries, men with still partly feudal estates and armies of loyal retainers. In those districts country folk were not yet involved with the money economy centered at London; and they were relatively untouched by puritan propaganda.

Looking at the two forces thus opposed to one another, an observer might have estimated that initial advantage would lie with the king, long-term advantage with the Parliament. The king's forces included some gentlemen with real military experience and at least one commander of spectacular ability: that was Rupert, Prince Palatine, the king's nephew, who brought to his uncle's cause a dashing troop of cavalry and a quick grasp of strategy that were unique in this war fought mostly by self-taught amateurs.[15] Still in the king's favor, the private

14. A cold account, based on "interest," of how Englishmen took sides glosses over the agony of families divided, friends turned enemies, and sensitive men forced to choose between two repugnant alternatives. Lucius Cary Viscount Falkland, whose friendship with Sir Henry Morison had inspired Ben Jonson to a famous ode, reluctantly sided with the king; but he died in an early skirmish, not without suspicion of having deliberately sought his death. For him, as for many Englishmen, the civil war was a tragedy, whoever won it.

15. Rupert was the son of James's daughter Elizabeth, who had married Frederick the Elector Palatine, and whom James had refused to help in their hour of need (above, p. 208). In addition to his soldierly skills (and he was as good with ships as with horses), Rupert was strikingly handsome,

troops assembled from tenants on great estates usually had the rudiments of military training—knew the butt end from the muzzle of a gun. And they were passionately loyal. To raise money for the king's cause, many a country gentleman melted down the heavy silver plate that had been in the family for generations, while the ladies of the house tearfully donated their rings and jewelry. The privileged classes rallied, as in honor they were bound, to the fountain of privilege, the wellhead of honor.

On the other side, the forces supporting Parliament came from the richest and most populous sections of the land, but they included few trained commanders or practiced soldiers. Prentices and shopkeepers were more at ease with yardsticks than with pikes or muskets. Indeed, there were men in the country—Oliver Cromwell knew where to find them—who would make better soldiers even than the gentry; but it would take time to recruit them. In the first stages, the Parliament's soldiers were a largely inept, half-hearted lot, and the cause was saved only by the city of London, its devotedly Puritan citizens, and its access to large supplies of credit. After their first burst of generous enthusiasm, the king's partisans had nothing more to give; after the first bumbling failures of the parliamentary armies, city merchants simply floated another loan and hired a better army. In describing the two parties of combatants, one must always recall that a large part of the population stood by, in almost complete indifference, as the civil war unfolded before them. Occasionally we hear of spontaneous semi-organizations called "Clubmen" who appeared briefly near battlefields, taking no sides, but expressing their sentiments in crude, hand-lettered signs. One of these said, memorably, "If You Take Our Cattle, We Will Give You Battle." In the struggle between privilege and money, that was as close to involvement as many Englishmen wanted to come.

Since it lasted less than three years, the military side of the war is soon described. The king struck quickly at London, but at the battle of Edgehill (23 October 1642) he was checked; further advance on London was stalled when the "trained bands" (a kind of urban, once-a-week militia) marched out to Turnham Green and proved so formidable that the king withdrew to Oxford (November 1642). With one army under the earl of Newcastle in the north, another under Sir Ralph Hopton in the west, and his own base at Oxford in the center, the king tried throughout 1643 to tighten a ring around London. He was frustrated, mostly by stiff resistance in urban centers like Hull, Gloucester, and Plymouth. Late in 1643, Parliament, feeling the need of Scottish help, negotiated a carefully ambiguous and shady treaty which the Scots interpreted as a promise to establish Presbyterianism. Under auspices of this treaty, a joint force of Scottish Presby-

---

artistically gifted, and extremely intelligent; his diplomatic instincts were good, he made discoveries in chemistry and metallurgy, and took part in founding the Hudson's Bay Company. Charles, who did not know what intelligence was, mistook Rupert's intelligence for disloyalty. It is an interesting, if futile, speculation to consider how different English history might have been had the uncle been a cavalry commander and the nephew a king.

terians and English parliamentarians attacked and defeated the main royalist army of the north at Marston Moor near York (2 July 1644). It was the last battle on English soil in which bands of retainers played a major role; the earl of Newcastle's "White Coats" held the royalist center, and held it heroically, dying on the field to the last man. But no sooner was victory won than the agreement underlying it started to disintegrate. The Scottish army had not done well at Marston Moor; the decisive force had been the army of the Eastern Association, raised and led by Oliver Cromwell. These were for the most part Puritans from the East Anglia countryside; they were the germ of what was soon to be called the New Model Army; and they wanted neither Anglican government as formed by Archbishop Laud nor Presbyterian government as exemplified in the Scottish kirk. Like Robert Browne before them (see above, p. 163), they wanted each separate congregation to make independent choice of its own form of worship; and so they were called sometimes independents, sometimes congregationalists.

These troopers of Cromwell's, who made their debut by smashing Rupert's "invincible" cavalry at Marston Moor, were unique among seventeenth-century soldiers in being motivated not by personal greed or by feudal loyalty but by religious principles. Like Cromwell, they had a strong sense of God's hidden hand directing their actions toward an end known only to Himself. Instead of carousing the night before a battle, they sang psalms; they carried Bibles in the pockets of their greatcoats, and read them as they waited to charge the enemy; after their first sweep across the field, they did not scatter to collect spoils, but held ranks, right-about-faced, and charged again. They were terrible warriors, often uncouth in their speech, with a passion for metaphors out of the Old Testament; but when they smote the Philistine hip and thigh, or sent the Amalekite groveling in the dust, few men needed an interpreter to get the point. Their success at Marston Moor led to remodeling the entire army to get rid of inefficient or half-hearted commanders. Early military leaders had preserved the polite fiction that they were fighting to rescue Charles Stuart from evil advisers who had misled him. Many worried that they might meet him face to face on the field, when they would have to decide between kneeling before their liege lord and shooting to kill. Cromwell and men of his ilk felt no such distress. Their loyalty was to the Lord of Hosts, and Charles Stuart, if he opposed that dread commander, would be met with saber and horse pistol, as well as the next man.

Thus the help of the Scots was rejected as unnecessary and actually offensive to those native troops on whom Parliament was determined to rely. The last full-scale battle of the civil war was fought at Naseby about twenty miles east of Coventry, 14 June 1645. Both armies were small by modern standards (10,000 men for the king, 13,000 for Parliament); but the field was won by discipline, not numbers, and it was won decisively. Naseby annihilated the king's last concentrations of human and material resources.[16]

16. The war decided at Naseby is sometimes called the first civil war; the brief second civil war, between the New Model Army and a Presbyterian-royalist coalition, ended at the battle of Preston

TROUBLES OF A SETTLEMENT

Two pressing problems remained: what to do with Charles Stuart, still at liberty but no longer effectively king? and what to do with those God-fearing, strong-minded warriors whom Cromwell had summoned and who now refused to lie down quietly and go away? The latter question was part of a larger one. For the first time in history, a majority of the English population, wholly untrained in such matters, was being asked to consider and decide its own destiny. When Parliament curtailed the power of the bishops in 1641, censorship of printed material disappeared too; the result was a perfect flood of pamphlets, tracts, broadsides, sermons, and miscellaneous persuasives on current events. (A book-seller named George Thomason started collecting them in 1641, and twenty years later, when he stopped, had more than 23,000.) This flood of propaganda, to which the semiliterate and semisane contributed alongside a literary genius like John Milton, had its effect on the army, as on the population at large. Hundreds of different religious sects sprang up; thousands of different opinions, on an infinite variety of topics, started to be aired.[17] Some were sensible, some silly. But the new habit of common folk reading and thinking about public affairs created for the first time a force very powerful, though intangible and hard to measure; we know it as public opinion.

Soldiers of the New Model Army had, on the whole, reasonable and practical ideas, being under the predominant influence of a liberal London group known as the Levellers. Their program was not as radical as that name implies. They wanted thorough electoral reform and a wider franchise, equality before the law, popular elections of sheriffs and JPs, total abolition of monarchy, the state church, and the House of Lords—briefly, a liberal secular democracy tempered by concern for property rights. (Far to the left of the Levellers was the smaller, more ephemeral community of Diggers, who agitated for immediate universal communism.) But even the moderate Levellers were too radical for Cromwell. By threats, arrests, and a single summary execution, he broke the back of a potential revolt in the army and hounded the Levellers out of existence. From then on, though grumblings continued, Cromwell kept his left-wing critics so busy in Ireland and Scotland that they had no chance to organize. And though sects continued to proliferate, some restraints were placed even on them. In 1656 a

(August 1648). Relatively unimportant in itself, the second civil war knit bonds between Presbyterians and royalists that would become significant in 1660.

17. A few of these seventeenth-century sects, among them the Quakers and Congregationalists, still survive. Among the many which did not were the picturesque Ranters, Seekers, Muggletonians, Adamites, and Fifth Monarchy Men. Local preachers and teachers, with theologies too idiosyncratic even to have a name, sprang up and flourished briefly. The more wild-eyed of these enthusiasts commonly laid claim to some form of special inspiration; they had been touched by an Inner Light which enabled them to identify the Antichrist, foretell the Second Coming, or otherwise give voice to the Divine Will. Amid this welter of confused and extravagant claims, many sensible and practical reforms were proposed, most of which got lost in the shuffle.

Quaker named James Nayler was terribly punished for intimating a comparison between himself and Jesus.[18] Perhaps the punishment was deliberately made severe so it would not have to be repeated. For the Puritans were not eager to persecute each other. As long as they stayed out of politics and avoided offending public opinion too grossly, the sects were not much bothered by Cromwell or his government.

THE INCONVENIENT KING

Charles Stuart was a special problem, tougher in many ways when he did not have an army than when he did. After Naseby, Charles retreated to Oxford, and when Oxford was on the verge of surrender (May 1646), he turned himself over to the Scots, supposing that as they had been disappointed in the treaty before Marston Moor, they might restore him to the throne in return for his establishing Presbyterianism in England—for a while. (That "for a while" was typical of Charles's dealings under duress. If he could have sided frankly and fully with any one faction, he might have had a chance to get his throne back. But all his dealing and bargaining aimed only at making his enemies quarrel with one another, so he could get the crown on his own terms. He was an instinctive, inveterate equivocator.) The Scots held him for about a year, then as part of a larger bargain turned him over to Parliament, with whom he was negotiating when, on 3 June 1647, he was seized by the army and held in the palace at Hampton Court. With the army (i.e., Cromwell) he might have made a deal, except that he was simultaneously and secretly negotiating with the Scots. On November 11, the king escaped from Hampton Court, with the rumored connivance of Cromwell,[19] and fled to Carisbrooke castle on the Isle of Wight. There he proceeded to drive the last nails in his own coffin. In December 1647, he signed an agreement with the Scots promising three years of Presbyterianism in England in return for a military invasion leading to his restoration. The Scottish invasion actually came off in July 1648 and at Preston, in August, was crushed with contemptuous ease. The whole story of Charles's complicity then became public, to the fury, not only of Cromwell, but of all English patriots. That a king of England should conspire with foreigners (and the Scots were not only foreigners but long-time enemies) was the last straw. A peace party, largely but not exclusively presbyterian, still wanted to negotiate with the king; but Cromwell sent Colonel John Pride into

18. Nayler's actual offense was that in October 1655 he rode naked into Bristol on a mule surrounded by followers who sang, "Hosannah! Holy, holy! Lord God of Sabaoth!" It was an imitation or parody of Christ's entry into Jerusalem. He was twice whipped (once in London, once in Bristol), branded, had his tongue bored with a red-hot iron, and was sentenced to two years at hard labor.

19. Cromwell knew Charles was not to be trusted, and probably calculated that if he was given a moment's freedom, he would entangle himself in plots so tricky that when exposed they would discredit him and lead to his execution. That was how it worked out; but that Cromwell planned it that way is only probable.

the commons with a file of soldiers, and they forcibly expelled more than a hundred members. The move was known as "Pride's Purge" (pun intended); the shrunken house that remained was universally and derisively called "The Rump." They promptly constituted themselves a court to try the king for treason. As with the trials of Strafford and Laud, the charges were feebly sustained, and the court doubtfully legitimate at best. Indeed, the very idea of a king being traitor to himself had its absurd side. The king was bullied by his accusers and judges, humiliated and silenced when he tried to speak in his own defense. But his whole bearing in these last days of his troubled life was noble and dignified. He died, he said, for the rights of subjects and monarchs under the law, and for the rights and privileges of the church of England, as established by his ancestors. His last word on the scaffold, spoken so softly that only Bishop Juxon who stood next to him could hear it, was the simple, mysterious word, "Remember." His execution took place on 30 January 1649. He had been a weak, foolish, and narrow man, but the style with which he went to his death redeemed every failing. Hard-eyed Andrew Marvell wrote, in his "Horatian Ode," the ultimate tribute:

> He nothing common did or mean
> Upon that memorable scene.

THE CULTURE OF THE STUART COURTS

The forty-five turbulent and tragic years of the first two Stuarts were for England years of intense intellectual ferment and radical literary change. Within this period fall the last and greatest plays of Shakespeare, the prophetic scientific declamations of Francis Bacon, and the first poetic masterpieces of John Milton. Within these years, English philosophy as a discipline separate from theology sprang to vigorous life; English history and biography, if not absolutely new crafts, revived and produced their first classics; the art of the masque flourished and declined; while during the civil wars periodical journalism emerged into the world, a birth no less portentous for being strikingly ugly. Oriental and Biblical studies, antiquarian research, the theology of the church fathers, classical philology, the arts of astronomy and celestial navigation, anatomy, and mathematics all experienced decisive advances. For the first time in history, England had, in Inigo Jones, an architect worthy of a European reputation.[20] Gilbert's ground-breaking study of magnetism a little antedates the first Stuart, William Harvey's classic study of the action of the heart practically coincides with the coronation of the

20. Monumental building had taken place in medieval England, witness spectacular cathedrals like those of Ely and Wells (both built gradually between the eleventh and the fourteenth centuries); but these are associated with the plans of no specific architect. While studying in Italy, Jones experienced the influence of Andrea Palladio, whose neoclassic style he carried into the north of Europe for the first time. He also occupied a place of prime importance in the history of the English masque.

second. Englishmen of the Stuart era traveled through the Middle East, colonized America and the West Indies, established trade relations with Russia, India, and the Spice Islands, even made a first tentative appearance in the Chinese port of Canton. When we add to these active enterprisers a group of devotional poets unequaled in Europe, a dozen dramatists "second string" only by comparison with Shakespeare,[21] the most learned and eloquent preachers known to the English pulpit, numerous madrigalists and song writers of whom Orlando Gibbons and Thomas Campion are still well known, plus mythographers, chronologists, translators, popular moralists, character writers, balladeers, satirists, essayists, philosophers, and psychologists, we get some notion of the zesty activity of this nation, amounting to a scant five million or so inhabitants. Not for nothing did Milton describe his countrymen in "Areopagitica" as

a nation not slow and dull but of a quick, ingenious and piercing spirit, acute to invent, subtle and sinewy to discourse, not beneath the reach of any point, the highest that human capacity can soar to.

The importance of the Stuart court to England's cultural life in the early century is hard to overstate. Not only the monarchs but the lords and ladies who flocked round the court thought it part of their social function to inspire writers, to be writers themselves if they were able, and to reward writers with social prestige and material patronage. Especially that sort of writing which we distinguish as *belles lettres* was the work of court people, done for court people, to court standards of taste. Donne published hardly any poems during his life, yet he reached everyone who (for a complex and demanding poet) mattered, because manuscript collections of his verse circulated around court and were freely transcribed. Masques were put on mostly at court, for a single performance, before a select audience; the general public was excluded. Lancelot Andrewes was known as a court preacher; his power to squeeze the doctrinal marrow out of a tiny text, word by word and sometimes syllable by syllable, would have stupefied an unlearned audience. So would his custom of citing freely in the original Latin, Greek, or Hebrew. He was not showing off: far from it. He was addressing his intellectual peers, who wanted the last and best word on a text from the most precious book in the world. A whole area of literature by Englishmen, about which we rarely think in these unlanguaged days, was written in a dead tongue, Latin. John Barclay's political romance *Argenis* (1621) gained wide popularity in its original Latin. When King James visited Cambridge in 1615, he was entertained with a Latin comedy, *Ignoramus;* the male lead mimicked Sir Edward Coke so skillfully that his majesty nearly laughed himself into an apoplexy. Even Milton's poem "Lycidas," when it appeared in 1637, could hardly have been

---

21. Whether Jonson is the second figure of the first rank or the first of the second will always be disputed. The names of Webster, Ford, Tourneur, Middleton, Beaumont, Fletcher, Marston, Massinger, Dekker, Chapman, and Shirley may stand here for a whole constellation of dramatic achievement, inferior to nothing in the language.

read outside a narrow circle of the learned. The volume in which it was printed bore the title *Iuxta Eduardo King,* and of the thirty-six poems, just thirteen were in English (three were in Greek, the rest in Latin). And without explanatory notes, even an English poem like "Lycidas" required a good classical background to understand it.

> O fountain Arethuse, and thou honored flood,
> Smooth-sliding Mincius, crowned with vocal reeds—

the nexus joining these two far-separated watercourses has nothing to do with the streams themselves, it is the fact that Theocritus in Alexandria and Virgil in Rome wrote poetry naming the brooks (that's why the reeds are "vocal"). It is a nice example of what George Herbert, in his poem "Jordan I," called "catching the sense at two removes."

"METAPHYSICALS" AND "CAVALIERS"

The metaphysical poets of the seventeenth century never realized that they amounted to a "school" or, for that matter, that they were metaphysical. The word was first applied to some of them by Dryden and Dr. Johnson long after the poets themselves were dead; at first, it implied nothing more than "abstruse." For the poets and their contemporaries, "strong lines" were the distinguishing feature of their style. Such lines employed powerful metaphors, used for structure, not ornament; they were intellectually difficult, and deliberately so. Much less appeal than before was made to traditional decorative mythologies and stock Petrarchan properties, such as frozen hearts, Cupid's arrows, etc. And sometimes, though not always, strong lines made use of colloquial diction and rough metrics—and not only in traditional love lyrics. The devotional verse of Donne, Herbert, Vaughan, and Crashaw is the most substantial body of such writing in English; the tense and resistant style of metaphysical verse lent itself particularly well to sacred themes. Because the style put such heavy pressures on language, even verse celebrating secular ladies tended to take on vaguely blasphemous overtones. Above all, it was their rejection of "the poetic"—mere prettiness—that gave the metaphysical poets their staying power. Their gift for the abrupt and striking phrase, the hard, witty thought thrown off in an apparently careless colloquialism, delighted twentieth-century readers who had wearied of Victorian high seriousness. Donne is, of course, the chief master of this style, and it was Professor Grierson's edition of Donne's poems (1912) which touched off the revival of the metaphysical poets in our time.

But as we move away from Donne himself, the metaphysical element in the metaphysical poets rapidly evaporates. George Herbert has some strong lines, but his most characteristic verses are quiet in their intensity, almost self-effacing. Henry Vaughan and Thomas Traherne are visionary poets, absorbed in the radiance of an inner landscape. Richard Crashaw is commonly described as a "baroque" poet; the word, adapted from art criticism, is not without literary meaning,[22] but it has little relevance to other metaphysical poets or to the metaphysical style in general. Marvell is a poet of serious wit, like Donne, but his wit takes the form of drollery, and he writes pages on end without a strong line or a violent metaphor. Abraham Cowley is not a wit at all. In fact, metaphysical style, being rooted in tensions and pressures of the mind, was too personal and various to make for a proper "school." In anthologies and critical studies, the label is rarely attached to the same group of poets; each editor defines the group differently, which may make us wonder how much of a group it really was. We may envision a single deep anxiety radiating a variety of expressions. The court and church, as they had long been established, were in deep crisis; metaphysical poetry was one mode in which some men, some of the time, expressed that anxiety.[23] One could also think of it as an extension and intensification of the compressed, abstruse, and anxious poetry written under Elizabeth by George Chapman and Fulke Greville.

The central figure among the poets of the early Stuart courts was the laureate, Ben Jonson. He wrote many of the royal masques, he was master of the grave, sententious poem of compliment, and he enjoyed the adulation of fellow poets, who were mostly his juniors. They christened themselves "The Tribe of Ben," and among their numbers were Robert Herrick, Thomas Carew, Richard Lovelace, Sir John Suckling, and Thomas Randolph, to name no more. What they shared with Ben was a preference for clear, measured verse, modeled on classic precedents. Being smooth and graceful often turned, among these courtly songsters, to being casual and conversational. Some, like Herrick, wrote tiny verses on tiny topics. But as a group they were unsympathetic to the anxiety and strain of the metaphysical poets; instead of strong lines, they cultivated smooth surfaces. Suckling, professing utter indifference to the art of poetry, wrote that he

> Prized black eyes, or a lucky hit
> At bowls, above all the trophies of wit.

The rhyme seems to come along just as accidentally as a strike on the bowling green; the girl's black eyes are no more valuable than a bit of luck in the game,

22. The baroque, of which the sculptor and architect Gianlorenzo Bernini was the greatest exponent, is a weighty, agitated style, stirring the emotions of the viewer by a blend of illusionism, light, color, and motion. It often combines erotic with religious feeling, leading sometimes to disquieting responses. For an intelligent, determined, but not always convincing effort to apply art-historical categories to Renaissance poetry, see SFR, D.21.

23. Symptomatic of the same anxiety was an Anglican drift toward monastic ideals. At Little Gidding, Nicholas Ferrar and his family established a private retreat for contemplation, prayer, and intricate handicrafts like needlecraft and fine bookbinding. It was a gentle and inoffensive option; but Puritans were enraged at this withdrawal from the world. Denounced as an "Arminian nunnery," Little Gidding was broken up as soon as the Puritans could get at it. But weaving oneself into a circlet of contemplation was a frequent pattern of metaphysical thought.

though both are worth more than poetic reputation. Still, we note that it's a poem he's writing, and writing rather deftly.

The ideal of being careless and masterly in their verses served the cavalier poets well when they wrote, as they generally did, of love—or rather, of sex. The court of Charles I was strait-laced indeed compared with that of his son Charles II after the Restoration; but all the cavalier poets professed libertinism. Sir John Suckling is a cheery little flirt whose piping voice and tripping meters mimic the more cynical moods of Donne. But the erotic poetry of Carew ("A Rapture," "A Second Rapture") is tougher stuff; it foreshadows the hard porn of the earl of Rochester some forty years later; and both can be seen as stages in the progressive degeneration of that ideal courtier whom Sir Philip Sidney had described and exemplified.

MASQUES AND PLAYS

As they represented the aristocracy's heroic dream life, Stuart masques gave vivid expression to the courtly ethos.[24] They were static, superficial, spectacular pageants, rich in costume, scenery, and song, held together by a very casual story line. Heroic virtue was the ideal they generally proposed, but virtue so reconciled with pleasure, so instinctive and natural in the enactors of it, as to require no effort. Vice was no less absolute than virtue; the masques enact a contrast, not a conflict, between the two. Deformity displays itself in the anti-masque, and disappears without struggle or confusion before the radiant vision of order presented by the final intricate dances of the masquers. Metamorphosis or transformation is thus a frequent theme; and the final triumph is commonly climaxed by an act of fealty and homage on the part of the masquers to the supreme figure of honor in the audience. Unlike dramas, masques maintain no sharp division between audience and actors. In a final celebration, the masquers, without quite abandoning their mythic identities or openly resuming their everyday persons, bring forward all their combined identities in a single act of obeisance, uniting in one gesture the principles of loyalty, courtesy, honor. If they did not derive from that Neoplatonism which was widely diffused through court circles (Cardinal Bembo gives it eloquent voice in the last book of Castiglione's *Courtier;* Spenser and the youthful Milton give it an English cast in their verses), the masques generally harmonized with it unforcedly.

The typical masque is unlocalized in time and space; it takes place Somewhere and Anytime. The distance between this dream world and the actuality of everyday London was partly bridged by the drama, which had good commercial reasons for keeping its feet on the ground and its audiences on the edge of their

---

24. Masques grew out of courtly festivals and ceremonies of the early Renaissance—tournaments, triumphs, joyous entries, marriage feasts, and the like. Socially, they were quite distinct from the early miracle plays and of course the later professional theaters.

seats. London itself provided no small part of the drama's material; London audiences were conscious of themselves and of their city as dramatic spectacles. Jonson's low-life comedies (*The Alchemist, Bartholomew Fair, A Tale of a Tub*) seem intent on cramming their stages with as much street life as they can.[25] *The Shoemaker's Holiday* (1600) by Dekker and *The Knight of the Burning Pestle* (1613) by Beaumont and Fletcher make affectionate fun of character types whom the audience could find in real life a five-minutes' walk from the theater. As they had been doing for years, playwrights took their plots from mythology, from continental collections of short stories, and sometimes from their own imaginations. In the collaborative work of Beaumont and Fletcher, as in the last "romantic" comedies of Shakespeare, we find a new emphasis being placed on spectacle, song, fantasy. There is a full-fledged masque toward the end of *The Tempest* and in *The Winter's Tale* a parody scene is played out where Mopsa and Dorcas (the simple-minded audience) repeatedly ask Autolycus if his ridiculous ballads are true. Oh, yes, they are indeed, he says, very true. Shakespeare underlines his self-mockery by making a bit of the action take place on the seacoast of Bohemia, which is landlocked; unity of time he disposes of by putting a sixteen-year interlude in the middle of his play. The fantasy is clearly deliberate, the play playful.

Another sort of drama popular in the early century may require more explanation: these are dramas of murder, incest, and madness, actions generally set in Italy or Spain, the Catholic countries. Perhaps they owe something to the bloodthirsty Senecan dramas of earlier days and to traditional tragedies of revenge. But they are subtler in their psychology, and in their fitful, luminous poetry. Examples are *The White Divell* and *The Duchess of Malfi* (1612, 1614) by John Webster, *The Broken Heart* and *'Tis Pity She's a Whore* (both 1633) by John Ford, and Thomas Middleton's *The Changeling* (1623?). With just one partial exception, the duchess of Malfi, the characters in these plays have no heroic aspirations; rather, they go to their deaths as if snarled in a hopeless web of stifling circumstance. Death itself is much dwelt on beforehand, in all its grisly details and particulars; madmen wail, dead hands are passed around in the darkness. The mood of the plays is singularly airless and oppressive; "macabre" and "ghoulish" are adjectives that have been freely invoked. But this gloom is lit intermittently by flashes of poetic eloquence; the plots may seem stagy and improbable, but the individual scenes are alive with imaginative energy. Where did these nightmare visions come from, and why were they so acceptable to seventeenth-century audiences? We must beware of thinking that audiences enjoy morbid plays because their personal lives are morbid; still, the passionate, som-

25. The comedy of "humors" applies to this picturesque pageant the standard psychological theory of the time. Moral eccentrics like Voltore or Morose suffer from an excess of one humor or another; their purgation takes place in the course of the play's action and might be therapeutic for the audience as well. Instruction and correction which would have been considered absurdly presumptuous in a masque were accepted as natural and normal in a play.

ber melancholy of these Jacobean tragedies is a cultural fact to be pondered, as was noted at the beginning of this chapter.

PROSE: ORNATE STYLE

Loosely speaking, the prose of the early seventeenth century can be divided into ornate and plain. Euphuism (above, p. 172) enjoyed its brief hour and vanished not quite without a trace. In its place succeeded, on the one hand, the rolling periods and measured deliberation of writers like Hooker and Raleigh; on the other hand, a clipped, irregular prose style, concise and abrupt, known as "the Senecan amble."

Ornate style relied, naturally, on several different sorts of adornment. One line of descent was from Cicero, whose oratorical sentences, formally balanced and suspended through long periods, keep one waiting for the moment when, after much circling and qualification, they wind down to their terminus. Hooker is fond of such extended and balanced sentences:

Because therefore want of the knowledge of God is cause of all iniquity among men, as contrariwise the very ground of all our happiness and the seed of whatsoever perfect virtue groweth from us is a right opinion touching things divine, this kind of knowledge we may justly set down for the first and chiefest thing which God imparteth unto his people, and our duty of receiving this at his merciful hands, for the first of those religious offices wherewith we publicly honor him on earth (*Of the Laws of Ecclesiastical Polity*, Book V).

The sentence, like some of Milton's, may be compared to a tree, with wide-spreading roots in the preliminary subordinates, wide-spreading branches in the concluding consequences, the whole strongly tied together with a powerful double-duty affirmation, "we may justly set down."

A little less formal control, a little more driving energy, but the same pattern of extended, elevated assertion is displayed in a famous passage from Raleigh's *History of the World:*

Oh eloquent, just and mighty death! whom none could advise, thou hast persuaded; what none hath dared, thou hast done; and whom all the world hath flattered, thou only hast cast out of the world and despised. Thou hast drawn together all the far-stretched greatness, all the pride, cruelty, and ambitions of man, and covered it all over with these two narrow words, *Hic jacet.*

It is clear from both these passages that the ornate style was well adapted to, and no doubt it was partly derived from, pulpit oratory. Seventeenth-century preachers developed its resources according to their various temperaments. Donne, for example, can never resist wringing and twisting an idea through all its possible paradoxes in order to bring it to a climax:

Adam sinned and I suffer; I forfeited before I had any possession or could claim any interest; I had a punishment before I had a being, and God was displeased with me before I was I; I was built up scarce 50 years ago in my mother's womb, and I was cast down almost 6,000 years ago in Adam's loins; I was born in the last age of the world, and died in the first. [Sermon of 24 February 1625]

Later preachers sometimes adapted the lofty device of the epic simile to the occasions of the pulpit; Jeremy Taylor, a famous Anglican elocutionist of the mid-century, was particularly noted for his "So have I seen" passages which introduced extended comparisons with clouds, birds, trees, and other natural phenomena into his moral discourses.

   Ornate style could be turned equally well to secular ends. Sir Thomas Browne was a Norwich physician with a temperament that combined skepticism in philosophy with an active faith in religion. The technical name for this position is *fideism* (from Latin *fides*, faith), and among its other exponents are Montaigne, Charron, and John Dryden. Browne needed supernatural faith because of the uncertainty of human knowledge; he proved his faith by deliberately losing himself in uncertainties. And to express the weakness of the human mind before the dark immensities of the universe, he resorted to a prose at once symphonic and witty—metaphysical in its wit, grandiose in the reach of its imagery. The best known of his books is the first, an account of his religious position published in 1643 as *Religio Medici*.[26] But Browne is an addictive taste, and the true devotee will not be content with anything less than the vast *Pseudodoxia Epidemica,* or *Vulgar Errors* (1646). Like Robert Burton's ragbag encyclopedia, this is an enormous compilation of ancient beliefs and observations, mostly ridiculous and outmoded. The pretext is that by exploring these foolish beliefs we will arrive at a true one; but more often the errors are explored for their own sake. It was Browne's special delight to wander through the curious lore of the past, musing on the follies of human belief and the marvelous ways of the Creator. Old-fashioned even in his own day, Browne was one of the remarkable minds of the century—a deeply private man who could wind the cocoon of his intricate thought around even a trivial topic, and make of it something fascinating.

PROSE: PLAIN STYLE

Plain style is exemplified early in the century by the *Essays* of Francis Bacon. Picking up his essay "Of Riches," we find ourselves in another world:

26. In English, *A Doctor's Faith;* the book was startling because fideism is not often found in Protestant churches. If one deprecates reason to build up faith, there's no reason not to put one's faith in the most authoritative of all churches, the Roman Catholic. Browne didn't, because for him as a provincial Englishman, the natural church was the national one. He had to think out his position while studying medicine at Montpellier in a Catholic land; if he had been born in such a land, his fideism left him no reason not to conform with the custom of the country. Puritans, who placed their faith in Scripture, not the church, would certainly consider such a position scandalous.

I cannot call riches better than the baggage of virtue. The Roman word is better, *impedi-menta*. For as the baggage is to an army, so is riches to virtue. It cannot be spared or left behind, but it hindereth the march; yea, and the care of it sometimes loseth or disturbeth the victory. Of great riches, there is no real use, except it be in the distribution; the rest is but conceit.

These abrupt, impersonal discourses, as dry and concise as if generated by a computer, were first published in 1597, and continued to be revised and augmented till 1625. Bacon's immediate predecessor in writing essays was Michel de Montaigne, but his greater debt was to the Roman dramatist, moralist, and philosophic letter writer Seneca the Younger. Montaigne is an open, a confessional writer; his program for the *Essais* was to write of the only subject he knew well, himself, and to do so by stripping himself morally naked. Bacon is a guarded writer; his essays are so pithy and impersonal that many of the sayings in them have become proverbial. They seem to express the wisdom of the folk, not of an individual. Above all, as he combines prudent morality with a shrewd sense of business, Bacon's emphasis is practical. He solves the religious problems so important in his day mainly by ignoring them, and provides his reader with advice as free from spiritual overtones as if written by a pagan philosopher. In this respect, as in many others, Bacon's mind was a remarkable mix of old and new. His little book *On the Wisdom of the Ancients* interprets mythological tales in the complex allegorical mode that had been traditional since the middle ages. It is only in an extraordinary fragment, "The New Atlantis," that we get a powerful measure of the prophetic quality of Bacon's thought.

With its choppy sentences and avoidance of long, balanced suspensions, Bacon's prose strikes us as an artful avoidance of art; for simple, natural garrulity, we turn to the work of a word-intoxicated Oxford scholar, Robert Burton, who published in 1621 the first edition of his *Anatomy of Melancholy*. Burton's book, though ostensibly a medical treatise, is much like Montaigne's collection of personal essays. Like Montaigne, Burton is absorbed in himself. He was an indefatigable reader, and by patching into successive editions of his book every thought or phrase he encountered, he effectively converted his book into his personal existence. Indeed, the books of both men continued to grow after their physical deaths, because both left behind copy for further annotated and augmented editions. And finally, both Burton and Montaigne are humorists, as Bacon never was. Burton's central subject being a mania for study, and the cure for his disease being more and more study, he seems to be caught like a hamster in a wheel, running ever faster and faster to get nowhere. Yet behind his wild accumulation of quotations lies a wise and subtle mind, which recognizes its own absurdity, and finds a wry sanity in that recognition.

Both Browne and Burton are very present in their writing; in fact self-display is a prime purpose of their writing. Most plain prose of the early century was less complicated by this interest. Without reflecting very consciously on the form of his prose, Izaak Walton wrote a number of graceful contemporary biographies, as James Howell wrote a number of letters, ostensibly private, but really designed to exercise his line of easy, unpretentious patter. He lost no time in publishing them, in four volumes. Ben Jonson was our first English poet to write close literary comment and criticism. Like most early criticism, it is unsystematic. Ben writes as he may be supposed to have spoken over a tankard of ale at the "Mermaid," bluntly and briefly, on topics that struck his fancy, on specific poets or poems. It is plain talk by a sensible man, not composed or artful prose, but his very self and voice. Would that we had equivalent material from Shakespeare! There was a vogue in the early century for "characters," which were compressed accounts, witty or malicious if possible, of some individual or social type. Being immovably static, characters never developed toward fiction, though they did enter into the writing of history. Many people wrote informal letters, since collected. Scandal about the courts of James and Charles Stuart was plentiful, though covert; in later, safer centuries it was made public. Similarly, Edward Herbert, brother of George the poet, wrote an autobiography, not published till the eighteenth century. And throughout this period we may hear, as in the background, a steady drum roll of popular preachers, expounding, exhorting, and in the process forging a flexible and familiar idiom of English prose. Because they disliked ceremonies, the Puritans laid particular emphasis on preaching. Even when still in the church of England, they could and did speak (with certain reserves) from the pulpit; their cumulative effect was incalculable. The memories of these "learned and painful" divines are now largely lost, but some of their volumes survive, to awe us with a sense of their irrepressible volubility (SFR, E.20)

SCIENTISTS AND PURITANS

From different points of view, but to converging effect, the advocates of scientific research and of religious reform consciously sought simplicity in prose style. From the first, Bacon pointed his followers in that direction. His criticism of previous philosophy had been that too much of it was merely verbal; the new philosophers would report in the plainest possible language precisely what they had observed and nothing else. Thomas Hobbes is in the spirit of Bacon when at the beginning of every demonstration he defines as exactly as possible the words he is going to use. Much of the important scientific work of the age, for example Harvey's 1628 study of the action of the heart, was recorded in Latin for an international readership. But to the extent English was used, it was increasingly a simple, clear, literal English. Very influential in this respect was the action of Sir Thomas Gresham, Queen Elizabeth's principal financial agent, who in his will established a set of free public lectureships in London. One lecture was to be given each day of the week on the seven subjects of astronomy, geometry, medicine, law, divinity, rhetoric, and music; and the lectures were to be in

English. That was a great rarity. From their inauguration in 1597, the Gresham lectures attracted, out of the commercial population of London, a lively and practical-minded audience. Many, perhaps most, were puritan by conviction, as well as scientifically oriented.[27] They formed the nucleus of a vernacular scientific culture that spread its contacts through the kingdom. When in 1614 that remarkable and isolated mathematician John Napier, alone in his remote Scottish castle, invented logarithms, it was the men of Gresham College who translated his Latin into English, adapted his ideas to navigational calculations, and made his invention a national possession. Out of the Gresham lectures grew that "Invisible College" which afterward became the Royal Society of London for Improving Natural Knowledge; its ranks included men with scientific interests quite regardless of their political or religious affiliations; and it deliberately inculcated simplicity and directness of language.

Puritans not only participated in the scientific movements of the age, they had on their own account an interest in using plain prose. If they were to bring the word of God to the unlearned majority, they had to write as plainly and clearly as possible. Many puritan preachers were fond of stirring metaphors and vehement, incremental rhythms; their preaching aimed to stir up the "zeal" of their hearers. Some also tended to lace their daily conversation with Biblical phrases and analogies; it set them apart as the elect and specially holy people. But at the same time, they had to preach and write plainly in order to be understood; the humbler the audience, the simpler the prose required to reach them. After the outbreak of civil war, when a torrent of proselytizing sects and pamphlets was released on the people, writers had to compete with one another to catch and hold public attention. Though the government of England never became anything like a democracy, a tremendous shift took place in the direction of popular values. In the course of it, ornate prose and metaphysical verse faded together from the center of public attention, and a simpler style, both in prose and poetry, became a widely accepted norm.

27. Some puritans welcomed the scientific revival because they thought it a stage preliminary to the second coming of Christ; though by scientific standards their motivations were odd, their contributions were often real. Daniel 12:4 encouraged them.

Nicholas Hilliard's languishing lover (with hand pressed to his throbbing heart and dreamy, inward expression) is clearly experiencing both the thorns and the flowers of love—and more of the former. But the elegance of his stance and the easy grace with which he drapes his cloak over the suffering organ should keep us from feeling too sorry for him. In Hilliard's exquisite miniature, he is about five and a half inches tall. The original of the picture is in the Victoria and Albert Museum.

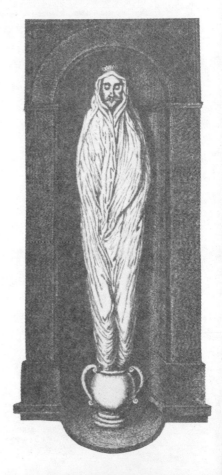

When he felt his end approaching, John Donne had his portrait painted, dressed in his shroud. From that picture, now long lost, a wraithlike statue was made for Donne's tomb in old St. Paul's; and that statue, though scorched by the flames of the 1666 fire, still stands in modern St. Paul's. Donne's obsession with death, like that of his contemporary on the tragic stage, John Webster, sank deeply and reverberated widely in his literary personality. Though to our sunlit age it may appear morbid, this death relish imparts a dark splendor to the imagination of both writers, a different tonality of which can be sensed in the writing of Sir Thomas Browne. It is a special quality of the period, and one which calls for sensitive imaginative assessment.

The greatest sculptor of the early seventeenth century was Gianlorenzo Bernini, and Charles I wanted to be immortalized by him. But Bernini would not come to England, and Charles could not go abroad. The problem was solved when Sir Anthony Van Dyck painted this triple protrait of the monarch, and sent it to Bernini in Rome. Working from the portrait, Bernini molded a bust and shipped it to England—where, before the century was out, it was destroyed in a fire. But Van Dyck's work survives and lends its strong though silent voice to our judgment of Charles I and the sort of man he was.

Wenceslas Hollar, a Czech engraver of genius, was uprooted from his native country by the wars of religion. He caught the notice of the earl of Arundel and came to England with him about 1637. His work proved popular in England, and, though much cheated by the booksellers, he never returned home. To his skill we owe the best representations extant of seventeenth-century England, its people, its buildings, its scenery, and many works of art which survive in no other form. His *Ornatus Muliebris Anglicanus* (1640) is devoted entirely to English women of every class and condition.

Sir Peter Lely, a visiting and ultimately a naturalized Dutchman, was the great portrait painter of the Restoration period; his portraits of Charles II's stable of sleepy-eyed, warm-breasted mistresses are a feature of Hampton Court. But Nell Gwyn was not formally a "beauty"; the perky animation that made her the foremost comedienne of her generation could not be caught by the Dutchman. Gutter-bred, illiterate, reckless, generous, and out-spoken, she was also vulnerable—as Charles recognized when, on his deathbed, he begged his brother to "Let not poor Nelly starve." To James's credit, the request was honored; Nelly and her bastard son the duke of Saint Albans were well provided for for as long as they lived.

Old St. Paul's, the church that Shakespeare knew, started to rise on the site of an even earlier church some time in the eleventh century, and over the years grew very gradually. But in 1561 the steeple, which stands proud and high in the present picture, was hit by a bolt of lightning from a clear blue sky and destroyed, never to be rebuilt. Over the next century, Paul's was subject to a great deal of abuse, tempered by occasional efforts at reconstruction; but the great fire of 1666 completely ruined the old church, and the present St. Paul's was built early in the eighteenth century from plans drawn by Sir Christopher Wren.

(Facing page) Sir Christopher Wren, who rebuilt so much of London after the fire of 1666 lies buried in the greatest of his achievements, St. Paul's Cathedral, under a proud Latin epitaph, the last part of which translates, "If you want to see his monument, look around you." Actually, the present spacious and noble structure does not represent Wren's original intent very well. He planned something much closer to a classical temple; ecclesiastical and puritan complaints forced alteration of his designs, and the building erected between 1675 and 1710 represents a compromise. But it was a happy compromise because Wren, as consummate a diplomat as he was an engineer, twisted it as far in the direction of his own tastes as he possibly could. The statue in the foreground is that of Queen Anne.

A musketeer in the civil wars carried not only sword, body armor, and musket, but a stand on which to rest his heavy weapon and a bandelier holding charges of powder and a bag full of bullets. But to civilians who had been plundered by them, the soldiers looked more like this caricature—with a pot for a helmet, a spitted chicken and a duck for trophies, bottles and sausages dangling from his person.

9

Commonwealth and Restoration (1649–1688)

ONE PERIOD OR TWO?

The "periods" into which English history pretends to divide itself, and which this book with its chapter divisions tries to simulate, are by no means cut and dried—none less so than the second half of the seventeenth century. The forty-year span covered by the Commonwealth-Protectorate (1649–1660) and the Restoration (1660–1688) is commonly presented as two distinct periods, but it can also be seen as a single age of experiment and adjustment, aiming in different ways to cope with the consequences of two revolutionary acts: cutting off the king's head, and abolishing the government of the church by bishops. Two very different governments held power during these forty years; but no government was able to create, or even try to create, the sort of authoritarian state and comprehensive, disciplined church that had been the ideal in England before 1640. Let us, then, first try to look at the period as a whole, before turning back and inspecting its parts.

THE SPLINTERING OF THE CHURCH

Prospects of a unified church evaporated first. Decades of Puritan propaganda had conditioned Englishmen to think that as soon as the proud prelates of Anglicanism were crushed, a strong and unified church would emerge, a phalanx of purified saints marching against Satan and his minions. Nothing of the sort occurred. Though defeated, episcopalians retained considerable power in the land; and the prospect of a tightly disciplined Presbyterian church appalled many who had opposed the bishops because *their* discipline was too strong. One group of bossy churchmen looked much like another. John Milton spoke in part for such men when he wrote in a famous sonnet "On the New Forcers of Conscience," "New presbyter is but old priest writ large." Puritans who had been united by hatred of bishops found they could agree on nothing else; their wranglings were encouraged by those who thought a strong church government worse than a weak one, and no church government the best of all.[1]

Episcopacy had been abolished, "root and branch," but episcopalian ministers survived, as lecturers or private chaplains, as school teachers or as exiles, in exactly the same status as the sects they had once despised. In place of the single state church there were now a hundred quarreling, aspiring churchlets, each promising sure salvation, each thundering anathema on its rivals. To make one of them the exclusive national church with power to persecute the others was unthinkable; to let them co-exist, granting freedom of opinion to all but power to none, and requiring all to behave civilly in public, was a half measure. It fully satisfied nobody, because each sect wanted exclusive privileges for itself; but to get toleration for themselves they had to concede it to others. Thus the idea of a single national church, comprehending everybody in one creed and one organization, perished from sheer impracticality. Instead of a single church in England, there were many. After the Restoration of 1660, Anglicanism became the established church again, but it was favored, not compulsory. If one did not like Anglicanism, one could join another church; if one were of another communion but wanted the privileges that accompanied Anglicanism, one could see the light, or pretend to, and be admitted to the fold. Under the Puritans, Anglican parsons lost their jobs, but nobody persecuted them for heresy, because heresy was undefinable; under the Restoration, sectarians suffered some legal penalties, but they were easily evaded by the cynical and ambitious, over the years they were gradually relaxed, and before long they practically disappeared.[2] Roman Catholics and socially unpopular sects like Quakers and evangelical Baptists suffered pen-

1. Weakening church government would leave the state free to make what rules it chose; the position, foreshadowed by Wyclif (above, p. 70), was known after a sixteenth-century Swiss theologian as Erastianism. John Selden, the great oriental scholar, was a convinced Erastian, who deliberately used his immense learning to confuse the Puritan divines in their efforts to settle on a new form of church government. The *Table Talk* of Selden, collected by a disciple, is one of the sharpest little books of the age.

2. Certain official positions were closed to sectarians, and they could not attend the universities. But the penalties concealed some real advantages. Being disqualified for public office left wealthy sectarians free to concentrate on becoming wealthier; being barred from the universities let young sectarians escape a classical curriculum that many found arid, and roam the greener fields of engineering and science.

alties; Anglicans enjoyed some special advantages. But as these discriminations faded, England increasingly was a community within which different creeds were admitted.

Religious toleration may fade imperceptibly into religious indifference. Persecutors and martyrs share the virtue, if it is a virtue, of taking their beliefs seriously. Having lost all their disciplinary powers and most of the remaining income that Henry VIII had not snatched, having discredited themselves by failing to agree on any major question of scriptural interpretation, English churchmen were subject during the last half of the century to increasing contempt from laymen. Pragmatism brought peace of a sort, but it was the peace of the weak.

CONSOLIDATION OF SOCIAL POWERS

In politics as well the story is one of increasing compromise. Though to many Puritan partisans, including Milton, the collapse of Cromwell's regime in 1660 looked like the end of the world, it was far from that. For twenty years of civil war and Stuart exile, royalists had been under pressure to sell their estates. The market had been depressed, the chief buyers parliamentary generals or city merchants, who had access to cash and credit. After the Restoration, there was no general review of these transactions; the new landowners, former parliamentarians, remained in possession of their estates, and became a powerful force in the land. Restless, radical Puritans who had made the 1640 revolution became less restless and radical (as well as less puritan) when absorbed into the influential class of landowners and county magnates. But their ties to the moneyed interests of London city were not forgotten. Under the Restoration, city people and their semi-ruralized friends became the center of power and authority in England, while the court faded to a hollow show.[3] Charles II, called back from his travels by the magnates and always an idle man by nature, became their easy puppet; and when his brother James (who had succeeded to the throne in 1685) turned intransigent, the moneyed and landed classes who now ruled England tossed him off the throne with contemptuous ease. That was the Glorious or Bloodless Revolution of 1688. It not only ended (except for brief, abortive episodes in 1715 and 1745) the troubled story of the house of Stuart in England, it established England's destiny for the future as that of a limited constitutional monarchy controlled by propertied classes operating through Parliament.

3. It is true that the aristocracy, after passing through a serious crisis in the first half of the century (SFR, E.28), soon regained its strength. It is also true that with newly rich, newly titled men like George Monk duke of Albemarle, Anthony Ashley Cooper earl of Shaftesbury, and Sir George Downing, the baronet from Massachusetts, in its ranks, it was not the same aristocracy after the crisis as before. Of the thirty men in Charles II's privy council (1661), no fewer than twelve had fought against his father. Forgiving and forgetting, which the new king had promised to do, and actually did, was commonly said to involve forgiving his enemies and forgetting his friends.

PRAGMATISM

Religious compromise led to skepticism, political compromise to the rule of expediency. The new age tends to ask of innovative proposals, not whether they are true or agreeable to the word of God, but how in practice they work. Abroad, Cromwell's vigorous foreign policy laid the foundations of English trade supremacy; even those who thought the murderer of Charles I a fearful villain had to be impressed with the material prosperity he brought to the land. After the Restoration, when the dynamic puritan spirit could no longer busy itself building the kingdom of God on earth, practical undertakings became the order of the day; they suggest where the old energy was now flowing. A man like Daniel Defoe, had he been born in 1609 rather than 1659, would certainly have become a Puritan divine; instead, we find him writing (1698) an *Essay on Projects* typical of the age in its practical concerns. Banks and credit unions, insurance companies, humane treatment of the insane, better education for women, more sensible bankruptcy laws—such were some of Defoe's projects. As he wrote, other men of his temper were devising similar sensible, limited enterprises. Newspapers were started to keep people minimally informed, joint-stock companies were organized, some effort was made to light city streets and even to clear a bit of their immemorial garbage. Canals were dug in a small way, and a few toll roads established; they cost more but offered a chance for higher speeds—seven miles an hour, maybe, instead of two.

Polite sanction for these practical activities was supplied by the Royal Society of London for Improving Natural Knowledge. The learned gentlemen did not think it beneath them to investigate physical phenomena; they rather gloried in being useful. Men of humbler station needed no further encouragement. Puritanism invited them to labor in their callings; labor they did, and in large numbers they prospered. Complaints are loud in the latter part of the century that clever, aggressive men of no background are squeezing into the forefront of national affairs, shoving aside the old families with their established values. There is no period of English history when this has not been happening; but in the last half of the seventeenth century, it happened on a larger scale, and over a shorter time span, than ever before.[4]

PARTY POLITICS

One social invention of the age has been so completely domesticated now that we may forget what an original and difficult achievement it was at first: political

4. Apart from the vague and awkward locution "middle class," there is no English word equivalent to the French *bourgeoisie*. Because English aristocrats and gentry were less exclusive, the middle class in England was less sharply defined than in France; perhaps, in a nation of shopkeepers, it was also larger. The lack of a term is in any case remarkable; for it was the unmistakable *bourgeoisie* of England who pushed to the fore in the course of the seventeenth century.

parties were a creation of the late seventeenth century, and represented, in softened form, the division between parliamentary and royalist factions. Whigs got their name from "Whiggamore," a slang term for Scottish Presbyterians, while Tories got theirs from a Gaelic term for Irish Catholic outlaws. The names point up a loose tendency for Whigs to favor puritans, parliament, and the moneyed interest, while Tories stood for the established church, the king's prerogative, and the hereditary landed interest. But the parties were not war parties, they were interest groups. Family ties and connections, always strong in England, softened and diffused party conflicts; local interests did something to determine a man's allegiance, and so did his social status.[5] More important still, both parties quickly learned the magnetic power of patronage. Political fanaticism was softened by new opportunities for political profiteering.

THE PLAIN, THE VULGAR, THE SUPERFICIAL

An age dominated by practical commercial enterprise had pronounced effects on literature and literary standards. When theaters, effectually closed by the puritans in 1642, were revived after 1660, they were limited by royal patent to at most two, while management was no longer in the hands of the companies (as in Shakespeare's time) but was pre-empted by businessmen who put authors under contract and told them what to write. They found it profitable to flood the stage with flashy scenery and gaudy costumes, to encourage melodrama in tragedy and smut in comedy, and to fill the theater with jugglers, acrobats, and dancers. Actresses appeared on the English stage, not to open a new career for women, but because sex appeal was the most salable of commodities. More subtle and complex was the transition in poetry. The poetry of the metaphysicals had been inward and private; to follow it, one had to work one's way into the poet's inmost feelings. During the middle years of the century, this strenuous, inward style gave way to a poetry of plain statement formally patterned—a poetry of verbal point and antithesis rather than strenuous metaphorical action. "Profundity" went out of style, in poetry as in the pulpit; strained analogies and interpretive subtleties were no longer the vogue. Even philosophy, in the person of the third earl of Shaftesbury, began cultivating a genteel superficiality from which John Locke was not entirely free.[6] Like religious and political systems, philosophical sys-

5. Never cast in concrete, English social status was destabilized further by the mixing effect of the wars and by ready access to and from the colonies. Moll Flanders (in Defoe's novel) was a pickpocket, a jailbird, and not much better than a whore; but she became rich and respectable in Virginia, where one of her neighbors could have been a Mr. Washington of Northamptonshire, grandfather of George; whether out of discontent or ambition, he had emigrated in 1658.

6. It's arguable that philosophy became superficial because science (the science of Newton and his great French predecessor Descartes) had taken over and in effect disposed of so many of its previous concerns. The ordered mechanical universe described by Newton had its human counterpart in the ordered mechanical psychology of Locke, which described the mind as a blank sheet of paper

tems too were discredited; good manners, good humor, personal candor, and intellectual skepticism seemed like better guides to social behavior. Literary criticism began distinguishing between the solid "sense" of a work and the "fancy" or "wit" with which it was adorned. The new bald truths of mechanical science were partly responsible for this dichotomy, which would have made no sense at all to Donne; the new habit of thought marked the beginning of that "dissociation of sensibility" which T. S. Eliot would baptize and deplore in the twentieth century. (Eliot took the phrase from Rémy de Gourmont, but applied it for the first time to figures and periods of English literature.) An immediate consequence in the seventeenth century was the development of a formal artificial language of literary decoration: poetic diction, as it later came to be called. It was one strategy by which poetry was able to survive, after a fashion, in a gathering age of prose.

WITHOUT A KING, WITHOUT A COURT:
ENGLAND UNDER CROMWELL

Horror and dismay, throughout England and Europe, greeted the news that Charles I, an anointed king, had been beheaded. Milton spoke up boldly in defense of the regicide, with discourses in Latin and English; but his was an isolated voice. Most people, puritan supporters included, were simply appalled. Under the circumstances, it behooved Cromwell to move swiftly and decisively; that, in fact, was his special talent. In a series of quick, smashing blows, he put down incipient revolt in his army, and crossed the Irish sea to crush (1649) a Catholic revolt in that unhappy island. So cruel were his methods, so ruthless his soldiers on this occasion, that "the curse of Cromwell" (which cannot be pronounced in all its malignant detail in less than an hour) has become a byword in Ireland. But Cromwell could not linger even to finish his conquest; leaving the bloody mop-up to his lieutenants, he rushed back to Scotland, and in two overwhelming battles (Dunbar, 1650; Worcester, 1651) completed the subjugation of that kingdom. These are the victories celebrated, perhaps too complacently, in Andrew Marvell's "Horatian Ode" addressed to Cromwell. As seen by puritan Englishmen, they were splendid victories. But, as Marvell deftly intimated, one crucial victory continued to elude the puritan general: that over his own party in the

---

written on by experience—experience, obviously, of the mechanical universe. Where in this blind concatenation of bumped particles (atoms) was there room for religion, ethics, or even any sort of active consciousness? Berkeley (see below, p. 285) thought there was none. In fact, the compromise worked out by roughly homogenizing Locke with Newton lasted more than a century, fostering much fine scientific work, some coarse but practical government theory, and some extremely limited efforts at psychology. Its inherent contradictions, rendered acute by Hume, would finally be transcended by the German philosopher Immanuel Kant (below, p. 338). Meanwhile, a minority strain of republican thought stemming from the Cromwellian commonwealth remained quietly alive to nourish sentiments which in the colonies led to the American revolution (SFR, F.23).

House of Commons. Though they had been purged of dissenters, though Cromwell was patient with them, surviving members of the Long Parliament could agree on nothing except their own political power. When they undertook (April 1653) to pass a bill declaring themselves permanently elected and absolute judges of who should be elected in future, they went too far. In a rage, Cromwell stormed into the House, abused the members, and calling in a file of troopers, dismissed in contempt the last representative body in England. Some thought and called this the behavior of an ambitious tyrant; it was also possible to take Cromwell at his word when he cried out to the departing members, "It is you that have forced me to this; for I have sought the Lord night and day that he would rather slay me than put me upon the doing of this work!''

Reluctant tyrant though he might be, with the old king dead, his son exiled to France, and Parliament dismissed, Cromwell ruled by force of arms and nothing else. The title he took of "Lord Protector," though familiar to history, was absurd under the circumstances. It implied a king in his minority who needed protection; but who was a greater enemy to kings than Cromwell himself? Protector of whom from what? men might have asked; and also, Who was to protect England from her protector? They were unanswerable questions, but Cromwell was an unanswerable ruler, and rule he did, with his customary energy, for the four years of life that were left to him. It was, on the whole, enlightened rule. Cromwell persecuted no men for their religious opinions, not even Roman Catholics. He encouraged learning, reformed the currency, moved to bind Ireland and Scotland more closely to England, and vigorously stimulated foreign trade. His revitalized navy not only harassed the traditional enemy, Spain, but undertook a successful war against the Dutch, whose commercial power blocked expanding English trade. Though generally deplored as a usurper, Cromwell won universal respect on the Continent as a spokesman for the Protestant cause. In 1655 the Inquisition induced the duke of Savoy to take action against an obscure Protestant sect, the Waldenses, living in the valleys of the Piedmont; an atrocious persecution resulted, against which Cromwell mounted a stiff protest. The secretary who drafted his formal diplomatic letter (in Latin, naturally) was John Milton; and Milton's mighty sonnet "On the Late Massacres in Piedmont" is simply the content of that letter condensed into poetry.

But though Cromwell could rule, and on the whole successfully, he could not consolidate his power into institutions capable of lasting beyond his lifetime. He confessed as much by resorting to makeshift expedients, such as dividing England into eleven arbitrary units and place a Major General over each. The Major Generals were no doubt able men, and their functions were familiar, a little more exalted than those of JP's, but similar. As strangers and interlopers, however, they were resented; being unfamiliar with the local people and local customs, responsible only to the central administration, they soon came to be hated. One of their typical blunders was to close alehouses all over England; the step seems small, but nothing was more likely to put a thirsty August harvester in a mood to revolt. Unpopular though it was, the regime could not be directly challenged as long as Cromwell lived; but when he died, in 1658, the protectorate simply disintegrated. From sheer lack of imagination, ineffectual Richard Cromwell was pushed into his father's place; but already the power brokers were dealing behind his back with agents of Charles Stuart, the future Charles II, who had only to sit still in France and wait to be returned to his father's throne.[7] Everyone who had not actually taken part in the execution of Charles I saw something to gain from his son's return. And so, on 26 May, 1660, a tall, dark, sardonic stranger landed, amid tumultuous acclaim, at the port of Dover. He was presented with a handsome Bible which he solemnly kissed and declared to be "the thing he loved above all things in the world." Thereupon he was duly transported to Whitehall where, amid general rejoicing, he was installed as King Charles II.

LITERATURE MARKING TIME

Periods of social strife and radical experiment don't generally produce much literature, and the two decades from 1640 to 1660 bear out that rule. More remarkable than the paucity of literature in the period is the fact that most writers were active enemies of the puritan regime. Sir William Davenant and Abraham Cowley, both royalist agents, published epic poems (*Gondibert*, 1651; *Davideis*, 1656); Henry Vaughan and Richard Lovelace, both soldiers for the king, produced collections of verse (1650, 1659); while, from their exiles in Paris and Rome, Thomas Hobbes published his authoritarian political philosophy (*Leviathan*, 1651) and Richard Crashaw his scandalously Catholic poems (*The Delights of the Muses*, 1648, and *Carmen Deo Nostro*, 1652). As if to spite the puritans who had just let him out of jail, Sir Thomas Urquhart published in 1653 his bawdy translation of Rabelais; and among the anglicans, dispossessed but not silenced, we note Thomas Fuller, the witty church historian, Jeremy Taylor, the preacher and popular moralist, and Izaak Walton, the gentle biographer and fishing enthusiast. By comparison with the rich literary life in and around the Stuart courts, this is not a massive list; but it puts to shame the puritan record for the same period, an almost perfect literary blank.[8] Of the two major literary figures with puritan sympathies, Andrew Marvell published almost nothing, and Milton,

7. "Power brokers" is a vague modern phrase for some quiet, cautious, influential men; the contemporary word, equally vague, was "grandees." Their reticence equaled their power; they were not chance takers. Aubrey the scandalmonger tells a revealing story about General George Monk, the decisive Presbyterian leader. He had, it seems, been keeping company with a lady, Nan Clarges; her brother came calling, to say she had given birth to a child. "What sort?" "A boy." "Then she is my wife." The careful man rose to be duke of Albemarle.

8. Intellectually, there was more stirring. In addition to the informal meetings of scientists which would turn into the Royal Society, a group of social philosophers headed by James Harington began meeting toward the end of the interregnum, under the name of the "Rota Club." They liked to sit at a round table, but the name also alluded to their most prominent idea. Reflecting on the late revolu-

though meditating gigantic projects, confined himself to prose controversy. Yet the interregnum was not by any means a waste period of literary time. Sir Edmund Waller and Sir John Denham developed and practiced the writing of smooth, antithetical "heroic" couplets;[9] and this was no slight achievement. When writers of the Restoration picked up the couplet form, they found it ready to use; one has only to compare Dryden's couplets, in point of smooth and controlled power, with those of Ben Jonson, to see the difference. And, all during this period of the interregnum the idea of *Paradise Lost* was growing and deepening within the mind of John Milton.

RESTORATION COMPROMISES

The new king was thirty years old, an exceedingly fine gentleman, and a practiced dissimulator. He had spent his adult life wandering around the Continent, dependent on the generosity of foreign monarchs, and intriguing with English exiles to get his throne back. Though few people knew it in 1660, Charles was a secret Catholic; but he had more than once committed himself to establish Presbyterianism in England, and was now, as king, obliged to wear the mask of Anglicanism. He was a sensual man, with a royal appetite for mistresses, whom he neither concealed nor encouraged to conceal themselves. The wife whom in 1662 he was obliged to take (she was a princess of Portugal) he regarded as a minor nuisance, and he left her to her own devices while he sought amusement elsewhere.[10] An angry mob once attacked the coach of Nell Gwyn under the impression that she was the Catholic duchess of Portsmouth. Nell stuck her head out the coach window and shouted, "Hold, good people, hold! I am the *protestant* whore!" Charles, who loved her cockney impudence, simply guffawed over the episode. Posterity has sometimes referred to him as "The Merry Monarch"; a frequent nickname in his own day was "Old Rowley." Marvell wrote of him, in an anonymous satire,

---

tion, they saw its motive force as a major shift of economic power, to which political power had to adjust, if not by rotation, then by violence. Facilitating such rotation, by limiting tenures of land and office and by holding frequent popular elections, was the substance of their positive program—for which see Harington's ill-written but insightful book *Oceana* (1656).

This realistic social analysis reminds us that among the politically minded puritans the work of Niccolò Machiavelli enjoyed great popularity. They read *The Prince*, not altogether inaccurately, as a book exposing the deceits and cruelties of princes. To some puritans the Florentine was known as "the divine Machiavelli."

9. "Heroic" couplets because used in the stilted and oratorical tragedies that were the vogue during the Restoration; from the elevation of the characters and style, they were called "heroic" tragedies.

10. In addition to a lot of ready cash which Charles badly needed, Catherine of Braganza brought to England, as part of her dowry, the port and island of Bombay in India and the port of Tangier in north Africa. Major building blocks of the British Empire were thus formed from the disintegrating colonial system of Portugal.

The poor Priapus king, led by the nose,
Looks as a thing set up to scare the crows.

Marvell was a keen man; he saw weakness in the king where many saw only wickedness.

Except for his pleasures, Charles was extremely lazy; he enjoyed being king, and was determined not to be "sent on his travels" again, but he never tried to work very hard at his job. Accordingly, his ministers, particularly the earl of Clarendon, who as Edward Hyde had been one of the staunchest and most sensible advisers of Charles I, carried much of the burden. But Clarendon was too strict and principled to please Charles long; in 1667 he was dismissed, disgraced, and sent into exile, while Charles entered into secret negotiations with France which culminated in his receiving an annual pension from the king of France of £200,000. This was one way for an English king to render himself independent of parliament; but it simply confirms the ramshackle, unprincipled nature of the Restoration settlement.

It was said above that the Restoration could be lumped with the commonwealth-protectorate as a single period of constitutional experiment, and so it can. But for people at the time, the two periods differed as day from night. A licentious, frivolous king on the throne contrasted sharply with all those gloomy, dogmatic puritans before 1660. Charles and the courtiers who had shared his exile brought from France new styles, new manners, new ideas. Even folly changed its motley coat; a stage booby like Sir Fopling Flutter of Etherege's comedy *The Man of Mode* is far removed from Shakespeare's clowns, more sophisticated in his verbal wit, more subtle in his affectations. A crucial change is the popular attitude toward the clergy. Under Charles I they had been makers of opinion, pillars of authority for the cause they espoused; under Charles II, they were often the objects of contempt and ridicule. The tone of society changed as luxury and display, no longer shameful, became openly avowed principles of conduct. After the chill austerity of the puritan winter, ladies blossomed forth in splendid gowns of satin and lace, while gentlemen donned velvet coats aglitter with braid, and covered their pates with long, curly wigs.

And the manners of the court were, let us say, free. The shorthand diary of Samuel Pepys is a precious social document in giving us a picture of this raffish court set in the midst of a rough seaport town. Pepys came from a puritan, middle-class background and earned his living as a navy bureaucrat. Though at first his post was humble, with time it became more important and better-paid; but for the nine years he kept his diary, Pepys never lost his outsider's view of the court, his eye for a fine lady, or his nose for gossip. John Evelyn also kept a diary, and for a long period; but as he was more gentlemanly himself, he didn't notice as much as Pepys or record it as closely. The fresh naïveté of Pepys's sensibility was another legacy to English literature from the age of Cromwell.

Indeed, if we take our image of Restoration life from the comic dramatists of the age, we may think of society as consisting of handsome, swaggering bucks and generously proportioned young ladies, all rich and idle, all with just one and the same thing on their superficial little minds. But Restoration comedy, though apparently it mirrors quite well the actual court of Charles II,[11] does not recognize the wider world outside court circles. There we find profound though unspectacular changes taking place across the land and in foreign relations as well; often they are not reversals of commonwealth ideas, but extensions of them.

Restoration governments encouraged foreign trade; they were cautious of monopolies which limited domestic enterprise; they accepted the abolition of feudal land tenures, especially the irksome custom of wardship described above (p. 205); they lifted restrictions on commerce into which the old guild system had slipped; they re-established the JPs and gave them generous powers, including the power to fix agricultural wages. Thus graced with royal favor, the already prosperous landowners prospered still more. It isn't too much to say that Restoration policy encouraged all the prosperous and powerful classes, while neglecting all the weak and underprivileged. Whether they were the traditionally poor or the new poor who had backed a losing cause in the civil wars didn't much matter. Those who had much tended to get more; those who had little got even less. With government help in the shape of the very effective Navigation Acts (that of 1660 simply renewed and expanded that of 1651), the merchants and importers of London trebled the size of the merchant marine and overawed their competition. Trade with colonies (in India, Africa, the Americas) became increasingly valuable to the nation. Since medieval times, trade in wool and woolen cloth had been at the heart of England's commercial activity; now, with many raw materials entering England to be processed there and shipped elsewhere, or simply to be trans-shipped, the economy was more widely based and secure.

In 1666 a vast fire devastated more than 400 densely built acres in the heart of London city, ruining St. Paul's, over 80 churches, and more than 10,000 houses. Superstitious folk saw it as God's warning against the sins of the city, and in hard, practical terms, the fire represented a tough test of the town's economic resilience. But London rose from her ashes, more splendid than before. Sir Christopher Wren was given a chance, such as architects only dream of, to rebuild a major cathedral and half a hundred churches. And so vigorously did the work proceed, that less than a year later, when Dryden published a poem of instant history, *Annus Mirabilis* ("The Wonderful Year"), he boldly predicted the city's glorious future:

11. Charles Lamb in a well-known essay on "The Artificial Comedy of the Last Century" (1822), argued that the Restoration dramatists created "a world of themselves," having nothing to do with the real one. However valid as a means of dodging pious disapproval, the notion is not very accurate historically. Some recent owlish commentary has proposed that Restoration comedy carried not only a moral but a theological message; it is criticism which destroys excellent comedy to build from the ruins third-rate prissy moralizing.

Me-thinks already from this chymic flame
I see a city of more precious mold:
Rich as the town which gives the Indies name,
Wih silver paved, and all divine with gold.[12]

THE PURITANS' PROGRESS

Inevitably, puritans and ex-puritans shared in the commercial prosperity of the land. Under Cromwell, many had learned the indispensable arts of administration; if they had a lot of money in their pockets and a little tact on their tongues, they gained easy entree to the social system, even to Restoration governments. At home, the puritan code of worldly asceticism led them to spend little; at the office, they worked hard; naturally, they accumulated much. Their minds proved vigorous and practical. Prominent supporters of Cromwell, who after the Restoration sensed that foreign travel would be good for their health, studied the ways in which things were done abroad, and returned to teach their English neighbors profitable lessons about farming and trade. Puritan beliefs were no bar to success in business. Despite laws forbidding it, puritan ministers ejected from their livings found a substitute calling in teaching; in great numbers, and after 1688 quite openly, they established academies, and such good instruction did they provide that before long even anglican families began sending their children to academies run by dissenters.[13] Above all, the vast body of puritans, who in 1660 had been dreaded as potential revolutionaries only waiting for a chance to murder Charles II as they had murdered Charles I, managed during the Restoration to improve their image drastically. They did so by suffering with patient heroism—"the better fortitude [as Milton called it] / Of patience and heroic martyrdom"—the various and often brutal punishments inflicted on them by a vengeful Parliament, a fearful anglican clergy, and a hostile magistracy. Harassed as they were by these enemies, the nonconformists exemplified as a group that passive obedience to higher authority which royalists had often preached and rarely practiced. In Scotland, where Presbyterianism had sunk deep roots, puritan sufferings were most acute. Episcopacy returned under cruel and unprincipled renegades like James Sharp and the duke of Lauderdale; government decisions affecting Scotland were all made in London and sustained by ferocious acts of legal and military repression. Sporadic revolts took place, emigrations (to northern Ireland), assassinations; Stuart "policy" included raising an army of highlanders and turn-

12. Mexico City gave its name to Mexico, which for Dryden was part of the West Indies. Puritan doomsayers, drawing on the book of Revelations, had predicted that 1666 would be "the year of the beast," that is, of the anti-Christ; the fire and plague had seemed to justify them. Dryden's imagery suggests the exact contrary, the coming of the New Jerusalem.

13. *Dissenters* and *nonconformists* are alternate names for Protestants (mostly of puritan persuasion) who dissent from or won't conform with the church of England. Catholics who do the same thing are called *recusants*, from Latin *recusare*, to refuse.

ing them loose to plunder lowland farmers in the hope of fomenting a racial war that would disintegrate the whole nation. Such behavior from a king claiming Scottish blood taught many bitter lessons to the Scots; and south of the Tweed were others, on whom the lesson was not lost. But for the time being, the wretched nation could only suffer and submit.

In England, though the two Conventicle Acts (1664, 1670) made it a crime for any five people (members of the same family excepted) to meet in a private house "under color of" religion, neither informers nor militiamen could really enforce the law. The Five Mile Act of 1665, piled atop the Act of Uniformity (1662), imposed oaths of loyalty to the Anglican church upon everyone in holy orders, and forbade anyone declining the oaths to approach within five miles of a corporate town: it exiled nonconformists to the countryside.[14] Another law forbade them to teach, either as schoolmasters or private tutors. But all these ferocious laws were irregularly and only partially enforced. Many violations were simply winked at; and where persecution was carried out, it often proved self-defeating. John Bunyan was flung into Bedford jail for twelve long years because he insisted on preaching the word of Christ in competition with the Anglican clergymen of the area; his treatment was bitterly unfair, but he submitted, put pen to paper, and wrote in his gloomy cell, not only an autobiography to rank with Saint Augustine's *Confessions* (he called it *Grace Abounding to the Chief of Sinners*), but the book by which he is still known, *A Pilgrim's Progress.*[15] George Fox, a founder of Quakerism, refused to remove his hat before the magistrate because he thought it an act of idolatry. But he turned his trial at the Lancashire assizes of 1663 into an exhibition of Christian magnanimity, praying in a voice of thunder for those who reviled him, and demanding that the Holy Bible, which had taught him to behave as he did, be sent to jail with him. Such tactics, which were those of the early Christian martyrs, were irresistible in a community professing to be Christian; the nonconformists won wide public sympathy.

Dissenters appeared especially innocent and honorable members of the community when their behavior was contrasted with that of the Roman Catholics. Charles as a secret Catholic himself and a secret pensioner of Louis XIV was

14. Without much flexing of principles, Presbyterian ministers of high character and vast popular influence, such as Richard Baxter and Edmund Calamy, could have been accommodated within the establishment. By driving them out, the Restoration bishops inflicted an unintended but deadly wound on their own cause. Though too radical for the Anglicans of their day, these sincere and respectable men provided effective leadership for the dissenting community, which grew rapidly under their care. About 1675 there were fewer than 200,000 dissenters in a population approaching 5 million souls; that was under 4 percent. By 1850, 175 years later, the figures among churchgoers were about 50–50, though the proportion of nonchurchgoers had also increased.

15. Meticulous accuracy would distinguish Bunyan's long twelve-year stay in Bedford jail, during which he wrote *Grace Abounding* and as many as eight other books, from a later and shorter jailing in 1675, when he wrote *Pilgrim's Progress.* When free, he was such a busy and popular preacher that he wrote nothing but sermons; jail cells, horrible in themselves and particularly to Bunyan, a devoted family man, were the seminaries of all his enduring books.

constantly trying to favor Catholics at the expense of the Anglican church. His ultimate aim, unavowed but spelled out in secret treaties, was to return to England to the Catholic fold, using foreign money and foreign armies to do so. Messengers from Oliva, head of the Jesuit order in Rome, dodged in and out of court, telling Charles how to manage domestic matters in the interest of France and when to abandon his Protestant allies on the Continent. Partly in reaction to these intrigues, partly on their own merits, and partly because their sober, businesslike habits tended to enrich them almost as fast as an extravagant court life impoverished fine gentlemen, the dissenters gradually became an influential and respected force in public life. Marvell put a popular view of the court in a nutshell:

> This isle was well reformed, and gained renown
> Whilst the brave Tudors wore the imperial crown;
> But since the royal race of Stuarts came,
> It has recoiled to popery and shame.

DISCONTENTS AND CONSPIRACIES

Changes that occurred gradually and quietly in social life had violent repercussions in politics; it was an age of deep animosities and suspicions. Two striking expressions of this fact were the deteriorating relations between Charles and his Parliaments and the many plots hatched by or attributed to violent Catholics or radical puritans.

When the first Restoration Parliament assembled in 1661, someone remarked to Charles that the members were very young; no matter, said the new monarch, he would keep them till they all had beards. What he knew was simply that he would never again get such a group of committed royalists; in fact, he kept his first Parliament in session, with frequent recesses, from May 1661 to January 1679. In the first flush of their enthusiasm, the Parliament actually did give the king all it seemed he could ask. To avoid squabbles over "supply," such as had plagued his father and grandfather, they voted the king a splendid annual income of £1,200,000 for life. And they were so fierce against dissenters that Clarendon, fearing to render his old opponents desperate, had to restrain the hotheads.[16] But experience with Charles changed many minds. Splendid as it was, that annual allowance could not be stretched to maintain both the troop of Charles's mistresses and the troop of soldiers that he considered necessary as his "royal guard." To many Englishmen these royal regiments looked suspiciously like a standing army; and English traditions were against standing armies. Presbyterians who

---

16. Clarendon, raised in the gentler era before the war, had many friends in the party which ultimately sided with the Parliament; he also honored as a man of principle the Declaration of Breda (April 1660) in which Charles, as a way to get his throne back, promised wide toleration and few reprisals. The furious royalists of the later 1660s didn't care what Charles had promised; they wanted their pound of flesh.

had cooperated in bringing Charles back were disappointed at being relegated among the sects; Charles thought their religion "ungentlemanly," and had the covenant, to which during his exile he had solemnly subscribed, burned by the common hangman. Royalists who had lost their estates during the civil wars were bitter at not getting them back. Churchmen who thought the established church should have a monopoly of religious life were upset at a proposed royal "declaration of indulgence" (26 December, 1662), opening the way for more sectarian and Catholic privileges than they had a mind to. But the real murmurs of popular anger began when, in 1665, Charles allowed the nation to drift into another war with the Dutch. (It is during a battle of this war that Dryden imagines the dialogue of his "Essay of Dramatic Poesy" as taking place.) Just like Cromwell's earlier war with the Dutch, Charles's was commercial in its motivation. But the inevitable comparison with Cromwell worked entirely to Charles's disadvantage. In 1658 Cromwell's aggressive tactics had enabled England to seize the French port of Dunkirk; in 1662, Charles's supine policies and need for money led him to sell Cromwell's conquest back to the French. (Seizure of New Amsterdam, now New York City, in 1664, did nothing to counterbalance the earlier loss; the American colony was too remote and trivial to count.) By the time open war broke out with the Dutch in 1665, the English navy had been allowed to deteriorate, ships were rotten, seamen sullen, commanders halfhearted; the whole enterprise was doomed to fiasco. On 13 June, 1667, the Dutch admiral De Ruyter sailed boldly up the Thames, and burned several English warships in the dockyards at Chatham. Charles kept carefully out of sight, but to show his unconcern let it be known "that he was very cheerful that night at supper with his mistresses." Popular rumor declared the fleet was in such bad shape only because Charles had appropriated to his own selfish purposes much of the money Parliament had voted for its upkeep. Inevitably, the treaty signed with the Dutch on July 21 was a setback for England; Charles, however, did not care, since public anger over the scandal enabled him to get rid of Clarendon, as he had long wanted to do.[17]

Further distrust and disillusion set in when Charles negotiated a Triple Alliance of Protestant powers (Holland and Sweden were the other two partners) in order to get a grant of £800,000 from Parliament; he immediately undercut this gesture by secretly inviting Louis XIV to attack the Dutch, promising to do nothing to help them. Then, hoping to capitalize on England's commercial jealousy of Holland, Charles started still another Dutch war (March 1672–February

17. Exiled to France, Clarendon devoted his time to completing that *History of the Rebellion and Civil Wars* which he had begun in the midst of the events it describes. The book was not published till 1704, and then clumsily; it reached its final form only in the late nineteenth century. But from the first it was influential as a history with a political philosophy coherent in itself and shaping a coherent account of historical events (SFR, E. 16). The profits of Clarendon's history, which were considerable, went to establish the Clarendon Press, a division of the Oxford University Press still famous for the elegance and accuracy of its products.

1674); but it stirred little enthusiasm because the Dutch at that point were heroically standing off the immense military power of the French, and Charles was suspected of stabbing Protestants in the back to gratify Catholics.[18] Suspicions deepened even further when the king, in 1672, issued a second "declaration of indulgence" for all dissenters and Catholics. Ostensibly, this was a liberal and tolerant gesture; in fact, as Parliament suspected, its aim was to strengthen the Catholics at the expense of the other creeds. Faced with a general protest, the king withdrew his declaration, and Parliament followed up by passing the Test Act, which required all persons holding public employment to renounce the Catholic faith on oath, and to receive the sacrament according to the rites of the church of England. Three high members of Charles's administration, including his brother James, heir to the throne, refused the oath and were deprived of office.

Amid these deepening quarrels, a quiet, important private event was overshadowed by a loud, empty public one. Without fanfare, Mary, the elder daughter of James Stuart, was married in 1677 to William of Orange, bulwark of the Protestant cause in Holland (and, coincidentally, a grandson of Charles I). Hardly regarded at the time, this marriage became supremely important eleven years later when, with Charles II dead and James II deposed, England started to look for a Protestant in the line of succession. In Mary and her husband William they found not one but two such sovereigns, who would ease the transition to Queen Anne and then to the house of Hanover with its four successive Georges.

But the wedding of William and Mary was quickly overshadowed by the first of those horrifying "plots" which racked England during the last quarter of the seventeenth century. This was the so-called "Popish Plot," and it consisted (on the say-so of those who vouched for it) of a scheme to kill Charles and replace him with James. This would have been an idiotic project, since (as we now know, though contemporaries did not) Charles was already a covert Catholic. What is more, the chief authority for this "plot," a man named Titus Oates, was a pathological liar.[19] But his story, absurd in itself, seemed to be confirmed by a set of striking accidents. In 1678, Oates told his story (or one of his stories, for he changed them constantly) to a magistrate, Sir Edmond Berry Godfrey, who within the month was found murdered. Several men hanged for the murder, but on perjured testimony, and to this day nobody knows who did in Sir Edmond or why. But popular opinion naturally declared that the Catholics had killed him, to hush up the story of the plot. Then Oates brought charges against one Coleman, secretary to the duchess of York, wife of James Stuart; and among Cole-

18. For years Charles Stuart ran a double or triple foreign policy, systematically going behind the back of one set of officials to negotiate a contrary set of secret treaties with another. Keeping the whole tangle straight was a virtuoso feat of memory, though it doesn't say much for the king's rudimentary honesty (SFR, E.23).

19. Grotesque in appearance, uncouth in speech, Oates had been dismissed, on a variety of pretexts, from assorted colleges and posts; the real reason for most of these episodes seems to have been his homosexuality (SFR, E.13).

man's letters addressed to Jesuit agents abroad were found distinctly incriminating phrases, proof of malignant intent if not actual conspiracy.

Many people, including King Charles, did not believe Oates for an instant; on the witness stand he frequently revealed himself as a shifty liar. But his story roused a storm of fury against the Catholics, for which Charles himself, with his many duplicities, was partly responsible. In addition, the flames of religious hatred were fanned by an unscrupulous opposition led by the first earl of Shaftesbury. That nobleman, who is represented as "Achitophel" in Dryden's savage satire on the plot, *Absalom and Achitophel* (1681), was too intelligent to believe in Oates. But he saw a chance to stir hatred against popery, and so to get James excluded from succession to the throne. Shaftesbury himself had been on both sides in the civil war, and he was one of the "grandees" who brought Charles II back from exile; he had a knack for being on the winning, or at least the popular, side. As head of the residual republicans and spokesman of the Presbyterians, he now appointed himself defender of the Protestant cause; had he succeeded, he would have been able to dictate policy to the man he had chosen to supplant James as Charles's successor.

The problem was urgent because Charles, though splendidly prolific of bastards by his various mistresses, had no heir by his legal wife Catherine of Braganza. Shaftesbury hoped to install as heir and successor one of Charles's illegitimate but Protestant children, James Scott, duke of Monmouth. He is the "Absalom" of Dryden's satire. Personally, he was a vain, foolish, brave young man, handsome and appealing. Shaftesbury hoped, by accusing James of complicity in the Popish Plot, and demonstrating Monmouth's popularity, to push the young man to the head of the succession line. The scheme did not work; Charles was not to be manipulated that way, and in the end Monmouth and Shaftesbury lost more than they gained by the "Popish Plot." When public opinion turned against them, they resorted to desperate measures and at last lost their heads—Shaftesbury only in metaphor, young Monmouth in literal fact. While the Plot had the country in an uproar, James, the central figure of it, was kept discreetly out of sight in Europe or Scotland; but when the story collapsed, and the agitators puffing it fell under suspicion, James reappeared to encourage his brother in a campaign of reprisals and repressions. Toward the end of 1682, Shaftesbury fled to Holland, where within a few months he died; as for Monmouth, he tried a futile plot of his own (the Rye House Plot) and then, when James had ascended the throne, made a last forlorn attempt to cross the channel, invade southwest England, and seize royal power. Captured almost at once, he was just as promptly beheaded, in 1685; the greater tragedy was the slaughter that hanging judge Jeffreys made among his deluded followers.[20] An ultimate

20. At the Winchester assizes of 1685, judge George Jeffreys sentenced over 300 of Monmouth's followers to the gallows and sold over 1,000 more into slavery in the Barbados (one of the lucky few who escaped prosecution was Daniel Defoe). Dissenters loathed Jeffreys for his cruelty to them, and King James, whose tool he was, readily let him shoulder the blame. He has therefore had a very bad press; but, on the evidence, he was a pretty bad man and deserved most of the infamy he got.

irony of this muddled young man's story is that he was probably not the son of Charles Stuart at all; his mother, Lucy Walter, was as promiscuous as she was beautiful, and Monmouth was very likely the son of another man.

Scares over the Popish Plot, which had the kingdom in turmoil for years and resulted in the deaths of a number of innocent people, were followed by other scares. The "Meal Tub" Plot of 1679 was so called because the incriminating documents were planted, and found, in a flour bin; the "Rye House" Plot of 1683 got its name because Charles was to be abducted and hidden in a house of that name. All these plots were exposed and their contrivers punished, often savagely. But public reaction to them favored King Charles; for the first time in years, he became a truly popular king. As a result, he started to move toward an intractable authoritarian position, more dangerous to England than any of the exploded plots. Then, unexpectedly, on 6 February, 1685, he died after a short illness. He was but fifty-four years old, and died an avowed member of the Catholic church to which, for many years, he had secretly subscribed. His brother James succeeded to the throne, not quite without incident. In Scotland the earl of Argyll mounted a brief, futile insurrection, and Monmouth's harebrained landing in the west country had to be put down. But in the main throughout the land, James's accession as the first frankly Catholic monarch since Mary Tudor was accepted, if not welcomed. James had promised that there would be no persecutions, and to that promise he actually kept; but Englishmen had yet to learn what twists he could give to the laudable doctrine of universal toleration.

LAST OF THE STUARTS

James Stuart was neither an intelligent nor, in his last years, a brave man; he suffered the additional liability, which never bothered his brother, of being an honest one. During his short reign, he did little which did not directly contribute to the shortening of it. He began by allowing Judge Jeffreys to blacken the west country with gallows laden with Monmouth's unfortunate followers. He prohibited his clergy from preaching against Catholicism, and roughly pressured his judges to exempt Catholics from that Test Act which Parliament viewed as its own special achievement. He enlarged the standing army, which everyone mistrusted, and stationed it just outside London as a threat to the Protestant population. He systematically promoted Catholics to positions of command and authority; and wherever he could, he replaced the heads of colleges in the two universities with known Catholics. When he issued in 1687 a declaration of indulgence to all Catholics and dissenters, he meant it to appear an even-handed gesture, but in fact it meant bare tolerance for dissenters, open preference for Catholics, and humiliation for the "established" church of England. Events abroad conspired to make James a figure of fear and hate in England. In 1685, Louis XIV revoked the edict of Nantes, under which, since 1598, French Protestants had enjoyed a limited and qualified religious liberty. Thousands of the most ambitious and intelligent workers in France were thus uprooted because of their religious beliefs. Many came to England and Ireland, where their skill as weavers was in demand; they brought with them tales of Catholic persecution which could only increase the revulsion toward James felt by his Protestant subjects.

Another unlucky event for James involved the question of his successor. After all, James was only three years younger than Charles; passionate Protestants might hope, though uncharitably, that he would die before long. While he had had eight children by his first wife (she was Anne, the earl of Clarendon's daughter), only two daughters, Mary and Anne, survived; and both were Protestants. They would normally succeed at his death, the elder first. But in 1673, his first wife dead, James had remarried, this time the Catholic Mary of Modena; and by her, after fifteen barren years, in 1688, he unexpectedly had a son, James Francis Edward Stuart. The son automatically took precedence over all daughters; and the son was inevitably going to be raised as a Catholic. England was faced, not with the brief inconvenience of a single elderly Catholic king, but with the prospect of a long line of Catholic rulers. Against all the evidence, many folk refused to believe the new babe was a legitimate child of James and Mary. It was a foundling, they said, slipped into the queen's bedchamber by devious Catholic plotters. The facts were against them; but the depth of their despair at the prospect of a Catholic succession was apparent.

Finally, James made his climactic mistake when in April 1688 he ordered all the Anglican bishops to read his declaration of indulgence (for Catholics and dissenters) from the pulpits of their diocesan churches—and thus in fact to advocate a measure that most of them detested. In an ideal world, with an ideal history or none at all, the ideal of universal toleration might have been welcome. In 1688 the bishops were being asked to surrender an institution and a position for which many of them had fought and sacrificed. They were being asked to grant equal rights to two fierce competitors of whose intolerance they were convinced and at whose hands many of them had suffered. They knew that equality for all meant preference for just one, and that the most dreaded, of the three groups. The wonder is not that seven bishops refused to read James's declaration, but that nineteen others obeyed.

Instantly the recalcitrant bishops were national heroes. Lawyers scrambled to defend them from the government's prosecution, and their acquittal was greeted with wild rejoicings. Meanwhile a number of powerful leaders, official and unofficial like the "grandees" who had brought back Charles II, had been secretly in touch with William of Orange.[21] He was the son of Charles I's daughter Mary,

---

21. To this day Protestants in Ireland are called *Orangemen*, green being the color of the Catholic party. *Jacobites* are the Tory fraction that remained loyal to James (Latin, *Jacobus*) after his abdication, and to his descendants. A Jacobite in the church would likely be a *nonjuror*, one who refused to take the oath of allegiance to William. While William was alive, his partisans were *Williamites*; after 1714, and the advent of George I, they supported the house of Hanover, and were therefore *Hanoverians*.

his wife Mary was elder daughter of James; his Protestantism, like hers, was unquestioned. With strong guarantees of a popular welcome William crossed the channel unopposed, while James, stripped of all support, only tried to escape to France. Even that he did not do very well; he was caught and arrested, but William, sensibly judging that he would be more of a nuisance in England, let him go again. The whole transaction, being without precedent, left a lot of loose legal ends, but the lawyers, never at a loss for a formula, decided that James had "abdicated." The proclamation of William and Mary as joint sovereigns (13 February, 1689) concluded the Glorious Revolution of 1688. It concluded also the effective history of the house of Stuart in England, and resolved finally, just a century after the victory over the Spanish Armada, that snarl of quarrels between monarch and Parliament which defeat of the Armada had unleashed. From now on there could be no doubt that on all major issues between these two branches of government, the voice of Parliament would prevail.

THE BOOK BUSINESS

Until 1640, literary activity centered on the royal court, catering to courtly tastes and interests; under the commonwealth, without a court, literary production languished or subsisted on courtly memories. With the return of Charles II, literary society again sprang up in and around the court; but it was relatively thin and deliberately exclusive. Outside its closed circle now swirled new, strange currents of thought and expression such as had hardly existed before. The sheer bulk of English publication had increased radically during the pamphlet wars. People far beyond the traditional range of the "cultured classes" got into the way of reading books; with a wider and more diverse audience to appeal to, more publishers entered the field, responding to more various interests. To be sure, censorship of the press continued through the Restoration period (it was abolished only in 1694), but without any effort to maintain the old Laudian uniformity. Even rules about obscenity were hard to enforce when the king himself applauded the most obscene plays his playwrights could contrive or his mistresses could perform. Accordingly, publication flourished. To reach the new audiences, men wrote more clearly than before, with fewer strained metaphors and less complicated allusions; for such plain, vigorous writing, a large public and a large market were available.

The traditional name for a publisher was a "bookseller"; the same man was likely to fill both functions, and sell in the front of his shop the books he printed in the back. Advertisements directed the reader who wanted a certain book to proceed to the publisher's house, and it was clearly in the bookseller's interest to have there other books of the same sort—by the same author, in the same political vein, or of the same sectarian persuasion. A bookseller who sensed that a particular book might sell well could suggest that an author write it, or even stake the author to an advance while he wrote it. Booksellers thus built up stables of authors. During the later years of the century, we find many "Miscellanies" being published; they were collections of brief writings or translations loosely related to a common theme. In such cases the bookseller was also a maker of books; the idea was his, he assembled the contributors, paid them a pittance, and put out the book as "by several hands." The appetite for miscellaneous information was unbounded, and it resulted in a number of publishing innovations. About 1690 a publisher named John Dunton started a weekly magazine called *The Athenian Mercury,* the contents of which were controlled by its subscribers. They sent in questions on medicine, etiquette, natural history, mechanics, and sex, which Dunton (a "Dear Abby" before her time) tried to answer. Another innovation was the practice of publishing by subscription. Before producing a book, the publisher circulated among the gentry a prospectus; those who subscribed in advance got a copy and had their names printed on a special sheet as patrons of the enterprise. Such a list of patrons by no means prevented the author from dedicating the book as a whole to a distinguished man, and the several sections to several other distinguished men, from all of whom he might expect gratifications.[22] Dryden published after this fashion his translation of the *Complete Works of Virgil* (1697); though not the first to publish by subscription, he was one of the best-known authors to do so.

Behind all these experimental publishing arrangements can be sensed a polite but nasty struggle between publishers who, thinking themselves employers of authors, wanted to pay them as little as possible, and authors who, thinking publishers mere tradesmen and hucksters, wanted more rewards for themselves. Dunton invented a way to get floods of free copy from his readers; the vogue of translation was in good measure a passion for cheap copy, translators being the coolies and fellaheen of the literary industry; while publishing by subscription was a way of milking the author's social connections in order to eliminate the publisher's risks. Though they were at a great disadvantage before the booksellers, and many of them wrote for starvation wages, a few authors did actually manage to live by their pens; the most distinguished among them was John Dryden.

DRYDEN IN HIS AGE

Like Ben Jonson before him, Dryden laid the foundations of his modest fortune in the theater. After some early apprentice work—clumsy and obscene in comedy, but dignified and impressive in the lofty vein of "heroic" tragedy—he had

---

22. The dark side of patronage showed through the cudgeling Dryden received in 1679 from bullies hired by the earl of Rochester. Noblemen who rewarded what they liked could punish what they did not like, as Voltaire would rediscover forty-five years later. The law took no notice of such episodes. In fact, Dryden was innocent of the slur Rochester resented, but he had no recourse at all.

the good fortune, about 1667, to be placed on retainer as a writer for one of the two theaters, and for the next fourteen years wrote mainly plays. In 1670 he was appointed poet laureate, as Jonson had also been, and held that post till 1688 when he was deprived of it because of his recently declared Catholic faith. The work he did in translation, during the last decade of his life, was an obvious effort to make up for loss of his laureate's pension. Apart from his work for the theater, Dryden's production of poetry was sporadic and occasional; he was superb at writing verses of formal compliment and voicing grave, judicious sentiments on solemn occasions. The satires by which he is now best known rose out of public events, and expressed the keen judgment of his basically conservative character. Throughout his life he wrote a great deal of critical prose, dealing with his craft; it is supple, sustained, but never ponderous discourse, rippling with wit and sharp with raillery. Dryden was our first complete man of letters, with all the virtues and limitations that term implies—a social writer, in and of his time, agile, intelligent, and on the dry side. "Dry" is an adjective that applies to champagne as well as dust. Still, if we could recall someone from the seventeenth century for an hour's conversation, Donne, Cromwell, and Sir Thomas Browne would come long before Dryden on our list.

Dryden's thought was once neglected and his character tarnished by the imputation that he was simply a selfish turncoat. For a fact, if we look at the record in outline form, there may seem to be something to the charge. In 1659 he published a laudatory poem to the memory of Cromwell, in 1660 an enthusiastic poem of welcome to Charles II. In 1682 he published a poem supporting the Anglican creed, but after converting to Catholicism in 1685 (the very year of James II's accession), he published in 1687 a poetical argument in behalf of his new faith. These successive changes, if not necessarily those of a mere opportunist, were liable to that interpretation; and as Dryden was a man who gave no quarter in controversy, so he got none from his contemporaries. Only recently, as the influence of skeptical traditions on Dryden's mind was more fully studied, has a steady logical progression become apparent in his thought (SFR, E.27). He was a deeply skeptical man, more fond of balancing one alternative against another than of declaring any categorical conclusions. He was a professional man of letters, who took it as his business to gratify the audiences of his plays and the readers of his books—responsive, therefore, to the moods of that nation which he once described as

> . . . a headstrong, moody, murmuring race
> As ever tried the extent and stretch of grace;
> God's pampered people, whom, debauched with ease,
> No king could govern, nor no God could please.

His skepticism helped him to adopt fashionable literary styles, even those for which he had no natural aptitude, and to turn his immense rhetorical skills to many different ends; and a certain natural impetus of language drove him to carry all modes to extremes. His bawdy comedies are bawdier and cruder than anyone else's, his satires more cutting, his tragedies more grandiloquent. But behind Dryden's cleverness in manipulating rhetoric and attitudes (before Auden, he was the cleverest discursive poet in English) he was seeking a deeper certainty to which he could submit. When he found an ultimate faith, he became a fideist, like Browne. Dryden's conversion to Catholicism, in 1685, cost him dearly in 1688, but he never wavered in his new faith. His unshakable achievement was the establishment for English, in both poetry and prose, of a flexible yet dignified mode of argumentative discourse. It was once customary to apply to Dryden the old saying about the emperor Augustus, that he found Rome brick and left it marble; if that implies the addition of an element of veneering, let the imputation stand.

THE KALEIDOSCOPE OF RESTORATION WRITING

Though Dryden was a professional writer, most of his contemporaries were not; the comic dramatists of the Restoration looked with disdain, real or affected, on the very idea of writing for a living. George Etherege, William Wycherley, and William Congreve were all fine gentlemen by profession (that is, they had none); and Congreve, who abruptly stopped writing at the height of his powers when he was just thirty, proclaimed the utmost contempt for a literary reputation.[23] Most of the Restoration court poets were equally scornful of fame; they published anonymously or posthumously, and a few of them, like the earl of Mulgrave, got splendid literary reputations by being careful to publish the next thing to nothing at all. It's true that Dryden dominated the courtly writers of the Restoration as Ben Jonson dominated an earlier generation; it is also true that he had a less rich and various realm to dominate.

Outside court circles, it was another story. Science, theoretical and applied, occupied a greater proportion of the printed books than ever before. The discoveries of Boyle in chemistry and physics, of Newton in optics and mechanics, of Tyson and Collins in comparative anatomy, of Hooke, Halley, Flamsteed, and (of course) Newton in astronomy, of Wallis in algebra and Hooke again in microscopy can only suggest the extent and character of this explosion of knowledge.[24] With Richard Bentley a new order of precision entered the study of the

23. The plays of these comic authors all deal with comfortably rich and politely promiscuous people. The characters pursue sex and money with high intelligence, glossy manners, and total indifference to moral scruple. Of the group Etherege has the lightest, most casual touch; Congreve is the most witty and poished stylist; while Wycherley's was the most strong and forthright mind. The best satiric play of the Restoration is a merry, malicious slander on Dryden, concocted by the duke of Buckingham and others, under the title of *The Rehearsal*.

24. Though Bacon and Boyle are conspicuous exceptions to this rule, science in the seventeenth century was mainly rational and deductive; mathematics, optics, and astronomy were the preferred fields. The eighteenth century, more empirical in its approach, made crucial discoveries in physics, chemistry, and mechanics.

classical languages; with Clarendon's *History of the Rebellion,* history graduated from the stage of anecdote and chronicle to the level of philosophical analysis. Thomas Burnet published, in *The Sacred History of the Earth* (1684), a rhapsodic and visionary effort to reconcile geology with Genesis; Inigo Jones and Dr. Walter Charlton published books on Stonehenge, that huge enigma of ancient rocks on Salisbury plain. The science of social statistics was invented by Sir William Petty and refined by Charles Davenant, son of a poet laureate. Practical proposals for doing practical jobs more efficiently sprouted like mushrooms.

Classes of society not previously represented in the world of letters began to make themselves heard. John Bunyan the religious tinker, wrote in a tradition which invited him to seem less literate then he perhaps was. Still, his was a fullthroated voice from levels of society and levels of consciousness that before the rebellion had remained unprobed,

> . . . one morning, as I did lie in my bed, I was, as at other times, most fiercely assaulted with this temptation, to *sell and part with Christ;* the wicked suggestion still running in my mind, *Sell him, sell him, sell him,* as fast as a man could speak; against which also in my mind, as at other times, I answered, No, no, not for thousands, thousands, thousands, at least twenty times together; but at last, after much striving, even until I was almost out of breath, I felt this thought pass through my heart, *Let him go if he will!* and I thought also that I felt my heart freely consent thereto. Oh, the diligence of Satan! Oh, the desperateness of man's heart!

For many years, popular ballads had been printed on single sheets and sold in the streets, sometimes by the singer; in the late seventeenth century, broadsheets began to be used for other purposes: to press programs of social reform, to make satirical attacks, to present the lives of famous criminals, or simply to amuse a casual reader. The novel was slow in developing, but rogue stories exercised perennial fascination; *The English Rogue* by Richard Head and Francis Kirkman (1665) is half translation and the rest plagiarism, but a readable production for all that. Hesitantly and uncertainly, a group of women affiliated with the court began writing and (more rarely) publishing verse. Anne Killigrew, who died very young but was memorialized in a splendid ode by Dryden, was a painter as well as an occasional poet. Katherine Phillips was known to her rather precious circle of admirers as "the matchless Orinda"; and Anne Finch, later countess of Winchelsea, liked (for poetic purposes) to describe her husband as "Daphnis," herself as "Ardelia." The pastoral names and imitative styles of these amateurs bespeak a certain thinness of inspiration. But a tougher and more interesting figure, Mrs. Aphra Behn, became England's first professional woman writer, because she was able to tap deeper veins of feeling and tackle the larger forms of drama and fiction. Mrs. Behn's personal life apparently resembled that of a Defoe heroine, and her fifteen stage comedies include some pretty coarse work. But in *Oroonoko, or the History of the Royal Slave* (1678), she drew on childhood memories (she had grown up in Surinam, South America), humanitarian sentiments, and perhaps her own sense of feminine oppression to produce a prose fiction resembling *Uncle Tom's Cabin* nearly two centuries before its time. The prevalence of a simple forceful prose style, and the ready availability of printing presses opened the door to materials previously thought too ephemeral for print. The ominous birth of a six-legged calf in Worcester, the prophetic dream of a housewife in Hampshire, the appearance of a ghost in Canterbury, and a thousand other bits of folk gossip now rose to the dignity of print. This was the common material of everyday vulgar life out of which fiction would some day be made—a slowly accumulating compost which would spring to life through the novel's wonderful power to adopt points of view which make the inherently trivial seem supremely significant.

MILTON AND THE MODERNS

Apart from the literary, and sometimes subliterary, marketplace, remote from the mutual-admiration circles of the court, the greatest literary work of the Restoration came to maturity in solitude and entered the world obscurely. In 1667, a tumultuous year still shaking from the great fire of London, the second Dutch war, and a frightful epidemic of the plague, blind John Milton published the supreme epic poem of the modern age. Its printer was Samuel Simmons, a humble craftsman who had never before dealt in literature, and the time could scarcely have been less propitious for a heroic poem on religious themes. Just a few years before (1663–1664) a smart, malicious man named Samuel Butler had published to great acclaim the first burlesque poem in English,[25] a satire on puritanism and knight-errantry titled *Hudibras*. The vogue for burlesque had begun in France, but quickly caught hold in England, where mockery of heroic ideals exactly suited the cynical temper of the Restoration court. Milton's poem not only ran counter to that fashionable current; it was solemn, religious, and explicitly puritan in theme; in style, it was complex and allusive, when the age was all for clarity and simplicity; and it used the unfashionable medium of blank verse, quite unfamiliar outside of drama, and even there no longer *à la mode*. Despite all these handicaps, and much dislike of the author for his defense of the regicides, *Paradise Lost* made slow but steady headway. Dryden and Sir John Denham lent generous support, and there was enough readership to call for a second edition in 1674. Milton took advantage of it to divide the original ten books into the present twelve, and to add explanatory "arguments," for easier reading. But otherwise he did not much alter his first version. A final volume of verse, containing *Paradise Regained* and *Samson Agonistes*, had appeared in 1671; and in November of 1674 Milton died. The dramatic rise in his reputation came after

25. Burlesque writing (from Italian *burla*, a joke) exploits a ludicrous incongruity between a heroic theme and a vulgar or ridiculous manner of treatment. The word's association with the art of strip-tease is largely twentieth century.

1688 when John Somers, a lawyer who had taken an important hand in the Glorious Revolution, persuaded a publisher, Jacob Tonson, to buy the rights to Milton's poetry. Unlike Simmons the first printer, Tonson knew his way around the world of literary politics, and he "pushed" Milton vigorously. The temper of the times changed, as the witty cynicism of Restoration comedy played itself out—its departure speeded by attacks from outraged moralists. In the early eighteenth century, a powerful set of appreciative essays by Joseph Addison launched Milton's reputation on a triumphal course which would not be checked, even temporarily, till the early twentieth century.

Possession of an epic poem which could challenge comparison with those of Homer and Virgil was a heady experience for those who took pride in English literature. World-wide and across the centuries, epic was the oldest, rarest, and loftiest form of verse; to have equaled the ancients in their chosen form but in modern idiom gave to the English language a special cachet. It was a kind of coming of age. The language was becoming too various now to have a traceable course of development; it had a variety of traditions to follow or work against. Its users were becoming more assured in their handling of its different qualities, in their development of individual styles. Apologetic attitudes toward our weak and ephemeral modern idiom faded rapidly. One old-fashioned admirer of *Paradise Lost* did actually translate it into Latin hexameters, as another man, with a bit more reason, translated Locke's *Essay Concerning Human Understanding* into the international language of philosophy, Latin again. But the books themselves stood, and stood permanently, as everyone knew they would, on the solid ground of the English tongue.

Not by any means coincidentally, the last part of the century witnessed a renewal in England of a verbal dispute which had already produced a number of interesting books in France: the so-called quarrel between the ancients and the moderns. In its first form, the question was whether modern writers were better or worse than ancient ones. Was Homer an inspired barbarian, describing the deeds of "heroes" who, if we could really meet them, would strike us as bloodthirsty oafs? Or have we, in putting on the traits of civilization, lost the true nobility and dignity of our ancestors? Have we outgrown our classic forefathers or instead degenerated from them?

Both in France and England, the question was answered in contrasting ways by different people, as perhaps it always will be. In France, clever Charles Perrault espoused the cause of the moderns, learned Boileau that of the ancients; and there, where the field of dispute was largely literary, one may think that Boileau had the better of it. To say that in Jean Chapelain the society of Louis XIV boasted a better poet than either Homer or Virgil—especially when one was incapable of reading Homer in the Greek—was to invite brutal ridicule. But in England the controversy was less strictly literary; it shifted to a question of general knowledge, a comparison of ancient and modern learning. Mr. William Wotton and Dr. Richard Bentley upheld the cause of the moderns; Sir William

Temple, Charles Boyle, and (in the controversy's last stages) Jonathan Swift sustained the ancients. And though it will always be a question who had the better of the slanging match, on the substantive issues it's impossible to doubt that the moderns scored decisively. They could point to modern studies in anatomy, astronomy, and medicine, in algebra, physics, geometry, and calculus, to the microscope, the telescope, North and South America: of all these matters the ancients had been either comparatively or absolutely ignorant. Bentley was even prepared to carry the war into the enemy's territory by proving (conclusively, had his antagonists been learned enough to understand his arguments) that the letters of Phalaris and the fables of Aesop—held up to his admiration as inimitable works of ancient writers—were in fact late forgeries by undistinguished hands in a degenerate period of antiquity. Positively and negatively, the "moderns" clearly had the best of it.

Yet, like most word-wars, the quarrel between the patrons of the ancients and the patrons of the moderns ended indecisively. In the history of critical thought, it has a certain importance, just now coming to be appreciated as we try in our turn to grasp that slippery word "modern." But for the history of the Restoration, two aspects of the story stand out. First is the instinctive turn of the "modern" partisans in England to make their case, not on literary grounds, but on the footing of scientific and technical knowledge. There, in what we may call the "cumulative" disciplines, they could show that modern men had far outdistanced their classic forebears. That was grounds for a national mood of confidence which is in itself the second important thing evidenced by the ancients-versus-moderns controversy. For a small nation, still groping after its political status in the big world, still racked with the jealousies of a civil war, to challenge comparison with the classic civilizations of Greece and Rome was an extraordinary event. Louis XIV, at the head of a solidly organized and immensely powerful empire, might better do it. But the mood of the English after 1688 can be summed up in the word they applied to that revolution, "glorious." They had won a large charter for their future enterprises, and were confident now of exploiting it to the full. Not without reason is the new era sometimes called "The Age of Exuberance."

10

The Settlement of '88 and Queen Anne (1688–1714)

The life of an average Englishman under King William and Queen Mary resembled the life of a modern man, living three hundred years later, more closely than it did the life of an equivalent man living in 1588, just a hundred years earlier. English people had come more than halfway into the modern world, shedding in the process many residual practices from the middle ages. For instance, men now wore something like the modern costume, with coat, vest, and breeches; trunk hose and codpieces were no more, body armor was purely ceremonial, and few men carried swords in the streets. Shoes took the place of heavy boots, except on long journeys. Though early postal services had all been to and from London, in the last decade of the seventeenth century "cross posts" were begun, to carry letters, say, from Bristol to York without passing through the capital. Leather clothing was now seen only in the backwoods, and cotton had started to replace wool in daily wear. A completely indigenous silk industry was out of the question, but England was only a few years away from its first silk-spinning factory.[1] The language of 1688 was far closer to our modern English

---

1. People who wore cotton clothing were, in the early days, sometimes assaulted in the streets by angry exponents of the wool trade. The English silk industry resulted from an act of industrial espionage; John Lombe went to Italy, early in the eighteenth century, to find the jealously guarded secret of Italian machinery for making very fine threads. He returned with the secret and his life, but

than to Elizabethan speech; thee's and thou's had largely disappeared, "Master" gave way to "Mr.," and "Mistress" to "Mrs."—the latter now an abreviation of a word that cannot be spelled, or if spelled, missus, is only a joke. Before 1688 many words dropped out of the English language as others entered; hardly any that were current then are not also current now. The vocabulary has increased enormously, mainly by the addition of new names for new things; most recent additions are technical terms. The core words of the language, which make up most of our everyday speech, have remained remarkably constant.

Outside the circle of its voluntary membership, the power of the church to define sin and punish sinners, severely exercised by Elizabethan and early Stuart bishops, had almost vanished by the eighteenth century. The well-behaved nonconformist, however bizarre his theology, had nothing to fear from the discipline of the established church. Judicial torture was no more, and the more brutal forms of punishment (burning alive and pressing to death) were rapidly disappearing. Houses had glass in their windows, not oiled paper, carpets on the floor, not rushes; people sat on upholstered chairs, not wooden benches. Tea, chocolate, and coffee, unknown a century before, had become common beverages. After 1688 the ordinary man could attend the church of his choice or none at all; he could read any newspaper he wanted, keep his money in a bank or invest it in a joint-stock enterprise, insure his life or property, and pay his debts with a bill of exchange. His diet was far better than it had been a hundred years before; fresh meat was available throughout the year, and even some vegetables in winter. The humble cabbage, which Ben Jonson mentions as an exotic import from Holland, had been domesticated in England. So had the plebeian turnip, and that nobler vegetable, asparagus.

Girls were no longer bought and sold on the money market, as routinely, as callously as before; in middle-class circles at least, married love was an ideal, not just a bad joke as we see it, vestigially, in Restoration comedy. Dictionaries, compilations, and compendia of useful knowledge started to be published, more and better than ever before. Foreigners like M. Saint-Evremond came to dwell among the English and learn their ways; wealthy young Englishmen, in greater numbers than before, embarked as part of their education on the grand tour of the Continent, where they learned to admire (just like their modern counterparts) what they had been taught was admirable. Returning home, they brought as souvenirs a few phrases of French or Italian, a print, coin, or copy of a famous painting. Instead of wooden trenchers and pewter pots, the average family now began to use at table china crockery and glass goblets.[2] Knife and fork, which

---

died shortly after; he had been poisoned, some said, by vengeful Italians. His brother set up an immense factory on an island in the river Derwent, operated it successfully, and added domestic silks to the array of British finery.

2. We noted above (p. 106) the coming of the first paper mill to England; about the same time, in the later sixteenth century, manufacture of glass began. Venetian immigrants brought the craft; early factories were nomadic, because they burned up all the fuel around them, and then moved on.

used to be luxury devices, used only by the upper classes, now became commonplace. (A century before, even a gentleman like Montaigne regularly ate with his fingers and used plenty of napkins afterward.) The water closet, an object of wonder and ridicule in Elizabeth's day, became less remarkable, though not by any means to be taken for granted; even stately homes might still rely on chamberpots. An extreme of luxury was hot and cold running water; only one nobleman enjoyed that luxury. But thousands of families now welcomed the practice of setting aside a separate room for a kitchen: a pot or spit over the living-room fireplace no longer sufficed. As recently as the sixteenth century, the chimney itself had been a novelty in poor men's houses; so was the idea of sleeping in a proper bed with a pillow instead of on a sack of husks using a log to support the head. Now comfort, if not luxury, was available to most folk of the rank of yeoman or above. The art of conversation, whether formalized in clubs or salons, or simply flowing from the meeting of congenial minds, flourished in a society which admired voluntary associations and freedom from dogma.

THE GRIM WORLD OF THE VERY POOR

We must not idealize the early eighteenth century. Much that the age accepted without question would horrify and disgust us today. Streets were still filthy, ill-lit, unpaved, noisy, and dangerous. The parodic last lines of Swift's "Description of a City Shower" give us a capsule scene:

> Sweepings from butchers' stalls, dung, guts, and blood,
> Drowned puppies, stinking sprats, all drenched in mud,
> Dead cats and turnip tops come tumbling down the flood.

Or, for a fuller account, one might turn to John Gay's fine antipoetical poem in three books, titled *Trivia, or the Art of Walking the Streets of London* (1716). Though much idealized by poets, the country for working folk was no less grim than the city. Everywhere the unpropertied, unprivileged classes lived in squalor and died wretchedly of filth, disease, cold, a string of afflictions, the real name of which was neglect. They had no voice in politics (only the propertied could vote) and no redress if they fell foul of the law in the person of a puffy, choleric justice of the peace. For the theft of a single shilling's worth of goods, mere children could be hanged or transported for life; lesser punishments, such as lash and pillory, were often but steps on the way to debtor's prison, bridewell, or— final destination of most human refuse—the loathsome workhouse. Even if they kept clear of the law, the fate of the poor was cruel. Wages were low, hours of work long, the bare necessities hard to come by. Many a poor person who would actually have liked to go to church could not attend for lack of decent clothing;

---

on. Goblets, beakers, and similar small table ware made up most of the early production; window panes came later.

rags and bare feet were so frequent as to cause little comment. Even then, and all the more nowadays, students looking at the statistics must admit they do not see how these people survived. Part of the answer is simply that many did not; life expectancy among the poor was under thirty-five years. Any effort to improve their condition by collective action met with ferocious repression. Parson and squire, church and state, agreed solemnly or savagely that, if only for their own good, the poor must be kept from the unforgivable sin of disobedience.

Obvious alternatives to a life of drab drudgery were, depending on one's sex, to turn highwayman or whore; these traditional callings attracted so many aspirants that John Gay, in his *Beggar's Opera* (1728), used their harum-scarum arrangements as an image of the larger society that he considered just about equally brutal and lawless. Apart from out-and-out criminals, many dispossessed families from the countryside drifted into cities, where they lived anonymously and desperately in slums, fighting, thieving, begging, and doing the odd job. Two new additions to England's diet contributed to their depravation: gin and potatoes. Gin, which replaced beer or ale in the diet of these unhappy people, not only intoxicates faster and more thoroughly, it has far less nutritive value. (Beer contains some protein and carbohydrates, and in the old days, when it was stronger than it is now, contained even more.) As for potatoes, their story is told in the popular names for them, "The Root of Misery," and sometimes "The Root of Extreme Unction." A diet of potatoes will in fact keep one alive, but just barely. A slum population, fed on potatoes and devoted to gin, marginally employed, and not far from starvation, made for social instability. For the first time in the early 18th century, we start hearing of the "mob," short for *mobile vulgus*, meaning in Latin restless herd. A London mob, easily roused by a demagogue of either right or left, but not easily manipulated after that because its members had their own resentments and aspirations, could be an ugly thing; we hear increasingly of riots, lynchings, and lootings in the century to come. For a while we also hear about voluntary associations of well-meaning folk who wanted to improve the condition of the poor by making them sober, devout, and docile. The Society for the Reformation of Manners, the Society for the Promotion of Christian Knowledge, and other such societies doubtless did some good in some circumstances. But they soon got a bad name, because their morality was an obvious social pacifier, and also because they used informers to report on the profane and promiscuous. Such behavior did not sit kindly with the poor, or for that matter with the well-to-do, who relished not at all the prospect of being arraigned for their moral failings before a committee of pious upstarts. Accordingly, the unregenerate poor were commonly allowed to remain unregenerate, until the mighty wind of the Methodist revival began to blow among them toward the middle of the 18th century. To be poor was probably to be bad; and that put you beyond the pale. Even the radical sects, which had once expressed the social aspirations and dreams of society's broken and rejected, lay for the most part torpid during the early century.

THE POWERS OF THE RICH

The active conflicts of the new age took place between two different parties of privilege and power. Tories represented the landed interest, especially small independent landowners hostile to central government as such (Squire Western in Fielding's *Tom Jones* is the type). They strongly upheld the church of England, and a fringe on the far right still hankered to bring back the Stuarts, in other words they were Jacobites. Anglican clergymen who took seriously their oath of allegiance to James were in a particularly awkward fix; they had to think William, Mary, and all their successors were usurpers. Those who refused to swear allegiance to the new line (the nonjurors) thus wound up suffering for their loyalty to a king who had done his best to destroy them. As for the Whigs, though they included some big landlords (land, as the best and safest investment, was the natural destination of all large sums of money), basically they represented the moneyed interest—that is, the predominantly London merchants, bankers, and shipping magnates; hence they identified with the dissenting community, especially the Presbyterians. Whigs were creators of the Bank of England and the national debt; in the early century, they tended to be a war party because war served their commercial interests, while the Tories were a peace party because they did not want to pay war taxes. Both parties were powerful, and the main theater of their conflict was the House of Commons, now the unquestioned center of government authority. Five times King William tried in the early years of his reign to veto acts of Parliament, and five times he failed. His successor Queen Anne tried just once; and that was the last time any English monarch ever made such an attempt. As for the parliament-men, they made no bones about it: they represented, not Englishmen in general, but their own moneyed class; they depended neither on the king's pleasure nor the general public's; their function was to protect the liberty of the subject, by which they meant the property of the propertied. They declared as much, repeatedly; what they were reciting was the central teaching of their patron saint, John Locke, in his *Second Treatise of Civil Government*. [3]

Money called the tune; moralists described its working as shameless greed. Shameless it really was. Most men whose opinion counted (men of property, that is) saw nothing wrong with giving property predominant rights in the kingdom. The only question was what sort of property, old land or new money, was most entitled. Both Swift and Pope, who stood for the traditional values, saw personal honor, dignity, morality, even individuality itself, being swallowed up in the tides of corruption and greed. [4] For the Whigs, who had made the Glorious

3. In medieval times, property typically followed social status: a baron would be given estates to carry out his duties as the king's vassal. By the seventeenth and eighteenth centuries, a big landowner, whatever the source of his money, could generally get a title and a seat in the House of Lords. Status, in other words, was following property. This was a tremendous turnaround.

4. Though at any given point it may be convenient to distinguish the moneyed from the landed interest, throughout the eighteenth century the first was constantly becoming the second. The mag-

Revolution and controlled most of the governments resulting from it, used their money with a crassness that was almost splendid. Hardly anything was not for sale, whether decorations, offices, titles, estates, seats in Parliament, commissions in the army, or sinecures in the church. Christianity was openly mocked, not only in the street talk of the mob and the salons of the cultured, but on the public stage and in the public press. Dr. John Eachard wrote a tough, funny book *On the Contempt of the Clergy* (1670); the fact needed little demonstration, the prime cause of it he found to lie in the wretched poverty of churchmen, which led to secondary failings, such as ignorance and servility.[5] A little later, Jonathan Swift added new dimensions to the discussion in a book which showed his utter contempt of those modern hack authors, facile, greedy, superficial, conceited, whom he saw as trying to worm into the places of the now-despised clergy. *A Tale of a Tub*, written in 1697, published in 1704, is a book so savage in its wit, so far-reaching in its implications, that it may fairly be said to have written a massive FINIS to the seventeenth century. Everything that century stood for— the pursuit of an assured, exclusive way to salvation, belief in the value of deep, encyclopedic learning, individualist zeal or enthusiasm— Swift tears to shreds and tramples underfoot. After so devastating an explosion of destructive hatred, we have to find ourselves in a new world.

BALANCING FRIENDS AND FOES

When he was invited to become William III of England, William of Orange was thirty-eight years old, but with the political and military experience of a much older man. His father had been the leader of an unsuccessful coup, and was in official disgrace when he died of smallpox just eight days before William was born; the boy grew up among enemies, physically frail and indeed deformed, a lonely, suspicious, and cold-faced young man.[6] At the early age of twenty-two, he was called to lead the Dutch in their resistance to the French armies of Louis XIV (1672). Henceforth he was the European symbol of Protestant defiance of Catholic aggression. Repeating a famous tactic of the sixteenth century war with

---

nates who made the revolution of 1688 were mainly money men (examples are Baron Somers, Sir Charles Duncombe, and Charles Montague, who became earl of Halifax); but they and their friends were not slow in converting their money into landed estates—which solidified their political power, and led to the consolidation of the so-called "Whig oligarchy."

5. Contempt for the clergy could be remarkably frank and brutal. Lord Halifax was far famed for the elegance and polish of his manners; but when his chaplain ventured to pray for him in public "as his Lord and Patron," the noble lord asked if he could not be content to play the fool, but he must let the world know whose fool he was. For a strongly colored but not overdrawn contrast between the upper and lower clergy of the English church, see Macaulay's *History of England,* Chapter III. The entire chapter of this famous book is well worth reading, not only as polished, eloquent history, but as literature. It is a formal portait, full-length, of the age.

6. William was great-grandson to William the Silent, sixteenth-century founder of the Dutch republic, whose implacable resistance to Philip of Spain was almost as notable as his devotion to religious toleration. See above, p. 154.

Spain, he opened dykes and flooded the countryside to block enemy advances. He had sworn, he said, to die in the last ditch rather than surrender his country; and this was not just rhetoric. Holland being much smaller than France, William depended heavily on his allies, and therefore had to keep in touch with public affairs throughout Europe. He was hardly surprised when asked to replace his father-in-law as king of England, nor at all averse to doing so. Primarily he wanted to be king of England in order to wage more effective war in defense of Holland. Not everyone in England saw this as an unmixed blessing, but it was a clear sign of the Dutchman's stubborn character.

William's first tasks, upon arriving in England, were to reward the friends who had invited him over and to secure the land from external foes. He was more successful at the latter job than the former. The immediate danger was Ireland. Since Cromwell's cruel campaign of 1649, Irish Catholics had gradually and unofficially regained a good deal of power in the southern part of their island. Not so in the north, where Scottish colonists, planted by Elizabeth and James I, had been steadily reinforced by ex-soldiers from Puritan armies and refugees from Restoration atrocities. If James were to regain his kingdom, it would have to be through southern Ireland; and thither, as soon as he had assembled a few French soldiers, he proceeded. His first step was to organize a mass persecution of Protestants, such as he had often been accused of plotting in England. William, with a small but disciplined army, crossed the Irish sea, picked up reinforcements in Ulster, and seized the offensive. On 1 July, 1690,[7] he crossed the river Boyne to attack and destroy James's Irish army in a battle still vivid in Irish minds today. This may have been the last major battle to be decided by the personal characters of the commanders. William was tough, clear-headed, and perfectly brave; James dithered and fled the field before battle was even joined. (His embittered troops, such as survived, promptly christened him "dirty James," Seamus-a-Cacagh.)[8] A final peace treaty was negotiated at Limerick; though it was ostensibly generous, its application was very cruel. The Irish have always denounced it as a piece of British perfidy, and it was so harsh that thousands of ex-soldiers promptly fled their native land to take service abroad. The Irish call them, poetically, "wild geese," and over the next two centuries we repeatedly meet with Irish names in exotic contexts: O'Donnell, duke of Tetuan, in Spain; MacMahon, marshal of France; Meagher of the sword in North America; Bernardo O'Higgins in South America; Irishmen in Russia, Austria, Naples. A brigade of Irish exiles mounted the charge at Fontenoy (1745) which won that classic battle for the French against the English.[9] They wrote a heroic legend;

7. This was 1 July Old Style, 11 July New Style; see below, fn. on the calendar, p. 314.

8. When he was a younger man, James had been a competent, even at times a distinguished military commander. In his last years it is possible that he was the victim of a degenerative mental or nervous disorder. For a Stuart, he lived unusually long (1633-1701).

9. An officer of the Irish Brigade, Captain Richard Hennessy, son of James Hennessy, esquire, of Ballymacmoy in the County Cork, settled in France after Fontenoy, and started a famous cognac company. To this day, Hennessy Three-Star Brandy ranks among the finest that France produces. Living well is said to be the best revenge.

but the constant emigration from Ireland of her strongest and most enterprising men helped bleed the country white.

In fact the land that the wild geese left behind was utterly prostrate. After three devastations in less than a century (those of Elizabeth, Cromwell, and now William) Ireland was helpless before her conqueror; and English policy showed no mercy. If, as has been said, the English learned the art of empire by making all their mistakes on Ireland first, the early eighteenth century would offer much evidence in point. All Irish industries which showed the slightest sign of competing with English industries were aborted or strangled at birth. Absentee landlords racked exorbitant rents out of Irish tenants while an English Parliament denied those tenants recourse to export markets. Poverty, ignorance, filth, and disease were universal; world travelers declared they had never anywhere seen such desolate, miserable countryside as in Ireland. In the English Parliament there was even a move (fortunately defeated) to prevent Irish people from fishing in the sea, except in English boats. As a rule, officials of the Irish Protestant church and those of the English government spent only a bare minimum of time in the districts for which they were supposedly responsible. Literal starvation was very common among the people; yet, out of Irish taxes, the English Parliament bestowed liberal pensions on Germans and Englishmen. Only in the latter half of the eighteenth century when England (because of foreign wars and industrial expansion) had special need for the products of Irish agriculture, did a little prosperity come to Ireland. And even then it remained a bitter irony that while the land was exporting beef, butter, and bacon for English consumption, the peasants who raised these good things had to subsist on potatoes and turnips.

TROUBLE WITH THE CHURCH

At rewarding his friends William was less successful than at crushing his foes. A sore point was the church, which he had promised to maintain, but did not maintain as much as it expected. Generally, it was the nonconformists who prospered under his policies, while the Anglican church, which in 1688 for once in its long career had come close to heroism, stood by and saw its shadow grow ever less. William—or, rather, his Parliament, for he cared little about the domestic affairs of his new nation—began by establishing Presbyterianism as the state religion of Scotland and passing in England the Toleration Act (1689) which gave new status and security to the dissenters. What most disturbed Anglicans about this new arrangement was that it narrowed the gap between the "established" church and the various competing sects. What, traditionalists asked, was the advantage of being the established church, when all the little sects in the land enjoyed practically the same rights and privileges? It was particularly infuriating that the power structure of the church, the bishops and archbishops appointed by William, seemed ready and eager to give away the church's privileged position. For the new regime systematically promoted "moderate" churchmen (i.e., those tolerant of dissenters) and systematically neglected those whose devotion to the church they served seemed somehow "immoderate."[10] The lower clergy, poorer than ever because of inflation, and resenting that poverty because of the commercial affluence around them, tended to become bitterly Tory and narrowly devoted to the church, not as a universal body of believers, but as a corporation of clerics. Some of them were, not religious, but ecclesiastical bigots.

Meanwhile, the dissenters outside the church were busily eating away at its privileges. The Test Act of 1673 had forbidden them to hold public office unless they were communicants of the church of England. After 1688 numbers of them started to evade this rule by a practice called Occasional Conformity. To qualify for office they attended Anglican services as the law required, just twice a year. The rest of the time they went, either secretly or publicly, to worship at a nonconformist conventicle or chapel. This was clearly making a mockery of the statute and of the authority of the English church as well; it was bitterly resented, and those who most resented it soon came to be known as the high-church party.[11] Twice an act forbidding occasional conformity was passed by the House of Commons, and twice it was rejected by the House of Lords, where low-church bishops like Gilbert Burnet (who was at least one-third Presbyterian) joined with Whigs of the dissenting persuasion to prevent its passage. Only under the Tory administration in the last years of Queen Anne did the act finally pass, and then after only seven years it was repealed.

THE WARS OF LOUIS XIV

A second focus of opposition to William was the string of expensive continental wars in which he and his Whig advisers involved England. Increasingly these wars had to be fought by professional soldiers, whose payrolls had an instant impact on English tax rolls. War had always been the ruination of English budgets and of the regimes forced to live by them. William was able to support his enormous and expensive enterprises abroad only through the establishment of the Bank of England (1694) and another, associated novelty, the funding of a

10. Most of the early openings that William had to fill were created when churchmen loyal to James II, Jacobites, refused the oath of allegiance to William. These nonjurors numbered about 400, including Sancroft, archbishop of Canterbury, and seven other bishops, as well as a number of able, high-principled men in lesser positions. Though they made up less than 4 percent of the total clergy, their dismissal represented a serious loss to the English church.

11. Low-church Anglicans minimize the episcopal authority and ritual elements which antagonize Presbyterians and other nonconformists because they are like the usages of Rome; broad-church (latitudinarian) Anglicans seek to gather as many differing opinions as possible within a formula acceptable to all. High-church Anglicans are sometimes called Anglo-Catholics. The terms "low-church" and "high-church" came into use early in the eighteenth century, "broad-church" not till the middle of the nineteenth; all three terms designate tendencies in the church which can be seen as early as the sixteenth century.

national debt. The fact that very few people could understand what these financial operations were all about softened to some extent the anguish of the war's cost. But where the cost could be identified, it was resented. William had a little habit of rewarding Dutch officers who had served him well (and sometimes only abroad) with English titles, estates, and pensions. Dislike of foreigners rose to such a pitch that Daniel Defoe, who as a dissenter supported William, felt impelled to write a rough, vigorous poem, "The True-Born Englishman" (1701), pointing out that the English people were themselves a mixed and miscellaneous breed, so that a "true-born Englishman" was inherently a ridiculous idea.

True-born or not, William was scarcely an endearing personality, and would probably have been liked even less if wars and diplomacy had not kept him abroad for a full third of his reign. These Williamite wars form part of a long series, lasting from 1667 to 1713; they have separate names and were separated by brief intervals of truce, but really constitute a single long-drawn-out conflict. The crucial figure in all of them is Louis XIV, who was king of France from 1643 till he died in 1715 after the longest reign of any monarch in European history. Louis was vain, ambitious, and impatient of ministers; he had at his disposal an immense bureaucracy and the finest armies of Europe. His lifelong series of conflicts started in 1667 with an attack on Holland aimed at regaining some territories claimed by his wife; with the help of Charles II's navy, he fairly won this engagement. A second Dutch war of 1672–1678 brought William of Orange to the forefront of Holland's defenders, and ended in something like a draw. Then in the following decade, while France was weakening herself by expelling her Protestants (this was the revocation, in 1685, of the edict of Nantes), William moved to accept the English throne, and so to transform England from a partial ally of France into a dangerous foe. When hostilities resumed almost immediately after 1688, France faced not only Holland but England and Sweden as well, the three nations united in a grand alliance known, from the city where the papers were signed, as the League of Augsburg. Power had shifted decisively, and Protestant success on the field of battle was crowned by the treaty (or, as it should have been called, the truce) of Ryswick in 1697. But just three years later the balance was again upset when Carlos II, king of Spain, died, leaving the question of his successor completely up in the air.[12] Louis claimed on behalf of his grandson Philip, a member of the house of Bourbon, as against a Hapsburg candidate, Karl, archduke of Austria. As a matter of sad fact, Philip, who became the fifth Spanish king of that name, was little better than a cretin; but in these dynastic struggles, nothing counted for less than personal abilities. The War of the Spanish Succession was fought by the grand alliance that William assembled to prevent France from acquiring, through dynastic alliance with Spain,

12. As noted above, p. 117, the Carlos who ruled Spain in the mid-sixteenth century was Carlos I of Spain, though as Holy Roman emperor he was Carlos V. Carlos II of Spain (d. 1700) showed the results of Hapsburg inbreeding over many generations; he was invalid, imbecilic, and fortunately short-lived.

overwhelming military and economic power in Europe. King William died in 1702, but under the political and diplomatic leadership of John Churchill, first duke of Marlborough, the war was fought, not to outright victory (for Philip remained, babbling, on his throne), but to the exhaustion of all the participants. A complex, far-reaching compromise of the many issues was reached at the secretly negotiated treaty of Utrecht (1713), which was probably more a victory for England than a defeat, more a defeat for Louis than a victory, and unquestionably a sellout of England's many allies.

Such, in capsule form, is an outline story of this intricate complex of hideously bloody, hideously expensive, clumsily fought wars. The result, though apparently ambiguous, was actually decisive. At their beginning, England was a third-rate power, divided domestically and insignificant abroad; at their end, she was the first power of Europe. France lost not only territory but the initiative; the causes she represented—Catholicism, so far as it was a persecuting, predatory force, and centralized autocracy—suffered international setbacks. Whether the game was worth the candle we had better not ask.

The war began small and got steadily bigger. As it developed, ever-vaster and more miscellaneous armies of Dutch, Germans, Austrians, Swedes, Italians, Catalonians, and assorted freebooters had to be assembled for annual campaigns against the French. Command responsibility was strangely and almost fatally divided among the officers of the alliance; military and diplomatic decisions of utmost complexity had to be made in light of a strategy which was never clear to more than a few people, and not acceptable to all of them. All this complex business devolved, partly before the death of William but entirely afterward, on the duke of Marlborough. He was so important a man, and so typical of his age, that a brief outline of his career is in order.

A MAN OF THE AGE: MARLBOROUGH

He was born John Churchill, son of Winston Churchill (the twentieth century statesman was a descendant of the same family), and turned early to a military career, serving both Charles II and James II in their feeble and not very creditable efforts to help the French against the Dutch. James, who was much impressed with Churchill's soldierly qualities, employed him on confidential missions and rewarded him generously with military rank and a title. Churchill, never backward, accepted whatever posts and prizes James saw fit to offer. But he was one of the first to make secret overtures to William; and when, in 1688, James sent him with 5,000 men to intercept the invading Dutch, at the last minute Lieutenant General Churchill faded into the night and deserted to the enemy camp.

Though glad to have the timely help of Marlborough, William was not eager to trust his new friend implicitly, and within a few years it was discovered that Marlborough was corresponding with King James, telling him the strategic plans of the Williamite regime he was ostensibly serving. Probably Marlborough had no large-scale treason in mind; while the 1688 settlement was new and apparently insecure, many prominent Englishmen found it desirable to keep on good terms with the pretender, just in case.[13] Even so, Marlborough could not be trusted; though given dignities and admitted to the king's councils, he did not, under William, exercise any important military command. But in 1702, just as William was preparing to enter on the War of the Spanish Succession, an apparently minor accident ended his career. While he was reviewing troops, William's horse stepped in a mole-hole, stumbled, and threw the royal rider. Complications set in, and the king died shortly, to the delight of his many enemies, who drank bumper toasts to "the little gentleman in the black velvet coat"—the mole. Since Queen Mary had died in 1694, William's successor could only be Anne, younger daughter of James II.

Queen Anne and her quiet consort, George, prince of Denmark, continued the war policies of William, and promoted Marlborough to captain general of English troops at home and abroad; he was promptly made commander in chief of the united forces of the alliance. Some of his instant favor with Anne, Marlborough owed to his own talents; some he also owed to the fact that his wife Sarah was an intimate friend and companion of the new queen. The two Churchills worked as a team, she guarding his interests at court, he building a magnificent reputation as soldier and diplomat abroad. The art of war, as practiced in the early eighteenth century, was in one of its drabber and less exciting phases. The power of artillery and cavalry, as demonstrated in the sixteenth and seventeenth centuries, had provoked a counterdevelopment in the art of defensive fortifications, of which the acknowledged master was Louis's servant, Marshal Sebastien de Vauban. Especially in the flat country of Holland and northern France, these earthwork fortifications of his were hard to attack. Months of time, thousands of men, and long wagon-trainloads of supplies were poured into protracted sieges;[14] but because these actions served to expand Dutch territory, the Dutch officers who were Marlborough's supposed subordinates tried hard to limit him to them. On the other hand, the Austrian contingent cared nothing for Dutch dirt, they wanted only to get Archduke Karl on the throne of Spain; while Marlborough, who was supremely confident of his talents as a field commander, wanted to strike at the heart of France and defeat the enemy in a war of maneuver. Divided councils made slow work. But in 1704 Marlborough got, or rather took, a splendid chance to fight his kind of war. Louis sent an army eastward to advance down the Dan-

13. Jacobite sympathizers were not always serious, but the Jacobites were; an ugly little plot to assassinate William and recall James was uncovered in 1696. Probably it could never have succeeded, but that was hard to know at the time, and the project itself, if launched full-scale, would have cost thousands of lives, whether successful or not.

14. It was in an early one of these sieges, that of Namur in 1695, that "my uncle Toby" (in Sterne's novel, *Tristram Shandy*) suffered that obscure and crucial wound in the groin which brought depair to the heart of the widow Wadman. See below, p. 334.

ube, capture Vienna, and so defeat the Hapsburg candidate on his home ground. To satisfy his cautious Dutch partners, Marlborough had to pretend to be attacking Alsace, but he slipped away on his own, marched his motley, multinational army through the Black Forest with amazing speed, cut off the French armies at Blenheim, and there in cooperation with the Austrian commander, Prince Eugene, inflicted on them a crushing defeat. It was an occasion for national rejoicing; Joseph Addison was hired to write a triumphal poem, "The Campaign," which was not quite the most pompous such poem ever written. And tangible rewards, much more to the general's liking, were soon added. Parliament bestowed on him the splendid estate of Woodstock, near Oxford, and voted to build on it, at public expense, a house for the general. They meant to be generous, but even they did not expect the duke to erect a structure as gigantic as Blenheim Palace, with its acres of rooms and miles of formal gardens. It still stands, a massive pile, the only English equivalent of Versailles.

Part of the national exuberance over Blenheim was due to war enthusiasm, part also to hopes for an early end to hostilities. But in the year following, the Dutch and their allies among the German states hindered Marlborough from forcing the war to a decision; Louis had time to regroup his armies and reinforce his defenses; the war dragged on. 1706 was a good year, because Louis's generals grew impatient and attacked Marlborough directly. He met them in the open field at Ramillies in Belgium, not far from Namur, and defeated them roundly; but once again the rest of the year was spent in mopping up and consolidating Dutch gains, while Louis was given time to recuperate. The same story was repeated at Oudenarde in 1708; but Malplaquet, in 1709, was a different matter. Technically, the allies won the battle, but at the cost of inordinate losses. When the French were fighting, not for the vanity of Louis XIV, but for their homeland, it became apparent, they would fight savagely. The point of the war, never very clear, was starting to get lost.

Meanwhile, things had not gone well for the general on the home front. His wife was displaced as Anne's intimate by a cousin, Abigail (Hill) Masham, and instead of a friendly monarch, Marlborough had to deal with a bitter enemy. Whether the new favorite deliberately fostered jealousies is unclear; but the queen and the haughty duchess of Marlborough were soon at daggers drawn. At the same time the Tories, who had never been enthusiastic for the war, came to power, partly on religious issues, partly on the strength of a growing tax revolt. They began to insinuate that Marlborough was prolonging the war for his own financial advantage. The sting in the charge was that Marlborough and his staff had made enormous fortunes from their service on the continent; Blenheim palace was but one of many magnificent country seats constructed out of profitable peculation in the war.[15] The soldiers who fought the duke's battles were, of

15. "Peculation" may be too strong a word here; generals in those days were given money to hire armies, and thought rather peculiar if they didn't make a personal profit on the deal. Public opinion was more scandalized at the amount of money Marlborough made, than at the way he made it, though charges of double-dealing with allies and even enemies were also voiced.

course, another story; as he never hesitated to say, they were the scum of the earth, and like scum he cast them aside, though the cynical betrayals involved in the treaty of Utrecht (1713) were not his responsibility. Before then, by the end of 1711, Marlborough himself had served his turn and been cast aside by the new Tory ministry. Though never actually brought to trial, as some of the Whig ministers were, he found life in England so disagreeable that he never returned to occupy his splendid palace till after the death of Anne in 1714. By then he was sixty-four years old and in ill health, so he was neither forced to account for his immense fortune, nor able to enjoy it.

TORY RULE AND THE REASONS FOR IT

The revolution of 1688 had been, in the main, the work of Whigs, and the advent of George I in 1714 ushered in a half century of unchallenged Whig supremacy, so the politics of the age of Anne, in which Tories played a predominant role, call for some explanation. For one thing, in the first parliaments of William the Whigs overreached themselves; they did not make it easy for the new king to feel grateful. They imposed on the monarchs they had created a bill of rights, declaring in thirteen trenchant articles their right to free speech, free elections, and freedom from arbitrary taxation. They also kept the new king short of money. He was voted an annual income of only £700,000 a year, about half what Charles had had;[16] and Whig parliaments would vote extra supply only for a fixed period of time, generally brief. William wanted a big army for use abroad, but the Whigs, with their prejudice against standing armies, cut the army budget while padding that of the navy, which was useful in protecting English trade. Much against the will of the king, who regarded English politics as a distraction from the serious business of defending Holland, the Whigs passed an act requiring that a new parliament be convened every three years. All these, and other lesser restrictions, sometimes expressed in a way that William found downright humiliating, turned the monarch against those whiggish supporters to whom originally he owed his throne. His dilemma was a peculiar one. As a particularly urbane and subtle Whig, the earl of Sunderland, once took occasion to remind him, "it is true that the Tories are better friends to monarchy than the Whigs are, but then your majesty is to consider that you are not their monarch." And in fact anybody who really took a high view of royal authority and kingly prerogative would have been committed to King James.

Thus the king chose his ministers among both Tories and Whigs, balancing the two parties against one another for his own advantage. But one striking reversal had taken place as a result of the 1688 revolution: before that date, the ances-

16. These sums sound large, but they were intended for much more than household expenses. Out of his annual stipend the king was supposed to maintain the diplomatic corps and the secret service, award a whole system of pensions (what is now called the "civil list"), support the royal guards, and keep up many royal buildings of a purely ceremonial character.

tors of the Whigs had been the country party, party of outsiders, while the ancestors of the Tories had been the court party, party of privileged insiders. Now things were quite reversed. Bishops were whiggish, the House of Commons dominated by Tories; the ministry, the king's close advisers, were Whigs, the opposition was Tory. Because of William's frequent absences from the country, Whigs were thought of, not just as supporting his policy, but as making it. For as long as Mary lived, she acted as co-ruler; but when she died in 1694, a group of Whig lords known as the Junto were appointed to act in the king's absence. In the country they gained some credit for his successes, but they also shared in his unpopularity; and since they often had to restrain his naturally autocratic temper, they were not much rewarded by his affection. So long as the nation remained at war, and the Whigs were able to meet the demands of a swollen military budget, they remained in power, though precariously.

But the peace of Ryswick in 1697 was the downfall of the Junto. Many Whigs were dismissed from office, others failed of election, and an attempt was made to impeach their leaders, Orford, Halifax, and Somers, before the House of Lords. Such trials were almost routine when power changed hands in those early days of the two-party system; and the charges were dropped this time. But Queen Anne heartily mistrusted and disliked Whigs. She thought they had tried to dominate William, and she was sure they had been rude to her personally in the days when her favorite, Marlborough, was suspected of treason. Also, being deeply attached to the church, she worried lest the Whigs' connection with the dissenters might put the church in danger. Still, in spite of her hostility, Whigs gradually gained positions in the administration during the early years of the queen's reign. But their support of the long, expensive war was draining their strength throughout the country; people were weary of taxation, and two unrelated incidents in 1710 and 1711 tipped the scales of power. In 1710 the Whigs tried to prosecute a clergyman named Henry Sacheverell for preaching and publishing two violent sermons declaring the church to be in danger from occasional conformists and their protectors, whiggish politicians. Though in a court of law the prosecution obtained a conviction of Sacheverell, in the court of public opinion the Tories won a smashing victory; the mob rioted in their behalf, and the voters returned them triumphantly to office. Their success at the polls was confirmed next year when a French refugee accused of treasonable acts against England stabbed and tried to kill Robert Harley, head of the Tory party. Both episodes enabled the Tories to appear before the public as patriots sustaining English institutions against conspirators at home and assassins from abroad. Thus the four last years of the queen were years of Tory dominance. Even in the House of Lords, whiggish control came to an end during the debates over the treaty of Utrecht, when the queen, to get it passed, created out of hand twelve new peers, freshly minted and ready to vote the Tory line.

We are particularly lucky in having for the first three years of the Tory ministry the personal London diary of Jonathan Swift, in the form of his *Journal to*

Stella (first published in 1766). Swift, who was personally friendly with all the Tory leaders, wrote the journal as a series of very private letters to his friend Esther Johnson in Dublin.[17] The letters are full of baby talk, private jokes, mock scoldings, and self-ridicule, as well as political gossip. No closer view of political craftsmen at work survives from that age; but the real fascination of the *Journal* lies in the glimpses it gives of Jonathan Swift himself, who was alternately and sometimes simultaneously the toughest and tenderest of men.

The Tories in office found they were rowing against a strong tide. They concluded the peace of Utrecht, but to nobody's satisfaction; England's allies felt betrayed, and all the long labors of Marlborough yielded but scant rewards. In 1711 an act was passed against occasional conformity, and three years later an act "against schism," which sought to give the established church an absolute monopoly of the education of the young. The last act particularly might have had important effects, and probably for ill rather than good; but as the Tories disappeared from the seats of power in 1714, not to reappear there for many years, their acts proved ephemeral.[18]

THE COMING OF THE HOUSE OF HANOVER

A constant preoccupation of the period 1688–1714 was the question of succession: who should come next as monarch of England? William and Mary were childless. Anne and her husband Prince George promised to have a cornucopia of offspring, but no fewer than ten of her pregnancies miscarried, four of her children died in infancy, and only William, born in 1689, promised to live and become a ruler. When he too died, in 1700, Parliament had to make a decision, and by the Act of Settlement (1701) they declared the heir to the throne to be Sophia, electress of Hanover.[19] Sophia entered the picture because she was granddaughter of James I through his daughter Elizabeth, who had married Frederick the Elector Palatine (above, p. 208). Sophia herself was the wife of Ernest Augustus, elector of Hanover; she was staunchly Protestant, and had male chil-

17. Much prurient speculation has been invested in the relation between Swift and Stella. He was a fascinating, frigid man who hated intimacy; her side of the story is untold. She was thirteen years younger than he; though they lived for some years in the same house, they were never together except in the presence of a third party. That they were married is unlikely; that they were secretly intimate, impossible.

18. One step of lasting importance Anne was able to take in behalf of the church. Ancient and onerous taxes known as first fruits and tenths had been collected from the clergy, by the pope before the Reformation, by the crown after it. In 1704 Anne assigned these moneys, known henceforth as "Queen Anne's Bounty," to a fund for augmenting the salaries of the poorer clergy. They had been a slush fund, used by Charles II for disgraceful purposes; now they contributed directly to the morale and well-being of the church. It was a mighty turnaround.

19. Hanover is a flat, sandy district in northwest Germany, between modern Holland and modern Denmark; an elector is one of the German princes, originally seven in number, who alone can' elect the Holy Roman emperor.

dren, also Protestant. Three of them died in the continental wars, but three survived, and the eldest of these became next in line for the English throne when his mother Sophia herself died just two months before Queen Anne. All these calculations were complicated enough in themselves, but they were made worse by the intrigues of the Stuarts exiled in France, by the latent loyalty of many Englishmen to the Stuart line, and by the neurotic reluctance of Anne even to contemplate a successor. One of the lesser reasons for her dislike of Whigs was that, in their eagerness to establish a Protestant succession, they were constantly suggesting visits by Hanoverian dignitaries to the English court. Anne successfully fought them off, and in consequence when George I became king of England in 1714, he had never set foot on the island, and spoke not a word of English. He had, however, served with Marlborough at Blenheim, and had come darkly to understand that Whigs were good people. Hence, for reasons almost as confused and accidental as those of Anne, but to exactly the opposite effect, he favored Whigs during his reign as blindly as she had favored Tories.

Had the cause of the exiled Stuarts depended only on James II, they would have presented no threat at all to the Hanover succession. After his defeat at the Boyne, James Stuart showed an unexpected side to his character by retiring to a life of religious seclusion. But his last-minute son James (later nicknamed the Old Pretender to distinguish him from *his* son, "Bonnie Prince Charlie," the Young Pretender), though debauched, was a man of some ambition; he kept in touch with his English friends, and they with him. Prospects of a second restoration were not in fact as hopeless as we now (with the help of historical hindsight) suppose they were. Whigs continually reproached Tories with Jacobite sympathies, and were right in their charges more often than they could prove. Not even Whigs were always free from suspicion of playing a double game. Generally, the "outs" in English politics, whatever their creed, tended to look on the Stuarts as a chance, remote but not to be neglected, for getting back "in."

How much these hedgers and intriguers were willing actually to risk on the Stuart cause would be shown in 1715, when a real effort was made to set the Old Pretender on the throne. Meanwhile, the government of Queen Anne recognized, and moved to strengthen, a major weak point in the defenses of the kingdom, Scotland. The Stuarts had been kings of Scotland long before they had been kings of England; any Stuart attack on England would be likely to start in Scotland. Thus in 1707 English and Scottish commissioners met to negotiate an Act of Union between the two countries; it provided for uniform trade and taxation laws, a single parliament, interchangeable citizenship. As usual, different judgments have been passed on the outcome; to many Scots, the English embrace seemed not far from the kiss of death. But for the Scottish negotiators, there were no real alternatives; they did not want a Catholic king, which a Stuart would certainly be, and economic self-sufficiency was out of the question. The union was never very popular in Scotland, yet the eighteenth century (whether because or in spite of it) was a period of fresh prosperity and cultural achievement in that northern land. As for the security the English wanted, they got some of it, but, as events were to prove, not very much. The Act of Union, like the outcome of the long wars against Louis, is an ungainly, important historical fact; it had all sorts of unforeseen and ambiguous consequences; nobody, looking back on it, can say categorically whether it was a good thing or a bad. But evidently, as England grew in power and complexity, new relations with her ethnic groupings were inevitable.

THE AGE OF ANNE AND ITS TASTES

Queen Anne was not a brilliant lady (had she been a commoner, the word "dull" might have been spoken), and she took little interest in art, literature, or music; she was not a patroness of the arts, and never cultivated the society of the witty or talented. For this thinness of mind she was not personally responsible; her life was wretched in its loneliness, its complex and divided responsibilities, its many personal misfortunes. Still, she was not a scintillating figure. All the more surprising is it, therefore, that her reign was notable for artistic achievement of many sorts. It was a flowering, not so much of thought as of taste, a sudden expansion of those civilized and personal arts that take a structure of thought for granted.

Luxury, polish, and urbanity were hallmarks of the new culture. These qualities were not accepted everywhere with enthusiasm; old-fashioned moralists looked with disapproval on so much worldly display, and social diagnosticians were reminded (as they periodically are) of the worst excesses of the decadent Roman Empire. They were answered by a recent arrival from Holland, Bernard de Mandeville, who had moved to England to work as a physician and to follow his hobby as a teller of disagreeable truths. *The Grumbling Hive,* also known by a later title as *The Fable of the Bees,* was first published in 1705; over the following years, Mandeville expanded, annotated, and defended it in a number of prose treatises. Basically a fable in doggerel verse, after the manner of La Fontaine, it describes a hive of most unedifying bees; they are greedy, gluttonous, ostentatious, dishonest to the core, and splendidly prosperous as a result. But they complain so much about everyone's dishonesty, that Jove at a stroke makes them all honest and virtuous. Instantly unemployment rises, trade shrinks, and prosperity dwindles, till the hive, helpless before its enemies, must retreat and live miserably in a hollow tree. Private Vices, Public Benefits; such was Mandeville's moral, expressed in a subtitle to later editions of the poem.[20] Like many so-called "immoral" books, it simply said openly what society had already done tacitly by converting a moral negative to a social positive.

20. Basil Willey, in *The Eighteenth Century Background* (VI, i) analyzes concisely and lucidly the clash of Mandeville's incompatible moral stances; the one ingredient missing from his account is Mandeville's obvious desire to make people uncomfortable.

As the social virtues (or vices) and the social values flourished, appetite for the heroic and the profound dwindled to affection for the intimate and the human. Light, conversational verse on familiar topics became the order of the day; the informal essay flourished, and little journalistic sketches began to appear, aiming simply to enliven an idle half hour in a coffee house. Amusement, which would be such a potent force in developing the novel, ceased to be a discreditable motive; the ground from which it springs, which is the condition of boredom, gained increasing recognition. New luxury led to new interest in arts other than literature. Both Harley and Somers, the Tory and Whig leaders, were collectors of books, prints, coins, and manuscripts; both were also associates of authors, not just lordly patrons, dropping a purse in response to an obsequious dedication, but close personal friends. The wealth of England's private citizens attracted to her shores artists and musicians, such as used formerly to come in search of royal patronage. George Friedrich Handel came from Germany, while painters like Sebastiano Ricci from Italy and Louis Laguerre from France joined established Dutchmen like Peter Lely and Godfrey Kneller. Working for the courts of Europe, these foreigners might have had larger commissions; for the merchant princes and landed proprietors of England they did work just as elegant though perhaps on a smaller scale. Most of the building of the age is of a human and humane dimension; it does not aim to stun or intimidate. The Wren churches which Sir Christopher built after the great fire of London were (with the obvious exception of St. Paul's) modest, even intimate, but always graceful structures. The style of furniture which is still known as "Queen Anne" brought new poise and lightness to English households; an age of heavy dark oak gave way to one of chaste and proportioned walnut. Of special interest to students of literature is the improvement in book design. The eighteenth century represents a lucid interval between the generally clumsy, plodding work done in the sixteenth and seventeenth centuries, and the absolutely miserable work done in the nineteenth century as a result of cheap paper and mechanical typesetters.[21] An eighteenth century book by Baskerville, Foulis, or their equivalents is likely to be printed on good rag paper, in large type, with fair wide margins, hand sewn, and bound in good leather. It will still be with us, mint-fresh and easy to read, when twenty generations of modern books have crumbled away from the acid in their own cheap paper.

A striking feature of the new era was the multiplication of private clubs and public coffee houses, where people could partake of "the cup that cheers but not inebriates," and also share in conversation more sustained and thoughtful than that of the old taverns. The opinions of ladies on matters of culture and general civilization began to be heard more frequently. Formal gardens, geometrically

21. As binders, nineteenth-century craftsmen often did beautiful work, and toward the end of the century art publishers like William Morris, consciously reacting against the general taste of the times, produced some fine printing. But as a rule the application to book production of high-speed mechanical processes led to utterly deplorable results.

patterned with gravel walks and boxwood hedges, provided a framework for relaxing strolls and gallant conversation between the sexes. It is a little curious that this cozy, sociable world of the well-to-do should have co-existed with the hideous degradation of the London mob and the clumsy, slow-moving imperialist wars on the Continent, but a little reflection may lead to the thought that each was the condition of the other.

THE DIMINISHED TONE

An age of social polish and formal manners is likely to be an age of prose. Whether or not this aphorism is categorically true, it was certainly true of the early eighteenth century. A change can be sensed very close to the year 1700 when Dryden died. Despite his fondness for concrete fact and polemical argument, Dryden is basically a poet of pomp and magnificence; no less than Milton (though using very different ingredients) he builds his verses into sweeping, cumulative paragraphs. After 1700 poetry seems to be written less in the old grandiose vein than in a tone of raillery or polite persiflage, such as the third earl of Shaftesbury had recommended for gentlemanly conversation. A neat and revealing exchange took place around an incident in the continental wars, when the troops of Louis XIV captured the fortress of Namur in 1692, and M. Boileau wrote a Pindaric ode on the victory in the heroic, inflated style. When William recaptured Namur from the French in 1695, Matthew Prior wrote a rollicking English ballad, answering Boileau's ode stanza for stanza:

Dix mille vaillans Alcides	Full fifteen thousand lusty fellows
Les bordant de toutes parts,	With fire and sword the fort maintain:
D'éclair au loin homicides	Each was a Hercules, you tell us,
Font pétiller leurs remparts:	Yet out they marched like common men.
Et dans son sein infidèle	Cannons above and mines below
Partout la terre y recèle	Did death and tombs for foes contrive:
Un feu prêt à s'élancer	Yet matters have been ordered so
Qui soudain perçant son gouffre	That most of us are still alive.
Ouvre un sepulchre de soufre	
A quiconque ose avancer.[22]	

The playfulness of the early eighteenth century is a constant. Its aim, as with Prior's handling of Boileau, is generally to deflate the pompous and overstuffed; a frequent method is to get readers to take the surface meaning seriously, and after they have swallowed, to explode it. Daniel Defoe's pamphlet, *The Shortest*

22. More or less literally translated, Boileau's stanza would read: Ten thousand valiant Hercules, / Assailing them from every side, / With fire scattering death afar, / Explode their ramparts in the air; / While in its treacherous entrails / The gloomy earth hides everywhere / A fire ready to leap forth, / Which, flashing from its cavern mouth, / Opens a sulphurous tomb for all / Who dare to let a footstep fall.

Way with the Dissenters (1702) recommended killing off the dissenters whole-sale; a lot of Tories, who wouldn't have minded doing just that, took the pamphlet seriously, and were enraged when they found that it was ironically intended, that in fact Defoe (a dissenter himself) had meant to parody their position. Simple readers were also taken in by the solemn manner and rational calculations of Swift's "Modest Proposal," and denounced the idea of killing and eating children as if the author had been serious. *Gulliver's Travels* (to look ahead a few years) has by now been bowdlerized into a children's classic; but, read with a full understanding of what it is saying, it is a cruel and cutting book indeed, strong medicine for most adults. Under the apparent simplicity and triviality of much early eighteenth-century writing there lies a vein of what the age called "drollery," and we distinguish into the several modes and tones of irony, genial or ferocious. The surface of such writing plays, subtly or broadly, against its substance.[23]

SWIFT AND HIS CIRCLE

Jonathan Swift was certainly the most powerful writer of the age of Queen Anne, though as he was born (1667) under Charles II and died (1745) in the era of George II, there is no reason to assign him narrowly to a single reign. Still, it was under Anne that he published (1704) his greatest, if not his best-known book, *A Tale of a Tub;* and during the reign of Anne he enjoyed most favor in government circles as the intimate ally of the Tory ministry of 1710–1714. About Swift the first thing to appreciate is that he was a passionate partisan, not only of the church of England at a moment when that organization seemed to be in deadly danger, but also of an organization we have scarcely mentioned, the Protestant Episcopal church of Ireland. When William won the battle of the Boyne, the Protestant church of Ireland was restored to its old position as the established church, the church to which tithes must be paid, in an overwhelmingly Catholic land. For Catholics the situation was bitter: they had to support a parson whose church they never attended and whose teachings they thought dangerous if not deadly to their salvation. (Many of them voluntarily taxed themselves a second time to pay a Catholic priest, whose function before the law was illegal, but for their consciences necessary.) Yet for the Protestant clergyman of any sensitivity, the situation was equally bad. To live, he had to accept tithes that he knew were being wrung from his unwilling neighbors; among them, he had little chance of

---

23. Mock-heroic and anti-epic are frequent in the early part of the century. Pope's *Rape of the Lock* (1714) and the Lilliput section of *Gulliver's Travels* (1726) are the best-known examples. We may add Garth's *Dispensary* (1698), John Philips's *The Splendid Shilling* (1701), and Fielding's *Tom Thumb* (1730). In the same way John Gay, deliberately lowering and vulgarizing the pastoral tone, produced, in *The Shepherd's Week* (1714) and *The Beggar's Opera* (1728), work more authentically poetic than most of the highfalutin "serious" pastorals of his age.

being respected and none of being liked; his ministry was doomed to fall on deaf ears or none at all. There is an old story that Swift, serving in the tiny parish of Laracor, used to read weekly prayers to an audience consisting of two persons, himself and the parish clerk: "Dearly beloved Roger, the spirit hath moved you and me in sundry places. . . ."

An outcast in Ireland and the partisan of a defensive and humiliated church in England, Swift always had in his spiritual complexion something of the garrison mentality, a grim sense of fighting to the last ditch. His *Argument against Abolishing Christianity in England* (1708) starts from the assumption that everybody wants to abolish Christianity and that real Christianity has in fact been abolished already. The only question remaining is whether a little nominal Christianity should be retained, for form's sake only, not because it will do any positive good but because it can't do much harm. As often in Swift's writing, his real opinion here is the one that everybody agrees is out of the question.

The true greatness of Swift as a prose stylist lies in the taut, nervous energy of his sentences; he was a man whose every word was alive with the instincts of attack and defense. Very often the severe conformist values for which he "stood" are deeply concealed behind the complacent masks of his bland and superficial narrators, but they give edge and bite to his writing. More explicit in their point of view were his Tory pamphlets on *The Conduct of the Allies* (1711) and *The Public Spirit of the Whigs* (1714); along with his writing of the Tory newssheet *The Examiner*, these polemics were of great service to the ministry. Swift was not unique as a political publicist, but he was unusually able, and though he refused money, he certainly expected some reward for his services. In this hope he was largely disappointed. Many men less able and less useful became bishops; but Swift was one of those too deeply devoted to the church to be given high office within her. His powerful London friends even had trouble getting him the deanery of St. Patrick's in Dublin, where he finished his days, increasingly lonely and embittered, not just at the dead-ending of his career, but at the loss of those few friends who were his chief refuge against an alien world. At the very beginning of his literary life, Swift took a stand (in *A Tale of a Tub*) against the "modern" spirit of progress, which he saw as fatuous and inane. From that position he never receded, and while his despair at the path mankind was taking grew ever deeper, his resources against that despair (games, trifling, intimacy) grew ever more hollow. Swift was not really a black humorist in our modern sense; most of his jokes were *against* despair, not expressions *of* despair. That they were sometimes personally cruel as well is not to be denied, but that was a quality of the age. Civilized as they were on the inside, the little closed circles of the age of Anne did not waste much sympathy on outsiders; Swift's mockery was sometimes like that of Voltaire, who said that if he had not been a writer, he would have murdered.

Swift's intimates in the literary clubs and societies of Dublin and London— Gay, Pope, Thomas Sheridan (grandfather of the dramatist), and Doctor John

Arbuthnot the literary physician—shared Swift's love of play but not his misanthropy. Among them, Alexander Pope was the nearest thing to Swift's intellectual equal, and his *Rape of the Lock* still preserves, as in cameo, the image of that festive, intimate, aristocratic society which, for a happy few, represented the age of Anne at its best. The ceremony of the coffee table, the reduction of war to a game of cards, of hell to a headache, and of religion to a pretty girl adoring herself in a mirror, all bespeak a miniaturized society. And yet, just as with *Gulliver's Travels* or *The Beggar's Opera*, a vein of grave irony runs through the poem, which is constantly reminding us how eggshell-thin, how terribly precarious, are the conventions on which civilized life rests. The writers of the age of Anne, perhaps because they were adjusting to the new fact of a pluralist community, were all fascinated with tricks of perspective, games involving various points of view. Big is seen in little, high in low, the remote in the here and now. Language moves us so subtly from one point of view to another, masks are so deftly manipulated, that we often understand only in retrospect how many and what disquieting questions have been left open behind that assured surface.

THE NEW COMPROMISERS

Joseph Addison and Richard Steele stood somewhat outside the Swift-Pope orbit, being Whigs rather than Tories, and assuming a rather different task than their high-flying brethren. This was nothing less than the creation of a new literature for an audience containing a major new component. Since the Restoration, a potential reading public of domesticated dissenters had grown up, ambitious of polite learning and social polish, but still retaining from their dissenting background an interest in serious morality and prudent, practical sense. Restoration drama, with its sexual innuendos and heartless hedonism, appalled them; Dryden's skepticism was as alien to them as his Catholicism; Milton was better, but he was very hard reading. About 1700 a "City poet," that is, a man of the commercial classes, ventured to publish a curious "Satire against Wit." Sir Richard Blackmore (he had been knighted by King William) was a physician by trade and an epic poet by hobby. In the intervals of his practice he had written a pair of pseudo-Miltonic poems on Arthurian themes, both strong contenders for the title of worst epic poem ever written, but popular with bourgeois readers who relished their sanctified morality and didn't mind their wooden versification. Thus emboldened, Sir Richard spoke out in his "Satire against Wit" for a general revolution in taste. As a principle of writing, he declared, wit was dangerous, immoral, and useless; in future literary work, it should be replaced by the principle of good sense.[24] And of that, he implied, examples might be found in his own works.

24. "Good sense" was or tended to become a very prosaic principle, and in eighteenth-century poetry it all too often prevailed. The age produced a great number of versified didactic treatises,

Needless to say, poor Sir Richard was overwhelmed with ridicule. He was said to dislike wit because he himself had not a spark of it, as indeed he didn't. His epics were said to bump and rumble because he wrote in his coach, trundling across London cobblestones on his medical rounds; he was called a quack in medicine and a botcher in verse. Every fine, careless gentleman in town, and some poets who were neither fine nor gentlemen, but who liked to ape modish manners, joined in; Sir Richard was pelted with epigrams till he was happy to go back to his practice and leave literary theory alone.

Yet for all this, Blackmore had called attention to a real deficiency in the writing of his day, and it was this lack that Addison and Steele moved to fill, quietly and undefiantly, a few years later. In 1707 Steele was appointed to edit the official gazette, a biweekly calendar containing mostly government news releases and formal notices. The job was innocuous, but Steele, a lively young Irishman, saw a way to make something more of it, and in 1709 started his own three-times-a-week paper, *The Tatler*. As its name implied, it included a gossip column, political news, and also an occasional column dealing with manners and morals. These last were what made the paper a hit. The moral lectures, which to our sophisticated ears sound commonplace, struck just the right note for the time. Steele was not writing down to his readers; he had strong moral convictions, and his way of expressing them, in good-mannered, earnest prose, neither dogmatic nor frivolous, sounded a chord that was widely appreciated. Before long he called on his old schoolfellow Addison for help, and between them they kept the *Tatler* going for nearly two years. It was followed almost at once by the *Spectator,* of which Addison was the principal author; and then the two friends combined to bring out (briefly) the *Guardian.* The general aim of all these journals, to instruct while entertaining, left the authors free to follow a wide range of paths. They might write a little story illustrating some foible of human nature or a descriptive sketch leading to a meditation; sometimes a straightforward character description, an essay in praise of married love, a piece on good taste in dress, or how to behave on Sunday, or how to read *Paradise Lost.* The tone was generally good-humored, conversational; the moral problems posed were not so hard as to be disagreeable, the wit was more often genial than biting. Addison and Steele wrote quite consciously for women as well as men; in those days, that meant their moral tone had to be softer and their style more appealing than that of hard-mouthed Swift. As it turned out, they did more to shape the taste of the future than did the greater, but narrower, man.

One clear sign of a shift in taste, perhaps in something deeper than taste, was

----

mechanistic in their philosophy as well as their versification. Blackmore's *Creation* (1712) and Moses Browne's *Essay on the Universe* (1735) may exemplify the high philosophic road; humbler accounts of useful activities are John Dyer's survey of the wool trade (*The Fleece, 1757*), poems on practical health precautions, poems on social dancing, and poems on field sports. In the same general vein, Erasmus Darwin, grandfather of Charles, wrote a verse treatise on vegetable reproduction, *The Loves of the Plants* (1789). To say it is better as biology than as poetry is not to say much.

to be seen on the stage, where the tough, worldly comedy of the Restoration was subject to direct challenge as early as 1698. Jeremy Collier, a nonjuring clergyman with a fine command of vulgar idiom, published in that year the first of several attacks on the immorality and profaneness of the English stage. Hardened sinners like Dryden were not stirred to instant contrition, but younger men, not so committed to the old style, began to modify the moral tone and emotional content of their comedies. George Farquhar was a bright and prolific young Irishman who never lived to celebrate his thirtieth birthday; but his last play, *The Beaux' Strategem* (1707), is commonly seen as inaugurating a new age of comedy. The raw materials are familiar, the combination is new. We are given a couple of disguised and penniless rakes seeking rich fortunes, and a pair of available girls, one nubile heiress, another young person married to an uncongenial brute. The usual deceptions and pairings-off occur; but before the heiress yields to her young rascal, he has a change of heart, admits his true identity, is enriched by the opportune death of a wealthy relative, and so marries his lady "honestly" and to the financial advantage of both. Meanwhile, the other lady is rescued by a handy brother from her sullen husband, given a generous dowry, and freed to marry the other adventurer, to everyone's delight. The new comedy, we note, preserves the matrimonial amenities: nobody beds down without a license. It also, and at a crucial point, makes the action rely on a character's sudden conversion to goodness and sincerity. Hearts of gold abound in what came to be called sentimental comedy. Of course, where most of the characters in a play are simple, sincere, and loving, the obstacles to their coming together and creating a happy ending in Act I, scene 1, must be very artificial. So they are in the typical sentimental comedy; and so, perforce, is the resolution of these difficulties. Oliver Goldsmith said, with great sharpness, that the popularity of sentimental comedy was firmly rooted in the fact that it was so easy to write. It was equally easy to watch. The new easy play appealed to the same middle-class audience that enjoyed Addison and Steele's new easy journalism. But a larger consideration is that during the early eighteenth century a major Christian doctrine dissolved and disappeared from men's consciousness: this was the dogma of original sin.

THE NEW GOODNESS OF MAN

Original sin, which underlay practically all the religious controversies of the seventeenth century, declares that man is radically defective at birth; his understanding is darkened, his will weakened, he has a strong inclination to evil (so run the words of the catechism). To gain salvation he needs supernatural faith based on special revelation, and the guidance either of the Scriptures or of a Christian church. Increasingly during the seventeeth century, Englishmen heard of a group called "Socinians," followers of the sixteenth century Polish-Italian theologians Faustus and Laelius Socinus, who held that the truths necessary to salvation were few, simple, and plain to the meanest understanding. A common formula (stemming from the quasi-Pauline Epistle to the Hebrews 11:6) was that one need believe no more than "that God is, and that He is a rewarder of them that seek Him." Later in the century, very similar beliefs began to be popular under the name of "deism." The deists phrased this minimal belief in a different way; they affirmed the sufficiency of "natural" religion, meaning that religious belief to which one could reach by unaided human reason. They denied, in other words, the need for special revelation.[25] The first founder of deism (though he never used the word) is generally reputed to have been Edward Herbert of Cherbury, brother of George Herbert the poet. But Herbert in his time was an isolated figure; the deist tendency gained strength only in the last years of the seventeenth and early years of the eighteenth century. Different individual deists always differed as to what truths the law of nature implanted in men's bosoms, and consequently as to what beliefs God required of men for their salvation. But the general tendency was to make them few and easy. On these terms it sometimes required more learning and ingenuity to be damned than to be saved; by definition, salvation came naturally to almost everybody.[26]

A belief in the inherent goodness of man is known to theologians as neo-Pelagianism, the revival of a doctrine first broached in the fifth century by the Welsh or Irish monk Pelagius. Pelagius himself was far removed from the position assumed by the eighteenth century deists; he held that man, by strenuous but unaided efforts, could attain moral perfection. The eighteenth century deists held that without much effort man was already instinctively and naturally good. A powerful influence in establishing this view, though he was not an avowed deist himself, was the third earl of Shaftesbury, the philosopher and esthete. (Grandson of the first earl of Shaftesbury, whom Dryden had caricatured as Achitophel, the third earl was an urbane and unpolitical invalid, who died in 1713 at

25. The titles of two influential deist books clearly display their contents. *Christianity Not Mysterious* by John Toland (1696) and *Christianity as Old as the Creation* by Matthew Tindal (1730) argue that all the essentials of Christianity are available to common sense; there is, therefore, no need of a special revelation attested by miracles, gospels, or a church (SFR, F.5).

26. An important side effect of the new belief in man's goodness was the new urgency of an old question concerning the origin of evil. For if man had not fallen through the tempting of the devil, if God was all-good, all-powerful, and all-knowing, why was the world in such a hideous mess? Pope confronted the problem in the *Essay on Man* (1733), Archbishop William King in a formal Latin treatise (*De Origine Mali*, 1702), and Doctor Pangloss (a caricature of the German philosopher Leibniz and his followers) in Voltaire's *Candide* (1759). Generally, the philosophical optimists noted above answered that the world *was* good, as good as it could be. (In capsule form, "This is the best of all possible worlds," and everything in it is a necessary evil.") By emphasizing the *impossibility* of things being better—because omitting plague germs, for example, would create a hideous gap in the world's perfect plenitude—they converted a creed of ostensible optimism into one of total despair. Nothing can be improved because things are already perfect. The human answer to this is obvious, and in time the logical answers became obvious too; but during the early eighteenth century, the problem continued to rankle.

the age of forty-two.) He ascribed great importance to our inherent, disinterested moral sense, common to all men, and accessible to all through a simple act of ingenuous, fair-minded reflection. The sentimental comedies breathe this atmosphere. The good characters are naturally and effortlessly good, by the mere prompting of their instincts; if the bad will look to their instincts, they will find that they are good too.

Finally, the importance of this new attitude to the development of the novel is clear. When the all-consuming struggle to avoid damnation and achieve salvation fades from men's awareness, the novel is freed to concentrate on those nuances of social behavior, those touches of natural good manners and flowerings of feeling which are its pecular province. More: the mobility of its point of view allows the novel to generate sympathy for the sinner in the very act of sin, to see, sometimes, the best of motives inside what from the outside look like the worst of deeds. Two groups of outcasts provided material for the newly developing novel: criminals and women. Only grudgingly had the classical forms of epic poem and heroic tragedy made room for the consciousness of such people; novels often placed them at the center. Novelists would hardly have ventured to do so without a sense of the innate value of human life. The greatest of the early English novels is hardly less than a parable of the human soul, virtuous by nature (its own nature and the Nature from which that springs) and untarnished by trials, achieving finally a sort of secular grace. It would be much too pretentious to call the author of *Tom Jones* a neo-Pelagian. But the whole tendency of Fielding's novel is to celebrate the natural goodness of Tom, a new Adam or Everyman even in drunkenness, lechery, and sexual servitude—until, by sheer natural goodness, he is brought into possession of Miss Sophia Western, who can be seen (if one has to be theological about it) as an embodiment of heavenly wisdom. Fielding never names his characters at random, and "Sophia" is Greek for "wisdom."

This, then, or something like it, was a comforting creed widely held in the early eighteenth century. It was more a mood than a creed; a tacit conviction that after the storm and fury of the seventeenth century, the cosmic machinery had been adequately adjusted, and no extra efforts were now called for on anyone's part. A bishop of the English church, Tillotson, in a deservedly famous sermon, assured his flock that God's commandments are not grievous, that every man who prepares his spiritual accounts in a prudent and practical way may count on finding a place in heaven. The world "place" in those days had the delicious implication of a sinecure, an official position with a handsome income and no work. The whole concept chimed beautifully with Newton's vision of an ordered universe moving with majestic precision under universal laws, as valid in the highest heavens as here at Woolsthorpe, down paths unshakably established at its first creation. God was a watchmaker; the metaphor was not Newton's, but was

27. Miracles, as exceptional divine interventions in the daily routine of the world's regular operation, greatly distressed the thinkers of the eighteenth century. There had been one great miracle at

implicit in his work. With miraculous skill, He had set the machine going;[27] we need but study it to recognize the divine wisdom of the Maker, and merely play our assigned roles in it, to keep His work operating and to earn for ourselves the reward of good and faithful servants.

One slight omission might have been, and in fact was, noted in the image of the world as ordered machine. There was really no room in it for mind or spirit. George Berkeley, bishop of Cloyne in the Protestant church of Ireland, moved to remedy the omission by striking at the root of the problem—that is, at materialism itself. For him the material world was simply a series of signs devised by a divine universal intelligence. Matter is in effect the language that God speaks, and which we can understand only so far as we recognize His intelligence moving behind it. Nothing can in fact *be* except as some intelligence, human or divine, perceives it. Vision is a form of creation. Berkeley thus stood materialism on its head.

Though he was the most genial and lucid of writers, common sense in the eighteenth century and since has made heavy weather of Berkeley's doctrine. Dr. Johnson imagined that by kicking a rock vigorously he had demonstrated the reality of matter, and so refuted the bishop; in fact, he hadn't even come close to Berkeley's argument. Like the doctor, most of Berkeley's opponents (he had no disciples) failed to make contact with his thought. But his emphasis on the active, creative power of vision was a striking exception in an age of materialism, when an image of the mind as passive, a mere blank sheet of paper to be written on by external experience, tended to prevail. His thought still rouses vivid reverberations in the imagination of our day, notably in Yeats and Joyce.

the Creation, they felt, and that was enough. Hume summarized the skeptical view in his "Essay on Miracles" (part of the *Enquiry Concerning Human Understanding*, 1748), when he concluded that "the Christian religion not only was at first attended with miracles, but even at this day cannot be believed by any reasonable person without one." That was turning the tables on the faithful, with a vengeance.

The "watchmaker argument," more respectably known as the argument from design, goes back at least to Cicero, *De natura deorum*, ii, 34. The application of the watch simile is said to have begun with John Ray and Robert Boyle (late seventeenth century), its general popularity with William Paley whose two volumes of *Evidences* (1794) and *Natural Theology* (1802) summarized lucidly the conventional theology of his day.

11

The Early Eighteenth Century: The Rising Novel (1714–1748)

Transitions of power in a monarchy are supposed to be automatic, but transitions from one royal family or dynasty to another are likely to be uneasy, especially when an active pretender lurks in the wings. George, the first English monarch of that name and the first of the house of Hanover, was neither strong nor popular when he was called to the throne in 1714, he being an unknown quantity in England and England being a nation utterly unfamiliar to him. If the pretender, James Francis Edward Stuart, son of James II, had been a wiser or luckier man, he might at this awkward juncture have asserted his claim with some chance of success. But at the crucial moment, he alienated many possible supporters, especially in Scotland, a largely Presbyterian nation, by defiantly proclaiming his Catholic faith. (He was Catholic, everybody knew it, but the time was wrong to insist on the fact.) His supporters in England and France had plotted an invasion, but were so careless about security that their plans were known to the government in London even before they had been concerted in Paris. Worst of all, Louis XIV, exhausted by a lifetime of immoderate business and immoderate pleasure, chose to die (1 September 1715) on the very eve of the projected Jacobite invasion, leaving as heir to the throne his great-grandson, a sickly five year old. The pretender's hope had always lain in military supply from France and solid support in Scotland. Both were now out of the question, yet something might have been accomplished had the pretender himself been a man of dash and decision. He was not. Queen Anne died on 1 August 1714, and George arrived, unchallenged, from Germany, in mid-September. Just about a year afterward the Highlands rose and an army was formed; but James Francis Edward did not arrive till mid-December, when his following was already starting to dwindle. He was a full sixteen months late to his rendezvous with destiny, and that lady does not like to be kept waiting. One small battle was fought at Preston in Lancashire and another in Perth; neither yielded the decisive victory the Jacobites required, and before the new year was a month old, the pretender was hurrying back to France. The Jacobite "coup" of 1715 was a total fiasco, its only real result being to confirm George I in his basic antipathy to Tories. From the day of his accession, the Whig supremacy lasted nearly half a century.

WHIGS AND THE PATHS OF PRUDENCE

As was only natural when the Tory party had backed itself into a corner, political conflicts tended henceforth to take place between shifting factions and rival leaders of the Whigs. Such conflicts were not negligible, but they were far smaller than the storms stirred up by James II and the foreign wars waged by Marlborough for William and Anne. At the end of the century, England would once more plunge into turmoil, with the American and French revolutions coming in quick succession on top of England's industrial transformation. But through the entire middle part of the century storms were few, and the ship of state, tacking a bit to take advantage of this breeze or that, enjoyed calm seas and prosperous voyage. Many of the lessons of the past had been learned, and their import was invariably moderation, caution, compromise. Since 1600 Britain's highly profitable oriental trade had been monopolized by the East India Company. Just after 1688, the Company went through a curious mini-revolution of its own, which (just like the greater revolution in the homeland) admitted a new group, the so-called "interlopers," to the seats of power. Then, just as at home, both groups settled down to the serious business of making money hand over fist. In spiritual as in secular life, peace prevailed. The government had learned not to persecute religious opinion; as if by common consent, Catholics and dissenters maintained what we now call a low profile. Fierce laws were still on the books against both groups, but they were rarely or never enforced. Within the church of England, the highest-flying churchmen had eliminated themselves by refusing to swear loyalty to William or by getting involved in Jacobite conspiracies; those who remained were comforted by the fact that, with rising agricultural prices, their tithes were worth more and more. Gradually a place in the church, which involved a decent position in society, very moderate duties, and no particular spiritual capacity, became an accepted destination for the younger son of a great house. And a deep quiet, not always distinguishable from torpor, settled over the religious life of the land.

Another major lesson had been learned from Marlborough's French wars; since it was apparent that wars invariably raised taxes, a policy of no wars at all was clearly the best. But if wars were necessary, then they should be fought to gain advantages in trade and commerce. Abroad, replacement of restive, ambitious Louis XIV by the boy who became slothful, lascivious Louis XV was, in British eyes, all to the good. Difficulties were bound to arise from the double sovereignty of the new English monarchs, like that of the early Norman kings. George I of England had not ceased to be elector of Hanover, and the survival of his little fief in the turmoil of European politics was a constant source of anxiety to him—more so, it often seemed, than the welfare of his English subjects. But his Whig ministers were careful from the first to limit English participation in foreign wars, thereby effectually capturing for themselves one of the strongest Tory arguments against Whig foreign policy. At the same time the English navy remained ready to support semi-official trading companies, and serve as a big chip in the territorial poker game that was constantly going on in Europe.

Finally, the Whig ministries of the eighteenth century had learned a major lesson about the uses of political patronage. It had long been customary for supporters of the king's policy to be rewarded with a well-paying place in the king's household. And there had never been a time when financial or territorial bigwigs did not have it in their power to name a relative or close personal friend to a sure seat in the House of Commons. Blocs of votes known as "interests" were thus built up in the names of various family groups. The modern principle of "one man one vote" was not so much as thought of in those days, nor was balloting secret. Only property holders voted, and electoral districts were defined by ancient, obsolete custom, so that districts with only a half-dozen voters ("rotten boroughs" as they came to be called) might return two members of parliament, while new towns with populations in the thousands returned none. Technically, London was entitled to only four members of parliament, but forty Londoners sat there, thirty-six of them nominally representing other districts but voting London interests on every issue. (To this day a man may represent a district without residing in it; but the scale of things has changed.) What we call "bribery," and the eighteenth century called "jobbing," was routine. Some votes could be bought for an office, others for a piece of land, the cheapest for a keg of ale and a drunken brawl on election eve. Thus it was not hard for a government of rich men, holding power over many years, to pick up a long list of supporters on whom it could depend because they owed their political existence to the government.

Parliament was only the center of a wide circle of influence or corruption—one could call it either. Positions in the administration and the civil service had to be filled, more than ever before, because a rich and powerful nation needed a numerous bureaucracy. Posts in government were handed out in return for political services rendered or to be rendered. (In our age of golden virtue, such practices are of course unknown, but in the eighteenth century they were quite common.) Offices of command in the army or navy were freely bought and sold, or granted to the kinfolk of influential politicians for values to be received. The quality of the service did not suffer as much as might have been expected; good as well as bad officers gained their commissions through the patronage system. But the system itself was corrupt, and it was deep-rooted. Judges, commissioners, surveyors, and assessors held their posts as a result of political favor, and were expected (so far as in them lay) to repay favor with favor. By replacing a single justice of the peace, the government could create for itself dozens of subordinate and docile officeholders. By naming his cousin to be parson of the parish church, Squire Snort could be sure of having sound doctrine preached every Sunday, with special warnings, as needed, for those who murmured against rent increases. The web of interest-groups spread in fine, almost invisible, threads along the complex patterns of English family groupings. Because daughters and younger sons were constantly splitting off (or being cut away) from the main trunk of the family tree, yet maintaining a sort of connection with it, they could be woven into wide, elastic webs of influence hardly a trace of which would appear on the public record. Alexander Pope, in a moral epistle to Lord Bathurst, once amused himself by imagining what would happen if statesmen, instead of being bribed with a tiny paper check or intangible understanding, had to take their bribes in real material goods:

> Oh! that such bulky bribes as all might see,
> Still, as of old, encumbered villainy! . . .
> A statesman's slumbers how this speech would spoil:
> "Sir, Spain has sent a thousand jars of oil;
> Huge bales of British cloth blockade the door;
> A hundred oxen at your levee roar."

But Pope, like a poet, exaggerated. Statesmen have to be bribed only when their interest conflicts with their principles; when the only principle they have is to follow their interest, a bare hint suffices.[1]

PROGRESS AND POVERTY

The first half of the eighteenth century was a period of steady but not explosive expansion. Like all pre-industrial societies, the country experienced only moderate growth in its economy, and like most societies without antiseptic techniques, its population was limited by a murderous rate of infant mortality. In London, the figures are estimated at between 40 and 60 percent; if they were

---

1. For a detailed demonstration that where influence is pervasive and open, bribery and secret venality are superfluous, consult Sir Lewis Namier, *The Structure of Politics at the Accession of George III* (SFR, F. 13). What underlay this absolute moral confidence in the virtue of corruption was a profound faith in reason and the reasonable class, identified by a process as frequent as it is comfortable and fallacious.

better in the country, it can only have been because there were fewer doctors there. The population of England and Wales was estimated at about 6 million souls in 1715, and apparently stayed fairly level during the first part of the century. But people were moving gradually from the south and east of England to the midland and northern counties. Hitherto, factories in which large numbers of people worked under one roof had been unusual in England; most labor was performed in private houses. Raw wool might, for example, be delivered by horseback to a worker's cottage, to be spun into thread or woven into cloth by a man and his family; their work would be picked up and paid for when the next instalment of new wool was delivered. Such cottage industries died out only slowly; but gradually the workmen were drawn to the northern counties where, with abundant water power to run many machines, several different processes could be performed under one roof. At first mills and their attendant towns located near waterfalls or where dams were easy to build.[2] Later, as steam engines were developed and applied to new uses (other than their first one of draining mines), and as coal became crucial, the towns spread across the countryside, and the people in them multiplied to create that population explosion which accompanied the industrial expansion of the later century. Meanwhile, England's industrial power grew in squalid little communities along riverbanks or around seaports— stinking, disease-ridden collections of hovels, inhabited by a despairing race of overburdened, illiterate laborers, men, women, and children harnessed to the machines for every waking hour, six days a week, fifty-two weeks a year, except for vacations on Good Friday and Christmas. We must mention these people here, because the literature of the age takes no account of them, and art knows not of their existence, unless in the more brutal engravings of Hogarth (active 1720–1764).

Things were little better for the poor man in the country. Improvements in farming techniques, of which the early eighteenth century saw many, worked against small freeholders and tenant farmers, because increased average yields caused landlords to demand higher rents, while only those with large quantities of capital could take advantage of the new methods. Waste and common lands of villages continued to be enclosed and consolidated into estates. During Tudor times, enclosures had generally aimed to replace plowmen with shepherds; that is the complaint in Sir Thomas More's *Utopia*. Not so now; crops made farmers prosper, and new systems of crop rotation joined with inventions like the seed drill, better cattle-breeding procedures, and new methods of transportation like canals, to make landlords prosperous and yeomen obsolete.[3] Oliver Goldsmith's

2. Early reliance on water power kept the working classes rural and scattered, hence hard to organize in unions or revolutionary parties. The same circumstance brought newly rich industrialists into close proximity, and often sharp hostility, with landed gentry.

3. The old agriculture had in many districts scarcely changed since medieval days: see above, p. 81. Lightening heavy soils by installing drainage lines and adding limestone in various forms made it possible to farm where men had never farmed before; but they were expensive improvements, and not widely applied.

nostalgic poem "The Deserted Village" (1770) has been complained of as describing an Irish, not an English village, and (with more justice) as sentimentalizing the old peasant life. But it shows feelingly the results of enclosures and depopulation—by-products both of a new agrobusiness which was driving subsistence farming from the land.

Above all, the agricultural interest profited by a set of Corn Laws passed by the first parliaments of William and Mary. "Corn" is the British name for cereal of any sort; what we call "corn" they call "maize"; and there had been corn laws in England for a long time. Those of the eighteenth century had two functions, both simple, both designed to favor the landowner. When the price of domestic grain was low, the government paid a bounty on exports, and so raised it; when the domestic price was high, imports from abroad were forbidden, to keep it high. The victim of these laws was the consumer, especially the laborer in one of the new industrial towns, who had no time, space, or skill to raise even a little garden of his own. When he went to market, he got less benefit from low prices and less relief from high prices, because of the Corn Laws. But, as we have emphasized, the law in this period took little account of the unpropertied man. In the countryside, the landowning class sponsored ferocious measures against poaching. For snaring a rabbit or spearing a salmon on a rich man's game preserve, many a hungry, ragged boy was sent to a living death in the colonies.[4] Others fell under the guns of game wardens who shot to kill, or fell victim to man-traps which could take a man's leg off at the knee. Snare lines were totally indiscriminate; a child walking in the woods and stepping on a wire could trigger a gun which killed anyone and anything along the line. Still other children could be sent to the workhouse for no crime but poverty, chained up to prevent escape, and forced to labor from sunup to sundown, not for a wage, but for a minimum diet, just enough scraps to keep them from starvation. But toward the upper levels of society, the law was very respectful. A tailor asking to be paid by a gentleman for whom he had made a suit declared rashly that he was as good a man as his customer; a court fined him a sum equal to the cost of the suit. Impertinence from the lower orders was not well thought of in the eighteenth century.

THE RISE OF ROBERT WALPOLE

After quelling the Jacobite rising in 1715, the government of George I got down to work. Its whiggish members clustered around two pairs of leaders, one the earl of Sunderland and General James Stanhope, the other Sir Robert Walpole

4. Because of their high mortality rate, Jamaica and the Barbados were good places to send convicts or social misfits; when Samuel Pepys's servant boy Waynman made too much trouble for his master, he went to the Barbados. Any time after 1619, convicts could be dumped on America (Virginia, where Moll Flanders went, or else Georgia); after 1776, it was the turn of Australia,

and his brother-in-law Charles Viscount Townshend. The four ministers operated in somewhat uneasy tandem. They agreed on partisan measures, such as nullifying recent Tory legislation and driving all Tories from office. Having found that calling new parliaments every three years kept the country in an uproar and made it expensive to hold a seat that had to be defended so often, they lengthened to seven years the term for which a parliament might sit. Stanhope, who knew his way through the tangled underbrush of European politics, negotiated a set of brilliant arrangements which, while they often brought England to the brink of war, allowed most of the actual fighting to be done by her allies, for whom she supplied financing. Meanwhile Walpole, responding to national concern over the huge debts left from Marlborough's wars, established a sinking fund to pay them off.[5] In the event, this national debt never did get paid off (they rarely do, and perhaps should not), but the existence of a plan to pay it off had a positive effect on public confidence.

On the other hand, a series of small, corrosive rifts between the Sunderland-Stanhope and the Walpole-Townshend groups widened toward a rupture. Walpole was for a more peaceful and conservative foreign policy; he also saw dangers in some of the more extreme domestic measures of the government. But above all, he wanted to be chief Whig leader himself. Accordingly, he and Townshend resigned and began to intrigue against the weakened government that remained in power. In this campaign, they made skillful and unscrupulous use of the prince of Wales, who was a natural rallying point for the opposition. Heir-apparent to the throne is always a delicate office, and the young German who was to become George II had much too stiff and limited a mind to appreciate its nuances. He was already on very bad terms with his father, as his son would later be with him; and Walpole skillfully exploited their differences, fostering the prince's pretensions, then casting him off abruptly while himself grasping at a strategic position in the much-weakened Stanhope government. The prince was furious, but Walpole had what he wanted. The government in which he was now serving had only to stumble a little, and he would be in a position to take over. The stumble turned out to be a terrific pratfall. The great South Sea bubble blew up and exploded in 1720; Walpole as the recognized financial expert was called on to clear up the mess; and once in the top office, he never left it for twenty years.

The South Sea Company had been formed in 1711 by Robert Harley, the Tory leader; its original aim was the modest and sensible one of trading with South America. (It had nothing to do with the South Seas as we know them, Tahiti,

---

where the first shipment arrived in 1788. A particularly ferocious act of 1723, which created no few than fifty new capital penalties for trespassing and poaching, was known as "The Black Act." Its effects were felt in England for over a century (SFR, F.24).

5. A sinking fund is an accumulation of money set aside from the regular budget to earn interest till it can be used to pay off a debt. When the debt is paid, it sinks to zero, hence its name. *The Oxford English Dictionary* gives 1724 as the first use of the term.

Samoa, and so forth.) But trade with South America, though it sounded allur-
ingly profitable, never came to much, because the Spanish, who had a monopoly
and wanted to hold it, obstructed the new company at every turn. Finding itself
with a lot of uninvested capital, the company moved into financing operations,
including climactically an attempt to take over a third part of the national debt.
(The East India Company and the Bank of England held the other two-thirds.)
On the surface, this made the company look like a wonderful investment; with a
little money, one could get in on the bonanza of the South American trade, while
enjoying the security of the national credit. During the first months of 1720,
speculators drove up the price of South Sea stock to dizzy heights; the company's
governors took in money and printed new stock certificates by the bale. Uncomprehending and inexperienced people invested their life savings, then lost everything when in August the market collapsed and the company defaulted. Only
Walpole was up to dealing with this crisis and the loss of confidence that resulted.
His path to power was eased when Stanhope the chief minister died of apoplexy
resulting from the stock-market crash. Walpole became treasurer and chancellor
of the exchequer with Townshend as his secretary of state. When the earl of
Sunderland died in 1722, Walpole remained sole and undisputed head of the
Whig party and the king's chief agent in governing England.[6]

Robert Walpole never had a good press with the writers of his day. In *The
Beggar's Opera,* John Gay mocked him in the person of Peachum, receiver-
general of stolen goods; Pope used him repeatedly as a corrupt symbol of ultimate infamy; Swift caricatured him as Flimnap, the mean, obsequious little minister of Lilliput. Indeed, his personal qualities were not such as would endear
him to literary men, whom, in turn, he did not much like. Tough and not very
imaginative, he was an incredibly hard worker. After twenty years in the House
of Commons, he knew its members intimately; he also knew the details of government bureaucracy as well as any man who ever lived. A good friend and a
determined enemy, he used the spoils of office without stint or shame for the
advantage of his friends, and he was his own best friend. He had few fixed
principles but a deep, instinctive awareness of what people wanted. In appear-

6. Though restive, Townshend stayed in political harness till 1730, when he broke with Walpole
and retired to his estate of Raynham in Norfolk, to become a gentleman farmer. He was one of the
first of this breed, and was ridiculed at first as "Turnip" Townshend; but turnips proved a thoroughly
profitable crop (especially the tough strain known as "Swedes"), and Townshend's example, reinforced by the deadly dullness of the Hanover courts, did much to keep the midcentury squirearchy
down on the farm. In the later century, T. W. Coke followed Townshend's lead, and made an
immense fortune by improving his estate, while his contemporary Robert Bakewell practiced an
intensive and well-publicized program of selective breeding to improve English sheep and cattle.
These new techniques ("new" in the sense of systematizing processes which had been haphazard
and tentative for a long time) involved very little new technology; what they did require was large
sums of capital and accurate records, carefully studied as a basis for planning. In the light soils of
Norfolk, results were spectacular; in the wet, heavy clays of the midlands and west country, agriculture lagged till the 1850s, when cheap drainage tile and machines for laying it made possible a second
wave of agricultural improvement.

ance, he was a hard-headed, hard-drinking, hard-working Norfolk squire, a rough sportsman, a crafty political manager, and a crude good fellow. (He like to talk bawdy in his family, he said, because it was a topic to which everyone could contribute.) He could also speak the language of money men and hold their trust. Yet there was at least one more side to him: he was a knowing and cosmopolitan collector of old masters. Many paintings, formerly in his country seat at Houghton, now hang in the major museums of Europe. For Swift and men of his stamp, Sir Robert was the epitome of vulgarity, no gentleman but a crass man of business. For the squires and traders of Georgian England, and for the first two Georges themselves, he was a supple, skillful servant. In Walpole we are for the first time entitled to see an English "prime minister," though the office would not be legally defined till the twentieth century.

THE REIGN OF SLY KING LOG

A listing of the accomplishments of Sir Robert Walpole's regime is perforce a recitation of negatives. He kept England out of war for a long time, neither surrendering her foreign possessions nor enhancing her prestige. He bestowed upon the colonies the ambiguous gift of "salutary neglect"; some of his successors would pay a bitter price for that neglect. About the crying need for reform of the poor laws and for changes in the inhuman penal system, he did nothing at all. He satisfied the landed interest by holding down the land tax, and tried to make up the lost revenue through an expanding set of excise taxes on imports, manufactures, and sales of specific commodities. He counted on these taxes not to offend the trading interests because they could be passed along to consumers; but here he miscalculated. Excise as such was hateful in England, the opposition blew up a storm of protest, and in 1733 Walpole's tax plan had to be dropped. Henceforth he had to make up the shortfall by drawing on that sinking fund for retiring the national debt which had been the cornerstone of his reputation. Because the economy was sound and the country healthy, because he was shrewd in balancing every necessary discontent with a gratuitous favor, the country jogged along comfortably enough under Walpole's rule. Yet there was something about it all to suggest that England was spending capital, maybe even mortagaging her future.

Two minor crises during the 1720s illustrate the deftness with which Sir Robert maintained his position. In 1722 a Birmingham iron merchant named William Wood was granted a royal patent to mint copper halfpence for use in Ireland. The shortage of small change there had long been a serious obstruction to business. But the secret aim of the patent was to make a tidy profit for the duchess of Kendal, née Ehrengarde Melusina, the king's elderly, ugly, ill-tempered, and avaricious mistress. Masquerading as a Dublin tradesman, Jonathan Swift attacked

the new coins in the so-called "Drapier's Letters," and forced their recall.[7]
Walpole, who had originally granted the patent, might have been embarrassed;
but his chief opponent at court, Lord Carteret (who enjoyed the inestimable
advantage of speaking German), overplayed his hand by complaining too loudly.
Walpole took urbane note of Carteret's interest in Irish currency, and suggested
that he reform the situation himself on the spot. To Ireland the reluctant Carteret
therefore went, as lord lieutenant; and there he stayed for six years, while his
political ambitions wilted.[8] As for the Irish, they continued to suffer that shortage of small coins which was the first cause of complaint. But, having enjoyed
one of their rare victories over the English, they idolized the dean of St. Patrick's
and added a new chapter to the Swift legend.

Another crisis in Walpole's administration occurred at the death of George I,
in 1727. There was never any question that the prince of Wales would succeed;
it was just as plain that he had not forgotten or forgiven the episode of 1718–
1719, when (as he saw it) Walpole had misled and then betrayed him. George
II, now forty-four years old, was a man of curious character, pedantic in details,
mechanical in the regularity of his habits, and close to helpless in the presence
of large or hard decisions. One of his favorite diversions was counting his money,
a single gold piece at a time. A minor slip in protocol, occurring in the morning,
would leave him distracted for the rest of the day. If he had once said or done
something, that was absolute authority for saying or doing it again.[9] So his outspoken dislike of Walpole was taken to mean that he would choose another
minister. But the man to whom he turned proved incapable even of writing an
acceptable inaugural speech; Walpole wrote a better one, and promised to secure
the king a larger income than his rival could promise. He also courted the good
will of Queen Caroline, whom George, despite his mistresses, adored and trusted
implicitly. (There is a story that Walpole, alluding in his rustic dialect to the
more influential of the royal couple once bragged "that he knew the right sow to

7. Much of Swift's argument against the new coinage rested on the fact that the new coins did not
contain a halfpenny's worth of copper. Of course they didn't. No coins, whatever the nation coining
them, necessarily contain metal equal to the face value, any more than bills are valued by the paper
they contain. Swift's point was fiscally absurd, though his management of the propaganda was
superb.

8. The story as told is instructive, accurate, but a bit incomplete. Carteret had got into political
hot water in Paris, where he had tried rather clumsily to marry off one of the king's second-string
mistresses to a French nobleman. Apart from that, the lord lieutenancy of Ireland was a traditional
post for shelving momentarily inconvenient politicians of high rank. In brief, Carteret might have
gone to Ireland even if he hadn't spoken out on Wood's halfpence. He was a relatively young man,
and returned, after Walpole's retirement, to head a brief administration under George II.

9. Like his father, George II spoke English only as a second language, and with a thick German
accent. For the arts he had little use, expressing himself contemptuously on the subject of "boets
and bainters." (Pope reciprocated with a wicked lick in the *Dunciad*: "Still Dunce the Second reigns
like Dunce the First.") His one aberration was a fondness for the music of Handel; if we now stand
at the singing of the "Hallelujah Chorus" in *Messiah* it is because George II was the first to do so.

take by the ear.'') George was a very hard man to move in the first place, but once he got used to relying on Walpole, he was unshakable. Thus Sir Robert was able to remain in office, using the power of patronage, his influence with the king, his skill in shunting off rivals, and his ability to straddle issues, long after a lesser politician would have fallen. After his 1733 defeat over the excise, he went on the defensive and came under increasing attack from a group of younger Whigs calling themselves "patriots." Yet he was able to hold onto power for nine more years, falling from place in 1742 only when he had been forced into a war of the sort he had spent most of his political life trying to avoid.

THE RISING FLOOD OF IMPERIAL AMBITIONS

What the "patriots" wanted was a more active and aggressive role for England in the tangled affairs of Europe. Stanhope's alliances with France, Spain, Holland, and the German states had worked well while, under the guise of a balance of power, they guaranteed English supremacy. Now France was embarking on expansionist adventures, while Spain opposed England's developing its trade in South America and the West Indies. That deteriorating position was one reason for opposing Walpole; another was his increasing vulnerability. Some of his close colleagues had retired, others went over to the opposition; Queen Caroline died in 1737;[10] and the minister's enemies multiplied daily. A violent, rhetorical young man named William Pitt appeared in the House of Commons, calling in explicit terms for a new war to expand England's trade. Already George II's son Frederick was gathering the opposition around him, as always happened under the Hanovers. Still Walpole hung on, until in 1739 he allowed himself to be pushed into a war with Spain, known picturesquely as that "of Jenkins's ear." In 1731 the ship *Rebecca,* Captain Robert Jenkins master, had been boarded by Spanish *guarda costas* on her way from the West Indies to England. The captain had resisted, they had cut off one of his ears; seven years had passed, but he flourished the ear before an indignant House of Commons, and the trifling event of 1731 led to war in 1739.

Wearily and against his will, Sir Robert entered on the war against Spain; though he prosecuted it half-heartedly, the Spaniards were in total disarray and soon collapsed, but within a year England had been forced into a wider and more complicated European melee. In 1742 Walpole resigned and by 1745 he was dead, partly of despair at seeing England caught up in what came to be called the War of the Austrian Succession. In its germ, this was a war of conquest by Friedrich (Frederick the Great) of Prussia against his neighbor Maria Theresa,

10. An episode from the queen's deathbed speaks volumes about George's sensitive character. Consoling her grief-stricken husband, who knelt in tears by her bed, the queen told him he must marry again. "No, no," cried the monarch in the depths of his sorrow; "I will have mistresses." "Ah, my God," replied the poor lady, "that's no hindrance (*cela n'empêche pas*)."

queen of Hungary. But these were relatively minor powers; the war was a war of allies. France, Spain, and Bavaria supported Prussia; England and Holland supported Austria and Hungary with occasional help from Saxony, Sardinia, and Russia. Various Italian city-states jumped into and out of the war on either side; the tangle of loyalties would take pages to describe. After years of neglect under Walpole, the English navy was in wretched trim, but it fought actions throughout the Mediterranean, off India, Panama, Chile, and Peru, in the East Indies and the Philippines; the hero of Smollett's first novel, *Roderick Random,* takes part in one of the Central American expeditions, and a gruesome shambles he makes it seem. A particular feature of the continental war was the way princes with armies sold the use of them to the highest bidder, while provinces were exchanged like horses at a fair. One Englishman at least seemed eager and perhaps even able to follow the twisted pattern of alliances and international bargains. Walpole's old rival Carteret returned from his lord lieutenancy in Ireland to become secretary of state; and in this office he plunged into a labyrinth of intrigue through which we need not try to follow him. His fellow ministers could not follow him; George II, though he liked and trusted him, could not understand what he was up to. And his policies produced no victories. Quite the contrary; as the annual bill for troops and subsidies rose to astronomical proportions, England and her allies lost battle after battle abroad. Spain was not a dangerous enemy, but Friedrich, with his meticulously drilled Prussians, was far stronger than Maria Theresa; and the one power to emerge dominant from the bloody fracas was France. Even against a weakened English navy, the French could not hold their own; but on land their armies, commanded by the superb Marshal de Saxe (a German by birth, as his name indicates), swept the board. At the pitched battle of Fontenoy (May 1745),[11] the French completely defeated the English; and the military weakness of England was so obvious that the Jacobites took heart and made one more desperate effort to replace the house of Hanover with the last, and, as it happened, the best of the Stuarts.

THE FORTY-FIVE, AND SCOTLAND'S FATE

The young pretender, Charles Edward Stuart, popularly known as Bonnie Prince Charlie, was what his father and grandfather should have been, a handsome, gallant man, worthy to be a king. In 1745 he was just twenty-five years old, as staunch a Catholic as any of his forebears (and therefore threatening to many Englishmen), but personally brave and a natural leader of men. His father was

11. A picturesque and unreliable legend has it that when the opposing armies were drawn up at Fontenoy, an English officer stepped forward, bowed with a flourish, and invited the French army to fire first. Just as politely, they demurred. The first English volley, which followed immediately, killed or wounded over 700 French troops. The combination of ceremonious manners with hideous brutality would have been pure eighteenth century—if the episode ever happened.

still alive and therefore the legitimate claimant, but politically he was a dead letter. By contrast with that father and with the stodgy, heavy-minded Hanoverians, Charles could not help showing to advantage. George II still did not speak good English; and though he never minded using English troops to protect his electorate, he gave preference and promotion to German officers, with whom he could carry on a conversation. The English government was freshly and not very firmly installed. Carteret having been ousted, the new minister was Henry Pelham, aided by his brother Thomas, duke of Newcastle; and both were at odds with George II, who loathed change of any sort. Thus the event of Fontenoy spurred Charles Edward to action, and unlike his father he was no laggard. In July, he landed in Scotland to sustain his cause in person; the Highlands rose with new enthusiasm, and after capturing Edinburgh Charles Edward found himself at the head of a very respectable army, numbering some 7,000 to 9,000 men. In September, this force won a decisive victory at Prestonpans over an English contingent led by sleepy Sir John Cope, and the way seemed open for an invasion of England. In fact the rebels got as far as Derby without any major fighting; but by then the government was recalling its veterans and mercenaries from the Continent. A well-trained, well-supplied army of English, Hessian, and Dutch troops barred the way south. The Highlanders fell back on Scotland, followed by a steadily growing English force under one of George II's sons, the duke of Cumberland. On the bleak, bare moor of Culloden, the final battle of the Stuart cause was fought, 16 April 1746; and there the dream ended. Charles made his escape, was hunted through the land by English redcoats but protected by his own folk, including the legendary heroine Flora MacDonald, and finally escaped to France. On the Continent he lived a life of intrigue and finally of drunkenness, dying at Rome in 1788, just one hundred years after his grandfather had been ejected from the English throne. The legends that he and his family left behind linger to this day; they are the stuff of countless ballads, novels, and folktales.[12] The "young chevalier" particularly is the paragon of gallant failures; nobody ever made a song like "Charlie Is My Darling" about George II.

Having crushed the rebellion of '45 and hanged every rebel they could catch, the English proceeded to destroy systematically the tribal culture of the Highlands. From time immemorial, the Highland folk had lived in their own warlike way, outside the English social and legal systems. Each of their many clans made and enforced its own rules; each was under the absolute rule of a single chief. Now English laws deprived the chieftain of his patriarchal authority, forbade the wearing of a plaid or tartan (badges, these, of clan membership), forbade the carrying of swords. The English introduced new schools with the obvious aim

12. By cooperating with the English conquerors, the house of Campbell earned the undying hatred and contempt of other Highland tribes; for a sample, see Robert Louis Stevenson's novel, *Kidnapped,* Chapter 12. On the positive side, William Collins wrote at the beginning of the year 1746 an exquisite elegy, "How sleep the brave," which might serve as appropriately for the defeated Jacobites as for those who defeated them.

of replacing Gaelic as the language of the people, and built new roads to reduce their isolation. Not all these programs were inherently bad, and some simply hastened a process which would have occurred anyway. But their effects were, first, to depopulate the Scottish Highlands for the advantage of America, and then to blend Scottish culture into the larger pattern of British ways.[13] The present movement for Scottish national independence dwells bitterly on memories of 1707 (the Act of Union) and 1745 (the crushing of the Highlands and their gallant Scottish chief).

One result of the two Jacobite risings, in '15 and '45, was unintentional but not unimportant. In both crises the dissenters of England stood rock-firm for the Protestant interest and the Hanoverian succession. Many Tory squires and high-church parsons who fancied themselves the backbone of the nation were less vigorous and explicit. Dissenters voted money and supplies; they also volunteered for the armies. Since by law no man could be an officer who had not subscribed the Thirty-nine Articles of the church of England, a dissenter who took a commission to save his country from invasion was technically in violation of the law. The only reward offered to dissenters, when the peril had subsided, was immunity from prosecution. Such incredible meanness on the part of the government could only redound to the popular advantage of the dissenters, and hasten their full integration into the mainstream of English political and social life.

Meanwhile, the War of the Austrian Succession, muddled in its inception, its management, and its conclusion, dragged wearily to an end. France and Prussia had clearly been the big gainers by it, but when the peacemakers finally sat down at Aix-la-Chapelle in 1748, everyone was so exhausted and most people were so confused by this most senseless of wars, that a shaky, untidy peace was all that could be huddled up. To many Englishmen, the peace of Utrecht in 1713–1714 had seemed a betrayal of Marlborough's battlefield victories; so in 1748 the peace of Aix-la-Chapelle seemed to many Frenchmen an ignoble betrayal of Saxe's battlefield victories. Actually, it wasn't even much of a peace. During the period when it was nominally in effect, Englishmen and Frenchmen continued to shoot at each other in the forests of America and on the vast alluvial plains of India. And eight years later, the irrepressible conflict between England and France was to resume full fury in the Seven Years' War. But as those events fall within the period dominated by the two strident, dramatic figures of William Pitt, father and son, we may pause here at mid-century to look back at the cultural character of an age which was essentially that of Robert Walpole.

13. Depopulation was hastened by recruiting young men into special Highland regiments for service in America; many settled there. In the nineteenth century, many Scotsmen thought the national accent ("burr") a badge of disgrace, and tried to eradicate it. This was true of men like Lord Jeffrey, editor of the *Edinburgh Review*, even when, in private or in their cups, they were masters of the comic story or poetic recitation, always delivered in broad Scots.

THE OPENING UP OF FICTION: DEFOE AND RICHARDSON

When English kings spoke only broken English and government business fell into the hands of coarse, money-minded managers like Sir Robert Walpole, literature largely ceased to look to the court for patronage, and became itself a business, the business of bookselling. Some vulgarizing of taste resulted, but less than might have been anticipated, because a new, middle level of readers came unforeseeably into being. Two strains of thought and feeling, once antithetical, converged to create a new audience for whom prose fiction, hitherto a very minor strain in English writing, proved congenial. On the one hand, puritans and ex-puritans raised their passion for introspection and self-analysis to the level of imaginative participation in the life of an imaginary character. Such a development was not easy for them. They had to learn not to worry that in fiction they were reading deliberate lies, and that in seeking worldly amusement they were neglecting their salvation. Easing these misgivings was a slow process, and accordingly in the early stages we find most fictions to be heavily laced with moral teaching, and a number of them pretending to be recitations of literal fact. On the other hand, "genteel" readers (that is, readers trained in the classical literatures with their emphasis on lofty, epic style and on mythological legends about gods and heroes) had difficulty lowering their sights to the adventures of modern characters with common manners and trivial problems. How could stories of thieves, footmen, bastards, and prostitutes possibly compete for a reader's interest with tales of princes, ladies, and mighty warriors? One way was to see the modern actor as a ludicrous contrast with heroes of old; the relatively new forms of burlesque and parody encouraged this response. But here too there were problems. It's not easy to build sympathy for a hero who is consistently ridiculous, and the jokes to be derived from his inferiority to Achilles and Aeneas, being predictable, soon become monotonous. As the puritans had to raise their imaginations to the level of fiction, so genteel readers had to overcome their disdain for low, modern materials. Before the two strains converged indistinguishably, there was a stage where they flowed separately; and here we may distinguish Daniel Defoe and Samuel Richardson, in the "serious" puritan tradition, from Henry Fielding and Tobias Smollett in the mock-heroic, "genteel" vein (SFR, F.11).

Defoe was sixty years old when he wrote, in 1719, his first proper novel, the famous *Robinson Crusoe*. Largely for moralistic purposes, he was working up a true story, the rudiments of which he had heard from Alexander Selkirk, the original castaway. Defoe's falling on this subject was partly but not altogether accidental. From youth, he had been something of a literary scavenger, writing satires, political propaganda (for both parties), entire newspapers, projects for reform, a ghost story, miscellaneous informal essays. The tale of Selkirk, who had been marooned for four years on an island off the coast of Chile, served Defoe as a frame on which to hang a typical puritan story of purification by trial.

Robinson on his solitary island is an independent man of spiritual business, managing shrewdly his limited capital and keeping carefully his spiritual account book in order to deserve his ultimate rewards. Striving and self-discipline are the essence of this program; it represents the heroic spirit in the common act, immense religious meaning in the humblest of everyday tasks. Having fallen into this vein of fiction, Defoe exploited it in a series of novels describing the lives of pirates, petty thieves, shoplifters, kept women, highwaymen, and soldiers of fortune. For all their variety, these fictions tell essentially the same story: it is the progress of a prudent and earnest soul into snares and moral pitfalls—Defoe soon found that he could hardly have too many of these—but finally through them. What sustains his protagonists is not so much religious faith as a sturdy spirit of practical enterprise. They are good business folk with a tiny bit of capital to invest and a determination to make it grow. Moll Flanders, for example, bargains like a pawnbroker for the use of her body. Nothing could be less romantic, nothing less tinged with sensuality, or for that matter with a consciousness of the seventh commandment. Moll is a merchant who knows the market, and scans every customer with a narrow eye. So cool and practical is she (and in this she is characteristic of Defoe's women) that some readers have suspected satiric intent or at least conscious humor. This does not seem to be so. Defoe was not a devious or witty man; he came from and moved all his life in classes which had never before expressed themselves in literature; their erotic life may well have been just as much a matter of stolid calculation as Defoe makes it seem. Among Defoe's many other books is a very revealing one titled *The Complete English Tradesman;* it is a heavily moralized set of instructions telling how to build and carry on a successful business. Its ambiguity lies in the fact that it explains in careful detail all the techniques of sharp practice, following each explanation with a sincere but perfunctory warning that such behavior is morally wrong. It is an effort to reconcile Christ with Mammon, and like all such efforts a little smudgy around the moral seams. But one thing it is not, and that is satirical. Satire would have been easy—for some, irresistible. But Defoe looks steadfastly at life and the compromises it imposes through the eyes of an earnest young shopkeeper trying to do all the business he possibly can while observing as much of the moral code as he must, and no more. One shouldn't impute satiric intent to Defoe's fiction without taking measure of the mind that wrote *The Complete English Tradesman.*

Such a book was by no means an accident in Defoe's career. Never quite a rogue nor quite respectable, he had sold woolen hose and run a brick factory, gone through the bankruptcy courts, stood in the pillory, been in and out of prison; though he was not without schooling, the college of hard knocks was the only one from which he ever graduated. He saw the world of the semicriminal who knows and aspires to something better, from the inside out. His art is to make a reader feel how easy and natural it was for the semicriminal to behave as he did. In good part he does this by closing our moral horizons and leading us down the narrow, walled streets of circumstance till suddenly, at a rising or turning, we look back, appalled, at where we have been.

Alongside Defoe's precarious, small-scale capitalists, may be set the heroine of Samuel Richardson's first novel *Pamela* (1740). Pamela Andrews too has a tiny, fragile bit of capital, her "virtue," very specifically defined as her maidenhead. Her employer, Mr. B., offers to take it away from her on very poor terms, she holds out vigorously till she can get him to offer better terms, to wit, marriage. Nobody has ever suspected satiric intent on Richardson's part; but the story has seemed irresistibly comic to many readers, who sense commercial motives on the young lady's part behind a masquerade of prudish virtue. This is not the way *Pamela* was first read by the many servant girls who bought it because the predicament with which it dealt—ruin or respectability, depending on how one played one's cards—was one which any of them might confront. It was certainly not the way Richardson meant his book to be read; he was seriously interested in the problem of distressed virtue, as he showed by returning to the same theme in his later novels, *Clarissa Harlowe* and *Sir Charles Grandison*. But comedy was a real potential of his early fiction.

In fact, Richardson was a psychological novelist who exercised in fictional form the old theological practice of casuistry, which is simply the resolution of difficult moral cases. By trade he had been a printer, but from youth his avocation was writing letters of moral counsel addressed to young ladies of the middling and lower social orders. His novels, the first of which appeared when he was fifty-one years old, took the form of letters delving at length into the complex feminine emotions of hope and apprehension aroused by the proximity of a magnetic male. Though not incapable of portraying a fine gentleman, Richardson could never see Lovelace, the seducer of Clarissa, from the inside, perhaps because he and his sort seemed to have no inside. But with Clarissa herself, as with Pamela and his other female subjects, Richardson was perfectly at home. It was as a guide to the wavering heart and soft conscience of frail females that he achieved his fame. Not only English but European reputation rewarded him; in France and Germany his novels were much read and widely influential. Richardson was the discoverer of the "ladies' novel," a genre that continued to flourish throughout the nineteenth century, producing masses of sentimental three-deckers for Mudie's Lending Library, and filling, to this day, the paperback shelves of drugstores and bus stations. But, looked at from another angle, Richardson's novels extended the work of Defoe, rendering deeper and subtler the analysis of minds that for centuries had been dismissed as trivial.

The arrival of women in the world of literature, as readers, writers, and figures with minds worthy of analysis, was a gradual but steady process, representing a major heritage from puritanism. Courtly literature, putting women on pedestals or toying with them as a gentleman's sexual playthings, granted them minimal identity outside of marriage and none inside. For the puritans, women were equal partners in marriage, business, and spiritual warfare, the serious tasks of salvation. But the sort of education that would enable women to compete with men in the erudite modes of literature remained very hard to come by. Dorothy Osborne, writing in the middle of the seventeenth century to her fiancé William Temple, reveals herself as a witty, playful, high-spirited woman; she is an excellent letter writer, one of the best of her age. Yet her spelling is very erratic, and her punctuation worse. When a woman of the upper classes had so much trouble with the rudiments, we may imagine how hard self-expression came to women less educated than she. But a few schools for girls were started under the Restoration, and by the middle of the eighteenth century we know that many women were reading novels and a few were writing them, as well as pursuing other literary activities. Lady Mary Wortley Montagu was an established maker of literary opinion, a formidable correspondent, and an early exponent of inoculation, about which she had learned when her husband was ambassador to Turkey. Mrs. Mary Manley produced several plays, published a wickedly satirical novel (*Memoirs from the New Atlantis,* 1709), and succeeded Swift as editor of the Tory newssheet, *The Examiner.* Mary Astell not only wrote a groundbreaking *Serious Proposal to the Ladies Wherein a Method Is Offered for the Improvement of Their Minds* (1697), but actually advocated the creation of a women's college. Queen Anne favored the proposal, and it might really have come to pass, but Bishop Burnet crushed the idea under his gaitered episcopal feet.

THE OTHER DELEGATION: FIELDING AND SMOLLETT

About Henry Fielding, who reacted to Richardson's sentimental psychological, and feminine novels by producing rowdy, comic, masculine novels of his own, it is useful to realize that he had a classical education (as Defoe and Richardson did not) and served his literary apprenticeship on the stage, writing satires, comedies of intrigue, and burlesques. This early work trained him to a different sort of vision entirely from that of Defoe and Richardson. They looked on life as at a tapestry, from which, with their help, the reader might pick out spiritual and religious principles of permanent, ennobling value. Fielding looked at life through a screen of classic fable and heroic narrative, of which the actions he described were diminished and ludicrous counterparts. Both Defoe and Fielding wrote about the famous criminal Jonathan Wild, who was hanged at Tyburn in 1725, but they wrote very differently. For Defoe, Wild is the model of a good man gone wrong; for Fielding he is a type of modern "greatness," the sort of great man that in a society without the classical moral standards people admire. Fielding's natural vein was irony, where Defoe and Richardson were single-minded. Fielding's feeling was of a Tory strain, not alien (in spite of his greater geniality) to that of Swift, Pope, and Gay; Defoe and Richardson were both in their different ways lay preachers of the dissenting persuasion.

Born into a lesser branch of a great house, Fielding was tossed young into the world, to live by his wits and his handsome features. He pursued heiresses, studied law, and wrote for the stage; like his later hero Tom Jones, he was a harum-scarum, unsettled, attractive fellow. In 1737 one of his plays reflected a little too sharply on the corrupt practices of Sir Robert Walpole, and was censored off the stage; Fielding returned to the law and after a time became a much-respected magistrate in London. His literary career resumed only when Samuel Richardson, with *Pamela,* offered him an irresistibly provoking target for satire. Fielding began by rewriting *Pamela* in miniature, retitling it *Shamela,* and providing for every episode in the original a brutal or vulgar interpretation. Shamela is not an innocent serving girl at all, she has already had one bastard by Parson Williams, who is a lecherous, sanctimonious hypocrite. The girl is a little prostitute, the man of God is her bully, and between them they are out to milk squire Booby (as Mr. B. of the original Richardson novel has been retitled) for every shilling he possesses. Fielding's burlesque is as broad and outspoken as Richardson is mealy-mouthed;[14] and it makes a hilarious little farce, though not much more. Fielding, however, saw at once that he had more material in hand than *Shamela* could use; so, without losing sight of Richardson, he began a full-length novel about the adventures of Pamela's brother. Joseph Andrews is just as chaste as his sister. His name is supposed to remind us of that Joseph in the Bible who had trouble with Potiphar's wife; he has to beat off the lecherous advances of Lady Booby. So long as he confines himself to this action, Fielding has not departed far from *Shamela;* but when Joseph is driven from Lady Booby's house, and sets off on a series of wanderings with "her" curate Mr. Abraham Adams, we enter on another world, of highwaymen and sheep stealers, of misers, rapists, derelicts. Parson Adams and Joseph Andrews form a duo reminiscent of Don Quixote and Sancho Panza in Fielding's favorite book. They ramble, they digress, they philosophize on life, tell stories, defend oppressed virtue, deplore selfishness, stumble from one mishap to another. Generous feelings and loving hearts triumph in the end, with the help of some handy fisticuffs and the timely intervention of Pamela Booby and her new husband, who, to serve the plot, are not boobies at all but generous and kindly folk.

The world of *Joseph Andrews* is very much that of *Tom Jones* (1749), Fielding's acknowledged masterpiece. Rigidified intellectual systems are represented, in this semi-allegorical novel, by Thwackum the man of religion who believes in original sin, and Square the philosopher who believes in natural law. Tom, who is all goodness of heart and generosity of feeling, has to make his way past these gargoyles, as well as those of an obtuse law and a selfish society in order

14. The difference in dialect between upper-class and middle-class people (abbreviated by Nancy Mitford as U and non-U people) is a constant in English society. County gentry talk broad and frank; the newly respectable tend to use timid euphemisms or what the eighteenth century called "cant." Sir Sampson Legend of Congreve's play *Love for Love,* and Squire Western of *Tom Jones* illustrate the full-mouthed dialect.

finally to reclaim his birthright and gain the hand of his Sophia. In the process he too rambles, from the woods of a west-country estate, from inn to inn through a series of comic adventures,[15] to the over-refined salons of aristocratic London; and from rude simplicity, through scapegrace predicaments, to full maturity as a man of prudence and good fortune. Fielding thought "Tom" the most ludicrous name in the world, and subjected his hero to a good deal of rough humor in the book. But he grew fond of his young man as the novel progressed, and so does the reader, until, by a trick familiar to Defoe, we find we have condoned more than we may be quite ready to condone. Fielding's manipulation of our sympathies sometimes looks crude (he intervenes in his own fictions more than is fashionable nowadays), but in fact much of it is real virtuoso work.

Tobias Smollett, whose first novel antedates by only three years Fielding's last, was a humorist like Fielding but notoriously lacking in the genial temperament. A Scotsman by birth, a physician by training, but a writer by deep natural inclination, Smollett kicked around the world as a young man and got kicked a good deal in return, sometimes pretty hard. His first novel, *Roderick Random* (1748), records at a rattling pace some of his adventures; they include service as a naval surgeon on a ghastly expedition to the West Indies, abduction by smugglers, attempts to seduce an heiress, misfortune at gambling, and encounters with miscellaneous rogues, cheats, rascals, and brutes. This first novel sold well, and was followed by others, rich in comic invention, yet always with a certain bite and bitterness to the humor. Smollett felt himself ill used by life and perhaps went out of his way to be so. Though he was an indefatigable worker and earned lots of money, he always managed to spend it faster than he could make it. Ultimately Smollett worked himself into a breakdown, to cure which he went to Italy; and there, mellowing a little and half-recognizing his own gruffness, he wrote his last and most enduring novel, *Humphry Clinker* (1771). The rambling, episodic story is told in letters, as are the psychological narratives of Richardson; but this is a novel of humors and social observation, like those of Fielding. Humphry Clinker himself is a minor character in the book, a semi-lettered Methodist postilion who is picked up almost accidentally by crusty, kindly old Matthew Bramble, his sister Tabitha, and their family associates, in the course of a rambling coach trip through England and Scotland. The pace is leisurely, the observations of human nature brusque and benevolent. The actions of the book are largely predictable, but its pleasures lie in its incidental observations, its dry and humane wit. In Matthew Bramble's recognition that good-hearted, simple-

15. Misadventures in inns, such as fistfights, bed-hoppings, and slop-emptyings, are a regular feature of early English fiction. English inns can hardly have been *that* lively, and it's probable that most of these hurly-burlies were modeled on *Don Quixote.* Another feature copied from Cervantes was the long interpolated narrative, recited by a secondary character; it interrupts but relates thematically to the main narrative. For the leisurely eighteenth century the fact that it slowed things down was all to the good.

minded Humphry is his own natural son, one can perhaps see a little more than a theatrical contrivance; this reconciling novel ends with something like a reconciliation of the two strains which went to make the novel itself.

FICTION AND THE BOOKSELLERS

From our modern point of view, Defoe, Richardson, Fielding, and Smollett are classics of the literature, and we may suppose that they delighted hundreds of thousands of readers, as Scott and Dickens would do a century later. No such thing. For most English folk of the eighteenth century leisure was scant, books expensive, and the habit of reading for amusement very strange indeed. The novels which today are available in cheap reprints for millions of readers were originally published in editions ranging from 1,000 to 3,000 copies, and did well if they sold out over a period of three or four years. Second editions were rare. Fielding's last novel, *Amelia,* was buoyed by the success of *Tom Jones,* and sold out quickly. But that was exceptional, and when he died soon after, the author (though he had been a prodigiously busy man, a magistrate, a pamphleteer, and the best-known novelist of his time) left barely enough property, even when his library had been sold, to pay his debts. His widow and children became the responsibility of his brother and his close friend Ralph Allen, the Squire Allworthy of *Tom Jones.*

Apart from the four major novelists, there were a number of lesser figures; yet there is something curiously desultory and occasional about eighteenth-century minor fiction. Young ladies wrote the odd novel, as Fanny Burney did *Evelina* (1778), on the margin of an active social life; though she tried several times to follow up the success of her first book, she was never able to do so. Under pressure of urgent monetary necessity, Dr. Johnson committed one quasi–novel, *Rasselas* (1759), and no more; Goldsmith did the same with *The Vicar of Wakefield* (1766). Robert Paltock produced in 1751 a curious pseudo–science fantasy about a flying man, *The Life and Adventures of Peter Wilkins;* John Cleland wrote in 1749 the first competent book of English pornography. Better known from its heroine as *Fanny Hill,* the *Memoirs of a Woman of Pleasure* was written with enough zest and art to retain an under-the-counter interest and influence well into the twentieth century.

Yet the eighteenth-century novel is quite as remarkable for the themes it avoided as for those it attempted. This was the great age of personalities in politics: there are no political novels. It was the age of family connections and family influence; there are no family chronicles. There is no contemporary fiction about the intrigues of '88, the Scottish revolt of '45, or the British presence in India, though in the nineteenth century Thackeray, Scott, and Kipling made splendid fictions from these materials. Thackeray particularly (in *Henry Esmond,* its sequel *The Virginians,* and *Barry Lyndon*) reaped a rich harvest where the eighteenth century had been able to glean very little. Evidently the novelists themselves were not yet ready to tackle big themes; the public was not ready for massive doses of make-believe on "serious" matters. And besides, the booksellers, powerful and conservative in their tastes, preferred books which had a more practical and enduring appeal. Multi-volume histories like those of Hume (1754–1761) and Gibbon (1776–1788) were good investments; they made handsome sets for library shelves. But volumes of sermons, as both Parson Adams (of *Joseph Andrews*) and the vicar of Wakefield discovered, were likely to be pronounced a drug on the market. Booksellers saw sure profits in projects like Dr. Johnson's *Dictionary* (1755) and those selections from the English poets for which he wrote a classic set of introductions (1779). In 1768 a "Society of Gentlemen in Scotland" began to publish, a volume at a time, the first edition of the *Encyclopaedia Britannica*.[16] But for the harum-scarum, Jack-of-all-trades literary artisans who scraped by in the garrets of Grub Street and tried to shark up writing jobs in the shallow waters of the trade, existence was wretched indeed. The desperate translator, the hack compiler of crime chronicles, the ill-paid political libeler all stood at the mercy of hardheaded printers and booksellers, who ground them unmercifully. Samuel Johnson's *Life of Richard Savage* (1743) is a feeling account of this existence, written by one who knew it all too well (SFR, F. 10).

ON THE FRINGE

Yet some developments were afoot to widen the literary public. Monthly magazines began to appear in the 1730s, first as compendia of snippets from the daily press (hence the word "magazine," meaning "storeroom"), then with special political coverage of their own and feature articles of a miscellaneous nature. After mid-century some of them attained circulations of as many as 10,000 copies, which might well mean a readership four or five times as great. In the course of the century a few libraries sprang up or were endowed, to assist in the circulation of books. Lydia Languish, the heroine of Sheridan's comedy *The Rivals,* has had her maid out all morning collecting junky French novels from the circulating libraries of Bath for her mistress's amusement. On a more serious level, Dr. John Williams, a public-spirited divine, left in his will (1729) money to establish a private-subscription library which flourishes to this day. In 1753 the British Museum was founded to house the collections of Sir Hans Sloane and Sir Robert Cotton; four years later, its library was much enriched by accessions from the royal collections, though the real explosion of its holdings did not begin till the early years of the nineteenth century, when Sir Anthony Panizzi became direc-

16. Inspirations for the *Britannica* were Louis Moréri's *Grand Dictionnaire Historique* (1674, translated into English later in the century), Pierre Bayle's *Dictionnaire Critique et Historique* (1697), and the immense, many-volumed, many-authored French *Encyclopédie* of which Denis Diderot served, throughout the middle of the eighteenth century, as guiding genius.

tor.[17] Cheap reprints of classic texts (the English poets and dramatists, the essayists, and even the novelists) started to appear only in the last years of the eighteenth century; free public libraries became widespread only in the last half of the nineteenth century. Thus the growth of a substantial reading public with an ingrained taste for print, though steady in the first part of the eighteenth century, remained very slow.

POETS OF THE AUGUSTAN AGE

Because of its novelty, the rise of fiction looms large in the literary landscape of the eighteenth century, but developments in the traditional genres were more appreciated at the time. Swift and Pope are commonly assigned to the age of Queen Anne, but both survived the queen by a full thirty years, and Pope particularly acquired a horde of imitators. Many of their names have now slipped into oblivion, but their emphasis on "correctness" of feeling and expression has earned for the period the title of the "Augustan Age" of English literature. The phrase implies a golden age when English, like Latin under the rule of the Emperor Augustus, attained its highest peak of purity and politeness. How well the parallel with Latin holds up is dubious or a little worse. But in one respect Pope and his friends did justify the adjective "Augustan." The figure of Horace, the urbane and moderate man of Augustan civilization, was very important to them; Pope imitated Horace repeatedly, and cast many of his reflections about eighteenth-century England in a form which invited the reader to see that they had also been the reflections of Horace about Rome in the first century B.C. Horatian unpretentiousness and good sense gave, as it were, the seal of ancient authenticity to the code of gentlemanly good humor which Pope's age took as an ideal. Those who made up good society in that age could not, as a rule, trace their blood lines very far back in history; English gentility therefore had to be proved in other ways,[18] one of which was knowledge of the classic tongues. They were to be learned chiefly at public schools and the universities, hence at considerable expense; once learned, they were practically useless and so constituted (like the bound feet of Chinese women) proof of status in a superior caste. In addition, a casual, friendly familiarity with Horace, Ovid, Propertius, and Tibullus implied a cos-

17. Sir Anthony was an unforeseen but precious reward for England's relatively liberal political stance after the Napoleonic wars. Driven from his native Modena by a reactionary regime, he became for his adopted land an administrator extraordinary—architect, collector of art objects, and book buyer without parallel.

18. In Europe a gentleman was defined arithmetically; he had to have a certain number of "quarterings," that is, of provably noble ancestors. But in England the best definition was that of Sir Thomas Smith in the sixteenth century: "Who can live idly and without manual labor, and will bear the port, charge, and countenance of a gentleman, he . . . shall be taken for a gentleman." In other words, if you have enough money, and set up for a gentleman, then you are one.

mopolitan, man-of-the-world attitude, far above parochial considerations. Clubs were much in vogue during the eighteenth century; to know the classic authors was to assume membership in a small but world-wide club of enlightened spirits. Not only poets, but some novelists made use of this ploy, and it is not altogether obsolete yet, except in the new world.

Not all poets, however, chose to follow the Augustan mode, and we should pause to note a few of them. James Thomson was a Scottish poet who made use of Miltonic blank verse for distinctly non-Miltonic ends. Between 1726 and 1730 he published a group of purely descriptive poems known collectively as *The Seasons;* they are, as it were, verbal landscape paintings, and reflect, even as they prefigure, an English interest in nature unadorned by the hand of man. John Dyer was another poet who worked in the descriptive mode (*Grongar Hill,* 1726); and Thomas Warton, more critic than poet, drew inspiration for some of his early verse from the work of Spenser, Milton, and Shakespeare, in a manner that has prompted some writers to call him a "pre-romantic." During the early eighteenth century the first notes were heard of a revival in Scottish vernacular poetry, even as the last sounds of ancient Irish minstrelsy were dying out. Allan Ramsay collected old songs and ballads, and like his greater successor Burns patched them together with verses of his own making; his is a genuine lyrical voice in a prevailingly unlyrical age, and *The Gentle Shepherd* (1725) made the obsolete pastoral live again. In Ireland, meanwhile, the last of the ancient Irish minstrels, blind Carolan, continued to improvise to his own accompaniment on the harp, till his death in 1738; the bardic tradition of which he was the last exponent reached far back into the darkness of prehistory, and it is pleasant to recall that among the little boys who listened, awe-struck, to the last of his epic lays, was one of Ireland's greatest writers, the youthful Oliver Goldsmith.

A special development of English poetry during the eighteenth century was an increase in the number and quality of English hymns. Perhaps the newly popular modes of opera and oratorio helped stir an interest in hymn writing and hymn performance; in any case, the form was deeply rooted in puritan tradition. One man particularly, a divine of the Independent persuasion named Isaac Watts, raised the whole art to a new level. Watts's hymns at their best combine simplicity with majesty to memorable effect. Some of them are still sung today, the best-known probably "O God, Our Help in Ages Past." But there were many others in Watts's vast output; Addison contributed one splendid hymn early in the century,[19] and toward its end William Cowper and John Newton added more. Though many of these hymns originated in dissenting communities, they were adopted by the established church as well, and did a good deal to relieve that spiritual dessication often considered characteristic of the eighteenth-century Anglican establishment.

19. If majesty can be found in deism, it will be found in Addison's ode, "The Spacious Firmament on High," inspired by Psalm 19, and first printed in *Spectator* No. 465.

BISHOP BUTLER AND THE METHODISTS

What we mean by Anglican "dessication" can best be illustrated by turning, not to the church's weaklings or sluggards, but to a man of genuine intellectual distinction and severe character, Bishop Joseph Butler. His chief book was *The Analogy of Religion Natural and Revealed to the Constitution and Course of Nature* (1736); it is a defense of Anglican doctrine directed primarily against the deists, whom, however, it never names. Butler's book assumes the limited deistic premises—i.e., the existence of a God, creator of the world, benevolently disposed toward man; it goes on to urge that no charge of unreasonableness can be brought against revealed religion which cannot be brought, with equal force, against natural religion, because the course of nature itself is not fully accessible to our reason. In natural knowledge, no less than in religion, we must be content with probabilities. But an analogy between the deficiencies of our natural knowledge and those of our Christian knowledge will suggest a common tendency in both, sufficient to guide us in estimating our religious duties in this world. Whether there is or is not an afterlife with rewards and punishments, Butler will not try to determine positively; the most he will say is that, based on what we know of this life, belief in an afterlife is not unreasonable. In formulas like this, the bishop combined radical skepticism with a strongly defensive posture in the matter of Christian faith. A parody of the position could reduce it to something like this: "You don't understand the nature of matter any better than you do the nature of the Trinity; so, on the probabilities, it's not unreasonable to believe in the Trinity." This is a pretty dour formula, not likely to bring much cheer to a man suffering under the fear of death. Personally, Butler was a kindly and modest man, popular with his brethren and with their flocks; among the beggars of England he was famous far and wide as a soft touch. But his creed offered few incentives to belief save caution, prudence, and acceptance of uncertainty as an unchangeable human condition. In the austere, limited accuracy of his prose and his personality, he reminds us of an ancient Roman stoic, surrounded by barbarian adherents of the new enthusiastic Christianity. His life, like his creed, had little hope but great dignity.[20]

The enthusiasts of Butler's day, and the great exception to the rule of religious apathy in the eighteenth century, were found in the movement known as Methodism, of which (though it left few directly literary memorials), we must here take brief account. Methodism was the creation of three men, John and Charles Wesley, and George Whitefield; in its early days, it represented a revivalist movement within the church of England, rather than a separate sect. The brothers Wesley had attended Oxford, had been ordained in the Anglican church, and had come under the influence of a magnetic nonjuror named William Law, before setting out in 1735 for Georgia, where they had high hopes of converting some

20. Among the literary essays of Walter Bagehot (*Collected Works*, London, 1965, Vol. I), will be found a long, serious, and very Butlerian analysis of Bishop Butler.

Indians. This proved impractical, but on shipboard and in Georgia itself they found a number of Moravian immigrants. These were Germans of a pietist tinge, nominally Lutheran, but insistent on the necessity of an active, powerful, individual faith. The Moravians did more to convert their new English friends than vice versa. From their experience in Georgia the Wesleys and Whitefield (who had joined them there) returned to England full of fervor for spreading the religion of Christ through the oppressed and neglected classes of England. The task was immense, and in performing it they were incredibly busy and successful. To the industrial towns of northern England, to the narrow coal-mining valleys of Wales, the Methodist preachers brought a thrilling message of personal redemption. Whitefield in particular was an amazing preacher. Because the churches of the establishment were closed to him, he spoke mostly in the open air; he preached seven days a week, as many as six times a day. Once he spoke to a gathering of 20,000 listeners, and made himself distinctly heard by them all. John Wesley was also a famous and indefatigable preacher, for whom no hamlet was too remote, no penitent too humble, and no mob, however threatening, too dangerous. (In Birmingham, he was pelted with mud as he preached, yet finished his sermon.) As he lived to almost ninety, it is estimated that he delivered in his lifetime nearly 40,000 sermons.

Though the Methodists sought out the humble and oppressed, the message they preached was far from revolutionary: what they taught was submission, industry, sobriety, and reform of the individual conscience. Emphasizing the supreme importance of saving faith, they sometimes mingled superstitious nonsense and quack medicine with their spiritual advice. And at a time when the system of child labor was at its worst, they spoke not a word about providing children with better education, let alone a chance for innocent play. On the contrary, they deplored both worldly learning and cheerful diversion as distractions from prayer and labor in one's calling.

Yet for all this, the impact of Methodism on the laboring classes of England was tremendous. We hear of vast throngs of coal-blackened miners listening hour after hour in silence to the Methodist preacher—the only sign of his hold on them being the grotesque white streaks left on their black cheeks by streams of penitent tears. Methodism rooted itself deeply in the life of the working class, assuming perforce the character of a sect. In fact, neither in doctrine nor discipline did the Methodists vary from the established church. The real objection to admitting them was social. They were of the great unwashed; they did not know how to behave or how to talk; they did not know or care who Horace was, or what Maecenas said to him. The chilly rationalism of the Anglican religion took no hold on their lives. All they had was sinful human hearts and obscure human feelings. The upper classes hardly recognized those attributes in themselves at all. A nice story is told of an eighteenth-century lady, who was advised by her gamekeeper of a gathering of Methodists outside the gate beyond her park. A footman was sent out to learn what they were doing, and returned to say they were praying for her ladyship. "Really," she said, with a sniff of disdain, "things have come to a pretty pass when religion starts interfering with a person's private life."[21]

THE AMENITIES OF LIFE—AND ITS DIVERSITIES

Being a confident oligarchy and eager to be a comfortable one, the ruling class did much private building, of fine rural seats and equally fine town houses. Georgian building is neat, genteel, but not pretentious; the basic material is brick or stone, the house rarely exceeds three stories, and has comfortable parlors rather than vast halls. The windows are many and symmetrically arranged, the door is generally crowned by an ornate fanlight. Inside, one is likely to find a central staircase of finely carved mahogany, high-ceilinged rooms with simple but elegantly proportioned fireplaces. During this period, the art of turning wood on a lathe was invented, which multipled decorative possibilities. A growing number of private coaches made for wider and better-paved streets. The spaciousness of Georgian building, its gift for framing human transactions in an architecture of civilized proportions, can be appreciated in the city of Dublin, where Merrion and Fitzwilliam Squares are models of Georgian civic arrangement. And in Edinburgh and Bath (not to mention the complex of Regent Street and Regent's Park in London), many of the same qualities are also evident.[22]

About 1705 the London fop Beau Nash established himself as reigning arbiter of manners in the city of Bath; he decreed codes of dress and comportment, erected a fine assembly room, encouraged civilized diversions while forbidding duels, and helped to develop, in this once rustic hamlet, a program of dignified urban planning, which in the 1730s received the ultimate accolade, when royalty came calling. In London, pleasure gardens like Vauxhall and Ranelagh provided elegant settings for light entertainment, casual or serious flirtation, and civilized frivolity; parks, malls, and promenades opened up the inner city.

Fine furniture was a special accomplishment of the eighteenth century, and throughout the entire century the family of Chippendale was busy producing

21. The saying has also been attributed to Lord Melbourne at the beginning of the nineteenth century. Nominally, the Methodists remained affiliated with the Anglican church till after Wesley's death in 1791; practically, when Wesley began ordaining bishops on his own in 1784, the two groups parted company.

22. The decline in standards of public taste from the mid-eighteenth to the mid-nineteenth century was precipitous; most of it resulted from the replacement of hand craftsmanship by steam-powered mass production. Furniture with machine-sawed joints had to be covered with overstuffed upholstery to conceal the crude workmanship; houses made from pattern books had to be covered with jigsaw gingerbread to conceal the poverty of the design. Sir George Young has said incisively that a future archaeologist lighting on two sites, one an eighteenth-century room, the other an interior of about 1840, could only infer a social catastrophe, the conquest and destruction of a higher social order by a lower one.

chairs, tables, and escritoires, which are to the craft of cabinetry what Stradivarius violins are in the world of fiddle making. Through the sale of a book of their designs, the Chippendale influence spread far beyond England; the founding fathers of America sat on chairs of Chippendale design, at least when they went into the very best society. The next generation would have the pleasure of using furniture designed by George Hepplewhite or Thomas Sheraton, less ornate than Chippendale's work, but equally slender and graceful. Luxury begot luxury; as the drinking of tea became common, the arts of silversmithing and porcelain manufacture became more refined. If people did not drink more than they used to, at least they became more attentive to what they were drinking. Claret and burgundy, as well as brandy, were imported from France, port and sherry from Portugal and Spain. Gentlemen became known, from their capacity to carry quantities of port, as two-bottle or three-bottle men. Fine ladies dressed in silken or velvet gowns touched with lace; they wore expensive synthetic perfumes, and puffed up their hair, in imitation of French fashions, into structures as intricate as castles. Gentlemen wore long, powdered wigs, and trimmed their coats with gold braid. Plain rural squires, who considered themselves blunt country folk, gorged on roast beef and drank themselves into a stupefied slumber after dinner. We get a glimpse of this rowdy, sensual world through the paintings and drawings of William Hogarth, whose pictures, done in series, often have a storytelling quality that allies them with the fiction of the age. The downward progress of the rake and the harlot, the contrast between an idle apprentice and an industrious one, are tales told in pictures every last detail of which contributes to the story or points the moral. Throughout, the art of Hogarth is an art of excess; his gift for zesty caricature and linear overstatement aligns him with his friend Fielding. What he saw in Georgian England is confirmed by other witnesses: it was a polite and rational elite standing on a boisterous, brutal foundation. Thomas Gainsborough and Sir Joshua Reynolds, painters very different from one another but alike in their skill at portraying fine ladies and dignified gentlemen, contrast with Hogarth's sordid images of *Gin Lane* and the last stages of *The Harlot's Progress*. Strolling the public streets, you would be as likely to encounter a bully with a cudgel as a fop in a silken suit; stepping outside from a club of congenial philosophers, you might encounter a press gang. Whether that haughty, elegant fellow was a fine gentleman or a gentleman of the road might be as hard to know as whether that patched, beribboned, and bescented creature was Lord Randall's miss or the duchess of Hautwater.

Here and there in the often rude squirearchy we find men of urbane tastes and intellectual interests. The society of Dilettanti, founded in 1733, assembled some of these amateurs and connoisseurs in a community more serious than its name implies; from time to time they sent forth expeditions to such ancient sites as Rome, Athens, and Palmyra, to record surviving monuments of the antique world. While Lancelot ("Capability") Brown invented a hundred touches of "natural" landscaping to accent the parkland groves and wooded vistas surrounding country estates, the earl of Burlington championed a Palladian (i.e., neoclassical) building style for the rural seats themselves. With the great empires and cosmopolitan cultures of the past, eighteenth-century oligarchs felt an instinctive sympathy; they were all enlightened together, and to make contact with other urbane aristocracies reinforced one's own sense of belonging. Naturally, only a few could belong. Just outside the park gates, in the open country, one would doubtless find a "bold, artful, surly, savage race"; and in the slums of borough and city, something a good deal worse—a dull, sodden, despairing, and misshapen race. But as reason taught one the existence of these unfortunates was part of the social plan, so it enabled one to forget without inconvenience their necessary and permanent misery. Snug materially and philosophically, your eighteenth-century fine gentleman might well look on the cosmos with a benign and complacent eye.[23]

23. Neatening up historical anomalies was an essential part of the eighteenth-century rationalism; one important change was made, about mid-century, in the calendar. Though in the calendar established by Julius Caesar, the new year had always begun on January 1, in the latter part of the twelfth century a calendar became standard which began the new year on the feast of the Annunciation, March 25. This calendar, known to us nowadays as Old Style, prevailed throughout Europe till 1582, when Pope Gregory XIII promulgated the Gregorian calendar, which once again started the new year on January 1. But England, being by now Protestant, refused to accept the pope's change, and so clung to the Old Style calendar till 1752. To bring the two calendars in line, the English started 1752 on the first of January and dropped eleven days between the second and the fourteenth of September. That straightened things out; but for the years when the Old Style prevailed (from the thirteenth halfway through the eighteenth centuries), modern historians write dates in the form "February 14, 1693 / 4"—that is, 1693 according to the Old Style, 1694 by the New. For Englishmen of 1693, the year didn't end till March 24; by our style of counting, it was over on the thirty-first of December.

For a man who protested against painting society portraits (he said he preferred landscapes),
Thomas Gainsborough was extraordinarily talented at it. His portrait of Mrs. Graham (1775) shows
this queenly young woman in all her finery, poised between classical columns on the right and the
deeper shades of a sunset forest on the left. The shimmering satins of her overskirt and the languid
flutter of her ostrich plumes contrast with the disdainful averted glance of a conscious "beauty."
Unlike most of his contemporaries, Gainsborough did not leave the draperies in his portraits to
an assistant; he painted the whole picture himself, and the effect he produced is proof of the pains
he took.

Since its founding in the thirteenth century, there is no period of English history when Oxford university has not been a-building. The result is a conglomeration of many styles, but the golden-brown limestone used for most of the buildings binds them effectively together. Unfortunately this stone does not weather well, especially under the corrosive effects of a modern industrial atmosphere, and many of the famous spires and towers now require repair or replacement. Among Oxford's most striking structures, the Sheldonian theater, the Radcliffe Camera, and the great Tom Tower of Christ Church gate are of the seventeenth and eighteenth centuries.

Blenheim Palace, the monumental structure that Sir John Vanbrugh erected near Oxford for the duke of Marlborough, took seventeen years to build, and inspired much malicious comment on its grandiose and weighty appearance. Originally it stood in the midst of a spacious formal garden, geometrical in its patterning, with neat hedges, clipped strees, shaven lawns, and gravel walks. But at the end of the eighteenth century, tastes changed, and Blenheim was relandscaped in the "natural" style of a park, with glades, groves, alleys, and a little lake. Then at the beginning of the twentieth century, tastes changed again, and now Blenheim is as formal and patterned as it was originally. Just as enormous, too.

The INDUSTRIOUS 'PRENTICE Lord-Mayor of London.

Proverbs CHAP: III Ver: 16.
*Length of days is in her right hand, and
in her left hand Riches and Honour.*

Much of Hogarth's popularity stemmed from his skill at pointing a moral and adorning a tale. The contrast of the Idle with the Industrious Prentice originates in an Elizabethan play *Eastward Ho*, on which Chapman, Jonson, and Marston collaborated. Every detail in this series of twelve plates contributes to the point. Bad Thomas Idle drinks, yawns at his work, and reads *Moll Flanders;* fired from his job, he is shanghaied onto a ship, returns to become a highwayman, takes up with a

The IDLE 'PRENTICE Executed at Tyburn.

trull, is betrayed by an informer, and hanged at Tyburn. His much less interesting counterpart Goodchild works hard at his trade, reads improving pamphlets, marries the boss's daughter, is created sheriff in time to sentence his old mate Idle, and finally rises to lord mayor just as his wretched counterpart is dragged off to the gallows.

Wedgwood pottery of classic design, like this example, was frankly intended for decorative, not practical, uses. Though it looks much bigger, the vase is only 7¾ inches high; its value is out of all proportion to its size. Wolf Mankowitz has written a snappy little story (*Make Me an Offer* [New York, 1953]) about the mania driving collectors of fine Wedgwood, and the wily intrigues to which they resort.

Though Andrea Palladio lived and worked in Italy during the sixteenth century, his most enduring influence was felt in England and America during the eighteenth. The spacious neoclassical villa called "Capra" or "La Rotunda" outside Vicenza was the model, not only for the earl of Burlington's Chiswick House (shown here, built in 1725), but for Thomas Jefferson's hilltop home in Charlottesville, Virginia, known as Monticello. (Jefferson even wanted to model the White House on the same pattern but was dissuaded.) While it was originally built in the country, Chiswick House and its spacious grounds have since been surrounded by London suburbs; it still houses part of Lord Burlington's rich art collection. Palladio's cool, proportioned, dignified style was exactly suited to appeal to a class of cosmopolitan and leisured gentry. Correct but not grandiose, a Palladian villa made manifest the owner's status while opening before him the park of his estate and the fields of his tenants.

12

The First Pitt and the Wars of Empire (1748–1789)

William Pitt was a new type in English politics, and as such had a hard time forcing his way into positions of power. His family was wealthy enough to get him into the House of Commons easily; but, once there, he had to impose his cold, forbidding character and his strident international views by sheer force of personality. Pitt's grandfather, Thomas "Diamond" Pitt, had been an employee of the East India Company, and in that capacity governor of Madras in India. Somehow or other early in the eighteenth century he acquired an enormous diamond, which he sold to the duke of Orléans, then regent of Louis XV, at a markup of more than £100,000. (Even after cutting, Pitt's diamond weighed more than 136 carats; it is still to be seen in the Louvre, a blazing vision.) With that sum in pocket, "Diamond" Pitt returned to England and bought himself an estate in Cornwall along with a seat in the House of Commons.[1] William Pitt, second grandson of "Diamond" Pitt, was the only one of the family whom the old man liked. The boy was not strong, suffering even as a child from gout,

1. When people talked about "rotten boroughs," Old Sarum, for which Pitt sat, was the stock example. It was the land where Salisbury once stood. After the town was moved in the thirteenth century, and its last ruins were demolished in the seventeenth century, the four or five farmers who still grazed sheep on the open fields still sent representatives to Parliament, as if there was still somebody there to represent. There was: it was Thomas Pitt, the Cornwall plutocrat.

which was to torture him all his life; he was also of a moody temper, given to bursts of wild enthusiasm and deep depression, which with the years became more extreme.

PITT OUT OF OFFICE AND IN

His father and grandfather having died within a year of one another (1726, 1727), Pitt as a younger son decided on a career in the army, and bought a commission in the dragoons; but within a few years a seat at Old Sarum fell vacant, and he entered Parliament (1735). Here he discovered a talent for oratory which made him both feared and admired. Not that he was ever well liked by anybody. He was a proud, formal man with a single overwhelming idea, the two faces of which were ambition for England's commercial empire, and hatred of France which stood in the way of it. Accordingly, he became a "patriot." Walpole's compromises were odious to him, and his attacks on them became so fierce that the government took the special step of having him dismissed from the army. But there was no silencing Pitt; he continued to thunder against the subordination of English interests to those of Hanover (wounding deeply, in the process, the sensibilities of George II). He also denounced Walpole as a public malefactor and double-dyed criminal. As often occurs with the moral indignation of politicians, Pitt's cries against the rascal in power were largely recommendations of himself, and he took pains to build his own popularity. But Pitt once in office proved a very different man from Pitt out of office. Having got a place, he set about placating the ruffled feelings of George II and making himself indispensable by carrying out policies he had previously denounced. He also did a good deal of lying low.

The "stupid" peace of Aix-la-Chapelle in 1748 provided a respite for both England and France to build up their resources and rearrange their alliances in preparation for the climactic Seven Years' War (1756–1763). In this period of partial peace and military retrenchment, Pitt remained obscure; by nature he was an extreme man, not at his best in peacetime. In fact his hard temper led him to oppose a major reversal of English foreign policy which would in future have immense beneficial consequences. On the Continent, England's traditional allies against France had long been Holland and Austria; but a series of complex negotiations (which Pitt opposed) led England in 1756 into an alliance with Prussia, led by their new king Friedrich, not yet, but soon to be nicknamed "Frederick the Great." Against Prussia and England were now united Austria, France, Sweden, Russia, and perhaps Spain. When war began, there was every reason to feel that England's position had deteriorated; for Prussia, a small nation, until recently quite unproven in arms, stood practically alone against the entire remainder of the Continent. But Friedrich's armies were tough, well trained, and fanatically loyal; the king himself was one of the great strategic commanders of history.

While Friedrich fought the land battles, year after year, with sickening casualty lists, England sent subsidies and supplies to help the Prussians, but devoted her primary energies to fighting a naval and colonial, that is, a commercial war. For this decision and its execution William Pitt was largely responsible. On strategic grounds, there was much to be said for it. England did not have the army to fight a major land war, and by blockading the French her navy could radically reduce their power. And from an economic point of view, the decision was shrewd indeed. The land war beggared most of the participants, and drained their best manpower; though ostensibly victorious, Friedrich had to rebuild his nation practically from scratch. Meanwhile England's naval and colonial efforts established the British Empire.

With the duke of Newcastle, a fussy, detail-minded man, heading the government, the war began badly; before the year 1756 was out, a series of naval disasters in the Mediterranean made imperative new leadership in London. George's deep mistrust of Pitt had to be overcome, but he had no one else to turn to, and Pitt assumed strategic command of a global war, as he had wanted to do all along. He was not shy about asserting his merit: "I am sure I can save the country, and nobody else can," he said simply. The only excuse for such arrogance is being right; Pitt was right. He was a born war leader, and allowed no foolish consistency to distract him from the task. He had spoken harshly about Friedrich and the Hanoverian electorate; now he sent timely aid to the first, and repudiated the shameful treaty of Kloster-Seven which had effectually surrendered the second. After flowing strongly against England and Prussia in 1756 and early 1757, the tide of the war started to turn. Friedrich's battle-scarred veterans defeated a French and Austrian force at Rossbach, another Austrian army at Leuthen, and the Russians at Zorndorf. Meanwhile in America (where the war was known as the French and Indian War), an initial defeat at Fort Duquesne (Pittsburgh), where General Braddock led his army into deadly ambush, was avenged by a series of campaigns which pushed north from New York toward Canada and west through Pennsylvania toward the Ohio valley. Traveling slowly from India came news that heroic Robert Clive, with a vastly inferior force, had routed at Plassey the nawab of Bengal with his French allies. Thereby vast amounts of booty and the whole district around Calcutta fell into British hands. There were lesser victories in the West Indies and along the coast of Africa, and no pronounced defeats anywhere; it was a good year for the war.

But 1759 capped the climax; from every corner of the globe came fresh news of England's successful arms; all year long, the cathedral bells were kept ringing to celebrate new triumphs. In North America, Lord Amherst captured the important base of Louisburg on the tip of Cape Breton island, from which in the autumn of the year General Wolfe was able to push up the St. Lawrence and in a heroic assault, fatal to himself, his opponent Montcalm, and also to French power in Canada, capture the city of Quebec. In India, successive defeats at sea isolated the chief French trading post at Pondicherry (it was left hanging on the vine, and dropped off a few years later), while the nearby English post of Madras was liberated from French siege. The French had hoped, while the English fleet was thus dispersed around the globe, to invade the island directly; but a combination of massive blows—at Le Havre in July, at the Mediterranean fleet in August, at Quiberon Bay on south Brittany in November—put an end to that plan. For the rest of the war, the French fleet never ventured to sea again.

It was a season of fabulous triumphs around the globe, and Pitt got the lion's share of the credit. Unquestionably, he was a good commander in chief, with the qualities of wide vision and quick decision needed for the job; he was also lucky to have outstanding subordinates, like Clive in India, Sir Edward Hawke and Lord George Anson in the navy. Personally, however, most people found Pitt to be pompous, vain, and aloof, even if awe-inspiring. He could be mean and vindictive as well as heroic, and he was always temperamental. One consequence of his policies could not be ignored: he was a prodigious spender. Continents and subcontinents were the prizes for which he played; but £13,000,000 was the price for the victories of 1759, more than £15,000,000 had to be found for the following year, and nearly £20,000,000 for 1761. That was five times the prewar budget. A movement for peace and economy was just starting to be felt in England when suddenly, in October 1760, George II died. The event was important because George III, who immediately succeeded, loathed the war and hated Pitt.

A NEW KING, A DIFFERENT ENGLAND

George II was seventy-seven when he died; his grandson, George III, was just twenty-two when he succeeded. Frederick, prince of Wales and father of the new king, had himself eagerly anticipated succeeding to the throne; but in 1751, he caught a cold which became pleurisy and killed him. Frederick's moral character, his political behavior, and for that matter the legitimacy of his birth were much maligned at the time, not least by his loving parents: Sir George Young, most allusive and informed of recent commentators, has tried to make out that he was a good sort, though of a rather bad lot.[2] In any case, when George II died nine years later, it was Frederick's eldest son who became king as George III. A well-educated, idealistic young man, he enjoyed the advantage of speaking English as a first language. But he also suffered from the conviction, amounting almost to obsession, that his grandfather had been dominated by politicians who used him for their own ends. George III was determined to be his own man; he therefore appointed as secretary of state his own Scottish tutor, John Stuart, third

2. The best evidence of Frederick's popularity is the street song from which Sir George takes his title, *Poor Fred*. After pointing out, not uncheerfully, that poor Fred is dead and there's nothing more to be said, the song proceeds with considerable relish to list all the rest of the royal family, whom the singers would *rather* see dead.

earl of Bute, who had been a close friend of the late Frederick. To be sure, the king and his new minister could not immediately break off Pitt's war; indeed, when Spain entered the conflict in support of France, it was somewhat prolonged. But in debates over Spain's last-minute belligerency and over the terms of peace, Pitt took such a high hand that he was finally forced to resign in October 1761. Bute proceeded to make peace with France on the best terms he could get, and they were good indeed, for England's position was strong. When, after much wrangling, the treaty was signed in February 1763, it represented a decisive victory for the interests of England. In terms of territory won and lost, the peace terms decreed significant moves everywhere but in Europe. France lost heavily in India and America; England gained correspondingly. But hidden shifts of power were even more important than real-estate transactions. France was so impoverished internally, so curtailed in her trade and foreign expansion, that the Seven Years' War, in conjunction with the American Revolution to which it led, may fairly be ranked among the latent causes of the French Revolution which broke out a quarter century later. England, which had spent so much money on the defense of the American colonies, now had to ask that they contribute to their own security. Hence the Stamp Act, various excise taxes, and constraints on future expansions, which led toward the American Revolution of 1776. Particularly deep-seated and long-range in their impact were the major changes, amounting cumulatively to a revolution, that war imposed on the industrial and transport machinery of England.

Most apparent were changes in transport. After 1,500 years of neglect, English roads were indescribably bad. Huge boulders and bottomless sloughs of mud were only the obvious obstacles; many roads had worn deep tracks in the dirt, with steep, hedge-crowned banks on either side. Two coaches meeting in such a bottleneck could not pass; sometimes not even two packhorses could get by. The road was no more than a miry trail; and, being below the level of the surrounding land, it converted in a rainstorm to an instant drainage ditch. Slowness in mobilizing armies to meet the Scottish threat of '45 advertised the need for road building, and a major program, which lasted through the rest of the century, got under way about 1760.[3] Simultaneously, though only coincidentally, began an even more valuable program of canal building. James Brindley, self-taught mechanic and engineer, built the first canal, which cut the cost of coal in Manchester by half, and made a fortune for his employer the duke of Bridgewater; this was but one in a chain of linked enterprises, which spread rapidly through

___

3. "Blind Jack of Knaresborough" (John Metcalf) was one of the most remarkable figures in this program. Working alone, and using a calculating system of his own that he could never explain, he laid out and supervised the building of a network of turnpikes in his native Yorkshire. He was also a soldier (in '45) and an itinerant horse dealer; he rode to hounds, dealt in timber and hay, smuggled, played at cards, took tremendous cross-country hikes, and lived to the age of ninety-three, leaving behind him direct descendants almost to that number. From the age of six he had been stone blind (SFR, F.16).

the midlands. There the headwaters of the Trent, the Severn, the Dee, the Aire, and the Mersey converge; by connecting their upper ends, deepening their channels, and constructing new waterways, engineers could create corridors of slow but cheap transport for the heavy goods just now becoming supremely important.[4] Coal mines were linked with deposits of iron ore, corn growers gained easier access to shippers, factories got better sources of supply as well as handier markets. Better roads made conventional travel quicker; canals made heavy goods move in quantity to places which had never before been physically or commercially feasible.

Statistics for late eighteenth-century industry are unreliable and hard to interpret. The "industrial revolution" did not take place at any one time or spot; nobody saw it happening. It was the culmination of slow, diffused forces long at work in the fabric of society. But a revolution it was, perhaps the richest in consequences, immediate and remote, of any revolution in human history. At its heart was the Lancashire cotton industry. In America and India, Great Britain now held the two greatest sources of raw cotton in the world; neither colony had, or was allowed to have, any machinery for processing the fiber. That machinery England invented, kept, and improved. The flying shuttle had been invented by John Kay in 1733; it made possible the weaving of cloth wider than the stretch of the operative's arms. The spinning jenny invented by Hargreaves in 1766 allowed a single worker to spin as many as sixteen threads at once; Arkwright improved it in 1768, and Cartwright's power loom before long enabled weavers to keep up with spinners. The result was a flood of cheap cotton textiles for foreign as well as domestic markets; and the climactic changes came late in the century, with the application of steam power (which, in terms of the energy-source, was really coal power) to all these machines. That meant moving most of the work from cottages to factories, where new and largely disagreeable forms of industrial discipline were called for. But in terms of growing production, the consequences were spectacular; over the last half of the century, England's exports of finished cottons multiplied fiftyfold.

The other industrial complex that fueled the industrial revolution was the iron-steel-coal combination.[5] Basic to the whole technical development was the discovery by Abraham Darby, early in the eighteenth century, of a way to make cast iron by melting the ore with coke made from coal; the novelty lay in minimizing the effect of coal sulphur, which previously had made the iron too brittle. Thereafter new inventions came thick and fast. Payn and Hanbury developed a

---

4. A fully laden packhorse can carry, at best, about 300 pounds; the same animal, set on a towpath and harnessed to a barge, can move up to fifty tons along a canal. The efficiency differential is better than 1 to 300.

5. In this field English industry enjoyed two special advantages. By a legal ruling of 1568, minerals found on a property (gold and silver excepted) belonged to the landowner; squires were therefore eager to discover coal and iron. Also the human energies of the lower middle classes, nonconformists particularly, turned naturally to commerce and industry.

method of rolling iron into thin sheets, Huntsman invented (about 1750) the crucible process of making steel, and in 1784 Henry Cort devised the reverberatory puddling furnace, which solved for good the problem of coal sulphur. Not only did production of iron multiply twelvefold during the eighteenth century; new techniques for making it coincided with new uses for the material and new means for working it to close tolerances. Fractions of a millimeter are no trifling matter in wartime, since weapons of greater range and accuracy enable one side to shoot at the other without being shot at themselves. In addition, iron machinery of increasing precision and complexity was at the heart of the explosive cotton industry. Under pressure of this drive toward mass production and standardization, England's exports doubled and redoubled; the demands of a war economy could not help spurring the process forward, regardless of social consequences. Horace Walpole in 1760 thought Sheffield "one of the foulest towns in England"; by the end of the century, Robert Southey could suggest many rivals for the honor (SFR, G.15). Population and pollution advanced hand in hand; poverty for the many and prosperity for the few seemed just as inexorably linked.

Less easy to explain is the spurt in population. After rising gradually but steadily over the centuries (for the half century 1700–1750, the increase was about 20 percent), the population shot up by nearly 50 percent in the next fifty years from 1750–1801.[6] This was a vast increase, more impressive in actual numbers than in percentage figures. From fewer than 6,500,000 souls in 1750, England and Wales rose to nearly 9,000,000 in 1801. Yet the first of the public-health measures which might have explained this mighty surge dates from the last years of the eighteenth century. Jenner started work on his program of smallpox vaccination in 1798; and the whole discipline of bacteriology remained unknown till the middle of the nineteenth century. Indeed, whatever was known theoretically about disease in the eighteenth century stood little chance of being applied to the pullulating populations of factory towns. England's population grew amid filth and squalor, it grew at a spectacular rate and in spite of deprivations appalling to contemplate. Why it did so remains a question for philosophers.[7] In any case,

6. Whether the root cause was a rise in the birth rate or a decline in the death rate nobody has yet proved. Though cholera remained a threat, epidemics of plague diminished; perhaps this was because the black rat, a city dweller with a population of vagrant fleas, was supplanted by the brown field rat, with a population of fleas that stay close to the rat's nest. The germs of plague are, of course, spread by fleas living on rats; but many factors besides plague entered into the death rate. All population figures prior to the first English census of 1801 are rough approximations, based on parish records and other fragmentary materials.

7. Increase of population prompted an Anglican cleric, Thomas Malthus, to publish in 1798 the first edition of his *Essay on the Principle of Population:* the last version he revised appeared in 1816, nearly twenty years later. Malthus argued that population naturally increases faster than the food available to feed it; hence vice, war, and misery (to which in later editions of the *Essay* he added "moral restraint") are really advantageous, as they prevent overpopulation and starvation. The book became celebrated because prosperous readers thought it showed the ill consequences of spending money to improve the lot of the poor. Malthus was neither a moral monster nor particularly original,

the worst social consequences were not to appear for several more decades; we note here merely the beginning, awesome enough in truth, of a long, dark process (SFR, F.14, 15).

AN AGE OF RAGE: WILKES AND THE MINISTRY

After peace papers were signed at Fontainebleau early in 1763, George III and his favorite, Lord Bute, now secretary of the treasury, might have anticipated a period of relatively smooth sailing. But it was not to be. Several years earlier, Bute had trod on the toes of the most reckless, vitriolic politician of his day, an MP named John Wilkes. Wilkes was a tough, bawdy fellow with a squint, a leer, and a gift of gab; he never took himself too seriously, but he had many friends among the radical Whigs of the City, and he knew how to play the London mob. He went after Bute, who as a Scotsman was odious to Londoners, in a paper ominously titled *The North Briton;* and he flayed his man with the most cruel and exquisite ingenuity known to an age skilled in political torture. Wilkes savaged Bute for some real things that he had done, and just as much for being Scottish, which was a handy stick to beat him with; and before the ink was fairly dry on the peace settlement, he had driven the wretched man from office. In his official capacity Bute was replaced by George Grenville, known to that point chiefly as Pitt's brother-in-law; but as a personal friend, the departed minister retained ready access to the king. This made for much jealousy; Grenville suspected secret influence and grew positively unbalanced on the subject of Bute. So the world was treated to the unedifying spectacle of Bute conferring with the king while the prime minister waited outside, then scuttling down the back stairs as the minister advanced through the front door.

One cannot properly use the word "Tory" to describe Bute or "Whig" to describe Grenville, who, though very conservative, was probably of that ilk. Neither was really a party man; that was why George selected them. Convinced that his grandfather had been victimized by parties, he tried hard to pick counselors without strong party ties—Tories because the party was generally in disarray, or Whigs of several different factions and few dogmatic convictions. The trouble was that such counselors tended to be men without political strength or ability. Apart from being (very often) obtuse personally, George's advisers rarely enjoyed the confidence of the House of Commons; and Pitt, who had that confidence, refused to lend his name to any government, except, perhaps, one of his own making. For a long time, George would have none of that. So at a crucial period of its history, the nation wandered and wavered.

Meanwhile Wilkes, who had briefly fallen silent at the resignation of Bute,

---

and his central thesis, as stated, took inadequate account of technical improvements in food production and birth control; but his book was yet another stimulus to the thought of Charles Darwin (below, p. 418).

came out with one more issue of *The North Briton,* the famous No. 45 of 23 April 1763, which attacked Bute, Grenville, and in effect the king himself. This broadside was not the action of a single individual; Wilkes had constituted himself spokesman for a group of truculent left-wing Whigs who were radically discontented with the flow of things under George III. They were persistent men with forceful views, and they did not play by the old political rules; they appealed instead to public opinion, which they sometimes inflamed before appealing to it. The Grenville government felt it had to silence "that devil Wilkes" (it was George III's phrase), and so proceeded against *North Briton* No. 45 as a seditious libel.[8] Wilkes fought off the charges for a while; but then he pressed his luck too far by reprinting, not only No. 45, but an obscene parody on Pope by a friend of his. The "Essay on Woman" was bad enough in itself; it was also fitted out with notes purporting to be by the bishop of Gloucester. This was going too far. Early in 1764 the government got Wilkes expelled from the Commons, retried him on the old libel and new obscenity charges, and got a conviction. Rather than go to jail, where he would likely have died from a wound recently received in a duel, Wilkes fled to France. With the help of an allowance from his whiggish friends in London, he remained there, a declared outlaw, for the next five years or so. He did not leave without a flick of his caustic wit. When a London lady one evening invited him to take part in a game of whist, he declined, saying, "Dear madam, do not ask me. I am so ignorant that I cannot tell a king from a knave."[9]

THE AMERICAN PROBLEM: WAR CLOUDS AND A STORM

But an impudent gadfly like Wilkes always comes back; and when he returned, in 1768, the American question was much inflamed; his case was thus complicated by the fact that he and his fellow radicals supported the American cause, and were supported in turn by American opinion. Wilkes began his new campaign by getting most of his old sentence annulled, then ran for Parliament again.

---

8. "Sedition" came in because No. 45 attacked one of George's speeches in Parliament, and so was alleged to violate the treason statutes. Wilkes declared in defense that such speeches, as everybody now knew (see above, p. 295), were written by the ministers, and to attack them was not to attack royalty itself.

9. This period of Wilkesite agitation is one of the uglier ages of literary involvement in English politics. Among Wilkes's allies was a rough and reckless satiric poet named Charles Churchill, who began by attacking the English stage, went on to assail William Hogarth, and ended his brief career the declared enemy of practically everybody. The same surly character appears in an anonymous writer calling himself "Junius," who between 1769 and 1772 published a savage set of political letters aimed at destroying the ministry of the duke of Grafton. Who "Junius" really was remained, for long, a mystery; it's now supposed he was Sir Philip Francis. In any case, over the two or three years of his activity, "Junius" showed himself a master of invective, abuse, and slanderous innuendo. There is something very reptilian about this writer (SFR, F.19).

No sooner was he elected than the government had him expelled. He ran again, was again elected, and again expelled. Within a month the process was repeated. Finally, after a fourth Wilkes victory, the government declared that all votes cast for him were void, and accordingly his opponent (who had received only a handful) was elected. This made a mockery of the election process, and a storm of indignation broke all across the country. The simple numbers "45" were chalked on every wall, and everywhere the cry of "Wilkes and liberty" was heard. What people meant by it was clear in the way slogans usually are, broadly. The issues were freedom of speech and freedom of choice in elections. These were old battles, many times fought and many times won in the past. What gave sharpness to the Wilkes agitation was that it cast George III and his government as enemies of liberty in England at a time when they were being fiercely assailed as enemies of liberty in America.

Whether George III was really an enemy of freedom anywhere is a still unsettled question. Certainly in Bute and Grenville he chose, to advise him, two of the least imaginative, least liberal-minded men in his realm. But his program for dividing the Whig oligarchy and ruling without the constrictions of party and patronage was not illiberal in itself. Within the horizon of his political vision, he tried a variety of governments; under less trying circumstances, one or other of them might have held together long enough to accomplish something. What made the situation desperate if not hopeless was a number of conjoined and conflicting inheritances from the past. For one thing, a strain of thought stemming from the civil wars and commonwealth of seventeenth-century England lingered in the country and animated the colonists; it proclaimed the right of all Englishmen to have a say through their representatives in making the laws and imposing the taxes to which they would be subject. But this liberal, semidemocratic tradition came into direct conflict with the economic philosophy of mercantilism by which the relation of mother country to colonies had long been governed. Mercantilist thought assumed as a matter of course that the mother country was to make all economic decisions for and about the colonies, and in her own interest. Thus, the Americans might make pig iron for use by British manufacturers, but not finished ironware. Newfoundland was not to be settled at all, ever; its function would be to serve as a resupply and relief station for fishing vessels on the Grand Banks. Such decisions, governmental in show but really dictated by English commercial interests, hung like a dark cloud over all the colonists. Yet though theory had been ominous, practice was generally weak. The English government which claimed a right of absolute decision over the colonies had historically made few decisions of any sort, leaving the colonies to grow, diversified and wild, pretty much as they would. After years of what one could call either freedom or neglect, both tempered by vague threats, the Americans had become a truculent and quarrelsome breed.

The recent Seven Years' War, successful though it was, exacerbated relations between the English and their American colonies. British strategy had depended heavily on blockading French trade, and Americans had not only dealt with blockade-runners, they had not scrupled to run the blockade themselves. After the war, English landowners who for years had been heavily taxed—in good part, as they saw it, for defense of the colonies—tried to shift the burden. As a first step, they tried to revive a long-dormant tax on imports of molasses and sugar from the West Indies, largely for the making of rum. In 1763, Grenville's government cut the tax rate in half but proposed actually to collect duty. Yankee seafarers, who combined the parsimony of country storekeepers with the brutality of slave traders and a dash of the piratical spirit, naturally protested and did their best to evade the levy.

Just as important was the issue of westward expansion. An obvious occasion of future conflict was the country west of the Alleghenies, where place names like Detroit, Des Moines, and Eau Claire still remain in evidence that the French settled here first. Since recent experience indicated that the British would have to fight any future wars, and pay for them, they tried to forestall such trouble by drawing a line beyond which American expansion was not to pass. This Proclamation Line was announced in 1763; it ran along the ridges of the Alleghenies, and served a second purpose in tightening England's monopoly of colonial trade. Clearly, if there were no western or southern limit to America, England would have a much harder time policing the trade of her bumptious, burgeoning possession. But the Proclamation Line infuriated frontiersmen, as the Sugar Tax enraged merchant seamen.

Taxing the colonies, limiting their industries, and controlling their expansion led by a process too familiar to be described to American protests, complaints, remonstrances, and demonstrations. The British responded with acts of repression and reprisal. The first shots of the War of American Independence were fired at Lexington, Massachusetts (April 1775); the Continental Congress declared the independence of the colonies (2 July 1776); the war which followed, though to all intents it ended with the surrender of Lord Cornwallis at Yorktown (October 1781), was not officially terminated till the signing of the treaty of Paris (September 1783).

Into the details of this intricate, wide-ranging, yet often desultory war, space forbids our entering. For England, the struggle was never all-absorbing. Only a fraction of the navy was ever sent to the American theater, mostly second-line troops and commanders were employed, and the war was often prosecuted halfheartedly. Some idealists wanted the Americans to win because their cause seemed just, cynics doubted the colonies would ever repay the cost of holding them. The struggle took place at a great distance, it was diffused across a vast continent; news reports were belated and uncertain. Indeed, the British could and did occupy major cities up and down the coast: Boston, New York, Philadelphia, Charleston. But as long as General Washington could maintain an army in the field, the American cause was not lost. A turning point took place when General Burgoyne with a little army of 3,500 troops was cut off and forced to surrender at Saratoga (October 1777). Word of this event enabled the American envoy to France, Ben Franklin, to bring France in on the American side, at first only with moral support, but then with trained soldiers, an invaluable naval force, and the inspiring presence of the Marquis de Lafayette. A year after France, Spain joined in, and a new alliance of the Baltic countries threatened to take part as well. Few of these welcome allies were motivated by enthusiasm for American liberty, so much as by hatred of England; but England could not hope to stand against them all, and the ministry of Lord North, without explicitly conceding defeat, began looking for a way out.[10]

As the war of attrition ground slowly to an end, its last days were marked by an outburst of rage and violence on the part of the London mob for which no single explanation will properly account. The spark that set off the explosion was an act of 1778 to give Roman Catholics limited relief from the strict but no longer enforced laws against them. It was a small step, and not unenlightened. But it set off protests in Scotland, traditionally anti-Catholic, and they spread among the London poor, for whom foreigners, Catholics, and the wealthy were all, equally and just about interchangeably, objects of hostility and resentment. Roused by a hysteric named Lord George Gordon, the mob quickly got out of hand (June 1780). They burned down Catholic chapels and looted the houses of well-known Catholics; then Newgate Prison and the Bank of England were assaulted. Distilleries drew the mob next, where some rioters died of choking down unlimited alcohol, and others, befuddled, could not escape the burning buildings. During the week that the mob ran wild, hundreds of mostly inoffensive people were kicked or hacked or burned to death. Finally, troops were brought in to restore a minimum of order. The Gordon riots (which were brilliantly described by Dickens, long after the event, in *Barnaby Rudge*) had no coherent rationale or purpose; they were mainly an outburst of working-class rage and frustration at "the system." Like the far milder Peasant Revolt of 1381 (above, p. 68), the Gordon riots were less significant in themselves than for what they revealed about the state of the popular mind. It was not by any means a reassuring revelation, least of all to men like Wilkes, who had thought themselves "radicals." *That* radical they were not prepared to be.

CRISIS IN THE EAST

While the American colonies were breaking free in the west, Britain was also faced by painful dilemmas in her relations with the east. The "conquest" of

---

10. Pressure of space and familiarity of the material have led this book to a deliberate scanting of the American struggle for independence. Among the many books on the subject, the student is referred for further details to J. C. Miller, *The Origins of the American Revolution* (Palo Alto, 1943); E. Robson, *The American Revolution* (London, 1955); and P. Mackesy, *The War for America 1775–1783* (London, 1964).

India had never been planned out in London; officially, indeed, the British government was not in India at all. For almost two hundred years the East India Company had been sending out agents to organize trading operations, while operating in government matters behind a screen of native puppet rulers. Of these there was no lack; but behind the many sultans, rajahs, wazirs, and nawabs, the controlling force in the land was the company's chief agent. During the later eighteenth century the post was held by Robert Clive and his successor Warren Hastings. Both started their careers in India as "writers," that is, clerks in charge of trading posts or factories employing native workers; both learned the complex art of surviving in India by imitating a wonderfully dexterous French predecessor, Joseph Dupleix. Both were victims, and in some measure beneficiaries, of a system which practically required company agents to plunder the natives and native governments. Clive discovered early in his career that he was essentially a soldier; Hastings was always an administrator. Both fell victim to essentially the same problem as plagued British agents in America: the home office was eager to receive profits from the colonies, but took no interest in the way they were made, till trouble blew up. Then the only demand was for scapegoats. Both Clive and Hastings were held responsible for the faults of a system they had both tried to reform; their fiercest accusers were men who had themselves been profiting by the unreformed system.

Like America, India was immense, unhealthy, and highly profitable. Most of the bold young Englishmen who went out in those early days did not come back; those who did return came back rich, to be known among their envious neighbors as "nabobs."[11] The perils of the land were quite as great as its riches. India was a welter of competing creeds, conflicting empires, enormous wealth, and immemorial, grinding poverty. Without warning, vast armies could rise up and sweep across the countryside; they might consist (one could never be sure) of furious fanatics who would fight to the last man, or of bewildered peasants who would run like sheep. Sanitary conditions were everywhere frightful; famines and epidemic diseases carried off the population by millions, and with them all but the hardiest or luckiest Europeans. Survival was a gamble against heavy odds.

All the company's agents in India were paid very little, and expected to make their main income by trading on their own; so long as the company's main business was actual trading, this led to scandalous maltreatment of the natives, but nothing really to disturb British complacency. But the Seven Years' War roused Dupleix to attempt the establishment of French hegemony over the subcontinent; and the English, who had discovered in Clive a military genius where they thought they had only a clerk, were bound to respond. As a result of his audacious victories (Arcot, 1751; Plassey, 1757), Clive established Mohammed Ali and

11. The word "nabob" was made popular by a comedy of Samuel Foote (1772); in passing, it may remind us how much English vocabulary owes to the oriental experience: words like pundit and pajama, divan, calico, brahmin, bazaar, juggernaut, sacred cows and white elephants, thugs, and a thousand others which we use today without giving a passing thought to their source (SFR, F.20).

Jafar Ali Khan as puppet rulers of vast districts in and around Bengal and its new capital city Calcutta. So liberal were the terms dictated to these native "governors" that Indians were allowed to do all the work of administration, while agents of the company assumed the pleasing labor of tax collection. London speculators, most of them completely ignorant of India, saw this as a no-lose situation, and promptly bid up the stock of the company to absurdly inflated levels. But in 1770 a catastrophic famine struck the land, wiping out a full third of the population; and before the survivors had recovered, they underwent a number of invasions by tough Mahratta tribesmen from west and central India, leading to still more dangerous incursions by the powerful Hyder Ali of Mysore and his son Tippoo.

Against these successive waves of danger and misfortune, the company's agents, now under the leadership of Warren Hastings, fought successful defensive battles. But, inevitably, company profits disappointed the speculators; and this frustration, combined with the first stirrings of moral awareness over the way native populations were being treated in India, raised questions about the entire conduct of the company. Dissatisfied employees returned from the east to testify, first against Clive (who, under pressure of parliamentary inquiry, killed himself) and then against his successor Hastings, who after a seven-year trial (1788–1795) during which he was ferociously denounced by Edmund Burke, was finally acquitted of all charges. Whether it was fair to judge, in comfortable London, by the cool light of historical hindsight, men who had acted in a corrupt and desperate situation, on imperfect knowledge and in great urgency, may be doubted. But history cares nothing for fairness; the trials of Clive and Hastings blighted their names, but brought to light conditions in India which made government controls inevitable. An early step in this direction was the Regulating Act passed by Lord North's administration in 1773; but it required constant oversight, and the overseers themselves had to be watched carefully. The India Act of 1784 was better; it functioned fairly effectively till 1858, when the crown took over the East India Company completely. None of these changes altered the basic fact that British presence in India always served exploitative ends. But during the nineteenth century, we hear more of civil servants, teachers, missionaries, and career military men going out, and less of "nabobs" coming back. And in passing, it may be added that Warren Hastings, who knew India intimately and loved it, was largely responsible for opening to Western scholarship the treasuries of ancient Sanskrit and that wisdom of the East which became so prestigious in the nineteenth century and the twentieth, so far.

PITT THE YOUNGER

Loss of the American war resulted, by the inexorable logic of politics, in dismissal of the North government (1782). With true Hanover stubbornness, George III clung to hope for victory in America long after everyone else had abandoned it; but when hope was gone, even he saw that Lord North must go. Most of the alternatives were hateful to him; he shuffled them and jockeyed among them, as was his custom. But late in 1783 he fell on a young man after his own heart, who also had the skill (which none of his previous ministers possessed) to dominate the House of Commons. William Pitt, second son of George's old bugbear the earl of Chatham, was just twenty-four years old when he became prime minister. He bore his father's name, and had many of his father's traits and talents, as well as some of his weaknesses. Burke, hearing him speak, said "This is not a chip off the old block, it is the old block itself." The phrase was meant admiringly; but there was an undertone to it that might have given pause. Pitt had some of his father's hard, limited temper; he was grave, reserved, prudent far beyond his years; he was a masterly debater and a master of parliamentary procedure. But his human imagination was limited. History would, before long, bring him up against social forces that he could comprehend no better than could the block to which Burke compared him.

The first years of young Pitt's administration were, however, years of peace and relative prosperity. A steady hand at the helm moved the nation's business forward quietly but quickly. A program of administrative reform, unspectacular but sustained, eliminated many sinecures and streamlined antiquated procedures. Useless offices went unfilled; clerks who had not notched a pen for years were suddenly asked to scratch for their salaries; duplicate records were eliminated. One at a time, but to great cumulative effect, Pitt tore down trade barriers and negotiated reciprocal customs treaties, even with the hereditary enemy, France. (His policies were much influenced by his reading of Adam Smith, whose book *The Wealth of Nations*, published in 1776 and further noticed below, strongly backed free trade.) He took steps to reduce the national debt. Though beaten in the Commons on a few of his first proposals (especially a program of electoral reform that would, if carried, have taken much of the sting out of the Reform Bill disputes of 1832), he quickly learned how to manage the House. He became adept at preparing his votes, relaxing the reins on routine matters to tighten them more effectively on crucial issues, controlling the parties firmly yet flexibly, and establishing a working majority that soon gave him power beyond that enjoyed even by Walpole at the high noon of his popularity.

Thus matters stood when in the fall of 1788, King George, while being driven through the royal park at Windsor, called on the coachman to stop, descended from the royal carriage and, approaching a large oak tree, addressed it as the king of Prussia.[12] He was out of his mind, and clearly incapable of performing the duties of his office. The prince of Wales, ever alert, asked to be appointed

12. As with many of history's picturesque stories, this one is a bit suspect. The one eye-and-ear witness was a man not without malice toward George. But though the details are questionable, the general state of the king's wits is not. Modern pathology has given his disease a name, porphyria, but has not altered the important circumstance. Though George was cared for by the most enlightened French physician of the day, Philippe Pinel, he never could achieve more than a temporary remission of the disease.

regent immediately, and was supported by the opposition under the leadership of Charles James Fox. What unnerved the British public in this conjunction was that the prince (bored to desperation by the dreary court of his dull father) had made himself known as the greatest rake and roué in Europe; while Fox (with perhaps less excuse) was a heavy drinker and compulsive gambler, who had already thrown away several fortunes, and was suspected of having corrupted the prince. Pitt, a man of severe morality himself, assumed the role of guardian to his ailing and virtuous sovereign. Three months of scuffling in Parliament ensued; the new regent was about to be proclaimed, in February 1789, when the king returned to his senses as abruptly as he had left them.[13] Amid general rejoicing the monarch and his vindicated prime minister attended thanksgiving services at St. Paul's cathedral; the horizon was once more unclouded, and all prospects fair. And then, on 5 May 1789, the states-general of France assembled for the first time in 175 years, not knowing what precisely they were to do, or even who they were, but destined to take the first steps leading to the French Revolution, greatest of modern European cataclysms. A new day was about to dawn in Europe; the morning skies were fiery and ominous.

THE CULTURAL MAGNETISM OF FRANCE

In outlining the history of the later eighteenth century, it has not been easy or natural to make many allusions to the literary life of the age. No major figures stood forth to support political leaders with their pen like Swift, to satirize them like Dryden, or to point out shocking social conditions like Dickens. Though Burke (who is an exception to almost all the rules) took an active part in the politics of his age, it was as an orator before the House of Commons, not as an imaginative writer appealing to a book-buying audience. Such writers had their private political views. But no literary figure addressed the nation through the medium of his art concerning the Seven Years' War, the struggles in India, or the American problem. The industrial transformation of England is not mirrored in English literature till many years after its inception. Imperial issues were perhaps too enormous and too complex to be addressed in heroic couplets or compressed into a personal narrative such as the novel could then handle. Even writers for the stage kept their tone light and the range of their observation domestic. In the biography of Richard Brinsley Sheridan we observe an absolute division between his literary career, up to the age of thirty, and his political career for the next thirty-six years, during which, as a writer for the stage, he is all but mute. Dryden, with a confidence verging on the foolhardy, had tried to make a heroic historical poem, "Annus Mirabilis," out of yesterday's headlines, the big events of 1666. By the late eighteenth century, the scale of public actions had widened

13. The prince of Wales did not become prince regent till 1811, when his father was judged definitely and permanently insane; he did not become king, as George IV, till 1820.

as the confidence of authors to deal with them shrank. England entered on her imperial era without an imperial poet or imaginative writer; indeed, to judge from the literature of the day, the eyes of the nation were riveted either on the remote historical past or on her great historical rival across the channel (SFR, X.2).

It is a curious fact that as England moved toward economic and political empire, she focused her cultural imagination on France, an inveterate enemy tottering toward a catastrophic revolution of her own. Yet both the French court, the most sophisticated and luxurious in Europe, and French intellectual circles (the group known as *philosophes*) exercised a marked fascination on English writers. Edward Gibbon, the historian of the declining Roman Empire, wrote and spoke French before he did English, and a mere glance at his footnotes will reveal how heavily he leaned on the publications of the Académie des Inscriptions and other French learned societies. Oliver Goldsmith's *Citizen of the World* (1762), in which a visiting Chinese comments on the oddities of the English, is clearly modeled on M. de Montesquieu's *Lettres persanes* (1721), in which a pair of visiting Persians comment on the strange institutions of the French. Adam Smith, Scottish economist and political philosopher, drew the basic ideas for his massive treatise on *The Wealth of Nations* (1776) from two of the *philosophes,* Quesnay and Turgot, with whom he had studied a decade earlier. Lord Chesterfield, author of the famous *Letters* written for the instruction of his illegitimate son, was at least half a Frenchman, and drew both his manners (which were exquisite) and his morals (which were dubious) from the example of the French court. Boswell, before he settled for doing the biography of Johnson, thought of doing that of Voltaire, and visited Ferney to consult with the sage. Horace Walpole, son of Sir Robert and in his own right England's best writer of familiar letters, never failed to rise to the top of his form when his correspondent was Madame du Deffand in Paris. Lord Hervey and his friend Lady Mary Wortley Montagu were also voluminous writers of letters and memoirs; neither of them set pen to paper without a jealous glance toward the achievements of Madame de Sévigné the supreme French letter writer, and the duc de Saint-Simon, most distinguished of memoir writers.

Until the disillusions of the French Revolution, liberal and radical thinkers in England were particularly indebted to the *philosophes,* who can be described in a capsule phrase as anti-absolutist neo-pagan ideologists. Clustering around Denis Diderot and his project for a new encyclopedia, they numbered in their enlightened company Condorcet, Condillac, d'Alembert, d'Holbach, Helvétius, and Friedrich Baron Grimm—along with their assorted mistresses and patronesses like Mme. Geoffrin, Mme. du Deffand, Mlle. de Lespinasse, Mme. d'Épinay, and numerous other birds of passage. Such a brilliant assemblage of witty and learned people existed nowhere else in Europe; and various as they were, a remarkable thing is the extent to which they agreed in meaning much the same thing by rationalism in religion and rational reform of the social order. If the eighteenth century in France was the century of lights, of the enlightenment, the center of that illumination was the group of *philosophes* in Paris. Loosely attached to it, sometimes in, sometimes out of the circle, were two much greater men, Voltaire and Rousseau. Neither can be summed up in terms of the creed of the *philosophes;* Rousseau in particular requires our special attention later in connection with the romantic movement. But they shed the glitter of their minds on the group in Paris; seeing them in conjunction with the brilliance of the French court, in the company of artists, sculptors, architects, and musicians, we need not wonder that this sparkling civilization fascinated the English. There has been space to note only a few of those writers who reflected French influence, stylistic as well as intellectual. It was a specially potent influence because it built directly on the "correct" literary tastes inculcated by the Augustan writers of the earlier century.

GOTHIC FADS AND FASHIONS

All the more remarkable is it, therefore, to find an independent taste growing up among the English for the exact opposite of the enlightenment—that is, for the Gothic dark.[14] Neither in Paris salons nor at court in Versailles could anyone have learned to admire Gothic building or write a Gothic novel. Odder yet, the men who introduced this Gothic taste to England were no strangers to France; Horace Walpole we noted as Mme. du Deffand's favorite correspondent, and William Beckford wrote *Vathek,* his one novel, in French before he translated it into English almost as an afterthought. But it was Walpole's shocker, *The Castle of Otranto* (1764) which inaugurated the Gothic mode in fiction. The story, which takes place in the thirteenth century, involves a wicked usurper, a haunted castle, an ancient curse, an innocent virgin; like the fat boy in *Pickwick,* the author is

14. Like many other words, "Gothic" has undergone tremendous changes in its connotations. The original Goths were Germanic tribes which from the third to the fifth centuries sometimes attacked and sometimes supported the declining Roman Empire. Compared with Huns and Vandals, Goths were relatively civilized barbarians; but in the seventeenth and early eighteenth centuries, the word's connotations were entirely negative. "Ah, rustic," says Millamant (in Congreve's *The Way of the World*), "ruder than Gothic!" It is a put-down of oafish Sir Wilful Witwoud; *rough, uncivilized,* and *benighted* are some of the implications. About this time, the word started to be applied to all the architecture between late Roman or Romanesque building and the revival of classic modes in the Renaissance: a feature of most building in this period is use of the pointed arch. The buildings of ancient Rome, says John Evelyn, "were demolished by the Goths or Vandals, who introduced their own licentious style, now called modern or Gothic." From "licentious" (i.e., lawless), new overtones attached themselves to the word, such as *extravagant, strong,* and *wild,* but also *primitive-therefore-authentic.* Not to be overlooked among the new meanings of "Gothic" is the latent concept of *dark.* Gothic novels took place in the "Dark Ages," in somber castles, amid clouds of mystery, and often at night. Gothic churches were admired for their religious gloom; and stained-glass windows, which historically were introduced to suggest the radiance of divine light, began to be admired for the dim, reverential obscurity they created.

out to make our flesh crawl. *Vathek* (1786) is oriental in flavoring, and evokes a good deal of diablerie as well as exotic eastern femininity; it too aims at eerie effects. Before the century was out, creaky stairs and rattling chains, mysterious curses, demonic possessions, and lustful villains lurking in secret passageways became as familiar to novel readers as they are in horror movies. *The Mysteries of Udolpho* (1794) by Mrs. Ann Radcliffe may represent the vogue at its height; *Northanger Abbey* (1818) by Jane Austen was an astringent corrective.

The vogue for Gothic passed beyond sensational novels to influence English taste in general. Both Walpole and Beckford, being blessed with independent fortunes, built what they thought were Gothic residences, Walpole's Strawberry Hill stuffed with curios like a museum, Beckford's Fonthill Abbey as gigantic as a cathedral. Neither structure showed much knowledge of what medieval Gothic was really like; both would be called "kitschy" nowadays, that is, pretentious and bogus. But they were symbols of a new taste which would burgeon in the nineteenth century; the rebuilt houses of Parliament (1840) and the Albert Memorial (1876) are high-water marks of what came to be known as the Gothic revival.[15] Many strains entered into a new vein of antiquarian-nostalgic concern for the past. Starting in 1763, excavations at the site of Pompeii brought to light more and more of the ancient Roman town buried by the ashes of Vesuvius in the year 79. Familiar strains of neoclassicism (the poetry of Pope, the paintings of Poussin) had represented the Roman world as pure, austere, dignified, rational; Pompeii exposed a more human side of Rome, a wild and picturesque aspect of Roman ruins. A Gothic Rome was a new Rome; and nobody did more to popularize that view of the ancient city than Giovanni Battista Piranesi, whose gigantically exaggerated engravings of Roman ruins entranced tourists from northern Europe. Engravings by the Cavalier Piranesi accompanied every Englishman returning from his Grand Tour; no other artist has ever made the Eternal City look so ruinous or so Gothic in her ruins. (And, we may add in passing, no fictional presentation of the ancient world ever made it look and sound so Gothic as Bulwer-Lytton's melodramatic *Last Days of Pompeii* [1834].)

SOFT GOTHIC: GRAVEYARD POETS AND SENTIMENTAL NOVELISTS

On the fringes of what we call "hard" Gothic (macabre novels and eerie medieval properties) we can distinguish several zones of "soft" Gothic feeling. These are shadowy regions where, as the glittering clarity of the rational enlightenment shaded toward darkness, writers found it agreeable to cultivate the obscure but not violent sentiments of nostalgia and melancholy. The retrospectively titled

15. The ancient houses of parliament burned to the ground in 1834, when a bonfire of tally sticks, rendered obsolete by reformation of the court of exchequer, got out of control. Sir Charles Barry and A. W. Pugin supervised the reconstruction in Gothic style. The Albert Memorial honored Victoria's deceased husband (see below, p. 385).

"graveyard school" of poetry emerged about mid-century. In 1743 Robert Blair and Edward Young published almost simultaneous poems in the sepulchral vein ("The Grave," "Night Thoughts"), and about the same time Thomas Gray began, though he did not publish till 1750, the most famous poem in the genre, his "Elegy Written in a Country Churchyard." Everything about this stately procession of general sentiments is gentle, reflective, reconciled; humble merit and proud ambition are leveled before the ultimate fact of mortality. The "Elegy" is not a Gothic poem, far from it; rather, it is a poem of potentially Gothic feelings being softened and humanized; perhaps these are among the reasons for its timeless popularity.

Indulgence in the emotions for their own sake, though not specifically in a Gothic context, marked a short-lived fad in the writing of the later century. "Sentimental" novels, like the sentimental comedies that preceded them, exaggerated and exploited the benevolent and pathetic sentiments of mankind as ruthlessly as the Gothic writers exploited chills and shivers. A lady in *The Fool of Quality* by Henry Brooke (1766) is forgiven for a "lapse" which she has never committed, but is so overcome with her feelings that she expires on the spot. The ecstatic hero of Henry Mackenzie's *Man of Feeling* (1771) cannot sustain the shock when his lady admits she is not wholly indifferent to him; he too drops dead. Marlow, the tongue-tied hero of Goldsmith's play *She Stoops to Conquer* (1773), and Faulkland, the equally bashful subaltern of Sheridan's play *The Rivals* (1775), are both victims of their own seething subterranean sentiments. Goldsmith and Sheridan protested in their prologues against the excesses of the sentimental fad, yet both, even in their best work, fell victim to it. These prosy, posturing fellows remain blots on the last playable comedies England would produce for better than a century. Bob Acres is the real hero of Sheridan's comedy, as Tony Lumpkin is of Goldsmith's.

SEARCHERS FOR THE SELF

Cultivation of pathos and the spontaneous ebullition of sympathy were characteristic of Laurence Sterne and his two fictional mouthpieces. Mr. Yorick (the name is a pun on the city of York where Sterne was a clergyman, as well as an allusion to Hamlet's graveyard jester) and Tristram Shandy repeatedly fall victim to interruption and digression from their own emotional impulses; after a while it becomes clear that that is what they are inviting. Both Sterne's novels, *A Sentimental Journey* and *Tristram Shandy,* are unstructured, consisting of digressions from a merely nominal objective. Sterne is a master of pretext and innuendo; his best joke is to circle persistently but to all appearances unconsciously around some explicit erotic point that he never makes. He provokes, tantalizes, delays; he interrupts, and then interrupts the interruptions, as if planlessness were his only plan. Thus his books are literally endless. At one point in the exposition of his life and opinions (Volume IV, Chapter 13), Tristram Shandy pauses to calculate that describing the first full day of his existence on earth has required a full year of the author's writing time. He is obviously losing ground to himself, at the rate of 364 days to 1, and by proceeding further can only get further from his conclusion. The very act of Tristram's conception was marred by a fatal and prophetic interruption; the deficiency of nose caused by an accident at his delivery has left him rudderless on the ocean of life. Writing simply adds to the complications of his existence. In a word, the novel makes comic capital of the insubstantiality of fictional character, and the artificiality of linear plot. For a long time, *Tristram Shandy* was thought to be an amusing eccentricity in the history of prose fiction, but in the twentieth century, when the established solidities again turned hollow, the vaudeville of the book has revived as an important influence.

VICTIMS AND IMPOSTORS

By freeing the fleeting impulses of his duplicitous emotional self, Sterne floated a fictional cockleshell on their choppy, uneven waters. A number of other authors in the troubled late eighteenth century sank beneath the waves, had trouble with their wits, were in fact lodged for periods of time in asylums. William Collins and William Cowper, Christopher Smart, Charles Lamb the essayist, and (a little later in the nineteenth century) John Clare all had to be confined. They were writers of quite different sorts, most of them well educated and some with access to perfectly respectable positions in society. (One should also add a caution that the Age of Reason was much quicker to confine people in asylums, and did so on much slighter grounds, than we nowadays think civilized.) Still, for some sensitive and imaginative folk, the reasonable life of rational calculation and social conformity, leading to the happy conviction that "whatever is is right," clearly left something to be desired. What these people felt was a need, beyond common sense, for something extravagantly and personally reassuring; it was a need which simply could not be met by the philosophy of Mr. Locke and the theology of Bishop Butler.

William Cowper's terror of the everyday world was both personal and symptomatic. He was born of good family and university-educated; in his early thirties he was nominated by a cousin for a clerkship in the House of Lords. Cowper was a capable scholar with a law degree; he had no competitors; the post involved no duties; to get it, he had only to make a token appearance before a committee. Everything was routine; perhaps that was what horrified Cowper, who simply could not face the ordeal. He tried, ineffectually, to commit suicide, with poison, knife, rope; on the morning of the interview, his cousin found him huddled in a corner, his eyes shut, babbling to himself, "I am damned, I am damned, I am damned." "Come, come, Mr. Cowper," said the cousin sensibly, "this will never do—'' and in short order the poet was committed to an asylum. After some months he was released, when a kindly religious family named Unwin volunteered to care for him; and indeed, when he was not threatened with social position, Cowper was the most genial and agreeable of men. He was talented too as a poet, if not of high passions and stormy amours, of gentle, humorous observation. Yet the abyss was never far from him, and the mere prospect of social responsibility could drive him mad again. One of his most poignant and compressed poems is "The Castaway," in which the sailor, lost overboard in a storm, shrieking, struggling, and at last sinking silently into the depths, is Cowper himself. The poem achieves a pathos both profound and unlabored; it suggests the cavernous depths of guilt and darkness over which the enlightened eighteenth century tried to build its sunny summerhouse of civilized discourse.

The high-pressure, tightly ordered world that set Sterne to capering, drove Cowper mad, and forced William Blake into an imaginary antiworld of his own (below, p. 364) invited other writers to redefine themselves radically. Thomas Chatterton, born to poverty and obscurity in Bristol (1752), imagined himself into the person of Thomas Rowley, a satirical monk of the fifteenth century, whose "manuscripts" Chatterton professed to have discovered. As forgeries, his poems were not very convincing; but as poems, they were remarkable achievements, not just for a schoolboy but by any standards. Chatterton sought patrons, sought employment for his amazingly versatile pen; many recognized, or said they recognized, his talent; but nobody encouraged him in the one way that really counted for a boy who was dying of hunger. While patrons hesitated, and publishers withheld payment, Chatterton, "the marvellous boy" as Wordsworth called him, committed suicide by arsenic in August 1770, three months before his eighteenth birthday. His failure to make a mark as the "Gothic" Rowley might have been merely comic had it not involved as well the cruel loss of the boy-genius Chatterton.

With James MacPherson and his production of the poems of "Ossian" we turn from black tragedy to broad farce. MacPherson was a literary Scot who knew a bit of Gaelic; in the early 1760s, he brought forth no fewer than three volumes purporting to be translations from the writings of a third-century warrior-bard named Ossian or Uisin, son of Fingal or Finn (above, p. 19). MacPherson's story about the source of his poems was strange, but not on the face of it impossible. Everyone knew the ancient Scots and Picts had bards. Most early manuscripts survive in ragged fragments; three complete volumes from the third century would be most improbable; but the poems of "Ossian" were grand poems, if rather vague, and readers tended to hope, rather than believe, they were genuine. Indeed, for many years romantics throughout England and Europe continued to sigh over the sublime sorrows of Ossian. Goethe's hero, the melancholy Werther (1774), found it degrading that someone should ask if he "liked" Ossian; of course he adored, he worshiped, such a noble soul. In 1798, Napoleon carried a copy of Ossian (in the Italian translation by Cesarotti) on his expedition to Egypt; he read it by moonlight under the inscrutable gaze of the sphinx, or so his publicity-people said. But long before that romantic moment, hardheaded Dr. Johnson suspected a forgery and demanded copies of the Gaelic originals. What he got from MacPherson was evasions, equivocations, and, unfortunately, personal threats. Nothing worked. MacPherson in fact had originals for only a few of his translations; most of the poems were his own eighteenth-century idea of what a third-century bard might have written. Like the poems of "Rowley," they were frauds, but exceedingly well done. The French have a kinder word for the same thing: *pastiches*.

This frequent impulse to shed one's identity and slip into a new one may be related, by those who like to speculate about such things, to the pressures of a mechanical philosophy professed by an "enlightened" society. In the history of English literature, it is a quite exceptional event which would have been portentous even if not accompanied and followed (as it was) by massive social dislocations and explosions.

THE SCOTTISH RENAISSANCE

The period covered by this chapter is, of course, the age of Dr. Samuel Johnson, yet the name of that massive and pervasive spirit has hardly been pronounced. And before he appears, the intermediate figure of Boswell reminds us that something must be said of a Scottish literary renaissance in the late eighteenth century. This is more than a matter of the odd poet like Allan Ramsay, or the novelist like Smollett, born in Scotland and truculent about his origins, but a Londoner most of his life. A rich and various cultural life, Scottish in origin and rooted in Scottish society, grew up around Edinburgh, "the Athens of the North." We can only note briefly a few of the more famous names, starting with Adam Smith, professor of moral philosophy at Glasgow, and later at Edinburgh the center of a congenial, convivial society of thinkers. Smith himself was an idealist in his moral philosophy, a realist in his political economy; it is the latter which has survived. His massive treatise on economics, *The Wealth of Nations,* was published in the fateful year 1776; it is a weighty and complex book, but its two dominant ideas are clear and simple. Smith argues the advantages of division of labor and the consequent necessity of free trade. These were the ideas of the future, not because Smith proposed them, but because English capitalism and an English government headed by the younger Pitt, were prepared to implement them. France, where the ideas had their origin, could not or would not use them.[16]

16. During the years 1764–1766, Smith lived as tutor to the duke of Buccleuch amid the company of the French *philosophes*. He was particularly influenced by the economic theories of Quesnay and Turgot, both strong exponents of free trade, neither able to influence the fatally restrictive policies of the old regime. (Turgot ultimately rose to the office of comptroller general, but was hamstrung by intrigues and driven from office by the stupidity of Marie Antoinette.) Smith's work on *The Wealth of Nations*, apparently begun before this French interlude, occupied the decade that followed it.

Smith's close friend and associate was the philosopher and historian David Hume. Hume's importance as a thinker is too great to be explored fully here; he is one of the seminal thinkers, but we must limit ourselves to noting one fundamental shift in philosophy that resulted from his devastating skepticism. He squeezed, one could say, the empirical method of Locke into such a tight logical impasse that only the transcendental philosophy of Immanuel Kant (see above, p. 236) offered an escape. As a young man, Hume grasped firmly the first principle of Locke's system, that the mind can have distinct impressions of distinct facts; but he could conceive of no way in which it could make any real connection between facts. I see, for example, the black billiard ball hit the white one, and I see the white one move; but I have no way, apart from guesses based on previous experience, to know that the impact of the black ball causes the motion of the white one. Under the cold scrutiny of Hume's skeptical eye, the world of experience shrank to a set of meaningless atoms bumping into one another incomprehensibly in the void. You might say Hume atomized the atomistic view of the world; the new philosophy, if there was to be one, would have to start, not by looking at matter, but by looking into the nature of the mind and its energies.[17]

Smith and Hume are the great names of the Scottish Enlightenment, but there are many others. Lord Kames was an influential legal scholar, logician, and systematizer of critical method; Lord Monboddo, derided in his own time as an eccentric lawyer, proved eventually to be the first of the anthropologists and an anticipator in major ways of the discoveries of Charles Darwin. Principal William Robertson ranks with Hume and Gibbon among the historians; while Thomas Reid, Adam Ferguson, and Sir William Hamilton make up a set of moral philosophers and metaphysicians of which any nation could be proud.

A recurrent dream of eighteenth century critics living in a sophisticated, enlightened era, was that a simple, passionate poet of the people might emerge to speak nature's language, outpourings of the untutored heart. The minute he appeared on the literary scene, it was clear that the inspired plowboy Robert Burns qualified for this position, and perhaps for others as well. Burns had little formal education (and just as well for him), but he was steeped in the traditional poetry of Scotland, its ballads and folksongs. Much of his own work consisted of mending, patching, and extending poems written originally by some anonymous figure of the past. What he did, in fact, was not unlike what MacPherson had done in creating "Ossian," except that he did not falsify history, and he improved almost everything he touched. One need only compare his songs with the originals to see how little he took, how much he gave. (The third volume of the "Centenary" edition of Burns's poems, edited by Henley and Henderson,

17. For a close analysis of Hume's skepticism, see Leslie Stephen, *A History of English Thought in the Eighteenth Century* (London, 1876), vol. I, pp. 309–343; Norman K. Smith, in *The Philosophy of David Hume* (London, 1964), casts fresh light on the intentional backgrounds of Hume's thinking.

1896–1897, explores many of these comparisons.) And in his own work, the strength and boldness of his inspiration are unmistakable. "The Jolly Beggars" is only one of his masterpieces; its ragged roisterers, roaring the chorus of their defiance at respectable society, could only be the work of Burns:

> A fig for those by law protected,
>   Liberty's a glorious feast;
> Courts for cowards were erected,
>   Churches built to please the priest.

Among those he called the "unco guid," the prissy and strait-laced of Scotland, Burns naturally had no good name. He liked the lasses, just about all of them, and in no particular order; and he liked his glass. Undoubtedly when they yearned for a "natural" and a "national" poet, the good critics of Scotland had in mind someone a little more decorous in his habits. But the Burns they actually got remains to this day one of the few poets in the world whose birthday is celebrated, proudly and joyously, wherever his countrymen foregather. January 25 is the day.[18]

JOHNSON

Dr. Johnson, whom we are bound to find at the center of the age, bulks large because we know so much about him, especially the last twenty years of his life: he met Boswell in 1762 and died in 1783. But his early years were no less colorful, and much more productive, than his days as a literary dictator of London. Johnson's youth was made miserable by abject poverty, by the scrofulous disease which disfigured his face, and by the grotesque nervous tics and mannerisms which made it hard for him to get jobs teaching school or to appear in good society. For years he drudged obscurely at the trade of literature, often acclaimed critically, rarely rewarded financially. His tragedy *Irene* (1736) was respected but not popular; his poems, "London" (1738) and "The Vanity of Human Wishes" (1749); a biography, *The Life of Richard Savage* (1744); and a moral novel, *Rasselas* (1759) barely kept him solvent. From 1750 to 1752 he wrote a set of informal essays, *The Rambler;* he recorded parliamentary debates for a magazine, freely inventing most of the speeches; he wrote articles, reviews, sketches, and between 1747 and 1755 he was engaged on the herculean labor of preparing, almost singlehanded, his two-volume dictionary of the English language. For a man whose besetting vice was sloth, this was an immense quantity

18. One other untutored poet of Scotland merits mention. Jane or Jean Elliot was the daughter of a Scottish gentleman; one day she fell into a discussion with her brother about the battle of Flodden Field fought two and a half centuries before. Though neither had ever written a poem, they agreed to try ballads on the subject. Hers, titled "The Flowers of the Forest," was instantly, widely, and permanently acclaimed. Many hearers refused to believe it was not a sixteenth-century original. Jane Elliot never again in her entire life wrote a single poem.

of hard work; and with the possible exception of *Irene,* none of it is second-rate. Yet had Johnson died before his meeting with Boswell and the gathering of the literary group which he dominated so long, he would hardly merit extensive mention in a literary history of England. An important circumstance underlying Johnson's late flowering was severely practical. Through the interest of the earl of Bute, he received at the accession of George III a government pension. It was not a large sum of money (£300 per year), but it was enough to take the edge off Johnson's poverty; it enabled him to spend more time in talk with his friends, and that in turn helped render his written style more relaxed and colloquial. The Johnson we remember and cite continually, two centuries after his death, is pre-eminently Boswell's Johnson and the Johnson of his last major work, "The Lives of the English Poets."[19]

Talking was good for Johnson; it concentrated, instead of diluting, his thought. In the company of his friends, who included Goldsmith, Sheridan, Burke, Gibbon, Sir Joshua Reynolds the painter, David Garrick the actor, and the indispensable, irrepressible Boswell, the full Johnsonian character flowered. "His" literary club was originally the notion of Sir Joshua Reynolds, but because Johnson so dominated the conversation, it soon came to be thought of as the Doctor's.[20] Originally it met weekly at the "Turk's Head" tavern in Soho, then later, as it grew in size, it met less frequently and at a variety of different public houses. Johnson was not a self-conscious conversational "dictator," but his opinions were trenchant, and many of them retain tonic vigor to this day: "You must clear your mind of cant" ought to be heard more often in twentieth-century America than, alas, it is. But Johnson also had a special gift for reaching to the heart of a literary question. What he declares is often only the robust common sense of the matter; but it's wonderful to observe how often literary criticism, to

19. For sheer entertainment, hardly anything written about Johnson equals the *Journal of a Tour to the Hebrides,* which Boswell published in 1785, describing a trip to the northern islands taken by the two friends in 1773. They were looking for the "primitive," and found it—so much of it that bits of civilization, when encountered, were very welcome indeed. Boswell had many contacts with the Scottish lairds, who put up the visiting party in their homes; the rest of the time they stayed, for worse or for better, in common inns. On occasion, they really had to rough it. Boswell and Johnson were pioneers; within a few years, when war and revolution had closed off the Continent, "touring" of a less adventurous sort became very much the British thing. In the early nineteenth century, one William Gilpin wrote a series of guidebooks to different districts, instructing the tourist where to find picturesque views, ruins, places with literary or historical associations, etc. A well-known parody of this vogue was *Dr. Syntax in Search of the Picturesque* (1809) with doggerel verses by William Combe and drawings by Thomas Rowlandson, a caricaturist of genius (SFR, G.21).

Boswell's printed version of the *Tour* was much less vivid and human than his original version, scribbled in the course of the trip itself. The manuscript was discovered, with many more of Boswell's personal papers, in Castle Malahide near Dublin by Colonel Ralph Isham; the full text, published in 1936, is more extensive by about a third than the printed version. Concise and unobtrusive footnotes enable one to compare the two versions—a revealing and amusing exercise.

20. Because of poverty, Johnson had failed to complete his degree at Oxford; his doctorates were honorary, from Trinity College, Dublin (1765), and from Oxford (1775).

this day, even when ultimately it disagrees with Johnson, finds his remarks the most direct path to the central issues. What Johnson lays down as the last word on a subject often turns out to be something much better, the opening step of a new and capacious argument with very modern implications.

The charm of the Doctor and his circle remains inexhaustible. As in all good literary groups, the brilliance, and sometimes even the deficiencies, of one participant bring out unexpected facets in the character of another. But the deepest part of Johnson's character he saved for his privacy, his diaries, and his prayers. They are moving documents. Had Johnson been simply a crusty old Tory who knocked down all his opponents, we should no longer care much about him. Even kindly feelings beneath that gruff exterior would be just another commonplace. But Boswell—the kind of young man who goes around asking his elders "What shall I be when I grow up?"—had the genius and sensitivity to divine a kindred soul, almost as lost and frightened as his own, inside Dr. Johnson. The Doctor's hunger for the comforts of companionship, his terrors and superstitions beyond the comfortable space available to civilized reassurance, contrast amazingly with his public powers of confidence and decorum. Even here, at the heart of the heart of the enlightenment, we find a consciousness haunted by intimations of powers it cannot use and obligations it is helpless to fulfill.

13

Revolution, Romanticism, Reaction (1789–1815)

About the nature and meaning of the French Revolution of 1789 opinions have varied wildly since the day it began (SFR, X.20). Sympathizers hailed it as the dawn of a new day for humanity, enemies deplored it as inciting class war, anarchy, tyranny. It promised unlimited individual freedom and led to the rigidly organized modern state; it proclaimed the brotherhood of man and enforced the idea with musketry and cannon fire; both capitalists and communists claim its authority for their doctrines; in France it is still the fundamental issue from which modern social conflicts spring and to which they can all be reduced. Throughout western Europe it is the mainspring of modern history.

BLACK STORM OR BRIGHT NEW DAY?

For better or worse, those who lived through the revolution experienced it as a soul-shaking experience. It began with a meeting, called by a bankrupt monarch, of the three traditional estates of the realm. These were representatives of the 100,000 clergy, the 250,000 nobles, and the third estate, which was everybody else, in the neighborhood of 24,000,000 souls. They were to consider a condition of the kingdom which everyone saw to be difficult and many thought intolerable.

For the privileged, the question from the start was how to keep the third estate from correcting too many of the abuses which had piled up, unreformed and unquestioned, since feudal times. A few superficial changes were acceptable to the monarch and even to the more arrogant aristocrats. But the middle-class lawyers who headed up the third estate wanted more, and more basic, reforms; to get them, they demanded that the third estate should have as many representatives as the other two orders combined, and that voting should be by individuals rather than by orders (when the third would be automatically outvoted two to one). After much legal wrangling, representatives of the third constituted themselves a National Assembly and began to meet separately, welcoming members from the two privileged orders but acting essentially on their own. Some liberal nobles and clergy did join them, and they united in rejecting an order of the king to dissolve. Suspicion that the aristocrats were preparing an armed coup against the National Assembly led on July 14, 1789, to the storming of the Bastille by the armed and furious populace of Paris. In itself, the Bastille was an anachronism; it was an ancient fortress, weakly guarded, and holding only seven prisoners (among them, curious to note, the marquis de Sade).[1] But it was a hated symbol, and its taking by a mob of enraged slum dwellers showed the revolution starting to escape from its first leaders, the middle-class liberals. Soon the nation was covered with a network of revolutionary committees, in close contact with one another and with the National Assembly. Their avowed aim was to watch for a widely anticipated aristocratic plot; in fact the committees became a substitute government, replacing the old one outright or taking over its business and leaving it as an empty shell. In autumn of 1789 the National Assembly declared its democratic principles in a Declaration of the Rights of Man.[2]

At first the French Revolution aroused much sympathy in England. The French court had been extravagant and frivolous, social privilege far greater than in England, taxation unjust beyond belief, and the poor more abject than humane English opinion thought decent. (A 1790 survey showed 40 percent of the French population living below the poverty level, and a third of these absolute paupers, with no resource but begging.) Some Englishmen saw in Louis XVI a figure like the seventeenth-century Stuarts and in the patriots demanding reform French equivalents to John Hampden and Oliver Cromwell. Dr. Richard Price, a nonconformist minister, was only one of many to preach (November 1789) exultant

1. The king put people in the Bastille by sending them a *lettre de cachet,* a royal order; families sometimes asked to have a troublesome member lodged there. Over the years some eight hundred authors, printers, and booksellers had also been jailed there, plus thousands of copies of the suppressed *Encyclopédie.* The seven actual prisoners of 1789 give no idea of the Bastille's symbolic magnitude.

2. The "rights of man" were founded on a half-defined but widely invoked "law of nature," to which Rousseau, in his "Second Discourse on Inequality," made frequent appeal. (Modern "human rights" are akin.) A neat and useful untangling of the many meanings attached to the word "nature" at this crisis of human thought will be found in Basil Willey, *The Eighteenth-Century Background* (XI, I).

sermons on the overthrow of the French monarchy and the new glorious liberties to follow. Somewhat later, during 1791 and 1792, William Wordsworth would share, in very similar spirit, enthusiasm over the rebirth of the French nation.[3] But Price was more extreme than most when he argued that, as the French had cashiered their king for misconduct, so Englishmen, acting on the principles of 1688, might do likewise. Price was answered by Edmund Burke, whose *Reflections on the Revolution in France* (1790) set forth the classic conservative position which was to prevail in England. Burke argued that the ''rights of man'' were schematic and doctrinaire ideas, and that reform, not revolution, was a proper cure for social abuses; he went on to prophesy that the revolution would shortly lead to anarchy and then to tyranny.

Unhappily, Burke was not far wrong. The French aristocrats clung, with arrogant tenacity, to their privileges—feudal rights, monopolies of office, exemption from taxes; and to defend these, they organized private armies at home and called in princely armies from abroad. As the revolution spread beyond the middle class into the proletariat and that dark three-quarters of the French population known as the peasantry, hatreds buried for years rose to the surface. Tax collectors and grain profiteers were lynched first; then class hatred brought manor houses and chateaux throughout the country under siege. The other privileged order, the clergy, came under suspicion; radical opinions and acts of ferocious violence spread like wildfire. In August 1792, the Swiss guard protecting the royal palace of the Tuileries was attacked by a mob and torn to bits; in September, wholesale massacres began in the Paris prisons, crowded with royalists and suspected royalists; in January 1793, the king was guillotined;[4] and as part of the systematic executions known as the Reign of Terror, his queen, Marie Antoinette, followed him to the scaffold in October. Whatever their provocations, the revolutionaries in their bloody reprisals went far beyond anything civilized opinion could tolerate. People were executed on rumors, because their hands were not calloused, because they had a Latin book; caught in the street by a mob, they could be hanged from the nearest lamp-post or hacked to pieces with knives. The daily procession of carts from prison to guillotine was a spectacle to delight every sadist in Paris. Scenes of horror like these turned English opinion against the

3. Few middle-class supporters of the revolution took to the trenches in its behalf. Joseph Priestley, a unitarian minister in Birmingham and also a notable chemist, migrated to Pennsylvania after a mob looted his laboratory. William Godwin's two-volume *Political Justice* (1794), though radical enough to please young Shelley, sold for three guineas—reason enough for the government to ignore it. By contrast, the work of Tom Paine was direct, popular, and sustained in its appeal. In *Common Sense* (1776), he had already championed the American Revolution; now, in direct opposition to Burke, he took up the cause of the French in *The Rights of Man* (1791). Both pamphlets were enormously effective, and their simple, trenchant prose strongly influenced later radical writers like Hazlitt and Cobbett.

4. The guillotine was a beheading machine, adapted from Renaissance models by Dr. Joseph Guillotin. The doctor is said to have died on his own machine, but this is a case of the wish supplanting the fact. He died in bed in 1814.

revolution and against many liberal ideas as such; for too many years, the French example converted England into a bulwark of reaction, at home and abroad. A state of war between the two countries was declared early in 1793.

But, much as they loathed the turn the revolution was taking, the English could take little practical action against it. Many aristocrats fleeing the terror crossed the Rhine into Germany, where they persuaded Austria and some German princes to help them crush the revolution; and to these efforts the British extended a good deal of financial aid. But after initial successes on the borders, the exiled aristocrats and their allies were thrown back by a "nation in arms." The revolution mobilized for its support an avalanche of young men, mostly untrained, but furiously roused to defend the country. Bravery on the battlefield was instantly rewarded. Unlike the old army, the revolutionary army cared nothing for blue blood; it wanted only good men, and it got the bravest and best. Though undisciplined and untaught, they were quick, tireless, bold, inventive. Rallying from defeat, they drove allied armies out of the Low Countries, crossed the Rhine to destroy Austrian armies in Germany, and flung a band of ragged, excited boys across the Alps to defeat the Austrians in Italy. They crushed a dangerous rebellion in the western districts known as La Vendée, snuffed out half a dozen provincial rebellions, and wiped out a force of aristocrats who, with British help, tried a landing at Quiberon Bay in Brittany.

Meanwhile, the left-wing Jacobins in the National Assembly hounded to the scaffold the idealistic but ineffectual group named Girondins, and established themselves on the crest of the revolutionary wave.[5] But terror quickly turns on those who wield it, and on July 27, 1794, Robespierre, who had begun the terror and directed it, himself went to the guillotine. It was time for the revolution to pause and take stock. Militarily, things were not bad. France had repelled her enemies and transformed her raw militia into tough and seasoned fighting men. She had lost colonies, in the West Indies mostly; she had been blockaded, with considerable damage to her manufactures and more to her trade. But her social order was in shambles. The best educated and most experienced administrators had all been killed or driven out; the currency was worthless; feuding factions made the National Assembly a picture of confusion. Outsiders thought France would soon collapse in total anarchy. In fact, while the floor of the assembly was often chaotic, special committees had been writing a full program of intelligently designed and farsighted legislation. The laws were often enacted and then forgotten by an assembly intent on its faction fights. But after Robespierre's death, the need for a new central authority was apparent; and that authority, when it established itself, found a brilliant new program already in place, requir-

5. *Jacobins* were members of a revolutionary club, "The Society of the Friends of the Constitution," who met in a convent near the church of St. Jacques in Paris. As extreme French radicals, they are to be distinguished from the conservative English *Jacobites* who supported James II and his progeny after 1688. The *Girondins,* a liberal republican group, were so called because many of their leaders came from the Gironde, a district near Bordeaux.

ing only to be put into execution. The new authority, cradled in a new constitution and surrounded by an arabesque of representative bodies, was a five-man executive called the Directory. Though overwhelmingly approved by popular vote, the new Directory appeared tyrannical and oppressive to die-hard Jacobins; they rioted against it. But the Directory turned to a rising young general of artillery who, on 5 October 1795, fired into the Paris mob a charge of grapeshot that dispersed it, and established the Directory's authority beyond question. The officer was a Corsican, just twenty-six years old, named Napoleon Bonaparte. The Directory that rode to power on the carriages of his guns continued for four more years to govern France; but Bonaparte and his armies were the powers sustaining it, and when he chose to appear from behind its screen as First Consul (1799) and then Emperor (1804) there was no one to say him nay.

EVENTS IN ENGLAND

Because France held undisputed initiative through these years, it has been necessary to sketch quickly the chief events of the revolution and reaction. Events succeeded one another with breathless speed; from the first thunderclap of the Bastille to the coronation of an emperor, barely fifteen years elapsed. By contrast, life moved slowly in England under a government darkly suspicious of liberal change. The government of William Pitt, taking a firm stand against the revolution, directly opposed any politicians who seemed remotely sympathetic to it. To deal with suspected conspiracies, the government suspended *habeas corpus*, rendering radicals liable to indefinite imprisonment without trial. Other laws made any criticism of the government, even casual words in a tavern, an act of treason; and severe laws were enacted against working-class combinations of the kind that later became trade unions. Meanwhile, the British economy boomed on war orders and wartime prices. Britain had the most productive manufacturing plant in the world, and her full output went to equip British and allied armies wherever there was a chance of harrying the French. But for a long time French armies, under the deft direction of Napoleon, moved from end to end of Europe as they pleased, while the British navy held control of the seas and blockaded French ports. Twice, in 1797 and 1804, Napoleon seemed on the point of striking a mortal blow by invading across the channel. He assembled troops and transports, while on the other side the British built blockhouses and mobilized to repel the invader. But the blow never came, and Napoleon turned elsewhere. On the other hand, after the revolutionary French armies were created in 1792, neither Britain nor any of her allies ever came close to hitting at the heart of French land power.

Though splendid, Britain's victories at sea were mostly defensive. On 14 February 1797, Sir John Jervis caught a Spanish fleet off Cape St. Vincent and destroyed it; the Spanish had been on their way to help the French invasion of

England.[6] Another preventive strike knocked out France's mediterranean fleet in the battle of the Nile (1 August 1798), thereby crippling Napoleon's plans for an eastern empire. Still another defended the English blockade of French ports by invading the Baltic sea (April 1801) and overawing a coalition of northern powers. Climactically, England's most famous sailor, Horatio Lord Nelson, met the French fleet off Trafalgar on 21 October 1805, and at the cost of his own life destroyed it—thereby putting the last chance of an invasion completely out of sight (SFR, G.9). Victories like these were tonic for public opinion, and they made Nelson a national legend; but they left or seemed to leave French power on the Continent altogether untouched.

IRISH REVOLT AND REPRESSION

Meanwhile, events in Ireland took an ugly turn for Britain. During the American war, sympathy with the colonists joined with awareness of English difficulties to create in the Protestant Anglo-Irish establishment a move for greater independence. This was the result, not of impoverishment, but of prosperity. The eighteenth-century wars, as they increased the demand and raised the price for meat, grain, and dairy products, were a boon to Irish landlords. The prosperity of the upper class can be read to this day in the neoclassic townhouses of Dublin city and in palatial rural seats like Powerscourt, south of Dublin. But the reforms achieved during the early 1780s by Henry Flood and Henry Grattan proved more verbal than solid. In 1782, for instance, decisions of the Irish Parliament were freed from the veto power hitherto exercised by the English privy council; but the change was superficial, since most Irish people were still deprived, as Roman Catholics, of the right to vote. Catholic emancipation bills, which would have cut deeper, could not be passed; and though Pitt in 1785 proposed freedom of trade between Ireland and England, such a measure could never overcome English opposition. Standing frustrations of this sort were naturally inflamed by radical ideas flowing out of France after 1789. Early in the 1790s, a Protestant radical named Wolfe Tone joined with Catholic leaders like Napper Tandy to form the United Irishmen, an organization uniting both religious persuasions to obtain parliamentary reform in Ireland. That original aim was moderate; it soon gave way to the larger aim of expelling the British entirely, and then to the subversive aim of using French military force to do so.

Given the turbulence in France, the divisions in Ireland, and the fact of British power, such a plot was hard to execute. A first conspiracy was broken up in

6. In the brief security after Jervis's victory, two well-organized and curiously loyal naval mutinies broke out, at Spithead off Portsmouth, and the Nore in the Thames estuary (1797). Long-standing grievances over bad food, low pay, and brutal officers were responsible. The respectful mutineers won a remarkable victory in the first instance, but lost cohesion and were cruelly punished in the second (SFR, G.11).

1794–1795; in 1796 a French fleet which actually reached Bantry Bay was turned back by bad weather and inept French sailors. Finally, in 1798, just as Napoleon was turning his primary attention to Egypt, the Irish agents in France did get a minimal commitment from the Directory. Troops and ships were assigned for three small landing parties to be put ashore in different districts of Ireland. Expectation was that patriots would rise *en masse* to support them; and, indeed, there was some rallying in the countryside, long remembered in the ballad about "the boys of Wexford," who turned out with shillelaghs and pitchforks to fight British redcoats at Vinegar Hill (21 June 1798). But the insurrections were cruelly put down, invading French troops dispersed, local leaders either killed or captured. Tone committed suicide in prison the day before he was to be hanged; his associate, Lord Edward Fitzgerald, died of a wound received when he was captured.

One permanent result of the '98 rising, almost the only one, was final abolition of the Irish Parliament. Imperfect as it was, indeed disgraceful, the Irish Parliament had maintained a minimal awareness of Irish problems; when it was abolished by the Act of Union in 1801,[7] the Irish were recompensed with 100 seats in the British Commons, a corresponding number (28) in the House of Lords. But in Westminster they were a small minority before a majority five times as large, of whom few cared about Catholic emancipation and even fewer about Irish affairs. Thus the revolt of '98, in ending the one period of relative prosperity that modern Ireland has known, paved the way for the darkest events of the nineteenth century, the great potato famine and the depopulation it caused. It also drove William Pitt from office (1801); he had promised Catholic emancipation as a reward for union, and when he could not deliver, was honor-bound to resign.

A WAR OF EMPIRES

Pitt's weak and temporary successor as prime minister was Henry Addington, who engineered the equally weak and temporary peace of Amiens (March 1802). But Napoleon wanted only a truce, not a peace; the great war was renewed in May 1803, and just a year later Pitt was back as prime minister. The new war threatened England's social structure less fundamentally than the old one. Early in 1804, Napoleon suggested to the French senate that a move to declare him emperor would be very welcome. He protected himself against possible challenge by having the duc d'Enghien, most active among the descendants of the late king, kidnapped out of Germany and judicially murdered; and on 2 Decem-

7. Since a Parliament could be abolished only with its own consent, the British made open use of bribery in 1801. They may have been helped by the Protestant interest, which saw itself on the verge of being outnumbered by Catholics, whose emancipation was only a matter of time.

ber, in Nôtre Dame cathedral, he waved aside Pope Pius VII and set the crown on his own head as emperor of the French.

These acts gave evidence of growing megalomania in the emperor; they also destroyed forever the image of France as a revolutionary, democratic power. Henceforth, she was frankly imperialist; and instead of having the people with them when they "liberated" a new country, French soldiers were faced with growing hatred and active hostility. Still, for the moment, Napoleon was able to win smashing victories over England's allies in eastern Europe—over the Austrians and Russians at Austerlitz (1805), over the Prussians at Jena (1806), over the Russians again at Friedland (1807). But word of these stunning successes, in which Napoleon finally perfected that coordination of massed artillery preparation with furious infantry assaults on which his fame rested, reached England only as from a distance. Most of the novels of Jane Austen were written, and are supposed to take place, during the last years of the Napoleonic wars; it has often been remarked that she hardly notices them. Garrison soldiers of proper rank and naval officers of good family are among the matrimonial prospects contemplated by her young ladies; they provide gallant company at county balls. Actual warfare is kept the other side of a rather remote horizon; and the prospect that war would ever end must have seemed altogether visionary.

BONAPARTE'S RETREAT

But an over-aggressive decision of 1806 opened cracks in Napoleon's armor. Under the imposing name of a "Continental System," he decreed a counter-blockade against England; unable to invade, he would starve her out. All European nations were ordered to refuse British ships, decline British imports, and cease exporting to Britain. To enforce this counterblockade the emperor had to take steps, at opposite ends of his empire, which ultimately brought him down. These were the invasions of the Iberian peninsula (1807) and of Russia (1812); both grew out of the 1806 decision.

Alliance between England and Portugal went back to the fourteenth century; in the seventeenth, Charles II had married (not very happily, to be sure) a Portuguese princess. Napoleon disliked trade relations between the two countries as a breach of his "system"; after the destruction of his navy at Trafalgar, he also feared the British might land an expeditionary force. Accordingly, he decided to occupy Portugal, and arranged with Carlos IV the oxlike king of Spain, and his corrupt minister Godoy, to let French armies pass through Spain. But, finding the Iberian governments weak, the new emperor could not resist what looked like easy pickings. He talked the Spanish king into sending off the best of his army for garrison duty in the Baltic, then moved French troops, first into the frontier towns, next into the major cities of Spain. These were not citizen-soldiers any more; most had been fighting for ten or fifteen years, and they saw Spain as one more place like Italy or Germany where they could bully civilians and sweep up loot. But on 2 May 1808, the residents of Madrid began rioting against the foreigners to whom their own ruler had betrayed them; reprisals simply provoked them to greater fury, and the revolt spread across Spain. The entire royal family, along with Godoy (who was the king's devoted favorite, and doubled as the queen's lover), was thrown out. Napoleon installed his brother Joseph as king of Spain; but by now guerilla warfare had enveloped the whole peninsula, and the English were in a position to help out. Their expeditionary troops were put under command of two skillful generals, first Sir John Moore, then Sir Arthur Wellesley, who during the war was created duke of Wellington.

The Peninsular War, as it is known to history, was savage, destructive, and prolonged. Some formal battles were fought, but much of the struggle was impromptu back-street murder. Far from greeting the French as liberators, the common folk of Spain sniped at them from ambush and knifed them in the dark. Towns closed their gates to the French and fought them, with priests and women on the barricades, till nothing was left but rubble and corpses. The English armies, though small, built around Lisbon a triple wall of impregnable fortifications to serve as a base. French armies, lured into attacking them there, found themselves pinned down while around them the peasantry picked clean and burned bare the entire countryside. Then, when the sick, cold, and hungry French started to retreat, they were swarmed on by flying squadrons of British dragoons, bands of savage peasants, and irregular troops (half bandits, half militiamen) under local commanders.

Still, though the Peninsular War was a running sore on the French economy, draining troops and supplies from the imperial heartland, it would not by itself have brought Napoleon down. But as this war dragged on, Napoleon learned that on another front the Russians, whom he thought he had neutralized, were slipping back into the British trade orbit. Accordingly, in the summer of 1812, he invaded, confident that he could defeat Russia as easily as before. But Russian armies, aided by guerillas and partisans and fighting on their own soil, proved to be terrible opponents. After they had wearied and weakened the Grande Armée by strategic retreats and diversionary attacks, the Russians stood and fought with fierce determination at Smolensk and Borodino; though technically they won neither battle, they forced on Napoleon losses and delays he could ill afford. By the time he reached Moscow, his only hope lay in Russian capitulation, and there was no reason at all to capitulate. Even as the dreaded Russian winter settled down, the capital was put to the torch, and the long retreat began. Of its horrors we need not speak in detail; approximate figures suggest that, of the 700,000 troops with which he launched the invasion, Napoleon had lost, by the time he reached Paris again, more than 500,000.

And now all the enemies that Napoleon had made during his career of conquest rose against him at once. For years the Prussians had been smarting under

Napoleonic restrictions; they joined the victorious Russians and (after negotiations in which Napoleon's sense of political realities showed itself, for the first time, seriously clouded) the Austrians. A powerful contingent of Swedish soldiers joined in, and the battlefield was determined as eastern Germany. At first the emperor had some successes, but they were never decisive, and after Dresden (27 August 1813), he won no more battles. Leipzig (19 October) was an unrelieved disaster, and Napoleon retreated steadily westward, fighting rear-guard actions as he went. Meanwhile, Wellington's armies had broken out of their defensive positions in Portugal, capturing in two sieges of indescribable savagery Ciudad Rodrigo and Badajoz (January and April 1812). These were the gates to the rest of Spain, and before summer was out, Wellington had routed the French at Salamanca (22 July), entered Madrid (12 August), and was attacking Burgos in the northern mountains (19 September). From a minor nuisance on the fringe of a great empire, he had suddenly become a major factor, occupying a full half of Napoleon's available troops. In 1813 he drove Joseph Bonaparte ignominiously from the throne of Spain, and crossed the frontier to occupy Toulouse. While he was regrouping there, an allied coalition, driving from the east, pushed across the Rhine; and suddenly everything came apart at once. Holland and Switzerland declared their independence of France, marshals of France defected, Paris surrendered. At Fontainebleau, on 11 April 1814, the emperor signed a deed of abdication. He was allowed to set up a little toy court on the island of Elba, off Italy's west coast; and as the allied armies streamed into Paris, they carried with them an odd survivor from the age before the flood. He was Louis-Stanislas Xavier de Bourbon, younger brother by a year of the late Louis XVI. In 1814 he was fifty-nine years old, fat, gouty, weak, and timid. Still, such as he was, if Napoleon had been a usurper, Louis-Stanislas Xavier had to be legitimate king of France; he was therefore installed as Louis XVIII.[8]

One more episode in the thunderous career of Napoleon remains to be described, before we return to insular matters; but it is a fitting climax to a war of giants. After less than a year on Elba, Napoleon became aware that France was seething with discontent. Louis had deliberately antagonized the Napoleonic veterans and the new Napoleonic nobility; the allied powers, meeting to formalize peace at Vienna, were squabbling with one another, and threatening reprisals which stirred deep distress in France. Hesitation was never in Napoleon's nature; evading his guards, he slipped away and landed in Provence. Troops sent out to repel or capture him spontaneously joined his colors. On the nineteenth of March, 1815, he entered Paris in triumph, while Louis XVIII skulked sheepishly away to Ghent.

For just one hundred days, from 19 March to 22 June 1815, Napoleon again ruled in Paris. But he was not comfortable as the constitutional monarch he had

---

8. Louis XVII, son of Louis XVI and commonly known as the dauphin, lived to age ten and survived his father's execution by only two years, before dying (1795) in a Directory prison. Uncertainty over his fate produced a crop of nineteenth-century impostors, one of whom pops up in Mark Twain's novel *Huckleberry Finn*.

to pretend to want to be, and though he was only forty-five years old, many felt that his once superb powers of concentration were failing. The allies were, of course, assembling their forces as fast as possible, under the command of Wellington; given time, they could have outnumbered the French by two or three to one. In fact, Wellington's troops at Waterloo numbered some 42,000 German and Dutch infantrymen, stiffened by 21,000 English veterans of the peninsular war, who stood off Napoleon's 70,000 French till help could arrive from Blucher's 80,000 Prussians. It was the stand of the British regimental squares on the fatal eighteenth of June against the last desperate charge of Napoleon's old guard that decided the day. The French army broke, Napoleon abdicated again, and was sent into permanent exile on the remote South Atlantic island of Saint Helena.[9] The allied ministers returned to their interrupted conference at Vienna; and for the next century (with the single exception of the Crimean conflict of 1854–1856) England was not to fight another land war in Europe.

ENGLAND IN 1815

The nation that emerged in 1815, triumphant after a quarter century of war, was not constitutionally very different from the nation that entered the conflict. It was still dominated by landowners and their solid though not always presentable allies, industrialists and manufacturers. The ruling classes still ran the government very much as they chose, through their absolute domination of parliament, their monopoly of local offices, their control of the legal system. Absurdities of representation continued as before: sheep pastures devoid of human habitants sent two representatives to parliament, while flourishing cities sent none. The church of England retained its exclusive privileges; Catholics (including many whose grim determination at Waterloo had saved the nation) were still not allowed to vote. Dissenters could not take degrees at the universities, and the old seventeenth-century Test Act, barring them from public office, was still unrepealed though not always enforced. The court of chancery bumbled on (as in Dicken's novel *Bleak House*), still notoriously the slowest, most incompetent court in the realm. (Lord Eldon as chancellor controlled it for almost thirty years, during which he fought off any suggestion or even thought of change.) The exchequer still kept its financial records through a system of tally sticks and pipe rolls which had been obsolete in the fourteenth century. The chief law of the land was still the common law based on a deepening pile of interpretations and precedents growing every year less penetrable. Hundreds of different offenses, most trivial,

9. Many years before, when Napoleon was a schoolboy in Corsica, he kept a notebook of his studies in geography; it still survives, in the Laurentian library, in Florence, Italy. The last entry begins, "Saint Helena, a small island in the South Atlantic"—and then breaks off abruptly, as if under pressure of a premonition. The book was never written in again.

others obsolete, still carried the death penalty.[10] Branding of criminals had been abolished in the early reign of George III, but the punishment of the pillory remained on the books. Poaching still carried ferocious penalties; the laws against political protest were as tough as ever, maybe tougher. Newspapers were not only censored, they carried a heavy tax to keep them out of the hands of common folk. Peers of the realm still held almost all the cabinet and foreign service posts, and for most government sinecures only gentlemen were eligible. Workmen's "combinations," that is, unions, had been illegal during the war and were now tolerated, but not out of sympathy; experience had proved that repressive laws forced them underground where they were still effective and harder to keep track of.

Most of these accumulated anachronisms had long been complained of; but during the war most efforts at change, even those advocated by Pitt, had been stifled with the plea that social reform was dangerous when radical propaganda was rife. Besides, Burke's popular argument that the English constitution was an organic growth, proceeding by a logic of its own higher than mere logicality, tended to muffle criticism of any social anomaly, however gross. Always and instinctively, Burke gave preference to what had grown over what was made. For him the unwritten traditions of the constitution represented the cumulative wisdom of the race; to abandon any part of it for mere specious logic would be rash and foolish. Such words fell like music on the ears of many who had tangible reasons to be content with the present order of things.[11]

Indeed, as the British emerged into the full light of the nineteenth century, their rulers had good reason for complacency. Clearly, and by a great margin, they commanded the foremost industrial nation of Europe and the world. English manufacturing was successful world-wide in the traditional areas of wool, cotton, steel, and coal; its greatest triumphs lay ahead of it in the form of railroads, steamships, telecommunications, and cities which were not only productive but humane and attractive places to live. Having destroyed Napoleon and his European system, the British could afford to be moderate in restraining cynical reactionaries like Metternich of Austria, and evangelical autocrats like Czar Alexander of Russia. With reactionary governments in control of things from the Urals to

10. Forgery was still a hanging offense, but with a difference. In 1777 an admired London clergyman had been executed for this crime, despite popular agitation on his behalf. Now in the nineteenth century bankers themselves were pleading for a change in the law; their hearts had not softened, but the fact was that juries, knowing a guilty verdict meant death, would no longer convict, even on the plainest evidence.

11. One doesn't much exaggerate in using terms like "medieval organicism," or "bourgeois feudalism" to describe English government as it survived into the early nineteenth century. Reverence for the local interest, the standing privilege, adjusted—not without some jostling—to accommodate capitalist faith in the free operation of supply and demand. Loose as it is, and subject to abuse, there's no better word for the coalition of ruling classes and organs of opinion—parliament, magistracy, clergy, press, academics—than "the Establishment."

Gibraltar, the Continent could be left to police itself, and the less strictly the better.

The really serious problem confronting England after 1815 was not foreign but domestic; it was an accumulation of discontents put off or put down for decades and now crying out for redress. Industrial warfare had strengthened the manufacturing classes in their sense of national importance; contact with French rationalism and awareness of American democracy had worked their influence. Even those who profited by the old system were ready to concede its rottenness in many areas. When revolution was out of the picture, the nation was ready to consider reform. What nobody foresaw was that some of the reforms would have larger consequences than even revolutionaries could anticipate.

SOCIAL LIFE UNDER THE REGENCY: BUCKS AND SWELLS

Strolling through London during those halfway years when George III was incapable either of ruling or dying, an observer might have been struck by the docility with which the English still followed fashions set in France. As long as Marie Antoinette and Louis XVI held court at Versailles, their ornate and powdered elegance was the object of English imitation. But fashions changed as fast as political regimes in France. Under the Directory and when Napoleon was First Consul, France was trying to emulate the Roman Empire; accordingly, both French and English ladies changed to the severe and bewitching simplicity of a Greek robe most like a nightgown, cut very low in front, gathered with a simple ribbon just below the breasts, and falling in semi-transparent pleats to the ankle. With a bonnet for their neatly coiffed and beribboned heads, and low satin slippers for their feet, Jane Austen's young ladies may be supposed to have followed this free and natural fashion. The young men whom they pursue wear either uniforms or a civilian costume of tight breeches (often with a strap under the instep to keep them tight), a ruffled shirt with carefully folded neck-cloth, and a high-collared coat with broad shoulders and long tails. The prince regent was a fancy dresser in his slender days, though he could not keep up with his friend Beau Brummel, who raised masculine dress to a fine art and finally, under the title of *dandyism*, almost to the level of a religious cult. During the century, artists and men of letters like Byron, Stendhal, D'Orsay, Baudelaire, and Disraeli took turns at playing dandy. Though it was a fad, dandyism was more than a mere fad; in its elegance, idleness, and total effortless command of a situation, the dandy's stance suggests that of the artist, who by sheer knack of style imposes brilliance on the common things of life.[12]

The early nineteenth century has been called the age of elegance; it was also

12. A number of studies have tried to fix the dandy mystique, among them a few incisive pages in Baudelaire's "Peintre de la vie moderne," Barbey d'Aurevilly's study of Brummel from the 1860s, and Ellen Moers's modern study, *The Dandy* (1960).

the age of display. Because the upper ranks of society were now rich beyond precedent, life, on that level at least, was ostentatious and promiscuous. Lady Oxford produced children by so many different lovers that her family was popularly known as the Oxford Miscellany; the set in which she moved saw nothing exceptional in this. No young squire who wanted to be known as a blood came up to the university without a retinue of servants, a cellar full of bottles, a stable full of horses, and at least one mistress.[13] Regency bucks spent their lives shooting, gambling, drinking, chasing foxes through copses and ladies through bedrooms. The stately homes now became palatial in extent, staffed with regiments of housemaids and menservants, surrounded by miles of park patrolled by gamekeepers. When the diversions of the country palled, the genteel family moved to their townhouse for the "season," a round of balls, parties, and theatrical entertainments. In building and decoration, a curious restless eclecticism started to be felt, as if the new century were groping for a public mask to put on. Greco-Roman style continued to be used for London clubs, for the British Museum, or for a Birmingham town hall, but such a structure was likely to rub shoulders with a Gothic church on one side and a half-timbered Tudor manor house on the other. Furniture in the "Directory" and "Empire" styles followed classical models through French intermediaries, but there was also a vogue for Egyptian decoration, fruit of Napoleon's expedition to that land. When the regent erected a pleasure pavilion at Brighton, the channel town he was the first to popularize, he ordered the architect John Nash to build it in the Persian style. It still stands, an exotic pastel bubble of fantasy, with its onion domes, pagodas, and oriental decorations (SFR, G.7).

Collecting became a mania for well-to-do Englishmen. Lord Elgin was sent as ambassador to Constantinople; finding that Greece was under Turkish control, he took occasion to pick up all the friezes and pediment sculptures from the Parthenon. He shipped them to London where, in due course, the British government bought them. Despite more than a century of Greek protests, they still stand in the British Museum. Joseph Smith, sent by George III as consul to Venice, improved the shining hour by picking up all the Venetian paintings he could; after his return, he sold them to his sovereign for £20,000, and they still form part of the royal collections. Joseph Bonaparte, when kicked out as king of Spain, tried to carry off the best part of the Prado with him; he had the pictures cut out of their frames and stacked in a wagon like so many *crêpes*. But at Vittoria (21 June 1813) the collection fell into the hands of Wellington's army, and those canvasses not stolen or destroyed went to Britain, where many now hang in the National Gallery. Art buyers, art dealers, and art thieves were busy the length

13. By no coincidence, the two universities stood, at the turn of the century, close to the low point of their intellectual repute. Sons of the gentry attended to learn the fashionable vices; potential Anglican parsons picked up habits of servility like those of unspeakable Mr. Collins in *Pride and Prejudice*. On the other hand, dissenting academics and the universities of Scotland were centers of intellectual life.

and breadth of Europe; they did not serve Englishmen exclusively, but as the English had most money, that was where the best pickings went.

THE NEW POWER OF THE WORD

A social phenomenon of the eighteenth century rich in portents for the nineteenth was the rise of Edmund Burke, whose name has already occurred several times in connection with the French Revolution, and could well have been invoked in connection with the American struggle. Apart from his amazing talents, Burke was a novelty because he achieved political power and social status without massive money, the influence of a family, or the prestige of landed estates. He was the son of a Dublin lawyer, not very well educated at Trinity College, Dublin, and not very successful at the practice of law in London. For some years he scratched out a living on Grub Street, writing miscellaneous productions for the booksellers. But he had political and elocutionary abilities, which about 1765 brought him to the attention of the Whig leader, Lord Rockingham; and under the patronage of Rockingham he remained, till the latter's death in 1782. After that, and in spite of debts almost as magnificent as his estates, he was a leader in his own right.

In politics, Burke was a man of broad principles as well as Ciceronian amplitude of thought. His speech on conciliation with the American colonies (1775) recognized in the American principle of "no taxation without representation" a tenet of English law fundamental to the constitution; accordingly, he opposed the war against the Americans throughout its long, weary course. In 1790, on the other hand, his *Reflections on the Revolution in France* denounced the revolution and all its works (see above, p. 344). Some found the two positions hard to reconcile, but Burke's philosophy sharply distinguished abstract philosophical radicalism from respect for the organic principles of an established community. He could therefore endorse the ideas underlying one revolution and denounce those underlying the other with what looked like majestic independence. Indeed, there was something grand, even grandiose, about Burke; without actually being one, he lived and thought like a lord. His thought, though it led to no great political career, and indeed kept him for most of his life in the opposition, continues to have vital influences even today. And his example of a man rising to power by force of unaided intellect began to exercise its influence on the political life of the nation almost as soon as the wars with France were over.

Despite his lack of the wherewithal, Burke felt impelled to live like a great landed proprietor because the English social system laid great emphasis on aristocratic values; perhaps he was so subtle and intelligent in setting forth those values because he came to them as an outsider. At all events, in eighteenth-century England, land was the form of wealth carrying most privileges and admitting one most directly to positions of authority. Men grown wealthy by trade or through the professions were expected to launder their money by acquiring land with it before they (or preferably their sons or grandsons) presumed to a position among the king's ministers. There was some excuse for this view, especially at the time. Men who had fought their way up to ownership of factories or shipping companies tended to be fairly rough diamonds; tough survivors of a tough competition, they couldn't be expected to have the wide views and disinterested outlook of a good administrator. In addition, a lot of pure snobbery stood against them. Most good society held it against even an able conservative politician like George Canning (see below, p. 376) that his mother had been an actress. As a matter of fact, he never hesitated to use the same argument against others: they could not be good public servants because they were men of no background.

But early in the nineteenth century a new class of men came to the fore, emulating Burke in their reliance on the power of thought and language, but speaking for a new and utterly different set of values. They were not landowners, not capitalists, they had few family connections, held no public office and wished none, yet they wielded major influence on public affairs. They were philosophical journalists, word-men. Though sometimes comfortable, their backgrounds were never distinguished. Jeremy Bentham, for instance, was the son of a London attorney, wealthy but far from eminent; Thomas Macaulay's father was in trade and edited on the side an abolitionist journal; Francis Jeffrey and Henry Brougham were Edinburgh lawyers; James Mill was the son of a small-town Scottish shoemaker; and William Gifford, born a pauper in Devon, lived by manual labor before his gift for letters asserted itself. The rise of these men to influence was not concerted; the vehicle of their rise was a new sort of serious periodical, the review; and the advent of the review coincided with, though it was not directly caused by, major changes in the economics and technology of publication.

Basic to all these changes was the mushrooming population of the land. Here, for the first time, we can speak with assurance. After overcoming many superstitious objections, the first English census was held in 1801. It revealed a population of nearly 9 million in England and Wales alone. Ten years later the comparable figure stood at over 10 million, and in 1821 it was more than 12 million. That was a growth rate for the first decade of 14 percent and for the second of over 18 percent—phenomenal multiplication! (Counting Ireland and Scotland would have increased the figure for 1801 by 7 million, that for 1821 by 9 million, more or less.) Though schools were often poor, some of these new English speakers learned to read; a few became habitual readers. Periodicals sprang up to give them reading matter. During George's early reign, newspapers suffered from government disapproval; they were censored and taxed. But after 1815 the tax was not raised; it diminished, though slowly, and long before it was abolished, in 1855, most of its repressive effect had worn off.[14] For the wars created a huge appetite for news. Circulation figures boomed, and the Londoner had his choice, every morning, of half a dozen papers. Declining postal rates made it possible to circulate these papers beyond the metropolis; and new technology helped printers keep up with the demand. Early in the century, papermaking machines were imported from France, where they had been invented. Machine-made paper is not as good as hand-made paper, but it is cheaper and for many purposes just as practical. In 1814 steam power was first applied, by the *London Times*, to a printing press. By modern standards, production of 1,100 sheets an hour is paltry; for those days, and by comparison with hand presses, it was stupendous. Not only journalism, but literature too profited directly from the new technology. Back in 1774 a crucial liberating decision on the law of copyright had been made in the case of *Donaldson v. Beckett*. Under the old law of 1709 literary properties, almost all owned by booksellers rather than authors, were perpetual monopolies: they never lapsed. Men had been prosecuted for reprinting *Paradise Lost* more than seventy years after it was first published. The 1774 case put a time limit on copyright, after which a work entered the "public domain." As soon as the technology for cheap reprints became available, England was flooded with sixpenny paperbound books by Defoe, Swift, Shakespeare, Milton, Dryden, Congreve—all the great writers of the past. Schoolboys, though forced to assemble Latin verses in the classroom, got to read good English books in their spare time; sometimes the habit stuck (SFR, H.12).

On the wave of this new literacy and literary awareness, the reviews rode to popularity, carrying their contributors to positions of influence. These new publications were more serious than the old magazines, less miscellaneous; they paid better, granted a writer more space to develop his thoughts, and so got abler people to write for them. The many Scotsmen writing for the reviews were partly a result of the good general education offered by Scottish universities. Politically, the reviews took no common ground. The *Edinburgh Review*, started in 1802, was mostly Whig, the *Quarterly Review*, started in 1809, was Tory in tone. The *Westminster Review* was founded in 1824 with Jeremy Bentham's money and as his personal vehicle. Lacking party affiliation, it did not circulate widely, but its influence was often greater than that of the other reviews. It reached "the people who counted"; that was a popular phrase in the early century, one of those phrases that nobody can define but that in a loose way are very clear indeed.

The serious tone of the reviews rose from and in its turn deepened the seriousness of two new and potent movements in English society: evangelical religion and utilitarian philosophy. On paper they did not seem to have much in common, in practice they often overlapped.

14. Printers and publishers developed ingenious subterfuges for avoiding the tax; they posed effectively as martyrs to a cruel tyranny; and, above all, they strengthened their finances by selling advertisements, which made them less subject to government influence (SFR, G.23).

RESPECTABILITY AND REPRESSION

Evangelical (i.e., revivalist) religion had its roots in Methodism; it preached personal conversion and individual piety. Two forceful figures who helped inoculate the Anglican establishment with Methodist zeal were William Wilberforce, a wealthy Yorkshire philanthropist, and Hannah More, a tireless, tiresome lady with a small literary gift.[15] Their special crusades included Sabbatarianism (avoidance of any worldly activities on Sunday); hostility to the theater and to worldly literature as a whole; and the abolition of slavery. Like their Methodist precursors, the evangelicals were energetic, vehement, sincere. Among themselves, they had a way of referring to outsiders as "gentiles"; they talked freely of "converting" people who thought themselves perfectly good Christians already. On their special points they were a little crazy. When the French were threatening invasion, and Pitt had the militia drilling on Sunday (their only free day), Wilberforce objected. He said the Lord had sent the French only to show His displeasure at violation of the Sabbath, and would dismiss Napoleon elsewhere when the wicked practice ceased.

The new moral religion bore down hard on what it called "the mere animalism" of the lower classes; it rebuked, though more gently, the casual amorality of the rich; larger social evils hardly concerned it at all. Evangelicals might chide a rich man for playing cards or reading Shakespeare on Sunday, but not for sweating children in his factories through the week. They would not let the Lord's name be taken in vain, but did not notice if seamen were flogged to death, if Irish peasants starved, if poor women were forced onto the streets by starvation wages. Against chattel slavery, which was not one of England's pressing problems, they were, by their lights, successful. In 1807 Wilberforce got the slave trade outlawed (it moved immediately into foreign hands), and a bill emancipating all slaves on English soil passed in August 1833, a month after his death. But where the evangelicals might have trod on wealthy toes, they remained strangely silent. Rakes like Byron and generous-hearted men like Hazlitt and the Reverend Sydney Smith thought the new religiosity mere hypocrisy; and indeed, high-pressure virtue could only encourage the activities of Mrs. Grundy and her hateful neighbor, Nosey Parker. The Society for the Suppression of Vice, established in 1802, began a program of snooping and prosecuting which would climax, twenty years later, with an effort to suppress Shelley's *Queen Mab*. Against this sort of thing there were really violent objections. But sarcasms and sullen dislike were waved aside. The moral tone of society was changing, not from the top down or from the bottom up, but from the middle out, and among the sanctified young in reaction against their debauched elders. Personal honor being a worldly principle, the duel and the codes surrounding it largely disappeared from

15. Working with her sisters, Hannah More wrote tracts for the poor; they were simple, pious, and very popular. Cobbett caricatured them by saying they described "the celestial death of an evangelical mouse who, though starving, would not touch the master's cheese and bacon."

society. Drunkenness, no longer an amusing gentlemanly excess, became a personal disgrace.[16] Sunday schools, teetotal societies, and moral encouragement of the deserving poor became the special concern of voluntary societies, much like those of an earlier century (above, p. 261). Middle-class ladies set aside special days to visit the "unfortunate" and leave pious tracts for their edification. Abolishing the liquor trade was impractical but Sunday drinking could be stopped and was. From this period we start hearing of the grim, gloomy English Sunday, when all forms of work and play, down to whittling and whistling, were utterly taboo. The rule no longer holds, but from the war of Napoleon to that of Kaiser Wilhelm it was unbroken. Small changes in manners and mores accumulated toward the extreme prudery of Victorian times. In 1826, Sir Walter Scott's great-aunt asked her literary kinsman to send her the novels of Mrs. Aphra Behn, the Restoration pioneer; sixty years before, she had taken great pleasure in reading them aloud with a mixed company of friends. Now a single glance was enough. Mantled in blushes, she ordered the footman to burn the lot, and was left to muse on what had happened to standards of decency in her lifetime.

SOCIAL SCIENCE IN ACTION

Utilitarianism, forever associated with the name of Jeremy Bentham, and diametrically opposed to the philosophy of Burke, was not a mass movement, but a philosophical outlook emphasizing dispassionate discovery of facts and rational arrangement of institutions to accord with them. (An alternative name was philosophical radicalism—the word "radical," though not the concept, being a fresh recruit to the English language.) Its links with laissez-faire capitalism are obvious; it encouraged pursuit of enlightened self-interest, and valued a free marketplace, in ideas as well as commodities, as useful to that end. Like pragmatism, of which it is in effect a particular version, utilitarianism was not a body of beliefs, but an attitude toward belief. Though it influenced men of all persuasions from socialists to imperialists, it was particularly congenial to civil servants and bureaucrats, such as were increasingly required to guide the affairs of an expanding commercial empire. With growing impetus as England approached the mid-century, reforms and improvements in everyday institutions were proposed by Benthamites. Most were quite unglamorous; they were new drainage systems, penal institutions, legal codes, political and educational improvements. Nor was the personal part played in these matters by Jeremy Bentham instantly apparent. But very often indeed, the impetus for a simple practical change can be traced back to a

16. Sheridan, last of the old school, was picked up one night, incapable of navigation, and asked his name so he could be carried home. "Mr. Wilberforce," he replied, and fell asleep. But what was fun for Sheridan and his sort was sheer torment and nightmare for working-class families. Getting men to break the drink habit was fearfully hard, because there was no sort of home entertainment; the public house was the only center of light, warmth, and fun in the village (SFR, H.27).

lean, precise philosopher who sat in his London house ("The Hermitage"), talking quietly with a few choice associates (SFR, G. 10).

A sour tongue would describe both utilitarians and evangelicals as middle-class do-gooders. Though partial, the phrase is not wholly wrong. The two groups were also quietly united in their devotion to the lean goddess Abstinence. Whether in the name of Jehovah or of Political Economy, much of the advice handed down to working folk in the early nineteenth century had to do with not overindulging themselves. Rarely in their history have the English poor stood in less need of such advice.

THE "LOWER ORDERS"

During the wars, high agricultural prices had helped the landowner while military orders profited the manufacturer. When the French counterblockade cut off European markets, there were hard times, to be sure; some firms went bankrupt. But the survivors developed new markets in India and South America; some learned how to disguise their goods so they could be smuggled into Europe. A particular low point was reached in 1811–1812 when, after a run of bad harvests, the American war of 1812 cut off the chief supply of raw cotton. Midlands manufacturing towns felt the pinch, and some workers, feeling that the new mechanical processes of spinning and weaving caused their misery, embarked on a program of machine smashing.[17] Troops were sent out to repress them, and feelings ran high; but victories in the war, a better English harvest, and quick solution of the American troubles contributed to the return of "normality."

Not that "normality" implied much comfort for working folk. As the cotton industry migrated into factories run by steam power, workers had to migrate with it. Because machinery was expensive, owners tried to keep it running; that meant thirteen working hours a day, six days a week, for children as young as seven. Children were cheap; weekly wages averaged three shillings sixpence for boys, two shillings threepence for girls. Their fingers being small and flexible, children were quick at knotting up broken threads, and that was what they mostly did. After their thirteen hours of mill work, they had two hours of evening school, also in the mill; their day stretched from 6:00 A.M. to 9:00 P.M. A few humanitarians were heard to murmur that the schedule was a bit heavy, but the manufacturers, reinforced by the laissez-faire economists, stood firm: interfering with the free marketplace and the child's right to dispose of his labor would produce nothing but misery—bankruptcy for the employer, starvation for the child. Apart from the basic cruelty of child labor, the industrial towns that coagulated around

17. The machine breakers (known as "Luddites" after Ned Ludd, a Leicestershire precursor of doubtful sanity) remained active from 1811 through 1816. When caught, they were likely to be hanged, a policy against which Lord Byron protested generously if futilely in one of his few parliamentary speeches (February 1812).

factories were appalling places to live. Houses built for workers on minimal wages were naturally minimal houses, jerrybuilt shacks without plumbing or sewage facilities. Outhouse and waterwell stood side by side; street gutters overflowed with liquid filth. Epidemic diseases killed thousands; tuberculosis, malnutrition, gin, and despair did for others.[18]

Why then did workers flock to the miserable factory towns? Because, very often, things were worse in the country. Here and there no doubt the old folkways remained—the steady round of country chores, the homely village ceremonies, the handicraft and homestead existence celebrated as late as the novels of Thomas Hardy. In the north and west, ancient values persisted; we find Wordsworth honoring them in his pedlars, leech gatherers, and sturdy shepherds. But over the rest of England, war had spread a dark pall. High wartime grain prices had made it profitable to cultivate every foot of ground; big landholders gobbled up little ones, reducing yeomen to day laborers. The last bits of common land were enclosed, those few acres where the poor cotter had kept his pig or planted his garden, and which for him meant the difference between survival and starvation. A Parliament dominated by big landlords passed thousands of enclosure acts, each local in scope, the sum of them catastrophic to a way of life. And yet those who grabbed the land did not always profit by it; fields bought in 1812 when wheat sold at 125 shillings a quarter could not pay their mortgage in 1815 when wheat sank to half that price. The new landowner was often foreclosed before he was barely warm in his possession.

Farm labor was hard hit by a well-meant but cruel change in the poor law, begun in the district of Speenhamland in Berkshire and so named; it enabled magistrates to supplement farm wages out of taxes. Employers accordingly began to pay much less than a living wage, knowing that the taxes of their neighbors would be used to bring wages up to, and not one inch above, the barest level of non-starvation. When no longer able to drudge for this pittance, farm workers could be shipped off to the poorhouse. George Crabbe paints their wretched fate in the angry but not exaggerated lines of "The Village."[19] He knew; he had lived among them.

Yet at this moment the prosperity of England was the marvel of Europe. Singlehanded, she had financed twenty years of war against Napoleon; she had a

18. In 1837 the Manchester Statistical Society produced figures showing that Manchester gentry lived more than twice as long as laborers (thirty-eight years on average as against seventeen), but that in rural Rutland county both classes outlived even the Manchester gentry. Yet this was after the first sanitary reforms had been effected in Manchester, and Manchester was far from the worst of English towns. Let us not fail to exclaim over the existence of the Manchester Statistical Society; it was, of course, the work of Bentham and his disciples, and with others of the sort (a London Society dated from 1834) provided for the first time solid evidence on which to found social legislation.

19. Born to poverty in the backwater town of Aldeburgh, Sussex, Crabbe suffered degrading misery as a young man, till rescued in 1783 by Edmund Burke, who, on the strength of his dark, muscular poetry got him a post in the church. Most of Crabbe's blunt, direct verse takes the form of narratives; a little later, he would have written fiction. One of his poetic stories, "Peter Grimes," has been made into an opera, with music by Benjamin Britten.

practical monopoly on the world's carrying trade; her manufactures were so pre-eminent that British cottons, twice carried halfway around the world, could be sold in India more cheaply than the cheapest products of cheap Indian labor in the next village. Her buildings were as solid as her institutions, her credit unrivaled, her navy the strongest, by far, in the world. The question was, how long would her submerged classes accept being outcasts in their own land? The answer was not slow in coming.

THE REVOLUTION IN ENGLISH POETRY

In its early stages the revolution in France represented itself as the triumph of reason over superstition and privilege; an actress from the Comédie Française personated the Goddess Reason in a revolutionary festival, and received homage from the crowd. But in England the old regime had taken its stand, or so it said, on reason itself, the reason of John Locke and Isaac Newton. For those who sympathized with it, a new revolution must therefore be directed against reason and in behalf of something else. That "something else" was most often imagination. For the romantic poets imagination was a supreme organizing and unifying power; it went beyond merely recording and rearranging sense data to create both itself and the world that an individual could know. To see was to create, by composing exterior experience in accordance with basic principles which rise out of the mind in the process of composition. The way we see is who we are. Thus self-analysis became a prime ingredient of all poetry. Blake, exploring his mind, found in it a fearful symmetry to which the spiritual universe was exactly attuned; while Wordsworth created from the story of his own mind's growth and consolidation a poem of epic dimensions. Minds bottomless as mountain tarns need not labor or strain to meet the artificial standards of "correctness" devised by society; without urging or deliberate intent, they will feed themselves "in a wise passiveness." Whether in gentle rapport with nature or in stern, watchful opposition, the romantic poet uses her to define his ego. He seeks her among the naïve and humble, whose minds have not been corrupted by civilization and its oppressive uniformities; he seeks her in extremes of vice, crime, danger, anguish. But always it is the ego itself that fascinates him, as it fascinated the first arch-romantic, Jean-Jacques Rousseau. For as the mind-forged manacles of custom, convention, and conformity are discarded, each individual may hope to recover that birthright of giant strength and perfect innocence with which all men were originally endowed. "The Nature of my Work," Blake wrote, "is Visionary or Imaginative; it is an Endeavor to restore what the Ancients called the Golden Age" (SFR, G.18).

INTERIOR LANDSCAPES

Thus the mind's power to shape the cosmos, even to supplant it, became the primal theme of romantic poetry. Romanticism looked on nature, not for its own sake (as a rule), but as a mirror; it had nothing essential to do with falling in love, unless perhaps with oneself. Embarking together on *Lyrical Ballads* (1798), Wordsworth and Coleridge divided their labors; Wordsworth was to throw the light of imagination over ordinary events, Coleridge to make supernatural events seem dramatically convincing. Both actions illustrate the power of the mind and of the feelings with which it can transform experience. "Kubla Khan" is a vivid type of the mind as a sheltered, self-sufficient pleasure garden within which rises an intermittent dark river of subterranean poetry. In "The Prisoner of Chillon," Byron celebrates the mind's power to make a universe of absolutely minimal materials. Shelley's "Ode to the West Wind" glorifies the harmonies which the cosmic winds can elicit from the Aeolian harp of the poet's passive mind. Keats in the "Ode to Psyche" exults in the mind's ability to burrow deep into its own inner landscape and at the heart of it to discover a shrine, a refuge, a shelter of ultimate value. For all the poets, the mind was supreme; for some it was the only reality. When Blake read Wordsworth's lines in "The Excursion" describing how the individual mind and the external world are mutually fitted to one another, he found the doctrine all too tame and pale. In the margin, he wrote: "You shall not bring me down to believe such fitting & fitted. I know better & please your Lordship." For Blake, mind was nothing less than everything. ("Your Lordship" is a Blakean jab at Wordsworth's imperial assurance.)

Poetry which relied so heavily on inner insights and private intuitions confronted readers with special difficulties. Wordsworth was brutally parodied, Coleridge ridiculed, Keats savaged by the critics, and their friend Leigh Hunt treated like an offender against public decency, before the new style gradually made its way into the canon. Liberating though it might prove in the long run, the supremacy of the imagination shocked many early readers because it seemed a surrender, not only of dignity and decorum in literature, but of rationalism itself. The romantics were not, of course, known as romantics till long after most of them were dead, nor were the principles of their poetry fully grasped. While Blake was largely ignored, nicknames like "the Lake Poets" (Wordsworth and his friend Robert Southey), "the Cockney School" (Keats and his mentor Leigh Hunt), and "the Satanic School" (Byron the rake and Shelley the atheist) indicate both the hostility of the literary establishment and its failure to grasp the new phenomenon as a whole. For the polite, desultory reader of poetry during the century's first quarter, the best poets of the day were sensible men like Thomas Campbell and Samuel Rogers. At least they did not overtax plain readers with their imaginations.

SOME UNITY, MORE DIVERSITY

Though the romantic poets are sometimes divided into "generations"—the first generation Wordsworth and Coleridge, the second generation everybody else, with Blake set aside as a special case—this isn't a very helpful distinction. It is true that by 1803 Coleridge had finished his major poetic work, and by 1807 Wordsworth had done the same, while it wasn't till 1812 that Byron published his first major poem, *Childe Harold,* and Keats and Shelley both reached the climax of their poetic activity in 1819. Still, from first to last, this is a period of only twenty years or so, and "generations" in such a short period don't make much sense. Rather, we can think of the romantic poets as a circle, and not a very closely knit one. Though Blake always stood a little outside the group, among the others there were some close friendships, and a good deal of mutual appreciation. But the principle which united them—an exceptional concern for self-analysis and self-expression—also tended to divide them, and send each off on his own poetic path. It was a circle instinct with centrifugal forces.

As one can't generalize about the romantic poets, the best alternative may be to remind readers, swiftly and with inevitable omissions, of the range and variety of their achievements. They are commonly placed among the lyric voices of England, and this is right, for the direct personal expression of emotion was congenial to them all. From the tremendous gnomic utterances of Blake, which "see eternity in a grain of sand," through the wonderful opulent ease of Keats's great odes, to the poignant, often fragmentary outcries of Shelley (and we mustn't overlook the moving simplicities of Wordsworth's early laments and reveries), the romantics lifted the poetry of feeling almost to the pure sphere of music. In this field of lyric utterance they created a body of poetry unequaled since the Elizabethans, and permanently restructured the definition of what a poem can and should be.

But, aside from lyrics, Byron with "Manfred" and "Cain" (to mention no others), and Shelley with "The Cenci" wrote memorable closet dramas—so memorable that they have occasionally slipped out of the closet and onto the stage. Poems of descriptive meditation like "Tintern Abbey," brief poetic narratives like Wordsworth's "Michael" or Keats's "Lamia," and odes embodying dignified poetic discourse all had existed before the romantics took them in hand; they now took on new inwardness and elevation. To yoke Wordsworth's *The Prelude* with Byron's *Don Juan* may smack of perversity, but both can be seen as modern responses to the slow demise of the epic tradition, and one may get some interesting vibrations from placing Wordsworth's subtitle over Byron's poem: "The Growth of a Poet's Mind." Though he had predecessors among the religious enthusiasts and mystics of earlier centuries, Blake's tremendous cloudy prophecies stand largely apart from any support, literary or philosophical; they provide looming and enigmatic challenges to interpretive mountain climbers. (Blake, we note in passing, was as bold and original in the visual as in the verbal arts. The full dynamic energy of his designs can best be appreciated in London's Tate Gallery; but reproductions, as of his engravings illustrating the Book of Job, can suggest it.) Even relative literary failures, like Wordsworth's "Idiot Boy," are not without their interest when read with an eye to the potent principle that leads them to reject literary ingratiation.

In brief, romantic poetry offers a thick forest for exploration; not the least of its pleasures is the discovery of relatively atypical poems, like Byron's "Darkness" (on the end of the world), Blake's capering farce "An Island in the Moon," Shelley's grotesque "Swellfoot the Tyrant," and dozens of other remarkable poems which the exploring student will have the delight of discovering on his own.

PROSE AND THE VIRTUES OF CONSERVATISM

Political radicalism was the rule among the early romantic poets. Though some turned conservative later, to face ridicule as renegades, most supported the French Revolution (SFR, G.16, 17). Blake, Southey and Wordsworth in their youth, and Shelley were real enthusiasts. (On the Continent, it was not so; French romantics like Lamartine and Chateaubriand were royalist in their politics, and so was young Victor Hugo.) In prose, on the other hand, matters were more evenly balanced. Burke for the conservative and Tom Paine for the radical cause were ideally matched opponents—Burke majestic and philosophical, Paine sharp, clear, and quick. Conservative writers, notably William Gifford and George Canning, also cultivated the popular touch in a sharp satiric weekly called *The Anti-Jacobin*. But long range, the future of Burke's philosophy lay in prose fiction, where the spacious historical romanticism of Sir Walter Scott infused his vast audiences, almost imperceptibly, with a Burkean reverence for the past. On the other side, William Godwin (noted above, p. 344), finding that his cold and doctrinaire idealism had little popular appeal, also resorted to fiction. *Caleb Williams* (1794) was a suprisingly dramatic novel; but the qualities that made it effective as a story of crime and detection distracted from its impact as social propaganda. Many readers who enjoyed its lurid suspense must have overlooked entirely its philosophical point (the depravity of the rich, the moral nobility of the deprived). Still, it pointed a direction; and Godwin's wife Mary Wollstonecraft also tried her hand at fiction before and after her best-known book, the boldly conceived but turgidly written *Vindication of the Rights of Woman* (1792).[20] But writing fiction to support programmatic social ideals posed problems that fiction was not yet ready to confront. Despite wide differences of approach, the major novelists of the early nineteenth century—Walter Scott and Jane Austen in the first instance—agreed in accepting the structure of existing society as background and framework of their stories.

What Jane Austen would have thought of Mary Wollstonecraft's vindication

20. She died giving birth to a daughter Mary, who became Shelley's second wife and wrote, in *Frankenstein,* an early science-fiction thriller whose mythic reverberations have not even yet died away. The *Vindication,* Rousseauistic in its basic ideals despite frequent quarrels with specific ideas of Rousseau, was too outspoken for its time, and indeed for the whole nineteenth century. The relevance of both Burke and Wollstonecraft to major issues of our own day confirms the seminal importance of the French revolution for the history of the last two hundred years.

of her rights we shall unfortunately never know. That women should have, and that some of them do have, strong and sensible minds of their own, she certainly would have agreed. It is not by any petty cunning or insipid allurements that Elizabeth Bennet wins the devoted admiration of Fitzwilliam Darcy. On the other hand, the conditions under which Jane Austen wrote her novels—as a maiden aunt and domestic assistant in the household of her married sister, without a room of her own—might well have needed some vindication. Literary and for that matter social history would have been much enriched had the two women been able to comment on each other's books.

That they would ever have seen eye to eye is not to be expected; for Jane Austen's prevailing habit of mind is quietly ironic, not declamatory, her respect for property and propriety is deep, and she deliberately limits the field of her social observation. Once at the urging of a friend she hesitantly sent one of her novels to Scott, describing it, by deliberate contrast with his high-priced, best-selling, panoramic historical romances, as "a little bit (two inches wide) of ivory," on which she painted "with so fine a brush."[21] It is true that at first glance Jane Austen's novels appear minute and understated. They contain nothing about war, politics, religion, business, or the life of the working classes. Rather they deal with the domestic life of the small gentry, defined as people with an independent income, enabling them to keep a couple of servants, a couple of horses, and a carriage. The problems at the center of the novel are generally matrimonial; young ladies must be fitted out with suitable husbands. Some moderns read the stories as idylls of a cozy, secure world in which stable values prevail; but the severity of these values is as marked as their security. Harriet Smith, protegée of Emma Woodhouse, may fairly aspire to the hand of Mr. Elton the vicar, to that of Mr. George Knightley the squire, or even to that of Mr. Frank Churchill, who is in the way to inherit a very large fortune—so long as she is thought to be the illegitimate daughter of a great nobleman. But when she is found to be a mere tradesman's bastard, that disqualifies her to be anything but a farmer's wife, and lucky she is to find that rank:

She would be placed in the midst of those who loved her, and who had better sense than herself; retired enough for safety, and occupied enough for cheerfulness. She would never be led into temptation, nor left for it to find her out.

How fortunate that she was never permitted to rise higher! "The stain of illegitimacy, unbleached by nobility or wealth, would have been a stain indeed." Through a sentence like that ("unbleached," forsooth!) speaks the lucid and assured voice of the eighteenth century, with its strict social norms. There is a

21. All to Sir Walter's credit, he was and long remained deeply impressed with Jane Austen's quiet skills. He also admired and in some respects profited by the Irish tales of Maria Edgeworth. *Castle Rackrent* (1800), a mini-novel of a mere sixty-five pages, is not only a full tragicomedy in cameo, it presents a striking technical novelty in the transparent narrator Thady Quirk, who tells one story on the surface but allows another to show through from behind.

gentler side to Jane Austen as well; her comic touch can combine much affection with a little malice. But to read her as a cozy author is all wrong, and so is reading her as a bitter one. She was a strong, sensible woman with lucid, limited standards of social propriety.[22]

Sir Walter Scott grew up amid the romantic violence of border legend. Like many other literary Scots, he was trained to the law and all his life long held administrative legal positions around Edinburgh. But from early youth he loved to wander the countryside picking up old ballads and folk tales. Encouraged by examples of literary ballads from Germany and by Coleridge's ballad-romance of "Christabel," he worked up his indigenous Scottish materials into verse narratives, "The Lay of the Last Minstrel" (1805) and "Marmion" (1808). They were swift, picturesque tales of adventure, quickly popular and almost as quickly forgotten; even before writing them, Scott was already thinking of prose fiction, and to this he soon turned full time.

Scott's large and generous nature was the making of his novels and the ruin of his business life. He depicted heroic outlaws and flawless knights because he was a chivalric soul himself; the gusto with which he recreated the medieval past entranced readers in Europe and America as well as England.[23] By nature he was an avid worker who wrote three or four novels a year while turning out stories, biographies, articles, editions (Dryden and Swift), and collections of folk tales, meanwhile carrying on the business of his legal offices and entertaining crowds of visitors at his baronial estate, Abbotsford. But he was no businessman; his associates were shabby fellows for whose vast debts Scott insisted on making himself personally responsible. The novels he wrote under heavy financial pressure are the worse for the haste in which he wrote them; long passages of description and historic detail are barely animated by his weak heroes, his contrived plots. Yet, like his younger contemporary Balzac, Scott had the vitality of a great mythmaker. His incidental characters are often bywords in the mouths of those who have never read the books in which they figure.

Apart from his literary qualities, Scott as a professional novelist was a social phenomenon. He tapped—indeed, it might almost be said he created—the big market for prose fiction that was to make the novel, even down to the present, *the* pre-eminent literary form. Selling at a guinea or even more per volume, often gathered into handsome collections, patriotic yet picturesque, and chaste enough to pass even in strict Victorian families, Scott's novels gained a standing that

22. Of her six novels, mostly written for reading aloud to her family, Jane Austen published four between 1811 and 1816; two were published posthumously in 1818. All of them enjoyed a small but devoted readership till the early years of the twentieth century, when quite abruptly they began to be hailed as classics.

23. The vogue for Scott was apt to express itself in pseudo-medieval manors and towns named after Scott's books. There are half a dozen Waverley's in America and as many Woodstock's. Romantic masqueraders found the "dark ages" of medievalism very sympathetic terrain; they thought it fascinating because different from their world of crass commerce and machine production, also enticing because in its cultural idealisms, guilts, and repressions it was so similar.

not even Byron could approach. Abroad, Cooper in America, Manzoni in Italy, and Balzac in France were but a few of the major nineteenth-century writers who openly professed their indebtedness to Sir Walter. His was a spacious and potent influence.

A POTPOURRI OF PROSE

A garland of lesser prose writers may conclude this account of the early century. Thomas Love Peacock wrote witty, satiric caricature-novels (*Crotchet Castle,* 1831; *Nightmare Abbey,* 1818) from the point of view of a civilized, conservative hedonism. They are dry, playful, utterly unsentimental. At their best, Peacock's dialogues (they are novels only by courtesy) have the flavor of robust and opinionated conversation; within a page or two we will be tossed from modern education to the culinary virtues of salmon, from slavery in the West Indies to the points of fine wine and the iniquities of the reviews. The tone is crisp, the repartee rapid; it is civilized comedy. Matthew "Monk" Lewis and Charles Maturin produced Gothic novels of mystery and terror (*The Monk,* 1796; *Melmoth the Wanderer,* 1820); if they don't puzzle or frighten anybody any more, they can still entertain the idle hour. James Hogg, known from his origins as "the Ettrick shepherd," was mainly a Scottish poet, but also wrote a number of uneven romances and historical entertainments; best known is *The Private Memoirs and Confessions of a Justified Sinner* (1824), a schizophrenic Scots spooker. In Charles Lamb the informal essayist and Thomas de Quincey the autobiographer, we deal with figures of charm rather than grandeur, literary miniaturists. Like Montaigne the original essayist, Lamb devoted his brief humorous studies to exploring the quirks of his own character. But he does not cut deep; rather, he seems to be using his foibles to conceal his self, to be diverting us with mannerisms, stylistic and behavioral. He appeals, like Sterne, to our sense of sympathy and pathos. As for de Quincey, between drugs and poverty he lived his life on the shabby fringes, his one great strength being to know his infinite weakness. The immense cumulative periods and exotic inner panoramas of his prose serve to diminish his own figure like the infinite architectural spirals through which he imagined Piranesi climbing. Closely allied to these vast visions is de Quincey's image of London, perhaps the first literary landscape of the modern megalopolis with its endless crisscrossing canyons, valleys of dread through which forlorn children drift from one obscene abuse to another. Fifty years later Baudelaire would represent Paris in much the same light, and the picture has only darkened with time.

Another order of early nineteenth-century prose is the practical journalistic reporting of which William Hazlitt and William Cobbett were different exponents. Hazlitt's is a vigorous combative mind, frank in its prejudices, enthusiastic in its pleasures. To read him is to be continually renewed with a sense of present, material things—a windy landscape, a substantial book, plain good food. He has a plentiful supply of anecdotes and quotations from every quarter of the world's literature; he produces them for the occasion as a good talker should, not always with literal accuracy, but to the point. Like all good talkers, he sometimes repeats himself; but when his subject opens before him, few writers are more continuously entertaining. Reading Hazlitt, we are reminded of the England about to disappear, when one could hike down country lanes without fear of careening cars, when one could put up at country inns without reservations or credit cards, and when one could still talk about paintings, boxing matches, and roast beef as if they were all and equally parts of a civilized life.[24]

The most remarkable among the lesser prose writers of the early century is William Cobbett. He was a cranky, positive, self-taught laborer-turned-journalist, with a genius for getting into hot water and some talent for getting out. Good stiff fights stirred up Cobbett's circulation, and he deliberately sought them. He fought his way into the army and then out again, moved to America and opened a Philadelphia bookstore stocked mostly with material in praise of King George. Recognizing his own disposition, he adopted for a while the pen name of "Peter Porcupine." Back in England again, he began to write in the Tory interest, but gave his politics a radical twist appropriate to his audience and his interests, which were entirely populist. For many years, *Cobbett's Political Register* was a staple of the news in working-class and poor farmers' households. His prose was bold and graphic, his ideas concrete and immediate. He loved the land, loved to see it well worked, loved to talk crops, manures, and windbreaks with countrymen, Contrariwise, Cobbett loathed cities, calling London "the Wen," and the genteel establishment ruling England simply "the Thing." The best of his work was collected under the title *Rural Rides* (1830); it provides a vivid picture, in homely, precise detail, of a society and a set of social attitudes, that are no more.[25]

24. Though his sentences are short and his verbs active, so there is a great sense of briskness about the essays, Hazlitt's thought does not move fast. One feels the idea being hammered out, turned and heated and hammered again, as by a painstaking blacksmith.

Hazlitt was an inflexible man; after early sympathy, he quarreled with Wordsworth, Coleridge, and Southey over their increasing conservatism. His own admiration for Bonaparte never diminished, and he wrote an enthusiastic biography when enthusiasm was not the popular thing. Hazlitt's erotic life was also troubled; after divorcing his first wife, he fell in love with a cruel, sullen girl who inflicted on him miseries described in the curious *Liber Amoris* (1823), a foreshadowing in brief and in real life of Somerset Maugham's novel *Of Human Bondage* (1915).

25. At first glance, Cobbett seems choked by his many hatreds; in two sentences, he is likely to blackguard the government, the church, the Jews, the Quakers, stockjobbers and "tax eaters," paper money, depopulation (purely imaginary, this), foreigners, newspapers, and a bundle of grim enemies to whom he has assigned private names (e.g., "the Stern-Path-of-Duty Man"). But then he wins us back by writing a full page on the most beautiful tree he has ever seen, or a passage of adventure like the ride down Hawkley Hangar over Hindhead to Thursley (24 November 1822); it is fiercely energetic prose, sensitive yet humorous, writing which makes that of the "nature lovers" (Thoreau perhaps excepted) seem pale and timid.

Warships made of oak and powered by sails, like Nelson's flagship the *Victory,* had remarkably long lives. *Victory* had been in service for forty years before the battle of Trafalgar, and she is still to be seen (though dry-docked) in Portsmouth harbor. By modern standards she was small, measuring 186 feet in length, weighing a bit more than 2,000 tons, and carrying 100 guns, all muzzle loaders, with a range of about 1,200 yards at most. The best tactic for such a vessel, so equipped, was to haul alongside the enemy and try to sink her with repeated broadsides. At Trafalgar the British fought 27 ships of the line against 33 of the enemy; but British gunnery and seamanship were incomparably superior, hence the historic result.

This is a morning frock of the sort that Miss Jane Austen's young ladies may be supposed to have put on when they had no social engagements more pressing than a stroll in the neighborhood or a morning call on a lady acquaintance. The dress is of muslin, the hat of white pearl silk; primrose sandals and white kid gloves completed the ensemble, with whatever plain gold jewelry a lady chose to wear.

Alfred Count D'Orsay was not just a dandy; he was the man on whom other dandies modeled themselves. Though blessed with many talents—he sketched, sculpted, wrote, and had all the gifts of a diplomat, including judgment—he lived essentially on his charm. It brought him not only friendship with blades like Byron and the young Disraeli, but intimate acquaintance with the countess of Blessington and her elderly husband. For as long as the husband lived, they formed one of those equivocal *ménages à trois* in which cynics see nothing equivocal at all; afterward, D'Orsay and the countess lived in extravagant elegance until their money ran out; and then—in a final flourish of good taste, as it were—they quietly died. As the French say, it was *une belle sortie*, a graceful exit.

A man named Falkes once owned some land on the south side of the Thames in the borough of Lambeth. During the Restoration the grounds started to harbor, under the name of Falkes' Hall, a kind of amusement gallery, and in the eighteenth century a succession of smart entrepreneurs developed it into a major entertainment park called Vauxhall. Concerts, dances, variety shows, and spectacles provided the ostensible attractions; hankypanky, some innocent, some not so innocent, was understood to be a normal part of the sideshow. Rowlandson's drawing shows the gardens at the height of their popularity in the early nineteenth century. It should be added that Rowlandson was a man of Fielding's lusty temper; Thackeray, a more severe moralist, saw, and represented in chapter VI of *Vanity Fair,* a darker side of Vauxhall.

For centuries, a grandiose mystique has surrounded the hot mineral waters of spas like Bath, enabling them to attract fashionable high-livers who want to be fixed up so they can run down their health again. Well-heeled invalids require plenty of entertainment, and that attracts not only the healthy vacationer, but the ambitious young person in search of a wealthy spouse without too great a life expectation. The mixture of human types is a cartoonist's delight, as in this drawing by H. Repton, engraved by Rowlandson. The date is 1784; within a few years the costumes of the ladies will be much simplified, in the aftermath of the French Revolution.

The marbles brought to England from Greece by Lord Elgin included not only the massive figures of the pediment of the Parthenon, but the greater part of a frieze which used to run around the top of an inner room *(cella)* in which the great statue of Athena was kept. The frieze represented the Panathenaic procession, a public ceremonial at which all the citizens of Athens, wearing their best clothing and mounted on their most spirited horses, turned out in honor of the goddess. The snap and energy of these young horsemen are as crisp as they were 2,500 years ago; one can particularly admire the way the legs of the riders interweave with those of the horses in an almost audible syncopation of hoofbeats.

(Facing page) The three great furniture makers of eighteenth- and early nineteenth-century England were Chippendale, Hepplewhite, and Sheraton; as each had a chance to study and learn from the designs of the other, their work shows an increasing lightness of structure and freedom of movement, until in Sheraton the wood seems to float like fluently shaped ribbons of satin. For the process of change, which seems to be general among all cultures, if not universal, see George Kubler, *The Shape of Time* (Yale University Press, 1962).

William Beckford's outsize bogus abbey towered 260
feet in the air and was equipped with all the standard
pseudomedieval gadgets; money to build it came
from Beckford's father, who had garnered it from his
many Jamaican slaves. The great structure collapsed
in less time than it had taken to build; but by then,
Beckford (who had some common sense under his
flashy mannerisms) had sold it. These "Gothic"
structures, often prefabricated ruins stuffed with
freshly minted "antiques," were a brief but widespread vogue; like the Oriental Brighton pavilion and
the houses built to conform with the stricture's of
Mr. Ruskin's book about Venice, they suggest
a society looking for a false face to put on.

(Facing page) By setting up a residence there in 1786, George Prince of Wales brought fame and prosperity to Brighton, just south of London on the English Channel. The prince's first home was a modest house where he could visit conveniently with his unacknowledged wife, Mrs. Fitzherbert; soon he enlarged it, and after 1812, when George III was recognized as permanently insane, the new prince regent set John Nash to redesigning the structure into a pavilion in the Persian style. The Persians had a vogue in the early century; Tom Moore's poem "Lalla Rookh" (1817) was as authentically pseudo-Persian as Nash's pink bubble of fantasy by the choppy waters of the Channel.

Saint John wrote his Revelation or Apocalypse, the last book of the Bible, while exiled on the rocky little island of Patmos in the Aegean. His is a somber and often cloudy book, which foretells many tremendous trials and monstrous tribulations before men attain the final vision of the New Jerusalem. William Blake's *Angel of the Revelation* shows the angel dictating to John (the smaller figure writing in the foreground) the book that he in turn is to address to the seven churches of Asia (probably the seven horseback riders in the background). But Blake's angel is no tormented prophet of doom. Rather, he is a spiritual athlete, youthful, confident, gigantic, and supremely energetic, who gestures mankind upward toward transcendence. In the back of Blake's mind as he drew, may have been the famous Colossus of Rhodes, a huge statue of Helios, the sun god, which stood, not far in time or distance, from Saint John's isle of Patmos. The ancient statue raised aloft a beacon, and (according to legend) straddled the entry to the harbor, so that ships passing in or out had to sail between its giant legs.

14

Peace, Controversy, Reform (1815–1851)

The structure of English politics in the quarter century from 1790 to 1815 was both decentralized and homogenized to the point of being very hard to describe. At his first coming to power, William Pitt had been a Whig, even a reforming Whig; but the French Revolution and the need for national unity pushed him, his followers, and most of the nation into such a conservative stance that only Charles James Fox and a few followers remained on the parliamentary left; for long periods, their dispirited and isolated band withdrew from Parliament entirely. Thus political parties, their labels, slogans, and machinery, practically disappeared. Tories in particular sank into total obscurity; until George Canning deliberately revived the term after the war, nobody thought it worthwhile to call himself a Tory. Instead, the great Whig families, an oligarchy of entrenched landlords rooted in the land since 1688, held power in Parliament with the help of large and loyal followings. As patrons, they controlled boroughs and often county seats as well. No bright young man on whom they bestowed a seat was likely to displease his benefactor. Control was easily maintained because there were only about 400,000 voters to elect a Parliament governing (in 1820) a nation of 20 million. Thus Parliament represented the wealth much more than it did the people of Britain. Because party discipline was weak and local feelings were strong, few governments could manage consistent majorities on a number of different issues; coalitions and bargains had to be formed and reformed. Pitt was unusual in his ability to command the respect of other politicians and, when necessary, appeal over their heads to the country at large. While it periodically went through the forms of a national election (always expensive because high office was profitable to the holder), the country was governed from day to day in its routine business by local officials, meaning squires and those whom they appointed. Because many of these jobs were unsalaried, the holders of them were likely to be men of independent means with the views of their class. They were not disturbed by Parliament, where most bills, introduced by local members, concerned local matters. Parliament had been made supreme in 1688, everyone agreed, not to run the country, just to supervise it. Few of its actions infringed on the interests of the squirearchy. Any liberal idea slipping through the Commons could be certain of rejection by the House of Lords, which through the century maintained its intuitive devotion to the most reactionary positions available.

THE PEACE AND ITS DISCONTENTS

But the peace of 1815 created, as sudden peace often does, major dislocations. Slackening war orders, combined with abrupt demobilization, resulted in widespread unemployment. Though the hateful income tax had to be discontinued, servicing war debts remained a problem; land taxes, excise taxes, and house duties were ways, all disagreeable, of making up the needed sums. For centuries, England had been accustomed to fluctuations in the price of grain, depending on the harvest; these continued to be extreme, with a run of bad harvests and high prices between 1816 and 1819. But now, in addition, people found their lives subject to the fluctuations of an impersonal business cycle which nobody could understand or control. A momentary imbalance on the world market could throw thousands of unoffending laborers out of work at a moment's notice; invention of a new machine could reduce a whole countryside of traditional craftsmen to instant pauperdom. Poverty and depression on the Continent closed off markets earlier disrupted by the war. After the American war of 1812, trade possibilities with the United States opened up briefly, and a quick gust of trade with South America, largely financed by English bank credit, shook the sails: it collapsed in 1825 when several of the states that had just won their independence from Spain were forced to repudiate their debts.

As a result of these accumulating discontents, radical agitation spread across the English countryside; it reached so deeply into the agricultural laborers and urban proletarians that it terrified the ruling classes with visions of a home-grown French revolution.[1] Cheap but legal newspapers (Cobbett proudly called his sheet, priced low to avoid the tax, "twopenny trash") were supplemented by outspoken

---

1. Politics in the eighteenth century had been structured on the ideal of "vertical friendship," a mutual relation between patron and client, a model of which is Burke's dependence on and service to Lord Rockingham. After 1815 society is increasingly structured by the sharp division of social classes, their horizontal solidarity and vertical hostility amounting to what Marxists call "class consciousness" (SFR, G.22).

and sometimes illegal propaganda sheets. Their aim was to harness working-class discontent to specific institutional changes, of which the first and most crucial was reform of representation in the Commons. For seventeen turbulent years, from 1815, this was the vital issue on which laborers and mill owners, freeholders and city dwellers could agree. Imitating an early procedure of the French Revolution, the reformers initiated corresponding societies which coordinated propaganda activities nationwide. A little sporadic rioting occurred in Wales and Derbyshire, which the government put down with a heavy hand; but mostly the agitation was peaceful. On 16 August 1819, however, a major break took place when 50,000 Manchester demonstrators assembled outside town in St. Peter's Fields, to demand reform. Henry Hunt, the famous agitator, was to speak, but the magistrates ordered his arrest, and sent troops to effect it.[2] Whether from fear, inexperience, or natural brutality, a troop of cavalry charged the crowd, killing 11 and wounding 400. The episode was nicknamed "Peterloo" in derisive imitation of Waterloo; Shelley alludes to the violence in his savage sonnet, "England in 1819." As a result of this and other threatening incidents, the government cracked down on dissent, passing a package of laws known as the Six Acts to restrict public meetings and public propaganda.

BUILDING THE NEW ENGLAND

Though the situation grew less tense after 1819, repression had little to do with it; quite the contrary. The economic situation grew less bad; technical advances helped improve it. Digging canals and building railroads provided new employment and made transport so cheap that English manufactures could compete successfully around the world. Suddenly (and to the surprise of the railroaders who at first thought their lines fit only to haul heavy cargo), it became possible for a city worker to visit his country kin without spending days on the road and a week's wages. London newspapers could now circulate on the day of publication in cities outside the metropolis; in the race for news, carrier pigeons were used to speed the latest flash to the city desk. Between canals and railroads, mass production of uniform objects for sale on a national market started to be possible. Once connected by canal to their pits of fine clay in north Cornwall, the pottery works of Josiah Wedgwood at Burslem and Etruria near Hanley expanded to become a national industry. Their elegant porcelain products were so uniform that they could be confidently ordered from a national catalogue; they were so finely designed that they are still eagerly sought by collectors today.

Supplementing railroads and canals were highways, steadily improving since about 1760, and now approaching modern standards. The new style of road

2. There were as yet no police as we understand them; they would be invented, or rather adapted, from an Irish institution of Sir Robert Peel, in 1828. The two British slang names for a policeman, "bobby" and "peeler" both allude to Sir Robert.

building was simplicity itself: on a well-drained roadbed were laid six to ten inches of broken stones, compacted and leveled by a roller. At first the only binding was the grit and pebbles chipped off the stones themselves, and roads were built convex to make water flow into the ditches. Later an impervious asphalt coating was added (known, after its discoverer, as macadam); then roads could be built flat. On such a surface mail and passenger coaches could trot along at a stirring clip of eight to ten miles an hour, changing horses at intervals (hence "stage-coaches") and pausing at inns to refresh the passengers, not to mention the driver. The hero of Smollett's novel *Peregrine Pickle* (1751) took two days to reach Oxford from London by coach; in 1828 the same trip took just six hours. One cannot exaggerate the effect of improved transportation on English village life; it widened the villager's mental horizons and knit separate little thorps into larger communities. The quick, driving rhythms of a mechanical age imposed themselves on what was left of a leisured countryside. Sunday remained sacred, but a great number of traditional holidays were sacrificed to the steam engine, on the score that it was too expensive to bank fires and lower the pressures. Evangelicals tried to keep trains from running on Sundays, but were outvirtued by the engineers; cheap Sunday rates to temperance rallies and Sunday-school assemblies established the principle, and soon railroads were doing land-office business in weekend excursions to the country.[3]

Inventions were cumulative, one generating another. As trains became faster and more frequent, controlling their movements was seen to require an instant means of long-distance communication; hence the development of the electric telegraph in 1837 by Wheatstone and Cooke. The use of iron to make railroad tracks, and then of steel (twice as expensive, but sixteen times more durable), led inevitably to the building of metal bridges, and then (amazing the nonscientific) to iron barges and boats. Near Ellesmere a canal connecting the Severn with the Mersey river was led on a cast-iron aqueduct across the Vale of Llangollen; folk came from miles around to see the canal barges drifting quietly across the valley, 127 feet in the air. We cannot follow in detail the profusion of technical advances which filled the early nineteenth century with the rush and clatter of "development"; let it be understood that the process was continuous and constantly accelerating.[4] Early steam engines had to be crafted by hand; after 1850,

3. Mr. Slope, the intriguing, hypocritical chaplain in Trollope's *Barchester Towers* (1857), is understood to be an evangelical because he objects to railway trains running on Sundays. His is a late battle in a lost cause. Thomas Cook, founder of the travel agency that still bears his name, organized the first railway expedition to a temperance meeting (July 1841). Cook had been a dedicated temperance man himself, but saw a light of sorts, and after 1841 we hear of him primarily as a travel agent, hardly at all as a temperance reformer.

4. Experiments with steam locomotion lasted from 1800 to 1830; Richard Trevithick and George Stephenson were among the experimenters; tracks, traction, and the need for a high-pressure engine were the main hitches. The flanged wheel and multitubed boiler solved the big problems, and when the Liverpool-Manchester line opened in 1830, Stephenson's "Rocket" was able to draw a thirteen-ton train swiftly, safely, economically. No less impressive, the line promptly started to pay dividends

a new generation of engineers developed machine tools accurate to a thousandth of an inch, which reduced engine building to a swift, precise routine. Steam engines created a demand for coal which steam engines, as they drained and ventilated deep mines, helped to satisfy. Nothing symbolized the new era better than the railway lines—smoky, noisy, unprecedentedly swift—which cut through hills and over streams, overriding all the little green lanes and slow hedge-lined byways. Entire new cities (Crewe, Swindon) sprang up in open fields, devoted exclusively to servicing and repairing railway equipment. At the ceremonial opening of the Liverpool-Manchester line in 1830, an English politician of distinction, William Huskisson, was killed by a locomotive traveling at an unnerving 12 miles an hour; the event typified strains that would be placed on English imaginations by the new mechanisms. Lying heavy in the other balance were facts like the following: when a Norfolk farmer drove his fattened cattle to London, bullocks lost twenty-eight pounds apiece en route, sheep seven pounds; when he sent them by rail, they lost no weight, and he gained £600 a year.

Without these technical developments and the jobs they created, discontent would have been even sharper than it was; but a technical society was bound to create new and active classes, socially restless in the long run. Railroad builders and industrial magnates could not be expected to knuckle under before the landlord, and truckle like subservient tenants. The mixing that railroads introduced into social strata was inherently democratic in its effects; sensing this, titled landlords sometimes organized to prevent railroads from entering their districts. Thus, relieving one sort of social stress tended to generate other sorts. The government itself was in deep trouble; and the death of poor old George III in the first month of 1820 only deepened that trouble. For the prince regent who now succeeded as George IV was fifty-eight years old, obscenely fat, flagrantly immoral, grossly extravagant, and generally despised.[5] People had thought of George III as a decent, dull man, subject through no fault of his own to an incurable affliction; they looked on his son much less kindly. He was a most unattractive symbol of everything that was worst in the old order, a man so deeply hated that he hardly dared appear in public.

REFORMS WEAK AND STRONG

Evidently aware of their unpopularity, the conservatives who ruled England during the 1820s strove to appear liberal in all matters but the crucial one of parliamentary reform. The Six Acts inspired by Peterloo were soon allowed to lapse;

---

on its stock of 9 ½ percent per annum. Trevithick, a Cornish giant who started young and later built lines in Peru and Costa Rica, was the most picturesque and is now the least appreciated of these early inventors.

5. Indeed, the clandestine marriage of the regent with Mrs. Fitzherbert (15 December 1785) was the best part of his private life; but it made his "official" marriage with Caroline, ten years later, legally bigamous and altogether ignoble.

a free-trade policy was attempted; the first laws limiting child labor were passed. (The House of Commons thought eleven hours a day was reasonable; the Lords, ever generous, raised the number to twelve.) By the very simplest of decisions, the worst effects of the cruel game laws were mitigated.[6] During the late 1820s, London, particularly the district of Soho, started to receive many liberal refugees from reactionary regimes abroad. From Austrian-dominated Italy, for example, came the dramatic poet Ugo Foscolo, the great librarian Panizzi (above, p. 307), and a family named Rossetti, of whom more would be heard. About this period too we note in conservative circles the ripples of a paradoxical liberal stirring. It was a move to unite privileged landowners with the underprivileged poor in opposition to middle-class entrepreneurs. The concept was curiously chivalric; as put forward by a man named Kenelm Digby in a book titled *The Broad Stone of Honor* (1822), it seemed almost frivolous in its medieval romanticism. Yet when blended with Cobbett's rural populist feeling, it would later have its influence on Disraeli's brand of reforming Tory politics. Within only a few years Tory politicians would be sponsoring those powerful reports on industrial abuses out of which Friedrich Engels built his indictment of capitalism, *The Condition of the English Working Class in 1844*.

Blockage of parliamentary reform came to an abrupt end in 1827. Lord Liverpool, who for fifteen years had headed a do-nothing administration, suffered a stroke; his Tory successor George Canning died after only a few months in office.[7] The government of the duke of Wellington which succeeded, though reactionary, was narrow and for that reason subject to pressure. The first form of this pressure was a move to admit Irish Catholics (and so, by common logic, English Catholics as well) to public office. Twenty-five years earlier Pitt, seeing the need for this step, had given his word on it; now, under urging from the majestic Irish orator Daniel O'Connell and his Catholic Association, Parliament edged in successive votes closer and closer to the final decision.[8] Catholic emancipation was hateful to the sort of bigot who had taken part in the Gordon riots (above, p.

6. Most poached game had been sold secretly at high prices in the cities to meet middle-class demands for "noble" dishes. (Such animals were said to have been "shot with a silver bullet.") In 1831 public sale of game was legalized. When pheasants, grouse, and venison could be bought from lawful dealers, the price dropped sharply, and most of the temptations to poaching disappeared (SFR, G.14).

7. If Lord Liverpool had been present at the Creation, said a French wit, he would have cried, "Mon Dieu, conservons le chaos!" Canning, though deprived by fate of a major place in the history books, was a social portent. Son of a "bad" marriage (his mother an actress, his father disowned for marrying her), Canning was raised by a rich uncle, took service with Pitt, and during the years 1797–1798 made his name with his witty polemic for *The Anti-Jacobin*. As a literary man turned politician, Canning set a pattern that would be replicated in Disraeli, Bulwer-Lytton, and Macaulay; as a foreign minister (1822–1827), he set a policy of combining domestic conservatism with encouragement for national and liberal movements in Europe, which would be continued by Lord Palmerston for another half century.

8. The Catholic Association was a voluntary political-action group, backed by the hierarchy and in its heyday enrolling practically every Catholic in Ireland. Members pledged a penny a month to

326), also to George IV, who like all Hanovers owed his position to the Protestant, anti-Stuart interest. Wellington and his home secretary Robert Peel were in a position to put through Catholic emancipation only for the odd reason that they were both known to be firmly opposed to it. They had in fact no choice; given the violent state of popular opinion in Ireland, it was emancipation or civil war. King George grumbled and angry anti-Romanists cried out; but the reform was long overdue and averted major Irish violence. More importantly, it opened the door to a fundamental reform of the English electoral system. By yielding to Catholic emancipation in 1829, Wellington had divided his own party and strengthened the liberal Whigs.[9] Just at this point, and very conveniently for Whig purposes, George IV took occasion to die; new elections were necessary, and in the fall of 1830 Earl Grey formed a new government committed to basic electoral reform. Obstacles to such reform were the new king, William IV, the late George's brother; a group of irreconcilable Tories in the Commons; and, inevitably, the solidly Tory House of Lords. An oblique but potent argument for reform was provided by recent events in France: in July of 1830 the Bourbon monarchs who had been restored to the French throne just fifteen years before were roughly kicked off it. Three days of Paris street fighting sufficed to dispose of Charles X, the successor to Louis XVIII, with all his successors and accoutrements; in his place, the French installed Louis Philippe, "the bourgeois monarch." What had been done so easily in France might be done just as easily in England: it was a strong argument for preventive reform (SFR, G.12).

MODERNIZING PARLIAMENT

After all these preliminaries, the program of reform that the government placed before the Commons on 1 March 1831, seems to us remarkably mild, though many contemporaries thought it wildly radical. Some 60 boroughs, each with fewer than 2,000 inhabitants, were to lose both their parliamentary representatives; 47 others, with populations between 2,000 and 4,000 would lose one. The seats thus eliminated, 167 in all, would be given to more populous constituencies. Manchester, Birmingham, and five other large towns would now have two members apiece; so would four new districts in London. Of the counties, 26 would have their representation doubled; a number of representatives would be shifted from the south to the more populous north, from boroughs to counties, and from England itself to Scotland and Ireland.[10] But the reform was not as

---

support O'Connell's agitation, which consisted of getting elected to an office he wasn't legally qualified to hold, then challenging the government to disqualify him.

9. Glancing ahead a moment, we note that while Catholics entered Parliament in 1829, Jews were admitted ohly after 1860, avowed atheists not till 1888.

10. Scots were appreciably better represented than Irish, and Englishmen better than Scots; the south of England was still better represented than the north. Women, being voteless, were not represented at all.

thorough as it looked. Property qualifications and registration fees still limited the right to vote; the ballot was still not secret, so landlords could still supervise the voting of their tenants; corruption of electors was as easy as ever. Though the total electorate would be nearly doubled by the new bill from the 400,000 it had previously been, the population was now over 24 million, so voters were only a fraction of the whole society.

The 1832 reform bill was, thus, far from revolutionary; but pushing it through Parliament provoked so much resistance that a revolution was what it felt like. To become law, bills had to be read and voted on three times in each house. The reform bill narrowly passed its first two readings in the Commons, but stumbled when the king took advantage of a technicality and hastily dissolved Parliament. The reformers came back with a second bill and a larger majority. After three months of debate, the bill had passed its three readings in Commons (September 1831); the Lords, after five days' consideration, rejected it. Popular fury exploded in vast protest meetings, vaster petitions, occasional riots. In December the government introduced a third bill with the understanding that if it was vetoed in the Lords, King William would be asked to create enough new peers to pass it. (Queen Anne, it will be recalled, used this device to pass the treaty of Utrecht in 1713; it was Tory peers she created then, which made the precedent all the stronger in 1832. See above, p. 272.) Under such heavy pressure, the bill passed three readings in the Commons and two in the Lords; but there, infuriatingly, it stuck on another technicality. Seeking an escape hatch, William quibbled, and on 19 May 1832, the government resigned. At this point, revolution was a distinct possibility. Some people organized to stop paying taxes; others started a run on the banks by demanding all their money, immediately, in the form of gold. Government funds sank to new lows; popular leaders worked furiously to keep their followers from rioting in the streets; the nation was exhausted by the crisis. At last the Tories backed down; the bill was read for the third time in the Lords, and passed into law without any extra peers being created. And in fact the 1832 reform bill was a mighty event in English social history, less for what it did than for the mighty struggles over doing it.

For though Parliaments after 1832 were no more virtuous than those before, they did suddenly become busier and better informed. Having learned that Parliament was their creation, people started to hold the members more closely responsible. Early evidence of this was a reform of the poor law in 1834. For the needy themselves the "new poor law" was worse than the old. Because severe moralists wanted to make "honest labor" more attractive than pauperism, they refused to supply relief outside workhouses, and without deliberately trying to do so, made life wretched inside. *Oliver Twist,* which Dickens published in 1837–1838, must not be read as a literally factual account of life in a workhouse; but things were grim, especially for the children and the old. For rate payers, the new system was justified by its cheapness; administratively it replaced a jungle of local customs by a single uniform rule.[11] The tone of social life changed in less disagreeable ways. In 1835 the Municipal Corporations Act imposed major reforms on antiquated municipal constitutions; towns now had to hold elections from time to time and to maintain minimal services such as a police force. By their last-ditch opposition to the reform bill, the bishops in the House of Lords had earned themselves considerable ill will;[12] after 1832, enemies of the church were eager to crop its abuses, limit its privileges, and distribute its excess income through secular channels for secular purposes. Its friends rallied round the establishment and, correctly reading the temper of the times, reformed it themselves, so strictly that the ecclesiastics must have wondered if their open enemies could have done the job more thoroughly.

BENTHAM'S MEN ON THE COMMISSIONS

In much of this reforming, a favored exploratory instrument was the Parliamentary Commission, roughly equivalent in modern America to a congressional committee. By means of these commissions the reformed parliaments uncovered old injustices and proposed new remedies, one change often breeding several others. For example, repeal of the seventeenth-century Test and Corporation Acts, which barred dissenters from municipal office, had been accomplished in 1828; but the new Municipal Corporations Act opened fresh ways for them to move up the administrative ladder. Early efforts to limit the working hours of children were aided by antislavery arguments; demonstrably, slaves in Jamaica had been no worse off than free children in Lancashire. Freeing the first group led to freeing the second. But limiting the work hours of children required limiting the hours of adults, since all machinery had to stop when children were not present to tend it. Commissions to look into textile factories (1833) begot commissions on the dying craft of hand-loom weaving (1838), on the horrible conditions of miners (1842), and so on the public health of the laboring classes as a whole (1842). These commissions literally revolutionized English social life. They tended to be staffed by men of technical competence and administrative skill, rational and factual men owing their outlook to the philosophic school of Jeremy Bentham.[13] The conditions they documented for the world to see were

11. The earlier "Speenhamland" system, it will be recalled (above, p. 362), had been created by the magistrates of that one district, then copied by anyone who wanted to. The centralizing of administration that started in 1832 not only looks forward to the computerized welfare state but back to Cromwell's Major Generals and the hieratic authoritarianism of Laud and Strafford.

12. Even earlier, secular critics had not spared the church; the anonymous author of the *Extraordinary Black Book* (1831) is harsher on churchly fat cats, nepotists, and profiteers than he is on dealers in secular sinecures—and that is harsh indeed.

13. Dickens caricatured his idea of Benthamites in the figure of Gradgrind (*Hard Times*, 1854), and it's patent that in domestic situations a cold, factual man can be intolerable. But in the thick

often unknown and unimagined by respectable members of society. The rich lived in another world from the poor; that it was nasty in the factory towns or at the mine's pit face they knew, but how nasty they had no idea. As Christians many of them were appalled at what they learned; as Englishmen, they were ashamed. But above all, when they learned of the sanitary conditions, they were terrified. In the very year of the reform bill, 1832, an epidemic of cholera swept the land; the action of infectious diseases was understood just enough to make clear that an epidemic among slum dwellers could not be kept from spreading to the rich and genteel. Hence, in the long run, a series of acts and local ordinances establishing clean water supplies, adequate sewer facilities, and the minimal amenities.[14]

CHARTISM

In the late thirties and first years of the "hungry forties," England suffered a deep depression, one of the worst she has ever known. Bad harvests, high prices, widespread unemployment, and the onset of actual famine in Ireland were piled atop the squalor of the new cities and the miseries of the new poor law; such wholesale wretchedness in a country as rich and prosperous as England seemed to raise questions about the social order itself. Robert Owen's early and small experiments in cooperative socialism attracted great interest, and in 1834 he tried to enlarge his program into a Grand National Consolidated Trades Union. The Union collapsed, however; and from its pieces rose another working-class movement known from the "People's Charter" embodying its program as Chartism. The six demands of the Chartists were for (1) annual Parliaments, (2) universal male suffrage,[15] (3) equal electoral districts, (4) no property requirements for members of Parliament, (5) salaries for members of Parliament, and (6) the secret ballot. To advance these principles the Chartists organized mass meetings, moved giant petitions, proposed general strikes, and published much vigorous propaganda. They held a national convention; they generated broad popular support;

---

jungle of English social life, dispassionate fact finding was indispensable. More mischievous was the tendency of utilitarianism to unite with evangelical religion in disparaging any and all forms of imaginative activity. As they professed an interest in education, the utilitarians had a terrible effect on the school system, an effect still being felt in Herbert Spencer, who lived into the twentieth century and whom Carlyle described, very moderately, as "the most immeasurable ass in Christendom."

14. Chief pioneer in this work was a combative Benthamite (former secretary to the philosopher) named Edwin Chadwick. Chadwick had to be a fighter; the cost of replacing with cast-iron pipe all the old water-lines of tile, lead, or even wood, was formidable. London laid the first municipal sewage line in 1865; though far from serving the whole city, it was a great step forward from cesspools and open ditches or gutters.

15. William Lovett, a founding father of Chartism, wanted to include among the demands votes for women, but was assured by his fellows that the idea could not possibly be taken seriously.

they were widely regarded as a dangerous revolutionary force, and did their best to act the part. Yet their movement came to little. In 1838 and 1839, and again in 1842 and 1848, they stirred the masses to ominous rumblings; but none of their requests was ever granted or even seriously considered, and gradually their movement faded away (SFR, G.13, H.17). Partly this was because the leaders were vain and weak, partly because none of the demands involved bread-and-butter issues. Chartist leaders were too parliamentary in their ideas; they were also prone to bluster and bluff, which obscured real grievances and alienated possible sympathizers. To keep their cause alive, the leaders resorted to trick schemes for cooperative land purchase, and when they went bankrupt, Chartism faded from the scene. Its last gesture in 1848 was a monster petition to Parliament, with more than 3 million signatures attached. Inspection, however, revealed that many were forgeries or jokes: the duke of Wellington and "Mr. Punch," mascot of the comic weekly, had apparently signed the last Chartist manifesto.[16]

THE CORN LAW AGITATIONS

Out of the perceived failures of Chartism grew, about 1839, a new movement of agitation directed against the Corn Laws. This was a middle-class rather than a working-class movement, and it sprang from a perception that the economic power structure of the nation had shifted. When the Corn Laws were written in the 1690s, (see above, p. 291), agriculture had been England's primary interest; now it was only the third of England's interests, behind trade and manufacturing. Accordingly, opponents of the Corn Laws argued, it was absurd to protect landlords with tariffs which, by keeping food prices artificially high, limited trade and made manufactured goods more expensive. Better, instead, to abandon the ideal of self-sufficiency in foodstuffs, import them freely, and pay for them by exporting more manufactures. The argument had an obvious anti-aristocratic bias; titled landlords had installed the Corn Laws, bourgeois tradesmen would profit by their abolition. Had they been different men, the leaders of the anti–Corn Law agitation would have been vulnerable to the charge, which was brought against them anyway, of being mere moneygrubbers. With Richard Cobden and John Bright these charges would not stick; whatever else they might be, these were men of high principle and strict character. Cobden had sacrificed a lucrative career to advocate what he saw as good public policy; Bright was an earnest young man of Quaker background and democratic principles, sincere, even naïve in his devotion to free enterprise. Like the reform bill, repeal of the Corn Laws was debated through the land, with the rhetoric rising higher and higher. Passage

16. Aftermaths of the Chartist movement were many local mutual-improvement societies for working men. They met informally to discuss timely topics; in the absence of urgent political issues, they often turned to religious, philosophical, or literary themes. Their tone is dramatically described in Charles Kingsley's novel *Alton Locke, Tailor and Poet* (1850).

came in 1846 only when the prime minister, Sir Robert Peel, who had steadily opposed the measure, changed abruptly to support it—incurring from his own party the same sort of wrath as he and the duke of Wellington had known seventeen years before when they changed positions on Catholic emancipation.[17] As in 1829, Peel disapproved of the measure and even more of the language used in advocating it, but thought the country would be torn apart by continuing controversy. In fact, repeal of the Corn Laws showed that the war of words had been largely that. Corn prices did not drop far, imports increased marginally, landlords did not suffer much. In 1846 Peel's position was fortified by a bad harvest in England and news of the total failure of the potato crop in Ireland. This somber event marked the onset of the great Irish famine—before considering which we may look back to review a couple of major changes in the royal household. Major they were, but they had passed without much fanfare because, after the last years of George III's madness, the blighting unpopularity of George IV, and the shiftiness of William IV during the reform crisis, public indifference to the monarchy could only be welcome. When he was young and sane, George III could sometimes get from his governments more or less what he wanted; for the first forty years of the nineteenth century, British monarchs were better off not trying.

DYNASTIC MATTERS

William IV, who took over in 1830 for his unlamented brother, might have proved less inept had he come to the throne younger and better prepared. His career had been in the navy, he was sixty-five years old, and had become heir to the throne only three years before at the death of his older brother. Personally, William was a cheerful and hearty man, but, knowing little of political matters, he was timid and irresolute. In advocacy, he fretted his ministers to the point of exasperation, and when beaten on a point, he sulked. When he died in 1837, the crown devolved in the absence of direct heirs on his niece Victoria. She was the daughter of the duke of Kent, who died in 1820, the year after her birth; now, as the new queen, she was just eighteen, a conventional, demure, somewhat humorless young lady. To this point, she had spent her days under the thumb of her German mother and her mother's strong-minded adviser, Sir John Conroy.

17. The majestic authority of Peel's personality weighed heavily in these decisions; he would hold office, he said, "on no servile tenure," and that included subservience to his own stated principles. Under the English system, which allows a government to be turned out at any time on a vote of no confidence, this attitude was less autocratic than it would be in America. Peel's 1846 "betrayal" of protectionist principles not only lost him his office, but led to a deep reshuffling of parties; Peelites aligned themselves with Whigs as "liberals," the remaining Tories called themselves "conservatives." Of the two groups, liberals were much the stronger; over the next forty years (1845–1885) they were in office three-quarters of the time.

She looked very much like a weak young person, an impression which did not last long, for Victoria, in the tradition of English monarchs, actively disliked her parent, and soon dismissed both her mother and her mother's adviser to a safe distance. For herself, being young and unskilled in the world, she accepted the advice, personal and political, of the aging Whig leader, William Lamb Viscount Melbourne.

She could not have chosen better. At fifty-eight, Lord Melbourne was a kindly, polished, attractive man, raised in the casual moral traditions of the Whig aristocracy. His wife, Lady Caroline Lamb, had been one of Byron's more hectic and public mistresses, but she was dead now, burnt out a decade ago after a violent and pathetic career. Melbourne's witty, disabused, and not very dynamic view of people and politics made him an admirable instructor to a young and strikingly naïve queen. He had little use for the moralistic temper of the new age, dismaying signs of which he saw in Victoria herself. (At one point she told him determinedly that she wanted to be taught what was *right* and what was *wrong;* but the word *expedient* she never wanted to hear.) To the best of his ability, but not altogether effectively, Lord Melbourne tried to soften her stiff little mind. For three years he served, with great tact and devotion, as prime minister and private tutor to his youthful sovereign, and then, when it came time for her to marry, turned her over to her cousin and new husband, Albert, prince of Saxe-Coburg-Gotha. Melbourne lingered on as prime minister largely because the queen had a personal aversion to Sir Robert Peel: she found him stiff and cold.[18] But essentially her independent power as queen (and gradually she made herself a very strong monarch indeed) dates from her marriage in 1840. For in Albert she had found a man quite as moralistic as she was, also a pillar of domestic strength, a helpful administrative aide, and ultimately the focus of a mystique most fully expressed in Tennyson's *Idylls of the King,* a book dedicated to the prince consort. Compared to all these achievements, Albert's limitations (he was pompous, often sanctimonious, and mentally shallow) counted for little.[19]

BLACK FAMINE AND CRYSTAL PALACE

It is inevitable to describe in counterpoint the proudest achievement and the darkest shame of this age so rich in social contrasts. The achievement was a project of Albert's, the Great Exhibition of 1851; the shame was the Irish famine

18. Peel was not a genial man; Daniel O'Connell, who bore a grudge, compared his smile to the gleam on the silver plate of a coffin lid. But by contrast with Melbourne, he was a tremendous, day-and-night worker, familiar with the least details of government; in this respect he set an example for W. E. Gladstone.

19. As a foreigner, Albert faced much hostility in England, which was just starting to abate at the time of his death; he was most effective as a bridge for transmitting English constitutional liberalism to rulers on the Continent.

of 1845–1849. The famine provides a grim background to the exhibition; its roots sink deep into the past. Returning from Virginia in 1585 or 1586, Sir Walter Raleigh's agents brought with them tobacco and potatoes; both crops were cultivated on Sir Walter's estates near Cork, and became domesticated. Because it was cheap, and could be stored for months just by leaving it undug in the fields, the potato became a staple food. (Within the writer's recent memory, it was not uncommon to be served potato under four different guises at a single meal in a modest Irish restaurant.) Irish landlords were prevailingly Protestant absentee Englishmen, who through Irish agents and Irish tenants raised crops for English markets. In return for their labor, the tenants were allowed use of a field on which they raised potatoes for themselves. During the war boom, landlords put more fields into cultivation and hired more hands; some prosperity seeped down, and the Irish population increased rapidly. In 1672 the estimate was one and ⅔ million souls; it was nearly 4 million by 1791, and within fifty years it more than doubled to over 8 million in 1841. There were no Irish factories to employ these extra hands; they were crowding the rural slums, struggling for bits of land and scraps of food, even before the famine struck. The blight of 1845 was, therefore, devastating. In form, it was a fungus which rotted the leaves of growing plants, then spread down the stems and disintegrated the tubers. No variety of potato was resistant, no countermeasure was known. The fields turned black with a sickening stench; around them the peasantry too sickened and died. Those who could, the most prosperous and energetic, gathered their belongings in a bundle, and fled. Half a million went to England; Chartist leaders like Bronterre O'Brien and Feargus O'Connor advertised their origin in their names. But as England was hateful, many more went to America. They traveled in steerage, the cheapest and most miserable accommodations available; and in America they confronted new hostility: "No Irish Need Apply" was a sign frequently posted in hiring offices. But with time, the Irish Americans overcame their adversity, and prospered. A strong link was thus forged between Ireland and America, the latter often referred to, and justifiably, as "the greater Ireland overseas."

On the island itself, things went from bad to worse. Finding their fields less profitable, landlords evicted tenants; not surprisingly, tenants resorted for revenge to arson and murder. The hooded "Whiteboys" joined with the secret "Molly Maguires" in organizing rent strikes, barn burnings, cattle poisonings. When caught, they were hanged. Between the census of 1841 and that of 1851 a million and a half people disappeared from Ireland; emigration, disease, and starvation were the causes. No country in modern Europe has ever suffered such calamitous losses. What most enraged the Irish was that, even as they were starving, shipments of grain and foodstuffs continued to be made to England. They had to move under armed guard, but move they did; in the other direction, neither private charity nor public policy did anything effective to relieve Irish distress. Peel's Tory government of 1845–1847 did something to encourage imports of maize ("corn" in the North American sense of the word), and to initiate a program of public works. But when the Tories left office, the Whig administration of Lord John Russell decided to shift the burden of Irish relief to the propertied classes of Ireland. So far as those classes existed at all, they were practiced experts at tax evasion; in effect, the English government stood by while Irish families starved.

With the genocidal record of Elizabethan and Cromwellian England still festering in their minds, the Irish could be pardoned for seeing English behavior during the famine as deliberately vicious. But it was hardly so; rather, it can be traced to a duality at the heart of Jeremy Bentham, whose influence on politicians of all parties was strong. Hardly any economist doubted in that distant age that market forces must be allowed to operate freely; Bentham, who was himself a mild and benevolent person, doubted it less than anybody. Even those who deplored his influence and that of the laissez-faire economists followed their doctrines in practice. (The contrast with Christianity is curious; everybody professed that doctrine but nobody followed it, everybody followed utilitarianism and hardly anybody professed it.) Though inhuman, utilitarianism was not deliberately cruel. If Irish peasants starved, that was deplorable but, in the long run, less harmful to the general welfare than ill-considered interference with the law of supply and demand. Thus, like eighteenth-century optimism, nineteenth-century utilitarianism was willing to put up with many necessary present evils for the sake of a remote and abstract general welfare.

Irish miseries were not allowed to becloud English triumphs. The Great Exhibition was the inspiration of Prince Albert, that skater across the thin ice of general knowledge; it proved a triumphant success. It was a world's fair, an imperial exhibit, an amusement park, and a ballyhoo display all in one. The scale of the project was unprecedented, and the usual doomsayers had filled the air with ominous croaks. Nobody would attend, so the show would be a financial flop; too many people would come, so law and order would break down. Nothing of the sort happened. Six million visitors attended during the five months the exhibit was open; the profits realized made possible purchase of the grounds on which the Victoria and Albert Museum and the Royal Albert Concert Hall now stand.[20] Railroads transported visitors from the provinces, easily and quickly; light refreshments, catalogues, and rest rooms were provided; public order was never a problem. The Crystal Palace, in which the exhibits were housed, proved the hit of the show. Designed by Sir Joseph Paxton, it enclosed more than seventeen acres; giant elms flourished undisturbed within its spacious dimensions. Modular throughout, it was 1,848 feet long and 408 feet wide. Though cheap and quick to erect, it had the sort of tenacious indestructibility found only in

20. In Kensington Gardens stands a further monument to Albert: the Albert Memorial, designed by Sir Gilbert Scott after the crosses erected nearly six hundred years before by Edward I in memory of his wife, Eleanor of Castile. Completion of the Albert Memorial (1876) formalized the Gothic revival (above, p. 333). Incidentally, the book that Albert carries as he stands in his memorial is a copy of the catalogue of the Great Exhibition of 1851 (SFR, H.7).

"temporary" structures. After the Great Exhibition closed in Hyde Park, the palace was moved to Sydenham in the suburbs, where it stood till destroyed by lightning in 1943. Its functionalism, widely deplored at the time, provided a root inspiration for many modern architects.

Esthetically speaking, many of the exhibits in the great imperial bazaar of 1851 would qualify today for the chamber of horrors. Overstuffed furniture and gimcrack decoration, patent medicines, religious tracts, and Indian curries were jumbled in with ladies' corsets, brassbound steam engines, celluloid collars, and cast-iron whatnots for the genteel parlor. But the esthetic point was secondary. What the exhibition celebrated was the triumph of industry and commerce. And though the taste was uncertain or worse, there was something to celebrate in the sheer quantity of artifacts assembled within the glittering glass house in Hyde Park.

THE PRESSURE COOKER OF VICTORIAN "CULTURE"

Braggart patriots could exult over the exhibition for purely material reasons; it advertised the supremacy of the greatest commercial power on earth. But on the fringes of the main show, a shrewd visitor could observe other and better reasons for satisfaction. Among the reforms of the reforming forties, some had crept in which did not simply modify the machinery, but made the content of life more civilized for everybody.[21] The brutal sports of bull and bear baiting were abolished during the 1830s; cock fighting and rat killing (with terriers) diminished. The death penalty was restricted till only murder remained a capital crime. Public education improved slowly, and the University of London was gradually enabled to provide an alternative to the Anglican establishments of Oxford and Cambridge. After a long, painful climb through the ranks, Benjamin Disraeli's intelligence and eloquence raised him, around 1850, to leadership of the conservative party; it was a major step toward erasing primitive prejudices against the Jewish people. Prisons were made more sanitary, less corrupt, more humane; imprisonment for debt was eliminated by stages, and personal bankruptcy admitted as a legal procedure. In 1868 public hangings were abolished. The system of transporting convicts to exile in Australia broke down; it was too brutal, the Australians did not want any more hard cases, and besides discovery of Australian gold (at Ballarat in 1851) made punishment look too much like reward. Small matters revealed, even better than big ones, the temper of the times. For centuries English chimneys had been swept of their accumulated soot by tiny boys, only six or seven years old, who were forced to climb up flues as narrow as nine inches. Kidnapped by savage masters, beaten, starved, ragged, filthy, robbed of their occasional tips and often suffocated in the chimneys, they had long lived lives

---

21. The word "culture" and the ideal of being "cultivated" became widely diffused during the nineteenth century, till by Matthew Arnold's day they were almost ritual words, charms (SFR, H.2).

of infernal torment, till in the 1830s a parliamentary commission investigated their plight and brought partial relief. The cheap waterproof umbrella (a humble convenience, but in a damp climate very welcome) made life easier for millions. The divine drug was discovered which mitigates though it does not cure (nothing cures) the gout. Streets started to be lit at night by gas lamps; in private houses they were adopted more slowly, for fear of explosions. Competent police forces ceased to be rare and exceptional.

All these humane and civilizing changes were for the good, little as they helped the case of a miserable Irish laborer without a single potato to roast for his supper. But the "civilizing" of Victorian England also had dark consequences for the folk undergoing it. The morality that Victoria practiced and many Victorians preached was a stiff and oppressive doctrine. It divided society into the respectable and the non-respectable, with consequences equally disastrous for both. Too often, the respectable became priggish and sanctimonious, under the influence of popular morality like the *Proverbial Philosophy* of Martin Tupper (published serially from 1838 to 1867) and the unctuous adages of Samuel Smiles (*Self-Help,* 1859, is typical). C. E. Mudie established in 1852 his famous lending library; it was popular because Victorian families could be sure Mudie's books had all been censored in advance, it was infamous because publishers, recognizing Mudie's immense influence on sales, refused to consider any manuscript which was not milk-and-water in its "morality." Respectable taste was responsible for such monstrosities as the Reverend Thomas Bowdler's *Family Shakespeare* (1818), from which, in the editor's words, "all those words and expressions are omitted which cannot with propriety be read aloud in a family." Thus the Victorian evangelicals produced a kind of bloodless, sexless, sanitary domestic spirituality from which real life was, so far as possible, banished. We noted above the readiness of Mr. Wilberforce and his chosen people to make Christianity comfortable for the well-to-do while neglecting the massive problems of the poor. The developed doctrine of respectability formalized this contrast. Nowhere was the iron division between respectable and unrespectable more oppressive than for women. The married woman with a wealthy husband could be, if she chose, the angel in the house; her diabolic counterpart was the whore in the lane. Victorian society produced both types in quantity[22] (SFR, H.15).

Morally and esthetically, it was an age of surfaces. The taste of the developed nineteenth century was for the *genteel*—for plush carpets in airless drawing rooms, for overstuffed furniture and flat paintings of chubby children with cute morals appended; for machine-carved woodwork, chromolithography, wax flowers,

---

22. The phrase "angel in the house" is the title of a long seminarrative poem begun in 1854 by Coventry Patmore; it describes the courtship, marriage, and domestic bliss of Felix, an aspiring lawyer, and Honoria, daughter of a Salisbury dean. Though bad, the verse is bad on an edifying principle; it is an effort to show the holy in the humdrum, and achieves exactly the opposite effect. There was more to Patmore than this rosy, cozy domestic content; his "London Fete" is a rough, fierce poem protesting a public hanging at old Newgate prison.

stuffed birds, needlepoint, glass bricabrac, and three-decker novels in the parlor, while scullery maids wept despairingly in their dark closets under the stairs. With the repeal of the Corn Laws, England was said to mark a swing from the agricultural to the manufacturing interest; less dramatic but equally significant was a steady increase throughout the century in the number of white-collar workers, in clerks, teachers, civil servants, accountants, and paperwork people generally. Clerks swarm through the fiction of Dickens and Trollope; in Thackeray's novel *Pendennis* and in *David Copperfield* (published almost simultaneously just before 1850) the hack-hero or clerk-hero is splendidly metamorphosed into the hero-author. Respectability was, among other things, the doctrine of those who work with symbols on paper, not with living plants and animals (SFR, H.26).

TENNYSON, A BROODY SAGE

Though the decade after Waterloo belongs primarily to the romantic poets, they do not fill it very full. By 1821 Keats had run his short course, while Shelley and Byron, self-exiled in response to respectable British opinion (Shelley for his announced atheism, Byron for rumored incest with his half sister) spent their last years abroad. All three of these intense and passionate poets flashed through life like meteors; and after the death of Byron, who died in 1824 while trying to liberate Greece, English poetry fell silent for a time. But it was only six years before the next major voice was heard; it belonged to Alfred Tennyson, a refugee from the sullen feuds of a morbid north-country clergyman's family. Tennyson had a natural aptitude for gloomy rumination; early poems like "Mariana" and "The Lady of Shalott" are as remarkable for their air of stagnant and frustrated passion as for their feminine point of view. Their luxuriant sensual particularity implies careful study of Keats; but, unlike the poems of Keats, they are pageant-poems, with formal surfaces and a bold, recurrent design that suggests tapestry. The tortured and questioning "In Memoriam," which appeared in 1850, was both puzzling and impressive by contrast with this earlier work. It wove deeply personal themes into a loose pattern of far-reaching but inconclusive speculation, not without overtones of morbidity. Perhaps unfortunately for the poet, Queen Victoria had a corresponding streak of black despondency herself, as became all too evident after the death in 1861 of Prince Albert. In the circumstances of 1850, she took advantage of Wordsworth's death to name Tennyson, at the early age of forty-one, poet laureate.

Official recognition has not brought fresh inspiration to many laureates, and in Tennyson it encouraged a native tendency to pontificate on cosmic issues, while celebrating the triumphs of an age already rather too well pleased with itself. He liked to write sonorous, elevated poetry, and did it very well; it's been his misfortune that sonority and elevation in poetry are no longer highly prized. Another of his favorite strains of moral idealism has not worn at all well. It takes the form of a high-minded, high-strung young man whose high-flown passion is betrayed by a worldly and cynical young temptress.[23] This is the scenario of "Locksley Hall," it is the crucial action of Pelleas and Ettare in *Idylls of the King*. Victorian idealism, with its exaggerated emphasis on purity, admired the young man in this situation and deplored the lady; twentieth-century cynicism invites us to see the story from another angle.

Tennyson remains for us a remarkable craftsman with words and rhythms, a close observer of nature, a skilled evoker of murky moods; further, he was an excellent Latinist, who toyed with the classical meters, and used his historical imagination to develop the dramatic monologue, invoking classical characters to do so. It may seem odd that this semidramatic poetry should have risen to prominence when the drama itself was at the absolute nadir of its development. One of the reasons for that yawning depression was that Victorian audiences insisted on naïve morality and literal realism on the stage. Whether they would have appreciated subtleties of character or intricacies of comic plot can hardly be known since they were never given either. What they got was either broad burlesque, which ridiculed the conventions of the stage itself, or black-and-white melodrama.[24] Neither of these forms is without interest, but they are both forms of subtheater or antitheater. Quite possibly the undramatic inner theater of the poets, in their psychological monologues, was a reaction against the crude exteriority of the real stage as it then existed. But it was also a deepening of romanticism itself, an extension of that first romantic principle that the mind not only mirrors and modifies the world, but creates a world of its own.

LESSER VOICES

Browning is commonly joined with Tennyson to unite the two major Victorian poets; but this may imply more dialogue between the two than actually occurred. Browning's popularity waxed as Tennyson's waned, and came from a different class of readers. Only in the last part of the century did Browning win much general acceptance; in that quarter century from 1825 to 1850, major poetic voices are few, and Browning's is not yet one of them; he will appear in the next chapter. The turbulence of Walter Savage Landor's life echoed hardly at all through his poetry; it is terse, quiet, and in its chiseled concision seems written

23. The fashion for ranting virtue was set earlier by poets now mostly forgotten, such as Philip Bailey, George Gilfillan, and Sydney Dobell. Under the mocking name of the "Spasmodic School" they enjoyed a modest vogue till inevitable parody brought them down.

24. The exaggerated dialect of the old melodramas may be sampled in Thomas Campbell's poem "Gertrude of Wyoming" (Wyoming, Pennsylvania, that is), also in the fiction of Bulwer-Lytton (particularly funny in *The Last Days of Pompeii*), or firsthand in stage productions long vanished from the boards but lovingly collected by M. Willson Disher under the title *Blood and Thunder* (SFR, H.19). Any dyspepsia resulting from this turgid material can be cured by a short course of reading in the novels of T. L. Peacock.

to be carved in marble. In an age of men with good classical educations, Landor was outstanding for his grasp, not just of the languages but of the classical spirit; his epigrams and elegies, seeming slight, are tuned to the *Greek Anthology*. George Darley and Thomas Lovell Beddoes wrote some exquisite lyrics, imitating the fine proportions and also the shiver of mortality that haunts some Jacobean songs; neither created a substantial body of work. Tom Moore's sentimental Irishisms (*Irish Melodies,* 1807–1835) have enlivened many a barroom night; but as they lead simply to a smile, a sigh, and another drink, the Irish themselves have been inclined to regret them. John Clare is another occasional talent, whose diamonds were found, amid much rubble, only long years after his death. Among still smaller fry, we note Ebenezer Elliott, "the Corn Law rhymer," whose honest indignation and sympathy with the oppressed are reminiscent of George Crabbe; and Thomas Hood, who made his scanty living writing jokes, sketches, and puns but also wrote in serious vein vigorous poems of protest describing the hard life of the poor.

THE FAIR FIELD OF FICTION

These are all poets worth reading in and around, but the heavy work of the early century was in prose, and we need only mention (in addition to Scott, Jane Austen, and the essayists) the names of Dickens, Thackeray, Borrow, Carlyle, and Macaulay to see that this is where the big guns are lined up. The sort of seriocomic novel inaugurated by Dickens and Thackeray was a particularly succesful innovation. It appealed to a new audience, which it reached mainly through magazine serialization and with the help of many illustrations. The new magazines were not those intellectual quarterly reviews; they were, as a rule, monthlies designed for middle-class families, to whom they appealed with an abundance of fictional sentiment and few demands for concentrated thought.[25] Novelists enjoyed writing in monthly units, which spread out composition of a novel over a leisurely period, with a plum at the end in book publication. Episodes occupied an installment apiece; though that rather disintegrated the plot structure, hanging the novel on a theme or thesis gave it a compensating unity. Dickens has a workhouse novel, a chancery novel, an American novel, etc. Weeklies were harder to write serials for, but it could be done. Novelists became so important to periodicals that they started their own. Dickens founded, published, and wrote most of *Household Words* (1850); Thackeray helped found and edit the *Cornhill* (1860). When they were not (as in Thackeray's case) the same fellow, authors and illustrators worked together on these serializations, artists suggesting turns to the story, authors leaving points to be made by illustrators.

25. Though in the long run serialized novels might cost as much as a bound volume, readers did not feel the cost when it was experienced as a shilling an issue spread over a year and a half. They were buying books on the installment plan.

Two technical novelties eased this collaboration. Lithography, just invented in 1798, enabled the artist to draw directly on his stone without any intermediate artisan to blur the bold lines of his caricature.[26] And printers using steel engravings, first introduced in 1823, could get from a single plate enough impressions for an edition. Half satiric, half affectionate, dedicated to irreverent commentary on quirks and foibles of rich and poor alike, the new caricature and the new fiction had a lot in common. Pathos and irony were well within their range; anything like the heroic was not.

AMAZING MISTER DICKENS

An amused tone, a talent for drollery, and emphasis on mannerisms exactly suited the lively, inventive gifts of Dickens. He had the knack for impersonation of a good comedian; amateur theatricals and stage readings delighted him all his life. They delighted audiences as well; there are few periods when Dickens isn't carrying on at least three careers, as novelist, entertainer, and editor, any one of which would have occupied fully the average man. Like most comedians, he had in his closet a couple of skeletons—a ridiculous, improvident father and a nightmarish period of work, among rough boys in a dingy cellar, for a boot-blacking factory. For young Charles these were fearful experiences, but they also suggested many comical and melodramatic actions in his novels. Little of his immense experience was wasted on Dickens.

His popularity, which from the first was phenomenal, grew out of his vivid and contagious sense of fun. The publishers who suggested *Pickwick Papers* had in mind a series of ridiculous adventures by a group of cockneys who would go on sporting expeditions to the country and (knowing nothing about the sportsman's life) would make fools of themselves. There were safe precedents for this; Robert Surtees had done a series ridiculing a sportive grocer named George Jorrocks; but Dickens would have none of it. He knew little of field sports himself, and his good sense told him that jokes on such a theme would be snobbish and dull. Mr. Pickwick and his ambling menagerie of amiable eccentrics were an immense success when they appeared in serial form.[27] The plot was unpredict-

26. Across Europe, the early nineteenth century was the golden age of caricature. French artists like Daumier, Grandville, and Gavarni, English artists like Rowlandson, Gillray, and Cruikshank, raised swift, satiric drawing to a fine art. In Spain, Goya's bitter *Caprichos* touch the terrible and even the sublime. Caricature, it's arguable, had much in common with romanticism; it was contemporary, not classical, registering modern modes; it distorted the external world to show the artist's feeling toward it; it concentrated on moments of significant time. Baudelaire's writings on these matters are of great import to an understanding of the romantic movement; in their background lies Stendhal's 1823 manifesto, *Racine et Shakespeare*.

27. *Pickwick* was the first *new* novel to appear in monthly installments; reprints of older books had sometimes come out in sections. Though slow in picking up momentum, because it was tapping a new audience, *Pickwick* by the fifteenth episode was selling the then-enormous number of 40,000

able, the invention continuous, the flow of high spirits irresistible. The completed book was quite as successful commercially as the installments. Dickens was just twenty-five when the volume appeared in 1837; the *Quarterly Review* thought him certain to be a mere flash in the pan because his material was so vulgar. And in fact, compared with the historic grandeur of Scott and the cool, intelligent respectability of Miss Austen, Pickwick and his friends were low, very low. Had they been consistently ridiculed, that might have satisfied the *Quarterly;* but in the deeply felt prison scenes, Mr. Pickwick is not absurd or buffoonish at all; he rises, instead, to heights of moral grandeur. Dickens may have imitated in these scenes Goldsmith's *The Vicar of Wakefield;* but they were deepened by thoughts of his own prodigal father who, though he pretended to gentility, often descended along a trail of pawnshops and sponging houses to the abyss of debtor's prison. Though Dickens always altered his experiences before putting them into fiction, the traces can be followed in small as in large matters. For Mr. Alfred Jingle's jerky, incoherent manner of speech, Dickens evidently drew on his experience as a shorthand writer; he had been a first-rate legal reporter and had laughed over the disconnected shorthand phrases which in the final version would be fleshed out into normal English. To build a character out of such unconsidered trifles was the work of a born artist, and an artist of an altogether new sort.

Because Dickens was a young man of generous sympathies, his work from the start showed special concern for the oppressed and overburdened. Waifs, strays, and orphans are at the heart of his narratives; dispossessed of their proper social positions, they try to assert their rights, but cold moral monsters (Murdstone, Ralph Nickleby, Bounderby) push them back toward the ugly pit of the urban proletariat. Workhouses, boarding schools, law courts, and prisons are machines for repressing vital young innocents. These institutions stirred Dickens's deepest fear and loathing. His books touched the public conscience in general; their effect on specific reforms is less clear, but concerning matters like the prison system, his bitter pages can hardly have failed to have an effect. The stream of reforms proposed by John Howard in the late eighteenth century and pressed during the second and third decades of the nineteenth century by Mrs. Elizabeth Fry, drew strength from Dickens. On the other hand, his satire of chancery, in *Bleak House,* is quite out of date. The novel, though written in 1852–1853, is supposed to take place in 1827; historically accurate, it could have had little contemporary application (SFR, H.13).

More even than the individuals and institutions of London, Dickens used the giant city itself in his novels. As he started his career, the inner city was already

---

copies per issue. As a class, Dickens's readers were not literary sophisticates; they accepted unquestioningly a good deal of claptrap, and responded with floods of tears to passages of raw, overwritten sentiment, like the death of little Nell in *The Old Curiosity Shop* (1841). Dickens cultivated, and got, an immense amount of adulation. He needed it, and found it stimulating; but it was responsible for much that we find forced and shrill in that magnificent outpouring of invention.

starting to shrink a bit, while the district around the city—the county—was expanding rapidly. In the last part of the century the still more remote suburbs swelled gigantically, as railroad commuting made it feasible to live in the country while working in the city. Dickens is the particular poet of these outlying villages and waterfront suburbs which fill the Thames Valley and line the lower estuary. He knows their pubs and rooming houses, their semidetached villas and mist-shrouded fields. But he also knows the inner city, its swells and toffs and sharp-eyed clerks (of whom he was once one), its ragged boys and semicriminal dodgers. Very high up the social scale Dickens does not venture; a successful banker or established tradesman is about at the top of his social ladder. But from there on down, he knows everyone worth knowing, and anyone he doesn't know he's quick to invent. A visual image of this immense, filthy, busy London of his can be had by looking through Gustave Doré's collection of woodcuts, with text by Blanchard Jerrold, under the simple title, *London* (SFR, H.8). It is the city of 1870 that we have here, but it is not too different from the city of twenty or thirty years before.

THACKERAY AND GEORGE BORROW

Unlike Dickens, whose production is so prodigious that nothing under a volume could describe the kaleidoscopic range of his activities, William Makepeace Thackeray has become in our day essentially a man of one book. There is injustice here, for *Pendennis* (1849), *Henry Esmond* (1852), *The Newcomes* (1854), and *The Virginians* (1858) are all fine fictions, with complex plots, animated characters, and much acute social commentary; there are those who think *Henry Esmond*—botched ending and all—Thackeray's masterpiece. But for the general reading public, Thackeray is the author of *Vanity Fair* (1848) and the creator of one character in that book, Becky Sharp. Becky is what the nineteenth century used to call an "adventuress"; not exactly a scarlet woman, but equally far from being a woman of good repute. Whether, as the wife of Rawdon Crawley, she does or doesn't have an affair with Lord Steyne, Thackeray leaves carefully equivocal; but she gets into so many equivocal situations with so many men in whom she sees material advantage for herself that before long it's quite unequivocal what sort of girl she is. The "good" characters, Amelia Sedley and William Dobbin, are admittedly insipid figures when compared with flashy Becky Sharp; Dobbin's name alone is enough to suggest what Thackeray thought of them. Yet convention required that they be rewarded and Becky punished; and so, predictably, Thackeray brought it about. He had a basic fondness for rascals and schemers; they animate his plots and stir his wit, but he was careful to keep them at a distance, as if partly afraid of them. Thackeray himself is a more complex psychological study than any of his characters: a timid giant, one feels, who never fully unleashed his own energies. Perhaps his worst misfortune was being placed in direct competition with Dickens; at another period, he might have developed more boldly.

George Borrow's two novels (*Lavengro*, 1851; *The Romany Rye*, 1857) are two fragments of a single autobiographical fiction; they were cut in two by a printer, who stopped the author short in the midst of an episode, saying he had enough material for his first book. Borrow's peculiar combination of interests, his dry formal style and mysterious taciturnity make his books like no others. Because of the episodic way in which they are composed, his tales suggest without ever asserting conspiratorial profundities; yet his prose is not evocative or incantatory, but oddly flat. He was an original, who compounded himself out of an odd personal history.

In his youth Borrow had tried to support himself doing hack work for London publishers; that failing, he took to the open road and wandered cross-country in the company of tinkers, horse dealers, and gypsies. Having a good ear and the gift of tongues, he picked up the gypsy language, Romany; having a powerful frame and plenty of occasions to stand up for himself, he learned to box. The English Bible Society first employed him on a project to distribute Bibles in Spain. Catholic countries do not often welcome Protestant missionaries, suspecting that when they hand out Bibles, they will not be long in teaching a certain way of reading them. Spain in the early nineteenth century was very wild land indeed, torn by civil wars and infested by bandits. On foot and alone, Borrow made his way through the back country, having plenty of adventures and some real successes. Within the recall of men now living, there were still little Protestant communities in the hill country around León who preserved memories of this tall, straight-backed young Englishman with premature gray hair, who first brought them knowledge of the Bible.

Borrow's Spanish adventures, published as *The Bible in Spain* (1843), created a sensation in England; though his two novels were less successful, they remain the basis of his reputation today. They are very much outdoor books; the smell of the heath and the stable is on them. Like Cobbett, whom he admired, Borrow is a late voice of prerailroad, unclerkly England; his cart-drawn gypsies, telling fortunes, fixing fights, poisoning pigs, and pitching camp in the dingles are a last remnant of a lost way of life.

CARLYLE: THE IMPATIENT SAGE

Of all the nineteenth-century prose writers, Thomas Carlyle is hardest for us to reach. Hardly anything can be said of him that doesn't require a qualifying phrase beginning "but not." He was profoundly influenced by Scottish Presbyterianism, but not in an orthodox direction. He was a vehement moralist, but not in terms of any particular creed. He was a loud, rough writer, much given to overstatement, but not without subtleties of insight. He was a philosophical radical, but not in the service of any movement; in fact he often spoke the most reactionary language of the century. He harangued his readers as a sage and prophet, but not as a visionary like Blake. He was a Victorian evangelical revivalist without a very clear or present idea of God.

Everything in Carlyle's life was either hard by nature, or he made it so. The elder son of a poor Scottish family, he prepared to be a preacher but at the last minute gave it up, without acquiring any other distinct affiliation. He was poor, yet as the elder son responsible for helping out his eight siblings. Despite congenital incapacities, he prepared to marry the attractive and intelligent Jane Welsh; but with true Victorian scrupulosity, they first made over to her mother Miss Welsh's entire fortune, so the first six years of their marriage had to be spent in a bleak hut in the Scottish hamlet of Craigenputtock. Carlyle's first book of independent philosophy, *Sartor Resartus* (1833), was cast in the most indigestible form conceivable as a ragbag of autobiographical notes written by an imaginary German professor Diogenes Teufelsdrockh and assembled by an imaginary editor.[28] Publishers and readers alike were repelled by the odd presentation and boisterous tone; it was only slowly that the book's kernel of meaning became apparent. The strenuous energy of *Sartor Resartus* is something like its keynote. We must recognize that the world is changing and be intellectually agressive in keeping up with it—to that, or something not much larger than that, the main point reduces. Given this first premise, we find less trouble in grasping the extreme positions that Carlyle deduced from it. Being an individual stirrer of individual consciences, he disliked institutions, which lured men into attitudes of passive complacency. He admired natural aristocracies, and thought the naturally inferior (whom he defined perhaps too generously) ought to recognize them at once and knuckle under like good underlings. Except that he did not see Christianity as a slave religion, his position is like that of Nietzsche later in the century; like Nietzsche, he was a vitalist, preferring the heroic instincts over the merely rational mind. These relatively simple themes may be traced through his biographies of Cromwell and Frederick the Great, as well as his *History of the French Revolution*. Perhaps because they were simple, Carlyle's lay sermons were almost always built over a scaffolding of historical fact.

One of Carlyle's avowed tracts for the times, *Past and Present* (1843) is especially interesting in this regard. Written amid the great Chartist and Corn Law agitations, it contrasts medieval with modern England, much to the disadvantage of the latter. It is one of several books following this pattern to make this point. Carlyle took his text from the chronicle of Jocelin de Brakelond, then recently edited for the Camden Society of British antiquarians. Describing events of the twelfth and thirteenth centuries, Jocelin had emphasized the vigor of Samson, abbot of Bury St. Edmunds, in rebuilding the discipline of his abbey and encour-

---

28. *Sartor Resartus* is Latin for "The Tailor Retailored"; the professor's name means "God-Begotten Devil's-Dung." Clothes are symbols of ideas, so a retailored tailor is a philosophy rethought; the philosopher's name expresses the double nature of man, part divine, part diabolic.

aging the growth of the town. Taking Abbot Samson as his model of the active, practical, yet humanely minded man, Carlyle drew a contrast with the misery and social indifference of his own time. His cry was for a modern hero to do for modern England what Abbot Samson had done six and a half centuries before.[29]

Carlyle's idealizing of the past in order to denounce abuses of the present built tacitly on an earlier effort with religious and aesthetic rather than political overtones. In 1836 the architect Pugin, who would play a part in rebuilding the burnt-out houses of Parliament at Westminster (above, p. 333), published a little but influential book titled *Contrasts*. It placed side by side on opposing pages engravings of a medieval town and a modern city, the medieval town idealized, the modern town taken at its worst. Pugin was a Roman Catholic convert, and did not hesitate to rub sore points like the difference between the gracious Catholic almshouse and the brutal protestant workhouse. For Carlyle, whose residual Presbyterianism made him uneasy in the presence of "papistry," Pugin was best disregarded, and his point altered; Carlyle tried to distinguish morally responsible from morally irresponsible societies. For John Ruskin and William Morris, though both were partial Carlyleans, the point would be different again; they contrasted irresponsible capitalism with an egalitarian collectivity they saw in the future. Thus, with some misgivings, radical economic reform came to walk hand in hand with a medievally tinted Christian piety, under the rubric of Christian socialism. In the modern world, the two components do not mix well, if at all. But as they enable the propagandist to combine nostalgia for a past ideal with expectations of a transcendent future, their appeal is often deep.

MACAULAY AND THE MEN OF LETTERS

Thomas Babington Macaulay enters English history both as an actor in it and a writer about it. The son of an evangelical businessman, Macaulay was a prodigious child who learned languages in his cradle, spoke like Dr. Johnson when he was four,[30] and compiled at the age of eight a Compendium of Universal History. Born with the century, Macaulay seemed imbued with its positive thinking; at school, in the university, in Parliament, he was always a popular and much-admired man. Perhaps for this reason, he had remarkably few doubts or misgivings; Lord Melbourne once said quietly he would like to be as sure of any

29. Like the later sages Ruskin and Arnold, though using a different vocabulary, Carlyle urged the duty of a just society to develop the full human capacity of its members. In the abstract, everyone sees the merits of such an arrangement; bringing it about seems to require more than just one hero, perhaps a society of them, to be known, conceivably, as supermen.

30. A story is told that once, aged four, while he was paying a formal call with his parents, a servant accidentally spilled some hot coffee on his leg. Macaulay howled, like the baby he was; but after a while the hostess asked if he was feeling better. "I thank you, madam," replied the tot, "indeed, the agony has somewhat abated."

one thing as Macaulay was of everything. Because his father's business did badly, Macaulay had to seek office, and in office he did well; but his heart lay in writing, and as soon as he could, he left politics to live by his pen. Here too he was triumphant. For the magisterial reviews he wrote authoritative articles in return for imperial fees; for the *Encyclopaedia Britannica,* growing with each new edition in size and prestige, he wrote essays still recognized as classics of their kind; and his *History of England,* which appeared in five volumes between 1849 and 1861 (the last volume posthumously), was the most widely read book of its sort ever published.[31] All this success enabled Macaulay, a lifelong bachelor, to live in style at the Albany apartments in Piccadilly and hold conversational court among the London literati. The regal style came naturally to Macaulay; it was encouraged by a society without much background and with very little taste, which wanted to be told what to think. And it was also made possible by the changed conditions of the book trade. With new American readers in the millions, and the growth of literacy in England, the audience for books had multiplied manyfold. Copyright laws, which Dickens for one fought to get enforced, increased the value of literary properties, and released authors from that bondage to publishers which had afflicted even Dr. Johnson. George Borrow describes in the early chapters of *Lavengro* the last, hateful stages of that servitude; but his own novels, published under the more equitable scheme of copyrights and royalties, rendered his last years easy (SFR, H.12).

Dickens became a wealthy man through his writings; but Dickens was a very special case. The phenomenon of Macaulay calls our attention to the rise of a literary market place on which men who are not geniuses can find work for their pens. The great encyclopedias require informed articles; reviewing becomes a recognized craft, the reviewer's opinions often of more interest than the book that occasions them; editions, histories, biographies, and critical reappraisals start to multiply. All the secondary phenomena of literature proliferate; in their midst one finds now the man of letters—not a great artist, as a rule, nor yet a hack, but a laborer who may be worthy of his hire. Lord Macaulay was the first and lordliest of these; his example has given patronage to a numerous tribe.

IRISH WRITERS AND ENGLISH PAINTERS

Sydney Owenson lady Morgan, heads up an impressive group of nineteenth-century Irish writers (SFR, H.24). The first of her books appeared when the century was just four years old, and she was still active fifty years later. She was

31. Though it covers only the seventeen years from 1685 to the death of William III, Macaulay's *History* lays out a picture of England majestic in its outlines and precise in its details. It also defines in classic form a Whig philosophy of history. For years literary men in London spoke in hushed voices of the day Lord Macaulay was handed a single royalty check for £20,000. That was authorship!

an ardent patriot, a collector of folk tales and folk songs; her best-known novel is *The Wild Irish Girl* (1806). But she was also a European traveler, writing books on France and Italy which Lord Byron supported when the *Quarterly* savaged them. Lady Morgan, however, needed no help from his lordship, and her revenge on the *Quarterly* reviewer is a very sufficient example of literary vendetta honed to a fine edge.[32] Among her followers, Gerald Griffin wrote a novel called *The Collegians* (1829), best known through its stage adaptation by the mid-century actor-manager Dion Boucicault as *The Colleen Bawn*. Samuel Lover wrote novels of Irish humor and local color like *Rory O'More* and *Handy Andy;* while William Carleton, a greater talent, published under the sober title *Traits and Stories of the Irish Peasantry* (three volumes, 1830, 1833, 1834), vivid and vital studies of his native land. The brothers Banim (John and Michael) are another pair of Irish novelists, more dependent on Scott than they need have been, but with strong, dark imaginations. The brightest among the Irish novelists is Charles Lever, sometimes called, for his high spirits and adventurous fantasy, "the Irish Dickens." His novels, too many even to list by name, bubble with fresh animation; they are about hard-riding, hard-drinking squires and rakes and soldiers, careless and likeable fellows forever in scrapes, and about as good as adventure stories can aspire to be. Finally, in this too brief summary of the Irish literary scene, we come to the tragic figure of James Clarence Mangan, who died in 1849 at the age of just forty-six. Like Edgar Allan Poe, he had a passion for mystification and a weakness for drugs and alcohol; his lyrical gift was pure and melodic far beyond Poe's, and his poems live, not only in the concert hall, but in the popular mind. Though his work was uneven (much of it appeared in newspapers under pseudonyms), the best of it is among the most authentic poetry of the age. To say that Mangan died of starvation is inaccurate; he died of complications consequent upon malnutrition.

Amid the appalling bad taste that generally characterizes the mid-nineteenth century, it is pleasant to recall the work of two artists whose names stand higher today than even during their lives. John Constable and Joseph Turner were almost exact contemporaries (born in 1776 and 1775 respectively); both went their ways independently and in isolation from the prevailing taste of their times. Constable was a countryman from the flat fen land of East Anglia, where his father was a successful miller. Though he always wanted to be a painter, Constable met so many discouragements and had so few instructors, that he did not really find his own style till he was thirty-five. Some say it was a trip to Wordsworth's lake country that released his powers, but more likely he learned spontaneously if slowly to trust what his eyes told him about the wet, green Suffolk countryside. Constable's color was so fresh, it startled eyes grown used to the reddish browns that accumulate on old masters as varnish ages. Though he did not actually paint

---

32. In *Florence Macarthy* (1818) the figure of Con Crawley, a pretentious, half-educated fop, is Lady Morgan's portrait of the offending reviewer. As extra punishment for the victim, he doesn't appear till the second volume of this slow, talky novel.

in the open air, Constable did paint from oil sketches and pencil drawings made on the spot; with increasing boldness, he made his finished oils look like the swift, vivid sketches which recorded his first impressions. In landscapes, he rendered not only the leaves of trees, but glints of light left on them by a rain-shower; jokes were made at first about gallery-goers who got soaking wet by attending one of his shows. But a number of his paintings were hung and sold at the Paris salon of 1824; the great romantic painter Delacroix took a look at Constable's work and rushed back to his studio to repaint the picture on which he was working. It is commonly said that the French impressionists of the 1860s and 1870s owe something of their closeness to nature to the example of Constable. It is also true that by their time the possibility of carrying pigments in convenient zinc tubes had made it much easier to paint with oils in the open air.

Joseph Turner is the other great landscapist of the early century, and to his work the adjective "romantic" is more appropriate than it is to Constable's. He was born a Londoner, and though the son of a barber had more access than Constable to good pictures and established painters; accordingly, he was made a member of the Royal Academy in 1802, while Constable had to wait till 1829. Turner began his career as a water-colorist, and successfully; but around the turn of the century he began painting oils which public opinion (led by Sir George Beaumont, a wealthy and dogmatic amateur) denounced as "unfinished."[33] Viewers who wanted meticulous clear detail failed to see that Turner was out to render the grandiose aspects of nature, the cloud castles and misty forms of remote countrysides. As late as 1816 a smart ignoramus described Turner's work as "pictures of nothing, and very like." He continued on his way, however, and during the 1830s and 1840s spent much time in Venice, where his images of the city rising out of the mists of its lagoon are now generally recognized as supreme triumphs of his art. But his work was out of popular favor, and it was a surprise to him when in 1843 "A Graduate of Oxford," who turned out to be John Ruskin, hailed him in the first volume of a book called *Modern Painters* as one of the masters in the grand tradition. Truth to tell, there was something a little theatrical in Turner's vision of nature which appealed to a theatrical streak in Ruskin. But the splendor of Turner's visual rhetoric is no more to be questioned that that of Ruskin's verbal rhetoric; and in paintings like *The Fighting Téméraire* (1838) and *Rain, Steam, and Speed* (1844), he proposed a new way of seeing the glow and energy of modern industrial society. Both Constable and Turner left immense legacies of paintings to the nation, gifts without example or parallel in the history of the country. They are a major part of the heritage.

33. Nineteenth-century taste often made a fetish of close literal accuracy in art; painted animals should be anatomically exact, painted rocks geologically exact, down to the tiniest detail. Paintings were also expected to tell a story or even point a moral. Distractions of this sort often completely prevented the Victorians from seeing the paintings at which they thought they were looking.

Though canals and railroads, because of their novelty and efficiency, dominated the transportation picture of the early century, for many nineteenth-century folk the standard way of traveling was still by horse—either on horseback, in a rented carriage, or on the regularly scheduled mail coaches. Managing unfamiliar horses on unfamiliar roads called for some skill and experience; many of the comic misadventures of Mr. Pickwick and his friends involve refractory animals or roadside breakdowns. Robert Seymour and Hablot K. Browne ("Phiz") were the cartoonists who illustrated *Pickwick* (1836); their sketches were reproduced as steel-plate engravings.

Though small and not exactly a model of elegance, George Stephenson's "Rocket" locomotive was powerful and efficient. Stephenson had been making engines for fifteen years before he won the 1829 competition which put him in the forefront of British engineers and inaugurated, what could be called with equal truth, the age of steam or the age of coal.

The conquest of sail by steam in the annals of the Royal Navy is the theme of this 1838 painting by Turner: *The Fighting Téméraire Towed to Her Last Berth*. Against the backdrop of a flaming sunset, the ghostly old frigate is towed away by a squat, smoky, paddlewheeling tug. Dramatic, perhaps melodramatic in its spacious rhetoric, the painting is not ashamed to be making a big statement on a big theme. It is a heroic elegy for the wooden walls of England, which for two hundred fifty years (since the Armada) had defended the nation and were now forever obsolete.

Thomas Telford's canal bridge over the vale of Llangollen was one of the marvels of the age. It obviated the expense of building and operating ten or a dozen locks by carrying the canal smoothly across the 1,000-foot valley of the Dee. A special feature of the construction was a cast-iron trough for holding the canal waters themselves atop nineteen masonry arches. Sir Walter Scott called it "the most impressive work of art he had ever seen."

Our print is from the *Lives of the Engineers* by the positive-thinking Samuel Smiles (text, p. 387). For Smiles, the rise from poverty to wealth and fame of men like Telford was the very substance of the middle-class epic.

"Improvement makes straight roads," William Blake wrote; "but the crooked roads without improvement are roads of genius." Roaring, impatient railways had no time to pursue the roads of genius; they stamped their way into the very heart of ancient cities, dynamiting down whatever lay in their right of way, and creating a havoc that would only be equaled, a century later, by the automobile, with its reeking exhaust and insatiable demand for parking space.

A meager, ugly bust, a pair of tacky wives, vulgar signs and scrawled graffiti indicating popular disrespect—these mark the modern Episcopal tomb, as opposed to the austere dignity of a medieval prelate, in this plate from A. W. Pugin's *Contrasts* (1836). Everywhere, as Pugin sees it, the nineteenth-century world is ugly, penurious, and hateful, the fifteenth-century world is rich, gracious, and kindly. Though not a very balanced view of the two historical periods, *Contrasts* had a powerful effect as satire; and for those in society who plumed themselves on their "progress," it offered an astringent corrective.

The ugly side of industrialization showed itself in a polluted atmosphere, a brutalized working class, exploited children, cheap and shoddy goods, and a steadily declining standard of taste. The fate of the children—sometimes hitched like little animals to mine carts and savagely abused in the dark and lonely shafts—was particularly horrible till a measure of reform came with the Mines and Collieries Act of 1842. But the Dowlais iron works near Cardiff continued to blacken earth, sea, and sky, without the slightest effort at control or restriction, for decades to come.

As a picture of human misery, there is nothing to be added to this print of the Irish potato famine of 1847. In the print below a corpse is being dragged away on a manure cart—naked, because his rags have already been distributed, without a coffin because there is no money for one, and by a horse which looks as if he would die before he gets to the cemetery.

15

High Victorianism (1851–1887)

From the great exhibition of 1851 to the golden-jubilee celebration of Queen Victoria's reign in 1887, England's domestic economy and institutions developed peacefully and fast. The industrial plant grew along lines previously laid down, by steady increments, to spectacular effect. In 1848, 5,000 miles of railroad lines were in operation; in 1875, 14,500. In 1860 ships amounting to about 250,000 gross tons were added to the registry; in 1890, the annual increase was nearly a million tons, of which four-fifths were in steamers with steel hulls. The reform movements of the turbulent 1830s and 1840s had done their destined work and achieved decisive shifts of power, economic and political. Absolute predominance of the landed interest gave way to an unofficial and undefined sharing of power with the commercial and industrial classes. (Sir Robert Peel, for instance, was the son of a cotton manufacturer; William Ewart Gladstone was the son of a Liverpool merchant.) The franchise, widened in 1832, was widened further to admit working men (though not yet women); trade unions began to play a significant role in the social process.

Working out these shifts was a relatively undramatic process; the second reform bill of 1867 was far more radical than the first one of 1832, but it passed with far less furore. Queen Victoria, as she matured into the figure of an authoritarian matriarch surrounded by her nine children, grew steadily more severe and moralistic; always fond of referring to herself in the third person or through the imperial "we," she handled her ministers as she dominated her family. After the death in 1861 of Albert the prince consort, she went into an indefinite and (as it turned out) lifelong period of mourning;[1] it tinged the national life with that stiff and gloomy prudery which a later age thought typically "Victorian." On the Continent, and on the outskirts of British power, the story was very different. In 1848, revolutions all across Europe sent deposed monarchs, scared aristocrats, and failed revolutionaries—an odd, explosive mix—scurrying for the peaceful security of Britain. Among the revolutionaries was a German-Jewish journalist, already the author of a volcanic *Communist Manifesto*, who would spend the rest of his life working out the economic substructure of his ideology under the peaceful dome of the British Museum reading room. His name was Karl Marx.

Much of Britain's domestic tranquillity was due to the accumulation of what was slowly coming to be called an "empire." These foreign possessions were not invariably or even predominantly the result of conquest. Where the British had sent many colonists or established strong trade relations, they acquired political influence short in many ways of absolute sovereignty. Where their trade was menaced, they sometimes took over territories (either avidly or reluctantly) to protect it. The colonies themselves relied on the homeland for protection. And some regions, seeing the relative efficiency of British rule, actually petitioned for admission to the empire, as a better alternative to troubles they actually knew or had reason to dread. Thus British interests came to be affected by tribal wars in Africa, racial hatred between Russia and Turkey, nationalist hopes in the Balkans, commercial conflicts in China, and an American civil war—not to speak of ongoing troubles in Ireland and a murderous mutiny in India.[2] British diplomacy was involved deeply in all these struggles, and when diplomacy failed, the military were often summoned. Each of the situations was different from the other, and from each Britain's rulers took a different lesson. But learning to

1. Albert's death was almost certainly due to typhoid fever; Windsor Castle had an abominable sewage system, often deplored, never repaired. Ignorance of the basic laws of sanitation knew no boundaries of rank in those days.

2. The mix of formal with informal influence makes it hard to say how big the empire was at a given time. Sir Stamford Raffles bought the bare ground of Singapore from the sultan of Johore in 1819; less than a decade later, it was a thriving port and a colony. Though the British dominated many South American markets, they owned only a bit of land there. About 1840 Sir James Brooke got himself named, as much by hook as by crook, rajah of Sarawak, Borneo; a formal protectorate was declared only in 1888. Burma was swallowed gradually over a century; Fiji and the Malay States asked for admission to the empire in 1874; Cyprus came under British control (though not sovereignty) in 1878, to protect Suez when Turkey seemed threatened by Russia.

Emigration contributed largely to the growth of empire. Between 1853 and 1880, Britain sent out nearly 2.5 million emigrants. These were years of peace and prosperity at home; many who left were men of great enterprise, not losers or drifters at all. The government did not feel their departure as a crisis; on the contrary, men like Lord Durham and Edward Gibbon Wakefield did everything to facilitate and encourage emigration, which they saw as a long-term investment. That the colonies might someday become independent nations did not bother them; economic and cultural ties would remain. Thus British policy makers often distinguished sharply between their "white" and "colored" possessions—the first, safe partners, the second to be ruled by varying degrees of force (SFR, H.28).

govern a world empire was a long, slow process; though none of the various conflicts tested Britannia's full resources, cumulatively they represented a heavy drain on a small nation. When Victoria's jubilee was celebrated in 1887, it was an occasion for triumph and self-congratulation, but also for sober stock taking. The weight of empire was making itself felt.

IRISH AND CANADIAN GRIEVANCES: BLUNDERS IN CRIMEA

The famine and emigration that started in 1845 left Ireland in a state of depressed misery that hardened only slowly into active opposition. Though the 1848 revolts on the Continent sparked a corresponding rebellion in Ireland, it was an absurd fiasco; police constables put it down, and the leaders were exiled. But they kept in touch with each other and with sympathizers at home, until about 1858 an Irish liberation group was formed in America, under the name of the Fenian Brotherhood. Fenians had been a legendary group of ancient Irish warriors (above, p. 19), a kind of prehistoric Irish samurai. Modern Fenians were a secret organization with a disposition to violence. Hamstrung at first by spies and informers, they learned to organize in tight little cells, so that no member knew more than a few of his associates. While they limited themselves to occasional acts of terror in the dark Irish countryside, they disturbed but did not menace British rule. Yet they were not without influence. In the American Civil War, men who still thought themselves expatriate Irishmen gained practical military experience. They joined with the home-grown Fenians in an attempted seaborne landing on the Irish coast (1865), and when that failed, tried to invade Canada (1866 and 1870). Though these were nuisance raids, no more, they did stimulate the British rulers of Canada to allay the restlessness of this growing and increasingly prosperous colony. In 1867 Canada was granted dominion status, with a very large measure of self-government;[3] this paved the way for a rapid expansion into the Northwest Territories, a movement culminating in the transcontinental Canadian Pacific railway system. Thus the English-speaking majority within the community was increased manyfold, and the widening prosperity of this greater Canada eliminated permanently any possibility that Canada would be absorbed into the United States. But the French minority was not, and has not even yet been, permanently pacified. And similarly, the Fenians and the cause they represented survived in Ireland and, starting in 1880 made significant contributions to the home-rule campaigns of Charles Stewart Parnell. Their illegal, conspiratorial activity would

3. In the background of the 1867 decision lay a crucial report by Lord Durham (1839); it recommended the development of Canada toward increasing political independence combined with strengthened cultural and economic ties. Though not immediately implemented, the Durham report forecast policy not only in Canada, but in New Zealand, Australia, and the Cape Colony (British South Africa), thereby earning its author the nickname "Radical Jack."

combine with Parnell's legal, parliamentary campaign to provide a tricky set of problems for the British authorities.

A more bitter lesson was taught by the Crimean War of 1853–1856. The germ of this luckless struggle lay in a quarrel between France and Russia, in which Britain had no essential stake. Under terms of a long-forgotten treaty, France claimed the right to protect "visitors and pilgrims" passing through Turkey on their way to the Holy Land; on the basis of recent custom (though the actual number of overland pilgrims had dwindled to a mere trickle), Russia claimed the same right. Both powers had ulterior motives; they thought the Turks were a decadent power whom it would be easy to victimize once one got a foothold there. In fact, the Turks had recently begun a vigorous program of civil and military reform and were well able to take care, not only of passing pilgrims, but also of invading armies. Britain, however, thought herself obliged to make common cause with France, and so with Turkey, against Russia. In the early stages of the war, the Turks gave an unexpectedly good account of themselves; though their Black Sea fleet was destroyed at Sinope (30 November 1853), thereby drawing the English and French into active participation, their land forces more than held their own against those of the czar. When Austria threatened to join the allied cause, the Russians were forced (August 1854) to withdraw all their armies from the Turkish frontiers.

But Britain and France were not content with this standoff; they wanted to cripple Russia's power in the Black Sea by occupying the main Russian base, Sevastopol, on the Crimean peninsula. This proved harder than anyone had anticipated. Even before embarking, allied armies were suffering from cholera; when they reached the Crimea, they found the defenders solidly entrenched and roused to furious defense of the homeland. In October 1854, occurred the famous "Charge of the Light Brigade," when as a result of bungled orders, British cavalry carried out a hopeless frontal assault on massed artillery positions. Lord Tennyson's poem on the subject is not only a favorite piece for parlor recitation, it is technically pretty accurate; for the war was one of the first to be well reported, thanks, among other things, to the newly invented telegraph.[4]

Defeat at Balaklava and the savage but drawn battle of Inkerman ten days later made it inevitable that allied armies would have to stay in the Crimea over the bitter Russian winter. The worst of this was that a convoy bringing food and medical supplies had been lost in a storm. As a result, the British and French armies besieging Sevastopol suffered through a cruel Russian winter with inadequate supplies of every sort. Worse, the only hospital was more than 300 miles by sea from the battlefield, at Scutari, not far from Istanbul. It was a squalid,

---

4. The first submarine cable was laid across the channel in 1850, the first transatlantic cable in 1866. Victorian enthusiasts for the wonders of modern science made much of the telegraph; field commanders in the Crimea were less enthusiastic. The new gadget enabled the London War Office to pester them with detailed instructions and detailed inquiries about distracting trifles.

filthy old warehouse, infested with rats and roaches, and filled with a stench which alone defied men's powers of description. Into this inferno stepped a volunteer nurse, Florence Nightingale, with a small band of untrained assistants. Despite blind and stupid resistance from the Army Medical Corps, she reorganized the hospital with spectacular results. Before her arrival at Scutari, the mortality rate stood at over 40 percent, afterward it dropped as low as 2 percent. Her procedures were far from revolutionary, and by today's standards most of them were primitive; as long as she lived, she never accepted the doctrines of bacterial infection and antisepsis propounded in the 1850s and 1860s by Pasteur and Lister. But she brought to the suffering soldiers a regime of elementary sanitation, fresh air, clean food, and above all—that element for which even modern science has found no substitute—kind and gentle care. Miss Nightingale in action was a ruthless fanatic; to get what she wanted, she ripped through red tape, bullied, blackmailed, and pulled strings. In the process, she made herself the world's leading authority on hospital care and created the profession of nursing. And yet, for all her splendid achievements, three times as many British soldiers died of disease and the care they got in hospital as died on the field of battle (SFR, H.3).

In the fall of 1855, after savage battles through the suburbs and along the redoubts, Sevastopol fell to the allied armies, and ultimately peace was made with Russia. The war's lessons were not many, but it did teach the British (at the frightful cost of over 200,000 casualties) to stay out of land wars against enemies rich in manpower, regardless of British technical superiority. It was a lesson they were able to remember for most of the rest of the century.

INDIA, ITALY, DENMARK

The great Indian mutiny of 1857 taught other lessons. As noted above (p. 327), British presence in India had long depended on the East India Company, reformed in 1784 by the younger Pitt but still an active agent in Indian affairs, making treaties, hiring armies, and operating through its native puppets almost as a national government. In the company's armies, native troops (sepoys) outnumbered Europeans by nearly 8 to 1, and British officers, appointed through favoritism, were not always even minimally competent. It was, therefore, the height of imprudence for the company to annex as new territories the homelands of the very soldiers on whom the company's position depended. Yet they did worse. Evangelical Christianity impelled English governors to interfere increasingly with Indian religious beliefs. Some of the things they did were humane and (in our western eyes) right: they forbade the ancient practice of suttee or burning a widow on her husband's funeral pyre; they discouraged the practice of killing female children; they softened the harsh caste system by subjecting Brahmins to the same legal penalties as everyone else. But in all these matters they were going against the ingrained custom of the country; and in 1857 they made a ridiculous and unpardonable error by adopting the rifle invented by a Frenchman, Claude Minié.[5] Its heavy slug, long and pointed, was impelled by a cartridge, greased to facilitate the bullet's entry into the firing chamber. Before loading, the end of the cartridge had to be bitten off with the teeth. In India, all the sepoys objected to the grease on the cartridge, Hindus because they thought it was made of cattle suet, Moslems because they thought it was made of pig fat: each substance is taboo for one group. Weird as it seems, they were both right; the grease was made with pork *and* beef fat, and putting it in their mouths would defile Moslems and cause Hindus to lose caste forever. From such seeds, trifling in western eyes, tremendous for Indians, grew a mighty rebellion which roared like a monsoon across the subcontinent. While British administrators pulled back into garrisons or compounds, frantic young officers raced across the land to rally loyal troops, mostly Punjabis, Sikhs, and Gurkhas from the northern provinces. After deeds of awful cruelty and amazing heroism on both sides (the siege of Lucknow and the massacre of Cawnpore became legendary), the mutiny subsided. It had been a spontaneous rising, not an organized independence movement; many Indian states never took part in it. Still, the mutiny led to many changes, the first of which was demolition of the East India Company. The rebellion had been most violent in Bengal, where the company had long been strongest; its responsibility was clear. Abolishing its independent powers simplified channels of communication and command; it separated, at least nominally, money making from government. And the need for elementary tact in dealing with the Indian people was impressed on the British well enough to prolong their rule, for better or worse, almost another century.

Repressive in India, Britain assumed a relatively liberal stance in Europe, as evidenced by her support of the movement for Italian unification and liberation known as the Risorgimento (revival). This was a sustained program of agitation against the Austrians, who by the peace of Vienna had been assigned control of northern Italy, and against the reactionary petty princes whom they installed as puppets. Byron, Shelley, and Landor had sympathized with the early Italian rebels against this humiliating regime. These early patriots liked to call themselves "carbonari" (charcoal burners) because under that disguise they hid out in the mountains and forests. As they became more organized under the leadership of Giuseppe Mazzini, they also came more under the influence of liberal ideas from England; for the continental police often drove Mazzini to seek refuge in London. English liberalism inspired a steady drumfire of propaganda in Italy against Austrian absolutism and its clerical supporters. Nominally, Italy's liberal revolution of 1848 had the moral support of both France and England; but in fact the French were afraid of a strong, unified Italy, and demanded territorial concessions (the city of Nice, the district of Savoy) as the price of their help. England's

---

5. Many Civil War battles were fought with Minié rifles; the distinctive slugs, with a cup at the base, used to lie thick on the ground around Richmond, Virginia, and doubtless on other battlefields of the American war.

more disinterested influence won her many friends in Italy; and though the 1848 revolt was suppressed by the Austrians, and most of the patriot leaders again forced into exile, a few basic principles stood out. Italians would fight for their liberty, and with proper leadership heroically; Vittorio Emmanuele of Piedmont was the one political leader, as Giuseppe Garibaldi was the one military leader, around whom Italian patriots would rally. Thus when the crucial moment came in 1859, Garibaldi and his picked army of a thousand redshirts rolled through Italy from the south, even as the Piedmontese came down from the north, to squeeze out the Austrians. The reunification of Italy still faced many problems, because French troops maintained the traditional papal states in the center of the peninsula for some ten years. But in 1870 France herself collapsed under the Prussian onslaught, and French troops had to be withdrawn; after the formality of a plebiscite, Italian troops then occupied all the papal territory. In July of 1872, King Vittorio Emmanuele entered Rome to proclaim it the new capital of a united Italy.

In these many maneuvers, the British government, though careful to keep itself militarily uncommitted, played a consistently liberal role which won it much Italian good will. As foreign secretary, Lord John Russell made a forceful case for self-determination, and he was steadily backed up by the prime minister, Lord Palmerston. The creation of modern Italy was a triumph of British diplomacy. Yet when powers more dynamic than Italy and Austria were involved, Britain's influence on the Continent was very much subject to question. That was demonstrated during the 1860s by an ominous little dispute between Prussia and Denmark.

For many years the two provinces of Schleswig and Holstein had been ruled by the king of Denmark, Schleswig in the north largely Danish in its population, Holstein to the south mostly German. As a result of intricacies in the royal succession, the sovereignty of the two duchies came into question; and Bismarck, newly appointed chancellor of Prussia, decreed that they must both be German. The English prime minister Palmerston, conscious that the prince of Wales had just taken a Danish bride, issued an overbelligerent warning, implying that Britain would fight to help the Danes. This was quite impractical; Prussian troops invaded Denmark unopposed (February 1864) while England—along with France, Russia, and the other Scandinavian countries—stood helplessly by. Had Palmerston, whose penchant for taking independent action had long distressed Victoria, not talked so big beforehand, his failure to block this first little step of Prussian expansionism might have amounted to less; as it was, the Iron Chancellor and his staff got from the episode a strong sense of British weakness that led to further adventurism later.

AMERICA AND GERMANY

Two future rivals for the commercial supremacy enjoyed by Britain asserted their presence during the 1860s and 1870s in seismic wars from which Britain was able to stay aloof but whose consequences she could not escape. The American Civil War (1861-1865) posed particularly painful dilemmas. Having just taken a strong moral stand against slavery and the slave trade, Britain was bound to feel awkward about encouraging the Confederacy, with its "peculiar institution." But the south supplied much raw cotton for British mills; Federal blockade of southern ports was irksome to Britons, who saw themselves as guarantors of the freedom of the seas; in addition, the industrial north was just becoming a major commercial competitor for British markets. Direct intervention was out of the question, but there were strong temptations to recognize the Confederacy, a step which would pave the way for credits, maybe even a challenge to the blockade. In 1861 open conflict with the Federal government actually threatened, when a Federal gunboat stopped an English mail packet on the high seas to remove two Confederate diplomats; only careful editing by Prince Albert of a British protest averted the threat of war. But in the end the British preserved their neutrality and their friendship with the American government. As for the long-range consequences of the northern victory, they first made themselves felt in the 1870s, in the form of vast new agricultural imports. New lands had been opened up in the American West; new railroad and steamship lines cut shipping costs; and a flood of cheap American grain began devastating British agriculture even before American manufacturers began competing on world markets against British manufactured goods.

The Franco-Prussian War of 1870 disturbed British hegemony over Europe in a different and more dangerous way. The problem was not that the two parties went to war, but that the Prussians won such a swift and overwhelming victory. Until the war, Napoleon III, emperor of the French, had seemed an adequate counterbalance to a group of German states which had only recently been melded into a political unity. The collapse of France and abdication of the emperor seemed to leave an enormous vacuum of power in western Europe.[6] It also confronted the British with a German industrial machine more modern and dynamic than their own, a regime ambitious to acquire colonial territories, and a military establishment unmatched since the days of Napoleon I.

For Britain, the consequences of a new Europe were several. France, now no longer the Second Empire but officially the Third Republic,[7] could no longer be counted on as a major power, capable, for example, of defending the Suez Canal. Especially as France recovered swiftly from the humiliation of 1870, her friendship remained worth cultivating, and in the early twentieth century a close alli-

6. Louis Napoleon was a nephew of the great Napoleon; from childhood he cherished the faith that he too must be an emperor. Despite repeated failures and much ridicule, he finally rose to power as a result of the 1848 revolution that unseated Louis Philippe, "the bourgeois monarch." Napoleon III was an amazing melange of libertarian, imperialist, opportunist, tyrant, conspirator, and dreamer. Browning represents him in the monologue "Prince Hohenstiel-Schwangau" (1871).

7. The First Republic was formed by the revolution of 1789 and terminated by Bonaparte in 1804; the Second Republic, proclaimed in 1848, lasted only till 1852, when Louis Napoleon was proclaimed emperor; the Third Republic, born in 1871, lasted till the collapse of France in 1940. Since 1959 we have had the Fifth.

ance for mutual support (the so-called Entente Cordiale) made of the French commitment a keystone of British policy. But meanwhile, Germany's aggressive demand for more colonies triggered a wave of European imperialism; all the nations supposed they must get more undeveloped territories (generally in Africa), and tighten their hold on those they already possessed. In the long run, England's chief imperial rival was determined by the events of 1870 as Germany, and one may see that clash as a first giant step toward 1914. But for the moment, Victoria's many connections among the princes of Germany stood her in good stead. Wilhelm, the captor of Schleswig-Holstein and the conqueror of France, was not basically a ruthless man, though Bismarck's ascendancy made him seem such; his son Friedrich had married one of Victoria's daughters and imbibed from British statesmen, including Prince Albert, a strong taste for liberal principles. Thus British and liberal opinion looked forward, perhaps too complacently, to the day of his succession. In the event (to anticipate a few years), liberal Friedrich did not succeed his father till 1888. By then he was fifty-seven years old, and already suffering from cancer; he reigned only ninety-nine days before dying and giving way to *his* son, megalomaniac Wilhelm II, who precipitated Europe into the first World War.

ASIAN AND AFRICAN CONFLICTS

Throughout this period a string of lesser wars sputtered like firecrackers around the fringe of the empire. Some amounted to little more than police actions; others, though minor in themselves, bore the seeds of future troubles. There was a half-official river war of 1857–1860 in far-off China, a mere sideshow to the vast and murderous T'ai P'ing rebellion. It brought to China a Major Charles George Gordon, naïvely devout, profoundly egotistical, and brave as a lion; he was one of a new and growing class of English officers who, without abandoning their British rank or allegiance, took service with Britain's allies. In China, Gordon performed prodigies of valor in behalf of the old and crumbling Manchu dynasty, driving huge armies with a mere handful of soldiers, and crushing a major rebellion almost singlehandedly. These feats prepared him for further service in Egypt and the Sudan during the 1880s, service which culminated in his heroic, ill-advised, and ultimately fatal defense of Khartoum on the upper Nile against the armies of a Moslem fanatic, the mahdi (1884–1885).

During the 1860s and early 1870s, a complex of Balkan wars and risings resulted from efforts by the Serbians, Bulgarians, Montenegrans, and Romanians to free themselves from Turkey. These stirrings led in 1877 to yet another Russo-Turkish war, from which Britain and the European powers were sensible enough to abstain. The result proved favorable to the Russians; but at the treaty of San Stefano (1878) a British delegation managed, while weakening the Turkish Empire, to limit the gains made by Russia. The concern was to maintain a balance of power in the region; and, given the inherent violence and instability of the Balkans, it is remarkable that the 1878 compromise lasted, even if uneasily, through to the final cataclysm of June 1914, when assassination of the Austrian archduke at Sarajevo set off World War I.

Meanwhile the Turkish viceroy in Egypt, Ismail Pasha, took advantage of Turkey's many distractions to set himself up as Khedive of Egypt. (It was a refurbished title, meaning no one knew exactly what; but to Ismail Pasha it meant he was his own boss.) Among other projects, he inherited from his predecessors a half-dug canal across the isthmus of Suez, being built by the French engineer De Lesseps. Obstacles were many and immense; the khedive himself, a fellow much given to champagne and chorus girls, was not the least of them. Because of their eastern holdings, the British were bound to become involved sooner or later; but they were cautious, and bought into the enterprise only in 1875, when the canal had been six years completed, and the khedive had spent his way into the sloughs of ultimate bankruptcy.[8] Buying his share of the company's stock, as it was the largest single block, gave the British effective control of the canal; it also entangled them permanently in Middle Eastern politics. After propping up the Egyptian government for a while, they had to become the Egyptian government (it was Gladstone who took the step). And that led to complications of the sort that brought General Gordon to his end, fighting a fanatic's rebellion deep in the upper Sudan (SFR, H.3).

During the 1870s, as well, the full difficulties of Britain's position in South Africa started to make themselves felt. In the course of the Napoleonic wars, Cape Town had fallen into British hands, and England controlled the colony thereafter, even though most of the settlers were Dutch. Relations became strained during the 1830s, when the Dutch felt the English did not protect them adequately against marauding tribesmen; they were further aggrieved by Britain's abolition of slavery. Raids by Bantu tribesmen were in fact seriously destructive; and though the British promised compensation for liberated slaves, it was scant and hard to get. Impatient with English rule, the Dutch settlers (*Boers,* from the Dutch word for "farmers") moved out. Between 1836 and 1840 some 7,000 of them, a major part of the colony, migrated across the Orange river and its tributary the Vaal, north into the wide, rolling expanse of plain and hill country known as the Transvaal. Having shed British authority, they did not want to assume any new authority. The country was vast, settlers few; it was every man for himself. Though they declared themselves an independent nation, the Boers refused to pay taxes, build schools or roads, serve in armed forces, or live in peace with their black neighbors, whom they enslaved whenever they could. In 1876, Sir Theophilus Shepstone was sent north to investigate the Transvaal. He found that the state treasury contained twelve shillings sixpence, that neither an

---

8. As long as he had money or credit, the khedive spent with a lavishness that had few parallels even in the lavish nineteenth century. One good thing he achieved with his money was the commissioning of Verdi's opera *Aïda,* produced at Cairo in 1871 to celebrate the canal's opening.

army nor a police force existed, that the president was in despair, and that war with the ferocious Zulus living nearby was imminent. Sir Theophilus, a zealous imperialist himself, found nobody with authority enough to oppose annexation; and, taking lack of opposition for cheerful consent, he proclaimed annexation of the Transvaal on 12 April 1877. His action had two immediate consequences: the Boers began agitating against annexation, and the Zulus, instead of attacking the Boers, turned on the English instead. The Zulus (to whom Kipling referred, with his usual mixture of affection and contempt, as "Fuzzy-Wuzzies") turned out to be tough and wily warriors. Though no match for British regulars in the open field, they were adept at ambush and guerrilla attacks. Several campaigns were required to subdue them, while the Boers, standing aside, speculated disinterestedly on which of the belligerents would win. No sooner had the British settled the issue, than the Boers, not at all grateful, asserted their independence, and badly mauled several British detachments sent against them.

These Transvaal Boers were very tough customers—deadly shots with a rifle, daring horsemen, physically rugged, and skilled at living off the land. Banding together in small groups of neighbors, they formed mounted commando units deadly in their effectiveness. When men like these come to feel that they are an oppressed minority, they can be very dangerous. Mr. Gladstone, prime minister after 1880, was constitutionally incapable of standing against warriors whose moral and military position was so strong; accordingly, by a treaty of 22 March 1881, he granted the Boers—subject to a few vague verbal reservations—their total independence. Promptly the lucky Boers discovered gold in their territory. The strike was bigger than that of California, thirty-five years earlier; it brought outsiders pouring into the new nation, prospectors, settlers, speculators galore. They brought with them new ideas and ambitions, not very agreeable to the conservative, hard-headed Boers. They also brought money in large quantities; and out of the Transvaal gold fields, and still richer diamond mines, they made more money. But the Boers never ceased to mistrust these *Uitlanders* (foreigners), never granted them political rights, never saw them as anything but fodder for the tax collector. Thus, though the British government seemed to have done its best to disentangle itself from the Transvaal Boers, the stage was set for a bitter struggle in the future.

POLITICAL PORTRAITS

This long list of world-wide disputes, difficulties, and open wars in which Victorian England was involved demonstrates how enormous the imperial enterprise had now become. At home, things were so placid that Lord Palmerston once said wearily that practically all the thinkable legislation had now been written: "we cannot go on adding to the Statute Book *ad infinitum.*" With the rest of the world, Britain's relations, though still immensely profitable, were in various ways for various reasons, and sometimes importantly, out of control. The enterprise now dwarfed the men who proposed to manage it; not only had it swollen immeasurably, but the politicians who served or commanded it had lost in stature—shrinking in the powers of command as they were forced to rely more and more on the arts of ingratiation (SFR, H. 11).

For good or for evil, Pitt and Peel in the first part of the century had been decisive and masterful men. Viscount Palmerston would not pretend to play the courtier by consulting with Queen Victoria on her foreign policy; as long as he was foreign minister, he would make it, and he did. Waspish Sir John Russell followed a consistent if narrow Whig line, whether it led him into office or out of it; his fellow cabinet members often experienced some rude bumps and jolts when Sir John spoke his forthright mind. All these men were vigorous advocates of liberty, though they used that slippery word to mean very different things in different contexts. But on one point they were agreed, and that was the liberty of England's governors, to wit, themselves. They repeatedly declared their independence of the electorate and of party machinery, in ways that would be impossible at the end of the century. The new breed was represented by two political opponents, very different though equally enigmatic, strikingly supple in their political characters, and masters of the arts of popularity. William Ewart Gladstone, having begun as a conservative, finished his long career as the liberal *par excellence;* Benjamin Disraeli (known at the very end of his life as the earl of Beaconsfield), though he was a lifelong conservative, sponsored the most radical piece of legislation that the century would see.

Disraeli's career was the more spectacular. Centuries before, his family had been dispossessed from Spain by the Inquisition; they had prospered in Venice, and in the person of his grandfather Benjamin Disraeli had moved to England about the middle of the eighteenth century. This first Benjamin Disraeli made his fortune as a stockbroker in England; his son Isaac was a gentle, retiring scholar who, never quite at ease with his Judaism, converted to Christianity shortly after his father's death in 1816. Benjamin Disraeli the future statesman was accordingly baptized an Anglican when he was not yet thirteen years old. Disraeli was never allowed to forget his Jewish blood, nor did he have the least desire to do so; but it was a serious obstacle in the early stages of his career, and it is impossible not to see his gaudy dress, brilliantly paradoxical opinions, and extreme assurance as techniques of countering the prejudice against which he had, all his life, to struggle.

Without a formal education, Disraeli was from the first a prodigiously brilliant young man. He had the run of his father's splendid library; through his father, he had access to the world of publishing; and though he read law for several years in his late teens, he was even then trying his hand at literature. Fiction was his first and politics his second love; he never ceased to write, and in 1870, between two stints as prime minister, produced a lively and extremely successful novel, *Lothair.* For the moment, he had a reputation to make, and did so by publishing, when he was just twenty-two, a flashy, witty fiction about a political adventurer, *Vivian Grey*. The book caught public fancy, and Disraeli, by a display of green velvet trousers, elaborately ruffled shirts, ringed fingers and flashing wit, held it. He wrote more books, he traveled abroad, he moved in high society; and he tried to gain a foothold in the Tory party.

Why the Tory party? Two of his novels (*Coningsby*, 1844; *Sybil*, 1845) suggest some of the reasons. Disraeli had toured the factory districts of England, and had been appalled at the condition of the working classes. Seeing the terrible contrasts between rich and poor, and accepting the consequences of the reform bill, he saw the necessity for the Tories to be more than the party of property and privilege. Though the idea formed slowly in his mind, the germs of Tory democracy, even a sort of Tory radicalism (see above, p. 376), were growing there; he worked steadily, resourcefully, energetically to move his party that way. The shift was not easy. Disraeli had to endure several defeats before he gained a seat in the Commons; his maiden speech was an absurdity, and he had to serve for years in party ranks before rising to his first government post. Sir Robert Peel had no use for him; Disraeli reciprocated. During the 1846 debates over repeal of the Corn Laws, Disraeli took the offensive, and with his long-polished, now scathing oratory drove Peel from office. After a spell of Whig rule, Lord Derby accepted Disraeli in his 1852 cabinet, but the Tories seemed unable to hold power for long after winning it.[9] The government lasted less than a year, that of 1858–1859 little longer, and it was not till the session of 1866–1868 that Disraeli and his now disciplined body of conservatives got a chance to enact an important piece of legislation. The second reform bill of 1867 widened remarkably the franchise established in 1832; by cutting down sharply on property requirements, it added about a million new voters to the rolls. As the first reform bill had transferred some power from the landed to the propertied middle class, so the second bill went a long way toward enfranchising anyone at all who paid taxes. It was a strong measure, amazing to many even of the conservatives who carried it; Lord Derby (quoting from *Vivian Grey*) called it "a leap in the dark." But Disraeli had a vision of the future and a strong sense that after preaching Tory liberalism for so long, he was bound to do something spectacular in its behalf. He also admitted frankly that he wanted to "dish the Whigs"—that is, steal their thunder. Not one of these considerations would Sir Robert Peel ever have admitted. Perhaps they showed strength on Disraeli's part, perhaps weakness; they did not, in any case, prolong his term in office. For though Lord Derby retired early in 1868, leaving Disraeli as prime minister, within a year he had been unseated again.

Disraeli's one extended period of power came between 1874 and 1880, and it

9. Acute as the Tories often were, most people were unable to grasp their evolving principles or to reconcile their principles with their tactics. Of Derby's 1852 government, the *Edinburgh Review* said that it was "the first administration which reduced inconsistency to a system, and want of principle to a principle."

can't be said to have produced much major legislation or any striking shift of policy. Though his government carried out a few domestic reforms, its greatest achievements were purchase of the Suez Canal in 1875 and careful management, at the treaty of San Stefano, of the 1877 Russo-Turkish war. More symbolic than practical was the proclamation of Queen Victoria as empress of India in 1876. It had, as it was intended to have, a striking effect on the native populations; it had an equal effect on Victoria, who enjoyed the imperial style; for Disraeli himself, it translated into a title, as earl of Beaconsfield. But in concrete terms, it did not change much. For in fact, though Disraeli proclaimed imperialist goals, he did not during his time in office deliberately add a great deal to Britain's imperial holdings. His interest was in British prestige, not British expansion; expansion was both dangerous and expensive. He emphasized the major role of India in British foreign policy, and was led thereby to work against Russian influence in the east. (Hence Britain's interest in controlling Cyprus, the major addition of real estate during Disraeli's term in office.) But he had no large imperial policy, he just talked as if he did. Gladstone, though verbally more liberal, added quite as much to the empire as Disraeli did; and Lord Salisbury, conservative prime minister during the late 1880s and the 1890s, was the greatest imperialist of all.[10]

Thus Disraeli's record does not look very impressive, if judged on the basis of solid achievement. Most of his career was spent in opposition; no sustained legislative program stands to his credit. He was not a consistent thinker nor a complex one; many of his ideas were more popular than political, though personal popularity came only at the end of his life. But he created the myth of a greater England and the myth of Tory democracy, mingling benevolent imperialism with humanitarian reforms in a way which admittedly skimped many hard facts but inspired and directed men's larger aspirations (SFR, H.22).

GLADSTONE, A MYSTERY WRAPPED IN PLATITUDES

And so, at the center of Victorian political life, we come on the figure of Mr. Gladstone—demagogue, idealist, legislator of genius, and sanctimonious moralist—Mr. Gladstone, in whom the contradictions of the Victorian age are all writ large. Son of a wealthy Liverpool merchant, he studied the classical languages at Eton and Oxford, winning national fame even as an undergraduate for his feats of oratory in the Oxford Union. In Parliament he sat with the Tories, and his first speech was a defense of slavery as practiced on his father's plantation in Demerara, British Guiana. Characteristically, it endorsed emancipation in the abstract, but argued that freedom should be delayed till the slaves had acquired sound religious principles. Slaveowners found that easy to live with.

10. It's well to recall that the term "imperialism" had few invidious connotations till the twentieth century, when books by J. A. Hobson (1902) and V. I. Lenin (1916) made it synonymous with the predatory, decadent phase of capitalism. It is now a stock piece of abuse, used very loosely indeed.

Gladstone followed up by arguing that Jews were disqualified by their theological limitations (i.e., because they were not Christians) from sitting in Parliament. He also published a book arguing that an established Protestant church, being a vehicle of the truth, was good for England, and hence good for Ireland as well, where Protestants happened to be few. These were not very deep ideas; but Gladstone, while holding them, was also developing a detailed knowledge of the nation's economic life. His conversion to a liberal philosophy, begun in the late 1840s, was a slow, mysterious process. It was hastened by a visit to Italy in 1851; in Naples, the 1848 revolutions had failed, leaving the jails crowded with liberals and suspected liberals, by whose condition Gladstone was touched. Better evidence of a shift in his thinking came in 1853, after his attacks had brought down the Tory government over a budget concocted by Disraeli. Invited to construct one of his own, Gladstone produced what was widely hailed as a masterpiece among budgets. It reduced taxes for most Englishmen, encouraged trade, and kept the government solvent. New revenues came mostly from the propertied classes; they were increases in the inheritance and income taxes,[11] proposed as temporary, but prolonged by the costs of the Crimean War. Still, it was a popular budget, and by the standards of the day an equitable one. And over the next fifteen years, on issue after issue, Gladstone moved toward a liberal position. He supported parliamentary reform bills prior to that of 1867, and might have supported that too if it had not been proposed by his rival. Slowly but steadily, he worked toward a belief that the Protestant church of Ireland, as it represented a scant 12 percent of the people, must be disestablished. This contradicted his view of thirty years before, and Gladstone wrote a book to explain or at least excuse the change.

Once under way, his legislative momentum was awesome. The Irish church was disestablished in 1869; an Education Act of 1870 made elementary education all but universal. Most civil service jobs were made subject to competitive examination; religious restrictions at Oxford and Cambridge were sharply reduced.[12] The army was radically reformed; the punishment of flogging and the practice of puchasing commissions both went by the board; the term of enlistment was shortened, a system of reserves established. Starting in 1870, a set of important acts gave to married women new power over the money and children of a marriage; within a few years Girton and Newnham Colleges, for women, were opened at Cambridge. In 1872, after decades of agitation, the ballot was made secret; trade unions, legalized in 1871, multiplied rapidly in numbers and influence throughout the 1870s. At the center of these changes, encouraging

11. Previously levied only in wartime, the income tax was brought into the regular budget by Sir Robert Peel in 1842; though hateful (as we all know), it made possible elimination of many detailed, complex, and restrictive tariffs.

12. In 1854 and 1856 dissenters were admitted as students, though still barred from the M.A. degree, headships, professorships, and fellowships. In 1871 the Universities Test Act reserved only a few posts for Anglicans exclusively, and in 1877 equality was made absolute.

them and drawing strength from their success, was Mr. Gladstone. He cultivated the nonconformists and the working class, he took as his special concern the Irish, Scottish, and Welsh constituencies. His coaxing and urging, his flattery and imagination, his power to mobilize the popular imagination, brought the fabric of modern Britain into being. One element of this remarkable man's metamorphosis calls for special note: during the American Civil War, he addressed several gatherings of Lancashire cotton workers, who were suffering cruelly from the Federal blockade on cotton shipments.[13] He expected to find them blindly hostile to the north; on the contrary, despite their obvious self-interest, they recognized the evils inherent in slavery, and urged a strongly pro-northern position. Gladstone was, or pretended to be, impressed by their basic wisdom, and much of his subsequent respect for the unions was rooted in that experience.

PARNELL AND HOME RULE

Gladstone's reforms, amounting practically to an administrative revolution, were impressive, but for sheer drama they pale before the struggle over Irish home rule led by Charles Stewart Parnell. He was a Protestant landowner from the county Wicklow, educated at Cambridge, but committed to the cause of Irish independence. When he entered Parliament in 1875, the Irish delegation was led by Isaac Butt, a not very dynamic man. Parnell quickly took over and gave a new turn and a new bitterness to the Irish struggle. In Ireland itself he introduced a terrible new weapon, named after its first victim, an estate agent, Captain Charles Boycott. It is a shunning. The victim is isolated from all human contact; no man will buy from him, sell to him, speak to him, nod to him on the street; if his house burns, no man will lift a finger to help. He, his wife, and his children are simply stricken from the rolls of God's creatures. This awful weapon Parnell unleashed in the Irish countryside; and in the English Parliament he wielded another power, almost as deadly, of obstruction.

In America it would be called a "filibuster." The home-rulers, a minority of 86 in a Parliament of over 600, organized themselves to talk on anything or nothing for hours on end. They yielded the floor only to one another; they told stories, recited poems, discussed interminable absurdities in minute detail. The business of empire ground to a halt while they wasted days and weeks. The rules of the Commons allow a good deal of catcalling and rough invective; there were moments when Parnell held the floor alone while more than 500 infuriated members shrieked and howled abuse at him. He could not even try to speak; he could not for an instant sit down, since that would be to yield the floor. He stood still,

13. The figures are eloquent. From over a billion pounds of cotton in 1860, imports from the United States dropped in 1863 to barely 6 million pounds, shrinkage of nearly 99.5 percent. After the war, imports picked up, but only slowly; 1871 was the first year in which American imports again reached a billion pounds.

erect and defiant; and by standing alone against those blasts of hatred, held aloft the hopes of a nation.

The strategy of Parnell's campaign was to combine his own legal though obstructive agitation with insurrectionary acts by Fenians, Land Leaguers, and other extremists. Yielding to natural impatience, the English authorities jailed him, but only redoubled his authority in Ireland. Before so implacable a man, Mr. Gladstone crumbled, but gradually, as was his wont. A new Irish land law, granting tenants better terms than tenants had even in England, was passed by Parliament and accepted by Parnell; while still larger measures of conciliation were being discussed, in May 1882, two members of the English government were attacked in the Phoenix Park, Dublin, and murdered by a knife-wielding gang. The murders were the work, as it turned out, of a small fanatical group calling themselves the Irish Invincibles.[14] An informer turned up to point the finger of guilt, and five Invincibles were hanged. The informer, provided with a new identity and shipped off to South Africa, was murdered on shipboard by an implacable assassin; the assassin was promptly returned to England and hanged. Melodrama, it seemed, could go no further.

All this time Gladstone had been edging ever closer to home rule for Ireland; he was pushed further faster by the general election of 1885, which returned 335 liberals, 249 conservatives, and 86 Parnellites. With the Parnellites, Gladstone had a safe majority; if they joined the conservatives, parties would be exactly balanced. Under pressure, Gladstone announced conditionally for home rule; and the existence of a major party committed to home rule, even though, as it happened, that party held power only momentarily, led Parnell to tone down his own agitation. He was, in any case, busy suing the *London Times,* which in 1883 had published a letter purporting to show that Parnell knew of the Phoenix Park murders in advance, and approved them. Parnell declared the letter a forgery, and actually produced the forger, who under cross-examination broke down and confessed. While the wretched man fled in disgrace to Madrid where he blew his brains out, Parnell collected damages from the *Times,* and returned in triumph to Ireland, there to await Gladstone's next return to power. The final act of the tragedy was yet to be played out; the stage was set, the characters in place; two nations anxiously awaited the outcome.

RELIGION UNDER SIEGE: NEWMAN AND DARWIN

Two contrasting developments in religious life, a defensive reaction against modern liberal thought and a fresh wave of that thought, had important repercussions in the later century. On one hand, an ecclesiastical revival along conserva-

---

14. James Joyce, born in 1882, and seeing himself as the exponent of a new cold, hard style, felt affinities with Parnell and the Invincibles; he once spoke of his art as that "of the cold steelpen" (*Ulysses,* chap. 1).

tive lines took form in the Oxford Movement; on the other, long accepted religious doctrines were called into question by the "higher criticism" of foreign scholars like Strauss and Renan, while Charles Darwin's *Origin of Species* (1859) undermined not only the story of creation in Genesis but the whole time frame of the world, based upon it.

As an organized action, the Oxford or Tractarian Movement had a short life but an extended influence. It began in July of 1833 (a date significantly close to passage of the reform bill), with a sermon by John Keble protesting the church's submissive attitude before the government's recent outright abolition of ten Irish bishoprics. Was a church which conceded such power to the secular arm properly Christian at all? Keble thought not; under the bold title of "National Apostasy" the sermon was published and made a stir. Clerics like John Henry Newman, Edward Pusey, and Richard Froude rallied to the cause. They were all Oxonians committed to the "high" (i.e., ceremonial and ritualistic) wing of the church. Seeking to explain the church's abject weakness before the secular government, they soon found themselves forced to question the Reformation itself. Shortly began to appear a series of *Tracts for the Times,* which were widely discussed and much criticized, for they seemed to imply sympathy with Roman Catholicism, even to advocate national reunion with Rome. These suspicions were not wholly groundless. The tractarians upheld clerical celibacy, and clerical authority over the laity; they regretted the loose secularism of modern thought, and spoke nostalgically of the days when churchmen held a stricter hand on things. Newman brought matters to a head by publishing, as number 90 of *Tracts for the Times,* an argument that the Thirty-nine articles of the church of England were quite compatible with Roman Catholic theology properly understood. The articles themselves say there is a difference; but this, number 90 declared, was the result of Elizabethan misunderstandings of the Roman church's true position. The Reformation had not been necessary at all. A furore naturally resulted, Newman was badly shaken by it, and after resigning his positions in the church of England converted in 1845 to the church of Rome. That, of course, was far from the end of his career; he worked in Dublin to establish a Catholic university, he wrote, he taught, he preached. In 1864, Charles Kingsley, a vigorously anti-Catholic clergyman and novelist, went out of his way to attack Newman in an uncharitable if not slanderous magazine article. Newman for some time had been writing the story of his intellectual career; he needed to change very little to have a crushing refutation of Kingsley's clumsy charges of indifference to truth. The *Apologia pro vita sua* is Newman's masterpiece, not of polemic indeed, but of lucid, intimate, and transparently honest exposition. But by then the Oxford movement had mingled with larger intellectual currents, fading from sight as a separate social movement. Newman himself, though never fully accepted by Pius IX, was more sympathetic to Leo XIII, who appointed him cardinal in 1879; he died in 1890.

Long before that, the tide of secularism was in full flood, and for many Victorians the problem had become how to salvage a Christian ethic without any of the supernatural sanctions (faith, miracles, the resurrection) that had previously sustained it. Philological criticism, brought to bear on the text of the Bible, dissolved the probability that it was dictated by the Holy Spirit. David Strauss in 1835 and Ernest Renan in 1863 published lives of Jesus from which the supernatural had been eliminated as far as possible. Between 1830 and 1842 the French philosopher Auguste Comte put forth the outlines of his positive philosophy, a creed which in effect makes of sociology a substitute religion for purely rational men. It was quickly translated and eagerly read in England, where utilitarians like John Stuart Mill found much to admire in it.

Most devastating to the established religious belief was the quiet technical work of the naturalist Charles Darwin. His basic research had been done as early as 1831–1836 on a voyage around the world aboard H.M.S. *Beagle*. The journal of his trip and some of his geological observations were published soon after his return, but his main work, *The Origin of Species,* not till 1859. The book perturbed men most intimately by undermining their belief in themselves as a special divine creation; in this respect, it was distressing in much the same way as the findings of Copernicus and Galileo, during the Renaissance, that the earth was not the center of the universe. The chronology of the world was an academic question, but man's kinship with the other animals touched human dignity, or perhaps egotism.[15] Darwin himself was no iconoclast, nor even a proper publicist for his ideas. Thomas Henry Huxley carried most of that burden, and carried it well; Darwinian ideas spread through society, and can be seen at work and play, in Meredith's 1879 novel *The Egoist*. Often they were distorted or misapplied, notably by Herbert Spencer, in areas where they did active mischief. Social Darwinism, an extreme form of which proposes that we sterilize or kill the "unfit," while allowing only the "fit" to breed, has had a deservedly bad press. But Darwin's ideas, like those of Freud and Einstein, have outlived their own popular distortions and entered into the intellectual structure of our time (SFR, H.18).

THE SOLID SUBSTANCE OF ANTHONY TROLLOPE

In earlier ages, a discussion of literature had to begin with poetry, the primary literary form; about the middle of the nineteenth century, we change focus by speaking first of all about the novel. In the new age, though novels are still

15. Human dignity or pretension apart, Darwin's view of evolution seemed to reduce the universe to a utilitarian machine which valued any idea, ideal, or social practice only as it furthered brute survival. Like Marx and Freud after him, Darwin could be read as applying to human life a single mechanical measure. All three contributed, deliberately or otherwise, to dissolving the old humanist idea that man is the measure of all things.

deplored,[16] they are everywhere. Politicians temporarily out of office, civil servants in their spare time, bluestocking ladies, all write novels. Subsurface we note in passing a giant accumulation of literary garbage—penny dreadfuls, cheap pornography, scandal sheets, and accounts of sensational trials or crimes, slum literature, in a word. The novel was an indiscriminate form, if it was a form at all; it lent itself to everything. Dickens continued to produce fiction till the very hour of his death in 1870, and he was the supreme master. But over his last fifteen years, he started to have a rival, in productivity if not in imaginative energy, Anthony Trollope.

Trollope was the son of an improvident father and a sharp-tongued, independent mother. Fanny Trollope's book on *The Domestic Manners of the Americans* (1832) stirred cries of anguish from offended patriots, and still makes amusing reading. After a grum and truculent childhood, Anthony entered the postal service, aged eighteen, to be a clerk and inspector in Ireland. Out of this experience his first novels developed, making their way in the world, as Trollope did himself, slowly and painfully. He never did leave the postal service, rising under Sir Rowland Hill, who successfully introduced the penny post, to an important executive position in the London office. As an official, he was rude and egotistical, yet very competent, especially on tours of inspection, which he enjoyed. On the side, he wrote novels, producing at least one a year through the 1860s and 1870s. He also managed, three times a week in season, to indulge a passion for fox hunting, acquired in Ireland and exercised despite increasing years and weight. He traveled world-wide on postal business; he ran for parliament and kept a constant interest in politics; he married and raised a family; he played whist in good society, and had a wide circle of personal friends. How he found time to do all this, nobody, not even he, has fully explained. His novels, those dealing with the political world of Phineas Finn and the gentlemanly world of Plantagenet and Glencora Palliser, no less than those dealing with the imaginary county of Barsetshire, have a solidity of construction and a firm grasp of sensible human nature that still intrigue and hold readers. *Orley Farm* and *The Way We Live Now* are thought-provoking analyses of morality in a commercial culture; *The Eustace Diamonds* boasts a heroine as delightfully unscrupulous as Becky Sharp. Trollope is summer-vacation reading; his warmest admirer would not call his pace "dashing." But his books are solidly put together, as befits the world of fixed values and stable institutions that he describes; aided, perhaps, by a bit of nostalgia, they have regained in our time some of the popularity they had in their own.

16. Novels were thought to be idle in themselves and encouragements to idleness, immoral and incitements to immorality; some Victorian sages declared that young people would be better off in alehouses than demoralizing their minds in lending libraries. It was fashionable to denounce "bookishness," and to deplore reading which made the lower orders (working men, servants, women) discontent with their lot.

WOMEN ON A NEW SCALE: GEORGE ELIOT, THE BRONTËS

Mary Ann Evans, who wrote under the pen name George Eliot, spent her early years working free of a narrowly oppressive provincial Christianity imposed by her father. In the process she became widely learned—for a woman, in those days, unusually so. As she could free herself from the tyranny of religious conscience only by developing a more severe secular conscience, she also became one of the most rigorous and scrupulous of freethinkers. Her liberation from Christianity she celebrated by publishing in 1846 a translation of Strauss's *Life of Jesus;* but the scandal of her life began when, shortly after her father died, she formed an "irregular connection" with Mr. George Henry Lewes. Victorian society found this unspeakable, unthinkable. Mr. Lewes already had a wife, and so was not at legal liberty to remarry. But in every respect except the legal formality, Miss Evans and Mr. Lewes were wife and husband. Still, her "position" caused George Eliot many hours of earnest, anxious self-examination. Intellectually, she thought herself "free"; emotionally and spiritually, she clearly was not. It is a frequent theme of her fiction.

The novels, which started to appear in 1858 and reached a high-water mark with *Middlemarch* (1872), are all studies, almost casuistical in their moral intensity, of difficult cases of conscience. Passion is often set against formal duty, youthful idealism against the dusty responses of a conventional, uncomprehending world. The feminine characters of Jane Austen are, typically, respectable young ladies with modest domestic expectations; the characters of George Eliot, above all Dorothea Brooke of *Middlemarch,* are heroines seeking a destiny larger than their circumstances seem to allow. In these novels, women assume roles more active and dominant than in earlier fiction, are seen as creatures with more complex spiritual natures than they had been allowed to display.

Two of the most remarkable novelists of the age were sisters, Emily and Charlotte Brontë. They were children of a Yorkshire vicar who had in all five daughters and a son. But a blight hung over the old Haworth parsonage, which struck savagely at the children. Two of the daughters, aged just eleven and twelve, died abruptly, and the son, after a short, miserable career as a drunkard, died in 1848 when barely into his thirties. Emily died three months later, aged thirty, and Anne only a year after that, at twenty-nine. Something was wrong, hideously wrong, probably with the water supply at Haworth parsonage. Only Charlotte, who survived to edit her sisters' work, to care for her blind old father, and ultimately to marry, lived to the ripe age of thirty-nine.[17]

17. The Brontë family was first appreciated as a group when Mrs. Elizabeth Gaskell published in 1857 a life of Charlotte. Mrs. Gaskell was the author of an indignant industrial novel (*Mary Barton*, 1848) and some gentle small-town sketches (*Cranford*, 1853). But in describing the Brontës' early life (it is the best part of her book), she came indiscreetly close to the law of libel, and in its third edition the biography had to be somewhat "reworked by another hand." It still remains a fine vivid biography, perhaps the first of a woman by a woman in the language.

Emily was clearly the most gifted of the girls. Their first book appeared collectively and pseudonymously in 1846: *Poems by Currer, Ellis, and Acton Bell*. Of the poems in the volume, those by Emily are superior in quality and different in kind. Hard, clear, simple, and tragic, they have about them absolutely nothing of the lady poet. And Emily's novel, published next year as *Wuthering Heights*, is of a piece with the poetry. Unlike most Victorian novels, it is intensive, not extensive, not a social panorama or an essay on ethics, but a piece of dark fictional poetry focused on a single figure, the vengeful outcast Heathcliff. As his name suggests, he is a force of elemental nature; and the novel is one of passion in a sense far deeper and more impersonal than the tame, pale preference that unites most fictional personages. Catherine Earnshaw Linton is not fond of Heathcliff or devoted to him; she is united with him, in death as in life, for their misery as well as their joy, by a principle as fierce and impersonal as the storms that rage over Wuthering Heights. How this spinster daughter of a country parson came to know of passion on such a scale is one of the mysteries; but *Wuthering Heights*, neglected in its own time, is recognized today as one of the towering masterpieces of the nineteenth century.

Charlotte's chief novel, *Jane Eyre* (1847), has its attractions, but can scarcely be ranked with *Wuthering Heights*. The central figure is once more a dour, dark Byronic man; but Mr. Rochester's gruffness is common bad temper, not elemental ferocity. Jane encounters him when she takes service as governess to his natural daughter, duly falls in love, but flees Thornfield Hall when she learns that Mr. Rochester already has a wife, living though hopelessly insane. Not without touches of melodrama, both characters are tempered by the fires of suffering and repentance toward the redemptive condition of matrimony.

KNOTTY VICTORIANS: MEREDITH AND BROWNING

One can feel this convention of the happy domestic ending starting to constrict late nineteenth-century novelists,[18] and nowhere more than in George Meredith, who had one of the more restless, impatient minds among Victorian writers. Like Dickens and Trollope, Meredith was born outside "good" society; his father and grandfather had been tailors at the Portsmouth naval station. Socially, Meredith was "out," but he hankered to be "in," and was clever enough to recognize and ridicule his own unease. Such covert tensions were typical. His education was in Germany and in the free-lance literary world of London, where he worked first as a journalist and later as a publisher's reader.[19] His first marriage, to the

18. Dickens, we note, wrote two endings for *Great Expectations*, one (unhappy) for his conscience, the other for the public. But it is not till Samuel Butler's *The Way of All Flesh* (1903) that a novel culminates in a happy annulment.

19. With other amenities of a leisured age, this post is now largely obsolete. An intelligent man like Meredith, who read manuscripts for Chapman & Hall, influenced widely the literary taste of his

daughter of Thomas Love Peacock, was abominably unhappy; they separated agonizingly, and the story of that broken marriage is told, poignantly, in Meredith's sonnet sequence titled *Modern Love*. As a writer of prose fiction, Meredith first caught the public eye with *The Ordeal of Richard Feverel* (1859); it is one of those novels about growing up for which the Germans have a portmanteau word, *Bildungsroman*, meaning development novel. Richard Feverel's growing up is impeded by the "system" of his rigidly opinionated father; the tale is adorned with aphorisms and witticisms (for which Meredith had a raging weakness), mostly placed in the mouth of an ironic commentator, "Adrian the wise youth." But novel readers were a pampered and lazy tribe in those days; they wanted to be spoon-fed, and Meredith's gymnastic style discouraged them. Their general indifference to his work likewise discouraged him. He wrote steadily and carefully a train of excellent novels; they found discriminating readers but not many, while the lending libraries flooded publishers with orders for sentimental trash. Even *The Egoist* (1879), recognized today as the most absorbing and satisfying novel Meredith ever wrote, was not a truly popular success. It is a classic study of male chauvinism, produced at a time when women's rights were just attracting the attention of enlightened thinkers and of parliament. John Stuart Mill's powerful essay "On the Subjection of Women" had made a major impact, and petitions were starting to circulate, calling for female suffrage, the vote. But *The Egoist* is more than a feminist tract; it is scrupulous analysis of that gentlemanly ideal which fascinated even as it repelled Meredith; it is Darwinian social comedy; and it made a number of advances in the art of elliptical and laminated (i.e., perforated and many-leveled) storytelling.

Toward the end of his life, Meredith enjoyed more popular success, partly by outliving the other Victorian novelists, partly because of growing demand, in the late century, for a sage or moral teacher. The same quasi-religious ethical impulses that gathered around Emerson in America sought a magnetic center in English authors. Tennyson suffered from this popular passion for profound verities, surely not unrelated to the fading authority of the church; so too did "difficult" authors like Meredith and Robert Browning.

The only son of well-to-do parents (his father a banker of independent means), Browning had been before the public as a poet since the 1830s, and was well established though not widely read when in 1844 he made the acquaintance of Elizabeth Barrett, a recluse, an invalid, and a poet in her own right.[20] Miss Barrett's father had taken upon himself the decision that none of his children

---

time; even authors whom C & H decided not to print gratefully acknowledged Meredith's good advice.

20. Generous and gentle in its feelings, but not very stimulating intellectually, Miss Barrett's poetry reflects rather too faithfully the definition of "woman's nature" taken for granted by respectable Victorian society. On the other hand, the work of her contemporary Christina Rossetti, Dante Gabriel's sister, will bear comparison with that of Emily Brontë for its dark strength. The stripped severity of the poems is that of the psychic outcast.

should ever marry, a more than Turkish edict which made the courtship of the two poets precarious but did not prevent it. In 1846 they eloped and went off to Italy, where for the next fifteen years they lived in idyllic happiness. Old Mr. Barrett never forgave them, and made a point of returning his daughter's letters (often tear-stained pleas for forgiveness) unread and unopened. Such was the unlovely authority of the Victorian curmudgeon at his worst.

During the early 1840s, Browning had made some efforts to write for the London stage; but neither audiences nor producers tried to grasp the special qualities of his thought, and he gave up in disgust. His work was and remained, however, markedly dramatic, and the dramatic monologue became his favored vehicle. In 1855 he produced a major collection of poems in this form, *Men and Women*. An early poem, *Sordello,* had given the effect of crabbed and quirky obscurity; the character studies of *Men and Women* were both rich and accessible. Poems like "Fra Lippo Lippi" and "Andrea del Sarto" became, as it were, instant tourist classics: one could hardly visit the Uffizi without them. And after a long period of obscurity, Browning's reputation started to rise.

The death of his wife in 1861, though she had never been well, came as a cruel blow; Browning could never bear to revisit Florence, where they had been so happy together. But a return to England bore fruit in two more major volumes, *Dramatis Personae* (1864) and *The Ring and the Book* (1868). All Browning's poetry is more or less a tour de force; he delights in transforming the rough particulars of "prosaic" life into vivid, expressive verse. *The Ring and the Book,* telling a single story (of a lawsuit growing out of a grisly Renaissance murder) several times over from different points of view, is the climax of this method. Popular slang, legal jargon, theological technicalities, rage, jealousy, and utter purity of intent rub shoulders in this vast ragbag of a book; and the different angles cast continual glints of doubt on our assurance of knowing "the truth." Not without reason has Browning's work been granted seminal importance in developing the "modernist" idiom in poetry.

Toward the end of Browning's life, earnest readers started to form societies and collectively expound deep meanings from the master's verse. In fact, he was not a bard or seer and never pretended to be; it is his great and sufficient merit to have brought men and women into poetry, talking (as Falstaff says) like people of this world. Of course, "real people" in literature are simply triumphant illusions.

STUDIES IN SCARLET AND GRAY:
SWINBURNE, ROSSETTI, ARNOLD

Algernon Charles Swinburne, who rose in the poetic heavens like a rocket and subsided like a spent sparkler, had as much natural talent as any poet of the century. Born in 1837, he came of "good" family, his father a naval officer, his mother an earl's daughter; like a proper young gent, he attended Eton and Balliol College, Oxford. But physically Swinburne was small, with a huge head made to seem even huger by his mop of curly red hair; at school, he was singled out for a butt. Eton was a rough place in those days; Swinburne was bullied, beaten, and subjected to homosexual rape. Thus set on the path of sado-masochism and homosexuality, he rarely deviated from it. But his sexual ways did not prevent his acquiring more Greek than any English poet of his century save Shelley and Landor, plus a thorough knowledge of the Elizabethan and Jacobean dramatists. Having picked up French and Italian, he became familiar with the work of Baudelaire, Gautier, and Victor Hugo, and a little later with the work and person of Mazzini. Moving to London without completing his degree, he made the acquaintance of Dante Gabriel Rossetti and the group calling itself the Pre-Raphaelite Brotherhood.[21] These were clever, Bohemian young men, mostly painters but including some poets, who had found new ways to combine sensuality with religiosity. Rossetti, for instance, wrote poetry of high spiritual passion modeled on Dante's *Vita Nuova,* while also writing lazy, mocking, affectionate verses about the London whores whom he patronized and befriended. (Mr. Gladstone, in a very different spirit, also cared about whoredom; he would pick up the girls and take them home, where Mrs. Gladstone fed them tea and the prime minister tried to argue them out of the life. Rossetti was no reformer, but he was a kind and generous purchaser of their services.) Through Rossetti, Swinburne drifted deeper into dope, drunkenness, flagellation, and a rich array of pornographic fantasies. As therapy for worse habits, he was once maneuvered into an affair with the American actress Adah Isaacs Menken, but it did not take, though she may have suggested to him the idea of "Dolores, our lady of pain." Had these been just private eccentricities, they might have caused Swinburne no inconvenience; but he described his erotic hangups in explicit detail, as publicly as he could. Not surprisingly, both he and Rossetti were attacked in an article, "The Fleshly School of Poetry" (1871). The author was a Scot, Robert Buchanan, and the article led to a long quarrel culminating in a lawsuit.[22] But as Swinburne passed the age of forty, it became increasingly apparent to his friends that something must be done with or for him; he was turning up, incapable, in

21. The name was mostly a mystification. Rossetti and his friends had seen a book of engravings after paintings by Benozzo Gozzoli; they were detailed and sharp of outline, and they had been painted in the fifteenth century, before the time of Raphael. Mostly as a whim, the young men of the Pre-Raphaelite Brotherhood agreed to sign their paintings PRB. But they were also imitating a group of German painters, living in Rome and led by Johann Overbeck, who liked fifteenth-century painting because they thought it more devout than the "pagan" work of the High Renaissance. Among the Pre-Raphaelites were J. E. Millais, Holman Hunt, Thomas Woolner, and a little later William Morris and Edward Burne-Jones.

22. Buchanan, a far from clever man, attacked Rossetti more directly than Swinburne, in whose early work he might have found some real perversions and blasphemies. In their later work both Rossetti and Swinburne changed profoundly, Rossetti to a Tennysonian moralist, Swinburne to a shrill jingo patriot.

too many worse-than-dubious places. So he was taken in hand by Theodore Watts-Dunton, an unattached man of letters, under whose care he lived, secure from ill company but also from the muses, till 1909.

Swinburne's best poetry is found in his pseudo-Greek drama, *Atalanta in Calydon* (1865), the two volumes of *Poems and Ballads* (1866, 1878), and the mainly political *Songs before Sunrise* (1871). To modern tastes, Swinburne often seems in his poetry to be flogging the last drops of energy from an exhausted romanticism. The sensations he describes are extreme in themselves, and his verse exaggerates them; he often pours forth floods of words, used for their alliterative or rhythmic effect, but without care for their sense. His political views, revolutionary in youth, became downright reactionary with age. Yet he really had an extraordinary ear, and when he does not pound but lets the melody sing, few poets of his time can match him.

As poet and essayist both, Matthew Arnold rested on the middle ground of prudent and rational discourse. He was the son of an educator (Dr. Thomas Arnold, strenuous evangelical reformer of Rugby School), and was employed most of his life as an inspector of schools. The habit of teaching, earnestly, repetitively, discursively, has left its mark on his prevailingly serious prose and generally melancholy poetry. Arnold gave mournful expression to the Victorian sense of moral emptiness and undirection which followed the fading of religious faith. Where faith survived, as among the nonconformists, he felt it was narrow and parochial; for too many others, it was simply a dead letter. In a memorable phrase he described himself as "wandering between two worlds, one dead, / The other powerless to be born." "The Scholar Gypsy" is a poem about wanting to get lost, to free oneself from "the strong infection of our mental strife"; the extended metaphor with which it concludes combines nostalgia for the pristine classical world with a desire to encounter some shy, discreet barbarians, innocent but not pushy. "Dover Beach" evokes a gloomier aspect of getting lost in a darkening world of ignorant violence. Losing and getting lost were recurrent themes of this most civilized and thoughtful of late Victorian minds.

Arnold's earnest sense of moral responsibility kept his poetry (mostly written in the 1850s) from reaching heights or depths of personal feeling; always grave and thoughtful, it often celebrates the quiet richness of the countryside around Oxford. Arnold is one of the first poets to make deliberate use of homely names such as the two Hinkseys, Bagley wood, the Fyfield elm; far from being mere private allusions, they add welcome texture to Arnold's thoughtful but rarely opulent verse. (He committed one of the least speakable verse lines in English: "Who prop, thou ask'st, in these bad days, my mind?")

Written mostly in the latter part of his life, Arnold's essays did a great deal to establish what has to be called the genteel tradition. Culture in the form of humane letters, Arnold proposed, must take the place once held by religion in softening manners and energizing ideals. Nowadays, I think, we are a little less likely to look in literature for a guide to behavior or a talisman against ill fortune. We are also less confident of being able to recognize and make use of "the best that has been known and thought in the world." Arnold, as he foresaw, has dated; but though, like all the Victorian sages, he is remote, he is, in their company, one of the more humane, especially in his eloquent doubts and misgivings.[23]

ARITHMETIC AND PROPHECY: MILL AND RUSKIN

Victorian sages came in all sizes and shapes; one reason they were so assured in their various sagacities was that they were often preprogrammed for the role, none more so than John Stuart Mill. He was the son of James Mill, a dedicated Benthamite; in line with Victorian ideas of paternal discipline, he was raised to a system which in his case worked appallingly well. While learning Greek at the age of three (so that by eight he had read in the original Herodotus, Xenophon, and some dialogues of Plato), he also underwent a course of reading in the modern historians and political philosophers. Prolonged conversations with his father on abstract topics honed his infant mind to razor sharpness; while the task of afterward drawing up a résumé of these conversations helped him to organize his thoughts. Not surprisingly, this regimen produced a serious crisis of nerves as Mill entered his twenties; he recovered by reading the poets, particularly Wordsworth, who helped him, by a conscious, prolonged effort, to recover the fact of human emotion. But from the full searing effects of such a childhood, imposed upon him with the best of intentions, it may be doubted if he ever recovered completely.

Not that Mill grew up a cold and calculating monster; on the contrary. An administrative post in the East India Company gave him a regular salary and useful experience in practical government. His interest in social problems led to frequent essays for the reviews, an enormous correspondence, and a systematic book on *The Principles of Political Economy* (1848). Mill's principles grew steadily more liberal with time; his classic study *On Liberty,* primarily a defense of the rights of minorities, was published in 1859 (again!), and his vigorous essay "On the Subjection of Women" ten years later. He was encouraged in this liberal drift by the death of his father in 1836, and by his association with Harriet Taylor (Mrs. John Taylor). Wife of a London druggist and a lifelong invalid, Mrs. Taylor was Mill's intellectual companion and inspiration for twenty years until, her husband dying, they were able to marry in 1851. Mrs. Taylor was a woman of extraordinary mental powers, and in her ability to free Mill from the frozen wastes of his childhood, a woman of great generosity and vitality as well.

---

23. A slowly darkening mood in the later century was indicated by the rediscovery of Edward FitzGerald's adaptation of the *Rubáiyát* of Omar Khayyám. Originally published in 1859, it promptly sank into oblivion. But after FitzGerald's death in 1883, it slowly became, as it still remains, widely popular. Its weary and skeptical hedonism clearly meant more, twenty-five years later, than it had when Palmerston was prime minister and Albert prince consort.

Their marriage lasted just seven years, and after her death Mill lived chiefly in southern France, except for a three-year stint as member of parliament (1865–1868). All his life long, he remained a man of wide and vigorous interests, a practical as well as a speculative philosopher. His judicious approach to the questions of his time has made his works classics of middle-class humanitarian liberalism, in which capacity they continue to be both praised and attacked. (One oversimplifies Mill by considering him a mere libertarian; *On Liberty* should be balanced against the book on *Representative Government*, written two years later. It contains arguments against the secret ballot, against allowing illiterates or non-taxpayers to vote, and in favor of multiple voting by the educated. Mill is not to be summed up in a phrase.)

Very different from Mill, but equally the victim of an atrocious Victorian childhood, was the most oracular of the sages, John Ruskin.[24] Through a connection with the famous Pedro Domecq, Spanish bottler of sherry and brandy, his father had grown rich in the wine business. When he was thirty-three and she thirty-seven, Ruskin's father married his cousin, and the future sage was their only child. Both his parents being severe Scottish Calvinists, the boy was brought up in a strict and solitary environment, reading and memorizing long chapters of the Bible, forbidden toys and playmates, watched always, whipped sometimes, much encouraged to read the classics, write childish dramas, and appreciate natural scenery. He never learned to play a game, keep a pet, or tread a measure on the dance floor; though he was encouraged to look at art, his ideas of female anatomy were based on marble statues and plaster casts. His parents decided early that their child was a "genius," and tried, not without success, to persuade him of the fact. When, at the age of twenty, he entered Christ Church, Oxford, his mother, to the stunned amazement of the university community, moved to Oxford herself, so she could watch over her son's physical and moral development.

Ruskin began as a critic of art, and by an easy transition moved on to criticize the various cultures, moralities, and societies which produced, as he saw it, good or bad art. *Modern Painters,* the first volume of which appeared in 1843 as by "a Graduate of Oxford," suffered from no lack of confidence; the author denounced English ignorance in the field of art, and hailed the work of Turner, which had been on view for a number of years. Ruskin's Bible reading was evident in the prophetic fulminations of his prose; despite really limited experience of the world's art and even less experience of the world itself, he was given to sweeping generalizations, giant enthusiasms, and vitriolic hatreds. He liked to erect his personal tastes into universal aesthetic laws; and above all, he satis-

24. Ruskin's intellectual and emotional lives were violently entangled. Modern commentaries by John Rosenberg (*The Darkening Glass,* 1963) and Robert Hewison (*John Ruskin, the Argument of the Eye,* 1976) help us to be patient in reading the divagations of this extraordinary man, who was surely one of the greatest, as also one of the most troubled, minds of the century. Each reader must winnow the grain from the chaff with his own sieve; there is plenty of both.

fied a deep Victorian desire to identify aesthetic with moral values. By a process not unlike that of *Tristram Shandy, Modern Painters* grew over the years to five volumes; they include considerations of religious truth, the Crimean War, leaves and clouds, and the French peasantry of the Valais mountains. *The Seven Lamps of Architecture* (1849) is a lay sermon on the seven moral principles that Ruskin discovered in Gothic architecture; and *The Stones of Venice* (1851–1853) is a three-volume account of the rise and fall of the Gothic style in Venice. Ruskin's devotion to Gothic was rooted in the work of previous writers like Walpole, Beckford, and A. W. Pugin (above, pp. 333, 396). But unlike his predecessors, Ruskin was a magnetic teacher, and he had a remarkably sensitive eye for reading the nuances of architectural details. To this day a serious tourist visiting Venice is likely to carry a volume of Ruskin under his arm and ''read'' the building he is looking at as he reads Ruskin's eloquent text.

In 1851, Ruskin came to the rescue of the Pre-Raphaelite Brotherhood, under coarse and ignorant attack from Charles Dickens, among others; his intervention, though successful critically, led to misfortune when Effie (Euphemia) Ruskin, his wife of three years, fell in love with John Everett Millais of the Brotherhood. She was a beautiful, not very sophisticated girl, who had just vaguely suspected something was wrong when on their wedding night Ruskin, after alleging various excuses, said they would have to wait six years before they could have marital relations. (His excuses were all designed to conceal the plain fact that he was impotent, certainly with her, probably with anyone.) Millais opened her eyes, the marriage with Ruskin was annulled; Millais and Effie Gray were married, had eight children, and lived happily ever after. Poor Ruskin, doomed to erotic failure, went home to his parents. Later in life, he fell wretchedly in love with a girl thirty years his junior; her family objected and she herself, after several mental seizures, died in 1875, aged just twenty-five.

Personal miseries, however, did not deter Ruskin from an active career of writing and lecturing. After about 1860 he turned increasingly to working-class audiences, addressing them on topics like education, economics, beauty, morality, religion, work, truth, and the position of women in society. Elected Slade Professor of Art at Oxford in 1869, he continued to lecture there till 1884; his increasing involvement with Christian socialism led him to dissipate, on principle, most of his large inheritance. One of his most striking ventures was a socialist commune, St. George's Guild, to which he contributed generously; it flourished for a while, attracting students and intellectuals, as well as a few workers, then disintegrated.[25] Ruskin continued to be a patron of the working-class movement, though increasingly isolated for the last twenty years of his life by illness and uncertainties of temper.

25. It was the common fate of bourgeois efforts to bring high culture to the toiling masses that the better the culture they purveyed, the less working-class response they got. The Working Men's College established by F. D. Maurice in 1854 began hopefully, but soon found its clientele consisting almost entirely of folk ''in comfortable circumstances.''

THE WINDING DOWN OF AESTHETIC SOCIALISM:
WILLIAM MORRIS

Reforming society socially and politically seemed to many late Victorian idealists a necessary condition of reforming it aesthetically. Art could be genuine only when society was more authentic—more corporate, more organic, more egalitarian, less exploitative. Recasting the knotty, resistant world in a more humane mold was a daunting task, and nobody worked harder at both aspects of it than William Morris. Like Ruskin, he was independently wealthy, like Ruskin, but in a less isolated spirit, he worked frantically all of his life. More or less successively, he associated with the Pre-Raphaelites in their projects, labored in St. George's Guild, ran a large and successful studio of handicraft and decorative arts, and took part in organizing socialist meetings and demonstrations. He was a prolific author in verse and prose; his Kelmscott Press turned out magnificent editions of classic authors, rescuing the tradition of fine printing in England from the flood of Victorian bad taste. Nobody could have labored more valiantly in his chosen causes. Yet in effect Morris was serving two masters. Genteel, "aesthetic" people with a good deal of spare money bought his medievally inspired tapestries and handicrafts, read his medievally inspired poetry, collected his handprinted books. The "Morris chair" was found, not in working-class neighborhoods, but in the studies and studios of folk consciously devoted to composing for their pleasure what was called "the house beautiful." Such civilized and self-indulgent bourgeois had little to do with the mass demonstrations that Morris helped organize in the name of socialism. After the mass meeting of "Bloody Sunday," 13 November 1887, was broken up by the police, Morris spent his declining years at the apolitical activities which were the nearest thing he had to a real vocation. He was a finer and fuller man for the diversity of his interests, but too gentle for the new iron age of world politics just over the horizon.

Gothic crosses fronting a classical portico, Renaissance campaniles jumbled in with a railroad station, the whole enveloped in clouds of industrial steam and smoke—such was the center of Birmingham about 1886. Though the society had aspirations, cultural and religious, they were all but choked by the writhing, clutching jungle of commercial enterprises into which the city's true energies were absorbed.

Sloth, filth, crime, drunkenness, and immorality were the stigmata of the Victorian slum, last squalid burrow of the unrespectable. They are all summarized in the blackness of this print by Gustave Doré. The one flaring light in this eerie scene marks the public house, where cheap gin is available to mire the wretched slum dwellers even deeper in their moral and physical swamp.

Interior decoration was not the long suit of the Victorians, and the Great Exhibition of 1851 brought out the worst of their appetite for gaudy ingenuity. Bloated chairs and flashy whatnots competed with pianos made up to resemble a tropical rain forest. Even humble domestic implements like a cream ladle and a pair of scissors were belabored with "decoration" till it is impossible to imagine holding them in the hand, let alone keeping them clean.

John Ruskin was not personally responsible for all the architectural crimes committed in his name, but he did set before English designers the model of Venetian medieval building as morally and aesthetically right. In itself, the idea of using contrasting varieties of stone might not have been bad; but in connection with overwhelming quantities of pseudo-ecclesiastical gingerbread, it produced the sort of flashy, ragged structure we see here. Nowadays this kind of building has a certain "camp" appeal; bright people think it smart to admire what everyone else considers particularly terrible. But for this one there is not much to be said; hardly a bit of it is not ostentatiously bogus.

Built as a temporary structure to house a temporary exhibit, the enormous yet airy Crystal Palace attained international reputation and terrified conservatives (like the nameless narrator of Dostoevsky's *Notes from the Underground*) with visions of a new and oppressive mechanical civilization. In fact the structure was too advanced for its own day. Neither its metal-and-glass materials nor its modular construction would be much imitated for years to come. And by comparison with the average Victorian building, it was a model of free, light, and open design—as well as of transparent honesty in the use of its materials. John Ruskin absolutely loathed it.

When this photograph was taken in 1885, Queen Victoria had been on the throne for almost fifty years; she had been a widow since the death of Prince Albert almost twenty-five years before. Even as a girl, she had been a very serious and occasionally a self-important young person. It is not surprising that now, at the age of sixty-six, she had become a thoroughly formidable figure.

(*Who have not exactly "failed in literature and art."*)

R. G-D-S-T-NE—"Hm! Flippant!"   MR. D-S-R-LI—"Ha! Prosy."

Politicians who are also eloquent writers do not often match up so neatly as Disraeli and Gladstone. They did not like each other's writings any better than they liked one another's political principles—all of which was grist to the mill of the political cartoonists. Here, Disraeli is sniffing at Gladstone's book *Juventus Mundi* (1869), a study of Homer and the Homeric age, while Gladstone is equally contemptuous of Disraeli's novel *Lothair* (1870).

When Prince Albert died in 1861, George Gilbert Scott was asked to create a memorial for him in Kensington Gardens. Scott had already used the model of an "Eleanor cross" to design the Martyr's Memorial at Oxford, marking the spot where Ridley and Latimer were burned. His monument to Albert followed the same pattern, but it was 175 feet high, and fashioned for the most part of cast iron, a favorite Victorian building material. The work earned its designer a knighthood from his grateful queen and paved the way for many more commissions in the style known as "Victorian Gothic."

The evangelical morality of the Victorians divided women into angels and demons, nowhere more strikingly than in the work of Dante Gabriel Rossetti, who worshiped a few of the first sort, but consorted more frequently with those of the second. In his paintings, mouth-watering sirens of a particularly voluptuous character are found side by side with saintly and spiritual figures modeled on Dante's Beatrice. According to its title, this painting (dated 1873) portrays Lilith, the demonic and seductive temptress who in ancient Jewish folklore made so much trouble for Adam. In nineteenth-century contexts, Rossetti's picture is just another variant on the recurrent *femme-fatale* theme that runs through English imaginations from Keats to Swinburne. Mario Praz, in *The Romantic Agony* (1933, 1951), has chronicled its course.

William Morris opened new vistas before Victorian book designers by cutting his own type, drawing his own decorations, setting his books by hand, and printing them on the finest linen paper obtainable—in short, by consciously trying to make the best book possible. His edition of Chaucer, priced at a high £20, became an immediate collector's item and is hardly ever seen nowadays outside of rare book rooms and museums. It was a happy venture in being medieval without being self-consciously "Gothic." The illustrations were by Edward Burne-Jones, the Pre-Raphaelite.

16

Victorian Conservatism, Edwardian Liberalism, and World War I (1887–1919)

A dark, roaring, smoky inferno of industrial activity through which swarmed nests of antlike, laborious proletarians; a far-flung empire draining the riches of the world from jungles and deserts toward one little island in the North Sea; a center of the world's technology, industry, and finance, the mother of parliaments, the home of Shakespeare, free speech, free trade, and political gradualism: these were some of the images that Englishmen had of themselves as their nation entered the last decade of the nineteenth century. They were indeed a solid and confident people, the more so because under the leadership of Mr. Gladstone they seemed regularly able to solve problems as they emerged, or even to anticipate their emergence. The British pound, most solid of the world's currencies, was the universal medium of exchange; the British navy, still in a position to defeat any two of its potential opponents, ruled the waves; the upper classes, moving from one long weekend at a palatial country home to another, diverting themselves with sports, politics, gossip, and enormous meals, were the world's most urbane and assured people.

DARK CLOUDS ON THE DOMESTIC HORIZON

But things were not as secure as they seemed; and to find imminent dangers, one did not have to probe deeply beneath the surface of late Victorian England. Though the nation was rich, the rural countryside in many districts was disastrously poor. After 1870 a flood of cheap grain from America and Russia started pouring into Britain; free-trade doctrines left English farmers at the mercy of foreign competitors, and to make matters worse, advances in technology made it possible to send frozen meat from New Zealand and Australia. Thousands of farmers were forced off the land to seek work in the cities, just when the sharp depressions of the 1870s and 1880s were foreclosing new jobs in industry. Much of Britain's economic slowdown was due to new competition from foreign producers, primarily the rising economic powers of Germany and America; the depressions were ominous warnings that the sort of monopoly Britain had enjoyed earlier in the century could not be indefinitely maintained. And they provoked, not only scattered rioting in London, but protest parades of the unemployed— large, well-disciplined, but menacing demonstrations, which the trade unions and a scattering of radical parties organized to great effect. It's not to be supposed that the ruling classes of Britain were deeply or even seriously disturbed at this point by thoughts of revolution. If tenant-farmers in Scotland could no longer wring rent money from the stony soil, English landlords were perfectly ready to convert their acres into grouse-shooting preserves; the shouted slogans of marchers demanding jobs scarcely reached out into the suburbs where the great mass of the middle class now lived snugly. Yet the trade union movement was growing, not just in London, but through the "black country" of the north, the coal valleys of Wales, the cotton-mill country of Lancashire, and along the railroad lines, where transport workers were organizing. A third Reform Act (of 1884) and the so-called Redistribution Act of 1885, both passed by Gladstone's second administration, widened the franchise even further, yet left a curiously bad taste in the mouths of working men, who were starting to feel that having the vote wasn't, of itself, tantamount to having more of life's good things. In fact, combining economic plutocracy with political democracy was an awkward and perhaps dangerous experiment whose full implications nobody at the time could foresee;[1] but the British were committed to it, and while old habits of class

1. An exception should be made for one man speaking on one occasion. In June of 1885 Joseph Chamberlain, then but a radical member of the liberal party, said that property must pay a regular ransom for the security it enjoys in a democratic society. He was thinking of free education, a graduated income tax, help for small property holders, and access to local government; but implicit

subordination remained, while Gladstone held things together with his own peculiar mixture of statesmanship and charlatanry, and while the empire was still unweakened by direct attack from abroad, the structure stood and men thought it solid.

One factor sustaining it, which it's not fashionable to take seriously nowadays, was the British moral conscience, ingrained now by years of training and teaching and ethical examples. The lessons had been taught, not simply from pulpits, but by sages like Carlyle and Ruskin, by novelists like Dickens, by the poets; they had become second nature to the middle classes. Squalid as things were in the mining towns and waterfront slums of Victorian England, they would have been worse without the well-intentioned, sometimes misdirected efforts of myriad reformers, who probed and protested and cried aloud their conviction that such things must not be. From the late century date the Salvation Army for the recovery of drunkards and derelicts, the Royal Commission on Housing, which was but one of many organizations concerned with urban renewal, the Lord Mayor's Fund for the Unemployed, and numerous settlement houses for shedding both practical and spiritual light in the darkness of slum society. Middle-class charity was no effective substitute for institutional reform, such as was still years away, but it did pave the way for the creation of what Britain now possesses, an essentially middle-class socialist-welfare state.

Partly because Marxism stood outside, and in contemptuous opposition to mere bourgeois movements of social reform, the international socialist movement made more headway during the 1880s and 1890s (after the death of Marx himself in 1883) than it had done in all the years since the Communist Manifesto (1847). The special insight of Marxism is its identification of history's dynamic with the struggle of social classes. From this basic tenet derives the deep critical energy with which Marxists can lay bare the ideologies—that is, the philosophical rationalizations—which the privileged use to cloak their unavowed interests. Whether it ever will be equally successful in building the promised "classless" society which in theory is to transcend and replace all previous social orders, we had better wait and see. Meanwhile, the influence of Marxist thinking throughout the world can hardly be overstated; its vitality is shown as much in the variety of its theoretical exfoliations as in its geopolitical successes. The trouble is that Marxist activists, when successful, commonly give short shrift to doctrines other than their own. The major socialist powers of our day, among the most reactionary in the world, hold a dead hand on the revolutionary and inventive philosophy which first brought their secretive and conspiratorial ruling cliques into positions of authority. But in the late nineteenth century these crises were not yet at hand, and numerous socialist parties, some anarchist, some reformist, some Utopian, some conspiratorial, flourished in the cities of England. So long as the easier

---

in the view he formulated (which scandalized respectable opinion at the time) was nothing less than the entire welfare state, which since World War II has been the accepted form of British social life.

path of liberal socialism through gradual reform seemed to bring rewards, revolutionary ideologists remained a minority. When the soft line failed, the hard one was ready to supplant it.

THE COLLAPSE OF IRISH HOME RULE

Parnell's 1886 agreement with Gladstone for home rule in Ireland could have no practical effect till new parliamentary elections should again return the liberals to office; Gladstone, who saw an Irish settlement as the capstone of his career, was determined to regain power and put the measure through. But delay was dangerous for Parnell, and before the new elections were called, he suffered a deadly blow. Captain Willie O'Shea, bringing suit for divorce against his wife Katherine, named Parnell as co-respondent. Perhaps today this sort of thing would not make much stir. The unavoidable, undisguisable fact was that Parnell and Mrs. O'Shea had been carrying on a liaison since 1881. That it had been done with the knowledge and tacit consent of Captain O'Shea did not improve matters much. Perhaps Parnell and Gladstone might have worked the matter out between them, as men of the world; but both were responsible to political groups with very delicate moral consciences. Parnell, though he had never enjoyed enthusiastic backing from the Irish Catholic hierarchy, had never had to face their united, determined opposition; and Gladstone stood or fell by the opinion of the English nonconformists, who were the central pillar of his liberal party. Both groups agreed that Parnell had been "tainted" as a leader of the Irish people by the facts of his private life. He must go; and if he went (though nobody explicitly said so), the cause of home rule was dead. The leader was disowned by a majority of his own followers, amid scenes of unparalleled bitterness.[2] As soon as he legally could, Parnell married Mrs. O'Shea, but the damage was done. He fought manfully against ferocious opposition, and died, of exhaustion and despair, in the autumn of 1891.

With the death of Parnell, Ireland's mood relapsed into that muffled combination of despair, resentment, nostalgia, and recrimination which Joyce describes in his short story "Ivy Day in the Committee Room." The next determined step toward Irish independence would not be taken till Easter Day, 1916, when, under cover of the great war, the next little band of gallant, doomed Irishmen went forth to battle the British Empire—this time, however, not wholly in vain. Gladstone did return to Parliament for two years (1892–1894), but his majority was diminished, the old urgency was gone, and though he got home rule through the Commons, it was defeated overwhelmingly in the Lords. Gladstone resigned, rather to Queen Victoria's relief, and spent the short remainder of his life translating the odes of Horace and preparing an edition of Bishop Butler's *Analogy of*

2. Gangs of street urchins attacked Tim Healy, Parnell's ex-lieutenant; James Joyce's first literary endeavor was an oration, "Et Tu, Healy," which compared him to Brutus, the treacherous assassin of Caesar. Joyce's father thought so well of it, he had a copy printed up and sent to the pope.

Religion. For a statesman whose career has run its course there could be no better diversions.

THE SOUTH AFRICAN WAR: A TURNING POINT OF IMPERIALISM

The last years of the century saw the questions of Ireland and of domestic reform alike being subordinated to issues arising in South Africa and dealing particularly with the Dutch Boers of the Transvaal. We have noted the influx of foreigners (*Uitlanders*) into that territory as a result of the gold strikes of 1883–1886 (above, p. 410). Throughout the early 1890s they agitated to gain political rights from the Boers, but quite without success. On the face of it, their case was not bad. They were by now an absolute majority of the population; they owned at least half the land and most of the property; what they wanted was not absolute power, but some concessions. On the other hand, the Boers, having moved into this territory to get away from the British, not unnaturally resented their intrusion. Then the worst happened. Some tough, impatient Englishmen inside the Transvaal conspired with some equally tough Englishmen outside it to overthrow the government of president Paul Kruger. From Rhodesia Dr. L. S. Jameson in 1895 led an armed raiding party into the Transvaal; his action was taken with the knowledge and consent of Cecil Rhodes (though of few other Englishmen), and its aim was clearly to spark a rising of the *Uitlanders*.[3] As it fell out, the venture was a complete fiasco; Jameson was captured, Rhodes resigned his official positions. But Kruger was naturally furious; and Kaiser Wilhelm, never reluctant to make a bad matter worse, sent an uncouth message to Kruger, congratulating him on having crushed the raid without having to ask for help from "friendly" powers. Who those "friendly" powers were was not hard to guess. In 1899, the Boers, feeling they had much to gain and little to lose from violence, issued a series of impossible ultimatums which led directly to war.

In fighting South African Boers, the British confronted many of the same obstacles that would later face Americans in Vietnam. They had to deal with a force of agile and unpredictable soldiers, numbering nearly 80,000 men; they also had to cope with unfamiliar terrain which the enemy knew well, and with the popular spirit of a nation in arms. But on the face of things all the advantages seemed to lie with the British; they were vast, they were rich, they had a profes-

3. Son of a clergyman, Cecil Rhodes had made an enormous fortune in South African diamonds before he was nineteen; afterward, he explored the interior of the dark continent, and the galaxy of books at Oxford, deriving from both a dominant conviction about the destiny of the British Empire in unifying and civilizing the world. He was prime minister of the Cape Colony from 1890 till the raid of 1895; the last six years of his life were devoted to the land which long bore his name, Rhodesia. The munificent Rhodes scholarships were designed to fulfill, after his death, the ruling purpose of his life.

sional army and enormous numerical superiority. But the early, easy victories that had been expected never materialized; the British soon found themselves besieged in Mafeking, Kimberley, and Ladysmith, and it was only by mobilizing all the forces available to them that they were able to hang on there. For a while mobile squadrons of Boers commanded the whole hinterland, and threatened the British position in southeast Africa. But at last superior manpower and equipment began to tell; in March of 1900 the British occupied Bloemfontein and early in June Pretoria, capital of the Transvaal. By the rules of conventional war, the conflict should now have been over; already it had cost the British more in men and money than they had expected. In fact it dragged on, as a series of guerrilla actions and raids by flying columns, for another year and a half. The Boer generals were quick, tough, and tricky; they could get lost in the bush, then emerge miles away to hammer an unsuspecting British supply train. Slowly, as a result of much painful experience, the British learned how to divide up the country by long lines of blockhouses and strong points, and sweep it clean of guerrillas a section at a time. This was ugly work, expensive and dangerous; it left behind it a legacy of deep bitterness at the treatment of Boer prisoners, some 40,000 of whom were in concentration camps at the end of the war. English liberals, never enthusiastic about the war, protested conditions in these camps even while hostilities were in progress; as leader of the opposition, Sir Henry Campbell-Bannerman went so far as to say the British army was "using the methods of barbarism." While at the moment the phrase did not sit well with British public opinion, the Boers remembered it in Sir Henry's favor. After the war was over, when peace had been made and reconstruction was under way, the Boers were more ready to enter the new Union of South Africa because Campbell-Bannerman had risen by then to be prime minister. His conciliating influence was welcome and effective; and few wars fought so bitterly have reached such a speedy and generally acceptable resolution. Quite possibly, one reason was that both groups of whites were tiny minorities in an overwhelmingly black continent, and saw they had better stick together.

"THE QUEEN IS DEAD, LONG LIVE THE KING"

Meanwhile, on the twenty-second of January, 1901, after a reign just short of sixty-four years, Queen Victoria died. The prince of Wales, who succeeded as Edward VII, had for a long time been denied any share of the significant business of government; his mother had decided, years before, that he was not serious enough to be entrusted with anything but the ceremonial duties of the monarchy.[4]

4. She apparently held him responsible for the death of Albert, because the prince consort, just before his death, had been upset to learn that his son was having an affair with an actress. Albert was completely hysterical on the topic of sex, and what he died of was typhoid fever. But Victoria never forgave her son.

Being a man of some energy and intelligence condemned to a life of useless formalities, he naturally took to amusements of his own, which included actresses, gambling, drinking, yachting, and horse races. At the time of his accession, he was sixty years old and already ailing; his coronation had to be postponed because of a major operation. Still, despite his mother's best efforts, he was a man of good understanding; he was also jovial and kind-hearted. The end of an old reign and the beginning of a new, falling so close to the turn of the century and the end of a burdensome war, did something to change and lighten the mood of the country. For though in America the last decade of the nineteenth century was known as "the Gay Nineties," in Britain the same period is likely to be thought of as a period of glumness and depression (SFR, H.9).

THE GRAY NINETIES

These dark moods found frequent expression in literature. For example, Thomas Hardy was one of the major novelists of the period; he was a somber fatalist, whose studies of strong men crushed by a malignant fate which plays with diabolical skill on their inherent flaws are strong stuff, but not very lively. Novels like *The Mayor of Casterbridge* (1886) and *Jude the Obscure* (1896) are in the grand tradition of the Greek tragic stage, inexorable workings out of a fatal destiny against which the protagonists struggle valiantly. Hardy's books are also rich in feeling for the old pastoral English countryside, but there is nothing soft or nostalgic about them; like *Wuthering Heights,* they are rock-hard. After *Jude,* the most somber of his novels, Hardy gave up fiction entirely, and for the rest of his long life (he died in 1928) published only poetry. It was eloquent, chastened, and strong poetry, which has had a major influence on contemporary poetic practice, but not such massive, highly charged work as his novels.

Something of the same mood is felt in the poetry of A. E. Housman, a stoic pessimist whose Shropshire lads are almost predestined to be hanged for crime or killed in the army, but who meanwhile get what pleasure they can from drinking their ale and shouldering their burdens like men. Even tougher in their stern, unyielding stoicism were the poets W. E. Henley—best known for the lines of "Invictus"

> Under the bludgeonings of fate
> My head is bloody but unbowed—

and the extraordinary John Davidson, whose "Thirty Bob a Week" for the first time, almost, in English, looks at poverty from the inside out. It is a harsh vision of human decency being ground down by an inhuman system; without a touch of rhetoric, it is an appallingly honest and direct poem.[5]

Just as oppressive are the "naturalist" novels written in England during the

5. The grayness of 1890s London was not just metaphorical. Soft coal was the standard fuel for heating British homes. In winter, millions of chimneys poured forth sooty smoke to mingle with the

nineties under the general inspiration of the French author Émile Zola. George Moore's *Esther Waters* (1894) may fairly represent this class of fiction. It is the account of a humble, earnest, malleable serving girl, seduced and abandoned by a coarse fellow servant who rises in the world to become a racetrack tout and then a pub owner. Not being a bad fellow at heart, he takes in Esther and her son, but soon dies, and she returns to service. The novel ends, poignantly, when the dull little boy she has laboriously reared to manhood announces that he is about to enlist in the army. (With fine discretion, Moore says nothing further of his fate; but from what we know of his character, his destiny is inevitable.) It is a slow, beautiful novel, handling the most difficult of literary challenges, the depiction of ordinary people. George Moore, who cultivated the manners of a fop and the social life of a dilettante, was in fact a versatile and sensitive literary artist; *Esther Waters* is one of his most moving books.

Another novelist of the nineties who worked predominantly in gray was George Gissing; his early books are starkly realistic studies in poverty, misery, and the grubby life of the urban proletariat. Gissing himself was a man of sensitivity and learning, but he found literature a harsh mistress, partly as a result of his own limitations. He was not an evocative writer or a deep analyst of character; but he was a thoughtful, diligent literary craftsman, and the fact that his books did not sell, while much inferior hack work did, galled his pride. *New Grub Street* (1891) is his best-known novel, and its animus is clearly autobiographical. Edwin Reardon is an honorable if unpopular author, his friend Harold Biffen a novelist devoted to the "ignobly decent" side of life; they are both contrasted with Jasper Milvain, a crass, ambitious literary opportunist. The novel ends sourly, with the death of Reardon and the triumph of Milvain, who complacently marries his deceased rival's widow. One is reminded of the way in which, at the end of *Madame Bovary,* when all the minimally sensitive or intelligent people are dead, the pharmacist Homais is rewarded for his insufferable stupid complacency with the cross of the Legion of Honor.

Finally, we note as a true poet of the disillusioned nineties, a man whose best-known book was published only posthumously in 1903. Samuel Butler is often known, after one of his earlier books, as "Erewhon" Samuel Butler, to distinguish him from the seventeenth century "Hudibras" Samuel Butler. Son of a clergyman and grandson of a bishop, he was intended for the church himself, but fought his way clear by processes very much like those described in that posthumous, semi-autobiographical book of his, *The Way of All Flesh*. The struggle for his freedom was harsh, and left him with an appetite for disagreeable

---

heavy seasonal fogs and produce a choking atmosphere. James Thomson (namesake of the eighteenth-century writer of nature idylls: see above, p. 309) gave this somber aspect of London its enduring name in a popular poem, "The City of Dreadful Night" (1874). Thomson suffered from a despondent form of unbelief, as well as from melancholia, alcoholism, poverty, and chronic insomnia, all of which his dark, rhetorical poetry reflects. Once the two James Thomsons are clearly distinguished, their work offers interesting comparisons.

truths which made him one of the most stimulating and least liked men of his time. At first the break with the church and with his family traditions drove him abroad; he went, accordingly, to New Zealand, where he prospered as a sheep herder, then returned to England where, while dabbling in painting, art history, and music, he finally found his vocation as a writer. *Erewhon* ("Nowhere," more or less backward) is a bitterly satirical romance; several other clever but largely mistaken books criticize the Darwinian theory of natural selection (Butler believed, with Lamarck, in the inheritance of acquired characteristics); in addition to translating Homer into strong, colloquial prose, he wrote a provocative study, "The Authoress of the *Odyssey*." But most of his modern fame rests on *The Way of All Flesh*. It is a witty book about the blundering, painful process of growing up, and getting rid of the hypocritical nonsense one's elders press upon one as truth. Being genuinely tough-minded, it is one of the most useful examples of the *Bildungsroman* in English—perhaps a little more sour in its conclusion than some people may like, but astringently honest, like a sting planted by a mean little wasp in the soft white flesh of the Victorian era.[6]

DECADENTS

The "aesthetic" movement in England, its creed commonly summed up in the fuzzy formula "art for art's sake," seems far removed from the grubby naturalism we have been contemplating. Actually, in England as in France, the two tendencies coexisted closely. The "decadent" Huysmans was a near friend and associate of the "naturalist" Zola; and George Moore, no less than Oscar Wilde, combined a kind of provocative aestheticism with awareness of the ugly underside of the roaring metropolis. In fictions like Wilde's *The Picture of Dorian Gray* (1891),[7] and Robert Louis Stevenson's *The Strange Case of Dr. Jekyll and Mr. Hyde* (1886) we find remarkable intimations of a culture divided against itself—on the one side urbane, polished, and civilized, on the other dark, bestial, and degraded. One of H. G. Wells's earliest scientific fantasies, *The Time Machine* (1895) projects this division far into the future, when the human race will have divided itself into two distinct species, the airy, insubstantial upper-class Eloi,

---

6. Imaginative escapes from Victorian moral oppressiveness often took shape as the comic or absurd. A few examples are the fantasies of "Lewis Carroll" (*Alice's Adventures in Wonderland*, 1865; *Through the Looking-Glass*, 1872; "The Hunting of the Snark," 1876), the nonsense verse of Edward Lear (1846, 1870), and the genial satires of W. S. Gilbert and Sir Arthur Sullivan (1875–1896). These comic operas are known from the theater where they were produced as the "Savoy" or "Savoyard," or from the name of the producer as the "D'Oyly Carte" operettas. Behind and beneath these topsy-turvy fantasies lies a strong but buried music-hall tradition of burlesque: earthy travesties of fairy tales, stories from mythology, or Shakespearean dramas. The sane and sensible Mr. Overton, who guides Ernest Pontifex to moral balance in *The Way of All Flesh*, writes burlesques for a living.

7. Wilde's title surely echoes the title of Disraeli's youthful novel, *Vivian Grey* (see above, p. 412); in addition, "Dorian" was a code word of the time for homosexuality.

sunny and ephemeral as butterflies, and the sullen, underground Morlocks, who do all society's dirty work. During the nineties the two facets of society were recognized to be two sides of the same coin.

The "aesthetes" in English literature, who only gradually assumed the more provocative title of "decadents," took much of their inspiration from the poets of France (Gautier and Baudelaire, a little later Verlaine and Mallarmé); but also from a mild-mannered, retiring Oxford don, Walter Pater. The concept of the "Renaissance," first popularized by the German art-historian Jakob Burckhardt (1860), attracted Pater from the time he gave up his early expectations of entering the church. He wrote studies of artists like Leonardo, Michelangelo, and Botticelli, also of figures like the prodigious polymath Pico della Mirandola, the poet Joachim du Bellay, and the art historian Winckelmann. These were published in 1873, with a conclusion which asserted in essence a philosophy of refined hedonism. We are given only so many fleeting impressions in this life, Pater proposes; the purpose of philosophy or speculative culture is to help us select from among these impressions those of the greatest intensity, "to be present always at the focus where the greatest number of vital forces unite in their purest energy." This cultivation of experience for its own sake was more shocking to the evangelical Victorians than it is likely to appear to us. Pater withdrew his conclusion from the second edition of his book, and published some years later (1885) a much softer book of self-explanation called *Marius the Epicurean*. Marius does not burn with a hard gemlike flame, as the earlier book had proposed one should do; at most, he glows gently. His meditations, which are the substance of the book, lead him gradually almost as far as Christianity, concluding a little short of the goal. But Pater's refined literary style and quiet, studious life made him something of a cult figure at Oxford; he gained the acquaintance of Ruskin and the later Pre-Raphaelites (William Morris and Edward Burne-Jones) to their mutual advantage; and undergraduates like Oscar Wilde came under the influence of his mannered and slightly precious talk.

Wilde was the prodigiously talented son of a famous Dublin surgeon; he won prizes for poetry at Oxford and acquired, even as a youth, a vaguely scandalous reputation for affected aesthetic posturing.[8] After taking his degree, he moved on to become a busy London editor as well as a famous essayist, conversationalist, and writer of entertainments. About his whole glittering and unfortunate career there clings an aura of the mythical and the misunderstood, so that it isn't easy to decide just how important a figure Wilde was. As a poet, he was certainly a minor figure, much of his work vitiated by the vices of his time, florid rhetoric and sentimentality. His one novel, *The Picture of Dorian Gray* (1891), was complained of as immoral; with its weighty insistence on the wages of sin, it probably strikes us now as too heavily moralistic. His play *Salomé* survives

8. He was parodied by Gilbert and Sullivan as the poet Bunthorne in the operetta *Patience* as early as 1881.

chiefly as the libretto of an opera by Richard Strauss; without the music, its flat characters and slow action would hardly hold the stage. His real talent was for artificial comedy, and there he is hardly surpassed even by Congreve. *The Importance of Being Earnest* (1895) is a brittle ballet of frank absurdities and affectations that, when acted with the requisite lightness of touch, achieves that effect of perfect artifice which is the next-to-highest potential of the theater. In a less formal way, Wilde also achieved real greatness in his critical essays and scattered epigrams. Apparently superficial and obviously effortless, these sayings very often had the quality of true parables: the more one thought about them, the more complex and interesting the ideas they turned out to contain.[9] A last set of uncertainties rises from this paradoxical circumstance: Wilde was a very capable publicist for a set of attitudes that were essentially inward, esoteric, and unavowed. His was an amazingly complex, superficial, and richly intuitive mind.

Complicating the whole matter of Wilde's real stature is the public and publicized scandal of his trial and conviction, in 1895, on charges of homosexual conduct. The trial was recklessly invited by Wilde himself, almost as an act of deliberate self-destruction. The marquis of Queensberry (a burly sportsman whose name is associated with the rules of boxing) grew incensed at Wilde's intimacy with his son, Lord Alfred Douglas, and publicly denounced Wilde as a homosexual. Against all advice, Wilde sued for libel; the inevitable defense was that the charge was true, and it was. Not only was the libel suit lost, the publicity ensured that Wilde would be prosecuted criminally, under the old and generally ignored statute still in force. He was convicted and sentenced to two years at hard labor, an experience of which he wrote bitterly in "The Ballad of Reading Gaol"; after his release, he went abroad under the gaudy name of Sebastian Melmoth,[10] to compose a self-pitying apologia, *De Profundis,* to indulge his taste for street boys, and to die in a seedy Paris hotel (1900).

9. "We live, I regret to say, in an age of surfaces," says Lady Bracknell. It is a passing joke about the importance of money; a flick at the speaker, who is herself concerned chiefly with appearances; a scoff at the audience, which has been entertained with nothing but shows; and a jeer at solemn moralists who had brought this charge repeatedly against Wilde and other "aesthetes." But it also contains more truth about the Victorian age than many a long essay by the Victorian sages. As noted above, a frequent imaginative theme of the age was fair surfaces and the nasty things hidden just beneath them, mostly clandestine and sometimes perverted sex (SFR, H.15).

Apart from a few melodramas and burlesques, Wilde's effervescent comedies were the first worthwhile writing for the English theater since Goldsmith and Sheridan. For this blight the ministry of virtue was largely responsible. Its withering force can be judged from the story of one Charlotte Elizabeth Browne, whose moral constitution was almost shattered by perusal of *The Merchant of Venice.* Fortunately she recovered, to banish from her shelves all wordly literature of every description, and to celebrate her own resulting indescribable purity in *Personal Recollections* (1841). One shudders to think what might have happened if she had fallen upon *Othello,* a drama so horribly corrupt that Reverend Bowdler (above, p. 387) could not even try to purify it for family reading. He relegated the play to the dungeon of an appendix, where the father of the family could peruse it in the guilty secrecy of his study.

10. "Sebastian" because of Saint Sebastian, shot to death as a target for cruel archers, "Melmoth" from a Gothic novel by Charles Maturin, *Melmoth the Wanderer* (1820) (above, p. 369).

The Wilde case, spectacular and flamboyant like everything about Oscar Wilde, became a major turning point in the moral history of Britain. Wilde was by no means the saintly martyr to love and art that he proclaimed himself; but his punishment was savage, and his offense (as everybody knew) was a common one, commonly condoned. Nobody spoke out for many years yet to change the laws of England, but a great deal of pious cant and official hypocrisy went down the drain as a result of public sympathy for a brilliant career ruined by a private idiosyncrasy. There is every evidence, by the way, that Wilde was more brutally exploited by Lord Alfred Douglas than vice versa.

The aesthetic movement in England spread, of course, far more widely than to Oscar Wilde; following Swinburne and the Pre-Raphaelites, new schools of lyric poetry and of artistic design came into being. The Rhymers' Club was an informal gathering of London poets who contributed chiefly to two quarterly reviews, *The Savoy* and *The Yellow Book;* the illustrators of those reviews also formed a somewhat smaller group. Problems of technique fascinated the poets of the Rhymers' Club; they were concerned with cadences, phrasing, and imagery, above all in lyric poetry. On the whole, theirs were not bright or spontaneous voices; their prevailing mood was melancholy and weary. Ernest Dowson and Lionel Johnson both produced small volumes of chiseled austerities; but the group also included an untutored though eloquent young Irishman named William Butler Yeats, and the man who would provide Yeats with much of his early inspiration. Arthur Symons was just at work on his book on *The Symbolist Movement in Literature* (published 1899); for Yeats, whose foreign languages were always weak, the discovery of poets like Nerval, Laforgue, Verlaine, Mallarmé, and Maeterlinck had the effect of a revelation.

We should not fail to note among the contributors to *The Yellow Book* the short-lived but influential designer and illustrator Aubrey Beardsley (1872–1898). His work is patterned, linear, two-dimensional; it certainly owed something to the examples of William Morris and Wilde's American friend James McNeill Whistler, just as Whistler's work owed something to the example of colored Japanese woodcuts, recently starting to become known in the west. But above all Beardsley was influenced by a style of flat decorative drawing widely popular on the Continent under the name of *art nouveau*. The writhing lines and bold, posterlike quality of *art nouveau* style as exemplified by Beardsley add yet another facet of meaning to Lady Bracknell's casual joke about the 1890s as "an age of surfaces."

"Decadent" art was a European phenomenon during the 1890s; poets, painters and playwrights accepted the term gladly, sought it out as a term of distinction; and we can't leave English manifestations of the vogue without noting a certain paradox about it. Though they liked to advertise themselves as effete and languid scions of an exhausted tradition, the conscious decadents of the nineteenth century were the boldest and most imaginative inventors of their age. What they sought in decadence was not the cold, sterile formalism of the old, but the fresh, vigorous tonalities of new combinations. Weary and disillusioned as they seem, their work was far from representing the permanent exhaustion of anyone's sensibility. Abruptly with the coming of the new century, the mood changed to a brisker and more determined tempo; the heavy purple draperies and airless arrangements of aestheticism were shaken by a fresh breeze. Yet all the great figures of English modernism—Yeats, Joyce, Eliot, Pound—drew artistic inspiration from the aesthetes of the nineties, and proportionately less from the vigorous progressive voices of the early twentieth century, such as G. B. Shaw and H. G. Wells.

THE NEW LIBERALISM

England had little more than a decade of peace in the twentieth century before the whirlwind of World War I broke over her; and much of that little decade was overshadowed by the gathering storm. One sign of the new century's fresh mood was the run of liberal governments which, starting in 1905, assumed control of English affairs. They took command of an economy which was reasonably prosperous, though not expanding. Large numbers of Britons were leaving their native land to seek better opportunities in Canada, Australia, South Africa; those possessions also now absorbed large quantities of British investment capital. Such money was by no means lost forever; dividends returning to England constituted a kind of "invisible import" which made the economy much stronger than at first glance it appeared to be. Still, the slow, steady obsolescence of the British industrial plant was starting to worry many people. The very concept of "empire," with its implications of subordination and domination, had become less appealing; by a curious set of linguistic compromises the colonial conference of 1907 decided that future conferences would be called "imperial conferences," while the participants would no longer be called "colonies," but "dominions," and the "empire" would be known as the "commonwealth." This bit of fancywork with verbal cosmetics was part of a general diplomatic initiative to rally support world-wide for the threatening conflict with Germany.[11]

Two unpopular measures of the last conservative government (which left office in 1905) showed where the political strength of the new liberalism came from. The conservatives tried to introduce protective tariffs, and encountered strong objections from the working class, who feared higher living costs, and from the manufacturers, who feared retaliatory tariffs against their finished goods abroad. Again, an Education Act proposed by the conservatives would have shored up church-of-England schools, at the presumed expense of those under nonconfor-

11. During these prewar years, international peace trembled on a network of anxious threads. Russia's 1905 defeat at the hands of Japan meant to England that Germany's relative position in Europe was strengthened. A single German gunboat appearing off Agadir in Morocco (1911) created an intercontinental crisis, resolved only when Germany was given land in the Congo to compensate for France's acquisitions in North Africa.

mist auspices. Both these conservative measures resulted in an access of political strength to the liberals, who were further strengthened by an informal coalition with the newly emerging Labor party. There were only twenty-nine Labor members in the Parliament of 1905; their leader was a Scot named Ramsay MacDonald. But he made common cause with a radical Liberal wing under David Lloyd George, the eloquent Welshman, to gain a position of considerable power.

Thus the early twentieth century saw a renewal of that stream of liberal and reform legislation which had been apparent in the various governments of Mr. Gladstone. Trade unions won new rights to organize and to help one another financially. The principle of old-age pensions was established in 1906, though the amounts actually paid out were small at first; and an important unemployment-insurance measure fell into place five years later. In the realm of municipal administration all sorts of small, unspectacular, but important changes introduced efficiency and economy into the management of public utilities. The House of Lords, really vestigial now that the landed and aristocratic interests counted for so little, still retained its ancient habit of saying "No" to important legislation; its power to do so was clipped by the practical abolition of its veto.[12] Henceforth, if they did not like legislation coming out of the Commons, the Lords could delay it from taking effect for two years, but after that it became law, whether they liked it or not. England was not becoming an American-style republic, not by any means; even the Labor party recognized the value of the monarchy, and the death of Edward VII, in 1910, provoked universal, sincere mourning. But in characteristically gradual and flexible ways, she was adapting her ancient institutions to the ways of government by popular consent based on suffrage without property qualification. The trouble was, these liberal governments were increasingly weak, and the conflicts they had to confront were increasingly savage.

THE FABIANS: SOCIALISM WITH A DIFFERENCE

Important far beyond their actual numbers in realizing programs of liberal social reform were members of the small socialist fraction known as the Fabian Society. They got their name from the Roman general Fabius, who after the terrible defeat of Cannae took charge of the Roman armies and by a systematic campaign of harassment, delay, and avoidance finally brought about the destruction of

12. The battle to destroy the veto power of the Lords was fought with the traditional weapon, a threat to have the king create new peers sufficient to swamp the conservative majority. Five hundred was the figure named! But a new element was provided by the Irish party, who in return for a promise of home rule lent their strength to Mr. Herbert Asquith's Liberals, as previously, for the same reason, they had supported Gladstone. Bitterness over the nullification of the Lords channeled directly into intransigent defense of the Union (that is, the 1801 Act of Union) against the majority coalition in the Commons of Liberals and Irish Home-Rulers (SFR, I.4).

Hannibal. It was not, if truth be told, a very appropriate name; the Fabians did not pursue a strategy of delay or harassment, they were not even fighting a war. They believed essentially in the bureaucratic transformation of society; and to bring this about, they took vigorous part in local government whenever they could. They became aldermen, borough councillors, commissioners of the waterworks. Sidney Webb became an active and forceful member of the London County Council and the Royal Commission on Trade Union Law; his wife Beatrice served on the Royal Commission on the Poor Law; and George Bernard Shaw delighted to mount the hustings and hold forth in behalf of some special candidate for a post on the Sewer Commission. Apart from their participation in the nuts-and-bolts work of practical politics, the Fabians issued a series of important tracts on the issues of the day. They were clearly and forcefully written, to be understood by the socially minded graduates of workers' schools, trade academies, night schools, and extension courses—by the self-educated, in a word. They tied politics to the bread-and-butter issues of English life; and they were extremely effective. The class to which they appealed was growing by leaps and bounds. Between 1900 and 1914, membership in trade unions doubled. 'Enry Straker, John Tanner's chauffeur in Shaw's *Man and Superman*, is a new human type, sharply seen; he has lost his aitches, never to be recovered, but gained his self-respect as a graduate of the Polytechnic. In addition, a goodly number of purely secular secondary schools began turning out graduates destined, not for Oxford or Cambridge (traditional preserves of the upper classes), but for university colleges in the provinces. The young D. H. Lawrence may be taken as typical of this new class: the son of a coal miner, pushing his way through a teacher's college, naïve, aspiring, and very earnest. He portrays himself most vividly (and in himself a large group of his fellows) in the course of those conversational struggles with Miriam, which are such an appealing part of *Sons and Lovers*.

AN UGLY UNDERSIDE OF PROGRESS

Education, self-improvement, institutional reform, the first years of the twentieth century were stirring ones in these respects. Yet under all this idealism, we note a deep and disturbing note of growing violence, which manifested itself in strikes, in social agitation particularly for women's suffrage, and in the still-festering question of Irish home rule. The strikes were not particularly big or intolerably violent, but they manifested a tendency on the part of the unions toward syndicalism. Essentially, syndicalism is the use of unions, not for economic ends, but for political or symbolic purposes. Thus there was a great strike of the international seamen in 1911, which was timed to coincide with the coronation of George V, successor to Edward VII. It was orchestrated with a strike of the Merseyside shipbuilders near Liverpool, a strike so violent that troops were called out to keep order. Next year there were bitter strikes in the coal fields, especially in Wales, and again the troops were called out, while the government hastily pushed through a minimum wage for the miners. But that was far from a satisfactory solution, and in 1913, the coal miners combined with the railwaymen and the transport workers in what was called the "triple alliance." This was the real meaning of syndicalism, the unification of the country's basic industries in a single confederation so strong that it could, overnight, shut down the entire industrial enterprise. At that point, it was not unthinkable that the unions could take over the entire country; nobody had yet tried the effect of a general strike, and fantasy could play freely with its consequences. For the moment, though, this power remained in abeyance.

More savage and spectacular was the developing struggle by women for the right to vote. This agitation had begun in the middle of the nineteenth century; starting about 1870, annual petitions were presented to Parliament, containing each year more thousands and hundreds of thousands of signatures. Liberal Gladstone, not so liberal in this matter, threw his influence against a bill of 1870, and again defeated an amendment to the reform bill of 1884. Numerous other bills were brought forward during the years that followed, but all were talked down or died in committee.[13] Thus hopes were high when a liberal government came to power in 1905; but they were dashed when the liberals proved just as stubborn for male privilege as their nineteenth-century predecessors. About 1906, therefore, a new militant organization was formed by Mrs. Emmeline Pankhurst, her daughter Christabel, and their ferocious little ally Mrs. Annie Kenney. Their program was to interrupt political meetings, smash windows, set fires, destroy the mails, chain themselves to railings in the House of Commons—in a word, to disrupt. They were, of course, arrested and jailed, repeatedly. Many were gentle ladies, for whom the very idea of prison was terrible; but to prison they went with their sisters, and continued the agitation there. Some went on hunger strikes and had to be fed forcibly; but that was too crude a procedure for public opinion to tolerate. So hunger strikers were released when their health began to suffer, then rejailed when they had eaten their way back to good health. These were called "cat-and-mouse" tactics; and, shameful as they were, they continued to the very brink of the war. Whether the violence helped or hindered the cause of women's suffrage may be differently decided; but the bitterness of the struggle certainly soured the last years before the war.

Meanwhile, the Irish problem had entered a new phase. In 1912 the House of Commons at last got around to passing a bill granting Ireland home rule; the Lords could no longer veto it, though they could and did delay it. But now the problem of Ulster, familiar to this day, came suddenly to the fore. The northern counties of Ireland were furiously Protestant; they flatly refused to enter an inde-

13. Defeating the bills was bad enough, but the sniggering, complacent "jokes" that were used against an idea simple, sensible, and natural in itself added insult to injury. The suffragettes were unpardonably violent, but they had been unpardonably provoked.

pendent Ireland, within which they would be outnumbered by Catholics. The Catholic south would be satisfied with nothing less than the whole island. The liberals on the whole were disposed to grant it to them, supposing Protestant objections could be overcome; but the conservative leaders—Bonar Law in England, Sir Edward Carson in Ulster—set their feet in concrete. In speeches of atrocious ferocity, they encouraged the Ulster Protestants to oppose, by force if necessary and by means which clearly implied treason, the liberal-dominated Parliament's home-rule program. Tories, now calling themselves "Unionists," thus set the first example of that appeal to lawless violence which henceforth would mark, on both sides, agitation of the "Irish question." For the volunteer, vigilante army built by the orange lodges in the north was soon matched by an equivalent army in the south, followers mostly of Arthur Griffith's Sinn Fein party, early ancestors of the Irish Republican Army.[14] Theoretically, Parliament having voted home rule, the British army was supposed to "subdue" recalcitrant Ulster; but that might mean British troops firing on Protestant soldiers marching under the Union Jack—it was unthinkable. Rather than that, Unionist leaders proclaimed vociferously, British troops should mutiny. Under these tense circumstances, whether through a blunder or deliberately, a slovenly set of options— act or resign—was offered to British forces who were waiting at "the Curragh" (a garrison station just outside Dublin) before moving against Ulster. Grasping the occasion at once, most of the officers in command resigned on the spot, the troops were immobilized, and the whole issue remained in suspense. (The bill itself, having completed its formalities in September 1914 by receiving the royal assent, was suspended for the duration of the war.) How serious the whole matter was, and how bitter the conservatives felt, may be judged from the fact that early in 1914 they urged the House of Lords to reject the Army Annual Act, thereby almost depriving the government of any disciplined force at all, barely four months before, as it proved, a major war was to break out.

SHAW, WELLS, BENNETT

George Bernard Shaw published his first novel in 1886 and died more than sixty years later, in 1950; he might, accordingly, be considered in any one of three or four different "periods," but the height of his achievement and his influence fall in this decade before the war. Shaw was Dublin-born, but Protestant, indeed puritan, in his attitudes; no literary predecessor exercised as much influence on his mind as John Bunyan. His mother was a music teacher, and after they migrated

14. In Gaelic, "Sinn Fein" means "Ourselves Alone." Arthur Griffith was a Dublin agitator and publicist who had studied continental liberation movements and who (like Moses) lived just long enough to glimpse the promised land. He died in 1922, the year after the independence became an accomplished fact for the southern part of Ireland. The "orange lodges" (recalling William of Orange) were Masonic lodges, Protestant to a man.

to London, Shaw (who never bothered with a university education) turned his hand to musical and then to dramatic criticism. In both areas he was a sharp and intelligent commentator. Joining the Fabian Society, he polished his native wit in the give and take of street-corner political debate; and on the side, he wrote a number of unsuccessful novels which still make interesting if ungainly reading. But his real gift was for the stage; and his second play, *Mrs. Warren's Profession*, marked the beginning of a formidable career. It illustrates the two fundamental themes of Shaw's writing; the search for a true career or vocation, and the prostitution of people to money and the unjust social order it has built. In the old days, audiences were shocked because it alluded to bawdy houses; and they were repelled by the coldness of the conclusion in which Vivie Warren rejects domesticity and "love" in favor of actuarial tables. In fact the play is about the corruption of society as a whole; bawdy houses are simply a symbol of society. Sir George Crofts issues the basic challenge: "If you want to pick and choose your acquaintances on moral principles, you'd better clear out of this country." In effect, that's what Vivie does, so far as it's dramatically practical. She remains uncompromised, if maimed, using her own talents in her own way, and never to be deceived by aesthetic appearances, as Praed (the real villain of the piece, surrogate for the audience) will always be deceived, because that is what he wants.

These basic themes recur throughout Shaw's plays; like Henrik Ibsen, whom he greatly admired, he is a writer all of a piece. In *The Devil's Disciple*, Dick Dudgeon, who thought himself a soldier, turns out to be really a preacher, while Anthony Anderson, who had always thought himself a preacher, recognizes his real vocation as that of a soldier. In *Major Barbara*, Adolphus Cusins converts from a professor of Greek to a manufacturer of munitions while Barbara follows Vivie Warren in pitting her moral integrity against the munitions factory (emblematic of capitalism itself) which threatens to swallow her and her husband-to-be alive. Worship of the vital energy in people, and the vital economy which liberates the energy in people, was at the core of Shaw's artistic life. His own physical and spiritual energy was amazing, yet one can't help noting something a little hard and mechanical in the working of his mind. He never really was at his ease with female characters—they either have something strident and domineering about them, or they are sly deceivers intent on emasculating their men, like Candida in the play of that name, or Ann Whitefield in *Man and Superman*. Shaw's puritanism would not let him be satisfied with mere people; he was always hustling and huffing them to be something better.

H. G. Wells, briefly Shaw's colleague in the Fabian Society, was one of the brightest and strongest voices of the early century. The son of a professional cricket player, he was wretchedly apprenticed to a retailer of dry goods, worked his way through the Normal School of Science in South Kensington, and became a teacher, before turning to literature about 1893. Earlier in the century, Poe had written some stories that could be classed as science fiction, and in France Jules

Verne wrote practically nothing else; but Wells completely transformed the genre. He had an exuberant and grotesque imagination which could push prosaic factual observations to fascinating extremes. *The War of the Worlds,* which he published in 1898, was so realistic that when transformed into a radio play in the fall of 1938, it reduced the entire east coast of the United States to gibbering panic. Wells was more than a writer of fantasy; looking at the dull English establishment with fresh eyes and the impatience of a young rationalist, he found it absurd, nonsensical. *Ann Veronica* (1909) proposed libertarian views of the relation between the sexes; *Kipps* (1905) was a bitter satire on the stuffy and pretentious middle-class world into which an unexpected inheritance forces a naïve young man. Even more wide-ranging in its satire is Wells's masterpiece, *Tono-Bungay* (1909). The book is named after an absolutely worthless patent medicine which the narrator and his uncle foist on the public by means of idiotic slogans repeated over and over—in other words, a normal modern advertising campaign. Woven into this hilarious spoof are a splendid story of early experiments with aviation and (alas) a rather conventional love story. *Tono-Bungay* (the book, not the medicine) is a tonic for tired readers, full of energy and high spirits, ready to take on anybody or anything. It represents also the high point of Wells's art. He continued to write novels well into the 1930s, some of them tracts for the times. But his social expectations in the early century had been very high, his disappointments were correspondingly great, and these later books tend to be sour and sullen.

Like Wells and Shaw, Arnold Bennett emerged from the lower levels of the provincial middle class to become a professional man of letters. His native heath was the pottery district of Staffordshire, known as "the Five Towns."[15] They all lie near the original establishment of Josiah Wedgwood (above, p. 373) and within the smoky industrial region of the midlands. Bennett knew the plain, homely details of life in these shopkeeping, trade-oriented mill towns, and by reading French novelists like Flaubert and Zola learned how to make strong, realistic fiction out of drab materials. *The Old Wives' Tale* (1908) is one of his early and also one of his finest achievements; it follows the careers of two respectable, lower-middle-class sisters who manage to survive both the perils and the tedium of history until in old age they are reunited. The book describes thickly textured, precisely defined patterns of a life which does not run very deep or rise to any great heights of feeling, but is realized in great detail, and with more sympathy than appears on the surface. Bennett knew to perfection the texture of a provincial existence, and might have become a distinguished novelist in this vein. But he liked good living in expensive hotels, which he promptly turned into material for his fictions; and being as avid a businessman as Trollope, turned out a good many potboilers. Even his efficiency-expert habits became

15. The Five Towns used to be Tunstall, Burslem, Hanley, Longton, and Stoke-upon-Trent; the latter has now absorbed the first four into a united district.

grist to his mill, and he wrote self-help books like *How to Live on Twenty-four Hours a Day*, which rather obscured the glitter of his early achievements.

THUNDER ON THE RIGHT

Alone among these novelists of the early century, John Galsworthy came from, and stands for, the "establishment." He had passed through Harrow and Oxford, the very prototype of the handsome, tweedy aristocrat; and though he began as a satirist of his own class, the more he satirized it, the more attached to it he became. He worked both as a playwright and as a novelist; his plays made his early reputation, but as *The Forsyte Saga* unfolded its sinuous length, his fiction started to seem the more considerable achievement. It was perhaps inevitable that satire, sustained over so long a haul, should turn first to gentle chiding and then to positive affection. Galsworthy did not contribute much more than his younger contemporary, E. M. Forster, to the technical development of the English novel; there was little of the experimentalist in his temper; but, like Forster's, his was a cool, detached, and faintly ironic voice in a period of much hoarse exaggeration.

Though they were active on other fronts, one cannot consider G. K. Chesterton and Hilaire Belloc without first noting their position as lay apologists for religion in an increasingly secular, scientific age. They were both robust and entertaining men; it was no cloistered faith for which they spoke. They were journalists and polemicists of the very highest order; and when they had to do with an equally articulate atheist like G. B. Shaw, the intellectual sparks flew. (It was for the most part fencing, not fighting; a display of contrasting positions, hardly an attempt at changing minds.) Chesterton wrote much vigorous ballad poetry, in addition to detective stories (Father Brown was his detective), and many volumes of sparkling essays. He was an Anglican, getting steadily higher, till his conversion to Catholicism in 1922. Hilaire Belloc, as much French as English and a committed Catholic from birth, did his military service in France, but sat for some years in the English Parliament, supporting himself with a flood of popular books. He wrote biographies, histories, essays almost beyond number, and poems for grownups and children, sometimes for both at the same time. (The *Cautionary Tales*, ostensibly for children, are still read for their twinkling, ironic humor.) Belloc's *Path to Rome* (1902) also has a nostalgic interest these days, for it is the record of a cross-country hike across the Alps to the holy city, a pilgrimage performed and described in the highest of spirits, and now no longer possible or agreeable because of heavy vehicular traffic on the roads. In his miscellaneous writings, Belloc showed himself a natural debater, with an instinct for taking the opposite point of view. Even if one isn't convinced by his arguments, it's always interesting to see what a really athletic mind like his can find to say in defense of the late Stuarts or the old regime in prerevolutionary France.

VISITORS AND POETS

We pause to note as major additions to the stream of English fiction two figures from abroad, the American Henry James, and Joseph Conrad, *né* Korzeniowski, from Poland. Both contributed to the interiorizing and psychological turn being taken by the novel, James returning again and again to the theme of innocence and its paradoxical strength in the world of the knowing, Conrad dominated by a haunting sense of caring about honor in a world that had shed most of the codes. In Conrad we first encounter the figure of a sensitive and cultivated man who deliberately deprives himself of civilization's artificial supports and courts failure like a cherished mistress. He is the poet of a thin and scrappy culture flaking off a blind wall of underlying savagery. Perhaps this is why his world seems more closely akin to our own than the relatively convention-hobbled world of James.[16] Yet the intricacy of their craftsmanship brought them into sympathy, despite enormous differences of background; and though their position in English literature as narrowly defined remains (for different reasons) marginal, both contributed to our sense of the age as overflowing with riches.

In prose, it overflowed; in poetry, the flood has become a trickle. Yeats continued active through the period, but the greatest of his achievements date from the war period and directly after. Robert Bridges, though not without interest as a craftsman, is best remembered these days for having edited (nearly thirty years after the author's death) the poems of Gerard Manley Hopkins (1918). (Had they appeared when they were written, it seems probable, the stammering, urgent poems of Hopkins would have been greeted with the sort of ridicule from which even Browning was not exempt; coming out, as they did, alongside poems by Pound, Eliot, and the Futurists, they gained easy acceptance. Technically, they are very much of the early twentieth century, the age of fractured surfaces, though spiritually Hopkins belongs among the primmest of the Victorians.) Starting in 1912 and appearing at intervals till 1922, five volumes of *Georgian Poetry* by various hands were published. In a meticulously chosen phrase, George V once described himself as "just an ordinary chap," and though the *Georgian Poetry* volumes contained occasional memorable verses, too much of the material seemed to have been written by and for ordinary chaps. The tone of the poetry was generally relaxed, modest in dimension, and pastoral in its mode. Outside these anthologies, the major poetic achievement of the age was probably to be found in John Masefield's realistic narrative poems, such as *The Everlasting Mercy* (1911) and *Reynard the Fox* (1919). Despite some Salvation Army overtones, the first is a strong, gritty study of a hard case; the second is a Chaucerian

16. Conrad characters in real life were General Gordon, who died in a noble act of folly at Khartoum in 1885, and T. E. Lawrence, whose career in the Arabian revolt of 1916–1918 was a continual testing of himself against the sharp edge of death; literary analogues are to be found in Graham Greene and V. S. Naipaul.

description of a fox-hunting assemblage followed by a wild and scary chase, of which the fox is definitely the hero.

THE WATERSHED OF 1910

Around 1910 occurred a group of major unrelated episodes which made that date climacteric in the development of society's attitude toward itself. In 1910 Roger Fry mounted in the Grafton Galleries a show of post-impressionist painting, mostly from Paris, which created a sensation. These pictures (some of which later traveled to New York to become the famous Armory Show of 1913) included some early Cubist canvases by Picasso which, however mild by modern standards, shocked and amazed the expectations of English viewers. For they were not "realistic" at all; they deliberately distorted the human figure and broke the representational planes, till the canvas looked, not like a composed surface, but like a field of broken glass. Lady Bracknell's "surfaces" were shattered forever. A little earlier, in 1909, the Ballets Russes exploded in Paris, bringing with them the choreography of Fokine, the bold scenic designs of Bakst, and the broken phrasings, syncopated rhythms, and barbaric discords of Stravinsky's music. Almost at the same time Filippo Marinetti began preaching throughout Europe, and in England as well, a new aesthetic doctrine which he called "Futurism." The Futurists despised the rotten, genteel tradition, the code of middle-class manners and placatory gestures; they wanted to smash old surfaces and unleash new energies. Motion, noise, and violence were their themes—discords in music, and crude, ungrammatical force in writing. At their meetings (a favorite art form), Marinetti often howled long strings of nonsense syllables at the audience, to crack them out of their old thought patterns; and if a meeting broke up in a fist fight, that was evidence the audience got the point.[17] The new art, in a word, would not ingratiate, it would provoke.

Then in 1912, Constance Garnett published a translation of *The Brothers Karamazov*. This was not only the first English version of this novel; it was the first translation of a Dostoyevsky novel to be made from the Russian original. (All previous translations had been made from French versions by Victor Dérély.)

17. Later offshoots of Futurism, during and after the war, were the movements known as Dada and Surrealism; at a Dada exhibit of 1920 in Cologne, spectators were offered an axe with which to chop the art objects to pieces, the assumption being that they were so provocative, such a response would be inevitable, and fulfilling it healthy. Most spectators obliged with a will. Marinetti ultimately found an outlet for his cult of violence in the regime of Mussolini, of which he became the unofficial poet laureate. Surrealism, which emphasized release of all the artist's buried fantasies and repressions, had affinities with the artistic movement known as Expressionism, but laid greater emphasis on the grotesque, the macabre, and occasionally the absurd. Guillaume Apollinaire, killed miserably in the war, was a precursor of Surrealism; his farce, "Les mamelles de Tirésias," may have had an influence on Eliot's "The Waste Land."

Karamazov was gigantic, overwhelming in its direct emotional appeal; it made novelists like Henry James suddenly look timid and pale. Mrs. Garnett followed, two years later, with *Crime and Punishment;* and now the novels of Dostoyevsky, which for years had been dismissed as overstrained, hysterical, and exaggerated, seemed to express exactly the crises of the human soul in the modern world. Many established writers resented Dostoyevsky because his wrenching emotionality undermined what they thought the necessary nuances of fine art. Henry James was never reconciled, and Stevenson thought the less of him because of it; Conrad reacted with a visceral hatred which did not prevent him from visibly imitating *Crime and Punishment* in *Under Western Eyes.* D. H. Lawrence and Virginia Woolf proclaimed their emancipation from Dostoyevsky at the very moment when they were drawing intellectual sustenance most directly from him. It is not too much to say that in the last years before the war, this belated arrival of Dostoyevsky (who had died in 1881) completely changed the tonal register of English fiction, very much as a really good basso profundo can with a single note make other singers suddenly sound reedy and thin.[18]

THE RIPE SOCIETY OF PREWAR ENGLAND

Mrs. Woolf once remarked, fliply and accurately, that on or about December of 1910 human nature changed. It changed because of the events noted above; it changed also because society was changing, deeply and as a whole. If we survey Georgian society just before the dark hood of war closed over it, we shall find it, for one thing, amazingly rich and cosmopolitan. "Merchant princes" had long been a figure of speech; many English merchants and gentlemen whose money had originally been made in trade, were now richer than monarchs. They had their town houses and country houses, their shooting lodges, their steam yachts and motor cars. They wintered on the French Riviera, shot grouse in Scotland and elk in Norway, drank champagne in Claridge's and brandy in their Mayfair clubs; they invested from time to time, with the advice of their experts, in old masters. Their houses swarmed with parlormaids, housekeepers, footmen, butlers, lady's maids, cooks, scullery maids, and chauffeurs, their estates were alive with gamekeepers, groundskeepers, gardeners, ostlers, stableboys, and gentlemen's gentlemen. The energetic climbed mountains for sport, or galloped after the traditional fox; the lazy smoked cigars, talked languid politics, and ate themselves into heart attacks with ten-course dinners (SFR, X.12).

As a result of a few inconspicuous inventions, the world had suddenly shrunk

18. Before Dostoyevsky, Ivan Turgenyev had been the great Russian novelist, at least for the west. By training and by deliberate choice, he was much more westernized than Dostoyevsky; his novels, being more "literary," were accessible in a more familiar way. Tolstoy, an epic novelist strangely compounded with a religious fanatic, perhaps a saint, was too far out of the English vein to be much imitated, though he was from the first enormously admired.

in size. In 1910, that portentous year, the new wireless device of Signor Marconi was used to capture infamous Dr. Crippen, fleeing with his mistress after the murder of his wife, and supposing himself well out of it as his ship steamed peacefully up the St. Lawrence. Thanks to Marconi, he was hanged in Pentonville jail within the year. In 1909 M. Blériot made history by flying his gawky pusher biplane across the English channel; within a few years the feat was commonplace: even a woman (though still unable to cast a ballot) had accomplished it. The telephone and the telegraph made possible instant communication, especially within city limits. Some of Henry James's telegraphed replies to dinner invitations are as intricately qualified as the paragraphs of his later fictions. Automobiles were still playthings of the rich; as they roared down country lanes, scattering flocks of chickens, scaring horses, and raising clouds of dust, they were heartily cursed by poor folk. But taxes levied on them and on the gasoline they consumed helped to hard-surface the roads, and that was compensation of a sort. Newspapers were the common source of daily information; they included a cheap (vulgar as well as inexpensive) press with snappy captions and simplified explanations of intricate issues for the many, while the lordly *Times* was available for the edification, and boredom, of the establishment. Somebody parodied the style of a *Times* leader: "Not Really a Very Big Earthquake in Chile: Hardly Anybody Killed."

During these years just before the war, it seemed that Britain launched a major book as often as she launched a major battleship, and that was at least twice a year. To keep track of the proliferation, and to guide the bewildered reader, the *Times Literary Supplement* was launched in 1902, soon to become an opinion maker as authoritative as the old quarterlies and much more timely. The London Symphony Orchestra was founded in 1904, Sir Edward Elgar practically single-handed roused English symphonic composition from its long sleep, and in 1910 (again!) Ralph Vaughan Williams produced his first symphony. (His last, Number 9, made its debut when he was eighty-five.) The Tate Gallery of Painting opened its doors in 1897, and grew during these early years of the twentieth century to something like its present impressive dimensions. The first tennis tournament was held at Wimbledon in 1877, and over the years it grew in prestige and importance; the Davis Cup was first put up for competition in 1900. Cricket, always a favorite English pastime, became more serious and professional in the twentieth century; association football (known in America as "soccer") was the working man's game, and international matches, with Ireland, Wales, and Scotland as well as European countries, came to be attended by crowds of 100,000 and up, as they still are. At the level of popular entertainment, English music halls provided a peculiar mixture of slapstick, satire, ballading, pantomime, sentimentality, and nice naughtiness for which no other nation has an equivalent. English food was among the best in the world, and English cooks among the worst; foreigners found amusement in the observation that the English had eighty religions and only one sauce.

Among domestic conveniences, electric light was well established in the towns but less frequent in rural districts, where the need for it was greater. Central heating was slow in establishing a place for itself; even today, many British families which have it are reluctant to use it. But indoor sanitary facilities were becoming more frequent, while water-supply and sewage-disposal facilities of major towns were beginning to approximate modern standards. The scouting movement, started by Sir Robert Baden-Powell, hero of the South African war, provided healthy outdoor experiences for the young. After the elaborate corsets and bustles of the Victorian era, women started to rejoice in lighter and freer clothing; from time to time an ankle might even be glimpsed. And men's clothing too became more casual, as soft fedoras replaced hard stovepipes or derbys and loose tweeds became acceptable where once only morning coats would do. Nice girls still did not smoke in public; a divorced woman was still subject to considerable social suspicion and disapproval. Apart from domestic service, nursing, and teaching, not many women had jobs, and what jobs they had were generally menial and underpaid. But in many fundamental ways, prewar England looked like modern England (SFR, I.2).

THE MEN OF 1914

In the last minutes before war broke out, a group of young men came forward with new works which would prove to be the seeds of the modernist movement in years to come. They are known, rather inaccurately, as "the men of 1914"; they included T. S. Eliot, James Joyce, and Percy Wyndham Lewis. The inaccuracy of the designation is evident in that Eliot's first major poem "Prufrock," appeared in 1915, and Lewis's novel *Tarr* in 1918; only Joyce's book of short stories, *Dubliners*, actually appeared in 1914, and it had been written years earlier. Still, these men with their allies and associates, the expatriate American Ezra Pound and a tough young Cambridge philosopher, T. E. Hulme, were to make the literary taste of the future. We note here a few of the qualities they shared and which made them, from the first, a group. The surfaces of "Prufrock" are broken, its images hard, fragmented, and disparate; the poem's meaning must be constructed by assembling them. The stories of *Dubliners* are also hard, ironic, and often enigmatic; the reader is given implications, hints, suggestions, but forced to decide for himself about the basic themes. *Tarr* presented a hero with a remarkably cold and inhumane way of looking at the world, and presented him through sharp and clashing angles of vision. Pound was bound into the group by his emphasis on hard-edged and functional, not decorative, images; while Hulme (whose work was published only posthumously, after the war) proposed categorically that the literature of the new age would be hard of surface and classical in temper.

An older associate and early supporter of the "men of 1914," though not properly a member of their group, also published an important book in the year of crisis. Ford Madox Ford had been an editor of genius, a poet of talent, and the author of many bright but flawed fictions. In his dealings with people he was also a bit flawed, dealing lightly with the truth, and indiscriminately with the ladies. But in 1914 he got his extraordinary talents into line and produced, in *The Good Soldier*, a complex and moving novel. It was a breakthrough for him, and he followed it up during the 1920s with a king-sized tetralogy focusing on the life, mind, and persecutions of a hero named Christopher Tietjens. The five novels are commonly viewed as the solid armature of Ford's literary achievement. Their author, who belongs with Wyndham Lewis as a man whose life needs a good deal of forgiving, also belongs with Lewis as a man of intellectual talent and resource.

THE TERRIBLE WAR

But for the present literary and cultural matters were in abeyance; war was declared in August of 1914.[19] As a nation, the English welcomed it; they thought it would be over in a matter of weeks, or months at the most. They thought of themselves as teaching the arrogant Germans a "much-needed lesson." Rupert Brooke, an Oxford poet, wrote of going to war as a leap into clean, cold water; he was lucky enough to die before he learned what it was really like.

For in fact the British army was scandalously ill prepared to fight a major war; and the German armies were not only large, well trained, well supplied, and well directed, they consisted of first-class fighting men. The professional army that they had on hand the British sent as an expeditionary force into France, to turn back the invading Germans who had poured through Belgium and were threatening Paris. In a series of desperate engagements along the river Marne, French and British troops did throw the Germans back; and when they tried to advance again, British troops anchoring the left end of the long allied line stood and fought at Ypres, Belgium, despite casualties which practically wiped them out. After Ypres (October–November 1914), the British Expeditionary Force was

19. The occasion for war was the murder of Archduke Franz Ferdinand, heir apparent to the throne of Austro-Hungary, by Serbian nationalists; the Austrians, with German backing, made this a *casus belli* with the Serbians, who appealed to their protectors, the Russians; the Germans thereupon declared war upon the Russians and the French, who were their allies. The German invasion of Belgium, to get at the French, was the immediate occasion of England's entry into the conflict. In point of international law, the German invasion of Belgium was wholly unjustified; since 1839 a treaty engineered by Lord Palmerston and signed by England, France, Russia, Prussia, and Austria had guaranteed Belgian independence and neutrality. But influential German theorists like Count Alfred von Schlieffen and Friedrich von Bernhardi held that, between France and Russia, Germany's national existence was at stake—she must crush the first, ruthlessly and unscrupulously, in order to be able to dominate the second. A sensible emperor would not have listened to either adviser; but Wilhelm II was never described, even by his warmest admirers, as a sensible man (SFR, I.5).

strong enough to man only about 20 miles of the 450-mile front stretching from the English Channel to Switzerland; the rest was manned by the French. Kaiser Wilhelm had spoken of the English army as "contemptible," and they took up the name in pride, calling themselves "the old contemptibles." But the first few months of war came close to destroying them completely, though the kaiser had good reason to regret using that word.

More men were needed, and enlistment provided them; by year's end, nearly a million Britishers were under arms, and, if one counted expeditionary forces from the dominions and colonies, twice as many. They entered a struggle which had already settled into a stalemate. All along the western front, complex lines of trench were dug on both sides of no-man's land; that deadly territory was filled with barbed wire, machine guns were dug in and heavy artillery placed in the rear. During the three years that followed, though both sides launched massive offensives, using all the weapons they could devise—tanks, poison gas, planes, and rockets—neither was able to penetrate the defenses of the other to a depth of more than 20 miles.[20] Trench warfare was ghastly beyond any sort of warfare hitherto known; millions of men lived among rats and corpses, cowering in their trenches while giant shells crashed down on them, advancing bravely and futilely into withering machine-gun fire, dying in prolonged agonies on the barbed wire. Desperate generals contrived elaborate plans of attack, dependent on split-second timing, which collapsed in the first half hour, but had to be followed through blindly, at the cost of thousands of lives. Under such conditions, men disintegrated morally and physically; there were mutinies, suicides, desertions, and cases of officers shot by their own men.[21]

Censorship prevented any conception of these horrors from reaching Britain; most civilians, if they thought of the fighting, imagined men in red coats with long swords, galloping on white horses and crying "Charge!" Propaganda at home whipped up war hysteria to incredible self-destructive frenzies; Prince Louis Battenberg, the first sea lord whose brilliant initiatives had ensured the navy's readiness at the outbreak of war, was forced to resign, though he had been a British subject for nearly fifty years, because his title was German. (In 1917 the entire royal family had to change its name from Saxe-Coburg to Windsor; and Windsors they have been ever since.) R. B. Haldane, the minister of war who had done most to bring Britain's army to a state of relative preparedness, had in

20. The British army entered World War I with 63 operational airplanes and 80 motor vehicles. The first use of poison gas was by the Germans at the second battle of Ypres, April–May 1915. Gas was not a very effective weapon, being hard to control, especially on windy days; but as it blinded and suffocated the victim, its use was considered, and rightly, particularly horrible.

21. Many of the stupendous losses in the early months of the war were the consequence of a semireligious faith, on both sides, in the power of the offensive. The French were so committed to the doctrine of attack in August 1914, that some corps commanders expressed delight at not having any heavy artillery: it would just slow them up. Sickening casualties taught them a different lesson, and they started to use, for the first time, barbed wire and entrenching tools, the rudimentary means of self-protection.

his youth studied Hegelian metaphysics at Göttingen; he, too, was forced to resign. Beethoven was banished from the concert halls. Hysterical fantasies swept through the civilian population; an angel had descended from heaven at Mons to protect the British army, the German soldiers passing through Belgium spent all their time raping nuns and cutting off babies' hands.[22] Society ladies gave out white feathers (emblematic of cowardice) to any man wearing civilian clothes on the streets of London. Not the least of the real soldier's problems, when he did occasionally get leave to visit England, was his utter disgust at all this exaggerated and indecent patriotism.

Early in 1915 the British government, sensing stalemate in the west, tried to open a new front by attacking the narrow straits of the Dardanelles at Gallipoli; their aim was to capture Constantinople, unite with the Russians, and advance on Germany through the Balkans and Austria. But the expedition was not skilfully masked, Turkish defenses were unexpectedly strong, British warships blundered into a minefield, and after many casualties the necessity of withdrawing became obvious. Meanwhile the immense Russian armies which had been counted on to do much of the fighting, suffered one crushing defeat after another. The Germans did not want to invade or conquer Russia; she was too big. They did succeed in immobilizing the eastern front, which enabled them to shift many of their crack troops to the west. The best the British could do under the circumstances was to move their expeditionary force to Egypt, where they could guard the Suez Canal and hope to move north against the Turks with the help of T. E. Lawrence's guerrilla campaign behind Turkish lines.

On the home front, not everything was chaos and blundering. Enlistments filled the places of the "old contemptibles" and swelled the army beyond anything England had ever known. Canada and Australia contributed powerful expeditionary forces; and after January 1916, conscription was invoked (whether necessarily or not, there is some dispute) to keep the ranks full. As minister of munitions, David Lloyd George proved effective beyond anyone's expectations. One of England's top generals (Earl Haig) told him that two machine guns per battalion were plenty; the other (Lord Kitchener) said four would be more than adequate, anything more wasteful. Lloyd George told his suppliers: "Take Kitchener's figure. Square it. Multiply by two. Then double again for good luck." This was not just hearty enthusiasm; the first world war was a war of machine guns, as the second world war was fought with tanks and planes. Lloyd George had read the handwriting, and Britain during the last part of the war did have enough machine guns, as well as bullets to shoot from them, and shells for

22. This is not to imply that real atrocities were unknown in Belgium. Quite unable to see that their own presence in Belgium was illegal or worse, the Germans grew furious at any sign of "illegal" civilian resistance, and shot innocent hostages by the hundreds in reprisal. Entire towns which had not cooperated were looted and burned, including the famous university of Louvain, with its irreplaceable library. A curious counterpoint to this deliberately brutal behavior was the plaintive cry of many German propagandists: "Why doesn't anybody *like* us?"

artillery protection. But, as the anecdote illustrates, not even Lloyd George could manufacture imaginative and modern-minded generals. Most of the British high command had won their spurs in the Boer War, when flying columns of riflemen on horseback represented the ultimate weapon.[23] Their dream of success in this war was of tearing a hole in the German lines and pouring through it with troops of cavalry to spread across the interior of Germany as they had done in the Transvaal; with this fantasy in mind, 700,000 horses were kept behind the lines throughout the war, ready for use if the opportunity ever came.

The year 1916 began badly with the Easter rising in Dublin. It was a minor episode in itself, and put down without great losses on either side. But the martyrs of 1916 were far more influential in death than they had been in life;[24] it was particularly infuriating that Irish citizens should be shot down by British troops on Irish soil even after home rule had been granted in principle. The demand for immediate independence became truly popular as a result of the Easter rebellion.

At the end of May occurred the one direct naval confrontation of the war, the battle of Jutland, fought off the coast of Denmark by the massed fleets of England and Germany. Losses of men and ships favored the Germans by almost two to one; but as the British had immense numerical superiority to start with, they technically "won" the battle. The German fleet put back to its bases, and never again emerged in strength to challenge control of the seas. But in the two battles of the Somme (July and August), General Haig effectively squandered the vast civilian army that had been entrusted to his command. They were brave men, but they were slow in maneuver, they had not fully mastered the cruel rules of trench warfare, and they were commanded by dunderheads of suicidal stupidity. Led by lieutenants fresh from the public schools, they marched by battalions straight into enfilading machine-gun fire; and like wheat they were mowed down. On the first day of the Somme offensive the British army suffered casualties of 19,000 killed and 57,000 wounded, the greatest loss in a single day in British history.[25] A sensible command would have stopped at that point, and reassessed the whole strategy. In fact, the greatest conceivable victory along the Somme could hardly have done more than straighten out a bulge in the German lines.

23. As early as the American Civil War, alert military commanders realized that saber-wielding cavalry were helpless against sharpshooting riflemen. The Germans were slow in absorbing this lesson, but not as slow as the English.

24. British concern about the Irish rising was heightened by the fact that it had German backing, ineffectual though that was. Two days before the rising itself, Sir Roger Casement, once a British consul in Africa, was landed near Dublin from a German submarine. He had been trying to recruit Irish freedom fighters from prisoners of war in German camps; captured in Dublin by the British, he was promptly executed.

25. British infantrymen at the Somme had to carry 66 pounds of equipment when they charged; over the muddy terrain, these packs slowed them to a painful stumble. German losses were remotely comparable only because the high command, nearly as dumb as the British, insisted on launching counterattacks to recapture scraps of worthless terrain.

But the general staff was blind in one eye and refused to see out of the other; they paid no attention to casualty reports, but pushed stupidly forward till the end of November, when, the army being utterly exhausted, and having nothing to show for its staggering casualties, the offensive petered out (SFR, I.8).

During the winter of 1916–1917, the Germans put forward peace feelers which the Allies rejected; things, by now, were too embittered for any sort of negotiated settlement. On an all-out win-the-war program, Lloyd George became prime minister at the very end of 1916; and because he was a clever, unscrupulous, demogogic man, he got things moving. When shipping losses from German submarines became intolerable, Lloyd George stormed into the admiralty office, took over direction himself, and organized a system of convoys (packs of merchant vessels protected by destroyer escorts) which cut losses to less than one percent. His administration was heartened in April by American entry into the war; but American help was still far away. Her troop training had to start from scratch, and the whole economy had to be regeared to supply the needs of an expeditionary force. Meanwhile, Britain was still looking for a victory on the western front; but despite frightful slaughter at Arras, Vimy, and Passchendaele, little progress was made. Late in November, an attack with massed tanks actually did break German lines at Cambrai; but the victory was so completely unexpected that the allied command was in no position to follow it up, and within ten days the Germans had recovered all their lost ground. Meanwhile, however, world-shaking events had been taking place in eastern Europe. Following a revolt of the army and navy, Czar Nicholas II abdicated in Russia; a socialist government headed by Kerensky succeeded, and early in November it too was overthrown by the revolutionary Bolshevik party under the leadership of V. I. Lenin.[26] During the winter, the Bolsheviks stalled for time; they would not fight the Germans, neither would they accept the harsh peace terms the Germans wanted to impose. But on 3 March 1918, Trotsky signed the treaty of Brest-Litovsk, withdrawing Russia from the war, surrendering huge slices of Russian territory (far more than, after the armistice of November 1918 Russia was forced to give up) but also freeing all the German armies of the east to join in a climactic offensive against the allies in the west.

Before that last offensive began in the spring of 1918, Woodrow Wilson, the American president, proclaimed on the eighth of January the Fourteen Points for which he declared the United States was fighting, and which he thought should serve as the basis for ultimate peace. From the first ("open treaties openly arrived at") to the last ("a general association of nations to guarantee independence and territorial integrity to great and small states alike"), they were liberal and fair-

---

26. Lenin had been living as an exile in Zurich, Switzerland, during the war. Recognized by the German government as a useful disruptive agent (the Bolsheviks had steadily opposed participation by proletarians of any nationality in the imperialist war), he was shipped through Germany in a sealed train, like a deadly microbe, to bring down the Russian government. "Bolshevik" means simply "member of the majority." Their intraparty enemies were called "Mensheviks."

minded declarations of principle. How they would be applied remained, of course, to be seen.

For the moment, however, all energies had to be turned to stopping the last desperate offensive of the kaiser's armies. Throughout the spring, the Germans pushed forward, across the Somme, across the Marne; they captured Soissons, just thirty-seven miles from Paris. But there they stalled; and as American strength began to build up, the tide of battle turned. Once again, near Amiens, the British mounted an attack with massed tanks; once again, it succeeded. But this time, instead of trying to deepen the breach, Haig stopped short and attacked to right and left, where enemy lines had momentarily been drained of soldiers. There was no general breakthrough, but at Château-Thierry, Belleau Woods, and along the St.-Mihiel salient, American troops fought well; by 1919, it was clear, the Americans would have 5 million men in Europe.

And now the German Empire began crumbling, not on the western front, but in the demoralized and despairing east. Bulgaria and Turkey withdrew from the war, Austria and Hungary gave up. Four long years of British blockade, the strain of desperate military effort, and now despair of any victory at any time in the future, brought about a gradual but in the end total collapse. It had not been foreseen; as late as September, men in high places had been saying, despondently, ''We will none of us live to see the end of this war.'' It was not, in the last resort, a military victory, though indeed the German military situation was hopeless. It was, in essence, victory in a contest of attrition. One could not say with assurance which nation or group of nations ''won'' the war without saying, first and emphatically, that all of them lost it. From top to bottom, the Continent was a reeking shambles. A generation of young men had been butchered; every belligerent was tottering on the verge of bankruptcy; a way of life had disappeared. And for what? After the guns had fallen silent on the eleventh hour of the eleventh day of the eleventh month of the year 1918, the world waited for the peacemaking process to decide whether there had been any sense to it all.

17

Between Two Wars (1919–1939)

Slowly peace returned to a world exhausted, depleted, hungry, and ashamed of itself as after a long nightmare of bestiality. Like a burnt-out forest fire, which continues to flare up around the periphery after it is dead at the center, little wars continued to sputter and crackle along the edges of Europe. In Russia, Finland, and Hungary, whites continued to kill reds, and vice versa; in north Africa, the Spanish continued to fight a low-level, but nonetheless deadly war against a Moroccan independence movement that did not die down till halfway through the 1920s. Turkey continued at war with Greece, and in clearing the Anatolian peninsula of Greek settlers, many of whom had lived there for centuries, inflamed hatreds which themselves went back beyond the memory of man. The Irish, of whom there is always something to say, entered on the dark period of their "Troubles." But in central Europe there was relative peace, while the late combatants assembled at Versailles (1919) to survey the appalling damage and then to formalize a peace.

VERSAILLES AND REACTION TO THE WAR

The victorious powers who met at Versailles arrived there with very different expectations and commitments. Generally speaking, the fewer casualties they had suffered, the more idealistic they could be in their approach to peace. Woodrow Wilson for the United States (115,000 dead) still believed in the liberal

Fourteen Points he had set forth in January 1918; he also had visions of a league of nations, a kind of international parliament, and to get that he would sacrifice many immediate, short-range considerations. Lloyd George of Great Britain (three quarters of a million dead) occupied a middle ground; his fluent Welsh talent for verbal compromise left him as a buffer figure between extreme positions. And Georges Clemenceau, for France (a million and a half dead), pitched his tent on the far right; he was implacable and insatiable in his demand for revenge on Germany. Nicknamed "the Tiger," he was personally a hard and inflexible man; he recalled vividly that in 1871 after the Franco-Prussian War, the Germans had imposed a harsh peace on France. He was almost eighty years old and unyielding as flint before the pleas of Wilson to be more liberal. A hidden factor in the peace was that most of the powers had entered into secret agreements, either before the war, or during it, so that none of them was really a free agent. (The first of the Fourteen Points denounced secret treaties, and it was the first of the points to be violated.) Thus the ideal of a just peace was swamped in a torrent of demands for revenge. The terms imposed on Germany were not only cruel, they were impractical and self-defeating; instead of rendering Germany humble and weak, they made her defiant and vengeful. To begin with, the Germans were stripped of provinces in the west (Alsace, Lorraine, and most of Schleswig), provinces in the east (parts of Silesia and West Prussia, the city of Danzig), and all their overseas colonies. The Saar Valley, heart of Germany's industrial power, was internationalized, and the entire Rhineland demilitarized and turned over to French occupation troops. By land, sea, and air, Germany was totally disarmed; the German fleet, which surrendered at Scapa Flow in Scotland, but had been left in control of standby crews, was scuttled to the last ship by its embittered crewmen the instant they learned the contents of the treaty. And this was only the beginning. The Germans were required to restock French farms with new cattle, to replace ships, railroad lines, and rolling stock destroyed in the conflict, and to supply the French with free coal, because production from French mines had suffered. Finally, the Germans were ordered to pay enormous cash reparations; the sum, too hideous to be mentioned in the treaty itself, was fixed, two years later, at something like 33 billion dollars.[1]

Practically everything in this wretched peace settlement served to sow seeds of future trouble. Rewriting the map of eastern Europe left resentful minorities almost everywhere itching for revenge. To gain support from Arabs, the British had made promises which in the Balfour Declaration of 2 November 1917 they

1. Naturally, the Germans were infuriated at the time, and appealed to the Fourteen Points, which were far more liberal than the actual treaty turned out to be, and made no mention at all of reparations or unilateral disarmament of Germany. The first German representatives at Versailles refused to set their hands to the document, and had to be replaced with more docile agents. The United States Senate refused to ratify it, as well, and also refused its consent to join the League of Nations. America made a separate peace with Germany in 1921, but never did join the League, a step which doomed that organization almost from birth.

had to disavow in favor of earlier promises to establish a Jewish homeland. The partition of Ireland was another sore spot that was left to fester. But the heart of this vengeful and mischievous treaty was the humiliating conditions it imposed on Germany. The heavy reparations caused a ruinous inflation which wiped out the German mark completely; hardly any reparations were ever collected, and the crash of the German economy made it necessary for the United States to come forward with reconstruction aid (the Dawes Plan, 1924) before finally, in 1932, the whole business of war reparations was abandoned. Perhaps Hitler or someone like him would have seized control in any case; but the iniquities of the Versailles treaty provided him with an easy springboard to power. Those consequences should have been foreseen by the greedy, hate-filled old men who sat around the treaty table in 1919.

The obvious injustices of the peace contributed to a deep disillusion with the war, or any war, in every nation that had suffered from it. Public opinion in England was vulnerable to disillusion because war spirit at home had been whipped up to hysterical proportions, and because heavy censorship had protected the public from any real perception of existence in the trenches of Flanders. Since the seventeenth century, England had been lucky enough to know very little conflict at firsthand; the casualties of trench warfare were more and worse than anyone could conceive who had not actually been in the front lines. They were not simply physical mutilations (terrible as those were), but the complex of nervous traumas just becoming known as "shell shock"; and an even wider malaise was the disgust felt by many returning veterans for the armchair generals and home-front patriots who had sacrificed them so stupidly and then lied so grossly about the "heroism" of their sacrifice.

Embittered by their wartime service, the veterans met with fresh causes of disillusion on their return home; many found it hard to get a decent job. England's financial and commercial position had deteriorated radically during the war; competitors in neutral countries had captured many of her markets, and the colonies, which once could be depended on to absorb many of her exports, had now set up shop on their own. Exports of coal and textiles declined rapidly; taxation was heavier than ever, and inflation bore heavily on the working class. In 1921 the coal miners went out on strike, counting on support from their allies the railroad and transport workers; but Lloyd George, with a liberal's slipperiness in time of crisis, arranged for the coal miners to be abandoned by their allies, and so broke the strike. An immediate consequence was a sharp fall in the political strength of the Liberals, and a corresponding rise in the power of the Labor party. The party was not only stronger, for a time it became more radical, at least verbally. The Fabian socialists, with their program of administrative reform, popular education, and political gradualism, continued to be prominent; Bernard Shaw and his friends Beatrice and Sidney Webb remained active in the movement, though no longer as flamboyant and entertaining as in their youth. But in addition, the apparent success of the Soviet example, and a drumfire of propaganda to the effect that wars were the inevitable product of imperialist crisis, increased the influence within the trade-union movement of a Marxian communist fraction. Whether class warfare was preached or not, it was increasingly practiced; big unions and big business mobilized against one another, and militant factions both right and left began competing for the support of the still-undivided middle.

During the war large numbers of women had taken, for the first time, positions in industry. Work in a munitions factory, a hospital, or an office had been a patriotic duty; on occasion, it had also proved an exhilarating and liberating experience for women whose horizons had previously been bounded by housework and child care. After the war, with returning troops looking desperately for jobs, employment for women suffered a temporary setback; there were fewer women with jobs in 1921 than there had been in 1911. On the other hand, political and social freedoms won by women during the war could not be revoked. A timid act of 1918 had granted women over thirty the right to vote; ten years later, perhaps emboldened by the Nineteenth Amendment of the American constitution (1920), British voters finally, quietly, almost anticlimactically, conceded female suffrage. The cumbersome costumes of the prewar years, with their draggy skirts and floppy hats, gave way in the 1920s to the "flapper" look, the girl with a boyish figure who bobbed her hair, showed her knees, and smoked cigarettes in public. Manners became less formal, the precepts of conventional morality less binding. Life in the little village, with its narrow comedy of mutual gentility and everybody minding everybody else's business, became less constricting when the automobile provided a quick way out of town, and improved communications provided more amusements in town. Telephones and radios (invented by Bell in 1876 and Marconi in 1895) had been indispensable in wartime; now, after the peace, they became available to the civilian populace. Moving pictures, also an invention of the 1890s and now mostly made in America, brought the tinsel excitement of Hollywood into the quiet countryside; traditionalists deplored their vulgarity and sensationalism, but hardly anybody could object to the sharp decline in public drunkenness which followed their appearance. American jazz, on phonograph records primarily, but after 1927 in the movies as well, had a great vogue in England; and new dance steps—the tango, the shimmy, bunny hug, and turkey trot—quickly followed the music. In imitation of the great lover Rudolph Valentino, young men sleeked their hair to patent-leather smoothness, and played on ukeleles as they sang songs from Tin Pan Alley. In reaction to the horrors of the war, a wave of hectic and somewhat defiant gaiety swept the land, catching up the young, of the well-to-do classes at least, in a round of giddy parties and brittle, cynical chatter, well represented in the novels of Aldous Huxley and Evelyn Waugh. Not everyone joining these festivals had a dark wartime experience to forget; but the war was an excellent pretext for partying anyway, and to be solemn or portentous was to risk seeming "Victorian." Largely under the influence of Lytton Strachey (*Eminent Victorians*, 1918; *Queen Victoria*,

1921), that word suddenly acquired a great number of disagreeable overtones, *stuffy* and *hypocritical* being but the first. Overstuffed opinions about the lower orders, the lesser breeds, red-blooded manhood, and lily-white womanhood faded particularly fast. More than an age of gaiety, though they were that on the surface, the twenties were an age of cynicism. What had betrayed people was mostly the complacent surface of things; many of the age's typical patterns reduce to a determination not to be fooled again (SFR, I.7).

IRELAND AND INDIA: OLD PROBLEMS, NEW FACES

The Easter rising of 1916 in Dublin had been the work of a handful of men, to whom the general population remained apathetic. But martyrdom, perhaps because they have experienced so much of it, makes a profound emotional appeal to Irishmen. The Sinn Fein organization of Arthur Griffith, which had been active for more than a decade without attracting much popular support, suddenly became the majority party in southern Ireland. In the general elections of 1918, 73 of their candidates (out of a total of 102 Irish members) were elected to seats in the Parliament at Westminster.[2] But Sinn Fein refused to send any of them to sit in an English Parliament, where, as had always happened, their voices would be smothered by the voices of an English majority. Instead, they declared themselves the legal government of Ireland, and established themselves in Dublin, enforcing their authority through a volunteer military organization, the Irish Republican Army. The British reasserted their own power, to be exercised through the viceregal governor of Ireland and, in the last analysis, through the Royal Irish Constabulary. These were the traditional police forces of Ireland, but for the emergency they were reinforced with veterans of the European war, known from the special uniforms they wore as "Black and Tans." They were very hard-bitten men indeed. They had no training in police work, and they hated the Irish, who, though officially sympathetic to the allied cause, had, as they saw it, sat out the war. In their pursuit of IRA guerrilla fighters they abused the population savagely, as a result of which IRA men retaliated even more savagely. This was the period known in soft Irish understatement as the time of "the Troubles."

Popular support in Ireland, money from America, Parliament's 1912 vote, and a profound yearning in Britain to be done with the matter, made it inevitable that some form of home rule would prevail. But when, where, and how much were still questions over which men were ready to kill and die. At the core of the matter was the ulcer of Ulster. Many Protestants of that troubled district had no particular use for England, except as a shield to protect them from the hated Catholics of the south.[3] But protection from the south they must have. The south

2. Seventy-three seats represented every seat outside Ulster except four reserved to Dublin University (Trinity College), a traditional Protestant stronghold.

3. Before the war, Orange spokesmen had not hesitated to say outright that if Britain tried to include them in a united Ireland, they would seek aid from, or even secede to, Germany.

was no less resolute that home rule for Ireland meant home rule for all Ireland, and right away. The southern Irish were particularly blessed in their leaders, Arthur Griffith and Michael Collins (known as "the Big Fellow"), a New York stockbroker turned guerrilla commander and astute negotiator. But not even they were able to dent the rock-hard resistance of Ulster; and when Irish independence was at last negotiated (1921), Irish partition, like an ugly twin, insisted on being born with it. That was predictable, but less so was the infighting that broke out within the Irish movement itself, some members of which felt betrayed by a settlement less complete than they had wanted. In their disappointment, they assassinated Michael Collins, and birth of the new nation was marred not only by the pain of partition but by murder of its most intelligent and capable leader. Sinn Fein continued divided over Ireland's dominion status, the radicals refusing any association with the British crown, till 1927. Shortly after they decided to enter the government, their chief, Eamon de Valera, assumed national leadership, and the country, adopting a new constitution, retitled itself Eire. A final break with the commonwealth came directly after World War II, in 1948. To this day, some people in Eire are bitterly unreconciled to the partition which divides six of the nine Ulster counties from the rest of the island; by the same token, most people in northern Ireland are bitterly unreconciled to the idea of uniting with Eire (SFR, X.25).

In any brief account of relations between the Irish and the English, one runs the risk of exaggerating the antipathies—not between Catholic and Protestant fanatics, who for centuries have fought like Kilkenny cats, but on the part of ordinary folk. Eire is more like England in its everyday social life than it is like any other nation in the world. England has provided a regular market for Irish farm produce; and English hardware, like farm machinery, domestic appliances, and automobiles, is standard in Ireland. Because Ireland does not have a major industrial plant, Irishmen have long made a practice of crossing the channel to work for a time in English factories and offices, where they acquire rights under English social security laws. There is a small but influential Anglo-Irish community in southern Ireland; its journalistic spokesman is the respected *Irish Times*. During both world wars, many Irishmen served in the English forces as individual volunteers, though the country, in World War II, was officially neutral. Before terror attacks put an end to the practice, it was routine for Dublin housewives to make all-day shopping expeditions by rail to Belfast for items not readily available in the south. Irish entertainment, both radio and TV, is often piped in from Britain, though there are local programs as well; and Irish authors rely, perforce, for most of their audience on readers in England and America. Eire is a very small nation, about the size of West Virginia in area, with a total population about equal to that of metropolitan Boston. There are many things the Irish can do for themselves, but some they cannot; even in independence, and like it or not, they retain a special relation to England.[4]

4. As a matter of fact, after centuries of close if not always congenial interrelatedness, there is by now some Irish blood in most English folk, and vice versa. The Scots and the Welsh have also been

Another serious problem arose, after World War I, in India. Because Indians had contributed generously to the British war effort and needed encouragement to contribute further, the British cabinet announced in 1917 that the Indians should have a measure of self-government as soon as they were ready for it. But how does one demonstrate "readiness"? and whose judgment must be satisfied? During their years in India, the British had developed a corps of competent native civil servants, and had encouraged the growth of native colleges and universities. (These perhaps seem like elementary benefits to confer on a colonial possession; but not all colonizing powers did even so much.) On the other hand, Moslem-Hindu antipathies ran deep; the British could plead that India was not "ready" for self-government till the danger of racial and religious war had subsided. There was, therefore, a pretext for the British to go slow, and a reason for the Indians to feel impatient. But there was neither pretext nor reason for an episode such as occurred at Amritsar in 1919 when General Dyer ordered his troops to fire on a crowd of unarmed Indians demonstrating for independence. No fewer than 379 Indians were killed; the general, officially reprimanded, received a handsome purse of money from admirers in Britain.

These events brought forward, to head the recently formed Congress party in its agitations for independence, a tiny, charismatic lawyer named Mohandas Gandhi. The Jain religious sect into which Gandhi was born encouraged extreme ascetic practices; he was a lifelong teetotaler and vegetarian, ate the bare minimum necessary to sustain life, possessed nothing of his own, and rarely wore more than the plain white loincloth which is the garb of India's poorest folk. His law he had learned in England, but his techniques of popular agitation evolved from years of experience in South Africa, where he had gone to defend Indian immigrants against racial injustice. Nonviolence and passive resistance were at the heart of his strategy; they were techniques well adapted to use in India, with her enormous populations and deep religious traditions. Gandhi led campaign after campaign against the British presence in India, organizing boycotts of imported goods, encouraging refusal to pay taxes, and promoting protests in which thousands of demonstrators, by lying down in the streets, brought entire cities to a standstill. Colonial administrators, whose mentality has been etched in acid on the pages of E. M. Forster's novel, *A Passage to India,* simply had no notion of how to deal with the intangible power wielded by a man like Gandhi. In jailing him, as they did repeatedly, they deprived him of no wordly pleasures that he valued a rap; they simply increased his authority as a martyr and a holy man, while blackening their own image.

Frail, bald, and plain, Gandhi was one of the most powerful men in the world. From his jail cell he could cause governments to totter on their foundations, simply by refusing to eat; his hunger strikes carried a fearful threat to the British, for had they allowed the holy man to die, all India would have risen against them. As part of his campaign, Gandhi had adopted a symbolic spinning wheel,

partly homogenized, not only with the English but with one another; America is not the world's only melting pot.

with which he could make, in a few days, enough thread to weave himself a loincloth, demonstrating, thereby, his independence of the British textile industry. Gandhi sitting cross-legged and half naked on the bare ground before his spinning wheel exemplified, without a word being said, the terrible moral power of absolute humility. The poorest peasants flocked to see him, walking a thousand miles simply to lay eyes on the little man sitting in the yard of his prison. They came in silence, sat silently in his presence for an hour or so, then rose silently and departed, having seen what they came to see. The title "Mahatma" was bestowed on Gandhi, not by any official body, but by the people of India; it means "Great Soul." The Gandhi agitations continued to trouble British imperial power in India between the two wars; Gandhi and the other Congress leaders were imprisoned during most of the second war, and released only after, when Britain was eager to liberate a colony she could no longer afford. As it did in Ireland a quarter century before, freedom from empire meant for India a violent act of partition and assassination of a beloved leader. To the accompaniment of bloody rioting, Pakistan separated from India in 1947, and in 1948 Gandhi was killed by a fanatical Hindu assassin, just when the dream of his lifetime had been realized, even if not in the way he had wanted.

THE FIRST FASCISM

Though Italy had technically been on the "winning" side during World War I, and had figured among the victors at Versailles, she had not played a very heroic part in the struggle, and was not well rewarded at the settlement. After peace, the country's commercial life was in chaos; jobs were few, disillusion rife, and gangs of rightists and leftists were battling through the streets. No government seemed able to maintain even the rudiments of social order. Out of this chaos emerged an ex-socialist agitator, ex-soldier, at the head of a paramilitary organization calling itself the *Fascisti;* he was Benito Mussolini. In 1922 he marched on Rome at the head of his gang, and was asked by the figurehead king, Vittorio Emmanuele III, to take power. It was the first fascist regime of Europe.

Fascism takes its name from the *fasces* of Roman times, a bundle of rods tied together with an axe as a symbol of the unity and authority of the Roman state. Fascism was basically authoritarian nationalism, and its first step was to repress all dissent from whatever quarter. The party had been built out of street-fighting gangs, and its bully boys enjoyed beating up dissenters, torturing helpless victims by pouring castor oil down their throats, exiling them to the desolate Lipari Islands, or simply murdering them out of hand. Mussolini and the other fascist leaders preached a regimen of strict discipline; they emphasized physical fitness, tried to build up a sense of pride in the army, and whipped up the spirit of nationalism by holding mass meetings at which Mussolini ("Il Duce," as he styled himself, "The Leader") bellowed belligerent patriotic phrases at semi-hysterical audiences. A good deal of this "disciplinary" talk was bogus; behind their façade of hard arrogance, the *Fascisti* were grafters and opportunists, like cheap politicians everywhere. But foreigners took the exercise seriously; the story that Mussolini "made the trains run on time" was repeated by tourists as evidence of new national vitality. Conservative statesmen were impressed by the new Italian efficiency because they couldn't see behind it to the basic brutality and inefficiency of the regime. Mussolini solved his country's labor problems (by throwing union leaders into jail) and jacked up the nation's productivity figures (since they were the lowest in Europe to start with, that wasn't hard); he bragged about reviving the glories of the old Roman Empire and blustered against the decadent democracies. Even his goose-stepping army impressed some people, until it was tested in combat. But Mussolini was more a portent than an international force; though he was a pompous clown, his coming foreshadowed a new dark age of totalitarian politics, with brutal suppression, irrational propaganda, and glorification of war as the order of the day.

INDUSTRIAL WARFARE: BOOM AND BUST

In Britain itself, the 1920s were a time of sharp yet oddly muffled industrial hostility. Without any danger to their own precious skins, a great many men had made a great deal of money out of the war; there was every reason for bitterness on the part of those, like the coal miners and steel workers, who had endured the trenches and then come home to wage cuts and the dole. The Labor party was not yet strong enough to win elections or govern by itself; part of the time it was shackled by the need to placate its liberal allies, and part of the time it had to endure conservative rule. In 1925, the conservative government of Stanley Baldwin decided to return to the gold standard which had been abandoned in 1914; the result was to increase the value of the pound to its prewar level, consequently to make British exports more expensive. In an effort to remain competitive, British manufacturers tried to cut wages, and this led in 1926 to a general strike, the first ever attempted in Britain, and one of the few ever called in a modern industrial society. The strike's moral effect was tremendous; quietly and determinedly, thousands of workers downed tools and brought the nation's business to a halt. No trains ran, no newspapers published, nothing moved. It was an impressive demonstration of working-class solidarity. Yet the strike's actual effects fell far short of both the hopes and fears it had aroused. After ten days, the workers went back to work with little to show for their pains; the fabric of society stood as it had stood before; wages did not change all that much, and Britain's export markets continued to shrink. During the last years of the 1920s a measure of weak prosperity spread across the Atlantic from America, where the stock market was booming. But the collapse of the American market at the end of October 1929 marked the descent not only of Britain but of all Europe into the depths of a paralyzing depression.

Why the stock market goes up and comes down is proverbially mysterious.

The crash of 1929, men said, was due to a radical overexpansion of speculative credit leading to a general loss of confidence. In other words, men had thought the market was going up, but instead it went down. What this meant in Britain, where trade had never really returned to prewar levels, was a doubling of unemployment within the first year, the bankruptcy of many businesses, curtailment of credit, hasty devaluation of the pound, falling prices, lower wages, and economic stagnation. In America, the New Deal government of Franklin Roosevelt stepped forward in 1932 to moderate the economic crisis through programs of public works and deficit spending. England might have shortened her depression and softened its worst effects by the same means, but for two circumstances. Unlike the United States, Britain had in place a scheme of unemployment insurance; dating from 1911, it had been widened in 1920. The "dole" softened somewhat the impact of unemployment, hence less pressure was applied on the government to undertake special programs. Also the government was less active because of the weak character and awkward position of the prime minister, Ramsay MacDonald. As head of the Labor party, he led two successive governments which took office in June 1929 and August 1931; neither let him be master in his own house. In the first he was hamstrung by his alliance with the Liberals, and in the second, called a "national" government, he served as figurehead for an overwhelming majority of Tories, carrying out essentially Tory policies. Like Lloyd George before him, Ramsay MacDonald entered office with a reputation as a radical; like Lloyd George, he adapted to the establishment with a docility, not to say servility, that left his fellow Laborites groping for terms like "sellout" and "betrayal." MacDonald, a Labor man heading up a "national" government which was really conservative, did his own party and constituency far more harm than good. In the opposition role, he might have proposed measures to shorten or soften the depression, and he could certainly have given the English people a sense of alternative policies. But a "national" government seemed to close off all the channels of political dissent just when creative dissent was most needed.

At the root of England's economic problems lay a fundamental difficulty, which hardly anybody addressed with the necessary directness: it was obsolescence. Much of England's industrial plant had been built in the nineteenth century, after the stiff, inflexible fashion of the day; to change the flow processes in a plant, one would have to tear it down. That would be expensive, so it was never done; in the 1920s and 1930s many century-old English factories were still operating exactly as they had done from the first day. Now, however, they were in competition with newer plants in America, Germany, and Japan. In English mines, the thick veins of coal had been worked out; now miners had to wriggle through narrow corridors and hack coal off a face only a couple of feet high. Machinery could not fit there, yet coal mined with machines was what the miners had to compete with. Under pressure of such heavy competition, numbers of English enterprises simply died; plants were boarded up, workers laid off, and industrial towns faded to ghosts. This is the landscape of W. H. Auden's early poetry, a landscape of rusting machinery, sterile slag heaps, abandoned mine shafts, smokeless chimneys, and apathetic people.

THE LURE OF COMMUNISM, THE MENACE OF FASCISM

Economic depressions, which without any reason or purpose lay wholesale waste to human resources, strike frightful blows at an individual's self-esteem and so arouse bitter resentment. A society which kept millions of workers idle while allowing the environment to fester and deteriorate around them, which trained engineers for complex tasks and used them only to run elevators, could not help seeming criminally inept to those who suffered from it. England's failures were inevitably contrasted with the glowing successes, as they were represented, of the socialist system, now firmly established in the Soviet Union. The Soviets had no unemployment, none at all; it was a telling fact, and for the moment nobody suspected that a major reason was their incredible inefficiency in managing the labor force they had. Their standard of living was, admittedly, low, but they were raising it fast; one had only to wait, and they would, in their own phrase, "overtake and surpass" the stagnant west. On the international scene, the Soviet Union spoke up loudly for peace, and almost as loudly blamed the decadent capitalist system for the late imperialist war. On the evidence then available, both points were believable in the 1930s. The soviet system of forced labor camps was still well concealed, and stories about the forced collectivization of farms, with "liquidation" of the prosperous peasantry and millions of deaths from starvation, could be dismissed as mere propaganda. Stalin seemed a legitimate heir of Lenin, whose work had brought to a climax centuries of striving for human liberation. In 1936, Sidney and Beatrice Webb, early and staunch supporters of the Fabian Society, visited Russia and wrote a glowing report on the "new civilization" they discovered there. Like a lot of other liberals visiting Russia, they had seen a "Potemkin's village," consisting of stage props, false fronts, and contented proletarians from Central Casting. Since they were more naïve and credulous than most, being elderly and idealistic, they produced a report which in effect took seriously a phrase more often used since in bitter irony: "the worker's paradise."

Judged by its own self-description (and tight censorship prevented most of the facts from leaking out), Soviet Russia looked very good; its expressed ideals were liberal and humane, its occasional severities necessary but temporary expedients for achieving a classless and stateless society where compulsions of every sort would soon wither away. During the depression this was an easy line to swallow, not only because capitalist society was clearly in crisis, but because the rise of fascism on the European continent led the communists everywhere to tone down their own program of socialism under the dictatorship of the proletariat in favor of a united front of all peace-loving and democratic peoples. Thus the communists, vociferously proclaiming their devotion to the "united front," were able to assume leadership in the battle for bourgeois liberties they really despised because the growth of fascism on the Continent had assumed so menacing a character, and because the rulers of the west viewed its swelling power with such complacency. Like Mussolini, Hitler in Germany had begun as a petty agitator at the head of a gang of embittered veterans, toughs, and street fighters. His followers wore brown shirts and called themselves *Nazis* (an acronym formed from *Na*tionalso*zi*alistische Partei), where Mussolini's men wore black shirts and called themselves *Fascisti*. But their aspirations and techniques were much alike; they took much the same road to power; and though they agreed in despising France and England, who were responsible for the iniquities of the Versailles treaty, they were just as vociferous against the communists and the Soviet Union. From the start, Hitler made no secret of his desire to scrap the Versailles treaty, to repudiate the idea of Germany's war guilt, and to rearm his nation. Once in power (January 1933), he was as good as his word or better. He withdrew Germany from the League of Nations, withdrew from the Geneva disarmament conference, ordered a general conscription, abolished all opposition parties and shut down all opposition newspapers, took over all the provincial governments of Germany, cracked down on the last vestiges of dissent in the universities and the intellectual community, and in 1936 reoccupied the Rhineland, flatly defying the Versailles treaty and the western allies who had dictated it.

When Hitler moved into the Rhineland on March 7, 1936, he had not yet created a military force capable of standing up to a real allied army (the troops that marched in did not even have bullets in their guns), so his move was, in one sense, a gigantic gamble. But it was a very safe gamble indeed. The government of the United States had no presence in Europe, and had not signed the Versailles treaty in the first place. England and France were unprepared to act because pacifist sentiment in the west, growing out of disillusion with World War I, was still very strong; there was widespread conviction that the terms of Versailles really had been iniquitous. But, most important of all, influential conservatives in both England and France looked kindly on the fascist powers which they thought likely to prove tools useful in smashing the Soviet Union. For all these reasons, Hitler was permitted to rearm Germany, as Mussolini had already built up the military machine in Italy, while Britain and France did nothing to stop him and little to increase their own strength.

FIVE STEPS TOWARD WORLD WAR II

The fascist powers moved rapidly to expand their possessions, recruit new allies, accumulate the machinery of war, and train their armies in the realities of battle, all the while keeping the French, English, and Americans off their guard. Mussolini took the first step. In 1896, Ethiopia had successfully asserted her independence of an Italian "Empire" which consisted mostly of a few colonies in Africa; Mussolini determined to subjugate her again. The Ethiopian armies were small, ill-supplied, and poorly armed, so the Italians triumphantly bombed and shelled them into submission, driving the emperor, Haile Selassie, from his throne (1936). An equally feeble antagonist was the League of Nations, which deplored Mussolini's action and voted economic sanctions against Italy. They proved totally ineffectual, and the fascist powers laughed them to scorn.

A second step was the widening of the Axis (the German-Italian alliance) to include Japan. Already involved in a war aiming at the conquest of China, Japan was dominated by a militarist clique hostile to all liberal and radical ideas at home and eager to have a part in destroying and dismembering the Soviet Union abroad. Japan joined the Axis in 1936.

Then the Spanish civil war, which broke out in the same year, allowed Italy and Germany to give their troops some battle experience while supporting a fellow fascist and demonstrating the weakness and indecision of the western democracies. Francisco Franco was in revolt against the legitimate republican government of Spain, which had taken power after Alfonso XIII left the throne, by popular request, in 1931. Franco could not have been more explicitly fascist in his views, nor the Axis nations more explicit in their contempt for the democracies. But the governments of France and England, headed at this point by the conservatives Edouard Daladier and Neville Chamberlain, remained totally inert in the face of direct attacks on a fellow democracy. Indeed, they provided aid and comfort to the fascist enemy. Proclaiming their neutrality in the Spanish civil war, they announced an embargo on shipment of arms or aid to either side. Since the Axis powers were openly supplying the rebels with munitions, planes, troops, and all the materiel of war—and this intervention the democracies were neither willing nor able to interrupt—the only effect of the embargo was to cut off aid to democratic Spain, leaving her at the mercy of fascist armies, Spanish, Moorish, Italian, and German. Russia did something to help the loyalists, and antifascist volunteers from all around the world flocked to Spain via underground channels to support the Spanish republic; against heavy odds, the republican government held out till spring 1939, when resistance finally collapsed.

In the meanwhile, Hitler had taken yet another, a fourth, step toward war, when in March of 1938, after a long campaign of propaganda, terror, and assassination, Germany annexed Austria. At a stroke, this move (known in German as the *Anschluss*) radically increased the size of the German army and widened the base of German economic expansion. It also provided a springboard for Germany's next move to the east, into Czechoslovakia.

The pretext for moving into Czechoslovakia (stage five) was the existence of a small district of ethnic Germans in an area of the Czechoslovak republic known as the Sudeten. Hitler claimed that the Sudeten Germans, like the Rhinelanders and the Austrians, should be united in the greater Germany he was building. But Czechoslovakia, unlike his previous annexations, was overwhelmingly non-

German; it had a tough little army, a famous munitions plant (the Skoda works), an operative democracy, and a strong claim on the support of France and England, who in 1918 had been responsible for setting up the nation out of the ruins of the old Austro-Hungarian Empire. President Beneš stood firm against the Nazis and called on England and France for support. On the last day of September 1938 Neville Chamberlain flew to Munich to confer with Hitler; and in the first days of October, while Chamberlain returned to London with the triumphant news that he had negotiated "peace in our time," Hitler annexed the Sudetenland. Beneš resigned at once; and less than six months later, Hitler took possession of all Czechoslovakia. This time there was no pretense that oppressed German minorities were being returned to the Germanic embrace; the taking of Czechoslovakia was an act of outright conquest, and a clear signal that war was inevitable. No catchword ever died a quicker death than "peace in our time." It was instantly recognized as standing, not for peace, but appeasement.

Czechoslovakia extends nearly 500 miles in an east-west direction, from a point well to the west (and south) of Dresden in Germany to the border of the Ukraine in Russia. If one were a Russian who had listened to Hitler's ranting speeches, Czechoslovakia would look like a long spear pointed directly at the wheat fields of the Ukraine, a district popularly known as Russia's breadbasket. The complicity of the British and the French in pointing Hitler's aggressive energies toward Russia could not possibly escape Moscow's notice. Though the western powers were starting to grumble now about Hitler's insatiable appetite for new territory, they had taken few practical steps to stop him; they were prepared, evidently, to fight to the last Russian, but not to squander the more valuable lives of Englishmen and Frenchmen. Under the circumstances, the Soviet government moved to postpone its own entry into the conflict and gain time for its own preparations. On 23 August 1939, a treaty of nonaggression was announced between Nazi Germany and Soviet Russia. For the western world, it was a bombshell. At one stroke, Russia had freed Germany from the danger of having to fight a two-front war; she had left England and France, shockingly ill-prepared, to face the onslaught of the biggest and best-trained army in Europe. She had given a clear signal that Germany was free to attack Poland; indeed, the treaty almost certainly spelled out a plan for dividing Poland between Germany and Russia. Coming as it did after Moscow's many appeals to high principle, democratic values, the peace-loving forces, and so forth, the Nazi-Soviet pact was a shocking piece of cynical power politics. Yet it should have been foreseen as an inevitable response to the western policy of appeasing Hitler, of pointing him to the east and taking for granted that he would never move west. Russia had no reason to continue the united-front policy once it became clear there was nothing in England and France to unite with. Her bargain with Germany was uneasy and dangerous, but it bought nearly two years of time, during which she strengthened her western defenses, especially around Leningrad, at the expense of the recalcitrant Finns.

Meanwhile, for the west, the hour had struck. On 1 September 1939, German troops crossed the Polish border on the flimsiest of pretexts; in the most impressive demonstration yet of *blitzkrieg* (lightning war), coordinated columns of tanks and clouds of dive bombers tore the Polish armies to shreds. Soviet troops advanced from the east, and within a month Poland had ceased to exist. Britain and France immediately declared war on Germany; many of Britain's colonies followed suit, but Ireland declared her neutrality, and India demanded political independence as the price of her support, so leaders of the Congress party were silenced or jailed. Throughout Europe there was nothing but conscription and the training of armies, stringing of barbed wire, stockpiling of weapons, a closing down and tightening up of the amenities of civilized life. War was once again upon the peoples, and the struggle was clearly going to be a long one. The sensation was not unlike entering a dark tunnel without any assurance that one would ever come out again (SFR, I. 12).

CROSSCURRENTS OF THE TWENTIES AND THIRTIES

The many events of these crowded years between the wars have hardly left us time to sketch changes in mood which, though cumulatively important, were not marked by any decisive events. Most striking is the way in which fading responses to the first World War blended imperceptibly into anticipations of, and then preparations for, the second. The first stage (logically, if not always in time) was direct revulsion at what had happened, expressed in novels like Erich Maria Remarque's *All Quiet on the Western Front* (1928) and Richard Aldington's *Death of a Hero* (1929), plays like R. C. Sherriff's *Journey's End* (1929) and Maxwell Anderson's *What Price Glory?* (1924), realistic reportage like the several photographic compilations of Laurence Stallings, and bitter memoirs like Robert Graves's *Good-Bye to All That* (1929). During the 1930s a pacifist group headquartered at Oxford gained considerable publicity as exponents of a program called Moral Re-Armament. They took, and encouraged others to take, a pledge never to bear arms, offensive or defensive, under any circumstances. One could do this, and yet be strongly opposed to fascism, which was inherently aggressive; indeed, the united-fronters set the tone for this sort of ambiguity by urging strong measures against war and fascism, which clearly included strong threats of force and ultimately of war itself. Finally, as the need to contain and destroy fascism became more evident, along with the futility of half-measures in dealing with it, pacifism faded, though the ultimate goal of a peaceful world remained. Many of the young men who took the Oxford pledge in the middle 1930s, were volunteering, before the decade was out, for service in the RAF or the commando forces of elite raiders.

Throughout the period between the two wars, and especially after 1929, government bureaucracies grew steadily larger, stronger, and more expensive. Britain's income tax dates back to 1842 (the American version only to 1913); but the burden of two world conflicts, plus an increasing number of social services and government regulations requiring enforcement and inspection teams, led to new and staggering burdens of taxation. The presence of government boards and commissions in the everyday life of citizens multiplied manyfold during the period between the wars; some industries were actually nationalized, all were subject to increasing restriction and direction. Almost from the beginning, broadcasting was a public monopoly; after a short period of competition, overseas airlines were consolidated in a single government corporation, ancestor of the old BOAC, British Overseas Airways Corporation, now BA, British Airways.

As airplanes and airport facilities improved, their use expanded. World War I planes had been effective as observation platforms, and in dogfights with one another; but essentially, they were craft for daredevils. In America, with its vast distances, air mail was an obvious postwar development; in England, an equally obvious step was passenger transportation across the channel and ultimately to Africa, Canada, Australia, and the more remote dominions of the empire. Charles Lindbergh's flight from New York to Paris in May of 1927 gave tremendous impetus to the industry, though we should not forget the earlier (1919) flight of Alcock and Brown from Newfoundland to Ireland. But Lindbergh's flight inaugurated a technical development, very simple in itself, though not at all easy to build into pilot training. In fog or clouds, wherever they were without a horizon, pilots had to forget their lifelong habit of trusting to the pull of gravity in order to tell up from down, and depend entirely on their instruments. When blind flight was not only possible but routine, commercial aviation became possible. Motors promptly became lighter and stronger, variable-pitch propellers came into use along with retractable landing gear, streamlining was carried to lengths not hitherto imagined. With air travel, the world shrank; the English channel became a mere ditch, the Atlantic a not-much-bigger one.

Without much fanfare, science and technology flourished during the period between the wars. Some of this expansion derived from the wars themselves; hardly any of it was without influence on military techniques. Long gone were the days when lordly classicists dubbed the study of chemistry "Stinks," and banished it to the cellar of a single building at Oxford. During the 1920s and 1930s a steady stream of British physicists and chemists won Nobel prizes—not a staggering number in aggregate, but men of great distinction who attracted other men of distinction from the troubled Continent, as fascist terror darkened the horizon there. Physicists like Ernest Rutherford, J. J. Thomson, Sir Arthur Eddington, Sir James Jeans, and Patrick Blackett, in cooperation with many refugees of whom the most famous was Albert Einstein, not only contributed to the basic disciplines, but pointed the way toward development of the atomic bomb. They further pioneered in applying the laws of physics to the development of radar and submarine-detection devices. It was British mathematicians who, by sheer mental effort, broke Hitler's "unbreakable" code, and enabled the allies, during the later stages of World War II, to gain the incalculable advantage of knowing the enemy's plans long in advance.

Another set of influential continental imports consisted of the psychological theories and psychiatric practices of Sigmund Freud. These had been known in England since early in the century, first simply as social chatter, then with deepening understanding of their implications. (Freud's pioneering study on *The Interpretation of Dreams* was published in 1900; Dr. Ernest Jones founded the first of several English schools of psychoanalysis in 1913; and writers of fiction like D. H. Lawrence began almost immediately to make use of the new concepts.) In its most simplistic form, Freudianism was supposed to encourage people in discarding their inhibitions, but darker and more complex aspects of the doctrine soon revealed themselves. Freudianism invited people to see primitive and atavistic appetites lurking just below the surface of "civilized" observances. It destroyed wholesale once-unquestioned Victorian beliefs in the milk-and-water innocence of childhood, in the lofty sublimity of dreams, in the pure happiness of family life. Beneath all these ideal façades, Freudianism found lurking different manifestations of the same unchangeable, insatiable libido. First rejected as unbearably nasty, Freudian insights soon became the standard material of social discussion and literary representation (SFR, X.24).

Because government was becoming more and more the work of faceless bureaucracies, little reference has been made, in this discussion of England between the wars, to political parties, and almost none to the royal dynasty. In fact, party politics did not play a very large part in the governments of this period, when no party commanded a strong, solid majority or took a very positive position; compromises and coalitions made, and in the end muffled, most social issues. The Labor party was too conservative to accept, far less to propose, any effective opposition to the growth of fascism on the Continent; the conservatives were often in the forefront of moves to nationalize failing industries (mines and railroads), or to create government corporations in distressed areas. The prime minister, Ramsay MacDonald, was so blurry in his pronouncements that it was impossible to tell what, if anything, he meant.[5] Because there was so large an area of undistinguished consensus in the middle of the political spectrum, noisy and sometimes violent dissenting groups flourished on the fringes. On the right wing, Sir Oswald Mosley's British Union of Fascists sprang up during the mid-1930s, in pale imitation of Hitler and Mussolini; on the left wing, a small, vociferous party of communists and sympathizers wielded influence far beyond their numbers when they took up a truly popular cause like Spanish democracy. In a parliamentary way, both these parties were negligible; but in the war of ideologies that was racking Europe they counted, because they masked a few authentic, unscrupulous fanatics. In preparation for the war, spies, assassins, secret agents,

---

5. He spoke once of the necessity of "keeping in touch not only with progressive but with retrograding movements in our advance," and summed up his philosophy of government in the memorable words "Society goes on and on and on. It is the same with ideas."

and undercover operatives swarmed across Europe, in whose service, one could never be sure. Detective fictions by Graham Greene and Eric Ambler still preserve a flavor from the atmosphere of those days; the murder in 1940 of Leon Trotsky, axed to death in Mexico City by a fanatical gray terrorist in the service of Stalin's secret police, was but one well-publicized episode of many.

George V died in 1936 after a rule of just over twenty-five years; when his silver jubilee turned out to be a genuinely festive event, he was quite surprised; this was the occasion when he described himself as "really quite an ordinary sort of chap." He was indeed, and that may have been a major reason for his general popularity, as well as for his total lack of political influence. His successor, Edward VIII, had been in the limelight for many years, as prince of Wales. The world's most eligible bachelor and a man of great charm, he was famous as a bon vivant, world traveler, and enthusiastic though unstable horseman. Now at forty he assumed the responsibilities and restrictions of the throne; and very irksome he found them. What created a constitutional crisis, however, was the fact that he had fallen in love with an American woman, Mrs. Wallis Warfield Simpson, who had divorced her first husband and was in process of divorcing her second. The church of England hierarchy, led by the conservative archbishop of Canterbury, Cosmo Gordon Lang, took a dim view of divorce in general, and particularly of a woman with two divorces to her credit. The weighty and influential *London Times* was against the marriage, though craftily camouflaging its view as disapproval of American scandal sheets. Edward was determined; the church and the conservative government, under Stanley Baldwin, said no; of the royal family, some approved, others did not. After much backstage pulling and hauling, the decision was taken, and Edward abdicated the throne (even before the day of his coronation) in favor of his brother. The duke of York duly became king, 11 December 1936, as George VI; Edward had ruled less than a year. Naturally, these unprecedented events created a storm in the popular journalism of the day; but it soon died down, because, as duke and duchess of Windsor, Edward and his new wife kept out of the limelight, and because the approach of World War II made loyal adherence to the new king an imperative duty. On the other hand, the very archaic standards by which Edward's personal life had been judged only emphasized the status of the monarchy as a semisacred anachronism in British life.

"MODERN" LITERATURE: A SELF-DESTROYING CONCEPT

Modern, modernist, and post-modernist literature[6] we shall not undertake to treat here in any sort of detail. The material to be described is too vast and various,

6. Modern literature includes anything written in the last sixty-five years, the period 1914–1979. Modernist literature is a stylistic, not a chronological, category; it describes the work of Eliot, Joyce, Pound, and their followers, beginning in 1914 and trailing off in the late 1930s and early 1940s.

critical approaches are too numerous, and the authors of the age are likely to be too familiar, to render extended discussion possible or, if possible, worth-while. The aim will be simply to place the major authors of this period in some sort of temporal or conceptual framework.

Hardly any generation of poets has faced a more gruesome task of adaptation than those who came of age in the trenches of World War I. Nothing in their past, literary or otherwise, prepared them for the hideous, meaningless slaughterhouse into which they were thrust; most of them reacted with cries of anguished revulsion. It is common to place in contrast the boyish enthusiasm with which Rupert Brooke entered the war and the bitter disgust of poets like Siegfried Sassoon, Isaac Rosenberg, and Wilfred Owen, who knew trench warfare. But all the poets wrote under pressure of immediate circumstance, about bits and fragments of experience, without even a chance to get a perspective on it.[7] In fact, the war was too huge, brutal, and shapeless to be seen except in snapshot views, a further evidence of which is the fact that almost no good fiction dealt with the battle experience as such. The literature of the twenties is full of maimed and embittered veterans, but those who knew the facts of war took no delight in recreating them. Not even the so-called "glamor" services, such as the air force, which have since developed a rather elaborate mystique, produced any significant quantity of war writing. A major exception was the extraordinary book, at once adventure story and history, by T. E. Lawrence, "of Arabia." First published in 1921 as *The Seven Pillars of Wisdom,* and later condensed as *Revolt in the Desert* (1927), Lawrence's book describes a guerrilla war in which he organized Arab tribesmen of the Middle East for a campaign of raids against the Turkish empire, then allied with Germany in the war. Lawrence was a charismatic leader and resourceful tactician; he spoke Arabic like a native, and was tough enough to survive long camel treks across the burning desert sands. His work was exploding railroad lines, cutting communications, and harassing outposts in a war of constant maneuver and unceasing danger. His story was a classic narrative of adventure in the old nineteenth-century sense, of hardships overcome, loyalties tested under fire, resourcefulness, and daring. Nothing could have been further removed from the experience of the main armies in the trenches of France, except, perhaps, that Lawrence, like the fighting men elsewhere, was bitterly disillusioned by the terms of the peace that was supposed to crown his efforts.

Modernism in literature is related to Cubism and abstract expressionism in painting, and to the music of Stravinsky, Schoenberg, and Bartók. Anything that comes after modernism, that represents a reaction to it, or does not share its distinctive traits, is post-modernist. These are, needless to say, extremely loose and indefinite categories, sure to be modified or forgotten as soon as we get a better perspective on the recent literary past.

7. Edward Thomas, as he was relatively old when plunged into the maelstrom of war, showed some signs of being able to absorb the ghastly war experience into his subdued and thoughtful poetry without simply reacting to it. Unhappily, he was killed in April 1917, aged just thirty-nine.

JOYCE, ELIOT, LEWIS

Participants who survived the war sometimes survived it with a kind of seared vision from which they never altogether recovered. The major literary figures of the 1920s had been shaken by the conflict, spiritually wounded by it; but as a rule they had not been actual participants. T. S. Eliot in poetry and James Joyce in prose had both been formed in a literary sense by the symbolist movement in France. Both had published preliminary books before the war; and both were exempt from military service, Joyce as an Irishman and a lifelong objector, Eliot as an American and a man with serious health problems. Joyce's short-story collection *Dubliners*, published in 1914, had actually been written in the years 1904–1907; *A Portrait of the Artist* had been in process for a dozen years before it appeared in 1916. *Ulysses*, originally envisaged as a short story forming part of *Dubliners*, swelled during and after the war years to the dimensions not only of a novel but of a modern epic. Though ostensibly describing just the events of a single day in Dublin (16 June 1904), *Ulysses* aims to see the macrocosm in this microcosm, the world in this grain of sand; its central action is vision in depth. The mind which best sees this way is relaxed and intuitive, not hard and logical; it does not capture truth, but is invested by it. Of the book's three main characters, Stephen Dedalus has a keen, avid, and ultimately sterile mind; Leopold Bloom has a gross, inexact, and cliché-ridden mind; and Molly Bloom has a fluid, intuitive, and ultimately vital mind. It is in her formless, flowing, endlessly appetitive consciousness, which does not so much understand the world as identify with it, that the final words of the novel are formed.

Ulysses, considered too obscene to be published in England or America, first appeared in then-more-liberal France (1922); it baffled many readers, revolted others, and soon became the object of a cult. Its method of representing half-formed and apparently unarranged thoughts in the minds of its characters offered one obstacle for readers; its use of motifs complexly interrelated across hundreds of pages offered another; and its evocation of parallels with the *Odyssey* left readers groping as to whether its spirit was heroic, mock-heroic, or anti-heroic. Its range of encyclopedic learning, from the most esoteric to the most vulgar, stirred as much protest as its meticulously selective use of the four-letter words. Yet no book exercised more authority over the mind of its age. Its stature was diminished only when it was seen as a way station on the path toward the still less accessible *Finnegans Wake* (1939).

"The Waste Land," which also appeared in 1922, represented for Eliot a giant step forward from his prewar versing ("Prufrock" had appeared in *Poetry* magazine as early as 1915). Writing of the poem was made possible by Ezra Pound, who rescued Eliot from incipient nervous breakdown (a wretched marriage and long hours of drudgery in a bank were contributing causes), and sent him off for a couple of months in Switzerland; as we now know, Pound also helped to shape and prune the manuscript that Eliot brought back.[8] Like *Ulysses,* "The Waste Land" sees through the present to a backdrop of mythical narrative; like *Ulysses,* it maintains an ambiguous relation to epic tradition (the poem, someone said, is an epic with all the narrative parts left out); and like *Ulysses,* it baffled readers (above all, in those days before annotated editions) by the number and complexity of its allusions. Inevitably, with time and familiarity, the original sense of fragmentation and violent contrast that "The Waste Land" generated has softened; this sense of outrageous disorder, quite as much as its syncopated rhythms, gave Eliot's poem in its day a special feeling of modernity. One important secondary influence contributing to the poem's depth was the Cambridge school of anthropology which, in alliance with Jungian currents of psychoanalytic thought, sought evidence of profound archetypal patterns in primitive folk rituals and folk tales throughout the world. The jaunty energy of the poem's rhythms owes something to English music halls, something as well to the music of Igor Stravinsky, whose sophisticated, barbaric music for the Russian ballets mounted by Sergei Diaghilev (*Petrouchka, Firebird, Rite of Spring*) greatly impressed Eliot. Finally the Cubist and Futurist work of artists like Picasso, Braque, and their numerous followers can only have encouraged Eliot in that fracturing of representational surfaces which was one of the hallmarks of modernism.

Wyndham Lewis was the only one of the "men of 1914" actually to serve in the armed forces; he had done most of his critical blasting, under the influence of the Futurists, in the years before the war and had published the most "experimental" of his novels, *Tarr,* in 1918. Much of his postwar work consisted of laying down philosophical and political foundations for two massive satires, *The Childermass* (1928) and *The Apes of God* (1930). In these large and savage volumes Lewis arraigned the fashionable cliques and opinions of his time with so much personal venom that he shortly found himself, to his great satisfaction, a social and literary outcast. But though he had a special gift for being disagreeable, Lewis's general outlook was not too different from that of Eliot and Pound, both of whom assumed very conservative views with a predilection for fascism which did not stop quite short of endorsement. This tendency of the modernist movement to welcome the politics of elitism and even of violence is a trend to be noted; Marinetti and the Futurists set the trend, and Joyce was exceptional in not following it. The basic attitude may have derived from impatience with conventional liberal platitudes, from a passion for hard, authentic surfaces as opposed to mushy, idealistic rhetoric, from a horror of the outworn genteel tradition; in any event, we note it as a symptom, and perhaps something more. *The Revenge for Love,* which Lewis published in 1937, though marked by his usual political

8. Mrs. Valerie Eliot has edited a facsimile and transcript of the original drafts (they are in fact typescripts) of "The Waste Land," including the annotations of Ezra Pound (London: Faber & Faber, 1971). They confirm our sense that many of the poem's hard outlines and jagged discontinuities were the work of Pound.

animus, is spiritually a little softer and technically a good deal more conventional. Many think it Lewis's finest achievement in fiction.

LAWRENCE, HUXLEY, AND WAUGH

Like Eliot and Joyce, D. H. Lawrence had published before the war, had escaped its full impact, but emerged into the new uneasy light of peace as a prophet, healer, and mage. Both *Ulysses* and "The Waste Land" dealt centrally and explicitly with sex in a way that would have been unthinkable before the war; but it was largely failed, or sick, sex. Lawrence, a new primitivist, celebrated sex along with the other impulses and instincts of the unconscious, but without sex disgust. Lawrence's relation to modernism is ambiguous, to say the least; he does not fracture surfaces, make esoteric allusions, or tease the reader into building difficult connections between remote components of the fiction. Lawrence renders; he does not, typically, suggest. When he is observing directly and responding richly to what he observes, he is one of the most stimulating of writers; his books of travel and reportage are wonderfully vivid. But his preaching style is sometimes overemphatic; he hammers at words and concepts like a nonconformist preacher recently converted to the religion of sex. Even his masterpiece, *Women in Love* (1920), is not altogether free of these faults; and a thinly disguised fascist tract like *Kangaroo* (1923) makes very heavy reading these days. Lawrence was essentially romantic in his conviction that the relation between the sexes is a limitless frontier of exploration. In his personal life he left behind a swathe of burnt-out women who felt they had had the opportunity to explore this wonderful and ever-exciting world with Lawrence but had somehow failed him. Historical perspective suggests that some novelists as well may have been seduced by Lawrence's incantatory prose into supposing that sex is an inexhaustible topic.

Though he deplored the brittle, cynical literary society of his day, Lawrence was a part of it, a protégé of society bluestockings, a crony of editors, a center of his own little literary cenacle. The sterility he found in London literary circles evidently contributed to his restless search for a simple, natural existence in which the dark instincts of the blood would be fulfilled. Among his associates in London were two satirical, civilized novelists, whose cruel wit and mordant style of caricature served to represent, as well as to mock, the sophisticated, shallow world of upper Bohemia. Aldous Huxley and Evelyn Waugh were tough and cynical young men portraying a tough and cynical world, the funniest features of which were the occasional simpletons or fatheads who tried to live nineteenth-century lives. *Point Counter Point* (1928) was Huxley's most ambitious book; *Decline and Fall* (1928) disputes with *A Handful of Dust* (1934) for the position of Waugh's most amusing one. Comic negativism about the sterility of society thus played against Lawrence's romantic primitivism. But the cynicism of the bright young novelists was too arid to sustain them for long, and they moved off in different directions—Huxley toward eastern mysticism, under the guidance of a swami whom he met in Santa Monica, Waugh toward the pose of a Tory squire and snob, which had underlain his character all along.

BLOOMSBURY

The trades of communication (publishing, broadcasting, and nowadays television) are centralized even more strikingly in London than they are, across the Atlantic, in New York and Toronto. After the war, the tastemakers and opinion pronouncers clustered more intimately than ever before in the district around the British Museum known as Bloomsbury. Wyndham Lewis, who never got along well with anybody, stood outside Bloomsbury, making ferocious fun of it. But the "ins" were just as in as the "outs" were out. Virginia Woolf, her husband Leonard, and their friend Lytton Strachey, were very in; so were T. S. Eliot, J. M. Keynes the economist, Roger Fry the art critic, Lady Ottoline Morrell and the Honorable Victoria Sackville-West (when they condescended), the multi-talented Sitwell family (Edith, Osbert, and Sacheverell), E. M. Forster, Clive Bell, and a host of lesser lights. They were glittering, impenetrably smart people, liberal, agnostic, and very cosmopolitan; they made tastes, set fashions, and destroyed idols; they were on terms of intimate friendship and equally intimate enmity with one another; and of them all, Mrs. Woolf seems to be the one whose work has best stood the test of time. She wrote voluminously, not only the nine novels by which she is best known, but volumes of social criticism, a great number of literary essays, diaries, letters, and miscellaneous pieces. The daughter of Sir Leslie Stephen, a celebrity herself, and a lifelong associate of celebrities, Mrs. Woolf was a woman of immense refinement and intense, fragile sensitivities. Her awareness of life's nuances made the writing of her novels agonizingly painful; conventional forms of storytelling left no space for her sense of subliminal realities, and though she learned much from *Ulysses,* she resisted for a long time the less genteel aspects of Joyce's vision. Most readers feel her work succeeded best in *To the Lighthouse* (1927), though *Mrs. Dalloway* (1925) also has its partisans. Both books leave us with an intense sense of life, quivering and uneasy, surrounded by vast and difficult problematics—not only in the form of insensitive and limited males, but in the brutalities of common existence and everyday history. As the storm clouds of World War II gathered and her personal defenses weakened, Virginia Woolf gave way to despair, and in 1941 she committed suicide. Her last novel, *Between the Acts,* is not only beautiful and absurd in itself, but deeply moving as veiled revelation of a state of mind.

Just as sharply, though not as tragically abbreviated, was the novelistic career of E. M. Forster. He published four capable novels between 1905 and 1910, then nothing but short stories and critical studies till 1924, when *A Passage to*

India appeared. It was a major achievement, but his last till the posthumous *Maurice* (1971), which was remarkable only for its lack of fictional inventiveness and its theme of homosexual love, a theme which had lost most of its shock effect in the years since the book was written. That an established and acclaimed novelist should publish just one significant book over the last sixty years of his life is a fact to be remarked; the reasons for it are a matter for speculation, but it cannot help suggesting the drying up of that genteel, liberal tradition to which Forster was deeply and consciously committed.

OUTBACKS: IRELAND, SCOTLAND, WALES, AMERICA

During this period between wars new voices were raised from outlying districts and unprivileged classes of the British Isles and the English-speaking world. These were not conscious regionalists, nor were they self-conscious "primitives," but major spokesmen who took their place on the national stage, even as the literary culture of the home counties and the genteel classes seemed to wither and fade. Though Bernard Shaw continued to hold the London stage through the 1920s, an apparent successor appeared with a better knowledge of working-class realities and a darker view of ideology: this was Sean O'Casey, a self-taught Dubliner whose two great plays (*Juno and the Paycock*, 1925; *The Plough and the Stars*, 1926) grew out of the savage times of the Easter Rising and the Troubles. In the name of suffering, ignorant humanity, O'Casey protested bitterly against both the Irish freedom fighters and the English forces of repression. As a result, he shortly found it advisable to move to England. His four-volume autobiography, unlike most books of those dimensions on that subject, is consistently entertaining. Other self-taught Irish writers who came to the fore were James Stephens, Frank O'Connor, Liam O'Flaherty, and (a bit later) Brendan Behan. And the greatest autodidact of them all, William Butler Yeats, published in the twenty years between 1919 and 1939 almost all of the verse which has established his reputation as the supreme English poet of the modern era. For Yeats the arrival of modernism, with its hard surfaces and distanced symbols, was a precious gift of history. The old antithesis between his early "soft" poetry of Celtic vagueness and the later toughness and complexity is a great oversimplification; an apparently naïve and dreamy lyric like "Who Goes with Fergus?" (1899) is as knotty and thought-provoking as anything in the canon. But his experiences of "modernist" poetry, of Pound's vigorous criticism, and of the whole intellectual climate of the Troubles, were tonic for Yeats. His political sympathies drifted, in about the same measure as D. H. Lawrence's, in the direction of fascism. But his verse grew in simplicity and dignity of statement, even as it multiplied in complexity and severity of thought; no such voice has been heard in English literature since the great tragic dramas of Shakespeare, who also managed quite well without a university education.

Lesser but still distinctive voices were heard from Scotland in the persons of Edwin Muir and Hugh MacDiarmid (pen name of Christopher Grieve); both were largely self-taught, though to very different effects. Muir, born a poor boy on the outermost fringes of the northern isles, was a quiet and apparently traditional poet with a deep, mysterious sense of the pastness of the past. Belonging to no school and following no fashion, he wrote in the purest and simplest English of his age about a world outside time and place. His poems do not so much charm as they fascinate by a grave simplicity that leads us to the heart of a mystery, very much as Jorge Louis Borges likes to do in prose.[9] Hugh MacDiarmid on the other hand was a flamboyant rhetorical rebel who invented languages of his own and proclaimed his allegiance to provocative causes in order to assert his large poetical presence. Programmatic grandiloquence often overshadowed his quiet lyrical gifts; he may yet go down in history as the Victor Hugo *manqué* of Scottish letters.

Economically, no part of the country suffered more during the depression than the coal-mining districts of Wales; and as their very language faded away (only about a quarter of the people living in Wales itself understood it), one would have expected the vitality of their literary life to decline as well. Not so. Both in the Welsh tongue itself and in English, but making use of Welsh themes and materials, the little country remained one of the most active literary districts of England. Robert Graves drew on Welsh folklore for his mythological studies as well as for his poetry; Emlyn Williams made use of Welsh materials for his stage plays; and Richard Llewellyn (Lloyd) enjoyed great popular success with his moving account of growing up Welsh into an English culture (*How Green Was My Valley,* 1940). Less well known (naturally), but better evidence of the strength of the indigenous culture, were writers in the Welsh tongue proper, such as the poets Thomas Gwynn Jones and David Gwennalt Jones, the prose writers David John Williams, Edward Tegla Davies, and Thomas Rowland Hughes. We note also as lesser figures in the production of English fiction on Welsh themes storytellers like Caradoc Evans, Rhys Davies, and Jack Jones. Apart from their considerable interest as individuals, these writers provide evidence of the rich and vigorous cultural groundwork out of which sprang the unanticipated talent of a schoolboy poet in Swansea, Dylan Thomas.

Finally, though we can do no more than glance at them, we must call attention to a new class of provincial authors writing in English between the two wars, the Americans. One can't fail to note the shift in values when a large and influential

9. Muir and his wife Willa also exercised an extraordinary influence on English literature during the prewar and war years through their translations of the mysterious fictions of the Czech writer Franz Kafka. *The Castle* (1930) and *The Trial* (1937) appeared after the author's premature death (of tuberculosis, in 1924); their oppressive atmosphere, dreamlike illogic, and smooth, apparently lucid prose made them profoundly effective in an era, like the war, of public nightmare. (Kafka's fictions, left in fragmentary form and doomed by their author to destruction, had been assembled, edited, and published in 1925 and 1926 by his friend and executor Max Brod.)

body of English writing starts to come from outside the British Isles. During the nineteenth century, individual authors like Emerson, Longfellow, Poe, and Henry James had impinged from time to time on the British consciousness; but most of them were properly deferential before old world values, and those who were not could be easily shrugged off. During the 1920s and 1930s, a steady stream of novelists like Ernest Hemingway, Sinclair Lewis, William Faulkner, and Willa Cather demanded serious consideration; in addition to Eliot and Pound at the heart of literary London, the work of Robert Frost, E. E. Cummings, Wallace Stevens, and William Carlos Williams required and received careful attention. Literature written in England still remained, no doubt, the main current of the English tradition, but now it was one of many elements. American professors began to do important work in editing and expounding the texts of English literature; and very slowly the day passed when an American book could be dismissed with a patronizing sniff simply because it was American. From Australia and South Africa as well came novelists of world reputation; Samuel Beckett, an Irishman permanently resident in Paris, started to be heard from; and some of the most intriguing stories in English were written by a Danish noblewoman who had lived many years in Kenya, Baroness Karen Blixen-Finecke, who published under the names of Isak Dinesen and Pierre Andrézel.

MISCELLANEOUS

The achievements of English writers between the wars are too many and various to be neatly categorized; however one arranges them, one is left with a little pile of writers who don't quite "fit." Not that they are inferior for this reason. If anything, the contrary applies; a vast and various public made possible a wide range of literary activity. H. G. Wells, for example, known previously as an author of science-fiction books, turned much of his attention to a vast *Outline of History* (1919–1920); George Bernard Shaw published in 1928 not the least acute and sensible of his books, *The Intelligent Woman's Guide to Socialism and Capitalism*. Forrest Reid and Elizabeth Bowen published quiet, intense fiction in the Anglo-Irish tradition; Norman Douglas wrote, in *South Wind* (1917), at least one comic novel worthy of his genius. Ivy Compton-Burnett produced a number of acidulous fictions cast almost entirely in dialogue; and P. G. Wodehouse chronicled in many hilarious volumes the misadventures of empty-headed Bertie Wooster and his "gentleman's gentleman," the impeccable Jeeves. The art of the short story flourished under the care of James Joyce, D. H. Lawrence, and Katherine Mansfield; and Somerset Maugham, who had been active since the nineteenth century and who had published his masterpiece *Of Human Bondage* in 1915, continued to delight knowing readers with a scarcely veiled novel about Thomas Hardy and his sanctimonious idolaters, *Cakes and Ale* (1930).

In the background of the period lies a group of monumental intellectual undertakings, having little to do with one another, and not falling directly under the heading of *belles lettres* but contributing to the intellectual vitality of the age. Sir Winston Churchill's eloquent account of the events in which he had played so large a part earned him a Nobel prize for literature in 1953. Arnold Toynbee's ten-volume *Study of History* (1934–1954) sought a pattern in the risings and fallings of political power and spiritual vitality across the centuries and continents; it was an attempt at historical synthesis on the grandest scale ever contemplated. And the three volumes which Bertrand Russell and Alfred North Whitehead produced between 1903 and 1913 under the title of *Principia Mathematica* continued to exercise enormous influence upon English philosophers; in the very briefest of briefs, they represented an effort to identify logic with mathematics and to bring all mental and physical phenomena under the domain of this discipline.

Between the wars, literary criticism in English augmented in quantity and improved in quality, largely under the impulsion of T. S. Eliot. In a series of magisterial essays appearing originally in little magazines or in the *Times Literary Supplement,* he reversed the old romantic view of individual self-expression struggling for liberty from literary tradition; rather, he argued for modernity as influencing, and being in turn influenced intimately by, a living tradition from the past. His analyses of metaphysical poetry and Jacobean drama brought to the fore neglected areas of the literary record; while under his criticisms, the stock of Milton and Shelley fell dramatically on the literary marketplace. Above all, Eliot's example affected the tone of literary discourse. High-flown lyrical "appreciations" like those of Swinburne, and moral diatribes like those of Macaulay, disappeared quietly from literary commentary. Eliot's example was strongly reinforced by the work of I. A. Richards at Cambridge. *Practical Criticism* (1929) described an experiment in giving to a group of bright young readers an anonymous, undated, unexplained, and preferably unfamiliar text on which they were to comment. Analysis of the responses made clear how many irrelevant and distracting elements entered into poetic judgment, and, conversely, how few readers were able to recognize and respond directly to the specific qualities of the text. Richards's book exercised wide influence, not only on the writing of criticism, but on the teaching of literature in America as well as England. The close textual analysis performed by a brilliant and crotchety student, William Empson (*Seven Types of Ambiguity,* 1930), was one outcome of Richards's work; another speaks for itself in the title of F. R. Leavis's influential critical journal, *Scrutiny,* which enjoyed a vigorous life from 1932 to 1953.

Enormously prolific Robert Graves followed up the success of *I, Claudius* (1934) with several more classical pastiches; Ronald Firbank turned out extravagantly mannered charades, culminating in one *Concerning the Eccentricities of Cardinal Pirelli* (1926); and Radclyffe Hall scandalized good society with a frankly Lesbian novel, *The Well of Loneliness* (1928). The children's books of A. A. Milne and Kenneth Grahame have already outlasted many more mature efforts. We should not fail to remark the activities of numerous excellent translators, who brought not only Greek, Latin, and Chinese classics, but the poetry of Cavafy, Montale, and Mandelstam, the prose of Proust, Babel, and Mishima, plus a steady stream of current production, within the orbit of the English reading public. From Edgar Wallace to Dorothy Sayers and Agatha Christie, detective stories flourished throughout the period, and thrillers by Rafael Sabatini, Percival Wren, Dornford Yates, and others of that ilk were not in short supply. We note that even writers for the "high" culture (John Buchan, C. Day Lewis, and Graham Greene, for examples) often wrote on the side for the "low" one.

Unified more by personal acquaintance than by formal principles was a curiously temporary band of young men, mostly poets, who clustered together at Oxford during the 1930s. Their "leader" was W. H. Auden; their numbers included Stephen Spender, Cecil Day Lewis, Christopher Isherwood, Rex Warner, and Louis MacNeice. They were neither of the Bloomsbury crowd nor wholly alien to it in spirit, being (more or less in this order) bright, Marxist, Freudian, Christian, homosexual, jocose, and salvation-minded. Their writing was often jazzy, topical, and irreverent; it was always entertaining and versatile. Auden and Isherwood wrote a couple of poetical morality plays (*The Dog beneath the Skin*, 1935; *The Ascent of F6*, 1936); Auden and MacNeice a poetical travelogue, *Letters from Iceland*, 1937.[10] Spender, Day Lewis, Auden, and MacNeice published poetical collections of their own. Isherwood wrote sketches of foreign travel, including a series of stories about pre-Hitler Berlin; they became well known as the basis for the musical comedy and later the movie *Cabaret*. Warner was known for his semiallegorical novels in the manner of Kafka. They were all leftish during the 1930s, and (like an immense number of assorted radicals, liberals, and men of general good will throughout the world) supported the Spanish republic with almost religious fervor against its fascist aggressors. Auden's poem "Spain," published in 1937, is one of the most vigorous and militant poems of political dedication ever written. But when the world war broke out just two years later, Auden was already in America, where he sat out the war in relative comfort, becoming in the process a Christian tinged with the new existential philosophy and an American citizen. Just what was involved in Auden's apparent shifts of political and poetical character cannot readily be told. He was a subtle as well as a sensitive man, who regularly rewrote his early poetry in the light of his later convictions. Religious impulses were always strong within him, and he might well have argued that his changes were more apparent than real. In any event, the group within which he had played so large a part quickly disintegrated

10. *Letters from Iceland* merits more than passing notice; its combination of acrobatic poetry, travelogue information, informal diary, impudent satire, and general youthful high spirits, all illustrated with attractively amateurish photographs, is good evidence that poetry needn't be solemn or sublime. Sharp, intelligent fun has a place too.

and split up into its individual elements. They were able and interesting young men; but somehow they seemed to promise much more when they were a group during the thirties than they were able to perform as separate individuals thereafter. Perhaps, having looked at one Bloomsbury, they had taken a distaste for becoming another (SFR, I.3).

Picasso's *Man Smoking a Pipe* (1911) shows the sort of problem faced by English art lovers in the early days of modernism. Cubism shattered the surface of the "real" world, and with it all the old criteria based on "imitation." Instead of trying to act as a window on the world, the painting now set before its viewer a self-defined and self-limited structure of spatial relationships. Perhaps looking at these very new pictures would have been easier if English eyes had been better trained on the sort of intricate abstract design that ancient Irish monks imposed on the letters of the alphabet when they illuminated manuscripts like the Book of Kells.

No picture can represent the full nastiness of trench warfare on the western front, 1914–1918. Like the terror of violent death, the presence of mud and filth was inescapable. Men lived like rats amid the stench of death; and the feeling of heavy, hopeless futility in the face of a war machine that ground up young men steadily, unstoppably, senselessly, was as oppressive as the physical hardships themselves. The scene is the first battle of the Somme, July 1916—a battle which was lost on the very first day yet dragged on for four more agonizing months.

The bombing of London city by the German air force during the winter of 1940–1941 was too vast and complicated an operation to be represented in a single picture. High above the blacked-out city, squadrons of German bombers came under attack by batteries of anti-aircraft artillery. Almost lost in the dark and the distance, the planes could be traced from the ground mainly by their erratic, twisting vapor trails. Exploding anti-aircraft shells, looming barrage balloons, and the streaks of tracer bullets added to the chaos in the skies, while lurid fire, thudding bomb blasts, shattering glass, and collapsing masonry marked the devastation on the ground. At the time, it must have seemed the ruin could not be more complete. After decades of reconstruction the losses, though still serious, began to look less apocalyptic.

St. Michael's in Coventry was constructed in the fourteenth and fifteenth centuries, and became a cathedral church in 1918. Its lofty spire and pure Gothic style made it a priceless national treasure till, on 14 November 1940, the German air force bombed the entire structure to a hollow shell. The new cathedral was built right next to the ruins of the old one, joined to them by a porch and making dramatic use of the gaunt ruins as part of the new cathedral's lofty spatial effects.

The problem with the immense new dam across the Thames below London is that 99 percent of the time it is not only useless, it could (unless specially designed) impede the flow of river traffic into and out of one of the world's busiest ports. But for the occasional day when the North Sea backs up the estuary and threatens to drown all the low-lying parts of London, the new dam will raise a protective shield worth many times over its vast cost. Perhaps someday something of the same order will be created at Venice, where the need is even greater.

(Facing page) For the most part, London remains, as it has always been, a relatively low-built and conservatively designed city. But the visitor to central London will soon find the London Post Office Tower and Restaurant turning up on his horizon—spiky, aggressively functional, and curiously useful in orienting oneself amid the maze of streets. It stands in the little borough of Marylebone, forming the nub of the micro-link telephone network there. London's general post office is several miles to the east on Newgate Street, not far from St. Paul's cathedral.

18

World War II and After (1939–   )

The collapse of Poland under thunderous blows from Nazi Germany and Soviet Russia (September 1939) was followed by an ominous silence that on the western front lasted more than six months. During that lull, Russia and Germany managed to strengthen their strategic positions in two peripheral theaters. By invading Finland over the winter of 1939–1940, Russia strengthened the defenses of Leningrad; by capturing Norway in April 1940, Germany forestalled an allied beach head in the north. But along the main western front, stretching from Switzerland to the channel, there was practically no action at all. Behind massive defensive fortifications, known from the engineer who designed them as the Maginot line, French and British troops awaited a German attack. With her own naval strength and that of her allies, Britain could effectively blockade Germany; and Neville Chamberlain clung to a forlorn belief that the war would be short because the Nazis would presently "see reason." Besides, all the lessons of World War I seemed to point toward the supremacy of defense; thus the allies were content to lie low behind their tangled network of entrenchments, pillboxes, tank traps, and mine fields. But fortunately the British aircraft industry continued to tool up its factories and train its workers for mass production of fighters and bombers; only in this field were the British comparable in strength to their enemies, and aircraft were to be the major weapons of the new war.

WAR AND A WARRIOR

Long awaited, the Nazi attack burst suddenly in May of 1940, and it was over-whelming. Waves of dive bombers blasted holes in the allied defenses, through which poured columns of German tanks, the heavily armored and supremely mobile panzer divisions. Close behind the assault tanks followed fleets of trucks loaded with fuel, ammunition, repairmen, and replacement crews; once on the move, the panzer divisions never had to stop. Their long fingers reached out across the countryside, tearing enemy armies to shreds and leaving the pieces to be picked up later. They broke through Holland, Belgium, and Luxembourg to the north of the main Maginot line, drove the British Expeditionary Force back on the channel, and plunged southward irresistibly toward Paris, which they entered triumphantly on June 14. The French government promptly resigned, to be replaced by one under Pierre Laval and Philippe Pétain; and a week later the French signed an armistice, actually a treaty of surrender, with the Germans. Meanwhile the British fought fiercely and against heavy odds to extricate their troops from the Continent. Dunkirk was the port where they congregated; and to Dunkirk came a flotilla of naval vessels, small private boats, excursion craft, ferries, anything that could carry men. The RAF did what it could to fly cover, and though the ground troops cursed its inadequacy, the fact that nearly 350,000 men managed to get out indicates that it did a pretty good job. But those men left behind their artillery, their tanks, all their heavy equipment. Dunkirk was a little success on the fringe of a giant catastrophe. Meanwhile, Mussolini, seeing his chance to get a bit of the spoils, joined the war against England. But on the home front there was a spot of counterbalancing good news. Neville Chamberlain, discredited by his standing policy of appeasement and unpreparedness, was replaced as prime minister (10 May) by Winston Churchill.

Politically, Churchill had always been a maverick conservative, mistrusted by his own party without being much admired by any of the others. He had taken responsibility for the Gallipoli disaster of 1915 (above, p. 457), which was a heavy burden; he had earned the hostility of labor because of his attitudes during the general strike of 1926. When not in public office, he earned his living as a journalist; and this, though he was a member of the distinguished family made famous in the eighteenth century by the duke of Marlborough (above, p. 268), helped give him a somewhat flighty reputation.[1] He was not in fact a profound social thinker, not a supreme military strategist, not an impeccable administrator. But in the dark days of 1940–1941, he was the man of the hour because he was a fighter and a superb articulator of fighting moods. No matter that he was also a bit of an actor; most great national leaders are. His speeches had the force, the impetus, the crushing directness of hammer blows.

---

1. His mother, it is to be observed, was American; and his father, Lord Randolph Churchill, had a reputation of his own for erratic political judgments.

"Come, then," he told an audience in Manchester [27 January 1940]; "let us to the task, to the battle, to the toil—each to our part, each to our station. Fill the armies, rule the air, pour out the munitions, strangle the U-boats, sweep the mines, plough the land, build the ships, guard the streets, succour the wounded, uplift the downcast, and honor the brave. . . . There is not a week, nor a day, nor an hour to lose."

The power of these cumulative monosyllables, the force of their short rhythms and strong repetitions, was almost physical. Churchill's invective against the Axis leaders was beyond praise as well. When he called Hitler "a bloodthirsty little guttersnipe" or growled his famous warning to Mussolini that "the mills of the gods grind slow, but they grind ex*ceed*ing small," his contempt was blistering and his menace tangible. He was also totally dedicated to the war; and his conservatives often put into effect, for the sake of the war effort, measures they would have been quick to denounce in peacetime as "socialistic."

AN ARMADA IN THE AIR

From May of 1940 to June of 1941, Britain stood essentially alone against the German machine, protected by her navy and her air force. Like Napoleon before him, Hitler massed troops and assembled invasion vessels along the channel; but he could confront the British navy only if he could gain unchallenged control of the air, and this the Royal Air Force undertook to deny him. The ensuing "Battle of Britain" was not quite the David-and-Goliath struggle that it has been represented. Spitfire was superior and Hurricane equal to the best of the German fighter planes; many of the German bombers, though deadly at short range, could not operate effectively several hundred miles from home base. Every German plane shot down over Britain was a total loss, the pilot captured, the machine lost for good; whereas British pilots who parachuted to earth could generally be returned to combat, and damaged planes could be repaired or cannibalized for needed spare parts. Meanwhile, the aircraft builders of Britain worked themselves far beyond the point of blear-eyed exhaustion to provide replacements; and a heroic little group of flyers took to the air again and again, long after their faces were twitching and their hands shaking from battle fatigue. Finally, the British enjoyed a special technical advantage in the use of radar, by means of which they could spot enemy planes approaching England long before they crossed the coastline. Thus the defending squadrons could be scrambled aloft at the last minute, at the exact spot where they were needed. The Germans had some radar of their own, but it was not as good as the British radar, and they could not use it as effectively.

Yet for all this, the outcome of the Battle of Britain turned in good part on a series of lucky accidents. In its first stages, the air war was fought almost entirely between the two air forces; the Germans bombing British air fields and trying to destroy fighter planes in the air. But one night (24 August 1940) some German pilots got lost in the darkness and bombed London, causing some casualties: the British bomber command retaliated against Berlin, which Hitler had sworn to protect at all costs. Enraged at the civilian casualties in Berlin (which in fact were almost as accidental as those in London), Hitler ordered a shift in targeting from airbases to cities. There were many civilian casualties and enormous property loss in the raids that started September 7 and continued, whenever weather permitted, for the next two and a half months. But the attacks on English air bases largely ceased, just at the moment when (if the Germans had known it) they were on the point of success. Given a few days' respite, RAF regrouped and reorganized itself; the German high command supposed their foemen had been eliminated as an effective force, and on September 15 launched a giant daylight raid against London, without even the precaution of diversionary attacks. They were met by swarms of British fighters, who disrupted their formations and drove them in disorder back across the channel with heavy losses, losses at the most conservative estimate double those of the British. The tide had turned; and though the German air force continued to bomb British cities by night, Hitler within a month canceled his plans for invasion.

WAR BY HARASSMENT

From September 1940 to May 1941, the German air force steadily, systematically, with all the strength at its disposal, bombed English towns. Most of the attacks were directed against London, and they did terrible damage to the old city. The most deadly weapons were fire bombs, some equipped with an explosive component to discourage fire wardens from approaching them too boldly. As each was no bigger than a bottle of wine, thousands could be, and were, dropped over London quite indiscriminately. There was no possible way of aiming them. Many of the bigger bombs had delayed-action fuses of terrifying complexity which made the moment of explosion completely unpredictable; to the extent they could be aimed, they were aimed at communication centers, transportation hubs, major junctions of sewer lines. Fires above ground and explosions under ground rocked the city night and day. Pillars of smoke and piles of rubble were everywhere. On the night of December 29, St. Paul's stood, shaking, battered, but miraculously erect, in a sea of fire that stretched as far as the eye could see. Many Londoners sought shelter in the subways, where they found nauseous and disgusting conditions, but temporary safety; others hid in bomb shelters put up in the back yard, under railway trestles, or in cellars, where all too often they were buried under mountains of collapsing rubble. Thousands were killed outright, more thousands wounded or mutilated; three years of war would pass before the enemy killed as many of Britain's armed forces as he had killed of her civilians. But London was too big, tough, and resilient to be bombed into submission. The "blitz" was a terrible experience for the city, and one shouldn't imagine spunky little cockneys waking up after each night's destruction with a brave smile and a quip on their lips. Life in the embattled city was grim, bitter, ignoble; people crowded together in constant terror of their lives lost the last shreds of human dignity. But Hitler did not have the massive bomb power which would have obliterated London completely, as the British in February of 1945 would utterly obliterate the city of Dresden in a storm of fire.

Realizing the futility of bombing London further, the Nazis shifted the brunt of their attacks to provincial cities. Coventry in Warwickshire was an important center of the aircraft industry; on November 14, the Germans carried out against it what it was becoming fashionable to call a "saturation raid." The effect on a relatively small town was devastating; in addition to the cathedral, most of the shops and homes were destroyed, the population seemed stunned and demoralized. Yet the crucial element was the aircraft factories; and though most of their roofs were torn off or collapsed, the machinery within was little damaged (SFR, I.11). Workers returned, swathed in greatcoats and heavy boots, to stand in the open air before their humming lathes and automatic drills; within six weeks, production was back to normal. Other towns, like Bristol, Plymouth, Liverpool, Glasgow, and Hull, suffered terribly from the raids; for in London, when one neighborhood was bombed out, people could get pretty readily to another, but these smaller towns could be obliterated, to all intents and purposes, overnight. Still, the loss of one town or another could not bring England to her knees; and in an ultimate access of meanness, the Nazis set about a "Baedeker's tour" of England. Their bombers went from one cathedral town or beauty spot to another, from Exeter to Bath to Norwich to York, wrecking what they could. The raids were said to be reprisals for a British raid on Lübeck; but they went on long after the idea of reprisal had faded from view. They did nothing whatever to make the British think of surrender.

On the contrary. In the first six months of 1941, the government shipped 114,000 troops, including the country's only armored division, away from the homeland, around the Cape of Good Hope, and all the way to Egypt, where they would be in position to defend, not only Egypt and the Suez Canal, but the oil fields of the Middle East. To strip the country thus of its strongest ground forces must have seemed an act of boldness verging on folly; but Churchill judged the navy and air force to be capable of defending the homeland. By putting their armor into combat in the North African desert against the German tank expert Rommel, the British quickly learned their own weaknesses. Their first tanks were badly underpowered and undergunned; and they were terribly vulnerable to the German 88-millimeter cannon, which were generally used for anti-aircraft batteries, but could be leveled to serve as anti-tank artillery as well. Gradually, but only gradually, British tank designers learned what was needed; in the later stages of the war, British tanks were as good as any. Meanwhile, the war in North Africa seesawed back and forth, a war of maneuver and supply in which neither side seemed capable of striking a decisive blow.

Another source of anxiety was the German submarine campaign against British shipping in the sea lanes of the north Atlantic. The new U-boats were far more efficient than those of World War I; they moved faster, stayed submerged longer, and were often armed with deadly automatic mines as well as torpedoes. Early in 1941, losses to submarines became so heavy that Churchill had to prohibit publication of the statistics; they encouraged the Germans and dismayed Britishers who could feel, all too intimately, the shrinkage of the national food supply. But here too technology came to Britain's aid. Improved sonar devices made it possible to detect the submarines underwater; destroyer escorts equipped with powerful depth charges could then destroy them subsurface. Aircraft operating from small carriers could patrol the waters around convoys; they too had only to sight a submarine to be able to destroy it. Gradually the submarine menace came under control.

WARS ACROSS THE WORLD

Meanwhile, during the last part of 1941, two earth-shaking events completely upset the balance of power and gave the war a wholly new shape. On June 22, Nazi Germany abruptly and without declaration of war invaded Soviet Russia; and on December 7, Japanese naval air forces, attacking also without warning, destroyed the American fleet at its base in Pearl Harbor, Hawaii. Both attacks were crushingly successful in the short run, and the Japanese action had immediate disastrous consequences for the British Empire in the east, where Malaysia (including Singapore) was quickly overrun, Burma was invaded, and the Japanese stood ready to mount an attack on India itself. But in the long run both the invasion of Russia and the direct involvement of America in the war were major mistakes for the Axis. Russia proved much tougher for Hitler to conquer than he had supposed; and the power of America's industrial machine, once harnessed to the needs of war, overwhelmed the Axis powers beneath a hail of bombs and bullets.

These changes, however, were slow in making themselves felt, and 1942 was a very anxious year for the allied cause. Hitler, having been turned back at the gates of Moscow in late 1941, mounted a furious drive during the fall of 1942 across southern Russia toward the giant industrial city of Stalingrad. There, as winter winds swept across the steppes, Russian armies stood and fought through the ruined streets, gutted buildings, and in the very cellars, with spades and grenades and bayonets, till they had cut off and starved into surrender an entire army of invading Germans. Almost at the same time, the British army in Egypt, given newer, stronger tanks, and a dynamic, theatrical commander in General Bernard Montgomery, outfought the troops of Rommel at El Alamein, saving Egypt and the Suez, and forcing the Germans back through Libya toward their base in Tunisia. But this time the retreating Germans had a new enemy to confront; within a week after the final victory at El Alamein, a large force of British and American troops landed at Casablanca, Oran, and Algiers along the North African coastline. Consolidating their positions, they pressed east while Montgomery's veterans pushed west. The Germans fought skillfully and with great tenacity, but within six months they had been pushed out of Africa, and the allies, under the leadership of General Eisenhower, were in a position to assault, first Sicily, and then Italy itself. Simultaneously American naval power in the Pacific cracked the hard shell of Japanese strength in the decisive battle of Midway (3–6 June 1942); and as the Russian armies, victorious at Stalingrad, started their long push westward, it was possible to sense that the tide of war had definitely turned, that the Axis was everywhere on the defensive.

During the last three years of the war Britain definitely became a junior partner in a struggle that was being waged between the superpowers. She could not begin to match the quantity of Russian manpower or the industrial immensity of the United States. Yet her contributions to the final victory were far from negligible. British and dominion troops made up a large section of the army which advanced with agonizing slowness up the Italian peninsula, crushing in the process the miserable Mussolini. British raiders fought in Burma, and British heavy bombers struck, in ever-more-powerful raids, at German industrial centers. Most important of all, Britain herself became a staging area from which thousands of allied troops would pour across the channel, starting on D-Day, 6 June 1944, to attack German occupation forces in France, and ultimately to penetrate the German heartland. In these tremendous events, General Montgomery and the British Second Army played a major role, first anchoring the northern end of the allied line, and then, in a swift and daring sweep, driving forward to liberate most of Belgium and the Netherlands.

LAST FLARE-UPS AND EXPLOSIONS

Most people, by the winter of 1944, expected the regime of Hitler to collapse at any moment; and indeed, there were plots against Hitler among the generals, one of which cost the life of Rommel, the former German tank commander in North Africa. But a tough, tightly controlled regime like that of the Nazis does not collapse easily; and the Germans still had a couple of nasty surprises left for the allies. Two of these were technical in nature. In August of 1944, the Germans started to fire small, unmanned, jet-powered flying bombs at England. They carried a powerful warhead and flew at low altitudes but very fast until they ran out of fuel; then they dove to earth and exploded. Obviously they could not be aimed at a specific target. Some of them could be intercepted by fighters, others shot down by antiaircraft, still others tangled in barrage balloons. But enough of them reached London to damage further that already damaged city and to create a grisly number of casualties. Unlike earlier incendiaries, V-1's, as they came to be called, were not broadcast by thousands over the city; unlike the blockbusters of 1940–1941, they did not collapse entire buildings, except just at the point of impact. But around their point of impact, they blew out windows for a distance of a quarter mile, showering people indiscriminately with slivers of deadly flying glass. Then in September came a second generation of rockets, known as V-2; instead of buzzing along in the atmosphere, these larger and more fearful missiles rose in an arc and dove to earth faster than the speed of sound. They gave no warning because they made no noise; they could not possibly be defended against. They simply blew; one was dead before one knew that anything had happened. Had they had atomic warheads, the second World War would have ended with the victory of Hitler. As it was, much allied airpower had to be devoted to bombing launching pads in France and development centers at Peenemünde and Swinemünde in Pomerania.

Another technical threat that worried the allied command was German development of the jet engine. The fastest propeller-driven planes flew at about 400 miles per hour; jets could do 600 easily. Though Commander Frank Whittle of the RAF had developed an early jet engine, development lagged in Britain and America; the Germans were the first to fly a jet-powered combat plane, and its superior potential was obvious at once. Had they been able to get these planes into production and put any number of them in the air, they could certainly have dominated the skies again, and given the war an entirely different turn. To prevent this, the allies assiduously bombed the factories where the new planes were being assembled and managed to prevent most of them from taking to the air. Finally, German physics laboratories were just reaching, during the last years of the war, toward discoveries which would make possible the creation of the atomic bomb. Had they not driven away so many of their best scientists, starting with Einstein,[2] they might very well have wound up possessing the most powerful arsenal in the world, along with the most advanced delivery systems. Though badly hurt in late 1944, the Germans were extremely dangerous foemen; they had everything to gain by prolonging the war, if only by a few months.

Accordingly, during the deep winter of 1944 they assembled the last scrapings of their manpower—wounded veterans, young boys, service troops, old men— to mount a last desperate assault on allied lines in the Ardennes area of Belgium and northern France. The Battle of the Bulge (December 1944) was so called because it wedged a big bulge or salient into the area where the British and American sectors of the front met, near Bastogne. To strengthen their western offensive, the Germans stripped men from their battered and tattered armies in the east, leaving the Russians with an open road through Poland and east Prussia.

2. Professor Niels Bohr, the Danish physicist, was smuggled out of his Nazi-dominated homeland by a daring flight crew who nearly killed their precious cargo by flying him too high without adequate oxygen. Transferred from England to the United States with the vital calculations he had managed to bring along, Bohr became a crucial member of the research team at the University of Chicago, out of which grew the Manhattan Project at Los Alamos, New Mexico.

But all was to no avail; the allied lines in Belgium bent but did not break. And then in the spring of 1945 the allied armies began converging all at once on Berlin. Hitler fought to the end, finally committing suicide in a command bunker deep under the rubble of Berlin. On 4 May 1945, the German armies started to surrender, and on May 8 (V-E Day), the war in Europe was officially over.

REVELATIONS

Two frightful revelations in the immediate aftermath of the European war put a period to the struggle just concluded and inaugurated a new era. As the allied troops poured across German territory, they discovered at Buchenwald, Auschwitz, and Belsen concentration camps and machinery for the mass murder of the "inferior" races which corresponded to nothing in the worst nightmares of the human race. The systematic extermination of entire populations under circumstances of inconceivable bestiality seemed to open an abyss within every concept of civilized human nature. Propaganda during World War I, with its stories of raped nuns and bayoneted babies, had been exploded as untrue and left men cynical. But the evidence of the concentration camps was infinitely more horrible, and it could not be denied. The evidence was ghastly beyond expression. In one sense the concentration camps (where not only Jews but Gypsies, Poles, Russians, communists, dissidents, and "inferiors" of every breed were gassed en masse and burned in giant ovens) validated the entire war. It had been fought against an inhuman regime; the end of the struggle disclosed how much more inhuman it had been than anyone dared imagine. But the concentration camps also gave serious-minded people good reason to think of the black iniquities of human nature as such. They destroyed (if it still needed destroying) the last shred of complacent illusion about modern civilization and modern culture, making plain how easily the conventions of a courteous and kindly existence can collapse into a heart of primeval, barbaric darkness. More than 6 million souls perished in the camps.

Equally ominous for the future was the last great explosion of the dying war, the detonation over Hiroshima, Japan, on 6 August 1945, of the world's first atomic bomb. From one point of view, this was simply a single step forward in the long development of more powerful destructive machines. But so immense an explosive force, carried by a single airplane and released by a single hand, represented not just a change in measure or degree, but a whole new order of human violence. Even those who took part in creating it and were convinced that by shortening the war it would save millions of human lives were awed by the hideous potential of the bomb. Since the Renaissance, men had been steadily, confidently working to gain command of the forces of nature, supposing they would and could be used for human welfare. Suddenly, on 6 August 1945, the climactic step was taken—and its effect was to put the human race everywhere at the mercy of that "human" nature which had just shown its most monstrous face at Buchenwald, Auschwitz, and Belsen. No war in history ever ended more dramatically or more enigmatically than World War II.

THE ENGINEERING OF HOPE

Socially, the effect of the war on Britain was profound, far deeper than the effect of World War I. Because it was so largely a technological struggle, fought with intricate equipment made in factories and laboratories, the prestige and authority of the working and technically educated classes were enormously increased. The trade unions had proved themselves indispensable; their members quite naturally wanted more housing, more pensions, more vacations, more education for their kids. They maintained little tolerance for the caste system which in earlier days reserved all the good jobs for those who wore the old school tie or who spoke with the cultivated accents of Oxford and Cambridge. Besides, the war had been a great mixer of social classes. During the early days of the conflict, when massive air raids were feared, great numbers of children were moved out of cities and into relative safety in the country. Not many of them stayed throughout the war, but most of them learned at least a little about the possibilities of life outside their familiar industrial slums. At the height of the war, conscription of manpower, and womanpower as well, became an urgent necessity; that too had the effect of homogenizing the population. Not many heiresses drove tractors or planted turnips, but some people got to see what life was like for "the others." Thousands of people, rich and poor, whose houses had been bombed out had to find other quarters; English folk moved about during the war more than they had ever done before. In the Home Guard, in the Air Warden services, and above all under the fearful stress of the blitz, people got to know one another in different ways, and more closely, than the caste system had ever allowed them to do before. Ernie Bevin, burly and truculent head of the Trades Unions Congress who had begun life as a drayman (wagon driver), found that when it was a question of getting the job done, he saw eye to eye with Sir Winston Churchill, scion of the duke of Marlborough. Under pressure of war needs, labor gave unhesitatingly of its energies; factory workers often had to be restrained from exhausting themselves, in the face of an emergency, lest they be drained of energy for weeks to come. Employers too learned to abate their privileges and consult on managerial problems with their workers; the more farsighted of them realized, as Disraeli had realized before them, that in revolutionary times it is the best part of conservatives to direct where they can avoid opposing.

Partly under the impulse of thinking like this, partly out of genuine concern that the working class have a stake in winning the war, Churchill's government sponsored the production by Sir William Beveridge[3] of a major report on Britain's future, which appeared on the first of December 1942. Contemporaneous with the battles of El Alamein and Stalingrad, the Beveridge Report was almost as important in marking a turning point in the war. It proposed to unify almost all the existing health, welfare, and pension plans and to supplement them till they constituted a single system protecting the working folk of England against destitution "from the cradle to the grave." It was, in effect, a blueprint for the modern welfare state; and while most of the Tories who had sponsored the report were appalled by its implications, they could not resist its appeal. It was read world-wide; it stirred immense hopes; it confirmed the convictions of millions that they had a personal stake in the war. It was so important a document that Hitler strictly forbade his propagandists even to mention it. The popularity of the Beveridge Report, and the depth of the feelings it aroused, were very largely responsible for the crushing political defeat of Winston Churchill in the first postwar election (July 1945). He had been a great war leader; the nation was, and remained, passionately grateful to him. It was his initiative which had produced the Beveridge Report. But to implement it someone else, almost anyone else, would be required;[4] the Labor alternative was Clement Attlee, and he won a major victory at the polls.

REBUILDING BRITAIN

For six years (1945–1951) Attlee presided over a Labor government which did its best to foster a bold, if inevitably partial, venture at economic recovery. Things certainly went better than after the first World War, when "homes fit for heroes" turned into a bitter mockery for thousands of veterans who could find neither homes nor jobs. The wholesale bombings of World War II, without any such intent, turned out to have done a first-rate job of slum clearance; new flats and rows of semidetached houses, uninspired architecturally but practical and comfortable for folks who had known worse, filled the obliterated areas of towns and spread out into the suburbs. Churches and public buildings were restored, even when in the first awful moments they had seemed utterly unredeemable.

3. Sir William had been director of the London School of Economics and Social Science; more importantly, he was in the direct spiritual tradition of those nineteenth-century utilitarian philosophers who did such yeoman service in reforming English legal and administrative procedures during the first years of Victoria. See above, p. 379.

4. Emotionally, Churchill was a wider and more generous man than he could ever be intellectually; he loved his people, and he could draw forth their energies as could no one else. But he did not know their grievances, their intimate discontents; no more than once or twice in his life had he ever taken a bus or ridden in a subway. After World War I, when his political career was in a shambles, when he had no job or prospect of any, Churchill moved with his family to Cannes in southern France, where he spent his time painting. It was not the sort of experience to give a man sympathetic understanding of the need for unemployment insurance.

Oxford and Cambridge remained the centerpiece of the intellectual establishment;[5] and the provincial semi-vocational universities created during the nineteenth century (known from their prevailing architecture as "red brick" universities) also remained. But alongside them was created a new class of universities (known from *their* prevailing architecture as "white tile" institutions), which provided space for growing numbers of lower-middle-class and working-class students. Oxford and Cambridge themselves were much democratized by the creation of government scholarships, which brought into the hallowed halls many students from previously excluded classes. (A disturbing tendency which threatened to counteract Britain's new educational accomplishments was the so-called "brain drain." Attracted by higher salaries and more impressive research facilities, thousands of Britain's best scientific minds started during the 1950s and 1960s to emigrate either to America or to the dominions. Emigration was always a traditional way to climb the British social ladder; but the "brain drain" was quite different. The highly trained people Britain needed to keep if she were to revitalize her industry were leaving her shores in droves, most of them never to return. The drain would never be completely stopped; but by making special efforts to keep key personnel, British industries, in collaboration with the government, did something to slow it down.) A policy of national health insurance was installed and, despite many dire forebodings, turned out to work reasonably well, at least under conditions of prosperity. Those who could pay for private care continued to do so; but the National Health doctor was available to submerged groups of the population who had never known proper medical care before. In short, the Beveridge plan was put into effect; and for a while British exports of motorcars, aircraft engines, and motion pictures, as well as the traditional textiles and steel products, kept the national economy·buoyant.

DROPPING THE EMPIRE

As long as Germany, Italy, and Japan were prostrate or only slowly building up their economies, Britain held her position among the world's leaders. Piece by piece, of course, the British Empire had to be let go. It cost too much to maintain, and its maintenance was inconsistent with the principle of self-determination that the British had made one of their war aims. In 1947, after trying to get both Moslems and Hindus into a single state, the British government declared two separate dominions to be in existence, Hindu India and Moslem Pakistan, and tossed both onto the stormy seas of independence. About the same time New Zealand and Burma became independent, while Malaysia and Singapore were

5. The British penchant for allowing informal family connections to twine vinelike through and over official bodies is well illustrated in the academic establishment, where Huxleys, Darwins, Stephenses, and Trevelyans (to name no more) are intertwined in happy profusion. Sir Noel Annan, in a 1956 article titled "The Intellectual Aristocracy," was one of the first to draw explicit attention to this quiet, potent fact.

not long in following suit. Except for Hong Kong and a group of mostly tiny islands scattered across the vast Pacific, that substantially liquidated the British Empire in the orient. More severe complications attended the granting of independence to Britain's former possessions in Africa, and it can't be said, as of this writing, that the problems have been fully solved. Rhodesia (or, as it now is, Zimbabwe) has been much in the public eye; but the present situation in Uganda does not represent much of a triumph for democratic or any other civilized values. In letting go of their empire, the British had successes and failures; but they often had to act under acute pressure, with dwindling resources. The oldest and most bitter of their problems they still have not come close to solving: that, patently, is the question of a united Ireland. But elsewhere Little Britain was not long in becoming an accomplished fact. Even Churchill, when he returned for a last four years in power (1951–1955), had little to recommend to his people except economy and retrenchment.

The problems of living in a world only half committed to the rule of law were highlighted by two simultaneous crises in the fall of 1956. In the first, a many-sided, strangely halfhearted, and inconclusive struggle broke out over the Suez Canal. It was brought on by Egyptian president Gamel Abdul Nasser's nationalizing of the canal in retaliation for the canceling of American credits toward building the Aswan Dam across the Nile. The threat of closing the canal did not much bother distant America, but terrified England and France, who incited Israel to storm and take the Sinai. But the United States and the United Nations, along with influential bodies of public opinion in England and France, denounced the action as lawless. Invading troops withdrew in embarrassed confusion, while the British prime minister, Sir Anthony Eden, resigned in something close to disgrace. The canal was blocked for about a year, but ultimately reopened; the damage done to the moral prestige of England and France was not diminished by the fact that, in the second of these crises, the USSR crushed a popular revolt in Hungary. Though thousands were killed and hundreds of thousands forced into exile, Russia endured not even the mildest of rebukes. Evidently international law was starting to mean very different things, depending on where it was violated and who did the violating.

When George VI died in 1952, his daughter Elizabeth became queen, and the coincidence of names gave rise to predictions of "a new Elizabethan age." So far as that implied another Sir Francis Drake, another William Shakespeare, it hasn't come to pass. Elizabeth II, a respected lady, has presided over no great outpouring of public confidence, no flareup of literary imagination, and least of all over any bold revival of Britain's economic energies.

DEPRESSION

For after the early postwar years, the British economy fell on the leanest of lean times. Many explanations have been offered for the declining rate of production, the shrinkage of exports, the nagging problem of unemployment. The power of unions to obstruct and the overeagerness of government to regulate industry, uncertain and wavering tax policies, and the heavy pressure of foreign competition have been blamed for the slowdown; so have the costs of a welfare state, enormous growth of governmental bureaucracy at the county level, and the increasing reluctance of people to undertake productive work (as opposed to teaching, administering, entertaining, and providing luxuries or services). "Not enough workers" is the simple formula. Statistics can be cited supporting all these diagnoses and a good many others. But one sign that no adequate understanding of the problem has yet been reached is the failure of any political party to generate a convincing plan for dealing with it. A succession of generally able and well-meaning prime ministers representing both major parties has occupied No. 10 Downing Street since Winston Churchill retired for a last round of brandies and cigars. All would have liked nothing better during their terms of office than a decisive upturn in the nation's economic record; none was able to bring it off.[6] Labor was seriously divided between doctrinaire radicals, who were likely to think nationalization the cure for most economic problems, and hardbitten trade-unionists, who when they had negotiated high wages for minimal work took the line "I'm all right, Jack." Conservatives in England as elsewhere spoke much of unleashing the dynamism of private enterprise, but hamstrung themselves by their reluctance to interfere with the dead weight of private privilege. Thus the figures recording England's balance of payments, and consequently her currency reserves, continued steadily negative, while her per capita industrial production slipped from one of the highest to one of the lowest in Europe. Almost all the social diagnosticians agree that major parts of Britain's industrial plant are outmoded while her non-renewable resources, like coal and iron, are depleted to the point where they, and products manufactured with them, can no longer compete on the international market. Whether Mrs. Margaret Thatcher's conservative government will be able to mount the initiatives it has promised is, at the moment of writing (fall 1982) still dubious—though the longer recovery is delayed, the more doubtful it looks.

One potentially important development of the last few years calls for special note: it is the discovery and exploitation of sizable oil fields under the North Sea. With American technology and international capital, this oil supply promises, for a while at least, to make Britain independent of the OPEC cartel. But North Sea oil, like all fossil fuel, is a limited resource. Like France, England before the end of the century will probably be dependent for most of its energy on nuclear generators, some of which are already in place. Probably—it is a guess and no more—her future lies in the direction of small, high-technology enterprises requiring a very skilled work force and only modest amounts of energy

6. Their names, for the record, were Eden, Macmillan, Douglas-Home, Wilson, Callaghan, and Heath; their political complexion was prevailingly conservative. But Harold Wilson, the Labor man, was just as much the victim of circumstances as his conservative predecessors, though he had two gos at the job in 1964 and 1974.

and raw materials. But this obviously means entering some extremely competitive markets. It is possible that England, like France, will find that stripping off the appendages of colonies and possessions will leave her free to develop a more inventive and aggressive economy at home. The challenge is a greater one, and it is likely to be longer sustained, than those mounted by the Spanish in 1588, the French in 1804, or the Germans in 1940; but the tenacious and resourceful people on the little northern island will no doubt be found playing an important role in the world's affairs for years to come.

THE WRITERS WHO WEREN'T

The first World War, which was largely a stupid butchery carried out in the name of political objectives that were contemptible when they were not incomprehensible, produced or at least occasioned an immense flowering of literature, art, and culture generally. The powerful impulses of modernism, first felt around 1910, did not start to fade away till twenty years later; they still have not disappeared completely. During and after the first war, a sense of civilized surfaces being fractured by immense barbaric powers made the ironic stance and dislocated structures of modernism particularly appropriate. By contrast the second World War, being more intelligently waged, and for better ideals better defined, seemed to stimulate far less, and less interesting, literary production. No novel like *Ulysses*, no poem like "The Waste Land" is found in close proximity to World War II. A frequent cry of the age was "Where are all the war poets?" and the glum response had to be that there weren't very many, and they weren't very good.[7] Writers who had been active before the war, if they lived into or through it, as Yeats and Joyce did not, sometimes continued to produce. T. S. Eliot's service as a London air warden may be supposed to speak through section IV of "Little Gidding," the last of the meditative *Four Quartets*. Joyce Cary, an Irish Protestant novelist of enormous energy, published during the early years of the war a trio of related novels (*Herself Surprised, To Be a Pilgrim, The Horse's Mouth*) and during the 1950s another trilogy under the general title of *Prisoner of Grace*. But he was an uneven novelist and, since he was already fifty-three years old when the first novel of the first trilogy was published, hardly qualified as a fresh new voice. Graham Greene, who had written some excellent spy and adventure thrillers before the war, wrote in the course of it an even better one, *The Ministry of Fear* (1943); and "Henry Green" (Henry Vincent Yorke),

7. Robert Graves, who himself wrote nothing about the war, had a theory that poetry was incompatible with the internal combustion engine. It's also possible that the war, being more justifiable, more justified, and maybe even more just than its predecessor, attracted more sympathy from the writers, who channeled their feelings into active service. Most of the "war poets" of the first conflict were in fact bitterly antiwar poets; the problems of writing about a struggle to which one felt some degree of real commitment were greater.

who had written dry, complex comic fictions before the war, wrote a very good one during it, under the brief, compendious title, *Loving* (1945). Evelyn Waugh's gift for satiric comedy, long in evidence, manifested itself in *Put Out More Flags* (1942) before relapsing (with *Brideshead Revisited*, 1945) into pomposity and circumstance.

"George Orwell," the pen name of Eric Arthur Blair, was just coming into his own as a major satirist, with *Animal Farm* (1945) and *Nineteen Eighty-Four* (1949), when tuberculosis cut short his career. His was an authentic new voice of the war years, truculently honest, and accordingly pretty despondent about the future. Radicals like Orwell, who had been disillusioned about Soviet Russia and revolutionary politics in general, had a particularly hard row to hoe during the war. There was a period when criticism of the Soviet Union was considered more unpatriotic than criticism of one's own government.[8] On the other hand, anyone who had followed the twisting and turning of the communist "line" for more than a year or two could hardly help knowing that he was being used by a crude and unscrupulous gang of power politicians. The first result of this discovery was likely to be some bitterness, combined with deep self-questioning. Auden's Greenwich Village existentialism and Christopher Isherwood's California Vedanta provided quietist refuges for individual self-examination. Even John Strachey, once bellwether of the Marxist cause in England, started to proclaim individual moral principles that he would once have denounced as "bourgeois." Meanwhile, C. S. Lewis, long a belligerent controversialist for Christianity, enjoyed fresh accesses of popularity for the witty apologetics of *The Screwtape Letters* (1942); and J. R. R. Tolkien, slowly meditating an entire new world out of his Anglo-Saxon studies, produced in the *Lord of the Rings* tetralogy a cosmos exotic in its coloring but deeply Christian in its structure.[9]

NEW SIMPLICITIES

Dylan Thomas was a fresh new voice who started to be heard during the war; under the impressionistic title of "apocalyptic" poets, he gathered round him a small band of like-minded writers who expressed in violent metaphors, wrenched syntax, and vigorous rhythms a new semireligious version of English romanticism. Their outlook was only semireligious because most of the Apocalyptics

---

8. A particularly ugly event in the history of the war helped to change this climate of opinion. In August of 1944, Russian troops driving west into Poland came within a few miles of Warsaw, and the population there, seeing help within easy reach, rose against the Nazis. Stalin ordered his armies to stop and wait till the Nazis had exterminated the desperate Poles before resuming their advance.

9. Other Christian skirmishers of the period included the novelist, critic, and playwright Charles Williams, Malcolm Muggeridge once of *Punch*, and Dorothy Sayers the mystery writer. The group is miscellaneous, but spiced with imagination and on balance pleasantly free of unction. Perhaps they inherited from Hilaire Belloc and G. K. Chesterton the tradition of defending a forlorn hope with gallantry and gaiety. (See above, p. 449.)

seem to have followed Thomas in assuming a malignant deity, who after appropriate torture was bound to commit the world to Gehenna. Thomas mingled with this mythology a set of deep Freudian images and freewheeling allusions from his heteroclite reading in youth (Egyptology, cowboy fiction, and Anatole France) to produce powerful and orally vital poetry. But the mood, being violent and unstable, was hard to sustain; and Thomas's work had fallen off sharply, in quality as well as quantity, before he died prematurely in 1953.

Before leaving the period of the war proper, we should take note of a major publishing innovation growing out of wartime shortages. Lack of adequate newsprint led to production of large numbers of paperback books under the house name of "Penguin." Paperback books had been standard for years on the Continent; since 1840 the Leipzig house of Tauchnitz had been producing, for sale in continental railroad stations, paperback editions of English authors. Penguins were paperbound pocket books for domestic consumption; they were cheap, as durable as need be, and extremely handy. They sold well, and the publishers promptly expanded them into many fields—translations from the classics, musical scores, histories of art and architecture, book-length political tracts, and anthologies of poetry, as well as the traditional novels. Much of the cost of manufacturing a traditional book goes into the binding; Penguins were harbingers of that flood of paperbacks we now observe, which have transformed the economics of publishing.

Perhaps because complex ironic poetry and intricate symbolic fiction were well established before the war, writers during and directly after it seemed to move toward greater simplicity and directness. In so doing, they could hardly avoid treading in the footsteps of one predecessor or another. The romanticism of Dylan Thomas was noted above; after the war one started to hear from the so-called "angry young men" (John Osborne, John Wain, Kingsley Amis, among others), who expressed in forceful but basically traditional forms the resentments of working-class outsiders looking in. Plays like *Look Back in Anger* (1957) and novels like *Room at the Top* (1957) and *Lucky Jim* (1954) used language and vented attitudes which ruffled for a time the feathers of the extremely genteel; but, being mainly Dickensian in their inspiration, these indignant outbursts did little to alter permanently the course of English fiction. For some years during the 1950s and 1960s, the slow, substantial novels of Sir Charles Snow, essentially Trollopian in their social comment and their sober, middle-class realism, enjoyed considerable popularity. The influence of Joyce continued to be felt in linguistic deformations and games like those devised by novelist Anthony Burgess, poet John Lennon (of Beatles fame), and playwright Tom Stoppard. D. H. Lawrence is the root inspiration for Lawrence Durrell's 1957 *Alexandria Quartet* (four novels, *Justine, Balthazar, Mountolive, Clea*); Marcel Proust makes himself strongly felt behind Anthony Powell's many-volumed, low-keyed *Dance to the Music of Time* (1962–1975). During the fifties and sixties English poets like Donald Davie, Philip Larkin, and Thom Gunn—that group known informally as "the movement"—began writing verse in the restrained and rational vein which they consciously associated with Thomas Hardy. A poetry of limited social commentary isn't necessarily a step backward, but the movement poets contributed at least to a sense of literature marking time.

The arts are not incremental, of course. They are not bound to make "progress" in any particular direction, and it would be absurd to discount able and interesting work simply because it does not innovate in some hitherto untried direction. Hitherto untried directions are pretty scarce these days. But excellent writing in traditional forms and on traditional themes is so frequent, we hardly remark it. For many years now, Elizabeth Bowen, Iris Murdoch, Elizabeth Taylor, Muriel Spark, and Barbara Pym have been producing fiction so strong and sensitive, so witty and accomplished, that only the great volume of it discourages us from using the very highest words of commendation. Nevil Shute, C. S. Forrester, John Fowles, and John Le Carré may not be artists for the ages; but each is a skilled writer, deft, entertaining, and in the short run absorbing. As we enter the modern period, a literary historian is deprived of his two best supports, historical hindsight and the critical consensus. He may have ideas of his own about the important books of his own day, but his is just one man's opinion, not much better, if at all, than anybody else's. If he is, as he should be, an indiscriminate, inquisitive reader, he will be distracted in his judgment by all sorts of delightful but ephemeral or at any rate unpretending material. Daphne du Maurier's *Rebecca* will mingle in his memories with the short stories of Elizabeth Bowen, William Golding's *Lord of the Flies*, Cyril Connolly's *The Unquiet Grave*, the parodies of Max Beerbohm, Geoffrey Scott's enchanting *Portrait of Zelide*. One wouldn't bet one's bottom dollar on any of these books in a literary sweepstakes; but the history of literature is full of dark horses—Donne, for example, or Jane Austen—who after years of neglect came on in the late going to take the roses. If one could foretell which part of our current literary production posterity will find interesting, what dull decades would lie ahead![10]

AN ECLECTIC AGE?

Quite possibly, with the benefit of a few more generations of hindsight, historians will say with perfect assurance that British literature in the last half of the twentieth century showed few striking innovations and no grandiose achievements. For that matter, with possible exceptions for Germany and Latin Amer-

---

10. We shouldn't overlook the cheeky Beatles, who flashed across the pop-music firmament during the early 1960s; before their brash impudence and thudding rhythms many stiff walls of middle-class respectability came tumbling down. That social change may prove more permanent than their musical or literary accomplishments. A dark foretaste of the new society (half collectivist, half hooligan, grungy all the way) had already been offered by Anthony Burgess in *A Clockwork Orange* (1962).

ica, the postwar period throughout the world has not been notable for any major flowering of literary talents, any major extension of the literary potential. A conceivable reason for the dearth could be sought in the flowering of other arts, particularly movies, television, and radio. But it's not clear how this competition works to stifle literature. Even if many, perhaps most, people spend hours before the television set, there are still dozens of reading audiences, from the most vulgar to the most recherché; writers don't stop writing just because they can't all be millionaires *and* Nobelists too. If there is a flagging of invention, commercial circumstances seem like the least convincing of possible explanations.

Thin literary harvests are the more striking because in many respects modern Britain offers the aspect of a cultural bazaar. In painting and sculpture, never before the long suits of British creativity, talents as diverse as Graham Sutherland, Francis Bacon, Reg Butler, Jacob Epstein, Henry Moore, and Barbara Hepworth have achieved international reputations. In ballet and opera, where for decades they had been chiefly onlookers and followers, the British now contribute more richly than almost any other nation. British actors set a standard of excellence, particularly for North Americans. Their strong background in provincial repertory companies may be responsible, but their domination is all but complete. (Whether this is because or in spite of the dilapidation of their movie industry may be disputed.) As for British composers, since Sir Edward Elgar broke the ice, they have multiplied remarkably, both in numbers and prestige. Frederick Delius, Ralph Vaughan Williams, Benjamin Britten, and Sir William Walton provide a background of sustained achievement, on which younger composers are now building or against which they are reacting. Thus Britain is well represented today in fields where she rarely had important exponents before and less pre-eminent in the verbal arts, which were so long her special domain. This isn't necessarily a permanent condition. If, on the other hand, it derives (as one may suspect) from an exhausting of the big themes of traditional literature—the social, sexual, and money relations of people—then the imagination may be a long time renewing its charter.[11]

HIGH FOOLISHNESS: BECKETT

However solemnly one takes these somber considerations, a marginal but tough literature of exhaustion and survival can be observed on the fringe of the generally conservative mainstream. This is not a school but a random assemblage of writers who in different ways have adapted to arid climate and depleted soil; its

11. In a history of England, one may be excused for looking back to the fifteenth and early sixteenth centuries as a single long period of social transition when not only literary but artistic and architectural accomplishment in England sank very low indeed. Quite possibly we have passed through the horrors of our fourteenth century, stretched out for us from the French Revolution to the present, and now confront the diminished vitality and dreariness of an extended fifteenh century.

most commanding figure is the exiled Irish anchorite Samuel Beckett. Born a Protestant in Dublin, Beckett studied philosophy in Trinity College[12] before fleeing Ireland, first for London, then for Paris. During the war he dodged the Gestapo and after, in the solitude of his left-bank hideout, elaborated three semi-detached novels, *Molloy, Malone Dies,* and *The Unnamable.* They were published in French in the late 1940s, and translated into English, largely by the author himself. During the 1950s, his plays *Waiting for Godot* and *Endgame* (both also written in French and translated into English by the author) achieved international success which culminated in the award of the Nobel prize in 1969. Beckett's recurrent, almost obsessive, theme is the imminence of nothingness, the rupture of consciousness. Most of his characters are moribund; many are clinging to the last vestiges of sanity. All they can hold to is the faltering stream of their speech, the monologue of monotonous, oft-rehearsed questions and answers which is the sum of their perishing consciousness. As their hold on experience diminishes, words come slower and harder. *How It Is* (1964) reduces the drama of storytelling to its ultimate minimum. The speaker of this unpunctuated tale is discovered, wallowing face down in a sea of icy muck with a sack of tinned food tied to his neck; he encounters a similar creature whom he names Pim and with whom he communicates after a fashion by clawing him, hitting him over the head, and stabbing him in the buttocks with a can opener. After a while they separate. That makes a three-part story, grotesquely parodying the three parts of your basic novel (boy meets girl, gets girl, loses girl). Beckett is reported to have said that with this piece of writing he had murdered, or tried to murder, the novel. If that is how one sees life, if that is indeed how it is, there is every reason to assassinate, not only the novel, but every other variety of prettification in the world. Still, we observe that Beckett keeps on writing, sometimes wordless little mimes, but never without the most poignant eloquence. His vision of desolation is stripped and cruel; it is, at the same time, painfully funny. He is a tragic clown of almost unbelievable resource. Many readers feel that through him they come to touch something almost unique in modern life, a sense of the sacred.

A TIME TO STOP

The plays of Harold Pinter owe a good deal, especially in their construction, to the example of Beckett; that is, they are anti-action plays. For a long time noth-

---

12. Beckett's philosophical studies focused on the work of Descartes and his followers, especially the Belgian Arnold Geulincx. The fragile, almost accidental, thread by which consciousness retains its relation to matter is a recurrent theme in Beckett's work; the technical name is for this construct "occasionalism," and it leads (among other things) to a passive, inert view of life, oddly incongruous with Beckett's own brisk profusion of activities. A concise critical study of the philosophy has been made by David T. Hesla under the title *The Shape of Chaos* (1971).

ing, or at least nothing sensible, happens on the stage; dialogue repeats itself, rambles, falters, revives pointlessly. But between its aimless and disconnected parts a sense of menace or despair grows and gradually becomes manifest. It is a drama which deliberately fails to explain itself; the characters talk to conceal their thoughts from one another, and the audience comes to sense only gradually the pit of malignancy over which the play has stretched a thin net of dialogue. There's an element of melodrama in Pinter, not to be found in Beckett; people have been more apt to feel he brought them in touch with the nasty than with the holy. Still, he has been a potent influence on the London stage during the 1960s and 1970s, and may yet achieve more. This may well involve breaking away from the somewhat limited "theater of menace" to which hitherto Pinter has confined himself.

Ted Hughes is a poet well outside the "movement" and formally unrelated to Beckett. Yet like Beckett he inhabits a world stripped clean of all the edifying and comforting mythologies. His verse has a hard, unprettified strength about it, a gift for confronting raw existence and the imminent pressure of death; he has an affinity for tough, scrawny animals like crows, crabs, and soggy, enduring bovines. It is a bare, cold poetry, curiously right for readers who in the harsh modern weather want nothing to do with promissory rhetoric. The main consolation to be found in Hughes is his occasional turning, in meditative recollection, to thoughts of the pre-Saxon tribesmen who first worked the rough earth of Yorkshire and now lie buried in it. Interrogation of the entombed ancestors is a frequent feature of modern poetry, as one sees at once from Geoffrey Hill's *Mercian Hymns,* Ted Hughes's *Remains of Elmet,* and Seamus Heaney's tense, searching poems on the bog people. It is altogether fitting that we should end our long tale of England's interwoven history of political, social, and literary development with the latest and newest of her turns, back to the most deeply buried roots in the prehistory of the culture. There is no better place to look for renewal.

Appendix A
British Money and
Measures of Distance

Since 1971, British money has been calculated on the decimal system, with 100 pence to the pound; the pound has fluctuated from a bit more than 2 American dollars to a bit less, whatever dollars may be worth. Before 1971, the pound consisted of 20 shillings, each containing 12 pence, thus 240 pence to the pound. In paper money the change has not been great; 1-, 5-, and 10-pound notes constitute the mass of the bills under both the old and the new systems; nowadays, in addition, 20- and 50-pound notes have been added. But in the smaller coinage the change has been considerable and the simplification remarkable. Most notable is abolition of the shilling, which goes into retirement now with the mark (worth in its day two-thirds of a pound or 13 shillings 4 pence) and the angel (once worth 10 shillings but replaced by the 10-shilling note, now in its turn abolished). The guinea, an oddity of the old currency, amounted to a pound and a shilling; though it has not been minted since 1813, quality products (a suit from a good tailor, a piece of fine

Old	New
1 pound note	1 pound note
10 shilling (half-pound) note	50 pence
5 shilling (crown)	
2 ½ shilling (half crown)	12 pence
2 shilling (florin)	10 pence
1 shilling	5 pence
6 pence	
3 pence	1 penny
2 pence	
1 penny	½ penny
½ penny	
¼ penny	

silver, a rare book) are still generally priced in guineas. Colloquially, a pound used to be a quid, a shilling a bob, sixpence a tanner, a penny a copper. The common signs were £ for pound, s. for shilling, d. for a penny (from Latin *denarius*). A sum would normally be written £2.19.3, i.e., 2 pounds 19 shillings, 3 pence. That is Bloom's budget for 16 June 1904. In new currency, it would be about £2.96d.

What the pound was worth at any point in history is never easy to state. In the first part of the twentieth century, 1 pound equaled about 5 American dollars; but those dollars bought more than twice what 1983 dollars will buy. The value of the pound might be definable in terms of the goods and services it would purchase; but these too vary radically with special circumstances, wars, harvests, and the like. In a loose way, it's clear that money used to be worth much more than it is now. A Saxon penny was the biggest coin in general circulation; four of them would buy a sheep. When in Chapter III it was said that agricultural wages before the plague of 1348 were 2 or 3 pence a day, the point was perhaps not clear that for the farm laborer that meant an annual income of £3 to £4—at the modern ratio, $6 to $8 a year. However incredibly low his standard of living, however much he supplemented his cash income with produce from his own fields, that figure is impossible: the pound must have been worth much more than it is now, perhaps by a factor of several hundred. Hugh Latimer reports that in his day (the early 1500s) it was a common saying, "Oh, he's a rich man, he's worth £500." Probably he means, not fabulously, just comfortably rich; still, it's clear that the pound was a solid sum of money, equal perhaps to 400 or 500 American dollars of the year 1983.

In Jonson's *Alchemist*, Subtle tells Face that as an honest servant he had been a mere "livery-three-pound thrum"—that is, he had his uniform, food, and lodging, plus £3 a year. By cheating on household expenses, he had built up over the years, "a pretty stock, some twenty marks" about £13. Of course, the comic point of all this is the miserable sums involved in the lives of such squalid rascals. Forty pounds a year in independent income (generally rents) was the minimum requirement for a justice of the peace; it was also the sum fixed by King James at which a man could be forced to accept knighthood. It marked the threshold of gentry, and we must multiply it by 150 or 200 to get an equivalent in dollars. In 1661 that good bourgeois Samuel Pepys, just after he began working for the navy, calculated his worth at a modest £650; five years later, he was worth more than £6,000 and his annual income was about £3,000—cause for complacency. Of course, he was working for most of this income. Pepys was a rising and would become a very important official; but he never achieved a title or even knighthood because the smell of commerce had never been washed from his money by possession of land.

On a far humbler level, Joseph Andrews (in Fielding's novel, published 1742) worked as a footman in the house of Lady Booby for £8 a year; but he got his room, board, and livery in addition, plus the occasional tip. Among the comfortable classes again, Mr. Bennet of Jane Austen's *Pride and Prejudice* (1813) enjoyed an income of £2,000 a year (but he had a family of five nonearning females to support, and the income ceased at his death). Mr. Bingley had £4,000 per year of his own, Mr. Darcy close to £10,000; and this raises us close to the rarefied atmosphere of the aristocracy. In his deepest degradation David Copperfield (of Dickens's 1850 novel) worked in the warehouse of Murdstone & Grinby for 6 or 7 shillings a week (£15 to £18 a year). Mr. Murdstone paid extra for his lodging and laundry, but even so the boy was bitterly impoverished, though he had only himself to feed. When his father died, his mother was thought to be pretty well taken care of with £105 a year, a little less than £9 per month. Only a few years later, Dorothea

Brooke of *Middlemarch* (1872) is more than easy with £700 per year of her own; if she marries and has a son, he may inherit from her uncle as much as £3,000 per year in addition. That is high plutocracy for the folk of Tipton parish; one may estimate that Miss Brooke's pound is now worth between 20 and 50 American dollars of 1983 vintage. When John Davidson at the end of the century wrote of the horrors of being a clerk with a family at 30 bob a week, that stipend wouldn't work out much better than $1,500 to $3,750 of modern money. We see what he means.

Across the centuries, it's evident that money diminished in value; it's equally apparent that in every era there's been a gap between the poor and the rich. What money was worth depended heavily on which of those classes you belonged to. It also depended on where you lived. London was always very dear, and in the provinces (as is traditional everywhere) a small income went further. Finally, the value of money depended on the current rate of taxation. In the days of the Danegeld (ancestor of the modern income tax), nobody was rich except the Danes. Pitt introduced the modern income tax in 1798 as a war measure, Peel in 1842 made it a routine part of government financing; and it is one reason why an income of £10,000, though it was glorious aristocratic luxury for Mr. Fitzwilliam Darcy and his Elizabeth, does not today represent much more than solid middle-class comfort. For now, in addition to being heavily taxed, it's worth only twice the same number of current dollars.

The metric system, first adopted in France at the beginning of the nineteenth century and now standard throughout the European continent and Canada, is making the same sort of slow headway in Britain and Ireland that it is presently making in the United States. Scientific work is all done to metrical measurements, but the primary units of popular measure are still the traditional miles, feet, pounds, quarts, acres, etc. A basic formula for converting miles to kilometers is to multiply by 1.5 and add a bit. Thus, 10 miles is equal to about 16 kilometers, 100 miles to a bit more than 160 kilometers, and so forth. In the other direction, to convert kilometers to miles, divide by 2 and add a bit; 10 kilometers is about 6 miles, 100 kilometers is slightly more than 60 miles, and so forth. In old texts one may encounter now-obsolete units of mensuration, such as ells, hides, and leagues; but as these often vary from age to age and in different circumstances (a French league is quite different from a nautical league), no general rules can be given here.

Appendix B
The British Baronage

The English monarchy is hereditary, passing from father to elder son, to daughters in order of seniority if there is no son, to a brother if there are no children, and in default of direct descendants to collateral lines (cousins, nephews, nieces) in order of closeness. There have been breaks in the order of succession (1066, 1399, 1688), but so far as possible the usurpers always tried to paper over the break with a legitimate, i.e., a hereditary claim. When a queen succeeds and takes a husband, he does not become king unless he is in the line of blood succession; rather, he is named prince consort, as Albert was to Victoria. He may father kings, but is not one himself.

The original Saxon nobles were the king's thanes, ealdormen, or earls, who in return for booty, gifts, or landed estates provided the king with military service and counsel. The conqueror, arriving from France where feudalism was fully developed, added largely to this group. Archbishops and bishops, abbots and priors, who frequently held their land from the king though they might hold their office from the pope, served as counselors and very often in secular offices as well, as royal administrators. In addition, as the king distributed the lands of his new kingdom, he also distributed dignities to men who became known collectively as "the baronage." "Baron" in its root meaning signifies simply "man," and barons were the king's men. As the title was common, a distinction was early made between greater and lesser barons, the former gradually assuming loftier and more impressive titles. The king, no longer duke of Normandy, created the first English duke in 1337. "Marquess" or "marquis" was created in 1385 and "viscount" in 1440; though it's the oldest title of all, an "earl" now comes, in order of dignity and precedence, between a marquess and a viscount; only "baronets," created first in 1611, rank below barons in the scale of hereditary nobility.

Kings and queens are addressed as "Your Majesty," princes and princesses as "Your Highness," the other hereditary nobility as "My Lord," or "Your Lordship." When a commoner is created a peer (always by the monarch), he may select his own title; thus Disraeli became the earl of Beaconsfield after the district where his house stood; modest Clement Attlee, prime minister from 1945 to 1951, became simply Earl Attlee. Byron was the sixth baron of that line, by birth; Tennyson was created first Baron Tennyson. Peerages descend by primogeniture; they are given to a man with right of succession, they are not incidental to tenure of land—though when a man is given a peerage, he is sometimes given a pension or an estate to sustain the dignity. On the other hand, the children, even of a duke, are commoners unless they are specifically granted some other

The king and queen Prince and princess	(These are all of the royal line.)

Duke and duchess Marquess and marchioness Earl and countess Viscount and viscountess Baron and baroness Baronet and lady	(These may or may not be of the royal line, but are ordinarily remote from the succession.)

title or inherit their father's title from him. (Sons may enjoy the courtesy title "the Honorable," as daughters are referred to as "Lady" So and So; but these carry no social rank.) A peerage can be forfeited by act of attainder, as for example when a lord is convicted of treason; and, when forfeited, or lapsed for lack of a successor, can be bestowed on another family. Thus Robert Cecil was made in 1605 first earl of Salisbury in the third creation, the first creation dating from 1149, the second from 1337, the title having been in abeyance since 1539.

Scottish peers sat in the Parliament of Scotland, as English peers did in the Parliament of England till at the Act of Union (1707) Scots peers were granted 16 seats in the English House of Lords, to be filled by election. Similarly, Irish peers, when the Irish Parliament was abolished in 1801, were granted the right to elect 28 of their number to the House of Lords in Westminster. (Now that Eire is a separate nation, of course, this no longer applies.) On the seating of archbishops and bishops in the House of Lords, see Appendix C on the British church. For a genealogical guide through the tangled thickets of the aristocracy, see the classic compilation of Sir John Burke, known for brevity's sake as *Burke's Peerage*. The same author's *Landed Gentry* is popularly known in county society as "the stud book."

Below the hereditary peerage the chief title of honor is knight. Knighthood is not hereditary; it is generally a reward for services rendered. Though the word itself comes from Anglo-Saxon *cniht,* there seems to be some doubt whether knighthood amounted to much before the arrival of the Normans. The feudal system required military service as a condition of land tenure, and a man who came to serve his king at the head of an army of tenants required a title of authority and badges of identity—hence the title of knighthood and the coat of arms. During the Crusades, when men were far removed from their land (or had even sold it in order to go on crusade), more elaborate forms of fealty sprang up which soon expanded into the orders of knighthood. The Templars, Hospitallers, Knights of the Teutonic Order, Knights of Malta, and Knights of the Golden Fleece were but a few of these companionships; their similarity to the monastic and itinerant orders of friars was often remarked.

Gradually, with the rise of centralized government and the decline of feudal tenures, military knighthood became obsolete, and the rank largely honorific—sometimes it even degenerated into a scheme of the royal government for making money. For hundreds of years after its establishment in the fourteenth century, the order of the Garter was the only English order of knighthood, an exclusive courtly companionship. Then, during the late seventeenth, eighteenth, and nineteenth centuries, a number of additional orders were created—the Thistle, Saint Patrick, the Bath, Saint Michael and Saint George, plus a number of special Victorian and Indian orders. They retain the terminology, ceremony, and dignity of knighthood, but the military implications are all vestigial.

Knights are addressed as "Sir John"; their wives are "Lady Eleanor"; their children are commoners. The female equivalent of a knight bears the title of "Dame." The Order of Merit, instituted by Edward VII, does not carry the title of "knight" but is an equivalent recognition of distinguished achievement. The Distinguished Service Order and the Victoria Cross—DSO and VC—are the highest awards for military heroism. The OBE (Order of the British Empire) is awarded for distinguished services to the empire, either at home or abroad, by persons of either gender. It is but one of many special medals awarded for outstanding accomplishment in one form or another.

Appendix C
Anglican Ecclesiastical Offices

Britain consists of two archbishoprics or archepiscopal seats, one in Canterbury, the other in York; at the death of Theodore of Tarsus in 690, England was divided into fourteen dioceses, each under its bishop. There are now about forty diocesan or metropolitan bishops, having episcopal seats and geographical jurisdictions; there are also a certain number of suffragan (assistant) bishops, without right of succession, and coadjutor bishops, generally with right of succession. They are appointed by the diocesan bishop, and help in the work of the diocese when and as needed. Before 1878 all bishops were entitled as a matter of course to seats in the House of Lords; since that date, the number has been limited to 25, including the 2 archbishops, the bishops of London, Winchester, and Durham, and the next 20 bishops in order of seniority.

From the time of Henry VIII until recently, bishops were elected by the dean and chapter of the diocese, according to a rather special formula. When a vacancy occurred, the monarch after due consultation sent to the dean and chapter his royal permission to elect a new bishop; it was a form known as *congé d'éslire*. In a letter appended to this form was the name of the person to be elected. Thus the form of ecclesiastical freedom was preserved, alongside the reality of monarchical power. Nowadays, the matter is handled with more suavity; the dean and chapter get a little more input before the choice is finally made.

Deans are elected or appointed priests, generally made responsible for the material management of the church, conduct of services, and disposition of church property. They are either cathedral deans, presiding over a chapter, assisting the bishop; or else rural deans, inspecting throughout the diocese and maintaining discipline there. Chapters consist of the canons or prebends of a cathedral, i.e., the ecclesiastical staff; their secular counterpart is the vestry, a lay group elected from the parishioners for the conduct of mainly secular business. Deacons are the lowest of the three ecclesiastical orders (deacons, priests, bishops); they are commonly aspirants to the priesthood, serving an obligatory period of probation, at least a year, before formal ordination.

A candidate for office in the church selects his courses at the university with that end in view, and makes known his intention to the bishop of his diocese; having completed his courses and satisfied the bishop of his good character and serious vocation, he may be ordained, then serves a year in the diaconate. As for a living or benefice, i.e., a salaried post as minister to a congregation, that nowadays is often though not always in the gift of the church itself; a bishop appoints the new priest. But livings used frequently to be in the gift of a lay patron, the squire or lord of the manor. The right to make a presentation, an important property right in itself, was called an advowson. The local bishop exercised some control over appointments—the squire could not install a total ignoramus or a man of scandalous habits. But within the general limits laid down by the bishop, in accordance with the canons (i.e., church law), appointment to a living was in the gift of a squire. Thus it behooved a man who wanted a living in the church to cultivate and stay on the good side of a patron with livings to hand out. Technically speaking, a patron could not dismiss an incumbent who failed to please; but he could make things awfully unpleasant.

Ordinarily, the rector of a parish church would inhabit the parsonage attached to his living and collect the tithes annexed to it. (Nowadays the greater part of his income comes from the national government, which in lieu of tithes levies a land tax.) Until the early eighteenth century, he was bound to pay his first year's income to the monarch, as before the Reformation men had had to pay it to the pope; but by "Queen Anne's bounty," that payment was remitted. Attached to the parsonage may be a certain amount of farm land, known as the "glebe," which the minister may work himself or through a tenant. If he is ill, overburdened, or called away, he may arrange for a curate to perform his duties. In the old days, he could hold several different livings at once, which made him a pluralist; occasionally, while a living was vacant, he might hold it *in commendam*—that is, provisionally—but that privilege, obviously open to abuse, was abolished in 1836. In addition to his other duties, or sometimes as his sole function, a clergyman might, and still may, be appointed chaplain to some dignitary, lay or ecclesiastical, or in the armed forces. It was customary for clergymen to hold many academic positions in the schools and universities; for some academic positions, holy orders were actually required. Clergymen might also be wardens of charitable institutions, such as hospitals or old people's homes. The Anglican church still maintains a small number of contemplative establishments for laymen and clergy; as Puritan suspicions of the monastic ideal faded, periodic retreats for meditation and prayer became an accepted part of Anglican religious life.

As for the parson's ordinary duties, they consist, as they always have, of preaching and administering the sacrament, christening, marrying, and burying his parishioners, visiting the sick, giving alms to the poor, and providing those in need of it with spiritual guidance. He may have a sexton to help maintain the church grounds, a beadle to keep order during church service, a sacristan to care for the holy vessels, and a precentor, whose duties include supervision of the choir. Churchmen are still subject to the canons, those laws by which the church governs itself; and since 1827, when "benefit of clergy" was abolished, they are subject to the common law of the land as well. Periodically the church holds a convocation to consider its material and spiritual needs; for many years, convocation met when Parliament met, but this is no longer the rule. News of the church and of matters interesting to clergymen is disseminated through an ecclesiastical newspaper, the *Church Times*.

The information above applies exclusively to the British Episcopal (Anglican) church. Many other churches (Catholics, Presbyterians, Methodists, Baptists, Congregationalists, to name no others) maintain substantial communities in England; there is also a wide scattering of sects. Anglican communions are found in many different countries besides England. They preserve national autonomy, though they generally recognize the English church as first among equals and assemble every ten years at Lambeth to discuss church matters.

Suggestions for Further Reading

The historians of England, from the Venerable Bede to the scarcely less authoritative Mr. A. J. P. Taylor, march before the student, a majestic procession of predecessors, whom, at least in the mind's eye, it's useful briefly to review. There are the earl of Clarendon and Bishop Gilbert Burnet in the late seventeenth century, both historians of their own time, and the bishop in addition a historian of the Reformation. In mid-eighteenth century David Hume wrote (in reverse chronological order) the first complete national history, and in the early nineteenth century the industrious Henry Hallam produced a medieval history, a constitutional history, and a literary history which almost form a consecutive narration. Macaulay published his classically Whig and highly concentrated history almost at the same time as H. T. Buckle published his notably diffuse one. The *Constitutional History* of Bishop Stubbs, published in 1874–1878, carries a complex and technical development from Saxon to Tudor times. Samuel Rawson Gardiner devoted forty years and seventeen volumes to the Great Rebellion of the seventeenth century; J. A. Froude gave twelve volumes and fourteen years to the Reformation and the reign of Elizabeth. Finally, the French Elie Halévy is the classic historian—in six volumes—of the nineteenth century. It is worth calling to mind these great names (to which many more could be added) if only to manifest that English history is a much-plowed field which has been made to yield many crops. One can easily be oppressed by the great names of the tradition; one can also profit from their examples by building on or away from their achievements. No critical insight of T. S. Eliot's has better stood the test than his account of the taut, two-way, ever-shifting relation between tradition and the individual.

All history is abridgment, however, and a course of reading in the classic historians which would take years can be compressed sharply by consulting multivolume serial histories written by specialists in the different periods. Most spacious and imposing of these is the *Oxford History of England* in fourteen volumes as follows:

- Collingwood, R. G., Myres, J. N. L., *Roman Britain and the English Settlements*[1] (2d ed., 1937)
- Stenton, Sir Frank, *Anglo-Saxon England* (2d ed., 1947)
- Poole, A. L., *From Domesday Book to Magna Carta* (1951)
- Powicke, Sir Maurice, *The Thirteenth Century 1216–1307* (1953)

1. An ancillary volume by Peter Salway devoted solely to Roman Britain has recently (1981) been published under that title.

- McKisack, May, *The Fourteenth Century* (1959)
- Jacob, E. F., *The Fifteenth Century* (1961)
- Mackie, J. D., *The Earlier Tudors* (1952)
- Black, J. B., *The Reign of Elizabeth* (1936)
- Davies, Godfrey, *The Early Stuarts* (2d ed., 1959)
- Clark, G. N., *The Later Stuarts* (2d ed., 1955)
- Williams, Basil, *The Whig Supremacy* (2d ed., 1962)
- Watson, J. S., *The Reign of George III* (1960)
- Woodward, E. L., *The Age of Reform* (2d ed., 1962)
- Ensor, R. C. K., *England 1870–1914* (1936)

Sir Charles Oman edited for Methuen a similar, if less expansive, collection, the *History of England* in eight volumes, as follows:

- Oman, Sir Charles, *England before the Norman Conquest, Origins–1066*
- Davis, H. W. C., *England and the Normans and Angevins 1066–1272*
- Vickers, K. H., *England in the Later Middle Ages 1272–1485*
- Elton, G. R., *England under the Tudors 1485–1603*
- Trevelyan, G. M., *England under the Stuarts 1603–1714*
- Robertson, Sir C. G., *England under the Hanoverians 1714–1815*
- Marriott, Sir J. A. R., *England since Waterloo 1815–1900*
- Marriott, Sir J. A. R., *Modern England 1885–1945*

There are two paperback series, one by Penguin in nine volumes, the other by Norton in eight, the fourth of which, covering the sixteenth century, has yet to appear. (But, to compensate, Christopher Hill's *The Century of Revolution 1603–1714,* is a veritable diamond of a pocket history.) The two universities have put out multivolume histories of English literature as well. The *Cambridge History of English Literature,* first published in 1927 in fifteen volumes, is often useful for its bibliographies, but many of its critical judgments have, understandably, aged; the *Oxford History of English Literature,* begun in 1945 and projected for twelve volumes, still lacks the two parts of volume I (on English literature before the Norman Conquest and Middle English literature) and a promised volume II on the mid-nineteenth century. All these serial histories, political as well as literary, reflect the differing approaches, interests, and capacities of their different authors. Some of the volumes are classics, others little short of disasters; some are sharp and insightful, others barely animated bibliographies. The reader must pick his way through them with prudence, judging, not the different series as wholes, but the individual volumes within each.

Though the present listing omits all biographies of individuals, whether political or literary, a few series of biographical studies may be recommended. The English Men of Letters series was compiled near the end of the last century under the general editorship of John Morley; while generally outdated, the more than fifty studies include many ripely meditated assessments by commentators of importance in their own right. The English firm of Thames & Hudson publishes (alas, only for sale in Britain) a collection of short, illustrated studies under the general heading "So-and-so and His (Her) World." It includes both literary and political figures, and humanizes their often-abstract outlines by setting them in a social context. Additionally, the Critical Heritage series put out by Routledge Kegan Paul in England, by Barnes & Noble in America, presents the record of responses to an author's work, from first reviews to modern critical analyses; at present, there are more than sixty volumes in the series.

The American Historical Society published in 1961 a new version of its elderly *Guide to Historical Literature;* it is a critical bibliography covering all historical writings concerning all areas and periods of the world—hence more wide than deep. E. B. Graves edited a *Bibliography of English History to 1485* (Oxford, 1975) and the *Bibliography of British History* (Oxford, the Clarendon Press) has produced three volumes covering:

• *The Tudor Period,* ed. Conyers Read (1959)
• *The Stuart Period,* ed. Godfrey Davies (1928)
• *The Eighteenth Century,* ed. S. Pargellis and D. J. Medley (1951)

Writings on British History lists as they appear books and articles about Britain from 450 to 1914, but does not include anything written before 1935—it is a list of current production. The most comprehensive of literary bibliographies is the *New Cambridge Bibliography of English Literature,* edited by G. Watson and I. R. Willison. It can be supplemented by the updated bibliographies of a standard text like the *Norton Anthology of English Literature* and the annual bibliography of the Modern Language Association. The bibliographies of the *Oxford History of England* are outstanding, but even the paperback series of Penguin and Norton (though individual volumes vary widely) list enough material for future reading to occupy one's days and nights for years to come.

The more comprehensive they are, the less guidance bibliographies provide; they are most useful when one approaches them with a specific interest in mind. In the early stages, there is no economical substitute for the book hopping one does by reading first the latest book on a topic and then working back through the books to which that first book refers. Though individual biographies are omitted from the present list of suggested readings, it shouldn't be thought their importance in this process is negligible. Major biographies of major figures like Milton, Cromwell, Joyce, Gladstone, Dickens, Disraeli, Johnson, and Byron often represent, in their mingling of close particulars with more general considerations, our closest approach to the full texture of the past. Even the lives of humbler citizens—of a grumbling plowman, a humdrum merchant, an itinerant preacher—when we can recover them in any fullness, contribute to our full and intimate comprehension of an age. Without the diary of Samuel Pepys or Boswell's *Life of Johnson,* how gaunt and impoverished would be our picture of those two ages!

Between history as schematic arrangement and history as a kaleidoscope of rich but bewildering complexity, individual readers must mediate for themselves. The old style of history dealt more freely in generalizations than the new. It assumed the stability and uniformity of parties, sects, movements, institutions, abstract processes, and periods; it created entities like "Protestants," "Whigs," and even "the spirit of capitalism," and moved them confidently across the checkerboard of history. At its most naïve, it attributed to history a kind of immanent purpose, a yearning of all previous ages to become exactly like our own, and a division of all humanity into those who supported and those who opposed this spirit of "progress." That is what Professor Butterfield stigmatizes as "the Whig interpretation of history" (item X.19 below), and it is so deeply ingrained (especially in Americans), so "natural" in our political climate, that a deliberate effort must be made to escape from it.

Modern historians, suspicious of sweeping generalizations, are more apt to study family groupings, the temporary alliances known as "interests," the short-term behavior of actual people. They are interested in the close texture of the past rather than the large patterns that can be imposed on it. When we look hard at movements like "Puritanism" or parties like "the Whigs," they splinter into a number of frequently conflicting factions and individuals, few of whom are Puritan or Whiggish in the same way at the same time for very long. Putting a single faction, a single Parliament, or a single division in a single Parliament under the microscope, we can almost persuade ourselves that there are no large-scale patterns in history, and that long-term developments, if they exist, don't count for anything. The chief trouble with atomizing history so completely is that it becomes, under these circumstances, an incomprehensible jumble of particulars of which the mind cannot form or retain a model. Schematizing it completely, on the other hand, flattens out all those living and complex particulars which really mark the behavior of men and raise the study of history above the interest of a diagram or a formula. Two simple rules of thumb (unfortunately antithetical if not contradictory) are that one must learn as much as possible of history's gritty details and incorporate them as largely as possible in a coherent vision of the past. Reconciling these two imperatives—one of which looks toward the past chiefly for its own sake, the other chiefly for the sake of our modern understanding—is the art of creative or compositional reading. Without this resilient, constructive activity, the perusal of reading lists, however long and elaborate, is mere accumulation of inert materials, a toilsome vanity.

With these homilies out of the way, we may turn to a list of suggested readings. It is divided into nine chronological periods, with a tenth unit for books which are concerned with no particular period, or which, though useful as background, do not relate directly to English history or literature. About biographies one need only say that the student should read as many as he can. I've listed no editions of texts, collections or anthologies, or reprints of original historical documents, such as charters, treaties, and chronicles. For close critical studies, the reader is referred to the literary bibliographies. No historical fiction or fictionalized history. The emphasis of this book list, as of the book in which it appears, is on holding two weighty subjects in delicate, tremulous equipoise without violating the integrity of either. Numbering of entries within the different periods is for convenience of reference only, and carries no implication whatever of priority.

A. ROMANS, CELTS, AND SAXONS

1. Divine, David, *Hadrian's Wall* (Boston, 1969).
2. Margary, Ivan D., *Roman Roads in Britain* (London, 1967). More than you really want to know, but useful for details.
3. Scullard, H. H., *Roman Britain* (London, 1979). With exceptional illustrations.
4. Wacher, John, *Roman Britain* (London, 1978). A convenient survey.
5. Page, R. I., *Life in Anglo-Saxon England* (London, 1970).
6. Anderson, G. K., *The Literature of the Anglo-Saxons* (Princeton, 1949).
7. Alcock, Leslie, *Arthur's Britain, History and Archaeology* (Cambridge, 1956).
8. Blair, P. H., *An Introduction to Anglo-Saxon England* (Cambridge, 1956).
9. Rand, E. K., *Founders of the Middle Ages* (Cambridge, Mass., 1928). Clear and basic account of Saints Ambrose, Jerome, Benedict, Augustine, plus Boethius, Dante, and others.
10. Southern, R. W., *The Making of the Middle Ages 972–1204* (New Haven, 1959). In

972 Gerbert of Aurillac (later pope, as Silvester II) arrived in Rheims, bearing with him, it seems, knowledge of the Arabic numerals; 1204 marks the Latin conquest of Constantinople. A meticulous and deeply learned study.

11. Bede, *The Ecclesiastical History of the English Nation* (Penguin Books, 1955).
12. Adamson, J. W., *"The Illiterate Anglo-Saxon" and Other Essays* (Cambridge, 1946). He wasn't illiterate at all—at least many of him weren't.
13. Matthew, D. J. A., *The Norman Conquest* (New York, 1966). Rather scants the battle of Hastings but explores in detail the before and after.
14. Joyce, Patrick Weston, *A Smaller Social History of Ancient Ireland* (London, 1906). A work of infinite particularity and even more charm.
15. Hyde, Douglas, *A History of Irish Literature* (London, 1899).
16. *The Bayeux Tapestry*, reproduced in full by the Phaidon Press, with commentary by Sir Frank Stenton (London, 1957).
17. Bruce-Mitford, R., *The Sutton-Hoo Ship Burial: A Handbook* (London, 1972).

B. MEDIEVAL ENGLAND

1. Coulton, G. G., *Medieval Panorama* (Cambridge, 1938). See also his *Medieval Scene* (1930) and *Chaucer and His England* (1908).
2. Poole, A. L., ed., *Medieval England*, 2 vols. (Oxford, 1958). Nineteen essays by different hands, with copious bibliographies.
3. Platt, Colin, *Medieval England* (New York, 1978). An archaeological approach, with many elegant illustrations.
4. Knowles, Dom David, *The Monastic Order in England (943–1216), The Religious Orders in England (1216 through the Marian Restoration)*, 3 vols. (Cambridge, 1941 and 1959). Professor Knowles is the supreme authority on English monastic life.
5. Barrow, G. W. S., *Feudal Britain (1066–1314)* (London, 1956).
6. Hill, Sir Francis, *Medieval Lincoln* (Cambridge, 1948). A detailed account of what one medieval town was like, across the centuries. See also Hill's volumes on *Tudor and Stuart Lincoln* (1956) and *Victorian Lincoln* (1974).
7. Orwin, C. S., and Orwin, C. S., *The Open Fields* (Oxford, 1938). A painstaking study of medieval English agriculture as seen in a single Notts. manor.
8. Curtius, Ernst, *European Culture and the Latin Middle Ages*, trans. Willard Trask (New York: Harper Torchbooks, 1963). Weighty, erudite, and basic to an understanding of learned medieval culture.
9. Pollock, F., and Maitland, F. W., *The History of English Law before the Time of Edward I*, 2 vols. (Cambridge, 1923). Majestic and challenging to the nonlegal mind.
10. Ker, W. P., *Epic and Romance* (London, 1908). Deals with French, Icelandic, and Teutonic narratives, as well as *Beowulf;* indispensable background. See also, for an introductory survey, his *English Literature, Medieval* (1912).
11. Rashdall, Reverend Hastings, *The Universities of Europe in the Middle Ages*, vol. 3 (originally published 1895; rev. ed., Oxford, 1936).
12. Holt, J. C., *Magna Carta* (Cambridge, 1965).
13. Power, Eileen, *Medieval People* (London, 1924). Character studies.
14. Bennett, H. S., *Six Medieval Men and Women* (Cambridge, 1955). Most eminent of

Bennett's half dozen is Humphrey of Gloucester, the "good duke," but the humbler folk are good company too.

15. Flower, Robin, *The Irish Tradition* (Oxford, 1947). A short summary, packed with delightful examples of Irish poetry through the sixteenth century.
16. Owst, G. R., *Literature and Pulpit in Medieval England* (Cambridge, 1933). Copious in its detail and pleasantly testy with less informed scholars.
17. Turville-Petre, T., *The Alliterative Revival* (Cambridge, 1977).
18. Runciman, S., *A History of the Crusades*, 3 vols. (Cambridge, 1951–1954).
19. Jusserand, J. J., *English Wayfaring Life in the Middle Ages* (London, 1920, first published in 1895). Genial, jocose, detailed; antiquarianism verging on fine art.
20. Galbraith, V. H., *The Making of Domesday Book* (Oxford, 1961). Supplements and corrects the previous work of J. H. Round.

C. THE FIFTEENTH CENTURY

1. Weiss, Roberto, *Humanism in England during the Fifteenth Century*, 3d ed. (Oxford, 1967). Visiting and indigenous humanists, meticulously described.
2. Cohn, Norman, *The Pursuit of the Millennium* (New York: Harper Torchbooks, 1961). Traditions of radical dissent in the late middle ages and early Renaissance, with formidable bibliographies.
3. James Gairdner, ed., *Paston Letters 1422–1509*, 6 vols. (London, 1904). There are also abridgments of the correspondence of this voluble family.
4. Hodgart, M. J. C., *The Ballads* (New York, 1950). An introduction.
5. Lander, J. R., *Conflict and Stability in Fifteenth Century England* (London, 1969).
6. Blake, N. F., *Caxton and His World* (London, 1969).
7. Thomson, J. A. F., *The Later Lollards* (Oxford, 1965).
8. Mowat, R. B., *The Wars of the Roses 1377–1471* (London, 1914). Though showing signs of age, the lucid text is followed by genealogical tables and a good map.
9. Chambers, E. K., *The Medieval Stage*, 2 vols. (Oxford, 1903). Still the fundamental work on the topic.
10. Huizinga, Johan, *The Waning of the Middle Ages* (Garden City, N.Y.: Anchor Books, 1954). Largely concerned with the Low Countries and France, but fascinating to students of England as well.
11. Weston, Jessie L., *From Ritual to Romance* (Cambridge, 1920). Of interest to students of T. S. Eliot in addition to students of Arthurian legend.
12. Loomis, R. S., *The Development of Arthurian Romance* (New York: Harper Torchbooks, 1970). See also numerous earlier books by Loomis on Arthurian materials.
13. Brown, R. A., *English Medieval Castles* (London, 1954).
14. Bennett, H. S., *English Books and Readers (1475–1557)* (London, 1952).

D. THE TUDOR AGE

1. Bennett, H. S., *English Books and Readers (1558–1603)* (Cambridge, 1965).
2. Anglo, S., *Spectacle, Pageantry, and Early Tudor Policy* (Oxford, 1969).

3. Eisenstein, Elizabeth, *The Printing Press as an Agent of Change,* 2 vols. (Cambridge, 1979). Prolix, but frequently suggestive.

4. Dickens, A. G., *The English Reformation* (New York, 1964). Should be read in conjunction with his *Reformation and Society in Sixteenth Century Europe* (New York, 1966).

5. Wright, Louis B., *Middle-Class Culture in Elizabethan England* (Chapel Hill, 1935). The humus and compost from which Elizabethan literature partly sprang.

6. Haller, William, *Foxe's Book of Martyrs and the Elect Nation* (London, 1963).

7. Collinson, P., *The Elizabethan Puritan Movement* (London, 1966).

8. Morey, A., *The Catholic Subjects of Elizabeth I* (Totowa, N.J., 1978).

9. Harrison, William, *The Description of England,* ed. George Edelen (Ithaca, N.Y., 1968).

10. Harrison, G. B., *The Elizabethan Journals, being a record of those things most talked of during the years 1591–1603* (Ann Arbor, 1955).

11. Heath, Peter, *The English Parish Clergy on the Eve of the Reformation* (London, 1969). Especially intriguing on their mental and moral state.

12. Porter, H. C., *Reformation and Reaction in Tudor Cambridge* (Cambridge, 1958). Sharply and imaginatively written.

13. Neale, J. E., *Essays in Elizabethan History* (London, 1958). Valuable supplement to his standard biography, *Queen Elizabeth I* (1934).

14. Williams, Penry, *The Tudor Regime* (Oxford, 1979). Describes in detail how Elizabeth's government actually worked—who got to see the queen and how, who made up the budget, who formed the foreign policy, etc.

15. Hurstfield, Joel, *Freedom, Corruption, and Government in Elizabethan England* (London, 1973).

16. Burke, Peter, *The Renaissance Sense of the Past* (London, 1969). A crucial topic.

17. Andrews, K. R., *Elizabethan Privateering during the Spanish War* (Cambridge, 1964). Realistic account of a much sentimentalized activity.

18. Chambers, E. K., *The Elizabethan Stage,* 4 vols. (Oxford, 1923). The definitive study, massive in its detail.

19. Lewis, C. S., *The Allegory of Love* (Oxford, 1936). From the rise of courtly love through Spenser, with loving attention to the *Roman de la Rose* and Chaucer.

20. Tuve, Rosamond, *Elizabethan and Metaphysical Imagery* (Chicago, 1947).

21. Sypher Wylie, *Four Stages of Renaissance Style* (Anchor Books). "Renaissance," Mannerist, Baroque, and Neoclassical styles in art and literature.

22. Bradbrook, M. C., *The School of Night* (Cambridge, 1936). Raleigh and his friends.

23. Rowse, A. L., *Sir Walter Raleigh* (New York, 1962). Less about Raleigh than his brother-in-law, Sir Arthur Throckmorton, and the squirearchy he represents. Rowse is more respected as a historian (*The England of Elizabeth,* 1964; *The Expansion of Elizabethan England,* 1955; and *The Elizabethan Renaissance,* 1971) than as a student of Shakespeare.

24. In successive editions under successive editors, the Clarendon Press has issued in two handsome illustrated volumes *Shakespeare's England,* replete with social details, whether mentioned by Shakespeare or not.

25. M. S. Byrne, ed., *Lisle Letters,* 6 vols. (Chicago, 1981). Viscount Lisle, a natural son of Edward IV, lived from 1480 to 1542. His letters, many to his wife, present an intimate picture of court and family life.

26. Alpers, Paul, *The Poetry of "The Faerie Queene"* (Princeton, 1967).
27. Thomas, Keith, *Religion and the Decline of Magic* (London, 1971). Immense detail regarding the state of religious and superstitious belief in the sixteenth and seventeenth centuries.
28. Elton, G. R., *Reform and Renewal* (Cambridge Univ. Press, 1973). An intellectual and political portrait of a fascinating man, Thomas Cromwell.

E. THE STUART AGE

1. Wedgwood, C. V., *The Great Rebellion* in 2 vols.: *The King's Peace, 1637–1641* (New York, 1955) and *The King's War, 1641–1647* (New York, 1959).
2. Jones, R. F., *Ancients and Moderns, a Study of the Rise of the Scientific Movement in Seventeenth-Century England* (St. Louis, 1936).
3. Everitt, Alan, *Change in the Provinces: the Seventeenth Century* (Leicester, 1969). Concisely and brilliantly written, and packed with insights.
4. Pocock, J. G. A., *The Ancient Constitution and the Feudal Law* (Cambridge, 1957). Study of seventeenth-century ideas about the origins (if any) of the common law.
5. Underdown, David, *Pride's Purge* (Oxford, 1971). A close study, statistical in its detail, of the political eddies surrounding a single instant of history.
6. Hill, Christopher, *Economic Problems of the Church* (Oxford, 1956). Ostensibly a small, dry subject, actually shown to have wide and dramatic implications. Among Hill's many other books on the seventeenth century (in addition to *The Century of Revolution* for the Norton series), *Puritanism and Revolution* (1958), *Society and Puritanism in Pre-Revolutionary England* (1964), and *The Intellectual Origins of the English Revolution* (1965) all merit careful study.
7. Hook, Judith, *The Baroque Age in England* (London, 1976). Covers the period 1630–1730.
8. Parkes, Joan, *Travel in England in the Seventeenth Century* (Oxford, 1925). Full of detail about roads, coaches, inns, etc., and yields as well a vivid image of the society as a whole. Compare Jusserand, B.19.
9. Wilson, Charles, *England's Apprenticeship 1603–1673* (New York, 1965). Trade, industry, and economic development.
10. *Verney Letters and Papers down to the End of the Year 1639*, ed. J. Bruce for the Camden Society (London, 1853). A Buckinghamshire family of gentry.
11. Laslett, Peter, *The World We Have Lost* (New York, 1965). Preindustrial England, seen by a sociologist.
12. Thomson, Gladys Scott, *Life in a Noble Household 1641–1700* (London, 1937). The Bedfords and their domestic arrangements.
13. Kenyon, John, *The Popish Plot* (London, 1972). The episode itself and its implications; methodologically like Underdown, E.5.
14. Ashley, Maurice, *Life in Stuart England* (London, 1964). A brief survey.
15. Aubrey, John, *Brief Lives*, ed. Andrew Clark, 2 vols. (Oxford, 1898). Scandal and gossip from the seventeenth century. Similar material, but less juicy, may be gathered from his contemporaries Anthony a Wood and Thomas Hearne.
16. Feiling, Keith, *A History of the Tory Party* (Oxford, 1924). Old but still unchallenged.

17. Gooch, G. P., and Laski, Harold, *English Democratic Ideas in the Seventeenth Century* (Cambridge, 1927).
18. Knights, L. C., *Drama and Society in the Age of Jonson* (London, 1937).
19. Grierson, Sir H. J. C., *Cross-Currents in English Literature of the Seventeenth Century* (London, 1929).
20. Haller, William, *The Rise of Puritanism* (New York, 1938). A classic study of the propaganda campaign leading to the civil wars. Haller also edited *Tracts on Liberty 1638–1647*, crucial documents from the arguments rising out of the rebellion.
21. Hexter, J. H., *The Reign of King Pym* (Cambridge, Mass., 1941). Critical analysis of the parties in the early years of the long Parliament. Hexter's *Reappraisals in History* includes essays bearing on both the sixteenth and seventeenth centuries.
22. Notestein, Wallace, "The Winning of the Initiative in the House of Commons" (London, 1924), is a seminal lecture out of which many fat volumes have sprouted.
23. Ogg, David, *England in the Reign of Charles II*, 2 vols. (Oxford, 1934). Close account of the intrigues of this duplicitous reign.
24. Weber, Max, *The Protestant Ethic and the Spirit of Capitalism*, trans. Talcott Parsons from the German ed. of 1904 (London, 1930). Weber provided much of the inspiration for R. H. Tawney, *Religion and the Rise of Capitalism* (Mentor Books, 1954). The thesis was under dispute for a number of years, with attention focusing on the social character and political role of the gentry. Among the participants were H. R. Trevor-Roper, Lawrence Stone, and J. H. Hexter.
25. Westfall, Richard S., *Science and Religion in Seventeenth Century England* (New Haven, 1958).
26. Willey, Basil, *The Seventeenth Century Background* (Garden City, N.Y.: Anchor Books, 1953). Also by Willey are *The Eighteenth Century Background* and *Nineteenth Century Studies*.
27. Bredvold, Louis I., *The Intellectual Milieu of John Dryden* (Ann Arbor, 1934). A general view of skepticism and fideism in the century.
28. Stone, Lawrence, *The Crisis of the Aristocracy 1558–1641* (New York, 1965). Makes considerable effort at statistical particularity.

F. THE EIGHTEENTH CENTURY

1. Humphreys, A. R., *The Augustan World* (London, 1954).
2. J. H. Plumb, *The Origins of Political Stability in England 1675–1725* (Boston, 1967). *The First Four Georges*, by the same author, covers more territory less intensively.
3. Macaulay, T. B., *The History of England from the Reign of James II*, 5 vols. (New York, 1849). Chapter 3 particularly is an incomparable piece of historical description.
4. Baxter, Stephen, *William III and the Defense of European Liberty* (New York, 1966). Sees William in the perspective he would have preferred.
5. Stephen, Leslie, *A History of English Thought in the Eighteenth Century* (London, 1876). Lays special emphasis on the deists and skeptics. Stephen's *English Literature and Society in the Eighteenth Century* (1904) is less strenuous reading.
6. Mingay, G. E., *English Landed Society in the Eighteenth Century* (London, 1963). See especially Chapter 6, "The Landlords and Society."
7. Turberville, A. S., *English Men and Manners in the Eighteenth Century* (Oxford,

1926). On the model of *Shakespeare's England* (D.24) is Turberville's anthology, *Johnson's England*, in two plentiful volumes.

8. Marshall, Dorothy, *English People in the Eighteenth Century* (London, 1956). To be supplemented with her *Doctor Johnson's London* (1968).

9. Rudé, George, *Hanoverian London (1714–1808)* (London, 1971). Less a portrait than the biography of a city.

10. Rogers, Pat, *Grub Street* (London, 1972). The lane itself, its inhabitants, and its metaphorical meanings.

11. Watt, Ian, *The Rise of the Novel* (Berkeley, 1956, 1971). Focuses on the social circumstances.

12. Lovejoy, A. O., *The Great Chain of Being* (Cambridge, Mass., 1936). The image of a hierarchical and "full" cosmos as most strikingly expressed by Pope.

13. Namier, Sir Lewis, *The Structure of Politics at the Accession of George III*, rev. ed. (New York, 1957). By the same author, *England in the Age of the American Revolution*, rev. ed. (1961).

14. Mantoux, Paul, *The Industrial Revolution in the Eighteenth Century*, trans. from the French ed. of 1928 (New York: Harper, 1961).

15. Ashton, T. H., *The Industrial Revolution 1760–1830* (Oxford, 1948). A summary, concise and fluent, with good bibliographies.

16. Bagwell, Philip S., *The Transport Revolution from 1770* (London, 1874).

17. Chambers, J. D., and Mingay, G. E., *The Agricultural Revolution 1750–1880* (New York, 1966).

18. Clifford, J. L., ed., *Man versus Society in Eighteenth Century Britain* (Cambridge, 1968). Six aspects of the one theme.

19. Wardroper, John, *Kings, Lords, and Wicked Libellers, Satire and Protest 1760–1837* (London, 1973). With a great many malign caricatures.

20. Spear, Percival, *The Nabobs* (Gloucester, Mass., 1971). Englishmen as they were in India and after they came back.

21. Scott, Geoffrey, *The Portrait of Zélide* (New York, 1927). Gentle portrait of a difficile lady whom Boswell loved, but who couldn't adapt to the new vulgar ways of the nineteenth century.

22. Rudé, George, "The London 'Mob' of the Eighteenth Century," in *Paris and London in the 18th Century* (London, 1970).

23. Robbins, Caroline, *The Eighteenth Century Commonwealthman* (New York, 1959). A group of radical Whigs who preserved commonwealth principles through the eighteenth century and handed them on to the makers of the American Revolution.

24. Thompson, E. P., *Whigs and Hunters* (New York, 1976). The brutalities of the game laws (see below, G.14). They struck even at Alexander Pope's brother.

25. Deane, Phyllis, *The First Industrial Revolution*, 2d ed. (Cambridge, 1979). Describes lucidly and systematically the several distinct changes which came together to create the industrial revolution.

G. REVOLUTION AND REGENCY

1. Briggs, Asa, *The Making of Modern England 1783–1867* (New York, 1959).
2. Bryant, Arthur, *The Age of Elegance 1812–1822* (New York, 1950). Popular.

3. Kitson Clark, Sir George, *The Making of Victorian England* (Cambridge, Mass., 1962).

4. Brown, F. K., *Fathers of the Victorians* (Cambridge, 1961).

5. Jaeger, Muriel, *Before Victoria* (London, 1956).

6. Quinlan, Maurice J., *Victorian Prelude, a History of English Manners 1700–1830* (New York, 1941). All three of these books (4, 5, 6) see the regency in the perspective of the period that followed it.

7. White, R. J., *Life in Regency England* (London, 1963), with many illustrations. To be supplemented by reading in Byron's correspondence and perhaps *Jane Austen and Her World* by Marghanita Laski (1977).

8. Hazlitt, William, *The Spirit of the Age or Contemporary Portraits*, vol. II of the *Complete Works*, Centenary ed. (London, 1932). The title has been adapted by M. H. Abrams for an essay appearing in *Romanticism and Consciousness*, ed. Harold Bloom.

9. Marcus, G. J., *The Age of Nelson, the Royal Navy 1798–1815* (New York, 1971).

10. Halévy, Elie, *The Growth of Philosophical Radicalism*, trans. from the French ed. of 1901 (London, 1934). A study of Bentham and utilitarianism by the great French historian of the nineteenth century.

11. Manwaring, G. E., and Dobrée, Bonamy, *The Floating Republic* (New York, 1935). Touching and dramatic account of mutinies at Spithead and the Nore, 1797–1798.

12. Hobsbawm, E., and Rudé, G., *Captain Swing* (London, 1968). Describes a wave of agricultural riots and rural disturbances that swept England in 1830.

13. Hammond, J. L., and Hammond, Barbara, *The Age of the Chartists* (London, 1930). Generous in its sympathies, sometimes unsteady in its details.

14. Kirby, Chester, "English Game Law Reform" in *Essays in Modern English History in Honor of Wilbur Cortez Abbott* (Cambridge, Mass., 1941). An instance of extracting wide insights from a limited topic.

15. Southey, Robert, *Letters from England* (London, 1951; repr. of the 1807 ed.). An imaginary Spaniard writes home his impressions of contemporary England.

16. Woodring, Carl, *Politics in English Romantic Poetry* (Cambridge, Mass., 1970). Updates Brinton, item 17.

17. Brinton, Crane, *Political Ideas of the English Romanticists* (New York, 1926).

18. Abrams, M. H., *The Mirror and the Lamp* (Oxford, 1953). Analysis of the metaphors controlling the thought of the English romantic poets and their German predecessors; to be supplemented by the same author's *Natural Supernaturalism* (1971).

19. Erdman, David, *Blake: Prophet against Empire* (Princeton, 1954, 1979).

20. Lowes, J. L., *The Road to Xanadu* (Boston, 1927). On the backgrounds of Coleridge's poetry, a classic in a now somewhat dated mode of literary analysis.

21. Hussey, Christopher, *The Picturesque* (London, 1927). A special way of seeing and appreciating landscape (reflexive, as in Schiller's notion of "sentimental" poetry), prevalent in Europe between 1730 and 1830.

22. Thompson, E. P., *The Making of the English Working Class* (New York, 1964). The active creation of working-class-consciousness between 1780 and 1832.

23. Wiener, J. H., *The War of the Unstamped* (Ithaca, N.Y., 1969). Journalists and their struggle against the "tax on knowledge."

H. VICTORIANISM

1. Young, Sir G. M., *Early Victorian England*, 2 vols. (Oxford, 1934). Essays by several hands, including Sir George's allusive classic "Portrait of an Age."
2. Williams, Raymond, *Culture and Society 1780–1950* (Garden City, N.Y.: Anchor Books, 1958). Questions provocatively the meaning of that nineteenth-century code word "culture."
3. Strachey, Lytton, *Eminent Victorians* (London, 1918). Cardinal Manning, Florence Nightingale, Dr. Arnold, and General Gordon. A trendy book.
4. Wellman, Rita, *Victoria Royal* (New York, 1939). Flip and funny.
5. Somervell, D. C., *English Thought in the Nineteenth Century* (London, 1929).
6. Roberts, David, *Paternalism in Early Victorian England* (New Brunswick, 1979). It was pervasive, universal.
7. Eastlake, Sir Charles, *A History of the Gothic Revival* (London, 1872; repr. by American Life Foundation, 1975). With fascinating cuts.
8. Doré, Gustave, and Jerrold, Blanchard, *London, a Pilgrimage* (London, 1872; repr. by Dover Books, 1970). Images with a commentary.
9. Buckley, J. H., *The Victorian Temper* (Cambridge, Mass., 1951, 1969).
10. Houghton, Walter E., *The Victorian Frame of Mind 1830–1870* (London, 1957). Oddly arranged and less insightful than Buckley.
11. Bagehot, Walter, *The English Constitution* (London, 1867). An interesting and lucid account of how government really used to function. Written before the second reform bill, the book is best read with the lengthy foreword that Bagehot wrote for the second edition after passage of that bill.
12. Altick, R. D., *The English Common Reader 1800–1900* (Chicago, 1957, 1963). Publishing and reading practices in the nineteenth century, a ground-level view.
13. Holdsworth, William S., *Charles Dickens as a Legal Historian* (New Haven, 1928). A terse, cogent appreciation.
14. Taylor, A. J. P., *The Struggle for Mastery in Europe 1848–1918* (Oxford, 1954). Description, by a master historian, of the many vicissitudes of the European balance of power.
15. Marcus, Steven, *The Other Victorians* (New York, 1964). The seamy underside of a repressive society.
16. Briggs, Asa, *Victorian Cities* (London, 1963). See especially the chapters on Manchester and Birmingham. See also his *Victorian People* (Chicago, 1955).
17. Briggs, Asa, ed., *Chartist Studies* (New York, 1959). By several hands, with a concise and thoughtful summary by the general editor, pp. 188 ff.
18. Himmelfarb, Gertrude, *Darwin and the Darwinian Revolution* (New York, 1959). A close account of the new ideas and their reception.
19. Disher, M. Willson, *Blood and Thunder* (London, 1949). Victorian melodrama, plot summaries with dashing woodcuts.
20. Chambers, J. D., *The Workshop of the World* (London, 1961). Mid-Victorian industry.
21. Thompson, F. M. L., *English Landed Society in the Nineteenth Century* (London, 1963).
22. Feuchtwanger, E. J., *Disraeli, Democracy, and the Tory Party* (Oxford, 1968). Deals with Disraeli's last fifteen years, emphasizing the precariousness of his leadership.

23. Hiley, Michael, *Victorian Working Women* (Boston, 1980). An oppressed, neglected, almost invisible class.
24. Flanagan, Thomas, *The Irish Novelists* (New York, 1959). A reminder of several too-long-neglected talents.
25. Perkin, Harold, *The Origins of Modern English Society 1780–1880* (London, 1969).
26. Burn, W. L., *The Age of Equipoise (1852–1867)* (London, 1964). Despite its discouraging title and often allusive style, a book rich in episodes and insights.
27. Harrison, Brian, *Drink and the Victorians 1815–1872* (London, 1971). Especially shrewd in detailing the many social ramifications of boozing, which made the vow of abstinence so traumatic for many working men.
28. Eldridge, C. C., *Victorian Imperialism* (London, 1978). A clear introduction to a topic swarming with complications.

I. THE TWENTIETH CENTURY

1. Taylor, A. J. P., *English History 1914–1945* (New York, 1965).
2. Hynes, Samuel, *The Edwardian Turn of Mind* (Princeton, 1968).
3. Hynes, Samuel, *The Auden Generation* (London, 1976).
4. Dangerfield, George, *The Strange Death of Liberal England* (New York, 1935). Vivid and terrifying picture of the last years before World War I.
5. Tuchman, Barbara, *The Guns of August* (New York, 1962). The coming of the terrible war.
6. Seaman, L. C. B., *Life in Britain between Two Wars* (London, 1970).
7. Graves, Robert, and Hodge, Alan, *The Long Weekend, a Social History of Great Britain 1918–1939* (New York, 1941). Good fun.
8. Fussell, Paul, *The Great War and Modern Memory* (New York, 1975). A grave, sensitive, and terrifying study.
9. McElwee, William, *Britain's Locust Years 1918–1940* (London, 1962).
10. Daiches, David, *The Present Age in British Literature* (Bloomington, 1958). Rather more than half bibliography.
11. Longmate, Norman, *Air Raid, the Bombing of Coventry, 1940* (London, 1976). Describes the attack in full detail, discounting in the process a picturesque fable that Churchill had advance warning of it but refused to take countermeasures lest he compromise the British code-breaking operation, ULTRA. A good story but not, on the evidence, true.
12. Churchill, Winston, *The Second World War* (London, 1948–1954). Six volumes of memoirs, magisterial but still subject to the sifting process of critical historians.
13. Blythe, Ronald, *Akenfield, Portrait of an English Village* (London, 1969). Close study, much of it in their own words, of the inhabitants of an East Anglian village.
14. Alongside the Paston Letters, the Verney Letters, the Lisle Letters, and the Bedford papers (C.3, E.10, D.25, and E.12, above) must be listed the television series on PBS, *Upstairs, Downstairs*. As a full-length portrait of social attitudes and patterns from the Edwardian period through the market crash of 1929, it is unsurpassed. Though a work of fiction, not a collection of documents, it records in close detail a period as it was experienced by those who lived through it. Would that we had equivalent documentation for earlier periods!

X. BOOKS OUT OF SERIES

1. Randall, John Herman, Jr., *The Making of the Modern Mind* (Boston and New York, 1926). Creaky with age, but still a useful introductory synthesis.
2. Cassirer, Ernst, *The Philosophy of the Enlightenment,* trans. from the German ed. of 1932 (Princeton, 1951). Basic to the eighteenth century.
3. Cassirer, E., Kirsteller, P. O., and Randall, J. H. *The Renaissance Philosophy of Man* (Chicago: Phoenix Books, 1948). Selections from Petrarch, Valla, Ficino, Pico, Pomponazzi, and Vives with commentaries.
4. Thorndike, Lynn, *A History of Magic and Experimental Science,* 8 vols. (New York, 1929–1941).
5. Brown, P. Hume, *A History of Scotland* (Cambridge, 1899). An old classic to be updated by reference, for example, to Mitchison, Rosalind, *A History of Scotland* (1970).
6. Curtis, Edmund, *A History of Ireland* (London, 1950). Can be supplemented with Beckett, James C., *A Short History of Ireland* (1952). See also X.25, below.
7. Mercier, Vivian, *The Irish Comic Tradition* (Oxford, 1962). From the ninth century to the present day.
8. Lindsay, Maurice, *History of Scottish Literature* (London, 1977).
9. Lipson, Ephraim, *Economic History of England* (London, 1923–1931).
10. Cole, G. D. H., and Postgate, Raymond, *The Common People 1746–1946* (London, 1963).
11. Gregg, Pauline, *A Social and Economic History of Britain 1760–1970* (London, 1971).
12. Girouard, Mark, *Life in the English Country House* (New Haven, 1978). From medieval to modern times, with fascinating illustrations.
13. Auerbach, Eric, *Mimesis,* trans. from the German ed. of 1946 (Princeton, 1953). Close analysis of selected passages from Homer to Virginia Woolf, focusing on the changing concept of realism. Should be read in tandem with E. H. Gombrich, *Art and Illusion* (Princeton, 1960, 1969), also concerned with representation.
14. Burkhardt, Jacob, *The Civilization of the Renaissance in Italy* (New York: The Modern Library, n.d.). Despite its antiquity (1860), a vital classic.
15. Symonds, John Addington, *The Renaissance in Italy,* 7 vols. (London, 1875–1886).
16. Highet, Gilbert, *The Classical Tradition: Greek and Roman Influences on Western Literature* (New York, 1949).
17. Sandys, Sir John E., *A History of Classical Scholarship,* 3 vols. (Cambridge, 1903–1908).
18. Merz, John Theodore, *A History of European Thought in the Nineteenth Century,* 4 vols. (London, 1904–1912; repr. by Dover Books, 1960).
19. Butterfield, Herbert, *The Whig Interpretation of History* (London, 1931). A brief, astringent corrective for Whigs, conscious and unconscious.
20. The French Revolution is a lion in every historian's path. The French themselves, though they have innumerable histories of it, including multivolume works by Blanc, Michelet, Guizot, Taine, and Thiers, are not satisfied with any of them. Still less can English readers be complacent in possession of the rhapsodic Carlyle and his milder successors. All the same, the revolution must be squarely faced, and one could make a worse start than with the survey of available histories in the *Cambridge Modern History,* vol. 8, chap. 22, and the account of the revolution which follows it.

21. Roeder, Ralph, *Man of the Renaissance* (New York, 1933). Savonarola, Machiavelli, Castiglione, Aretino.
22. Gilson, Etienne, *History of Christian Philosophy in the Middle Ages* (New York, 1955). From the second century to the fifteenth. Though deep, yet clear, though gentle, yet not dull.
23. Hale, J. R., ed., *A Concise Encyclopaedia of the Italian Renaissance* (New York, 1981). Updates X.14 and X.15 above. Mostly about art, but deals informatively with many other topics as well.
24. A whole library of books and articles deal with Freud, Freudianism, the many revisions of Freudianism, and the impact of Freud on modern literature and art. One's reading might start with Frederick Hoffmann, *Freudianism and the Literary Mind*, 2d ed. (New York, 1957). The standard biography is by Ernest Jones. Hardly any major author has not been subject to one variety or another of Freudian interpretation.
25. Moody, T. W., and Martin, F. X., eds., *The Course of Irish History* (Cork, 1967). This series of twenty-one television talks on the history of Ireland, with extensive bibliographies appended, provides a popular introduction to a vast and complicated subject.
26. There ought to be a recommendable book—incisive, comprehensive, brief—describing the impact of modern science on the literary imagination. Apparently there is not. By "modern science" one would understand, first, the basic concepts of Einstein and their developments, especially the cosomology they entail; second, advances in biochemistry and microbial genetics; and third, computer technology and microprocessing. Science fiction has touched only minimally a few picturesque aspects of these earth-shaking developments; "serious" literature hardly so much. The subject may be a long time growing, but someday the book will have to be written.
27. Harvey, Sir Paul, *The Oxford Companion to English Literature*, in several editions since 1932. A handy compendium of basic facts concisely stated.

Index

ACKNOWLEDGMENTS

Watercolor of Stonehenge by John Constable, and miniature by Nicholas Hilliard Crown Copyright Victoria and Albert Museum. Photographs of dolmen, Hadrian's Wall, the Tower of London, Arundel Castle, Henry VII Chapel at Westminster, Compton Wynyates, Oxford University, Coventry Cathedral, and the London Post Office Tower courtesy of the British Tourist Authority. Roman Mosaic from The Metropolitan Museum of Art Purchase, 1938, Joseph Pulitzer Bequest. Mildenhall plate, Sutton Hoo helmet, woodcut of the Ark Royal, engraving of Nonesuch, engraving of Bankside, Wenceslaus Hollar's Old St. Paul's, and the photograph of the Elgin Marbles reproduced by permission of The Trustees of The British Museum. The book of Kells courtesy of Trinity College Library, Dublin. Reverse of the Tara Brooch photograph by the National Museum of Ireland, Dublin. Church of St. Laurence, Bradford-on-Avon courtesy of Drive Publications Ltd. Bayeux Tapestry courtesy of Archives Photographiques. Rievaulx Abbey and the suit of armor reproduction is with permission of the controller of Her Brittanic Majesty's Stationery Office. Wells Cathedral courtesy Sadea editore, Firenze. Medieval figures from Encyclopedia Britannica, 11th edition. Irish figures by John Speed courtesy of the Map Division, The New York Public Library, Astor, Lenox & Tilden Foundations. Hans Holbein's picture of Sir Thomas More from the Kunstmuseum, Basle. Hans Holbein's picture of King Henry VIII courtesy of the National Portrait Gallery, London. The Mary Rose (illustration from Anthony Anthony's roll, 1546) courtesy of Pepysian Library, Magdalene College. Armada courtesy of the University of California, Los Angeles, Library Photographic Services. Sketch by A. van Buchel after a drawing of the Swan Theatre by Johannes DeWitt courtesy of the University Library, Utrecht. Diagram of the Swan Theatre by C. Walter Hodges from THE NORTON ANTHOLOGY OF ENGLISH LITERATURE, 4th edition. Copyright © 1979, 1974, 1968, 1962 by W. W. Norton & Company, Inc. Inigo Jones designs for the Masque of Oberon by permission of The Trustees of the Chatsworth Settlement. Three-way portrait of Charles I by Sir Anthony Van Dyck from the Royal Collection at St. James Palace Copyright Reserved. Portrait of Nell Gwyn by Sir Peter Lely courtesy of the National Portrait Gallery, London. Wenceslaus Hollar engravings of women courtesy of The Newberry Library, Chicago. Photograph of New St. Paul's courtesy of A. F. Kersting. Woodcut of the English-Irish soldier from the British Library. Portrait of the Honorable Mrs. Graham by Thomas Gainsborough courtesy of the National Gallery of Scotland. Engravings of the Industrious and the Idle 'Prentice by Hogarth from The Metropolitan Museum of Art, Harris Brisbane Dick Fund, 1932. Photographs of Chiswick House, Brighton Pavillion, Holborn Viaduct, and Birmingham Center courtesy of the Royal Commission on Historical Monuments (England). J.M.W. Turner's painting of Lord Nelson's "Victory", and Rowlandson's engraving of Vauxhall Gardens from the Yale Center for British Art, Paul Mellon Collection. "Angel of the Revelation" by William Blake from the Metropolitan Museum of Art, Rogers Fund, 1914. Stephenson's "Rocket" from the Warder Collection. J.M.W. Turner's painting of the "Fighting Temeraire" courtesy of The Tate Gallery, London. Thomas Telford's Canal-Barge from Smiles Lives of the Engineers II, reprinted by Augustus M. Kelley, N.Y., 1968, in facsimile. Dowlais Iron Works courtesy of the Mary Evans Picture Library. Picture of child labor in the coal mines from the Children's Employment Commission Report, 1842. Pictures of the Potato famine in Ireland, Victorian piano, scissors, and ladle, and the Crystal Palace from the Illustrated London News Picture Library. Engraving of the statue in the Albert Memorial by W. Roffe, and photographs of Queen Victoria, London during World War II, and the dam across the Thames courtesy of Hulton Picture Library/Bettmann Archives. "Lady Lilith" by Dante Gabriel Rossetti courtesy of the Delaware Art Museum, Samuel & Mary R. Bancroft Memorial Collection. Page from the Kelmscott manuscript from the Spencer Collection, The New York Public Library, Astor, Lenox & Tilden Foundations. "Man with a Pipe" by Pablo Picasso courtesy of the Kimbell Art Museum, Fort Worth, Texas. Photograph of trench warfare during World War I courtesy of the Imperial War Museum, London.